# RICHARD WAGNER

# RICHARD WAGNER

## *Theory and Theatre*

Dieter Borchmeyer

Translated by Stewart Spencer

CLARENDON PRESS · OXFORD
1991

Oxford University Press, Walton Street, Oxford OX2 6DP
Oxford New York Toronto
Delhi Bombay Calcutta Madras Karachi
Petaling Jaya Singapore Hong Kong Tokyo
Nairobi Dar es Salaam Cape Town
Melbourne Auckland
and associated companies in
Berlin Ibadan

Oxford is a trade mark of Oxford University Press

Published in the United States
by Oxford University Press, New York

British Library Cataloguing in Publication Data
Data available

Library of Congress Cataloging in Publication Data
Richard Wagner, theory and theatre/Dieter Borchmeyer;
translated by Stewart Spencer.
Translation of Das Theater Richard Wagners.
Includes bibliographical references and index.
1. Wagner, Richard, 1813–1883—Criticism and interpretation.
2. Opera—19th century. I. Title.
ML410.W13B6913 1991 782.1′092—dc20 91–11653
ISBN 0–19–315322–X

Typeset by Litho Link Limited, Welshpool, Powys
Printed in Great Britain

# TRANSLATOR'S FOREWORD

References to Wagner's *Collected Writings* are included in the body of the text: roman numerals refer to the relevant volume, arabic numerals to the page. Volumes 1–10 are quoted according to the *Gesammelte Schriften und Dichtungen* (2nd edn.; Leipzig, 1888), volumes 11–16 according to the *Sämtliche Schriften und Dichtungen* (Leipzig, 1911–14). (These references have been retained in the English edition for purposes of orientation. All the passages from Wagner's prose writings have been newly translated, although earlier versions have occasionally been consulted and plundered where appropriate. Little would have been served, however, by including references to Ashton Ellis's eight-volume translation of the *Prose Works* (London, 1892–9), a translation as unedifying as it is unobtainable.) Cosima Wagner's *Diaries* are quoted, with permission, from Geoffrey Skelton's English translation (Collins, London, 1978–80), and are indicated in the text by the letters *CT*. Quotations from *Mein Leben* (*ML*) are taken from Andrew Gray's translation, edited by Mary Whittall (Cambridge, 1983). *WWV* = John Deathridge, Martin Geck, and Egon Voss (eds.), *Wagner Werkverzeichnis: Verzeichnis der musikalischen Werke Richard Wagners und ihrer Quellen* (Mainz, 1986).

And what is art, after all? It is like the lovely blue flames which now and again flicker over a fire, while everything going on beneath them is destruction, annihilation. But that art should provide a light during a period rich in deeds—that indeed is the dream.

Richard Wagner to Cosima, 21 December 1870.

# PREFACE

T. S. Eliot's poem *The Waste Land* (1922) is often regarded as the most quintessential and influential piece of English poetry of the first half of the twentieth century (it takes as its theme the breakdown of all sense of meaning in the world, and evokes the waste land of lost illusions which followed the upheavals of the First World War). It contains a number of lines in German—two original quotations from *Tristan und Isolde*, and reminiscences of *Das Rheingold* and *Götterdämmerung*. In the first part of the poem the memory of an erotic experience is linked with the Young Sailor's lines from the opening of *Tristan*:

> Frisch weht der Wind
> der Heimath zu:
> mein irisch Kind,
> wo weilest du?          (vii. 1.)

Later, the disillusionment brought about by love is associated with the line sung by Tristan's Shepherd, 'öd' und leer das Meer!' (vii. 58), a line redolent of the hopeless despair that marks the beginning of Act III— the setting is Tristan's ruined castle, itself now part of a waste land. Of course, no ship of hope sails into sight in Eliot's sea of desolation. In the third part of the poem the violated Thames-daughters echo Wagner's Rhinemaidens, singing 'the world's lullaby' from the beginning of *Das Rheingold* (*CT*, 17 July 1869), but subtly varying Wagner's onomatopoeic lines in order to give a deeply pessimistic gloss to their former tone of affirmation: 'Weialala leia | Wallala leialala', they sing, thus adding further to Eliot's 'heap of broken images'.

Lines of German verse in an English poem—an unusual phenomenon, made even more unusual by the fact that they were written by an opera composer. Yet what makes Wagner so unique in the history of music is that his influence, more than that of any other composer, extends far beyond the world of music, not only embodying an unfortunate chapter in the history of German ideas, but also leaving its mark on European literary history. Remarkably enough, Wagner's worldwide literary influence has been relatively ignored in Germany, where, with few exceptions, his literary impact has been slight. Indeed, Thomas Mann is the only major German author whose works reveal the same intense preoccupation with Wagner's music dramas as is found, for example, in the work of Gabriele D'Annunzio or in the writers of *fin de siècle* France.

Kurt Jäckel's monumental but unfinished study, *Richard Wagner in der französischen Literatur* (1931–2), Erwin Koppen's comprehensive survey, *Dekadenter Wagnerismus* (1973), which traces Wagner's influence as one of the cult figures of European *décadence*, and, finally, Raymond Furness's monograph, *Wagner and Literature* (1982), together with numerous individual studies of recent decades, have all shown how considerable, not to say preponderant, was Wagner's influence on European literature from the end of the nineteenth century onwards. Raymond Furness, in the introduction to his brilliant book, writes:

That a *musician* should have had such an overwhelming effect on *literature* is even more remarkable but the age was ready for a shift towards music in the arts, and it was Wagner who provided a unique and almost mystical stimulus. It was he more than any other artist who was able to fructify and enrich imaginative writing: it may safely be claimed that without Wagner the literature of at least a century would be immeasurably impoverished, as regards topics as well as structures.

The role which Wagner played more especially in late nineteenth-century French literature has been likened to the influence which Virgil exercised on the Middle Ages and which Shakespeare had on eighteenth-century Germany. (It is sufficient here to mention the names of Baudelaire, Mallarmé, and Verlaine.) That the literary history of *décadence* is, for the greater part, the history of French reactions to Wagner has already been mentioned. But it would also be true to say that scarcely any of France's major writers in the twentieth century have been unaffected by Wagner, even if that influence was purely negative. The *Wagnéromanie* of which Léon Daudet wrote in 1917 when recalling the years of his youth was an enthusiasm for Wagner triggered off less by the latter's music than by his metaphysics and poetry. It influenced almost every French writer of the early twentieth century, however violently some of them—one thinks of André Gide and Giraudoux, for example—may have sought to resist it. 'We are a generation that has Wagner in its blood', Claudel wrote to André Suarès in 1911. Claudel's attitude veered between passionate admiration and (especially during the 1930s) growing aversion, a change which is clear from the titles of his two essays on Wagner, *Richard Wagner: Rêverie d'un poète français*, published in 1926, and *Le Poison wagnérien* of twelve years later. Claudel embraces both extremes—on the one hand, that ardent *Wagnérisme* exemplified not only by Georges Duhamel and Romain Rolland but also, in part, by Marcel Proust, whose principal work, *A la recherche du temps perdu*, is shot through with countless allusions to Wagner, and, on the other, a no less vehement anti-Wagnerism, which won many converts among French intellectuals during the first half of the twentieth century, not least under the influence of the national socialist cult of Wagner.

Literary Wagnerism is also to be found in English and, above all, in Irish literature, where one thinks of writers such as Moore, Yeats, Shaw (whose *Perfect Wagnerite* has been of seminal importance for a whole new generation of writers and producers), and Joyce, whose *Ulysses* is perhaps even more indebted structurally to Wagner than is Proust's *magnissimum opus*. The fact that perhaps the three greatest novelists of the twentieth century—Marcel Proust, James Joyce, and Thomas Mann—were so clearly influenced by Wagner's works can hardly be fortuitous. Thomas Mann has written illuminatingly not only on the epic background of the Wagnerian music drama but also, and especially, on the leitmotif or 'symbolically allusive formula', and the affinities between the *Ring* and the great cyclical novels of both Balzac (whom Wagner admired immensely) and Zola (who in turn was influenced by Wagner). And it can be shown (as I hope to do in a later chapter) that Wagner's basic dramaturgical concepts are all grounded in the theory of the novel, and that his music dramas are crypto-novels, or (as he himself would have said) 'redeemed' novels.

In his later polemic against the composer, *Der Fall Wagner* (an essay which, for all its polemical zeal, contains a host of laudatory detail), Nietzsche advances the view that Wagner *'increased music's capacity for language to the point of making it immeasurable'*.[1] This is the essential key to understanding Wagner's 'poetry', a poetry which cannot be inferred from the linguistic material alone, but which must be sought, first and foremost, in the 'language' of his music. All who believe it possible to deny Wagner's status as a poet by drawing attention to certain singularities in his handling of *Stabreim* or to those passages which are traditionally, and rightly, described as bombastic are guilty of an error that was long since exposed as such by Nietzsche and Thomas Mann— and also by Wagner himself. In the fourth of his *Unzeitgemäße Betrachtungen*, entitled 'Richard Wagner in Bayreuth', Nietzsche observes that

Where this rarest of powers expresses itself [i.e. the power over the two worlds of poetic language and music, worlds which are 'as disparate in form, colour and articulation as they are in soul'], censure of individual excesses and singularities, or of the more frequent obscurities of expression and thought, will

[1] Friedrich Nietzsche, *Sämtliche Werke: Kritische Studienausgabe in 15 Bänden*, ed. Giorgio Colli and Mazzino Montinari (Munich, 1980), vi. 30; translated into English by Walter Kaufmann as 'The Case of Wagner', in *Basic Writings of Nietzsche* (New York, 1968), 629.

always be no more than petty and unfruitful . . . Before all, however, no one who reflects on Wagner as poet and sculptor of language should forget that none of the Wagnerian dramas is intended to be read, and thus they must not be importuned with the demands presented to the spoken drama.[2]

This is something which Wagner himself repeatedly stressed, and many were the times he suffered scruples about publishing his texts before setting them to music. In his *Epilogue to the 'Nibelung's Ring'*, for example, he writes: 'I had the completed poem printed at my own expense in a very small number of copies, which I then communicated to my closer and more distant acquaintances. My disinclination to see my poem treated and judged as a literary product was so pronounced that I expressly protested against this in a short preface . . .' (vi. 260–1). And in a letter to Mathilde Wesendonck of 15 April 1859, in which he mentions that he has been reading Goethe's *Tasso*, he insists that 'it was ill considered of me to have published *Tristan*. Between a poem that is intended entirely for music and a purely poetic theatre piece there must be such fundamental differences in design and execution that the former, viewed with the same eye as the latter, must remain wellnigh unintelligible in terms of its actual meaning, at least until such time as it is supplemented by the music.' The only exception, Wagner concedes, would be if the reader were 'so gifted' as to be able to add the musical dimension while reading the poem to himself.[3] Wagner leaves us in no doubt that, from an independent literary standpoint, his poem for *Tristan und Isolde* cannot be compared with the perfection of Goethe's *Tasso*.

Was Wagner a poet? It is a question which has often been asked and to which Wagner himself provided the answer: 'I am no poet,' he told Cosima on 22 January 1871, 'and I don't care at all if people reproach me for my choice of words; in my works the action is everything. To a certain extent it is a matter of indifference to me whether people understand my verses, since they will certainly understand my dramatic action.' Of the great scene between Alberich and Hagen in *Götterdämmerung* he said, not without a certain playful exuberance: 'It will have the effect of two strange animals conversing together—one understands nothing of it, but it is all interesting' (*CT*, 27 December 1873). Reduced intelligibility and 'blurred' linguistic expression are among the inescapable facts of operatic life, so that, borrowing from the language of quantum mechanics, one might perhaps speak of an uncertainty principle in music drama. Linguistic and musical expression can never be precisely defined.

---

[2] Nietzsche, *Sämtliche Werke*, i. 487–8; translated into English by R. J. Hollingdale as *Untimely Meditations: Richard Wagner in Bayreuth* (Cambridge, 1983), 238.

[3] *Richard Wagner an Mathilde Wesendonk: Tagebuchblätter und Briefe*, ed. Wolfgang Golther (Leipzig, 1914), 171.

Was Wagner therefore a pure musician? What would he himself have replied? 'R. persists in saying he himself is no musician', Cosima noted in her diary on 17 February 1876; similar remarks are repeated on page after page. If he refused to think of himself as a poet or as a musician, how in fact did he see himself? 'The main thing is that one should be out of the ordinary', he told Cosima on 16 August 1869. 'In me the accent lies on the conjunction of poet and musician; as a pure musician I would not be of much significance.' Indeed, his lifelong aversion to 'non-musicians' went so far that on one occasion he exclaimed: 'The musician who does nothing but write music from morning till night, entirely ignoring the world of ideas, must be an ox—he is missing far more than those who, knowing nothing of music, observe the rest of the world.' (*CT*, 17 January 1870.) And on other occasion, when considering whether to write a play on the death of Alexander the Great: 'If only I were not a musician! This wretched note-writing—into what category of uneducated people has it pitched me?' (*CT*, 18 March 1870.) Or, again: 'My pleasure begins only at the point where I cease to be a musician.' (*CT*, 1 November 1880.) There can scarcely have been a major composer in the history of music who has denied his profession so frequently and so vehemently. His use of words such as 'ox' and 'uneducated' shows that he viewed the pure musician as a product of that modern division of labour which had led to a decline in humanistic universal education and to the loss of human totality. For Wagner, by contrast, music was intended to become part of an integral process of education once again, while the 'musician' would find his ultimate justification as a *uomo universale*.

Wagner's oft-repeated claim that, as a mere musician, he was of no great significance is evidence of the inferiority which he felt in the presence of such great composers of instrumental music as Bach, Haydn, Mozart, and, above all, Beethoven. On one point, however, he regarded himself as unsurpassed, and that was in the 'conjunction' of music and poetry. What he meant by this was not the correlation between 'musical setting' and 'libretto' achieved by the fact that poet and composer were one and the same person, but what Hugo von Hofmannsthal once described as the 'pre-potency' of music in Wagner's dramatic poetry.[4] Even more important, however, is the 'literariness' of Wagner's music, a quality vouchsafed more especially by the quasi-linguistic semanticization of (leit)motifs which must be interpreted not as independent musical themes but as poetic clues or symbols which provide a framework of meaning. By associating musical and poetic means of expression in this kind of 'conjunction', Wagner has created an

[4] *Richard Strauss/Hugo von Hofmannsthal: Briefwechsel*, ed. Willi Schuh (Zurich, 1964), 240, letter from Hofmannsthal to Strauss of 24 Sept. 1913.

idiom whose evocatory potential and whose creative images and characters constitute poetry in a higher, not to say the highest, sense. As such, they cannot be interpreted by purely musicological methods. It is to Wagner's scenic and mythic imagination that the world theatre owes those characters, situations, and relationships which are among the greatest poetic achievements in the whole history of drama.

'It has always seemed to me absurd to question Wagner's poetic gifts', Thomas Mann wrote in 1937 in his lecture on the *Ring*.

What could be more poetically beautiful or profound than Wotan's relationship to Siegfried, the fatherly-mocking and condescending attachment of the god to the boy who will destroy him, the loving abdication of the old power in favour of the eternally youthful? The composer has the poet to thank for the marvellous sounds he finds here. But then again, how much the poet has to thank the composer for, and how often (it seems) the poet only really understands himself when he enlists the aid of his second language to interpret and amplify, the language that is for him the true repository of subliminal knowledge, beyond the reach of the word.[5]

Four years earlier, in his lecture *Leiden und Größe Richard Wagners*, Mann had already offered so convincing an assessment of Wagner's poetic ability in terms of its quality and its limitations that it is almost embarrassing to find over-zealous polemicists still repeating long-outworn beliefs. The poetry in Wagner's works, Mann argued, derived not from the purely linguistic element but from the integration of language, gesture, and music. 'Considered from a purely linguistic point of view [his works] often seem somewhat overblown and baroque, naive, with an air of grandiose and overbearing ineptitude: yet interspersed with passages of sheer genius, of a power, economy and elemental beauty that banish all doubt', he wrote in 1933, pointing especially to those 'flashes of linguistic genius scattered in among Wagner's dilettante audacities' which typify the *Ring*.[6]

'That Wagner's relationship to language differs from that of our great poets and writers, that it lacks the rigour and finesse that obtain wherever language is felt to be the highest good, the ordained medium of art', is clear, Mann observes,[7] when one considers Wagner as a prose writer. (One excepts in this context the short stories and articles which Wagner wrote in Paris and which, uniquely, betray his literary ambitions.) For Wagner, prose was, like the paper on which he wrote, merely a means to the end of communicating his ideas on aesthetics,

---

[5] Thomas Mann, *Wagner und unsere Zeit*, ed. Erika Mann (Frankfurt am Main, 1963), 147; translated into English by Allan Blunden as 'Richard Wagner and *Der Ring des Nibelungen*', in *Pro and contra Wagner* (London, 1985), 190–1.

[6] Ibid. 76; English trans., p. 104.

[7] Ibid.; English trans., p. 105.

dramaturgy, culture, and politics. He was never concerned with stylistic perfection. Time and again, the baroque magniloquence of his hypotactically structured prose reveals hiatuses and even solecisms which he did not feel the need to correct. While revising a manuscript, he once told Cosima that he was 'altering next to nothing in the style: "I am not a writer"' (*CT*, 22 July 1880). The poet who, in his music dramas, 'forced language back to a primordial state' (to quote Nietzsche[8]), reverted in his theoretical essays to that bureaucratic style which he himself was so quick to condemn in *Opera and Drama*. To cite Nietzsche again: 'a kind of reluctance on the part of the writer lies over [his essays] like a shadow, as though the artist is ashamed of intellectual demonstration'.[9] In his 1860 essay, *'Zukunftsmusik'*, Wagner himself observed that nothing could be 'more alien and more tormenting to an artistic nature' than to have to theorize. 'And so he does not abandon himself to it with that cool sense of calm which the professional theoretician necessarily has at his command; he is driven, rather, by a passionate impatience which prevents him from devoting the requisite time to a careful handling of questions of style'; and Wagner goes on to describe 'the sufferings caused by my painful excursion into the realm of speculative theory' (vii. 113–14).

Notwithstanding Wagner's proclaimed indifference to matters of style, his writings, and especially *Mein Leben*, contain passages of exceptional linguistic and epic strength: 'then the artificial, verbose and laboured periods vanish and there escape from him sentences and whole pages which are among the most beautiful in all German prose', Nietzsche wrote in 1876.[10] That Wagner's art of characterization was equally well adapted to the purely linguistic medium is shown by the grandiose portraits of Spontini, Rossini, Halévy, and others which adorn the pages of his autobiography. His exceptional ability to formulate graphic sentences is also attested by Cosima on almost every page of her *Diaries*.

By his own admission, Wagner wrote many of his essays, including *Opera and Drama*, more as an attempt at self-understanding than with the general public in mind. 'Such things are studies, explorations which one makes for one's own benefit, but which ought not to be published', he told Cosima on 4 June 1882 in connection with *Opera and Drama*. But it is precisely as 'studies' that Wagner's aesthetic and dramaturgical writings deserve to be numbered among the most fascinating essays on the theory of art to have been penned by any writer of the bourgeois age, not least because they dispense with that rigorously independent

---

[8] Nietzsche, *Sämtliche Werke*, i. 486; English trans. (Hollingdale, *Untimely Meditations*), p. 237.
[9] Ibid. 502; English trans., p. 248.
[10] Ibid.

theoretical approach which as a rule is not the concern of the practically minded artist.

The present book takes *Opera and Drama* as its starting-point, and seeks to analyse Wagner's aesthetic and dramaturgical 'system', including its self-contradictions, from a number of different points of view. The main emphases in what is, essentially, a comparative study will be placed on the dialectic tension between Wagner's aesthetic theory of 'dramaturgical' and 'absolute' music (an aesthetic outlook at odds with the theories of Hanslick and Nietzsche), on the grounding of his musical dramaturgy in the theory of the novel, on his concepts of a common style and an 'antique art-form', together with his multifaceted theory of improvisation with its origin in puppet shows and popular theatre, and, finally, his important contribution to Nietzsche's *Die Geburt der Tragödie*, a contribution which has hitherto been underestimated but which it is now possible to see in a new critical and historical light, thanks to the recent publication of Nietzsche's *Nachlaß*. Both here and elsewhere, Cosima Wagner's *Diaries*, first published in Germany in 1976–7, will be examined in detail from a number of philological and aesthetic viewpoints.

Inspired by Young Hegelian thinking, Wagner's aesthetic outlook is sociologically orientated in a way which often seems deterministic. It cannot be denied, of course, that, viewed from a modern perspective, his theory of social determinants in art is amateurish and often simply unacceptable; but it is a theory which, in its intentionality, is forward-looking and, in certain of its speculative insights, remarkably clear-sighted. The first part of the present study, which takes its title from one of Wagner's Paris essays, examines the composer's sociology of art in the context of his plans for theatrical reform, plans which, practical and Utopian by turns, culminated in the founding of a festival in Bayreuth which, by his own lights, represented more of a concession than an ideal.

The centre-piece of our study will of course be the chapters on Wagner's 'Romantic operas' and 'musical dramas'. Whereas some of these works will be considered from a limited standpoint (an exhaustive interpretation of the *Ring*, for example, would have been beyond the scope of the present book), others will be subjected to as comprehensive an overall interpretation as possible, drawing on Wagner's literary sketches and drafts. As with our exegesis of his theoretical writings, we shall be concerned not only with the works *per se*, they will also be examined against the background of world literature, and subjected to what might be termed the literary equivalent of spectrum analysis. In these chapters, too, we shall have the opportunity to compare Wagnerian theory and practice by examining the practical dramatic realization of those theories that were traced in the opening sections of this study. (To name only one example among many, the genesis of the Prize Song in *Die Meistersinger von Nürnberg* will be considered in the context of Wagner's theory of improvisation.)

The two points to which we shall have most frequent occasion to return are the influence on Wagner's thinking and imagination of classical art and mythology, and of the Greek way of life in general, and the indebtedness of his mode of thought to the classical Romantic tradition. Wagner was fond of denying his century. He had been born ten years too late, he told Cosima on 12 April 1879: 'he should have stood in the same relationship to Beethoven as Schubert did, and then he would also have been in touch with people like Carlyle and Schopenhauer; in music he had known Weber, but no writers or poets'. How much he regretted never having met Goethe (Wagner was 19 when the latter died, and had already written music for *Faust*, I) is clear from a dream which he recounted to Cosima on 15 February 1870: 'R. dreamed that he went walking with Goethe, conversed with him, and resolved to stay with him, "having found my mission in life in the company of such a man".' There was, however, one famous writer whom Wagner met and whose works had a deep and manifold influence on him—Ludwig Tieck, the last great survivor of the classical Romantic period, whom Wagner met in Berlin in 1847 and with whom he had a long and fruitful conversation.

In a notable conversation with Patrice Chéreau and Pierre Boulez in 1977, Carlo Schmid, a prominent social democratic politician and an important figure in the spread of literary ideas between Germany and France, described Wagner's work as the '*summa artium saeculi*'.[11] But, more than that, it is a summation of world theatre, and we may well be justified in regarding its creator as the most important artistic intermediary between German literature and a European public in the period between Heinrich Heine and Thomas Mann. The present study is intended to contribute to that understanding. Essentially it derives from the present author's book, *Das Theater Richard Wagners*, first published in Germany in 1982. It is not, however, a mere translation of the German original; substantial parts of it constitute an entirely new work. The two opening sections on Wagnerian theory—the first systematic account yet undertaken of Wagner's aesthetic outlook—are a shortened version of the German text: where cuts have been made, they affect those passages which are perhaps of less interest to the English-speaking reader. The third section, which deals with Wagner's dramatic œuvre, has been largely rewritten for an English audience. This is especially true of the chapter on *Die Feen* (which is entirely new),

---

[11] 'Mythologie und Ideologie', in *Die Programmhefte der Bayreuther Festspiele 1977*, iv. '*Das Rheingold*', 25–48, esp. p. 44.

the chapter on *Der fliegende Holländer* and the metamorphoses of the Ahasuerus myth, the chapter on *Tannhäuser*, and the second part of the chapter on *Parsifal*. The German edition also contained a fourth section on the influence of Wagnerian music theatre, including critical reactions to the composer on the part of Nietzsche, Thomas Mann, and Hugo von Hofmannsthal. Since it dealt exclusively with German literature, it has been omitted from the English edition. For much the same reasons the critical apparatus has been reduced in scope.

Wagner's aesthetic system is so heavily indebted to the German philosophical tradition that it may not always be easy for the Anglo-Saxon reader, unfamiliar with German literature, to follow Wagner's line of thought. Stewart Spencer, who over the years has translated a number of my articles for the Bayreuth Festival programmes and to whom I owe the English version of the present study, pointed out that it is difficult, for example, for the English reader to grasp exactly what Schiller means by his use of the word 'sentimental'. For a time I considered avoiding the term altogether in the English edition; only when I attempted to do so did it occur to me of what fundamental importance this concept was for Wagner. Thomas Mann described Schiller's treatise, *Über naive und sentimentalische Dichtung*, as the 'classic and comprehensive essay of the Germans', an essay 'which in fact contains all the others within it, thus rendering them superfluous' (*Goethe und Tolstoi*). 'Naïve' poetry, according to Schiller, is characterized by its oneness with nature, whereas 'sentimental' poetry presupposes an awareness that that oneness has been destroyed by culture and civilization. The sentimental poet, however, is unable to come to terms with his remoteness from nature, and uses the medium of reflection to rediscover the lost sense of oneness, which he posits as an 'ideal'. One could perhaps describe Wagner's *Ring* as a grandiose illustration of this same process. After all, the tetralogy conjures up the idyll of nature at the beginning of *Das Rheingold* before going on to depict the loss of our sense of oneness with nature and our repeated attempts to rediscover it. The sought-after unity or 'sentimental' ideal is hinted at in the motif of redemption with which the work concludes. In other words, the term 'sentimental' is used here not in the modern English (and German) sense, but is intended to indicate a reflective emotion or, more precisely, a feeling directed at something which has been lost. (It was in this sense of 'reflective emotion' that the term 'sentimental' was still understood in England in the eighteenth century.)

After this brief excursus on the history of ideas, it remains only to thank my publishers, and especially Bruce Phillips, for the commitment which they have shown in helping me to bring my ideas to the attention of an English-speaking audience. I should also like to thank my translator, Stewart Spencer, and all my English friends and supporters, particularly Raymond Furness and Terence James Reed, who have encouraged me in my work on Wagner over many years.

D.B.

# CONTENTS

III. WAGNER'S DRAMATIC POETRY

# I

## THE ARTIST AND HIS PUBLIC

It was under the foregoing title, in a French translation of course, that Wagner published the seventh of his Paris essays in the *Revue et Gazette musicale* of 1 April 1841.[1] Purporting to come from the posthumous papers of the first-person narrator of 'A Pilgrimage to Beethoven'—the narrator's death had been recounted in 'An End in Paris'—these semi-fictional, semi-theoretical *feuilletons* are unmistakably indebted in their inventiveness, style, and content to the German Romantic tradition of writers such as E. T. A. Hoffmann. They deal with a fundamental aesthetic problem to which Wagner was to return repeatedly in his theoretical writings up to and including his 1878 essay, 'Public and Popularity', and which is reflected, moreover, in those of his musical dramas that deal with the role of the artist. What is it that persuades the artist to express himself publicly, and how can the latter keep his talent unsullied in such an environment?

When I am on my own and my mind is full of musical noises which at last fuse into a melody revealing to me the essence of my being, so that my heart beats violently and my unseeing eyes shed heavenly tears of rapture, then I often tell myself what an utter fool I am not to be content to stay alone with this marvellous experience, what an utter fool to go rushing out with it to that horrible amorphous mass, the public. As though the right to exercise my talent depended upon its completely meaningless approval! (i. 180–1.)[2]

The paradox of having to sacrifice the product of artistic solitude to an indolent or uncouth public was one that Wagner considered and discussed on many later occasions, not least in conversation with Cosima while composing his final musical drama; and yet he never really came to a clear-cut answer. There was the same perplexity at the end of his

[1] The word *Öffentlichkeit*, translated here as the artist's 'public' or audience, assumes additional resonances in Wagner's later writings, where, under the influence of the Greek political ideal, it comes to mean public life in general, and implies that sense of community associated in Wagner's mind with the *res publica* or *polis*.
[2] English translation from Robert Jacobs and Geoffrey Skelton (eds.), *Wagner Writes from Paris* (London, 1973), 103.

life as there had been when he first embarked on his career as an artist more than four decades earlier. For over forty years he sought to create a 'public' which would draw the artist out of his isolation and become a receptacle for his work without leaving him feeling merely alienated. With each successive failure he rethought the problem from a different ideological and practical standpoint, but the end-result remained the same—scepticism and resignation.

# The Work of Art and the Market-Place: Festival or Repertory Theatre

> This is the kind of art that now fills the whole civilized world! Its true essence is industry, its moral aim to earn money, its aesthetic purport to entertain bored audiences.
>
> *Art and Revolution* (iii. 19).

In his 1841 article, 'The Artist and his Public', Wagner sought to attribute the artist's 'demonic secret of self-denial' or self-alienation to his 'urge to communicate'. This urge could not be the result of any feeling of social obligation, since 'of all people the genius is the least responsive to the call of duty; he can do nothing with it in his art'. Nor, Wagner went on, was he motivated by the need to win honour, a need which, although it encouraged virtuoso accomplishments, could not produce true works of art. Only 'the god-like impulse to communicate his own inner bliss to the hearts of all men' could explain and justify the artist's desire to communicate. But must the genius not immediately withdraw into himself when confronted by an indifferent, bored, vain, and ignorant audience bent only on enjoying itself, a public dominated by 'envious and corrupt reviewers', which saw itself as a market in which works of art were treated like consumer goods? If concern for his daily bread and the maintenance of his family were what motivated 'the labourer and craftsman' but not the genius, how was it that the latter was persuaded 'to hawk his most precious possession'? The true artist 'feels free', and therefore 'desires to be free in life, to have nothing to do with its necessities, to be borne along light-hearted, without a care in the world', precisely in order to be able 'to rejoice the world with his works'. But the pre-condition for freedom in modern society is money. That being so, there is nothing left for the man of genius but to 'seek a market for his creations' and come to terms with the institutions of a public that he despises. Money, of course, is 'a bribe from hell', and the effort to communicate and to win recognition from a third party whom the artist requires for the sake of his freedom, even if that third party proves to be a 'horrible amorphous mass', must involve him in an 'infamous quid pro quo' in which only the strongest can maintain his artistry unimpaired (i. 181–4).

The final part of the article is given over to a satirical account of the 'insane' genius who, convinced that he has created a work which will bring joy to the entire world, exchanges his solitary life-style for the public arena, and finds himself out of place in the world of convention and capital:

It has been taken for granted that you would be reasonable, that you would be prepared to make compromises. You urgently want a *succès*, do you not? Well, here it is guaranteed. You have only to make this and that slight adjustment: there is the singer, there the dancer, there the great virtuoso—go and arrange things with them. There they are standing by that wonderfully curtained doorway through which you have to pass in order to reach the great public. Don't you know that everyone who has trodden that blessed path has had to bring his little sacrifice?[1]

Wagner is as perspicacious as he is sharply satirical in the way in which he points out the ambiguity of the modern artist's existence. It is a life, he argues, that is determined by the marketable value of art. Indeed, the very independence of art, for all that the work of art cannot be reduced to a form of merchandise,[2] depends upon market distribution. The independent artist, able to secure his material livelihood by selling his works in sizeable quantities, is a product of the late eighteenth century. Only the growth of the art market allowed a distinction to be drawn between the artist's salaried appointment and those patrons who had previously subjected the work of art to alien purposes, restricting it to a canon of fixed forms and themes, and turning it into a vehicle of princely pomp. The autonomy of art is therefore bound up dialectically with our perception of it as a form of merchandise. As the imaginary author of 'The Artist and his Public' recognizes, the artist appears to be able to exercise his independence only as long as there is a paying public, a public which Wagner denigrates as such in countless other pamphlets.

Of course, Wagner realized that the independence of art is replaced by a new dependency once it is treated as a marketable product, and that the modern artist who is forced to think in terms of money is in a worse position than earlier artists who merely had to court the favour of princes. What kind of freedom is it that is interested in 'one thing only, namely, money' (i. 185)? There was a need, Wagner believed, to create a form of society which would make it possible for both man and artist to enjoy true autonomy unhampered by any further dialectical snares.

Wagner's ideology is made up of contradictions. There is no denying that, over a period of decades, revolutionary, reactionary, conservative,

[1] Robert Jacobs and Geoffrey Skelton (eds.), *Wagner Writes from Paris* (London, 1973), 108.
[2] See Jürgen Habermas, *Strukturwandel der Öffentlichkeit*, 3rd edn. (Neuwied and Berlin, 1968), 181.

authoritarian, liberal, and socialist tendencies are all to be found in Wagner's writings and *obiter dicta*, sometimes superseding each other, sometimes overlapping. But on one point, at least, he remained consistent, and that was his repeated attempt to free art from the vicious circle of a market mentality, and hence to destroy its mercantile aspect. His hope of a radical, revolutionary restructuring of society after 1848 was just as bound up with this goal as, say, his monarchical conception of an 'exempted' upper stratum of society which he hoped would come one day to enjoy a pure aesthetic education. (This latter view is advanced in the 1867–8 treatise, 'German Art and German Politics', which will be considered in greater detail below.) If, after 1864, Wagner yoked himself to a royal patron, it was not just the result of outward necessity (a necessity which caused him a good deal of anguish, as Cosima's *Diaries* show), it also reflected an ideological conviction that he had begun to articulate some time before.

There is a sense in which Wagner wanted to re-create the 'Weimar wonder' (viii. 38) of the relationship between Goethe and Grand Duke Carl August, a relationship which he found in idealized form in a work of Goethe's which he often reread, the 1788–90 verse play, *Torquato Tasso*. Wagner longed to be able to work in the same conditions as Goethe's Tasso at the Ferrara court, occupying a kind of no man's land between the older class-conscious system, dependent upon a court appointment and a patron, and a modern, independent existence in which the artist lived off the profits that accrued to him from his works, working for his art alone, subject to no alien authority when writing his poetry, freed from all cares concerning his material existence, and raised above 'life's narrow confines' to a position of 'beauteous freedom' (ll. 417–18). For Wagner, this form of existence must have seemed wellnigh ideal, not least if it cast cooling shadows over man's concrete existence. The sponsorship scheme devised to finance the Bayreuth Festival tried to retain certain features of the private character of patronage; as such, it was a conscious denial of the anonymity of the mercantile mentality and the audience associated with that mentality. The Bayreuth Patrons' Society as a collective sponsor! It was a matter of much regret to Wagner that this ideal had to be compromised when the Festival itself was realized. 'Everything is a compromise', he complained in conversation with Cosima on 8 April 1870 when royalties arrived from Hamburg, regretting the commercial 'sacrifice' involved in selling his early music dramas. It was 'terrible' that he had allowed *Lohengrin* and *Tannhäuser* to be treated as operas:

if I were independent, a man of means, I would not give my things to any theatre. There ought really to be a prytaneum set up in Germany, which would say to me, for instance: Your things will be produced everywhere, for that you will receive such and such an allowance, but the works will belong to the nation, for it is shameful to receive money for such things, to see them regarded as mere goods. (*CT*, 8 April 1870.)

The generic term 'opera' is used here as a synonym for 'artistic merchandise'. (The same is true of Wagner's use of the term 'literature', as we shall see shortly.) There could be no clearer indication than this that his concept of 'musical drama' is a conscious negation of commercial exploitation and of the market principle in general. As such, his reform of opera and drama presupposes social reform. Opera is distinguished from 'the art-work of the future' in much the same way that the 'magic jewel' described in the 1840 Paris essay 'The Virtuoso and the Artist', for which the miners of Salzburg and Bonn—Wagner is thinking here of Mozart and Beethoven, of course—were looking when they were buried alive in the depths of the mountain, differs from the 'rich veins of gold' upon which their successors have stumbled by chance (thus symbolizing the contrast between the artist and the virtuoso). In the same way, the Rhinegold differs from the ring that is forged from its gleaming metal. Even the deepest veins may be brought to the surface and become the object of common greed. And the same is true of the 'genius of music', symbolized here as the magic jewel. But neither this nor the buried miners can be rediscovered: instead, gold ducats are struck from the veins of ore (i. 167-72).

When art is divorced from its social function of sustaining religious ritual or courtly ceremonial and subjected to market forces, it loses its 'aura' in the specific sense given to that term by Walter Benjamin in his 1936 essay, *Das Kunstwerk im Zeitalter seiner technischen Reproduzierbarkeit*. This essay has a remarkable precursor in Wagner's letter to Franz Liszt in 1851, 'On the Goethe Foundation'. In both cases, the mercantile character of the work of art is ascribed to its reproducibility. Beginning with *The Art-Work of the Future* of 1849, Wagner repeatedly describes the disastrous change in the way in which the arts are disseminated and interpreted once the means for their mass production had been invented. On this point, too, he follows the Romantic tradition. August Wilhelm Schlegel, for example, in his 1803 essay, *Über Literatur, Kunst und Geist des Zeitalters*, had attributed the decline of poetry to printing and to the book market, arguing that the latter had supplanted what used to be the 'public' performance not only of dramatic poetry (in the theatre) but also of lyric poetry ('through singing') and epic verse-making ('on the lips of rhapsodes'), replacing them by 'solitary unsocial reading'. With the mass production of literary works instead of the unique or periodic performance of a single work of art, the listener's 'devotion' had yielded to the reader's 'distraction'.[3] (Walter Benjamin draws a contrast between this 'distraction' as 'a variant of social conduct' and 'diversion' or 'concentration' as a 'school for asocial behaviour' in order to lend legitimacy to the cinema—an art-form which exists only through reproduction—as the social art of the modern age. 'A man who concentrates before a work of art is absorbed by it. He enters into this work of art the way legend tells us of the Chinese painter when he viewed his finished painting. In contrast, the distracted mass absorbs the work of art.'[4])

Devotion and concentration, rather than distraction, should also characterize the audience's attitude towards the 'art-work of the future', but Wagner, in diametrical contrast to Benjamin, regards concentration, or inner composure, as the ideal mode of socio-artistic reception, while distraction is held to typify the attitude of the modern aesthetic 'egoist'. When market laws are revoked, art will once again become 'common' property, unlike the 'solitary poetic art' of the age of printing, an art which has lost its former elemental force and forfeited its ability to purify the senses and heighten moral sensitivities. Wagner gives graphic expression to this belief in the following satirical passage from his reform essay on *The Art-Work of the Future*:

Orpheus's lyric poetry would certainly not have reduced the savage beasts to silent supine devotion if the bard had merely given them printed poems to read: their ears must be enthralled by the sonorous notes that come from the heart, their voracious eyes be tamed by the singer's proud and graceful movements so that they instinctively recognize in him no mere object for their maw, no mere source of food, but an object worthy to be heard and seen, before they are able to devote their attention to his moralizing sentences. (iii. 103.)

It requires the live public performance of poetry to transform these savage beasts into neo-Kantians who, on an aesthetic level, respond with 'disinterested pleasure' to the sight of a beautiful human being.

As a result of their reproducibility, the arts, according to Wagner, have become what he describes sweepingly, and dismissively, as 'literature'. Literature is a form of art made possible by printing and marketing. 'We have no poetry, but only a poetic literature', he writes in the above-mentioned letter to Liszt. Like the generic description of

[3] August Wilhelm Schlegel, *Über Literatur, Kunst und Geist des Zeitalters: Eine Auswahl aus den kritischen Schriften*, ed. Franz Finke (Stuttgart, 1964), 79–80.

[4] Walter Benjamin, 'Das Kunstwerk im Zeitalter seiner technischen Reproduzierbarkeit', in *Illuminationen: Ausgewählte Schriften*, ed. Siegfried Unseld (Frankfurt, 1961), 171–4; translated into English by Harry Zohn as 'The Work of Art in the Age of Mechanical Reproduction', in *Illuminations* (London, 1973), 240–1.

'opera', 'literature' is all but synonymous with 'merchandise' here: 'through the medium of the book trade it is disseminated on the widest scale and converted into money'. It is in this sense that Wagner can speak of 'literary music' and describe even the visual arts as literature, since 'art-dealers' distribute works of visual art 'among the general public' in the form of 'copperplate engravings and lithographs'. None the less, the idea of an 'original', which 'consists of only *one* copy' and which cannot therefore be marketed in the same way as a reproduction, plays a far greater role in the visual arts than it does in poetry or music. The conviction 'that their artistic products consist of original copies which cannot be reproduced without sacrificing their essential artistic quality' (v. 6–7) presents visual artists with an almost insoluble problem of survival, since those artists who do not sell their works in the form of mass-produced articles are bound to lose their means of existence with the increasing decline in royal patronage. (It was partly to help visual artists overcome this economic problem that Liszt initiated the Goethe Foundation, a critical appraisal of which forms the burden of Wagner's open letter to him.)

Wagner's attempt to rid the work of art once and for all of its mercantile character meant investing it with the uniqueness of an original work of fine art. 'Even the most perfect reproduction of a work of art is lacking in one element', Walter Benjamin wrote, namely, 'its presence in time and space, its unique existence at the place where it happens to be'. This 'aura' of uniqueness, which Benjamin bases in cultic ritual,[5] is something that Wagner sought to re-create in the aesthetic ritual of a festival which drew a distinction between 'drama' and the commercially standardized repertory theatre.

It is in 'German Art and German Politics' of 1867–8 that Wagner gives most detailed expression to his social programme of 'exceptional, exempted performances'. The essay is as fanciful as it is ingenious in combining the erstwhile anarchist's revolutionary convictions with his later Utopian vision of a monarchical aristocracy. That republicanism and monarchism were by no means mutually exclusive even in the conceptual world of the Dresden revolutionary has long been known.[6] Wagner mentions his ideal of a 'monarchist republic' in his letter to

[5] Walter Benjamin, *Illuminationen* 151, 155; English trans., pp. 222, 225.

[6] See also Wagner's *Vaterlandsverein* speech, discussed below, and his letters to August von Lüttichau of 18 June and King Friedrich August II of Saxony of 21 June 1848. To describe the latter as an example of crass 'opportunism' (*Richard Wagner: Wie antisemitisch darf ein Künstler sein?* (Musikkonzepte 5; Munich, 1978), 78) betrays total ignorance of the historical background. On Wagner's idea of a 'monarchist republic', see e.g. Wermer Wolf's introduction to Richard Wagner, *Sämtliche Briefe* (Leipzig, 1970), ii. 36–40. The way in which Wagner's idea of a republican monarch is reflected in his conception of *Siegfrieds Tod* is discussed by Reinhold Brinkmann in 'Mythos—Geschichte—Natur: Zeitkonstellationen im *Ring*', in Stefan Kunze (ed.), *Richard Wagner: Von der Oper zum Musikdrama* (Berne and Munich, 1978), 61–77, esp. pp. 68–9.

Eduard Avenarius of 15 June 1848, and in so doing aligns himself with a respectable revolutionary tradition embodied in countless writings emanating from the circle of apologists of the French Revolution.[7] The 1867–8 treatise takes up many of the ideas of the 1848 Revolution, including the rejection of 'German restoration' and 'reaction', condemnation of the Carlsbad decrees (viii. 38–40), and the idea of a 'people's militia' (viii. 53). The final part of the essay envisages a kind of Utopia, not outside, but superior to, the existing national and social order. The state, the abolition of which Wagner had demanded and prophesied in *Opera and Drama*, is now acknowledged as the material basis of that ideal organization; it is like the foundering vessel from which Robinson Crusoe obtains the raw materials for his island existence, an existence which would not have been possible without the products of modern civilization.

The state, according to Wagner, 'represents absolute expediency', necessarily rejecting everything 'that cannot demonstrate an immediate utilitarian purpose'. That is why it is a mistake 'to attempt to make immediate demands on the state for the furtherance of art' (viii. 103). Perhaps Wagner was reminded here of Schiller's essay on aesthetics, 'Über die ästhetische Erziehung des Menschen', first published in 1795, in which the earlier writer had spoken of the 'absolute immunity' of art *vis-à-vis* a state that had 'caused the evil' it wanted to abolish. 'The political legislator can place a barrier around it, but he cannot hold sway within its confines.'[8] (In his 1879 essay, 'Shall We Hope?', Wagner called Schiller the 'first' writer to have 'recognized and described the modern constitution as . . . thoroughly inimical to art' (x. 121).)

Wagner stresses that the state as a 'utilitarian institution' is a product of late absolutism. He is thinking above all of the Prussian state as founded by Frederick the Great, a state whose aims and consequences were most sharply developed 'in the modern French imperial state'. 'Following the dissolution of the states of the Empire, all that remained was a patriarchal state based upon territorial possessions: it was the government's task to administer the country in such a way that it yielded the greatest possible returns as a mere inhabited territory.' (viii. 104.) In the Bavarian monarchy, Wagner continued, it was possible to discern a tendency to 'ennoble the aim of the state', a trend that revealed itself in a deeper understanding of the 'ideal meaning of the *monarchy*' (viii. 105). For Wagner, the ideality of the monarchy was the sole guarantee of

[7] See e.g. Gerhard Steiner (ed.), *Jakobinerschauspiel und Jakobinertheater* (Stuttgart, 1973), 14–15. Jacobin drama contains many similar ideas, as Brinkmann (see n. 6, above) has demonstrated in the case of the role allotted to the father of the gods in *Siegfrieds Tod*. (Cf. the idea of 'liberation from above' at the end of Beethoven's *Fidelio*.)

[8] Friedrich Schiller, *Sämtliche Werke*, ed. Gerhard Fricke and Herbert G. Göpfert, 3rd edn. (Munich, 1962), v. 593, 588.

theatrical reform, providing the only means by which art could fulfil its
proper destiny, a destiny which was to be found beyond the 'utilitarian
laws' (viii. 114) of modern society—in other words, beyond the principle
of the market-place; as long as art remained subject to that market
mentality, it was alienated from itself.

'The true meaning of the monarchy finds expression in that right of
pardon which is the Crown's prerogative.' The exceptional exercise of
clemency meant that the king was 'absolved of the law of expediency that
binds the entire state . . . As such, he represents the ideal of a negative
freedom which is all that the state recognizes and which lies at the heart
of all its aims.' (viii. 106–7.) Regarding the 'right of grace' as a
paradigmatic example of the monarch's role within and above the state,
Wagner extrapolates the idea of a social order at the head of society.
Orders are no longer conferred by mere royal grace; an 'actual
fellowship' will be created, 'exempt from the common law of utility by
dint of the pledge of joint self-sacrifice' (viii. 108–11).

But who is to belong to this 'exempted class' as the 'sphere of grace'?
Wagner believes that it should be made up, above all, of the aristocracy,
who would continue to lead a socially conscious existence in keeping
with their traditional role, while gratifying their restorational ambitions.
In this way, 'Germany would have retained a class now deemed
superfluous, nay, even harmful, and in doing so would derive an
immeasurably and actively beneficial force that was spiritual in
character'. Wagner reminds his reader that the aristocracy's traditional
ethos precluded them from gainful employment. Even as recently as the
eighteenth century the principle still held good that any member of the
aristocracy who was active in commercial circles forfeited his patent of
nobility. Conversely, those members of the bourgeoisie who were raised
to the nobility renounced their former financial activities. 'The rich
financier who no longer needs to carry on his business but who is
concerned only to enjoy his wealth and the leisure which that wealth has
made possible even sees in his patent of nobility the authorization that he
needs to give up his business.' (viii. 113.) The aristocracy's traditional
system of values frowned upon productive activity as a means of earning
capital. Their 'motto' was *otium cum dignitate*, or a career that 'aims at
heights of achievement which must remain remote from all purely
bourgeois aspirations and even from those of state bureaucracy'. (These
remarks of Wagner's, historically pertinent though they are, are truer, of
course, of the pre-revolutionary French aristocracy than they are of the
German nobility. In the Prussia of Frederick the Great, for example, it
was by no means regarded as socially disadvantageous for the hereditary
aristocracy to enter the civil service.) As a result of this reassessment of

his social role, the aristocrat 'enters of his own accord into that sphere which we have termed the actual sphere of royal grace' (viii. 113).

In the aristocracy's functionless role in the modern state (a functionlessness that follows from the abolition of privilege), Wagner sees the nobility's historical opportunity to continue a traditional way of life that is characterized by its 'exemption from the common law of utilitarianism'. The 'abandonment of its civic privileges' which this class has already been forced to countenance is, as it were, the 'sacrifice which inevitably attaches to every vow of ordination'; as such, it would secure the right of exemption. Its members would accede to this class by virtue of their wealth, and the fact that they were singled out by royal grace would 'encourage' them to use their material possessions for the higher, ideal aims of the community (viii. 114).

Together with the king, this class of persons exempted by royal grace would represent and foster the 'ideal', as opposed to the 'realistic', aim of the community: the 'beautiful' would be elevated over the 'utilitarian' (viii. 110, 118–19). The king and his new aristocracy would thus embody the 'aesthetic state' in the sense understood by Schiller, a state that was far above the world of constraint and utility. Or else they would form that 'class of people' which Schiller describes at the end of *Über naive und sentimentalische Dichtung* as ideally suited to an aesthetic education: it was a class 'which is active without working'; in other words, it acts without being gainfully employed,

combining within itself all the realities of life with the fewest possible of life's restraints, being borne along by the flood of events without falling prey to them. Only such a class as this can preserve that beautiful wholeness of human nature which is destroyed in the instant by every form of labour and which is uninterruptedly undermined by a life given over to work.[9]

Like Wagner, Schiller imagines a new kind of nobility: the aesthetic restoration of certain basic aristocratic values was, after all, an essential part of the social ideal of Weimar Classicism.[10] Wagner often reread and quoted from Schiller's essay, and must certainly have been conscious of the links between his own socio-Utopian ideas and those of his eighteenth-century predecessor.

It is instructive to compare Wagner's idea of an aristocratic élite with his 1848 Dresden address, *How Do Republican Aspirations Stand in Relation to the Monarchy?* Here he had his eye firmly fixed on ways of ensuring 'the extinction of every last glimmer of aristocratic privilege'.

[9] Ibid. 768.
[10] See Dieter Borchmeyer, *Höfische Gesellschaft und Französische Revolution bei Goethe: Adliges und bürgerliches Wertsystem im Urteil der Weimarer Klassik* (Kronberg, 1977).

Although these gentlemen of the nobility are no longer feudal lords who could enslave and torment us as their pleasure dictated, they should wipe out all offence and give up the final vestiges of a distinction which some sultry day might easily become a shirt of Nessus, burning them to the very bone, had they not cast it far away from them in time. (xii. 220.)

An integral part of 'humankind's emancipation' must be the 'emancipation of kingship' from the aristocracy and from a 'court which idly sustains the aristocracy'. In this way, the king would be directly dependent on the people and would thus become *the first and most genuine republican*' (xii. 225). By the time he came to write his treatise on 'German Art and German Politics', Wagner had rethought the function of the aristocracy, no longer seeing them as a barrier between the monarch and his people, and, instead of insisting upon their extinction, allowing them an aesthetic role. The ideal of a popular monarchy remained untouched. Together with the king, the newly exempted class would follow up the abolition of the commercial workaday theatre by superintending the rebirth of drama 'out of the spirit of the actual people' (viii. 65).

For the theatre to be perfect, it was necessary to 'reduce the number of theatrical performances', a reduction that ran counter, of course, to the principle of an uninterrupted turnover. The exemplary impact of drama that Wagner was striving to achieve could not be realized

in the daily concourse between theatre and public, and least of all on the basis of commercial interests . . . That example can be set only upon a soil that is wholly exempt from the needs and requirements of everyday theatrical practices, on a soil that can lie only in the sphere of what we have termed, in a broader sense, royal grace. A pre-condition here is that every aspect must be *out of the ordinary*, the greatest guarantee of which must, in the first instance, be its relative rarity . . . The commercialism that typifies all dealings between the theatre and its public would thus be wholly abolished: the spectator would no longer be led by a need for distraction following the day's exertions, rather would he be guided by the need for self-recollection following the distractions of an infrequent holiday; he would enter a special building remote from his usual haven of theatrical entertainment and opened only for the purpose of these extraordinary, exempt performances in order to forget, in the noblest sense, the toil of daily life for the sake of some far higher purpose. (viii. 122–3.)

In terms of both structure and organization, Wagner's theatre assumes the function of a classical temple and religious festival. Just as the temple, in accordance with its etymology as a 'place marked out', is an enclosed space set aside from the area used for agriculture and human settlement and regarded as the preserve of the gods, so the festival is a specific period of time outside those hours normally set aside for workaday concerns, a period, moreover, that involves no thought of financial exploitation.

In Wagner's projected festival theatre (here, of course, he was still thinking of Gottfried Semper's 1864 plans for a festival theatre in Munich), temple and cultic ritual are subsumed within a single aesthetic whole, hallowed space and time are rescued from the despotism of 'utilitarian law' and taken over by art, which, according to the 1880 treatise, 'Religion and Art', is uniquely able to 'salvage the kernel of religion' (x. 211). This tendency to treat art as a form of religion (and religion as a form of art) had gained increasing ground not only in aesthetics but also in theatre and museum architecture from the second half of the eighteenth century onwards, culminating in the festival concept that was ultimately realized in Bayreuth. Rarely, of course, has such a view of art, however problematical in terms not only of the idea behind it but, more especially, of its repercussions, been advanced with such socio-critical determination as we find in the case of Wagner: his opposition, after all, was directed against a society ruled by market principles, against time-wasting, and against the way in which even ostensibly 'priceless' goods increasingly assume the mass-produced character of marketable merchandise, merchandise always assessed according to its exchange value.

'German Art and German Politics' first saw the light of day in 1867 as a series of articles in the semi-official *Süddeutsche Presse*. However, the last two of the fifteen articles containing Wagner's vision of his theatre of the future remained unpublished until the 1870s, since the appearance of the thirteenth instalment was followed by an immediate ban on all further articles in the series—in spite of the king's initial enthusiasm for them. Doubtless Wagner's politico-cultural critique, which still contained clear signs of his revolutionary stance of 1848 alongside his remarkable vision of a new social élite, was too politically explosive for the articles' publication to be accepted without further ado in a state-run newspaper subsidized by the king himself. Wagner's politico-aesthetic tract could not be enjoyed as some vague future vision, since the wider Utopian view was repeatedly obscured by his detailed critique of the concrete contemporary situation.[11] This shifting perspective, in which an ideal overview that also takes in the present is combined with concrete proposals for improving the world (proposals that cannot be dismissed simply as insubstantial pipe-dreams), is characteristic of all Wagner's plans for reform. Here, indeed, is one of the principal reasons why his contemporaries found them uniquely unsettling.

[11] Wagner later attempted to interest various politicians in this series of articles. He even sent a copy to Bismarck, which, considering their anti-Prussian sentiments, showed a certain presumption on his part. Much to Wagner's astonishment, they aroused greater interest from the ultramontanist member of parliament Ludwig Windthorst, who in 1877 even entered into discussion with Wagner on the subject (the complete text had appeared in the meantime in Wagner's *Gesammelte Schriften*). See *CT*, 2 July 1877.

# 2

# A Theatre in the Provinces:
## Wagner's Plans for Reform and the 'German Spirit'

> But whenever a public state has successfully come into being
> through political zeal and good fortune, bringing satisfaction to all
> its members, it will not be long before the question is asked as how
> best to set up a popular festival which will fix the decisive moments
> of that success in an artistically appropriate manner and re-create
> what has taken place, allowing those events to live again in beautiful
> tranquillity, freed from the burden of privation and care.
>
> Gottfried Keller, 'Am Mythenstein'.

'In Germany it is really only the "provinces", certainly not the large
cities, which have produced anything', Wagner wrote in 1878 in his
introduction to the first number of the *Bayreuther Blätter* (x. 22). As early
as 1840, in his essay 'On German Music', he had already tried to explain
to the French readers of that article that, in a certain sense, 'all that is
peculiarly German . . . always remains provincial'. The composer who
'performed his works in Berlin would, for that very reason, remain
completely unknown in Vienna or Munich' (i. 153). (That this was no
exaggeration would be seen from the reception accorded to *Rienzi*
during the 1840s: the work's spectacular success was limited, in fact, to
Dresden.)

In other words, the works of German composers always remained
'provincial products', at least as long as their reputation abroad failed 'to
make an impact on Germany as a whole'. Germany's 'political structure'
made it especially difficult for opera composers to reach a wider
audience. Here we find Wagner harping on an old theme, namely, the
problems caused by Germany's fragmentation into thirty-nine
particularist states, and the 'lack of centralization' which meant that 'no
great work of national significance in music' would ever appear in
Germany. But, of course, he also saw a certain advantage in the
thoroughly 'provincial' character of German music:

The lack of centralization . . . is nevertheless also the reason why music among
Germans has always preserved its character of inwardness and truth. Precisely
because there is no great court which gathers to itself all Germany's artistic
resources in order to harness them to the pursuit of a single attainable goal —
precisely for this reason there are artists in every province who practise their

beloved art independently. The consequence of this is the diffusion of music all over the country, even to the most unlikely places, including the humblest cottages. (i. 153.)

Paradoxically, it seemed to be precisely this provinciality and the resultant 'inwardness' of German music that explained its universal significance. German music had, so to speak, transcended the nation and forged a link between the provinces and the greater world outside.

In Wagner's view, the paradigmatic example of a culture that was both provincial and universal was the Weimar Classicism of Goethe and Schiller, the 'Weimar wonder', as he himself called it (viii. 38). Goethe, too, had found the situation as paradoxical as it was symbolical, pointing out how Weimar had been 'chosen' in spite of, or because of, its smallness and politically lightweight character: 'Oh Weimar! thine was an especial fate: | Like Bethlehem in Judah, small and great!' ('Auf Miedings Tod', 1782.)[1] Provinciality and cosmopolitanism coincided here. (The reader will recall in this context Goethe's idea of 'world literature'.) The twinning of these two extremes has often been seen as the distinguishing mark of German artists in general. According to Thomas Mann's 1945 essay, *Deutschland und die Deutschen*, the link between 'cosmopolitanism and provincialism' was one of the salient features of the 'German character'.[2] With its juxtaposition of 'the provincialism of Kaisersaschern' and its 'outspoken cosmopolitanism of outlook' (to quote from chapter 20 of *Doktor Faustus*), the 'life of the German musician Adrian Leverkühn' seemed to Mann to encapsulate the character of every German musician. The extent to which such a combination of characteristics typifies Mann's own persona as a writer is clear from the address which he delivered in 1926 in homage to his home town of Lübeck, 'Lübeck als geistige Lebensform'.

In the fifteenth book of *Dichtung und Wahrheit* (1814) Goethe appealed to Justus Möser's *Patriotische Phantasien* of 1774–8 in support of his claim that the 'mass of small states' in Germany was not only evidence of 'fragmentation, anarchy, and impotence', but that, as such, it was 'highly desirable for the piecemeal spread of culture, meeting, as it does, the needs that arise from the geographical situation and particular nature of the individual provinces'.[3] He expressed a similar idea in conversation with Eckermann on 23 October 1828, insisting that the 'unity of Germany' was desirable from the standpoint of foreign policy, currency, trade, transport, and so on, but refusing to countenance the notion of a centralized unified state, 'with a single royal seat' fostering a culture that was supraregional. Of course, Goethe was

[1] See Dieter Borchmeyer, *Die Weimarer Klassik* (Königstein, 1980), 26 ff.
[2] Thomas Mann, *Gesammelte Werke*, 2nd edn. (Frankfurt, 1974), xi. 1129.
[3] *Goethes Werke*, ed. Erich Trunz (Hamburg, 1959), x. 52.

not blind to the disadvantages that would follow from the absence of a single 'centre of social culture'. A country lacking in 'general national culture', he wrote in his 1795 essay *Literarischer Sansculottismus*, was unlikely to produce any 'classical works'.[4]

This ambivalent attitude to German particularism, at least as it affected art, recurs in Wagner's writings, where similar terminology is used. For the historical and political reasons outlined above, he considers theatrical and cultural reform to be feasible only if undertaken at a provincial level. Indeed, he and Liszt almost had the opportunity to re-create the 'Weimar wonder' in the town of Weimar itself. Even if this hope was finally dashed, Weimar—the realization of a universal art in a provincial setting, safeguarded and encouraged by a princely patron who would ensure its material and intellectual independence—remained a cultural, political, and aesthetic ideal, providing him with a model for the Bayreuth Festival. When Liszt was appointed 'Grand Ducal Director of Music Extraordinary' in Weimar in 1842 (an appointment he did not take up full-time until 1848), he attempted to revive the great literary tradition that had been fostered under Grand Duke Carl August. This is clear not only from the symphonic poems and choral compositions that he wrote to words by Goethe and Schiller to mark their centenary celebrations in 1849 and 1859, but also from the Goethe Foundation that he planned to set up in 1850. This latter was intended to re-establish Weimar as a metropolis of art, to restore its reputation as a 'latter-day Athens', and to ensure not only that it exercised 'a centralizing influence in the field of literature and art', but that it safeguarded 'the character of German unity'.[5] (The proposed Goethe Foundation was the subject of Wagner's letter of 1851, discussed in the previous chapter, in which the composer considered the question of reform from a theoretical standpoint.)

Liszt's years in Weimar have been described as the town's Silver Age. 'There was a time', he wrote in valedictory mood in his testament of 14 September 1860, 'when I dreamt of a new period of art for Weimar, an age like that of Carl August, of which Wagner and I would have been the leaders, just as Goethe and Schiller were then'.[6] Ten years previously Liszt had conducted the first performance of the 'Romantic opera' *Lohengrin* in Weimar, an event which prompted Gérard de Nerval to comment that 'it is entirely in accord with the endeavours of the present Grand Duke to preserve that legacy of artistic outlook which has enabled Weimar to earn the name of "the Athens of Germany"'.[7] And

    [4] *Goethes Werke* xii. 240–1.
    [5] Herbert Greiner-Mai *et al.* (eds.), *Weimar im Urteil der Welt* (Berlin and Weimar, 1977), 233 (Liszt's letter to Grand Duke Carl Alexander of 3 February 1860).
    [6] Ibid. 236.                                                    [7] Ibid. 208.

Wagner himself wrote to Liszt from Zurich on 24 December 1850: 'Truly, dear friend, you have turned this little town of Weimar into a real source of fame for me.' During his years in exile Wagner not only received artistic encouragement from Weimar, he was also assisted financially, and Grand Duke Carl Alexander even lent his personal weight to Wagner's appeal for clemency. (The Grand Duke was also among the visitors who attended the first Bayreuth Festival in 1876.) Goethe's town narrowly missed becoming Wagner's, too.

At almost every stage of his artistic career Wagner drew up plans for theatrical reform, imposing a far-reaching vision of the future on the provincial conditions under which he found himself working. Wagner the starry-eyed idealist was never at a loss for systematized proposals, the very detail of which was clearly intended to avert the suspicion that his vision was merely Utopian. That his aims were not just visionary but also practical and responsive to present conditions is clear from the ultimate success of his Bayreuth venture, a success that met with astonished disbelief on the part of many contemporaries, who had regarded Wagner the theorist as a fantastical dreamer but who were now obliged to rank Bayreuth among the most striking achievements in the whole history of art. In his *Report to His Majesty King Ludwig II of Bavaria on a German School of Music to be Established in Munich*, presented in 1865, Wagner described the unifying aim that lay behind his various plans for reform: 'Moreover, at the various places where I have worked or stayed for any length of time, I have repeatedly striven to point out the road to reform with special reference to local conditions, indeed, with detailed regard to those said conditions, showing by practical suggestions how they might best be developed for the good of art.' (viii. 175.)

Wagner then goes on to mention his 'Plan for the Organization of a German National Theatre for the Kingdom of Saxony' (1848), the essay *A Theatre in Zurich* (1851), the open letter to Franz Liszt referred to above, 'On the Goethe Foundation', his plans for 'The Vienna Court Opera House' (1863), and, finally, and with particular satisfaction, his *Preface to the Publication of the Poem of the Stage Festival, 'Der Ring des Nibelungen'* (1862), which had ended with an invitation to some unknown German prince to underwrite the festival theatre in which he was planning to stage the tetralogy. The question with which he concluded that preface: 'Will this prince be found?' (vi. 281), was clearly intended to be a rhetorical one, and evidently expected a resigned 'No' by way of an answer. The response it received from Ludwig II was one for which Wagner had not dared to hope.

From a cultural and historical point of view, the most interesting of Wagner's reform projects was undoubtedly his plan for *A Theatre in*

*Zurich*, not least because it was the only one of his schemes that could
be based on an existing popular theatrical tradition. In other words, the
'popular spirit' from which, according to Wagner, all living drama
derives did not first have to be manufactured by artificial means. The
Zurich treatise has a remarkable counterpart in Gottfried Keller's 1861
essay, 'Am Mythenstein', which makes explicit reference to Wagner.
(Keller had been a member of Wagner's circle of friends during the
latter's years of exile in Zurich.) Inspired by the Schiller celebrations at
the Mythenstein on Lake Lucerne, Keller advances the idea for what
Adolf Muschg has termed a 'socially orientated total art-work'.[8] As such,
the idea has unmistakable parallels with Wagner's *Art-Work of the Future*
of 1849,[9] an essay with which Keller was as familiar as he was with
*A Theatre in Zurich*. In a letter to Wilhelm Baumgartner of September 1851 Keller declared himself in 'total agreement' with the ideas
contained in *A Theatre in Zurich*, adding that he was 'delighted' to find
his own hopes and ideas confirmed in this way. He had reservations only
about 'the ultimate consequences of Wagner's ideas about the art of the
future', namely, the belief that the dramatic work of total art (a goal
which Keller himself was hoping to achieve) would mean the definitive
disappearance of all the separate arts as individual genres.[10] If Keller
wholeheartedly approved of Wagner's Zurich project, while not
accepting his more general vision of the theatre to come, it was because
Wagner started out from those concrete, provincial, popular traditions
which, according to Keller, were part of the essential nature of myth.[11]
For Wagner, by contrast, *Volk* and myth were normally merged in a
timeless vacuum, remaining no more than an ideological, aesthetic
construct.

Whereas Wagner's aesthetic world was initially divorced from
audience reality, preferring to use the stage as a means of creating its
own aesthetically orientated public, Keller hoped that his own dramatic
festival would spring directly from the community and from the latter's
republican spirit. *Volk* and work of art must be as one; reality, the whole
civic world would, so to speak, themselves become the total work of art.
Keller's Mythenstein vision forms a theoretical counterpart to his
colourful account of a performance of *Wilhelm Tell* in *Der grüne Heinrich*,
in which not only the local citizens but the whole town and countryside,
including buildings, open spaces, rivers, meadows, and roads, all had a

    [8] Adolf Muschg, *Gottfried Keller* (Munich, 1977), 281.
    [9] See Johann Ulrich Saxer, *Gottfried Kellers Bemühungen um das Theater* (Winterthur, 1957). The
final chapter, 'Das Gesamtkunstwerk', contains a comparative survey of the theatrical Utopias of
Wagner and Keller.
    [10] Gottfried Keller, *Sämtliche Werke und ausgewählte Briefe*, ed. Clemens Heselhaus (Munich,
1958), iii. 1123.
    [11] See Saxer, *Kellers Bemühungen*, p. 170.

part to play. The open-air, popular theatre that is evoked here in epic form becomes a monumental political and aesthetic vision in his essay on the Mythenstein. Under the impression of the gymnastics displays, choral festivals, and shooting-matches in which the communal democratic spirit expressed itself at this time in Switzerland, Keller saw the 1859 Schiller celebrations (to quote Adolf Muschg) as

the nucleus of a festival on a national scale, a festival sustained by amateur choirs and drama groups and carried to every corner of the country, allowing the townsfolk to prepare for the festive element in their own existence; a festival that involves the gradual transformation of the Schillerian setting of the Rütli to a national fairground where working clothes and holiday clothes will be cut from a single cloth. It will be a total art-work, the bold transformation of a Romantic vision into republican practice, no doubt akin to Wagner's 'music of the future', yet not to be confused with it.

Anyone seeking a valid counterpart to this vision in Wagner's works will find it less in his theoretical writings than in the final scene of *Die Meistersinger*, a scene inspired not so much by Nuremberg customs as by Swiss choral festivals and, above all, by Zurich's *Sechseläuten*, a spring festival celebrated on the third Monday in April that includes a traditional procession of local guilds. It is here in *Die Meistersinger* that the festival first assumes the form of a spontaneous and popular *Gesamtkunstwerk*, integrating within itself that musical and poetical creation of the individual genius which is embodied in Walther's Prize Song. There is no doubt that the festival meadow scene foreshadows Wagner's ideal aesthetic goal. His own idea for a festival is, of course, far removed from this ideal goal, since it remains circumscribed by its practical realization in the historical here and now. Given a public that was hostile to art, the ideal festival could be re-created only synthetically on stage; it was no longer the festival that produced the drama, but the drama that produced the festival. That is why an imaginary barrier was used to divide off the stage from the reality shrouded in the darkness of the auditorium. The stage was not erected in the middle of the audience, as it was in the older popular or fairground theatre.

The following chapter will show how, in his writings, Wagner also espoused the idea of an alternative form of theatre, an alternative to which far too little attention has been paid hitherto. Although he refused to turn it into practical reality, it clearly prefigures his dramatic art of the future, involving a type of acting derived directly from the popular art of mimic improvisation. There is as yet no dividing line between the stage and the audience, or perhaps it would be truer to say that that barrier has now been broken down. An assessment of Wagner which fails to take account of this contradictory element in his concept of the theatre is bound to do him less than total justice.

Wagner's project for *A Theatre in Zurich* takes as its starting-point the composer's critique of the contemporary theatre in general and of 'grand opera' in particular. He draws a contrast between 'theatrical Paris' as 'the only real producer of modern dramatic literature' (v. 25), and a theatre which, unlike the existing institution in Zurich, would take account of popular local traditions. The dramatic art that was rooted in those traditions would effectively undermine the predominance of modern 'opera', which, for Wagner, was nothing but a form of rank vegetation flourishing amidst the decaying splendours of metropolitan, and especially French, civilization. It is at this point in his argument that Wagner finds himself in agreement with Keller. Drawing in part on Wagnerian terminology, Keller, like Wagner, would later reject the contemporary repertory theatre that could 'offer the popular theatre of the future nothing but discarded clothes, a fundamentally false style of declamation, and various other bad habits'. The following passage could just as easily have come from one of Wagner's essays, so close is it to the central ideas in his theory concerning the theatre:

A theatre which year in, year out is open seven days a week will lack all sense of ceremony, its festive purport will sink to the point where it is merely a means of killing time. Excessive enjoyment has created a particular type of theatre audience, an audience which as much resembles the common people as a cat resembles a lion, and which, while filled with silent disgust, hungrily devours the daily diet that is placed before it with indecent and indelicate haste.[12]

Wagner, too, seeks to revolutionize the theatre in the spirit of the same national and local institutions as those on which Keller had pinned his hopes. He points to public 'gymnastics competitions', to the 'widespread popularity of choral societies', and, above all, to the 'age-old popular tradition, handed down from father to son', of presenting plays at town and country festivals:

whatever the occasion for a public festival, be it cheerful or more solemn, there is a spontaneous desire . . . to organize processions in characteristic costumes: representations of scenes from the life of the people or from history, performed with great fidelity and natural eloquence, form the principal fare at these pageants. This movement in the direction of drama in popular culture finds even more decisive expression in those rural communities where plays are performed not only by the young but also by actors of maturer years. (v. 47.)

It is at this point, Wagner emphasizes, that the popular tradition coincides with drama as an art-form, the most graphic example of which is the rustic performance of Schiller's *Wilhelm Tell*, recounted in Keller's *Der grüne Heinrich*.

---

[12] Keller, *Sämtliche Werke*, iii. 984.

A theatre that was institutionally anchored in local traditions would cease to be 'an industrial organization which, in order to increase its earnings, offers its goods for sale as frequently and forcefully as possible; perhaps the theatre would then constitute the highest and most common point of social contact in public exposure to art' (v. 49). Were this ideal to be realized, Wagner even hoped that 'actors would gradually cease to be regarded as a separate caste cut off from our civic lives, rather would they be assimilated into an artistic community involving more or less the whole of civic society, according to the abilities and inclinations of its individual members'. The disappearance of actors as a class would mean an end to the distinction between 'art' and 'life'. 'We are closer than we think to this social humanizing of art or this artistic nurturing of society'; as 'proof of this claim', Wagner adduces the Swiss gymnastics displays, choral festivals, and drama festivals mentioned above (v. 46–7). There is no doubt that these thoughts were the direct inspiration behind Keller's idea for a republican festival; indeed, it could be claimed with some justice that Wagner anticipated Keller in every essential detail.

Among the various theatrical projects which Wagner drew up after the 1848 Revolution, the Zurich plan, seen simply as a conceptual construct, is by far the most convincing, since Wagner found a community here that, thanks to its manageable dimensions (and, one might add, thanks to its *polis*-like structure[13]) but not least because of the republican spirit that so often manifested itself in overtly theatrical form during these years, seemed to offer the most fertile ground for the survival of a plan for reform that was coloured by the experience of the Revolution. Certainly, Wagner's other plans for Dresden, Vienna, and, later, for Munich foundered on their conceptual inconsistencies and scarcely credible concessions. Basically, his idea for theatrical reform could be realized only in the provinces: it would inevitably have run into difficulties in the routine world of those metropolitan theatres that depended for their survival on so many commercial and social factors.

Wagner was no doubt constantly aware of this. Indeed, there could be no clearer demonstration of the fact than his 1862 preface to the poem of the *Ring*, in which the rural and social ambiance of the later Bayreuth Festival is prefigured with astonishing prescience; the passage in question almost reads like a description of Bayreuth and its surroundings (vi. 276–7), in spite of the fact that these lines were written long before he had the idea of turning the small Franconian town into the home of his dramatic ideal. How remarkable, moreover, that the very name of Bayreuth reminded Wagner of Switzerland! In his 1873 essay, *The Stage Festival Theatre in Bayreuth*, he points out the etymological link

---

[13] As we shall see below (pp. 59–72), the Greek model was the inspiration behind all of Wagner's plans to re-educate modern audiences.

between 'Reuth' (a clearing or a 'place reclaimed from the wilderness and made inhabitable') and the Rütli in 'ancient Switzerland', an etymology intended 'to invest the name of Bayreuth with a yet more beautiful and venerable significance' (ix. 332). As Keller's essay 'Am Mythenstein' makes clear, the Schillerian associations of the Rütli and its surrounding area played a significant symbolic role during the very period that Wagner was exiled in Zurich, encouraging a new republican and national awareness on the part of the Swiss confederates.

In his preface to the 1862 edition of the *Ring* poem Wagner specifies inner and outer distance from the standard repertory theatre as one of the conditions required to perform his tetralogy. The kind of remoteness he had in mind would be guaranteed, he went on, in one of the 'smaller towns in Germany'. Here an 'exceptional' audience could be brought together that would have nothing to do with 'actual metropolitan theatre audiences and their habits'. 'Here a temporary theatre would be run up, as simple as possible, perhaps built just of wood and calculated only in terms of the artistic suitability of its interior.' (vi. 273.) Wagner had already conceived his plan for a provisional theatre more than ten years earlier, when, in November 1851, he had written to Theodor Uhlig: 'The coming Revolution must necessarily put an end to this whole *theatrical business* of ours . . . I shall run up a theatre on the Rhine and send out invitations to a great dramatic festival: after a year's preparations I shall then perform my entire work within the space of four days.'[14]

Even at a somewhat later date, in his speech to mark the foundation-stone-laying ceremony in Bayreuth, and in the essay written to commemorate that event in 1873, Wagner was still speaking of a 'temporary theatre' that might remind his visitors of those 'festival halls run up in wood' which were 'sometimes erected in German towns for choral meetings and similar co-operative festivals and then taken down again immediately after the festival is over' (ix. 326). Being 'undecorated' (ix. 326), this theatre would have nothing to do with ostentation and social prestige, although Wagner did not exclude the possibility that it might be encased in a 'monumental superstructure' (ix. 328) at some point in the Utopian future when, 'through the spirit of music', architecture—associated with Amphion's lyre in the 'myth of urban development'—had been invested with a 'new-found significance'. With the emergence of an original 'German architectural style' to supersede the present syncretic approach, a wholly new 'architectonic ornamentalism' could then be allowed to develop, putting a definitive

---

[14] Richard Wagner, *Sämtliche Briefe*, ed. Gertrud Strobel and Werner Wolf (Leipzig, 1979), iv. 176; English translation from *Selected Letters of Richard Wagner*, ed. Stewart Spencer and Barry Millington (London, 1987), 234.

end to 'traditional ornaments'. But there was, he conceded, still 'a long way to go' before that would come about (ix. 342–3).

Wagner saw his 'temporary theatre' as a symbol of German history, inasmuch as 'every outward manifestation of the German character has for centuries been provisional' (ix. 329). He compares the German spirit with the God of the Old Testament, who for centuries lived in a tent until a temple was erected for him. The early 1870s, or *Gründerjahre*, were marked by a proliferation of monumentally ostentatious buildings run up by the *nouveaux riches*: it was certainly not for reasons of mere economy that Wagner now insisted that a theatre should have 'all the naïve simplicity of a makeshift structure' (ix. 343), and that it should dispense with every claim to ostentation. As such, it differs from that massive structure which was to prove the gods' undoing in the *Ring* (a work that was soon to be performed on the boards of this very theatre). The architectural style of the *Gründerjahre* is embodied not by Wagner's festival theatre but by Wotan's proud necropolis. How salutary Wagner found the contrast between what he regarded as the classical simplicity of the Bayreuth Festspielhaus and the grand official gestures of the Kaiserreich is clear from a remark recorded by Cosima Wagner on 29 July 1879. On seeing photographs of the golden wedding celebrations of the Emperor Wilhelm and Empress Augusta, he turned away in consternation and displeasure, his thoughts filled instead with his festival theatre: 'In contrast, our theatre in its simple grandeur!' (*CT*, 29 June 1879.)

Nor was Wagner willing to have his Bayreuth enterprise described as a 'national theatre'. 'Where is the "nation" that built this theatre for itself?' (ix. 328), he asked rhetorically, no doubt recalling the final section of Lessing's *Hamburgische Dramaturgie*, 'On the Well-Meaning Idea to Create a National Theatre for the Germans when We Germans Are not yet a Nation!' But to what extent was Wagner justified in using quotation marks to refer to the concept of a German 'nation' a year after the Second Reich had been founded? Had this question ever been put to him, he could have replied by quoting the very next sentence in Lessing's *Dramaturgie*: 'I am not speaking of the political constitution but merely of the moral character of the nation. One might almost say that its character consists in not wanting to have a character of its own. We are still the sworn imitators of all that is foreign, still the submissive admirers of the French whom we cannot admire enough.'[15] Indeed, the argument that Wagner was to develop in his speech to mark the foundation-stone-laying ceremony in Bayreuth tends in very much the same direction.

---

[15] *Lessings Werke*, ed. Georg Witkowski (Leipzig and Vienna, n.d.), v. 378.

In the same year that he wrote his essay on the Festspielhaus Wagner commented to Edouard Schuré: 'I am not to be counted among the ranks of the present-day patriots, for what a person can suffer under present conditions I am already suffering—I am, as it were, nailed on the cross of the German ideal.' (*CT*, 4 September 1873.) There is no denying, of course, that the Franco-Prussian War and the founding of the Second Reich filled Wagner for a time with a real chauvinist frenzy, encouraging him to forget his earlier federalist, anti-Prussian beliefs. He needed 'an emperor for the art of the future', he told Cosima on 12 December 1870, and asked her to write to Countess Bismarck to that effect. The poem of the *Ring*, with which he had wanted 'to make clear to the men of the Revolution the *meaning* of that Revolution, in its noblest sense',[16] was now intended to be viewed, so to speak, as the aesthetic counterpart of the German Kaiserreich. It was no accident, Cosima told Wagner on 20 June 1871, 'that his *Nibelungen* [i.e., the completion of the work] coincided with Germany's victories'. Her *Diaries* are littered with similar remarks.[17] (Wagner himself expressed himself much more cautiously.) What Cosima felt as wholly positive was to be repeated by Nietzsche in *Der Fall Wagner* (1888), but this time with critical intent: 'It is full of profound significance that the arrival of Wagner coincides in time with the arrival of the *"Reich"*.'[18]

By the mid-1870s at the latest it had already become clear to Wagner that his faith in the Reich was ill-founded. Time and again in conversation with Cosima he expressed his sense of shame at having committed this historical error. 'Our conversation leads him to his feelings of shame *vis-à-vis* C. Frantz and Schuré, both of whom saw— the one through knowledge, the other by instinct—what would become of the German Reich under Prussian leadership.' (*CT*, 7 October 1878.) The political journalist Constantin Frantz (1817–91) exerted a profound influence on Wagner's political thinking from the 1860s onwards. Even before 1870 the latter had already assimilated Frantz's federalist ideas and made them largely his own, and it was only when Frantz decisively rejected Prussian *kleindeutsch*[19] sovereignty, while remaining true to his basic self, that Wagner turned his back on him. Later, the composer came to see the error of his ways, and in 1878 he even placed the *Bayreuther Blätter* at Frantz's disposal, offering him an additional forum for his caustic critique of Bismarck. 'Few will have foreseen the speed with

---

[16] Wagner, *Sämtliche Briefe*, iv. 176. These lines were written in November 1851, when Wagner believed that it was only a matter of time before the Revolution broke out all over Europe.

[17] See *CT*, 12 July 1871 and 5 Jan. 1873.

[18] Friedrich Nietzsche, *Sämtliche Werke: Kritische Studienausgabe in 15 Bänden*, ed. Giorgio Colli and Mazzino Montinari (Munich, 1980), vi. 39; translated into English by Walter Kaufmann as 'The Case of Wagner', in *Basic Writings of Nietzsche* (New York, 1968), 636.

[19] The term *kleindeutsch* was used in the 19th century to denote the policy of unifying Germany to the exclusion of Austria.

which the barren concept of the Prussian state would be imposed upon us as the wisdom of the German Reich', Wagner wrote to Ludwig II on 10 February 1878, the same year in which he told Cosima: 'All ideas of Germany are just a dream' (*CT*, 10 November 1878). 'I expect nothing more from Germany', he confessed to her on 9 June 1880. Remarks like these recur with leitmotivic regularity in his conversations with Cosima during the final years of his life.

That the German spirit could find unsullied expression only outside the political sphere, in art, was a fundamental conviction to which Wagner returned with increasing fervour following his disillusionment with Bismarck's Reich in the 1870s. And that art, he argued, flourished best in the provinces. In 'German Art and German Politics' he quoted Schiller's 1803 poem, 'Die deutsche Muse', adding a detailed historical gloss (viii. 33):

> Kein Augustisch Alter blühte,
> Keines Medicäers Güte
>  Lächelte der deutschen Kunst,
> Sie ward nicht gepflegt vom Ruhme,
> Sie entfaltete die Blume
>  Nicht am Strahl der Fürstengunst.

> No blossoming Augustan Age,
> No Medicean patronage
>  On German art has ever smiled.
> Fame and glory ne'er she knew,
> Though fair as any flower that grew,
>  By princely grace was ne'er beguiled.

And in his diary jottings of 1865, published in 1878 under the title 'What is German?', we read: 'Only with the loss of external political power, i.e. with the abandoned significance of the Holy Roman Empire, whose demise we lament today as the decline of German glory: only now does the essential German character really begin to develop.' (x. 39.) There is no doubt that these lines recall the ending of *Die Meistersinger*: 'zerging' in Dunst | das heil'ge röm'sche Reich, | uns bliebe gleich | die heil'ge deutsche Kunst!' (Though should depart | the might of holy Rome, | no harm will come | to holy German art!) (vii. 271.) In his 1933 public lecture, *Die Leiden und Größe Richard Wagners*, Thomas Mann was certainly guilty of glossing over these lines when he insisted that they prove only 'how totally intellectual and apolitical Wagner's nationalism was: for they speak of a downright anarchic indifference to political structures, as long as German intellectual and spiritual values— "German Art"—are preserved intact'.[20]

---

[20] Thomas Mann, *Wagner und unsere Zeit*, ed. Erika Mann (Frankfurt, 1963), 113–14; translated into English by Allan Blunden as 'The Sorrows and Grandeur of Richard Wagner', in *Pro and contra Wagner* (London, 1985), 141. See also Reinhold Brinkmann, 'Über das kern-und Schlußwort

Earlier writers on Wagner appear not to have noticed that there is a striking parallel to the lines just quoted in Schiller's fragmentary poem, *Deutsche Größe*, written in 1797:[21] 'The Germans have established their own independent worth, quite apart from any political worth, and even if the Holy Roman Empire were to vanish into dust, German dignity would still remain unchallenged.'[22] Schiller's poetic fragment, although as yet unknown to Wagner, anticipates a number of the latter's essential ideas. This is no accident, since Wagner's idea of what is 'German' is clearly inspired by other remarks of Schiller's. Suffice it to mention here the *Xenien*, a collection of satirical epigrams written by Goethe and Schiller, and including *Deutscher Nationalcharakter* ('To form yourselves into a nation, you Germans, is a vain hope; | Develop, conversely, more freely as humans: this you can do') and *Das deutsche Reich* ('Germany? where does it lie? I can find no such country. | Where erudition begins, there must politics end').

In the fragment in question Schiller describes 'German dignity' as 'moral greatness, indwelling in the culture and character of that nation which is independent of its political destinies . . . While the political empire totters, the intellectual empire has grown ever securer and more perfect.' It is not therefore 'Germany's greatness | To conquer with the sword', but 'To enter into the spirit world' and win the 'freedom that comes from reason' for all the nations of the world. What we find Schiller advancing here is a kind of enlightened chiliastic national myth. The German, he writes, is

singled out by the world spirit and invited to work on the eternal task of educating mankind during the battle of our age and to retain what time brings with it. That is why he has hitherto adopted foreign ideas and retained them for himself. He has preserved all the precious things that have been produced by other ages and other nations, all that has come into being and disappeared with the passage of time, they are safe in his hands, the treasures of centuries.[23]

These lines remind one ineluctably of Hegel's idea of 'absolute knowledge', in which all previous forms of consciousness are subsumed and 'superseded'. But whereas, for Hegel, the goal of intellectual history has already been attained, Schiller locates absolute knowledge in a final, future phase of history. The 'day of the German' is 'the harvest-gathering of all time, when the circle of time is complete'.[24] In other

der *Meistersinger*', in Klaus Schulz (ed.), *Programmheft zur Neuinszenierung der 'Meistersinger' im Münchener Nationaltheater* (Munich, 1979), 82–91. The lines in question are quoted here in their (changing) context. According to Brinkmann, Thomas Mann's explanation is an optimistic over-interpretation.

[21] See Borchmeyer, *Die Weimarer Klassik*, p. 38.
[22] Friedrich Schiller, *Sämtliche Werke*, ed. Gerhard Fricke and Herbert G. Göpfert, 3rd edn. (Munich, 1962), i. 473.          [23] Ibid. 473–8.          [24] Ibid. 477.

words, the Germans are central to Schiller's eschatology, their language will be spoken throughout the world at the end of time, a Pentecostal language of the mind, so to speak, which will be intelligible to all mankind and which will replace the existing Babylonian confusion of tongues. In his 1860 essay, *'Zukunftsmusik'*, for example, where he makes explicit reference to the supranational aspirations of Goethe and Schiller, Wagner even goes so far as to identify German music with that 'universally intelligible language that is accessible to every nation' (vii. 95): Germany is the new Utopia! 'They belong to the day before yesterday and the day after tomorrow—*as yet they have no today*', Nietzsche was to write of the Germans in discussing the Overture to *Die Meistersinger* in *Jenseits von Gut und Böse*.[25]

In a letter to Nietzsche of 23 October 1872 Wagner declared that his thoughts on the question of 'What is German?' had led him increasingly towards the view that 'Germanness' was a 'purely metaphysical concept', but 'certainly something that is unique in the history of the world, its only possible counterpart being Judaism'. The voice one hears here is almost that of Fitelberg in chapter 37 of Thomas Mann's *Doktor Faustus*. But what persuades Fitelberg to think in terms of an elective affinity between the Germans and the Jews in the context of world history[26] is the very reason for Wagner's anti-Semitism: for Wagner, two metaphysical concepts cannot coexist. It is clear from the ending of his essay on Beethoven, written in 1870, that what Mann calls 'universal Germanness',[27] in other words, the Messianic extension of nationalist thinking (even if expressly opposed to all political nationalism and militarism, as was the case with Schiller, for example), involves the risk of misuse. The 'German spirit', we read here, is 'called upon' to 'bring happiness' to the nations of the earth. Proof of this is Beethoven's unprecedented impact in France. 'Bringing happiness to the world' is now described quite openly as 'conquering the world', a conquest that has provided the intellectual background for what is now being achieved by the German armed forces, namely, the supersession of French civilization by German culture. 'There, where our weapons now force a passage, at the very hearth of "brazen fashion", *his* [Beethoven's] genius had already begun the noblest conquest.' The apotheosis of the German spirit is abruptly transformed into an apology for military force. (What had Schiller written in his poetic fragment, *Deutsche Größe*? 'It is not

---

[25] Nietzsche, *Sämtliche Werke*, v. 180; English trans. (Kaufmann, *Basic Writings of Nietzsche*), p. 364.

[26] Nahum Goldmann has written of this kind of elective affinity, especially as it relates to a belief in the metaphysical principle of election, in an astonishing article entitled 'Warum der Nazi-Schock nicht enden darf: Über die Schizophrenie und Wahlverwandtschaften zweier Völker', *Die Zeit*, 2 Feb. 1979, p. 16.

[27] Mann, *Gesammelte Werke*, xi. 1138.

Germany's greatness | To conquer with the sword'.) Of course, in the final sentence of his essay Wagner stresses that 'He who brings the world happiness may claim yet higher rank than he who conquers it' (ix. 125–6), but the damage has already been done.

Following his disillusionment with the German Reich, Wagner wanted nothing more to do with 'world conquest'. 'We Germans will never become a world power', he told Cosima on 18 January 1880; their task would be a different one, 'to spread culture by colonization'. Here the concept of 'Germanness' appears once more in its apolitical, purely spiritual guise, in the form which had evolved in the provinces. During the final years of his life the provinces had narrowed in scope for Wagner. Germanness became more and more a mere dream for him, a dream he felt he could rediscover only in the great manifestations of German poetry and music of earlier centuries. 'There are no Germans', he assured Cosima in these and similar words in countless conversations (*CT*, 3 March 1879). Just as his Rienzi had felt himself to be 'the last surviving Roman', so Wagner finally came to believe, in his blacker moments, that he alone stood for all that was German.

# 3

## The Fascination of Punch and Judy:
## Wagner and the Popular Theatre

> He orchestrates, makes Fidi-music, as he says. Fidi [Siegfried] with us at lunch. Afterward with the three girls to the fair; great delight in the Punch and Judy show, whose director distinguishes himself through his lively (Silesian) accent, his puppets through their energetic movements.
>
> *CT*, 14 October 1870.

One of Wagner's chief aesthetic dogmas was that every major type of theatre developed out of the *Volksgeist* or popular spirit. For him, the prototypical stage was a platform or structure erected in the midst of the *Volk* and surrounded by spectators on at least three sides. Readers familiar with the Bayreuth Festspielhaus, with its strict separation of stage and auditorium, will regard such a claim as far-fetched, if not downright perverse. In fact, there are as many passages in Wagner's writings to refute this claim as there are to support it. It cannot be denied that his thinking was made up of two fundamental, and incompatible, views of the theatre, which were, however, to influence one another.

It may be claimed, at the risk of over-generalization, that Wagner's theatrical ideal presupposed the interaction of stage and auditorium in the case of the spoken theatre, and their strict separation in that of the musical drama. The reason for this is that Wagner considered music, as a specifically modern art, to be the ideal counterpart of corrupt contemporary civilization, a civilization which drama, issuing from it, was intended to counteract on a formal level, too; during the great periods of spoken drama, by contrast, and especially at the time of its earliest phase among the ancient Greeks, plays were the product of a 'beautiful public world' (iii. 29) that was in perfect harmony with art, so that the stage did not need to be cut off from its audience. Of course, this does not explain away all the difficulties and contradictions that are raised by Wagner's theatrical aesthetic. For would not the barrier between the stage and the auditorium inevitably disappear once the whole community were 're-aestheticized' by the spirit of music and of festival drama? There are, in fact, various suggestions in Wagner's writings that this ideal might one day be realized as the ultimate goal of his theatre of the future, most notably in the context of his remarkable theoretical attempts in the course of the early 1870s (in other words, when the Bayreuth Festival was still in the early planning stage) to turn the popular theatre, in its most naïve form, into the nucleus of a new type of theatre grounded in 'fixed improvisation'. Largely ignored by earlier writers on Wagner,[1] these experiments were to culminate in speculations about a *Faust* stage on which Goethe's *magnum opus* would at last receive a fitting production. By the mid-1870s this project had effectively been superseded by Wagner's Bayreuth plans, yet it remains an essential part of our total picture of the composer's theatrical cosmos, inspired, as it was, not least by his interest in the *Kasperltheater* or popular puppet shows.

In April 1871 Wagner and Cosima set off from Tribschen on a tour of Germany, the superficial highlights of which were their visit to Bayreuth (a visit which marked the initiation of their plans to establish a festival in the town) and Wagner's audience with Bismarck in Berlin. The last two days before their return to Switzerland were spent in Heidelberg, giving rise to an experience which Cosima described in her diary entry of 14 May as 'the nicest moment of our whole journey'. During the evening they had been walking in the direction of the Neckar Bridge when they suddenly heard loud laughter coming from the square. Attracted by the sound, they came upon a Punch and Judy show. 'I ask R[ichard]', Cosima noted in her inimitably stilted and pretentious German,

whether we should not visit it, and, since he assented, we had an evening of the most splendid entertainment. We stood there rooted to the spot till past 10 o'clock and drew veritable consolation from the various ideas and fancies; the folk wit of the Germans is still alive. Particularly delicious was the rapport between the audience (mainly little boys) and Kasperl, they talked to each other, and the smallest of the children joined in the action. Richard gave the woman with the collection box a florin, and that may well have spurred the man on, for he worked untiringly until at last Kasperl came on in a herald's cloak and said the show was at an end. Why? Because the lights were being 'spat out'.

Wagner was so fascinated by the puppet show that, on the following morning, before their departure, he 'tried to see Kasperl's master', but the man was not at home. When he asked a girl who was sitting next to the booth whether the puppeteer was from Heidelberg, he received the mysterious answer, 'No, from far away.'

Wagner's fascination with glove puppets is clearly due to the improvised interaction between the puppets and the audience, and to the latter's involvement in the action. One is inevitably reminded of

---

[1] This and the two following chapters are based on Dieter Borchmeyer, 'Inspiration durchs Kasperltheater: Richard Wagners Idee des improvisatorischen Dramas', *Euphorion*, 74 (1980), 113-33.

Goethe's encounter with the *commedia dell'arte* tradition in Venice in 1786: Goethe, too, was fascinated by the extempore interplay of stage and public, with the 'populace' as the 'basis on which everything else rests', for 'the spectators play too, and the crowd merges with the stage to form a single whole'.[2] The lasting quality of this encounter for Wagner emerges not only from Cosima's *Diaries*[3] (she herself, with Wagner's active encouragement, often gave puppet shows for her children, and in 1877 even *Das Rheingold* was performed with puppets), but above all from the essay *On Actors and Singers*, written in 1872, one of Wagner's most fascinating pieces in terms of both language and content. In a letter to Erwin Rohde of 25 October 1872 Friedrich Nietzsche, one of the essay's earliest and most enthusiastic admirers, who, having met the Wagners in Basle on the day after their departure from Heidelberg, must doubtless have heard of the previous day's puppet show,[4] praises the fact that 'a whole newly discovered field of aesthetics' had been opened up here.

The essay offers a gloomy picture of the world of German acting; even the 'popular theatre' is said to be in a state of decline as a result of the influence of the commercial theatre, so that 'the original, histrionic German popular spirit' was finally to be found only in the 'puppet shows seen at our fairgrounds'. Wagner was no doubt thinking of the Heidelberg episode when he wrote of his 'chance encounter with such a theatre':

In this puppeteer and in the utterly incomparable way in which he held me in a state of breathless suspense, while the audience in the street grew so passionately involved as seemingly to forget their everyday pursuits, the spirit of the theatre appeared before me, alive and well, for the first time in many years. With his improvisatory skills, this puppeteer was poet, theatre director, and actor in one, and, thanks to his magic, these poor puppets of his sprang into

[2] *Goethes Werke*, ed. Erich Trunz (Hamburg, 1959), ii. 78 (*Italienische Reise*). On Goethe's reactions to Italian comedy, see Walter Hinck, *Das deutsche Lustspiel des 17. und 18. Jahrhunderts und die italienische Komödie* (Stuttgart, 1965), 358 ff. Goethe's predilection for improvised comedy is clear even before his first visit to Italy. The Weimar amateur dramatic society was particularly fond of improvisation. See also the lengthy conversation on the subject of improvised acting and the advantages of masks and extempore delivery in Book 3 of *Wilhelm Meisters theatralische Sendung*. There seems little doubt that Goethe's fondness for improvised acting goes back to his childhood and to the impressions of puppets that he retained from that time. See the following chapter for Wagner's speculations on the puppet-play origins of *Faust*.

[3] See *CT*, 21 Jan., 23 Feb., 18 Dec., 24 Dec. 1869, 14 Oct. 1870, 14 May 1871, etc. See also n. 4, below.

[4] Nietzsche, in fact, had long been aware of the enthusiasm which Punch and Judy shows aroused in the Wagner household. When Wagner received the Order of Iftekhar from the Bey of Tunis shortly before Christmas 1869, he immediately put it to use as a decoration on the roof of the children's puppet theatre, a gesture which attests as much to his love of puppet shows as it does to his contempt for 'ridiculous' orders. On the preparations for Christmas Eve, Cosima reports that 'Professor Nietzsche comes in the morning and helps me set up the puppet theatre with Iftekhar on it' (*CT*, 18 and 24 Dec. 1869).

life before my eyes with all the truth of indestructible popular figures. He was able to hold our attention as long as he wanted, always with the same situation, constantly surprising us each time it recurred. And the principal means by which he did so was that remarkable, nay, demonic figure of the German 'Kasperl', a figure who, beginning with the calmly gluttonous 'Hans Wurst', becomes the invincible exorcist, worsting the wonderfully affected Count by dint of his irrefutable wit and intelligence, triumphing over every obstacle, and keeping all forms of Roman Law firmly at arm's length. I was unsuccessful in my attempts to meet the thaumaturge who presided over this most genuine of all theatrical entertainments ever to have come my way: in consequence I was probably spared the ordeal of having my judgement put to the test. (ix. 182.)

Here the improvising artist was 'poet, theatre director, and actor in one'. This remark of Wagner's is the key to understanding his enthusiasm for puppets and puppet shows. On 24 March 1871, shortly before his trip to Germany, he had completed his essay *On the Destiny of Opera*, which he read to a circle of artists at the Berlin Academy of Arts on 28 April. Here he developed the surprising theory that art was born from the spirit of improvisation, a theory which was to leave a lasting mark on his later essays and conversations. (There is scarcely a trace of such a theory in the great reform essays written in the years around 1850.) Improvisation is said to be the 'natural process at the origin of all art', but especially of drama and music. The origin of drama lay in 'mimic improvisation' and in the 'improvisatory mime' (ix. 142–3). It embodied the collective poetic *Volksgeist* or popular spirit which, for Wagner, as for Herder and the German Romantics, was the well-spring of every legitimate artistic expression.

Even as early as 1867–8, in his essay on 'German Art and German Politics', Wagner had backed up his theory that drama was born 'from the genuine popular spirit' by pointing to the way in which not only strolling players in the *commedia dell'arte* tradition but also minstrels and clowns had inspired and fructified all the major forms of drama, beginning with the legendary Thespians' cart of the ancient Greeks, through medieval mystery plays, to the great works of Spanish and English dramatic literature, all of which were suffused and sustained by the mimic art of the people or 'folk'. Again and again Wagner's thoughts come back to the 'ideal point of contact between the mime and the poet' (viii. 85). However much the poet may rebel against the mime, betraying the typical contempt for the theatre of those purely 'literary poets' for whom Wagner had no time, it is only through the mime that he can ever be generally effective. 'What places the art of the mime on such a low level in the eyes of other artists is the very thing that makes his achievements and influence so universal', namely, that every one of us, forced to play a variety of roles in life, feels 'related to the actor', with the result that he senses within himself 'a predisposition to show the selfsame skill'. (That this predisposition was egregiously evident in the case of Wagner, the born *histrio*, was the burden of Nietzsche's famous reproach.) But delight in mimic artistry and illusionistic 'imitation' constitutes the 'magic' and 'essential pleasure' of the theatre. It is not the poet but the vilified mime who influences our minds in the theatre. 'On this natural basis, the theatre could be compared to the outcome of a successful slaves' uprising or to the overturning of the relationship between a servant and his master.' (viii. 67–8.)

Wagner is keen to end the distinction between servant and master by granting both mime and poet their rightful due, thus enabling them both to achieve their highest potential. Accordingly, drama must never be isolated from mime and regarded as 'pure poetry'; rather, it must respond to that elemental and vital need that is satisfied by mime. Although the following quotation may appear to embody a 'materialist' aesthetic, it is by no means exceptional in Wagner's dramaturgical thinking, as the foregoing chapters ought to have shown. Among the most forward-looking elements in his theory of art is his constant derivation of aesthetic phenomena from more or less clearly defined social conditions: in his 1849 essay, *Art and Revolution*, Wagner himself had described his task as having to 'recognize art as a social product' (iii. 9). It is in this sense that he writes in 'German Art and German Politics' of the modern theatre:

The daily assault on his mental powers in furtherance of life's immediate utilitarian ends allows the bourgeois no time for aimless involvement in literature and art; all the greater, then, is his need to relax at some diverting entertainment, distracting in the better sense of the term and costing little or no preparation. This is the need. And it is to answer this need that the mime at once steps in; the public's need supplies him with a means of livelihood, just as hunger helps the baker. He knocks together his platform: and behold, there stands his theatre. Everything here is naïve and sincere: the mime proffers his art, the public rewards him for the entertainment which he grants them. Everything about this relationship is direct and immediate: the spectator is held transfixed by what he sees and hears before him; the narrative or story becomes an agreeably exciting fact: he laughs with the merry, weeps with the sad, and, suddenly aware of the deception that has been practised for his own amusement, claps his hands at the clever trick. It is upon this relationship and upon its exploitation for the highest ideal ends that the most sublime works of art of the greatest poets of every age are based. (viii. 116.)

This relationship between the mime and his public suffers, of course, from a 'shortcoming' which barely reveals itself in its naïve beginnings, but which, following the 'application of that law of utilitarianism which colours all civic dealings', leads to its total corruption: their relationship becomes subject to the law of supply and demand, and the theatre is ruined both morally and artistically as a result of commercialization. To the extent, however, that this 'fundamental defect' can be overcome, Wagner argues that it is that relationship 'in which the aesthetic susceptibility of the popular spirit expresses itself in its most naïve form as a genuine civic [one might almost say 'material'] need' which offers the most 'unique, incomparable, and utterly irreplaceable opportunity for the spiritual and moral forces of the people and its foremost minds to achieve the greatest common purpose and effectiveness' (viii. 116–17).

Wagner was to return to this train of thought three years later in his essay *On the Destiny of Opera*. Modern Spanish and English drama is said to have developed 'out of the genuine folk spirit, after the classicistic tendencies of each of these nations' learned poets had proved incapable of exerting any active influence' (ix. 135–6). Wagner sees the history of modern drama as a constant oscillation between a dramatic form which, arising spontaneously out of the folk spirit or art of mime, cannot, given the improvisatory nature of all mimic skills, be derived from any a priori aesthetic ideal, and 'literary drama', a genre sprung from purely aesthetic reflection, orientated towards Greek tragedy, and based upon a preconceived formal model. Even the plays of Goethe and Schiller tended at times to conform to the latter model, according to Wagner; in other words, a form of drama lacking in elemental mimic motivation.

Wagner was of the belief that every great dramatist of world literature since Aeschylus ('who stood at the centre of his sublime work of art . . . like the leader of the tragic chorus': ix. 142) achieved his position of greatness only by combining poetry with theatrical practice, the best example being 'that mysterious dramatist Shakespeare'. As countless entries in Cosima's *Diaries* make clear, Wagner's fascination with Shakespeare increased with the passing years: scarcely a day went by at Tribschen and Bayreuth without a reading from one of his plays. In his essay *On the Destiny of Opera* Wagner asserts that, as an '*actor* and *impresario*', Shakespeare rehearsed his plays under often makeshift conditions, and the same was true, he believed, of Lope de Vega, an 'almost no less wondrous' figure, whom he regarded even more highly than Calderón. (Among his contemporaries, only the Austrian dramatist Franz Grillparzer—Wagner's opposite in most respects and someone for whom he normally felt nothing but contempt—shared this view.) Among French classical writers, Wagner admired only 'the actor Molière', whom he played off against Corneille and Racine, describing the latter as 'poets of fashion' and as the authors of ostensibly purely academic literary plays that were circumscribed by the aesthetic formulas of neo-Classicism (ix. 141–2).

Wagner denies that the 'nature of drama' is primarily explicable from the point of view of the 'poet'. The 'dramatist' was 'no closer to the genuine poet than he is to the mime from whose innermost nature he will have to issue if, as poet, he wishes to hold up his mirror to life' (ix. 142). Just as in *Opera and Drama* (1851) Wagner had described the relationship of music to drama in his projected 'musical drama' as that of the 'means' to the 'end', so he uses a similar wording here in characterizing the relationship between the poem or libretto on the one hand and the drama on the other. The latter alone, to quote from *Opera and Drama* (iii. 231), was the 'aim of the expression', whereas the means by which that aim was achieved comprised mime, poetry, and music. (These latter combine to produce the *Gesamtkunstwerk* or 'total work of art', ostensibly re-creating the *mousike* of the Greeks in which poetry, music, and dance were not yet separated from one another.[5])

If the poet is to issue from the innermost nature of the mime, then he must study the latter's 'natural method', i.e., improvisation, and make it his own, 'so that the mime, in all its uniqueness, now enters the poet's higher consciousness'. Whereas the unconsciously creative folk spirit expresses itself in the improvisatory art of the mime, the poet, by contrast, remains calmly conscious (ix. 142). Wagner uses a concept here that had already played a significant role in Romantic poetry as the counterpart of unconscious imagination.[6] The supreme work of art would develop out of the interaction between the unconsciousness of the folk spirit and the consciousness of art, and that supreme work was drama, a form of *'fixed mimic improvisation'* (ix. 143) of a kind that Wagner found exemplified in Shakespeare's plays.

Although Wagner's idea of Shakespeare is marked by a number of historical and ideological misconceptions typical of his age, he appears to share the insights of more recent Shakespeare scholars on at least one essential point, namely, the belief that Shakespeare was strongly influenced by a pre-literary, mimic, popular culture that culminated in the improvisatory genius of the actor Richard Tarlton. Wagner's paradoxical notion of fixed improvisation seems not entirely

---

[5] See Wolfgang Schadewaldt, 'Richard Wagner und die Griechen', in Wieland Wagner (ed.), *Richard Wagner und das neue Bayreuth* (Munich, 1962), 149–74, esp. p. 161. In his essay 'On Musical Criticism' (v. 53–65) Wagner deals in some detail with the concept of Greek 'music'.

[6] On the significance of the concept of 'conscious recollection' or *'Besonnenheit'* in the writings of E. T. A. Hoffmann, see Klaus Kropfinger, *Wagner und Beethoven* (Regensburg, 1965), 54–5. On 16 June 1882 Cosima noted in her diary: 'Yesterday R. was emphatically in agreement with Jean Paul's statement that the artistic temperament is rooted in conscious recollection; he says it is true that conscious recollection does not provide inspiration—"all our present-day gentlemen compose self-consciously"—but it is necessary in recapturing the inspiration.' On the role of consciousness in the process of artistic creativity, see Wagner's famous letter to Eduard Hanslick of 1 Jan. 1847, in Richard Wagner, *Sämtliche Briefe*, ed. Gertrud Strobel and Werner Wolf (Leipzig, 1970), ii. 538; English translation from *Selected Letters of Richard Wagner*, ed. Stewart Spencer and Barry Millington (London, 1987), 134. See also Curt von Westernhagen, *Richard Wagner: Sein Werk, sein Wesen, seine Welt* (Zurich, 1956), 71–99.

inappropriate as an explanation of the structure of Shakespeare's plays, at least to the extent that the latter gave literary form to the popular traditions of his time.

Wagner gives concrete expression to his idea of mimic improvisation in his essay *On Actors and Singers* and in his open letter to Ernst Gettke of 9 November 1872 (published in volume 9 of his *Collected Writings* as 'A Letter to an Actor'):

Practise improvising scenes and whole plays. It is incontestable that the basis and heart of all mimic talent, all real acting ability, lies in improvisation. The dramatic writer who has never come to realize how powerful his works would be if only he could see them improvised can never have felt the true calling of dramatic poetry. The brilliant Gozzi declared that it was altogether impossible to specify how certain of his characters should be portrayed by using prose, still less by means of verse, and so he contented himself with indicating only the content of the scenes in question. Although he may have gone back to the very beginnings of dramatic art in adopting this procedure, they are none the less the beginnings of a genuine art to which it must always be possible to return, however advanced its later development, if the basis of art is not to dissolve into insubstantial artificiality. (ix. 262–3.)

Carlo Gozzi, whose indebtedness to the improvised acting skills of the *commedia dell'arte* tradition is justified here in dramaturgical terms, was a writer whom Wagner admired throughout his life. The libretto of Wagner's earliest completed opera, *Die Feen*, derives from Gozzi's *La donna serpente*, and, during the final decade of his life, there are repeated references to Gozzi in Cosima's *Diaries*. Wagner expressly defended him against his rival and close contemporary Carlo Goldoni (*CT*, 28 April 1878),[7] seeing him as a precursor of the 'art-work of the future' on the strength of his alleged opposition to 'literary production' (*CT*, 13 October 1872), i.e., a literary style of comedy.

In his essay *On Actors and Singers* Wagner discusses the 'artistic and social position' of actors, and even goes so far as to demand that the dramatist locate the starting-point of his art in the immediate circumstances of the mime's existence, including its utter triviality, since the 'entire nature' of the mime was that 'reproductiveness whose root we recognize as the impulse behind the most convincing imitation possible of other individuals and their behaviour in the events of everyday existence'. Anyone who felt called upon to become a dramatic poet 'should by no means overlook the lowest form of acting', for

here, where the mime convincingly imitates his landlord, the tapster, the commissioner of police, and all those other people with whom he is brought into

---

[7] Wagner was no doubt relying here on August Wilhelm Schlegel's *Vorlesungen über dramatische Kunst und Literatur*, the 16th lecture of which deals with Gozzi and Goldoni and with the difference between improvised acting and 'literary' comedy; see August Wilhelm Schlegel, *Kritische Schriften und Briefe*, ed. Edgar Lohner (Stuttgart, 1962–74), i. 248.

contact in the course of the day's tribulations, in order that he may avenge himself, of an evening, for all his suffering, while appearing to keep you in good humour: here the poet can learn more or less what Shakespeare learned before he turned his poor actors into heroes and monarchs. (ix. 216–17.)

Mime—the realistic reproduction of situations and characters from banal everyday existence because of an elemental need to imitate and caricature them—this is the root of all art, in Wagner's view, including the most sublime expressions of dramatic art. The art which does not issue from such subliterary origins remains sterile and artificial.

Among the demands which Wagner makes of the legitimate theatre, the most important was that it should be 'naturalistic in a mimico-dramatic sense'. As an expression of 'popular natural tendencies' it was at odds with the 'traditional dogma of classical criticism'. The latter had established a fixed 'stylistic model' that forced every drama—and especially the *tragédie classique* that flourished at the court of Louis XIV—into the strait-jacket of closed literary form (ix. 161, 191). So academic an art-form, categorized socially as a luxury art for 'well-to-do society', is contrasted with the popular mimic theatre of Shakespeare, a type of theatre whose starting-point was not the rank imagination of the aristocracy but the concrete, vital interests of the 'lower classes of society', those very classes whom Wagner hoped would 'purify and reform prevailing circumstances' (*CT*, 20 April 1869). In the case of Shakespeare, 'every stylistic model, i.e., every formal and expressive trend which was taken over from elsewhere or which was the result of conscious reflection', derived from the 'basic law' of mimic art (ix. 191). Thus Shakespeare's dramatic structures (to quote from Wagner's essay *On the Destiny of Opera*) 'defy assessment according to any standards yet to have been unambiguously derived from classical form' (ix. 136).

It cannot be denied, of course, that Wagner himself made this standard very much his own for a not inconsiderable period. His reform essays of the years around 1850, written against the background of an aesthetic outlook clearly indebted to Aeschylean tragedy, are typified at many points by what he describes as 'classical art-form'. Not until the early 1870s did the classical concept of 'unified form' (iv. 34) embodied by Greek tragedy (which, unlike modern neo-Classicism, was still entirely in harmony with the spirit of the people) begin to give way to the concept of open form as found in the Elizabethan theatre. There is no doubt that this change of emphasis was bound up with Wagner's experiences while working on the *Ring*. When he wrote *Opera and Drama*, the music drama for which he was preparing the ground theoretically was still *Siegfrieds Tod*. Only subsequently was this single drama expanded to become the four-part *Ring*.[8] Once Wagner had

[8] Thomas Mann offers an incomparable description of this creative process in his public lecture 'Richard Wagner und '*Der Ring des Nibelungen*', in *Wagner und unsere Zeit*, ed. Erika Mann

realized how impossible it was to compress his earlier outline into the
form of a single, closed drama, it was clearly only a matter of time before
a number of his notions concerning 'classical' form would be revised.
The essays with which we are mostly concerned here were written while
he was working on the second part of the tetralogy, and at many points
reflect Wagner's own creative experiences, including the impossibility of
proceeding according to some pre-existing formal model.

Wagner's enthusiasm for puppet shows, the genuine popular theatre,
and, above all, for Shakespeare during the early 1870s found expression
in a new theatrical ideal. Even in *Opera and Drama* he had dealt at some
length with the question of the Elizabethan stage, describing the manner
of 'setting the scene' as something merely 'suggested' and 'left to the
imagination'. But at this point he still regarded Tieck's idea of reviving
the Elizabethan stage as an aesthetic aberration (iv. 16–19). By the time
he came to write *On Actors and Singers* in 1872, however, Wagner's
thinking had undergone a remarkable change, inasmuch as he had now
moved far away from the absolutist claims of the theatre of illusion. His
ideal principle that drama should be 'naturalistic in a mimico-dramatic
sense' (a principle inspired by Shakespeare), he now derives from his
'reassessment of a *single* circumstance', namely,

> that Shakespeare's actors performed on a stage that was surrounded by
> spectactors on every side, whereas the modern stage, adopting the model of the
> Italians and French, presents the actors and sets from only one side, namely,
> from the front. What we see here is the academic theatre of the Renaissance,
> based upon a misconception of the classical stage, in which the stage is cut off
> from the audience by the orchestra. (ix. 191–2.)

What Wagner demanded in the case of Bayreuth would appear to be a
false development, at least in terms of the spoken theatre. Here the
audience no longer perceives the actor as a three-dimensional figure,
freely visible from every side, but as part of a 'theatrical picture . . .
which, according to the skill of the scene-painter, machinist, and
costume-designer, is now raised almost to the level of an independent
work of art'. Only on this kind of stage could that 'unnatural pathos'
thrive which dominated the acting style of Wagner's own time. If such
pathos were to have been presented on 'Shakespeare's primitive and
popular stage', a stage which 'dispensed with all the illusionistic
paraphernalia of sets and décor', and on which the 'economically
dressed' performers 'passed to and fro in front of the spectators, moving
in every direction, just as they would in everyday life', it would have been

(Frankfurt, 1963), 136–7; translated into English by Allan Blunden as 'Richard Wagner and *Der
Ring des Nibelungen*', in *Pro and contra Wagner* (London, 1985), 180. See also Carl Dahlhaus, *Richard
Wagners Musikdramen* (Velber, 1971), 85–8; translated into English by Mary Whittall as *Richard
Wagner's Music Dramas* (Cambridge, 1979), 84–7.

no more tolerable 'in such naked proximity' than were the 'affected actors' of Wagner's own day (ix. 192–3).

Throughout the 1870s Wagner returned again and again to thoughts of reviving Shakespeare's platform stage in a way appropriate to the nineteenth century. And each time he considered it, his ideas for reform would revolve around the work that seemed to him to be made for such an exercise, a work, moreover, which he regarded as the *ne plus ultra* of the art of the theatre, Goethe's *Faust*.

# 4

# The Idea of a 'Faust' Theatre

The origin and essence of every kind of theatre is mimic improvisation.

Thomas Mann, 'Versuch über das Theater'.

Wagner's first fascinated encounter with Goethe's *Faust* was one of the most fundamental aesthetic experiences of his life. It was an experience, moreover, which was to be repeated in different circumstances at various stages from early youth to ripe old age.[1] Countless remarks in his letters and conversations, together with frequent allusions to, or quotations from, the play in his theoretical writings, are eloquent testimony to a fascination which was not merely literary but musical, too: as early as 1831 — in other words, while Goethe was still alive — he wrote a series of *Sieben Kompositionen zu Goethes 'Faust'*, inspired by part I of Goethe's drama. They are immature and unimpressive pieces. On a wholly different level, by contrast, was his planned 'Faust' Symphony, of which, however, only the first movement was completed (1839–40).[2] When revising the piece in 1855, he retitled it *A Faust Overture*, the indefinite article apparently indicating that the work — arguably Wagner's most important purely instrumental piece — lays no claims to being regarded as the definitive accompaniment to Goethe's incommensurable poem.[3] The very fact that a piece originally planned as a symphony should have remained a fragment (a fact which Wagner concealed by publishing the opening movement as a separate overture) suggests that, like so many other composers before and after him, from Schumann to Busoni,

---

[1] See Dieter Borchmeyer, 'Goethes *Faust* in der Sicht Richard Wagners', in *Akten des 6. Internationalen Germanistenkongresses Basel 1980: Jahrbuch für Internationale Germanistik*, A. Kongreßbericht VIII/4 (Berne, 1980), 352–6. The present chapter is an expanded and amended version of the essential ideas advanced in that paper.

[2] See Egon Voss, *Richard Wagner und die Instrumentalmusik* (Wilhelmshaven, 1977), 66–87, 126–47, and *passim*.

[3] Ibid. 119: 'In the development from the first movement of the "Faust" Symphony to the Overture to Goethe's *Faust*, I and, finally, to *A Faust Overture*, there is unmistakable evidence that Wagner is withdrawing a certain claim.' See also John Deathridge, 'Richard Wagners Kompositionen zu Goethes *Faust*', *Jahrbuch der Bayerischen Staatsoper*, 5 (1982), 90–9. Deathridge examines Wagner's composition sketches to provide striking demonstration of how close the planned 'Faust' Symphony was to *Der fliegende Holländer*. In one of the sketches the themes associated with Gretchen and Senta have even become entwined, signalling their symbolic relationship in Wagner's imagination.

Wagner finally abandoned his search for a musical form that could have mirrored Goethe's universal work in all its poetical facets.

For Wagner, the only true musical equivalent of *Faust* was Beethoven's Ninth Symphony. When he conducted a performance of the work in Dresden in 1846, the programme notes that he drew up for the occasion included copious quotations from *Faust*, designed to assist the listener in tracing the Symphony's musical development (ii. 56–64). '*Faust* . . . and Beethoven's symphonies — those are the only things of which Germany can be proud', Wagner told Cosima on 3 September 1874; 'for *Faust* is utterly German, German in a popular sense, yet it embraces the whole world: it is the greatest of masterpieces'. Cosima objected: 'But not above Shakespeare.' To which Wagner replied: 'Shakespeare is the truest picture of the world. *Faust* is a commentary on that picture, a commentary on Shakespeare.'

Wagner's boundless admiration for *Faust*, and above all for part II, did not, of course, prevent him from criticizing it occasionally. The comparison with Shakespeare quoted above shows that he regarded *Faust* as a modern work, reflective in nature. Even as early as 1847, in his letter to Eduard Hanslick of 1 January, he had drawn a distinction between Goethe's two-part drama and the 'unconsciously created work of art' of earlier periods. But what still appears as a merit here was later to seem to represent a symptom of the modern poet's waning creative powers, especially when measured against the work of a Dante or Shakespeare. '*Faust* [is] much more valuable than the *Divina Commedia*', he told Cosima on 17 October 1876, while leaving no doubt that the later piece revealed 'less creative ability'. A few months later, while rereading *Faust*, he used a rising and falling curve to indicate the cultural development from Dante to Shakespeare and, finally, to Goethe: 'Shakespeare [belongs] to a culminating point in civilization; Goethe, no less great, to a time of decadence' (*CT*, 21 January 1877). It is striking that, on the frequent occasions when he used the term 'decadence', Wagner — who was later, of course, to become the idol of literary *décadence* — always invested the word with negative connotations, using it as a synonym for 'decline'.[4] Shakespeare's naïve creativity — 'naïve' in the Schillerian sense of unreflective oneness with nature — is contrasted with Goethe's greater 'artistic sense'. In the latter, 'one sees the great poet, how he arranges his material, how he shapes it'. Shakespeare, conversely, remains 'unfathomable' as a creative individual, a characteristic he shares with Homer: 'that is why people have the idea that neither Homer nor Shakespeare ever existed' (*CT*, 6 March 1880).

Wagner's most cogent critique of *Faust* comes in his letter to Mathilde

---

[4] See *CT*, 25 Oct. 1869, 6 Apr. 1878, 17 Feb., 16 Oct. 1880, 4 Feb., 27 June 1881, 1 Oct. 1882, and *passim*.

Wesendonck of 7 April 1858 in which he emphatically rejects her view that Faust is 'the most significant human type ever created by a poet'. For Wagner, by contrast, Faust represented 'a missed opportunity': 'and the opportunity that has been missed is nothing less than the unique chance of salvation and redemption' which Faust had forfeited by rejecting Gretchen. (Redemption, it will be remembered, was Wagner's lifelong preoccupation.) That this 'earlier omission' was made good in the 'final tableau' was something Wagner no longer found convincing. During his life on earth we see Faust only in the 'real world, the world of classical art', and, finally, at the high point of his life, 'in the practical world of industry', an 'objective' sphere divorced from the hero's inner life, whereas Wagner, on the basis of Schopenhauer's philosophy, sees life's central concern in that 'fellow-feeling' which supersedes the distinction between subject and object, internalizing external phenomena and allowing the individual to 'become the world itself'.[5]

Goethe's Faust sees his life's fulfilment in actively mastering the world of external phenomena, but this is an outlook which Wagner rejects, insisting rather that, 'Only inside, within us, only deep down does salvation dwell!' There is, of course, an evocation here of the final lines of the Rhinemaidens in *Das Rheingold*: 'Treulich und tief | ist's nur in der Tiefe . . .' (Trust and truth | dwell here in the depths: v. 268). For Wagner, Faust had come to personify the modern sense of alienation from self, a sense of dislocation which his music dramas, with their mythic enactment of redemption through love, in which subject and object merge as a single entity, are intended to supersede. (Of significance in this context are the reminiscences of the final tableau of *Faust* in *Tristan und Isolde*, reminiscences which will become clearer in the course of our interpretation of *Tristan* in a later chapter. Wagner's critical comments in his letter to Mathilde Wesendonck are poetically encoded in the erotic mystery of his *Tristan* poem.)

To 'attempt to turn Goethe's pitiful Faust into one of the noblest types of humankind' was an absurd undertaking, Wagner informed Mathilde. But at least from the mid-1860s onwards he was prepared to see *Faust*, both as a poem and as a work of the theatre, as the *ne plus ultra* of dramatic poetry: only Shakespeare was greater in his opinion, but Shakespeare was, in any case, in a class of his own. Cosima's *Diaries* document an almost uninterrupted interest in *Faust* during the final fourteen years of Wagner's life. 'Who will ever know enough of this work?', he asked himself on 14 November 1873; and in his essay *On Actors and Singers* (1872) he described it as 'the only truly German work,

---

[5] See Richard Wagner, *Briefe: Die Sammlung Burrell*, ed. John N. Burk (Frankfurt, 1953), 491–3; English translation from *Selected Letters of Richard Wagner*, ed. Stewart Spencer and Barry Millington (London, 1987), 382-3.

an original piece of the very highest poetic merit'. As we have already noted, Wagner's admiration was directed above all at 'the second part of the tragedy, which is as violently denounced as it is misunderstood', and which authorities on 'aesthetic criticism' felt entitled to parody (ix. 182–3, 214). Wagner was thinking here of *Faust*, III (1862), of course, by his former friend in Zurich, Friedrich Theodor Vischer. In the course of a conversation with Cosima on 4 June 1871, Wagner proposed a canon of works of world literature which he considered absolutely 'indispensable': it included Homer, Aeschylus, and Sophocles (but not Euripides, of whom Wagner was always sharply critical), Plato's *Symposium*, the whole of Shakespeare, Cervantes' *Don Quixote*, and—the only work of German literature to figure in the list—Goethe's *Faust*. (The omission of Dante's *Divina Commedia* was, no doubt, merely an oversight.)

Wagner's favourite section of *Faust*, and one that was capable of delighting him at each rereading, was the 'Classical Walpurgis Night',[6] the mythological humour of which was entirely typical, he felt, of 'our own outlook on the world' (*CT*, 6 December 1873). Again, 'all of it is dramatic, conceived for the stage, but without recalling what stages were like in a country with no popular art such as that possessed by the Greeks, who created a popular art for educated people' (*CT*, 8 August 1879). Wagner had no time for Goethe's mythic seriousness—of the whole of the Helen of Troy episode in part II, he admired only Mephisto's grotesque appearance as Phorkyas (*CT*, 7 December 1873), with its reverberations of the huge mythic wit of the 'Classical Walpurgis Night'; instead, his love was directed at the mythological satyr play. (Hence, it may be noted in passing, his enthusiasm for Aristophanes.)

In his 1937 public lecture, 'Richard Wagner and *Der Ring des Nibelungen*', Thomas Mann spoke of 'the ageing Wagner's selfless admiration for Goethe's Greek phantasmagoria', expressing his astonishment and delight at this encounter between two 'great creators of myths'. But Mann was unfamiliar with the remarks from the end of Wagner's life, and believed that it was only when the latter could place a certain distance between himself and the mythic poem of the *Ring* that he came to appreciate Goethe's sardonic treatment of myth. 'Nothing could be less Wagnerian than Goethe's ironical manner of invoking myth, and the "Classical Walpurgis Night" will have appealed little, if at all, to the youthful Wagner, the Wagner who was still completely bound up in his own work.'[7] That this is simply not true, and that Wagner read Goethe's phantasmagoria at the very time he was composing the *Ring*, is

---

[6] See *CT*, 7 Dec. 1873, 29 Jan. 1874, 1, 5 Dec. 1878, 8 Aug. 1879, 8 Apr. 1882, and *passim*.

[7] Thomas Mann, *Wagner und unsere Zeit*, ed. Erika Mann (Frankfurt, 1963), 131–2; translated into English by Allan Blunden as *Pro and contra Wagner* (London, 1985), 175–6.

clear from Cosima's *Diaries*. He certainly did not see his 'archetypally
German' figures as being as sharply contrasted with Goethe's
'archetypally European' mythic images as Thomas Mann believed.[8]
Greek myth was always allowed to shine through the outer layer of
Germanic myth.[9] And the tetralogy also contains enough comic and
ironic elements, in addition to its mood of tragic pathos, to remind us of
Goethe's 'mythological entertainment'.[10] Are the grotesque figures of
the Nibelung realm really so far removed from the sub-Olympian mythic
world of griffons, sphinxes, pygmies, and phorkyads? Mann's
hypothesis, that Wagner celebrated myth whereas Goethe played with it,
is evidently something of an over-simplification.

Wagner's paradoxical belief that the 'Classical Walpurgis Night' was
'a popular art for educated people' goes to the very heart of his
interpretation of *Faust* as a theatrical work. 'You know', he reminds the
readers of his essay *On Actors and Singers*, 'a puppet show inspired
Goethe to write his *Faust*!' (ix. 217.) And he was convinced that this had
left its mark on even the most elevated moments in part II. Time and
again in conversation with Cosima he drew her attention to passages
which revealed to him 'to what extent Goethe always had the puppet
show in mind' (*CT*, 7 November 1872), and how his characters were
'literally modelled on Kasperl' (*CT*, 17 September 1872). These
remarks are influenced, of course, by the puppet show he had seen in
Heidelberg in 1871, but even before this date he had told Cosima of his
remarkable plan to write his own *Kasperl* based on the Faust theme: 'R.
talks much about a *Kasperl* which he has in mind to write and compose.
The main characters are Kasperl and Wagner, Faust in the
background.' (*CT*, 23 February 1869; the Wagner referred to here is
Faust's famulus or servitor.)

Shortly before this, Wagner and Cosima had read the 'Faust Puppet
Play' (in Karl Simrock's version) 'amid hearty laughter, but with genuine
interest. Kasperl is so entirely different in kind from the Spanish
Grazioso or the Italian Harlequin, and what a striking testimony he is to
the dramatic talents of the Germans!' (*CT*, 21 January 1869.) Three
years later, in his essay *On Actors and Singers*, Wagner would describe
this type of puppet theatre as 'the nucleus of the German theatre' (ix.
182). Goethe's *Faust* was part of this tradition of the 'original German
theatre' and had nothing to do with the modern Italian or French
proscenium stage (ix. 182–3). As we have already noted, Cosima and her
children even rehearsed *Das Rheingold* in February 1877 for a

---

[8] Thomas Mann, *Wagner und unsere Zeit* 132; English trans., p. 176.

[9] See Wolfgang Schadewaldt, 'Richard Wagner und die Griechen', in Wieland Wagner (ed.),
*Richard Wagner und das neue Bayreuth* (Munich, 1962), 166–8.

[10] Mann, *Wagner und unsere Zeit*, 131–2; English trans. (Blunden, *Pro and contra Wagner*), p. 176.

performance with puppets. There is nothing sacrilegious, therefore, about Thomas Mann's description of the *Ring* as an 'ideal piece of puppet theatre': referring specifically to Wagner's account of puppets in his essay *On Actors and Singers* (which Wagner wrote when he was working on the *Ring*), Mann went on to ask whether it had 'not occurred to anybody that this Siegfried'—'this uncomplicated hero'—bore a striking resemblance to 'the little fellow who wields the slapstick in the fairground booth?'[11]

*Faust*'s affinity with puppet theatre also explained, in Wagner's view, the type of stage which Goethe had in mind. It was the typical form of the popular theatre discussed in the previous chapter, a type of theatre which, in keeping with what was originally the improvised action and reaction between actors and audience, eschewed any strict architectonic division between the audience area and the stage. Here Wagner was thinking above all of the Elizabethan stage and its Spanish equivalent. *Faust*, he argued in *On Actors and Singers*, could not be staged convincingly on the 'modern half-stage with its scenery presented to us only within a frame, *en face*', in other words, on a proscenium stage. 'Confronted by this stage, the spectator remains wholly inert and withdrawn, waiting for practical phantasmagorias to take place up there, right at the back, phantasmagorias intended to draw him into a world by which, however, he prefers to remain entirely untouched.' (ix. 194.)

Wagner is still thinking here of the spectator's active role in the improvised theatre, a theatre which can rely on his imaginative agility of mind and which, as a result, has no need of illusionistic designs, since it is sufficient for the scene of action to be 'meaningfully suggested'. For an adequate staging of Goethe's *Faust*, a 'fundamental change' was necessary, combining 'modern developments in the mechanical arts' with the 'simple architectural conditions of the Elizabethan theatre'. 'Thus, it would need only a brief appeal to the spectator's active imagination to transport him into the midst of that magic world where he might "travel cunning, swift as thought can tell, | From Heaven through the world and down to hell".' (ix. 194-5.)[12]

How Wagner imagined such a production, in which the events on stage would no longer be presented to the public from the front but 'press in upon the audience from all sides, as it were', is revealed by an astonishing passage in Cosima Wagner's diary for 7 November 1872. Here Wagner develops the idea of his own 'Faust' theatre which uses a

---

[11] Thomas Mann, *Gesammelte Werke*, 2nd edn. (Frankfurt, 1974), x. 42; translated into English by Allan Blunden as 'Essay on the Theatre', in *Pro and contra Wagner*, p. 31.

[12] Wagner's allusion is to the 'Prelude in the Theatre' from Goethe's *Faust*, quoted here from Philip Wayne's translation (Harmondsworth, 1949), 37. According to Wagner (*CT*, 24 July 1872), 'all the art of the future' was bound up with this 'Prelude'.

merely allusive, movable stage like a sort of a podium, 'as in a circus'. Some of the action would even take place 'behind the audience', since 'people turning around to watch would enliven the scene, and make the audience part of it'. The idea of a 'Faust' theatre—which might have been an alternative to the Bayreuth Festspielhaus with its realization of Wagner's other idea for the theatre—was one which he never gave up, even if, by concentrating on his own works and their scenic realization, he was left with no time or strength (and, above all, with no money) to convert this particular project into practical reality.

At the same time, it should not be forgotten that the two kinds of theatre which most influenced Wagner's thinking—the Attic amphitheatre and the Elizabethan stage—form the greatest possible contrast with the modern proscenium stage, a type of stage from which Wagner was unable to break free in Bayreuth, in spite of his bold and far-reaching plans to redesign the (spoken) theatre. The extent of his scepticism, however, is clear from his famous remark to Cosima: 'having created the invisible orchestra, I now feel like inventing the invisible theatre' (*CT*, 23 September 1878). The musical inspiration behind Wagner's dramatic ideal, moreover, derived far less from opera (which he dismissed as an artistic changeling) than from the, as it were, 'invisible theatre' of instrumental music, which, as is clear from his literary and theatrical interpretations of Beethoven's symphonies, he regarded as a kind of crypto-drama.[13] Of interest in this context are Wagner's frequent remarks, recorded in Cosima's *Diaries*, that after *Parsifal* he intended writing only symphonies.[14]

The extent to which Wagner imagined the performance of non-dramatic works of music as examples of 'invisible theatre' emerges from a fascinating passage in Cosima's *Diaries* in which he mentions his plan for a staged performance of Beethoven's *Missa solemnis*. His musical 'production' centred upon the same circus-like podium that was to have served as the principal acting area for his 'Faust' theatre. It was a stage that would do away with the distinction between the active performer and the passive spectator; as in the improvised theatre, there would be only 'participants'. 'He would like to place the orchestra in the middle of the hall', he told Cosima on 6 January 1872, 'with the chorus surrounding it as in a circus; everyone should join in the singing . . . for this music is not just to be listened to, the true impression is to be gained only by those who are swept along inside it . . . he says all music is designed for its executants.' We may safely assume that this idea for

[13] See Egon Voss's important and perceptive account of Wagner's 'symphonic ambitions', in *Wagner und die Instrumentalmusik*, esp. pp. 11–21, 153–81.

[14] *CT*, 28 Mar., 3, 5 Apr., 11 June, 22 Sept., 19 Nov. 1878, 22 Sept. 1879, 24 July, 14 Aug. 1880, 7, 9 Feb., 20 Mar., 13 Aug., 26 Nov., 11 Dec. 1881, 17 Dec. 1882; 10, 13 Jan., 9 Feb. 1883, and *passim*; see also *WWV*, p. 107.

merging the executants with the audience—with the listeners as a Dionysian chorus!—was conceived under the influence of Nietzsche's *Geburt der Tragödie* of 1872. It is none the less with some surprise that we find Wagner advocating the circus as the model for his ideal theatre, a theatre which transcends and transfigures not only the existing theatre and opera stage, but also the very theatre designed to stage his own musical dramas, with its well-defined barrier between actors and audience.

# 5

## 'Intentionally Random Creativity': Wagner's Theory of Fixed Improvisation

> Wagner's music, in the strict musical sense, is more improvisation than construction.
>
> Igor Stravinsky, *Poetics of Music*.

Wagner's intense preoccupation with Goethe's *Faust* during the 1870s was connected not least with the fact that he believed he had found in it a dramatic form which, unlike the structured model of ancient Greek tragedy, was particularly well adapted to his idea of fixed improvisation. Again and again in conversation with Cosima we find him referring to the 'barbarian advantages'[1] and 'barbarian style of composition' which, according to his letter to Schiller of 26 June 1797, Goethe had actively espoused in writing *Faust*, although he knew that, in doing so, he had offended against the 'highest demands' of artistic form as prescribed by the Greek classical ideal.[2] When, on 8 February 1872, Cosima once again mentioned those barbarian advantages 'on which Goethe says we must courageously insist', Wagner's reply was: 'Yes, *Faust*, the Ninth, Bach's Passions are barbarian works of that kind, that is to say, works of art which cannot be compared with a Greek Apollo or a Greek tragedy.' And to these he added his conception of 'the art-work of the future'. A few days later, on 19 February, he described *Faust* as 'just a sort of sketch, which Goethe himself looked upon in puzzlement, as a curiosity—he himself did not consider it a finished work of art'. The parallel with Beethoven's Ninth Symphony—for Wagner the apogee of all art—shows that this imperfection, when compared to the Greek aesthetic ideal, this 'barbarian' openness of form, was, in his view, evidence of a new and higher aesthetic law.

Wagner regarded Beethoven's late works as attempts, so to speak, to give fixed form to those improvisations and free fantasias at the piano

---

[1] Johann Wolfgang Goethe, *Gedenkausgabe der Werke, Briefe und Gespräche*, ed. Ernst Beutler, 2nd edn. (Zurich, 1961), xv. 1035. Goethe's remark on 'barbarian advantages' comes from the notes he wrote to accompany his translation of Diderot's *Le Neveu de Rameau*.

[2] On Goethe's concept of the barbarian, see Dieter Borchmeyer, 'Über eine ästhetische Aporie in Schillers Theorie der modernen Dichtung: Zu seinen "sentimentalischen Forderungen" an Goethes *Wilhelm Meister* und *Faust*', *Jahrbuch der deutschen Schillergesellschaft*, 22 (1978), 303–54, esp. pp. 323–4.

which his contemporaries had described in such eloquent terms. 'That is the tremendous thing about Beethoven, that in his last quartets he was able to remember and record improvisations, which could only be done through art of the highest, highest order.' (*CT*, 4 December 1870.) A little over a year before this, Wagner had made a similar claim for Bach: 'Certain features of Bach can only be explained by the fact that he was a great improviser and wanted to pin down what he was so lightly extemporizing.' (*CT*, 12 November 1869.) What appears to be inspired by the moment, extempore, sudden, and fortuitous, is therefore the product of the highest, conscious artistic intent. There seems to be an echo here of certain ideas on form that were dear to the German Romantics. Novalis, for example, had described poetry as 'intentionally random creativity', significantly drawing upon the image of a keyboard instrument to underline the idea: 'The poet needs things and words like keys, and the whole of poetry rests upon the active association of ideas — on independent, intentional, ideal, random creativity.'[3] The later Wagner's ideas on improvisation are doubtless Romantic in spirit, implying, as they do, the ability to break down all the limitations imposed by established norms, and, in keeping with Friedrich Schlegel's tenet in his *Gespräch über die Poesie* of 1800, to 'enter into the beautiful confusion of the imagination and return to the primal chaos of human nature'.[4]

The idea of improvisation does, in fact, occur among other German Romantics in a form very similar to that which is found in Wagner's speculations on the subject. In a letter to Ludwig Tieck of 11 January 1802, for example, Clemens Brentano set out his plan for a German improvised theatre modelled on the Italian *commedia dell'arte*.[5] But the most detailed account of the improvised theatre is to be found in the writings of Adam Müller, whose theories are closer to the later Wagner's aesthetic outlook than those of any other writer on the theory of the theatre. Here we find, succinctly expressed, both of Wagner's rival conceptions of the stage. Whereas in tragedy, 'stage and audience' were traditionally 'kept strictly apart', the audience at a comedy was directly

[3] Novalis, *Werke*, ed. Gerhard Schulz, 2nd edn. (Munich, 1981), 493. Even in *Opera and Drama* Wagner comes very close to Novalis in calling the poet 'the intentional portrayer of the spontaneous' (iv. 128). This parallel was first pointed out by Werner Vordtriede in his *Novalis und die französischen Symbolisten* (Stuttgart, 1963), 172.

[4] Friedrich Schlegel, *Kritische Schriften*, ed. Wolfdietrich Rasch (Munich, 1964), 502. On the quotations from Novalis and Friedrich Schlegel, and on the significance of the chaos motif in Romantic poetry, see Wolfgang Preisendanz, 'Zur Poetik der deutschen Romantik', in Hans Steffen (ed.), *Die deutsche Romantik* (Göttingen, 1967), 54–74.

[5] See Walter Hinck, *Das deutsche Lustspiel des 17. und 18. Jahrhunderts und die italienische Komödie* (Stuttgart, 1965), 387. For a comprehensive survey of the influence of the *commedia dell'arte* and puppet plays on E. T. A. Hoffmann (whose writings were familiar to Wagner from his early youth), see Heide Eilert, *Theater in der Erzählkunst: Eine Studie zum Werk E. T. A. Hoffmanns* (Tübingen, 1977), esp. pp. 11–13 (Gozzi), 55–64 (puppet plays), 65–86 (*commedia dell'arte*), and *passim*.

drawn into the action on stage. It was in comedy, accordingly, that
'genuine improvisation or extemporization' was 'truly apposite'. In
tragedy it was 'the stage alone that speaks', so that it was 'more in the
nature of a monologue, more monarchical', whereas comedy, thanks to
the interaction between stage and audience, was 'more in the nature of
a dialogue, more democratic'. (Wagner was unwilling to restrict this
'democratic' character to comedy, but preferred to extend it to cover
drama generally.) Müller saw that a time would come 'when real life in
the pit [i.e., auditorium] and the ideal life portrayed on stage are in such
close agreement . . . that the actors merely set the tone for a grand
dialogue between pit and stage' in which 'extempore spokesmen among
the audience' sought to influence the poet's work, while 'improvisers
upon the stage' came to his defence. The aim of such a republican
'universal comedy', the origins of which Müller, like Wagner, located
primarily in the Viennese popular theatre, would be 'for all to be
captivated by the immense life of poetry, rather than to sit outside,
looking in with cold and critical eyes' (an attitude conditioned by the
'peep-show principle of our theatre stages').[6] The dramaturgical maxims
of Müller and Wagner are as strikingly similar to one another as they are
radically different from the epic theatre of Bertolt Brecht, for all that
Brecht's aesthetic thinking was likewise aimed at overcoming the 'peep-
show principle'.

   In espousing improvisation, the German Romantics discovered 'the
archetypal form of a creative principle' which, in contrast to the closed
perfection of classical antiquity, validated the inspiration of the moment
at the expense of fixed, canonical artistic forms.[7] Whereas classical art
was 'a harmonic proclamation of the eternally fixed rules of a beautifully
ordered world' (to quote from August Wilhelm Schlegel's 'Lectures on
Dramatic Art and Literature' of 1811, the text of which Wagner studied
in detail), Romantic art was 'the expression of that secret movement
towards a chaos constantly striving for new and wondrous births, a chaos
concealed beneath the surface of our well-ordered creation, nay, in
creation's very womb: the quickening soul of original love moves here,
anew, upon the face of the waters'.[8]

   Of course, there is no doubt that the improvisation of pre-Romantic
music and extempore comedy was substantially different from what is
being described here. Improvised acting, like rhetoric before it, had

---

[6] Adam Heinrich Müller, *Vermittelnde Kritik: Aus Vorlesungen und Aufsätzen*, ed. Anton Krätli
(Zurich, 1968), 176–8 (irony, comedy, Aristophanes), 215 (Italian theatre, masks, extemporization):
'In tragedy the monarchical constitution is valid . . . Comedy, by contrast, is democratic poetry.' A
similar formulation is found in August Wilhelm Schlegel, *Vorlesungen über dramatische Kunst und
Literatur*, in *Kritische Schriften und Briefe*, ed. Edgar Lohner (Stuttgart, 1962–74), i. 133 (11th
lecture).
   [7] Hinck, *Das deutsche Lustspiel*, pp. 391–2.
   [8] Schlegel, *Schriften und Briefe*, ii. 112 (25th lecture).

developed within a well-established and wholly conventional framework,[9] whereas the Romantics, together with Wagner, opened up even that originally fixed framework to improvisation. For Wagner, accordingly, such improvisation or free extemporization was the way to break down conventional genres and forms, forms which, in music, included traditional periodic structure.[10] 'What is the thing written down as compared with the inspiration? What is notation in comparison with imagination?', Wagner asked Cosima on 4 December 1870, going on to reply: 'The former is governed by the specific laws of convention, the latter is free, boundless.' That is why the same advice applied to the musician as it did to the actor: 'Everybody should improvise, every good musician can produce something interesting in his improvisation. But writing it down is a quite different process; then it has to be turned into a sonata, a suite, and so on' — in other words, a conventional form — 'and it takes a lot to revitalize a familiar, defined form.' (*CT*, 22 January 1871.)

What Beethoven achieved through improvisation, Wagner set out to achieve in the sphere of drama: 'With me it is always drama which flouts conventions.' (*CT*, 4 December 1870.) And it was the 'art-work of the future' which was given the task of achieving this exceptional goal by merging musical and mimic-dramatic improvisation. In his 1871 essay, *On the Destiny of Opera*, Wagner defines 'the work of art that we ourselves envisage' as one that involves 'mimic and musical improvisation of consummate poetic value, fixed, moreover, by supreme artistic, conscious recollection' (ix. 149–50). Here we find Wagner taking up the thesis developed in his 1870 essay, *Beethoven*, where he had spoken of the 'archetypal affinity' between Shakespeare and Beethoven (ix. 106–12); but the question is now addressed from the point of view of the improvisatory nature of their art, allowing him to argue that the dramatic and musical form of their works would merge to create an 'uncommonly novel form' in which 'the four-square nature of conventional musical structure' would be superseded by 'an ideal arrangement of the highest freedom', just as the work's dramatic design, 'sublimely irregular when measured by the standards of antique drama', would appear 'almost in the light of a natural scene when set beside a work of architecture' (ix. 149).[11] In view of the effortful progress of

[9] 'What counts as art is not originality, but variation on familiar themes. Thus the *commedia dell'arte* has long shared one of the laws of rhetoric, namely, to derive the greatest possible effect from set themes and supplied forms.' (Hinck, *Das deutsche Lustspiel*, p. 6.)

[10] On the breakdown of classical periodic structure, especially in the *Ring*, see Carl Dahlhaus, *Richard Wagners Musikdramen* (Velber, 1971), 104–7; translated into English by Mary Whittall as *Richard Wagner's Music Dramas* (Cambridge, 1979), 106–9.

[11] On one occasion, however, Wagner did speak of the improvisatory character of Aeschylus's art: 'The remarkable thing about this truly great being is that one hardly notices the way it is done! It does not appear to be art at all, because it is in fact something much higher: improvisation.' (*CT*, 12 Jan. 1872.)

Wagner's music dramas from their earliest poetic sketches to their composition drafts and, finally, to the fully worked-out score,[12] his idea of an improvised theatre seems little more than the wistful vision of an art which, for all that it embodied his highest aesthetic aims, remained largely beyond his reach: the 'lost nature' of music, an ideal which he hoped the art-work of the future would rediscover through the medium of 'conscious recollection', remained inaccessible.

How difficult Wagner found it to improvise is clear from countless passages in Cosima's *Diaries* where he speaks of 'a kind of repulsion' when confronted by the task of writing out a full score (*CT*, 18 August 1871). 'My things give me pleasure only up to the first working out in ink, when the nebulous pencilled ideas suddenly emerge clearly and distinctly before my eyes.' (*CT*, 7 January 1871.) 'With me, composing is a curious affair; while thinking it up, I have it all in my mind, endless, but then comes the job of writing it down, and the mere physical actions get in the way. It becomes, "How did it go?" instead of "How is it?"; not "How is it to be?" but "How was it?"—and then having to search about till one finds it again.' (*CT*, 23 June 1871.)[13] Here, above all, he must have felt the lack of a facility that seemed almost second nature to composers such as Bach and Beethoven (and Franz Liszt, whom he never mentions, of course, in this context), namely, the ability to give immediate expression to musical ideas by improvising at the piano, a form of composition that is only one step away from the 'fixed improvisation' of the full score. But because Wagner was such a poor pianist, he was able to extemporize only on an imaginary keyboard. All the lengthier, therefore, was the process of giving 'fixed' and undistorted form to his initial inspiration.

Somewhat remarkably, Wagner repeatedly stressed that the business of 'journalism' and writing poetry caused him less effort than composing. 'How I should like now to write poetry!', he told Cosima on 10 May 1870: 'What easy, swift work—what is it compared with writing scores?' On the other hand, he no doubt felt that writing poetry—the literary conception of his music dramas—was equally remote from that improvisatory facility which he so much admired in Shakespeare or Lope de Vega. On one occasion, while discussing Roman comedy with Cosima, he remarked: 'We are all of us little Romans—Shakespeare was an Atellan!' (*CT*, 18 December 1872.)[14] (Atellan farce was a type of old

---

[12] See Stefan Kunze, 'Über den Kunstcharakter des Wagnerschen Musikdramas', in *Richard Wagner: Von der Oper zum Musikdrama* (Berne and Munich, 1978), 9–24, esp. pp. 14–24.

[13] In this context Cosima records Wagner as saying: 'It is incredible what a bungler I am . . . Mendelssohn would raise his hands in horror if he ever saw me composing.' (*CT*, 23 June 1871.) This passage provides evidence of a feeling of inferiority which Wagner the 'dilettante' was never able wholly to suppress in the face of professional composers.

[14] The conversation was inspired by Schlegel's 15th lecture on dramatic art, which had dealt with Atellan farce and Roman literary comedy.

Italian improvised comedy named after the small Campanian town of Atella: it later assumed a greater degree of stylization in the form of Roman literary comedy, although its stereotyped characters were to take on a new lease of life in the *commedia dell'arte*.) Here, then, is yet another example of the way in which the art of improvisation was the greatest of all the arts for Wagner.

It cannot be denied, of course, that Wagner frequently used the concept of improvisation in a purely metaphorical sense, and that the supposedly improvised design of the drama was due, rather, to its irregular form, just as the Romantic notion of random creativity actually involved precise calculation. The resultant structural principle was thus something of an aesthetic paradox. It was in this sense that, in his 'Essay on the Theatre' (1908), Thomas Mann characterized Wagner's art as 'fixed theatrical improvisation'.[15] What fascinated Wagner about improvisation was its 'spontaneousness' (to use one of his favourite words), in contrast to the predetermined norms and routine of a particular *'métier'*. One is reminded of Siegfried, spontaneousness incarnate, who forges the sword which Mime, trained smith though he is, is unable to fashion. Something that should apparently be reserved for the professional alone succeeds in an instant; indeed, the result is something that far exceeds the professional's capabilities. And this was something Wagner hoped for from improvisation. Ferruccio Busoni has said of improvisation that it 'would come closest to the essential nature of art if only it were within man's power to master inspiration extempore'.[16] However unreal the formulation, Busoni's ideal of controlled inspiration lies behind Wagner's paradox of fixed improvisation or calculated spontaneousness. Only on one occasion did he achieve this ideal in full, albeit in the realm of fiction: Walther's Prize Song in *Die Meistersinger* is in fact an example of fixed improvisation, as we shall see when we come to examine Wagner's musical comedy in due course.

One may add here that Wagner did actually believe that, in spite of all the self-confessed effort and calculation that went into composing, he was, in a certain sense, 'improvising' and working without being able to tell what was coming. Evidence of this is provided, for example, by a remark recorded by Cosima on 1 September 1871:

An improviser such as an actor must belong entirely to the present moment, never think of what is to come, indeed not even know it, as it were. The peculiar thing about me as an artist, for instance, is that I look on each detail as an entirety and never say to myself, 'Since this or that will follow, you must do thus and such, modulate like this or like that.' I think, 'Something will turn up.'

---

[15] Thomas Mann, *Gesammelte Werke*, 2nd edn. (Frankfurt, 1974), x. 37; translated into English by Allan Blunden as 'Essay on the Theatre', in *Pro and contra Wagner* (London, 1985), 29.
[16] Quoted in Alfred Brendel, *Musical Thoughts and After-Thoughts* (London, 1976), 109.

Otherwise I should be lost; and yet I know I am unconsciously obeying a plan. The so-called genius of form, on the other hand, reflects, 'This or that follows, so I must do such and such,' and he does it with ease.[17]

Wagner reveals himself here to be an epic musician through and through: in discussing the structural characteristics of the epic style, Goethe and Schiller had contrasted the individual detail and the autonomy of the parts with the principle of finality in dramatic poetry, where everything was strictly geared to what followed. Just as Wagner, in writing the *Ring*, allowed himself to be borne along by the momentum of the subject-matter and by the laws of its musical realization, epically transcending, as it were, the predetermined dramatic design of the work as laid down by *Siegfrieds Tod*, so he now refused on principle to acknowledge the a priori demands of 'form'.

What is implied by this refusal to acknowledge formal demands—this indifference to the fact that 'this or that follows'—is nothing less than the rejection of absolute music, in other words, music that is its own justification. From a more positive standpoint, it means that the music is determined by language and stage action, a system of priorities which may be described as the single most important principle behind Wagner's musico-dramatic praxis. The 'central maxim of Wagner's aesthetic theory', according to Carl Dahlhaus, is the principle that 'musical form' needs a *raison d'être*, which is the 'formal motive' of language or gesture.[18] In *Opera and Drama* in 1851 Wagner expressed this relationship between music and language using the metaphor of sexual polarity: '*Every musical organism is feminine by nature*, it exists only *to bring forth*, . . . the generative force lies *outside it*, and unless it be impregnated by this force it cannot bring forth.' Music must therefore receive 'the poet's generative seed' (iii. 314). Music can no longer force language to adopt its autonomous laws, but must adapt itself to suit that language in terms of both prosody and semantics. Wagner's aim was to replace the periodic structure of 'absolute music' with what he called the 'poetico-musical *period*' (iv. 154).[19] Whereas the absolute musician (Wagner's 'genius of form') can easily predict that this or that will follow, since he has only to conform to the formal patterns of his art, the element of predictability in the musical development necessarily disappears when the musician, so to speak, has to wait for the 'generative seed'; in other words, the poetic (or gesticulatory) motive. Music has lost

---

[17] In Wagner's eyes, Mendelssohn was the best example of a genius in matters of form who could compose with total ease (see n. 13, above).

[18] See Dahlhaus, *Wagners Musikdramen*, p. 112; English trans. (Whittall, *Wagner's Music Drama*), p. 115.

[19] See Carl Dahlhaus, 'Wagners Begriff der "dichterisch-musikalischen Periode"', in Walter Salmen (ed.), *Beiträge zur Geschichte der Musikanschauung im 19. Jahrhundert* (Regensburg, 1965), 179–87.

not only its absolute nature but also its providential status: the composer now proceeds very much on an extempore basis.

It seems to us that, behind Wagner's ideas on improvisation, there is an insight that is important, not least in terms of the sociology of art: improvisatory music and dramatic poetry are the radical antithesis of those works of art that have been denatured, as it were, by printing and by the book market; in other words, works which have become 'literature' in the sense discussed above. The improvised work, after all, cannot be reproduced and standardized like some consumer product; it stands and falls with the uniqueness of the moment that produced it, a part of that intransmutable 'here and now' in which poetry, music, and the scenic arts combine to form the 'total work of art'. This improvisatory inimitability has no part in the self-contained work, with its fixed written form, but only in its performance. As a result, Wagner even goes so far as to demand, in his essay *On Actors and Singers*, that the poet and creative artist should completely forget themselves and their work in favour of its mimic realization. The poet finds consummate expression not by objectifying himself in his work but by 'sacrificing himself' in favour of the mime (ix. 226).[20] The work of the creative artist finds its teleological justification only outside or beyond himself, in the improvisatory moment of presentation. This view is somewhat at odds, of course, with the image of Wagner as an artist obsessed with his own work, an image perpetuated by Thomas Mann, for example, who drew a distinction between Wagner and Goethe in which Goethe was seen as the artist more concerned with his life than with his work.[21] Certainly, it has nothing in common with the *idée fixe* of those anti-Wagnerians whose ignorance of their revered *Meister* allows them to imagine him as a vain and selfish bogyman decked out in a satin dressing-gown.

Wagner's idea that the actor should complement the poet is in part a provocative protest against the way in which the mime had been debased to the point of faithfully carrying out the commands of a 'literary poet' who saw himself as uniquely self-important. But it may also derive from his special affinity with the art of mime, an affinity which Nietzsche had begun by admiring in the fourth of his *Unzeitgemäße Betrachtungen*[22]

---

[20] This means that 'the poet forgets himself completely, to reappear in the mime, no longer as poet, but as the highest work of art won through the latter's self-realization'. Hence Wagner's conviction that 'the poet who is "called out in front of the curtain" at the end of the performance and who bows his acknowledgments to the audience' is an aesthetic absurdity, since the applause is directed at the mime alone. The 'exchange of his wondrous art for the spontaneous enthusiasm expressed in the audience's applause' is the 'natural law' and 'indispensable element' of his art (ix. 226).

[21] Thomas Mann, *Wagner und unsere Zeit*, ed. Erika Mann (Frankfurt, 1963), 56; translated into English by Allan Blunden as *Pro and contra Wagner* (London, 1985), 85.

[22] Friedrich Nietzsche, *Sämtliche Werke: Kritische Studienausgabe in 15 Bänden*, ed. Giorgio Colli and Mazzino Montinari (Munich, 1980), i. 467–8; translated into English by R. J. Hollingdale as *Untimely Meditations: Richard Wagner in Bayreuth* (Cambridge, 1983), 205.

(1876), but which later became the basis of his polemical attack in *Der Fall Wagner* (1888). 'The most enthusiastic mimomaniac of all time, also as a musician', Nietzsche called Wagner in *Die fröhliche Wissenschaft* of 1882.[23] If, by the time he came to write *Der Fall Wagner*, he was able to accuse Wagner of being 'an incomparable *histrio*, the greatest mime',[24] it was doubtless because he still recalled Wagner's essay *On Actors and Singers*, which he had once admired. But Wagner had drawn a clear distinction between the 'histrio' (ix. 213) and the 'comedian' (ix. 163–4, 180–1) on the one hand, and the genuine actor on the other. The latter was notable for the 'veracity' of his performance, since he did not obscure the borderline between appearance and truth, or between art and life; by virtue of the 'liberating consciousness of his acting', he aspired to that 'serenely cheerful' frame of mind (ix. 218–19) which Schiller described as the temper of appearance. The *histrio*, by contrast, sought to create a semblance of truth by means of deception.[25] In twisting Wagner's aims for his own polemical ends, Nietzsche has turned the composer's critique of the *histrio* into a criticism of the composer. In doing so, he merely serves to show, of course, how little he was able to break free from Wagner: even his repertory of invective is largely borrowed from Wagner's own aesthetic writings. 'That bad person has taken everything from me, even the weapons with which he now attacks me', Wagner himself observed in conversation with Cosima on 2 August 1878.

Wagner's idea of an improvised type of theatre no doubt goes far beyond the scope of his musico-dramatic praxis. It is notable that, in adopting a theoretical approach, he was advocating a concept of music theatre expressly at odds with the spirit and form of his works, a conception which reminds us, rather, of the musical and theoretical œuvre of a Ferruccio Busoni. In rejecting the music and the theatre of 'profundity, ethos, and metaphysics', Busoni felt himself to be Wagner's antithesis. And yet, at the very point at which he believed himself furthest from Wagner, he was in fact surprisingly close, namely, in his idea that improvisation was the highest form of artistic expression. 'Notation, the writing out of compositions, is primarily an ingenious expedient for catching an inspiration, with the purpose of exploiting it later. But notation is to improvisation as the portrait to the living model. It is for the interpreter to *resolve the rigidity of the signs* into the primitive emotion', he wrote in his *Entwurf einer neuen Ästhetik der Tonkunst*, first

[23] Nietzsche, *Sämtliche Werke* iii. 317; translated into English by Walter Kaufmann as *The Gay Science* (New York, 1974), 325.
[24] Ibid. vi. 30; translated into English by Walter Kaufmann as 'The Case of Wagner', in *Basic Writings of Nietzsche* (New York, 1968), 628.
[25] Prologue to Schiller's *Wallenstein* (1798), l. 137.

published in 1907.[26] The idea that the written notation preserves something originally improvised is as close to Wagner's theory of the early 1870s as the conviction that a work came into its own only at the moment of its performance; in other words, that improvisation was the beginning and end of every work of music, in the form of both the composer's initial creative impulse and the interpreter's extempore rendering of it. Busoni contrasted this rendition with the desire of certain 'lawgivers' for the performer to reproduce the 'rigidity of the signs', a dogmatic approach which argued that the performance was all the more perfect 'the more it stuck to the marks on the page'. Busoni, on the other hand, believed that 'what the composer's inspiration *necessarily* loses through notation, his interpreter should restore by his own'.[27] Owing its origins to improvisation, the musical performance should, as it were, lead back by a circular route to the origins of the piece.

The extempore origins of a work provided a link for both Busoni and Wagner between music and the legitimate theatre, so it is scarcely surprising to find the German-Italian composer drawing on themes and characters from the *teatro all'improvviso* for his music dramas, a type of traditional theatre which, from Atellan farce to *commedia dell'arte* and beyond (one thinks in our own day of the political improvised comedies of Dario Fo), has always been popular in Italy. The composer of *Arlecchino* and *Turandot* certainly could not have suspected that his own use of themes from Gozzi and the *commedia dell'arte* reflected a marked predilection on Wagner's part. Gozzi 'shared all the instinct of the people against the literary outlook', Wagner remarked on 13 October 1872 in the course of a conversation with Cosima, who, for her part, stressed how much Gozzi 'corresponds entirely with R.'s ideas of theatre'. Even less could Busoni have suspected that his musico-dramatic adaptation of the *Faust* theme sets out from premises that are closely bound up with Wagner's own thinking. Busoni's *Doktor Faust* is similarly inspired by puppet plays. In his prologue to the unfinished opera the poet points the same way out of these puppet-show beginnings as Goethe had done in *Faust*: for all its mystic excesses and self-absorption, the work of the great 'magician' followed 'the old traces', even if those traces were sublimated in such a way as to become an inimitable symbol of life. 'But what can a master do in the face of magicians?' All that remained for Busoni, once he had taken the painful decision to renounce his plans to set Goethe's *Faust* to music, was to go

---

[26] First published in Trieste in 1907 and reprinted in 1974; translated into English by Theodore Baker as *Sketch of a New Esthetic of Music* (New York, 1911), 15.

[27] Ibid. 22; English trans., p. 16. This view was vehemently rejected by Arnold Schoenberg in his *Anmerkungen* on Busoni's essay (Frankfurt, 1974).

behind the symbol, to return to the 'puppet origins' of the material, and, drawing on the naïve spirit of that puppet play, to breathe new life into the age-old theme.[28] Wagner, too, seems to have toyed with this same idea when proposing to write a *Faust* play as a musical puppet play, with Kasperl occupying centre stage (*CT*, 23 February 1869). No doubt this was merely a passing whim, but, faced with such a mass of evidence in support of our thesis that Wagner was inspired by puppet plays and improvised theatre, we would be wrong not to see in it a remark of paradigmatic import.

[28] Ferruccio Busoni, 'Doktor Faust', in *Spectaculum: Texte moderner Opern*, ed. Hans Heinrich Stuckenschmidt (Frankfurt, 1962), 10–11. See also Ferruccio Busoni, *Über die Möglichkeiten der Oper und über die Partitur des Doktor Faust* (Wiesbaden, 1967), 35–8; translated into English by Rosamond Ley as 'The Oneness of Music and the Possibilities of the Opera', and 'The Score of Doktor Faust', in *The Essence of Music and Other Papers* (New York, 1965), 1–16, 70–6.

# 6

# The Ideal Audience:
# The Greeks and 'The Art-Work of the Future'

We have no public life.

CT, 4 March 1874.

Wagner's theory of improvisation presupposes an ideal community which is not set apart from the artist in the way that the darkened auditorium is divorced from the brightly lit stage (thus symbolizing the alienation between art and reality), but which produces the work of art as a matter of course from within its midst, as an integral part of itself. It is a community, in short, which is not yet distinguished from that specific 'public' which makes up modern theatre audiences. The 'mystic abyss' (ix. 338) between stage and public in the Bayreuth Festspielhaus was a concession to modern necessity which should not be confused with Wagner's Utopian vision of the ideal relationship between the theatre and its audience. For him, the incarnation of that ideal was always Greek society as manifested in the Greater Dionysia and in the architecture of the country's amphitheatres.

In his essay *Art and Revolution*, written in 1849, Wagner contrasted the 'public art of modern Europe' with the 'public art of the Greeks' (iii. 23), concluding that art simply 'did not exist in modern public life'. The reasons for this provocative thesis were, he explained, as follows:

the art of the Greeks existed in the public consciousness, whereas art today survives only in the consciousness of the individual, the general public being *unconscious* of it. At the time when it flourished, the art of the Greeks was therefore *conservative*, since it was a valid and appropriate expression of public consciousness: with us, true art is *revolutionary*, since its very existence is at odds with the prevailing generality of mankind. (iii. 28.)

This contradistinction found expression in the polarization of stage and auditorium, whereas in the classical amphitheatre the latter had surrounded the stage on three of its sides. 'In the classical *orchestra*, almost wholly encircled by the amphitheatre, the tragic chorus stood, as it were, at the very heart of the audience', Wagner later wrote in 1872 in his essay *On Actors and Singers* (ix. 197). And this was the position which the stage must once again assume in the art-work of the future. Such a work of art would no longer be revolutionary (as it necessarily was in the prevailing circumstances), but would be '*conservative* once more' (iii. 35).

The audiences of Attic tragedy could still say to themselves, '*Tua res agitur*', as they watched the drama unfolding before them. 'For they rediscovered themselves in tragedy, finding here the noblest part of their innermost nature combined with the noblest parts of the general nature of the nation as a whole.' (iii. 12.) The Greek people,

> streaming in from the state assembly, from the Agora, from land, from sea, from military camps, and from the farthest regions, filled the amphitheatre with its thirty thousand places in order to see that most profound of all tragedies, *Prometheus*, each of its members finding inner harmony before this mightiest of works of art, gaining self-understanding, fathoming the meaning of his private actions, and merging in intimate oneness with the essence of all that was Greek, with his community, and with his god, so that, in the noblest, profoundest calm, all might once more live that life which but a few hours earlier they had lived in the most restless tumult and most disparate individuality. (iii. 11.)

The nation's ability to rediscover itself within the work of art, and the harmony between the theatre and the world of the audience, was grounded in the aesthetic organization of society as a whole. Public life in ancient Greek was still characterized by its sense of 'beauty' (iii. 29). Here we find Wagner drawing on one of the basic ideas of classical aesthetics, an idea advanced, most notably, by Schiller and Hegel. The latter, in his early lectures in Jena in 1805–6, had already described the Greek *polis* as a work of art, contrasting it with the reality of the modern state, which, he argued, was hostile to art: 'In olden times beautiful public life was a universal custom, beauty the direct union of the general and the particular, a work of art in which no one part was isolated from the whole.'[1]

This political concept of beauty, which recurs in a slightly different form in Hegel's later writings on aesthetics and on the history of philosophy and law, had already found expression in Schiller's epistolary essay of 1795, 'Über die ästhetische Erziehung des Menschen' (an essay which is also a kind of political propaedeutic).[2] Here, too, the Greek state is seen as a political work of art, contrasted with the modern bureaucratic state which, because of its abstract nature, is alienated from the concrete individual. Since beauty represents the union of the spiritually general with the materially specific, the modern state—which remains 'alien to its citizens, since feeling cannot find it anywhere'[3]— lacks all aesthetic justification.

---

[1] Georg Wilhelm Friedrich Hegel, *Jenenser Realphilosophie* (Leipzig, 1931), ii. 251.
[2] See Dieter Borchmeyer, *Die Weimarer Klassik* (Königstein, 1980), 203–11.
[3] Friedrich Schiller, *Sämtliche Werke*, ed. Gerhard Fricke and Herbert G. Göpfert, 3rd edn. (Munich, 1962), v. 585.

In his preface to *Die Braut von Messina*, written in 1803, Schiller gives a graphic account of the loss of that manifestly beautiful openness of public life which had distinguished the ancient Greek *polis*:

The palace of the kings is now closed, the courts of law have withdrawn from the gates of the town and are held inside houses, writing has displaced the living word, the populace itself, the sensuously living mass, has become the state, and hence an abstract concept, always assuming it does not operate as mere brute force, while the gods themselves withdraw within men's breasts.

The dramatist, however, cannot be allowed to tolerate this situation: he has to revive the beauty and openness of public life on stage[4] if he is to prevent tragedy from being reduced to an inappropriately private level, degenerating to mere specificity of action:

The poet must throw open the palaces again, he must bring the courts out of doors, he must raise up the gods again, he must restore that immediacy which has been destroyed by the artificial organization of real life, and he must cast off all that artificiality in and around man, an artificiality which prevents man from expressing his inner nature and his original character, just as the sculptor casts aside modern clothes, adopting none of man's outer attributes save that which reveals the highest of forms, which is the human form itself.[5]

Wagner read Schiller with avid interest, and there is no denying how close the foregoing thoughts are to his own reform essays. *Art and Revolution* and *The Art-Work of the Future* in particular describe the aesthetic world of the Greeks not only as the basis for the 'total art-work of tragedy' (iii. 12) but, at the same time, as a model for the type of society which Wagner hoped would result from 'mankind's great revolution' (iii. 29), which he believed was imminent, and which was, in brief, a pre-condition of the 'art-work of the future'. The spirit of the Greeks 'existed only in the public arena, in popular comradeship: the needs of this public constituted their cares'; to 'enjoy' that public life, 'the Greek set forth from his simple and unadorned domesticity; it would have struck him as shameful and base to indulge in sophisticated luxuriance and voluptuous pleasures behind the splendid walls of a private palace, leading the sort of existence that nowadays offers stock-market heroes the only meaning to life' (iii. 26). The Greek citizen entrusted his private domestic concerns to the care of a slave, so that his mind remained free for the political and aesthetic aims of public life.

In the case of the Greeks, it was the 'private individual' who was the slave, Karl Marx had written in his *Kritik der Hegelschen Rechtsphilosophie* of 1843, only a few years before Wagner's essay; 'the real private affair

---

[4] See Borchmeyer, *Weimarer Klassik*, 272–303 ('Schöne Öffentlichkeit: Schillers klassisches Drama').

[5] Schiller, *Sämtliche Werke*, ii. 820.

of the citizens, their real content', by contrast, was the *'res publica'*.[6] Similar thoughts had been expressed by Schiller in his 1790 Jena lecture, *Die Gesetzgebung des Lykurgus und Solon*: the arrangement 'whereby minds that were not distracted by any private cares could live for the state alone' had been made possible by the institution of slavery. In order that 'worries about work, or delight in domestic chores' would not distract peoples' thoughts from 'the interests of the fatherland', the Spartan lawgiver Lycurgus had decreed that the 'affairs of everyday life', namely, work at home and in the fields, should be entrusted to Helots.[7] As a result, the Greeks had no difficulty in reconciling their private lives with the interests of the community, since the private individual was not yet emancipated but remained a slave. In the modern world, by contrast, as Karl Marx and Friedrich Engels wrote in *Die heilige Familie* in 1844–5, the division of the individual into a private ('bourgeois') self and a public (*'citoyen'*) self meant that everyone was 'a member of the slave class and of the community at one and the same time'. Whereas the ancient Greek *polis* 'had slavery as its *natural basis*', the modern state was founded on *'emancipated slavery, bourgeois society'*.[8]

'We make a nation of Helots, and have no free citizens', Adam Ferguson had declared in his *Essay on the History of Civil Society*, written in 1767. It is a sentiment which Karl Marx was to cite in the opening volume of *Das Kapital* (1867), where he speaks of the way in which 'division of labour' affects 'not only the economical, but every other sphere of society, and everywhere lays the foundation of that all engrossing system of specialising and sorting men, that development in a man of one single faculty at the expense of all other faculties', which led to the loss of human totality.[9] 'The slave is not free, but the freeman has become a slave', Wagner affirms in *Art and Revolution* (iii. 27). There is little doubt that he is elaborating ideas from the circle of 'Linkshegeliäner' or Young Hegelians here, as well as those of Marx himself.[10] Slavery is described as 'the fateful turning-point in the whole

[6] Karl Marx, *Die Frühschriften*, ed. Siegfried Landshut (Stuttgart, 1964), 51; translated into English as 'Contribution to the Critique of Hegel's Philosophy of Law', in Karl Marx and Friedrich Engels, *Collected Works* (London, 1975), iii. 32.

[7] Schiller, *Sämtliche Werke*, iv. 811.

[8] Karl Marx and Friedrich Engels, *Die heilige Familie*, ed. Irving Fetscher (Frankfurt, 1967), 123, 129; translated into English as 'The Holy Family, or Critique of Critical Criticism', in Marx and Engels, *Collected Works*, iv. 113, 122.

[9] Karl Marx and Friedrich Engels, *Werke* (Berlin, 1970), xxiii. 375; translated into English by Samuel Moore and Edward Aveling as *Capital: A Critical Analysis of Capitalist Production* (London, 1887; repr. 1938), 347. The quotation from Adam Ferguson's *History of Civil Society* is from p. 285 of the 1767 edition.

[10] Martin Gregor-Dellin rightly stresses that it is inconceivable that, even if Wagner never mentions Marx's name, he was not introduced to Marx's writings by revolutionary friends such as

destiny of the world'. 'The slave, by sheer reason of the assumed necessity of his slavery, has exposed the nullity and transience of all the strength and beauty of exclusive Grecian manhood.' (iii. 26.) Wagner is clearly distancing himself from the traditional myth of Greece, which had ignored the material pre-condition for the ancient Greek's aesthetic wholeness. The institution of slavery is said to be 'history's sin against human nature' (iii. 27): the decline and fall of Greek culture and civilization had inevitably followed. Greece's élite lost its freedom and sense of totality, but this did not set men free; rather, it reduced them all to slavery.

This observation provides the starting-point for Wagner's critique of modern art, an art unworthy of its name, since, comprised of marketable goods which the artist sells in order to earn his livelihood, it is subject to the 'slavish' law of providing for his existence. (We are reminded here of Marx's remarks on the 'emancipated slavery' of a bourgeois market society divorced from the political sphere.)

Where the Greek artist was rewarded by success and public acclaim, in addition to his own delight in the work of art, the modern artist is maintained and—*paid*. And thus we come to the point where we are able to draw a sharp and clear distinction between the two: the public art of the Greeks was indeed *art*, ours is—artistic *handiwork*. (iii. 24.)

The Greek citizen had not deigned to devote his attention to any 'actual handicraft' or to 'acquiring life's so-called necessities'. 'His spirit lived only in the public sphere' (iii. 26), and it was to this public sphere that 'art' essentially belonged; only through its economic privatization did it become a handicraft, while the artist himself became an artisan and 'philistine'. This change had far-reaching consequences on the attitude he adopted when creating his art and on his relation to the work he produced:

The *artist* derives enjoyment not only from the object of his creative labour, but from the very act of creation, from his handling and moulding of his raw material; the work he produces is, in itself, a delightful and satisfying activity, certainly no toil. For the *artisan*, by contrast, it is the object of his effort alone which is important, the profit which his work will bring him; the energy which he expends gives him no pleasure, it is only a nuisance, an unavoidable necessity, a burden which he would gladly give over to a machine: if his work enthrals him it is only out of compulsion; that is why he is never mentally present when working, but always looking beyond his work to his goal, which he wants to reach as quickly as possible. (iii. 24–5.)

Bakunin and, later, Georg Herwegh; see Martin Gregor-Dellin, *Richard Wagner: Sein Leben, sein Werk, sein Jahrhundert* (Munich and Zurich, 1980), 357; translated into English by J. Maxwell Brownjohn as *Richard Wagner: His Life, his Work, his Century* (London, 1983), 242.

Wagner's antinomial contrast between the activities of the artist and those of the artisan mirrors exactly the distinction which Aristotle had drawn between action (*praxis*) and production (*poiesis*).[11] Whereas *praxis* is an activity that is its own justification, *poiesis* aims at a product that is separable from the process of production. To this material distinction, it has been customary, since Aristotle, to add a social distinction: the self-contained (chiefly political) action is the preserve of those who are free, while productive labour (producing objects for the free) is reserved for those who are not free. The sense of social precedence enjoyed by the aristocrat has always expressed itself, therefore, in his belief that he belongs to a non-working (but none the less 'active') class, while productive labour is the preserve of the 'lower' orders.

In *Das Kapital* labour is ascribed to the 'workman's will', which largely precludes any possibility of his being 'attracted by the nature of the work, and the mode in which it is carried on'; rather, he will be discouraged from 'enjoying it as something which gives play to his bodily and mental powers'. Its aim is to create a 'product', in the course of which 'the process disappears'.[12] In Wagner's view, this is emphatically not the case with the true artist. Although the latter aims to produce a piece of work, his activity is not completely subsumed by that 'object'; the very act of performing such an activity gives satisfaction to the executant. In contrast to this, the activity of the artisan remains work 'in the sweat of his brow', *labor improbus*, precisely because it is not an end in itself.

Wagner already seems to be equating manual work with modern alienated labour at this point, although he goes on to distinguish clearly between these two forms of activity:

Whereas the artisan's immediate object is merely to satisfy his own need, i.e., to provide his own home, his own chattels, clothing, and so on, his pleasure in the lasting value of these objects will gradually be joined by a desire to fashion the material in such a way as to appeal to his personal taste; once he has produced the most necessary items, his creative urge will address itself to less pressing needs before being raised to the level of artistic creativity; but if he gives away the produce of his toil and if only the abstract monetary value remains, his activity can never rise in character above that of a machine; he regards it only as toil, as sad and bitter labour. This latter is the fate of the slave of industry. (iii. 25.)

Although art, by its very nature, could hardly be further removed from alienated labour, it is none the less subject to the latter's constraints in modern society, and has therefore ceased to be art in the proper sense

[11] See Dieter Borchmeyer, *Höfische Gesellschaft und Französische Revolution bei Goethe: Adliges und bürgerliches Wertsystem im Urteil der Weimarer Klassik* (Kronberg, 1977), 10–12.

[12] Marx and Engels, *Werke*, pp. 193, 195; English trans. (Moore and Aveling), pp. 157, 160.

of the word. The artist who, like the labourer, sells his product as merchandise is lost to himself. It will be the task of the revolution, Wagner goes on, to restore him to himself, to free mankind in general 'from the slave's dishonouring yoke of universal labour', and to raise him to 'free artistic humanity' (iii. 30). And, just as the Greek used the slave, so he will use machines—'that artificial slave of free and creative man'— to overcome his 'worries' about his material existence (iii. 33).

'Must not art grow remote from the artist if the work itself, like some gifted child, no longer reflects on the father?', Ottilie wonders in Wagner's favourite novel, Goethe's *Die Wahlverwandtschaften*. The visual artist, in particular, had to suffer from the paradox that he was 'least able to make his own that which most belongs to him. His works forsake him, just as birds leave the nest in which they were hatched.' But it was the architect who suffered the 'strangest fate' in this respect. 'How often does he apply his whole mind, his whole bent, to designing rooms from which he must then exclude himself! The halls of kings owe him their splendour, but he is not there to enjoy their greatest effect.' This paradoxical separation of the product from the producer would not occur in a community which no longer obliged the artist to work for the private needs of the 'rich'—to whom he handed over 'not only the key to the palace but also all comfort and opulence without being able to enjoy any part of it'. Instead, he should be employed in the service of the community, of which he himself would be an integral part. 'And how much must art have been encouraged when its appointed concern was almost solely the public arena, that which belonged to all and hence to the artist, too!'[13] Goethe, of course, was thinking of Greek art here. This quotation from Ottilie's diary might almost have come from one of Wagner's essays, since the principal demand that he makes of art (the fulfilment of which ultimately legitimizes the concept) was that it should be 'the expression of a free, self-conscious community'; in other words, that it should not be 'subjected' to forces which prevented that community from 'developing freely and independently'. And the most baneful of those influences were not the Fathers of the Church or the princes of the realm (whom Wagner described as 'still respectable gentlemen'), but 'the captains of industry', who dragged art down to the level of a common business venture (iii. 18).

In Wagner's view, the most significant symbol and most perfect realization of a 'free community' was the *Gesamtkunstwerk* or 'total work of art', which he described in *The Art-Work of the Future* as 'the art-work of the people, a work which, in the form of Greek tragedy, 'enters upon the public arena of political life' (iii. 104). The concept of the 'total work of art' continues to be regarded as central to Wagner's aesthetic theory

---

[13] *Goethes Werke*, ed. Erich Trunz (Hamburg, 1959), vi. 374–5.

although it is one which he uses only in passing in his reform essays, where it scarcely enjoys the status of an accredited term. It occurs, rather, in a socio-Utopian context from which he was more or less to distance himself following his encounter with Schopenhauer's philosophy in 1854.[14] He often complained that not only his enemies but his supporters, too, tried repeatedly to pin him down to concepts such as the 'total work of art' or 'infinite melody' which he himself used only casually, or to others such as 'music drama' and 'leitmotif' for which he was not even responsible and of which he was more or less critical. Yet, even today, it is these concepts which are regarded as keys to an aesthetic understanding of his 'music dramas'. People were incapable of reading his essays properly, he noted with resignation in a letter to Liszt of 16 August 1853: 'It would otherwise be quite impossible for this unfortunate "special art" and "total art" to have emerged as the fruit of all my labours.' Popular opinion frequently associates the concept of the total work of art with the very thing that Wagner himself expressly rejected, namely, maximization of theatrical effect by merging all the different arts which constitute 'grand opera'.

Any discussion of Wagner must distinguish between two different concepts of the 'total work of art'. Where the term is expressly employed, it serves to define a cultural vision (the synthesis of all the arts) that goes far beyond its concrete artistic feasibility. But where a union of the arts is held out as a structurally constitutive principle of what he termed 'musical drama', as is the case in part II of *The Art-Work of the Future* (1849) or *Opera and Drama* (1851), what he meant here is simply the restoration of the 'original unity' of the 'three purely human art-forms', which he personifies as the 'primeval sisters' of dance, music, and poetry (iii. 67). United in the Greek concept of *mousike*, they embodied that integration of the mimic, linguistic, and musical dimensions which Wagner consistently espoused, notwithstanding the various shifts in his ideology and his 'conversion' from Feuerbach to Schopenhauer. It is only with regard to this sense of integration (rather than the additive effect of all the arts) that the concept of the total work of art can be invested with any concrete musico-dramatic meaning—assuming that we wish to use it at all, given that Wagner, significantly, refrained from quoting it in this context.

The present chapter is not the place to discuss the dramaturgical variant of this dubious concept. (A fuller account of it will be given in Part II, below.) Our concern here is with that visionary ideal of the 'total work of art' which Wagner had abandoned by 1854 at the latest. Its archetype, according to Wagner, was Greek tragedy. For him, it was the

---

[14] On the crisis in Wagner's idea of the total art-work following his reading of Schopenhauer, see Jack M. Stein, *Richard Wagner & the Synthesis of the Arts* (Detroit, 1960).

exact aesthetic counterpart of the communal way of life whose decline and fall was bound to herald the end of Greek tragedy as such once the latter had begun to disintegrate into the separate arts from which it was made up.

Hand in hand with the dissolution of the Athenian state came the downfall of tragedy. Just as the spirit of the community was fragmented in a thousand egotistical ways, so that great work of total art that is tragedy disintegrated into the individual components that it contained: on the ruins of tragedy, the writer of comedies, Aristophanes, wept in demented laughter [Wagner is referring here to Aristophanes' comic revenge on Euripides in *The Frogs*], and all impulse to create art finally stagnated in the face of philosophy's gloomy broodings as it pondered the reasons for the transience of human beauty and strength. (iii. 12.)

The disunification and independence of the arts stands in the same relation to modern social 'egoism' as their unity does to that 'communism' (iii. 70 and *passim*) which is seen as the social ideal embodied in the Greek *polis* and required for the art-work of the future. (Such 'communism' has, of course, nothing to do with the Communist Manifesto.)[15]

In *The Art-Work of the Future* Wagner compares the decline of the Greek total work of art with the myth of the Tower of Babel. Just as each of the nations involved went its own separate way 'when their languages grew confused and comprehension became impossible', so the individual arts grew separate and autonomous when the common political interest which united them aesthetically 'split into a thousand egotistical particularities' (iii. 76). Only when a free community had been restored (by revolutionary means) could the total work of art of the Greeks be replicated. The latter—and hence the 'art-work of the future'—was bound up with a genuine 'public' as such, i.e., a public that was no longer merely the 'common expression of general egoism' (iii. 127) (just as modern depoliticized bourgeois society inhabits the world of business deals and economic exploitation), but the *res publica* in which private and public interests coincided.

According to Wagner, the 'highest common work of art' could only be drama, since it alone communicated itself directly, via the senses, to a 'common public'. ('The public . . . always clings to what is immediate, to what is physical and real; indeed, it is essentially the give and take of the material world that constitutes what we mean when we use the word "public"': iii. 113.) Taking his example from the individual arts, Wagner holds out the possibility of their 'redemption' (iii. 122) in the musical drama, an act of redemption by virtue of which, it is argued, they will

[15] On the term 'communism', see Wagner's remarks in the introduction to vol. 3 of his *Gesammelte Schriften*, 4th edn. (Leipzig, 1911), 5–6, and also the first section of his fragmentary essay on 'Artists of the Future' (1849) 'On the Principle of Communism' (xii. 254–63).

achieve ultimate perfection. Architecture culminates in theatre architecture; the landscape-painter who has hitherto adorned 'the egoist's solitary interior wall' will henceforth 'fill the broad canvas of the tragic stage' with his work (iii. 150–4); while the miracle of Pygmalion's statue will repeat itself in sculpture when 'the spell on the stone is broken and it is transformed into the flesh and blood of a human being', namely, the dancer, the singing and speaking mime (iii. 140), and so on. In describing this act of self-repeal on the part of the individual arts, Wagner even goes so far as to appeal to the mystical Christian paradox of death as the one true life (iii. 122).

The total art-work of the future can be realized only in and by a *'community comprising all artists'* (iii. 162). The age of the 'individual genius' is past, therefore, according to the unfinished essay, 'Artists of the Future', which Wagner began to draft in 1849: 'all will participate actively in genius, genius will be communal' (xii. 264). Nowhere does it emerge more clearly that Wagner's concept of the 'total work of art', at least to the extent that it aims to combine *all* the arts, is merely an ideological construct which he soon abandoned and which has no material significance in terms of his dramaturgical praxis. This particular meaning is elaborated in only one of his essays, namely, *The Art-Work of the Future*. However, as Thomas Mann has already observed, the Utopian idea that all the arts would merge in drama contradicts Wagner's actual attitude to the arts as individual genres. The composer's numerous admiring remarks about works of 'absolute music', the visual arts, and, above all, literature show that he certainly did not regard them as in any way deficient or incapable of leading a true existence except in the afterlife of the 'total work of art'. Only by interpreting the term *Gesamtkunstwerk* in the sense outlined above, as a Utopian summation of the individual arts, will we share Thomas Mann's view that it represents 'the nineteenth century at its worst', a view that reflects the later writer's belief that art is 'entire and perfect in each of its manifestations'.[16] But this verdict barely affects Wagner's theory as it relates to the integration of gesture, poetry, and music, a theory crucial in determining the structure of the musical drama and one which he continued to hold even after he had renounced the Utopian vision of his revolutionary essays. In short, the ideology of the 'total work of art', at least after 1848, needs to be distinguished from its aesthetic and dramaturgical praxis.

Gottfried Semper, Wagner's friend and fellow-revolutionary at the time of the Dresden Uprising, and one of the most innovative architects of the new age, looked to architecture to achieve the very thing that

---

[16] Thomas Mann, *Wagner und unsere Zeit*, ed. Erika Mann (Frankfurt, 1963), 73; translated into English by Allan Blunden as *Pro and contra Wagner* (London, 1985), 101.

Wagner was looking for in the musical drama, namely, the integration and merging of the individual arts, including drama. The theatre now became the principal challenge to architecture, and here Wagner meets Semper half-way, not least as a result of his reading the latter's *Bemerkungen über vielfarbige Architektur und Skulptur bei den Alten* (1834), which left a decisive mark on his concept of the total art-work and of public life in Greece (see his 'In Recommendation of Gottfried Semper': xvi. 18–19). Whether we see architecture or drama as the determinative art remains an open question in the total art-work of the theatre, although it is undeniable that Semper's plan for a monumental festival theatre in Munich emphasized the architectonic aspect far more than Wagner could ever have wanted. For Wagner, the theatre, as we have seen, was never a self-advertising end in itself but a (modestly designed) means to an end, that end being the presentation of drama, as the architecture of the Bayreuth Festspielhaus makes abundantly clear.

It may be added that in 1851, in his letter to Franz Liszt 'On the Goethe Foundation', Wagner described the architectonic *Gesamtkunst-werk* combining the different visual arts as an entirely legitimate counterpart of the dramatic *Gesamtkunstwerk*, without in any way implying that the former, including the works of sculpture and painting that it embraced, should be 'superseded' by the musical drama, as he had insisted it should be two years previously in *The Art-Work of the Future*. Encouraged by the complementarity of the temporal arts in a musical drama which subsumed the 'fragmentary' genres of spoken theatre and opera, the painter and sculptor, he argued, should come to realize that their works, too, were merely 'fragments of art' that needed to be integrated into an all-encompassing spatial art:

It would then perhaps occur to them that they must likewise weld these fragments into a whole; and for this whole they would have to let the *architect* prescribe that law whose binding protection they continue to evade with such idle pride. As to the position of this architect who now suffers such neglect but who is the true poet of the visual arts, a man to whom the sculptor and painter must turn as the musician and performer turn to the actual poet—once he has thus been advanced to his worthiest office, we ourselves must then come to terms with his relationship towards that work of art which has now been realized by the poet. (v. 17.)

Wagner's total art-work is a quasi-political concept orientated towards the structure of the Greek *polis*: just as the individual was integrated into the community as a matter of course, not yet distinguishing his private interests from his public concerns, so the individual arts were integrated into the total art-work of tragedy. This latter formed, as it were, the *res publica* of the arts. Their fragmentation, therefore, meant that they became less public. This process of privatization culminates in the art market, which provides works of art which, denied to the community, gratify private needs on the part of the modern 'egoist'.

Even after his 'conversion' to Schopenhauer, it remained Wagner's ambition to re-establish the public nature of art by recombining its individual manifestations and by unifying a public that had been split into alienated egoists. But the way back to the Greeks was naturally barred. ('No, let us not become Greeks again', Wagner had already insisted in *Art and Revolution*: iii. 30.) What was important was to find a type of stage that borrowed from the model of Greek drama without neglecting conditions as they existed in the modern theatre. That there were, in Wagner's view, two fundamentally different routes to the theatre of the future will have become clear from the last two chapters. In realizing his own musical drama, the composer considered, but then rejected, the possibility of merging the stage area with the auditorium, insisting instead that 'reality should be separated from ideality' (ix. 337), and seeking to achieve that aim by means of the 'mystic abyss' (ix. 338) of the sunken, invisible orchestra. According to Wagner, the expression 'mystic abyss' was coined jointly by himself and Gottfried Semper. In his letter to King Ludwig's cabinet secretary, Franz von Pfistermeister, of 20 October 1865 Semper had demanded, entirely in keeping with Wagner's own ideas, that the projected festival theatre in Munich should incorporate 'the greatest possible distinction between the ideal world of the stage and the real world as represented by the spectator', insisting on 'the complete avoidance of any encroachment of reality on the realm of ideality'.[17]

In his 1872 essay, 'A Glance at the German Operatic Stage of Today', Wagner was sharply critical of those opera houses where there was 'no dividing line' between 'ostensible artistic events and those for whom those events are enacted. Both dissolve to form a concoction of the most loathsome kind, in which the conductor twirls his baton round as if stirring some modern witches' brew.' What Wagner praises elsewhere as a virtue of the architectural design of the Attic or Elizabethan stage appears here as a shortcoming: 'From nowhere can one obtain a view of the stage that does not also include a large section of the audience.' Why he condemns this in the modern theatre while praising it in its older counterpart becomes clear from the sentence that follows: 'The brightly lit forestage extends as far as the middle of the proscenium box: it is impossible to watch the prima donna here without having at the same time to take in the opera-glass of the opera-lover who sits there ogling

---

[17] See Dagobert Frey, 'Zuschauer und Bühne: Eine Untersuchung über das Realitätsproblem des Schauspiels', in *Kunstwissenschaftliche Grundfragen* (Vienna, 1946), 152–223, esp. pp. 208–9.

her.' (ix. 279.) An audience bent on pleasure, and divided up into separate boxes according to social class or degree, reflects the anti-artistic nature of modern cultural life: it is no longer 'public' in the classical sense of the word. The sight of such an audience is incompatible, therefore, with contemplation of the work of art, whereas the Greek audience, in Wagner's view, was, by its very nature, part of that work of art, so that there was no need for any dividing line between stage and spectator. We may conclude from this that, only when there is no longer an 'audience' in the pejorative sense in which Wagner almost always uses the word (i.e., an isolated body cut off from art), only when it is reintegrated into the *Volk* as a free community, will the eye no longer be aesthetically offended when it takes in both stage and audience at a single glance.

In his 1873 report on *The Stage Festival Theatre in Bayreuth* Wagner describes in some detail the 'relationship between the spectator and the stage picture' in his Bayreuth theatre (finally built by Otto Brückwald to Semper's adapted plans). It is striking that he seeks to characterize this relationship using classical concepts and mythic symbols in order to justify it to his own artistic conscience—not least because the theatre itself is so un-Greek, with a seating arrangement diametrically opposed to the all-encircling design of the Attic theatre:

Once he has taken his seat, the latter [the spectator] finds himself very much in an actual 'theatron', i.e., a room intended for no other purpose than for looking in, and, what is more important, for looking straight ahead. Between him and the picture to be looked at there is nothing clearly perceptible but merely a sense of distance that appears, as it were, to float and which is achieved by the architectonic arrangement of the two proscenium arches: it reveals the distant scene to him with the unapproachability of a dreamlike vision, while the spectral music, rising up from the 'mystic abyss' like vapours wafting up from the sacred primeval womb of Gaia beneath the Pythia's seat, transports him into that inspired state of clairvoyance in which the scenic picture becomes the truest reflection of life itself. (ix. 337–8.)

The stage as an oneiric vision, the spectator as a clairvoyant mystically transported to the world beyond the footlights and forced to gaze in one direction ('straight ahead'), the individual members of the audience united with each other and with the stage not by merging the stage with the living reality of the *Volk* but by collectively merging the audience with the illusionistic world of the drama—this concept of the theatre appears radically different from Wagner's other idea of the stage as outlined in the foregoing chapters. None the less, he continues, as before, to stress the democratic 'arrangement of the classical amphitheatre', which means that, for the first time since the Renaissance, 'our system of rows of boxes' is formally renounced (ix. 336–7). (The Bayreuth auditorium rises towards a single row of boxes structured around a series of pillars and surmounted by a small gallery.) Of course, the proscenium stage precludes any possibility of structuring the auditorium in the shape of a genuine circle, but offers, instead, a wedge-shaped or segmental arrangement, with steeply rising rows of seats designed to allow every member of the audience the same view of the stage.[18] Because 'the stage was used to its full depth', to quote Wagner, and because the forestage was now separated off from the *orchestra*, which had originally been placed in front of it for use by the chorus, 'there could be no question any longer of having an amphitheatre that would have extended some distance on either side and covered more than a full semicircle' (ix. 337). In this assimilation of the classical auditorium with the modern proscenium stage, we see how close to, and at the same time how remote from, the Greek ideal of 'public life' and of its aesthetic equivalent Wagner had now come in his theory and practice of the theatre.

[18] See Heinz Kindermann, *Bühne und Zuschauerraum: Ihre Zueinanderordnung seit der griechischen Antike* (Vienna, 1963), 41.

# II

## OPERA – SPOKEN THEATRE – MUSICAL DRAMA

'Is there any phenomenon that fills us with a more humiliating sense of the impotence of our own frivolous culture than the art of the *Hellenes*?', Wagner asks in *The Art-Work of the Future* (1849). 'Let us look to glorious Greek art, and infer from our inner understanding of it what the art-work of the future must be like.' (iii. 62.) For Wagner, the Greek *polis* was the prototype of the culture of the future and of those social conditions that would permit the true work of art to flourish in days to come. The 'theatre of ancient Athens' offered him 'a typical model' for the 'ideal relationship between theatre and public', he wrote in *'Zukunftsmusik'* in 1860 (vii. 99). At the same time, the *form* of Greek art represented the highest aesthetic norm for him, albeit with certain practical and artistic reservations and with whatever qualifications are necessary when drawing an analogy between two different cultural stages and two different artistic phenomena. Wagner repeatedly stressed that the classical work of art and the art-work of the future were not the same; indeed, that they were radically different from each other, emphasizing what was historically unique and unrepeatable about the aesthetic world of the ancient Greeks, a world to which we cannot and may not return. This is why we often find him defending formal principles such as improvisation even though they were fundamentally at odds with the classical norm, at least as he himself interpreted it.

Of course, even in cases such as these, Wagner's Hellenistic artistic conscience was still very much in evidence. Deviations from the Greek model are not so much justified as points of principle as tolerated as concessions to the modern state of the world and as a kind of alternative practice that does not affect the validity of what went before. On this point Wagner was in agreement with Goethe, whose comments on the 'barbarian advantages' of modern art—advantages which we cannot do without, even if they contradict the highest aesthetic ideal—he was fond of quoting in conversation with Cosima (*CT*, 8 February 1872 and *passim*). To a certain extent, Wagner was re-enacting the *querelle des anciens et des modernes*, a quarrel which had had such momentous consequences for the history of modern art but whose principles he himself was unable to reconcile. The 'ancients' were, so to speak, his book of saints in aesthetic matters, but his more immediate artistic guides were Beethoven and Shakespeare, whom he saw as the two greatest representatives of that period in modern art whose roots he traced back to the Christian Middle Ages. This double aesthetic orientation was not confined to his theoretical writings, but has also left its mark, for example, on the *Ring*, with its reciprocal interaction of 'classically' closed and 'Romantically' open dramaturgical structures.[1]

Wagner's backward glance in the direction of the Greeks was not the wistful gaze that expressed the hope, 'If only we could be like them!'. Rather, it was an appraising look, measuring the future by what was now past. Or, to take a different image, Wagner's return to the Greeks was the action of the athlete who draws back in order to gain momentum for a long jump or high jump. On this point he was at one with his antithetical opposite, Giuseppe Verdi, who, while working on *Falstaff*, was to write to his librettist, Arrigo Boito: 'Let us return to antiquity, it will be a step forward!'

---

[1] See Carl Dahlhaus, *Wagners Konzeption des musikalischen Dramas* (Regensburg, 1971), 25–33.

# 7

## In Search of a Lost Style:
## Wagner's Ideal of 'Classical Form'

'Antiquity is Antaeus in reverse; the higher that time raised it above its maternal soil, the more powerful it became.'

Hugo von Hofmannsthal, *Nachlaß*, 1920.

'Hellenism has the same value for us as the saints have for Catholics.'

Friedrich Nietzsche, *Nachlaß*, 1869.

In his open letter to Nietzsche of 12 June 1872 (a letter prompted by Ulrich von Wilamowitz-Moellendorff's critique of Nietzsche's *Die Geburt der Tragödie*) Wagner voices his enthusiasm for 'classical antiquity', dating his interest in the language, mythology, poetry, and history of ancient Greece from his childhood years. Although he had been denied a thorough philological training, he had, he goes on, gradually distilled 'an ideal perception of art' (ix. 296) from his study of antiquity—by which he invariably meant *Greek* antiquity. (In general he held a low opinion of Roman antiquity, which he was even led, on occasion, to dismiss altogether.) In *Mein Leben* he traces in detail the Greek influences on his view of the world and on his aesthetic thinking, and it is significant that, as with Hölderlin, whose *Hyperion* he naturally held in low esteem (*CT*, 24 December 1873 and *passim*), these influences were mixed with contemporary impressions gained during childhood, notably his enthusiasm for the Greek War of Independence.

My love for Greece, which later fell with enthusiasm upon the mythology and history of Ancient Hellas, thus originated in intense and painful interest in the events of the present. In later years, the story of the struggle of the Greeks against the Persians always revived my impressions of this modern revolt against the Turks. (*ML*, p. 12; English trans., p. 6.)

In his fifth year at the Nicolai School in Leipzig he even wrote 'a chorus in Greek about the most recent war of liberation' (*ML*, p. 42; English trans., p. 35).

Throughout his period as kapellmeister in Dresden and during his early years of exile in Switzerland Wagner's interest in Greek antiquity and classical archaeology reveals an altogether scholarly and professional thoroughness. (The individual stages of this interest have often been traced, most authoritatively perhaps by Wolfgang Schadewaldt.[1]) Wagner's real 'Greek year' was 1847, when he was working on the second complete draft of *Lohengrin*. In his autobiography he reports that his friends were 'amazed at that time to hear me talk with particular vivacity about Greek literature and history, but never about music'. He felt impelled to turn his attention to 'a new and systematic study of this all-important source of culture', and thus to give a greater and more objective sense of direction to his former youthful enthusiasm for 'these eternal elements of humanist education' (*ML*, pp. 352–3; English trans., p. 339).

The fact that Wagner's reading of Aeschylus coincided with the completion of *Lohengrin* and that he continued to draw on Germanic and medieval legend for his subject-matter even after 1847 is less surprising than might otherwise appear. For many antiquarians of his day, medieval research and classical philology went hand in inevitable hand: one thinks, for example, of Wagner's friend in Paris, Samuel Lehrs, who studied both ancient philology and medieval literature and who provided Wagner with ideas for *Tannhäuser*, *Lohengrin*, and *Die Meistersinger*.[2] Wagner himself justified his classical studies by expressly emphasizing his need to come to a deeper understanding of the Middle Ages:

In order to approach the real goal of these studies, Old and Middle High German, I began anew with Greek antiquity and was soon filled with such overwhelming enthusiasm for it that whenever I could be brought to talk, I would only show signs of animation if I could force the conversation around to that sphere. (*ML*, p. 353; English trans., p. 339.)

From classical antiquity Wagner passed logically to 'German antiquity' (*ML*, p. 356; English trans., p. 343). The extent to which he was influenced by the spirit of ancient Greece in his reinterpretation of these later texts (and hence also of those works that he adapted for his own dramatic ends) emerges not least from his 1851 *Communication to my Friends*, in which he draws attention to the Greek archetypes that lie behind the characters of his early music dramas—the Odysseus myth in *Der fliegende Holländer*, the myth of Zeus and Semele in *Lohengrin*, and so on.

From now on, the nucleus of Wagner's classical reading was to remain the *Oresteia*, a fascination which culminated in what was

[1] Wolfgang Schadewaldt, 'Richard Wagner und die Griechen', in Wieland Wagner (ed.), *Richard Wagner und das neue Bayreuth* (Munich, 1962), 149–74. A useful summary of Schadewaldt's writings, together with a number of independent insights into the influence of Greek ideas on Wagner's thinking, is contained in Hugh Lloyd-Jones, *Blood for the Ghosts: Classical Influences in the Nineteenth and Twentieth Centuries* (London, 1982), 126–42.

[2] See Schadewaldt, 'Wagner und die Griechen', p. 153.

evidently an overwhelming recitation of the tragedy in the Villa Angri in Naples in 1880. On 24 June 1880, in conversation with Cosima, he declared Aeschylus's trilogy to be 'the most perfect thing in every way, religious, philosophic, poetic, artistic'. According to *Mein Leben*, his initial encounter with Aeschylus in the summer of 1847 had left a decisive mark on his ideas concerning the theatre:

Droysen's eloquent commentaries [it was in Droysen's translation that Wagner read Aeschylus] in particular helped to bring the intoxicating vision of Attic tragedy so clearly before me that I could see the *Oresteia* with my mind's eye as if actually being performed, and its impact on me was indescribable. There was nothing to equal the exalted emotion evoked in me by *Agamemnon*; and to the close of *The Eumenides* I remained in a state of transport from which I have never really returned to become fully reconciled with modern literature. My ideas about the significance of drama, and especially of the theatre itself, were decisively moulded by these impressions. (*ML*, p. 356; English trans., pp. 342–3.)

Rarely has a leading creative artist of the modern period acknowledged his indebtness to Greek art with such unconditional and emphatic candour as Wagner does here in this homage to Attic tragedy. His reading of Droysen's translation of the *Oresteia* has left clear poetic traces on the *Ring*, not only in terms of the plot and the relationships between the various characters, where a wealth of parallels between Greek and Germanic myth may be discerned, but also on a linguistic level. (Droysen's translation even provided examples of the use of alliteration.[3])

That Wagner's interest in the Greeks remained vital and sustaining right up to the end of his life is impressively documented by Cosima's *Diaries*. Countless evenings at Tribschen and Wahnfried were spent reading classical writers, most notably Homer, Aeschylus, Plato, and Aristophanes (whom Wagner described as 'the greatest of Greek geniuses': *CT*, 31 December 1880). While rereading Droysen's life of Alexander the Great, Wagner remarked over lunch on 6 March 1870: 'If I were locked up in prison, I should ask only for Greek literature and things about Greece. From these people we derive joy; I am well aware that they did not dot all the *i*'s, but from them we learn happiness, they are without sin.' There are echoes here of that eighteenth-century view of Greece as a 'naïve' nation, a view which Wagner continued to hold in spite of the more recent, more realistic understanding of Greek civilization that he had acquired from the major scholarly writings of Johann Gustav Droysen, Friedrich Gottlieb Welcker, August Boeckh, and Karl Otfried Müller. And yet, for all these transfiguring statements,

[3] See Wolfgang Schadewaldt's articles, 'Richard Wagner und die Griechen', in *Die Programmhefte der Bayreuther Festspiele 1963*, iii. *'Die Meistersinger von Nürnberg'*, 24–44, and *Die Programmhefte der Bayreuther Festspiele 1964*, iii. *'Die Meistersinger von Nürnberg'*, 3–30.

it cannot be denied that in old age—inspired not least by Nietzsche's *Die Geburt der Tragödie*—Wagner came increasingly to see the Greeks as a 'sentimental' nation in Schiller's sense of the term.[4] On 13 June 1871, in the course of a conversation about Schopenhauer, he said of the Greeks: 'In the ancient world it was joy in overcoming misfortunes which inspired them; they acknowledged that life and the world were loathsome—"but I am stronger than they"; the strongest affirmation of the will.' There is no longer any room here for a 'naïve' interpretation of the Greeks.

How deeply Wagner's view of the world and his way of seeing things were influenced by Greek myth is attested not only by what he himself read and by the plans he drew up for his children's education (where the world of classical legend occupied a permanent place), but above all by the constant pointers to classical ideas that permeate his remarks on even the most everyday occurrences. Time and again he discovered Greek archetypes behind them, or else he played off the formal classical world against the prosaicness of modern life. 'At lunch R. catches sight of the old man whom we have engaged to pump out the water, which is still tainted with iron', Cosima reported on 8 May 1874, 'it reminds him of the maiden in the *Odyssey* who ground corn during the night. He is filled with pity: "The noise sounds primeval, it is like the squeaking of the spheres."' On another occasion, while the couple were out walking in Italy, Wagner 'suddenly points to a peasant pushing his barrow across the sun-drenched horizon: "A picture of antiquity", he exclaims.' (*CT*, 25 September 1880.) 'As I come down the steps from the *salon* [at Wahnfried] to join him and our friends he says, "Circe approaching Odysseus and his companions!"' (*CT*, 13 May 1882), and so on. Whether he was out walking, or at table, or engaged in various other everyday activities, he was constantly struck by such images, and sometimes even by phrases from the Homeric epics in the original Greek (see *CT*, 30 March 1878). On one occasion he even took it into his head to make an 'Apollo knot' for Cosima, but first, he told her, he intended to study 'etchings of the ancient Greeks' (*CT*, 30 June 1878). Wagner admired the way in which 'all these sagas continued to live in their [the Greeks'] thoughts; with us nothing now remains alive' (*CT*, 17 February 1879). Modern life, he lamented, was lacking in myth and form. 'People who learned nothing of the "ancient Greeks" in their childhood have no eye for beauty', he told Cosima on 4 May 1870. 'All

---

[4] The categories 'naïve' and 'sentimental' were proposed by Friedrich Schiller in his 1795–6 essay, *Über naive und sentimentalische Dichtung*. The naïve poet is at one with nature and tends towards realism. The sentimental poet is conscious of his separation from nature and longs to return to it; his poetry is idealistic. The terms are sometimes rendered into English as 'spontaneous' and 'reflective'. See also Preface, above.

my later feelings about the ugliness of our present world stem from looking at the illustrations in Moritz's mythology. [The *Götterlehre* of Karl Philipp Moritz, first published in 1791, had been of great significance for Goethe and Schiller, too.] Perseus with his fine helmet, but otherwise naked, delighted me and made me disgusted with our whole military system, with its buttoned-up uniforms plastered with decorations.'

Allusions to the myths and history of the Greeks recur repeatedly in Wagner's exegesis of musical works. On 11 March 1873, for example, he described Beethoven's Seventh Symphony as 'a complete portrait of a Dionysian festival':

At the start the herald and the tibia players, then the gathering people (the scale), after that the charming theme, whose swinging movement gives the idea of a procession, and so on. The Andante is the tragedy, the sacrifice of the god, memories of Zagreus, "you, too, have suffered", then the rustic celebrations, the vine-growers and other country people with their thyrsi, and to end with, the Bacchanalia.

Even contemporary issues were judged by classical standards. Bismarck and the politics of the Second Reich were scarcely calculated, of course, to inspire thoughts of ancient Greece, but Garibaldi, whom Wagner admired immensely and whom he saw in Italy in March 1882, was for him 'a classical figure [who] belonged to the time of Timoleon' (*CT*, 3 June 1882). It was to Plutarch, with whose age he felt such close affinity, that Wagner owed his picture of the Corinthian general. On 6 December 1881, for example, while 'thinking of a time and place in which he would like to have lived, he says it would be with Plutarch in Chaeroneia: he had been very close to the greatest and had experienced so much, then came under the wing of the Antonines, but always in Chaeroneia'.

Wagner's response to the mythology and art of ancient Greece was bound up with his wish to establish a viable modern art-form. Like Nietzsche at a later date, he was repeatedly troubled by the fact that the modern artist—and especially the German artist—could not turn for support to any normatively valid social and aesthetic form. 'If I had a question for the future', he told Cosima on 24 December 1872, 'it would be this: Will anything still come of the Germans? Will they find their form? This question I find of boundless interest.' And on 12 November 1879: 'We are no longer artists nowadays. The short stories of Lope and Cervantes may be insignificant, but what form they have! Whereas even Goethe and Schiller were always just searching, experimenting.' There is little doubt that it was while listening to remarks such as these that Nietzsche picked up many of the ideas that inform his discussion of the problem of form in German and Romance writers. Even his concept of dilettantism is already hinted at by Wagner. 'Talking again about E. T. A. Hoffmann, R. says he is always intrigued by the dilettantism in Germany, for to a certain extent all our greatest poets have been dilettantes, who produce sketches, in contrast to the Greeks, whose work always seems complete and assured.' (*CT*, 5 January 1871.) In the fourth of his *Unzeitgemäße Betrachtungen*, Nietzsche would later single out 'dilettantism' as a basic feature of Wagner's artistic development, too.[5]

Wagner's most revealing remark on the problem of national form is to be found in his 1860 essay, *'Zukunftsmusik'*, a work largely intended to introduce French readers to his aesthetic outlook:

It cannot be denied that at an early date the Romance nations of Europe came to enjoy one great advantage over the Germanic nations, and that advantage lay in their cultivation of *form*. While Italy, Spain, and France, in life as well as in art, were each evolving pleasing forms appropriate to their individual natures, such that those forms acquired a universally valid and legitimate application in every manifestation of life and art, Germany remained in a state of undeniable anarchy in this respect, a state which was scarcely concealed, but rather aggravated, by its attempts to use ready-made foreign forms for its own particular ends. The obvious disadvantage from which the German nation suffered in consequence in terms of everything concerning form (and how widely this extends!) very naturally inhibited the development of German art and literature, so that it is only since the second half of the last century in Germany that a movement has arisen comparable to what the Romance nations had achieved from the time of the Renaissance onwards. (vii. 93–4.)

In seeking its own unique form, the spirit of German art must begin by rejecting that 'Romance form' which it had merely imitated. (Wagner is doubtless thinking first and foremost of those 'rules' of French neo-Classical drama which had dominated the German stage up until the time of Lessing.) This was necessary, Wagner argued, not least because 'Romance form' had a specifically national stamp to it and was therefore bound to remain a foreign body in the art of any other nation.

According to Wagner, the 'German movement' of the late eighteenth century did not aim at establishing a specifically national 'German form'; rather, it followed the Greek model in seeking to constitute a 'purely human' art-form which would transcend all national boundaries.

The movement strove resolutely to discover an ideal, purely human form that did not belong exclusively to any single nationality. The distinctive significance of Goethe and Schiller, Germany's two greatest poets, was that, as never before

---

[5] Friedrich Nietzsche, *Sämtliche Werke: Kritische Studienausgabe in 15 Bänden*, ed. Giorgio Colli and Mazzino Montinari (Munich, 1980), i. 436; translated into English by R. J. Hollingdale as *Untimely Meditations: Richard Wagner in Bayreuth* (Cambridge, 1983), 200.

in the history of art, they concerned themselves with the problem of an ideal, purely human form of art in its most comprehensive sense, indeed, one might almost say that the quest for this form is the one essential component in all their creative endeavours. Rebelling against the constraints of a form which the Romance nations still regarded as binding, they succeeded in viewing that form objectively, perceiving not only its benefits but also its disadvantages, tracing it back to the origins of all European art, namely, Greek art, finding the necessary freedom to gain a full understanding of classical form, and thence setting out in search of an ideal art-form which, as one that was purely human and liberated from the constraints of narrower national conventions, was intended to turn those very conventions into something purely human, something that obeyed none but the most everlasting laws. (vii. 94.)

In his search for such a form, Wagner saw himself as the direct, legitimate heir of Weimar Classicism. On the one hand, therefore, he stresses the negative consequences of aesthetic anarchy, in other words, the loss of a universally binding, epoch-making style and formal principle that would have left their mark on all expressions of life and art. (It was a loss of which many aesthetic writers of the nineteenth century were aware, either as a matter of regret or, in the case of those who championed the emancipation of a more personal style, as a cause for celebration.[6]) On the other hand, Wagner sees in this loss a positive advantage in terms of artistic freedom. The ideal art-form which he was striving to achieve was intended to leave behind it all those limitations imposed on the creative artist by any strictly a priori form, such as that prescribed by Romance art, but at the same time he hoped that it would bring together all the advantages of a regulative stylistic principle. (This, in fact, was also one of the aims of Goethe and Schiller, as their correspondence repeatedly attests.)

The disadvantage under which the Germans have laboured hitherto when compared with the Romance nations would thus be turned to an advantage. Whereas the Frenchman, for instance, perfectly satisfied with a fully developed and self-contained form that is congruent in every part and willingly obeying its seemingly unalterable laws, feels that he is required only to reproduce that form in perpetuity and hence that he is bound (in a higher sense) to tolerate a certain stagnation of his inner creativity, the German, while fully admitting the advantages of such a position, would none the less perceive its serious shortcomings; its lack of freedom would not escape him, and there would open up the prospect of an ideal art-form in which the eternal validity of every single art-form would appear to him freed from the fetters of accident and untruth. (vii. 94–5.)

This ideal art-form, which, 'dispensing with the constraining element of a narrower nationality, would be universally understandable and

---

[6] See Wladimir Weidlé, *Die Sterblichkeit der Musen* (Stuttgart, 1958), 153ff.

accessible to every nation', could not be achieved, Wagner believed, in the field of literature, since the diversity of languages placed strict limitations on any cosmopolitan aim. Music alone—'a language immediately understandable to all mankind'—was the medium in which the ideality of form might best be realized (vii. 95). 'The only possible Church nowadays', Wagner told Cosima on 7 June 1874, ' is music, with Beethoven as the high priest.' Musical drama was, therefore, the culmination of the 'German movement' for him, or, more especially, the culmination of the aesthetic aspirations of Goethe and Schiller.

If it was 'classical form' which Wagner always saw as the ideal form of art, it was a Classicism indebted to eighteenth-century descriptions and interpretations. In his diary jottings, published in 1878 under the title 'What is German?', he argued that 'the concept of antiquity dates from the middle of the last century, in other words, from the time of Winckelmann and Lessing'. In advancing this viewpoint, Wagner was repeating an idea that many other writers had held since Schiller's day (see the latter's poetic fragment, *Deutsche Größe*, quoted on p. 26): the German spirit, being universal, was capable not only of subsuming all foreign elements within it, but also of 'comprehending and assimilating all that was foreign, all that was originally remote from it, and of doing so, moreover, in the utmost purity and objectivity of intuition'. This was especially true of classical antiquity, which, according to Wagner, was a specifically German concept, owing its existence to the alleged affinity between the Greek and German spirits. (This, too, was an idea often expressed by the adherents of Weimar Classicism.)

One may claim without exaggeration that antiquity would have remained unknown in its present universal significance, had the German spirit not recognized and explained it. The Italian appropriated those aspects of antiquity which he could imitate and reproduce; the Frenchman, in turn, borrowed from this reproduction whatever might flatter his national feeling for elegance of form: but the German was the first to recognize it in its purely human originality, divining in it a meaning wholly divorced from all utilitarian concerns and therefore uniquely suited to representing the purely human. Through its innermost understanding of the antique, the German spirit has acquired the ability to reproduce the purely human in turn in all its original freedom, not representing a particular subject by drawing upon some antique form, but creating a new and necessary form by drawing upon the antique view of the world. (x. 40–1.)

This final quotation shows that Wagner saw classical form not as something instantly applicable but merely as an incitement to discovering some 'new form'. He never lost sight of the historical distance between Greek antiquity and the nineteenth century. The former could not influence modern art *an sich*, but only when refracted by time and viewed in the light of our own contemporary concept of it. In this context, it is worth drawing attention to one of the most important essays by the later Wagner. Written in 1878 and entitled 'The Public in Space and Time', it takes as its starting-point the belief that even the greatest work of art is dependent upon its historical place and moment of creation, however much its influence may transcend the age that produced it.

Using the examples of Plato, Dante, Calderón, Renaissance painting, and the works of Mozart, Wagner demonstrates the way in which 'every individual phenomenon is subjected to the contingencies of time and space', a dependency which is 'tragic' for every artist of any significance (x. 92), since the essence of his art does not lie beyond his own time. Great art is not 'timeless', to quote the modern philistine phrase; it is both tied to a particular age and, at the same time, above all considerations of time. But to reduce a work of art to its timeless element, and to pass that element off as its true essence, is tantamount to divorcing it from the earth which gave it life. 'It is clear to us from Mozart's operas that the very quality by which they transcended their age brought with it the curious disadvantage that they were condemned to outlive that age, when the vital conditions that governed their conception and execution no longer existed.' Hence Wagner describes 'the seal of immortality' as 'a fatal gift'.

To what torments of existence is the departed soul of such a masterpiece exposed when tormented back to life by a modern theatrical medium for the delectation of a later generation! When we attend a performance of *Figaro* or *Don Giovanni* today, would we not rather the work had once lived a full and complete life, existing in our memory as a beautiful legend, than see its corpse resuscitated, abused, and forced to lead a life so wholly alien to it? (x. 96.)

For a modern audience, which takes it for granted that works of art from every period will always be available in the museum of the mind that today's culture industry has to offer, this is a provocative standpoint indeed. But, for Wagner, such a museum-like approach to works of art from the most disparate periods—an approach which treats them all as contemporaneous and invests them all with equal validity—was little short of preposterous. 'Nobody would be more surprised than Mozart to see things he wrote for an "academy" or a concert evening proclaimed as eternal masterpieces', Wagner told Cosima on 26 June 1882. The impression that a work made on later generations was, he believed, never more than a shadow of its impact on contemporaries. 'Even though the impression Shakespeare makes—on him, for example—is greater than on the public of his own time, it is no longer a living thing.' (*CT*, 17 November 1882.)

Even in his self-justificatory essay *A Communication to my Friends*, written in 1851, Wagner had had sharp words to say about that point of view which judged everything according to a single 'monumental standard' whereby 'artists and works of all ages and nations are piled up beside, or on top of, each other' without the differences between them being felt 'as something warm and living': 'for if our feelings are at all authentic, their simultaneous exhibition must be altogether insupportable—about as painfully unpleasant as if we were to hear Sebastian Bach performed alongside Beethoven' (iv. 244). This was still a paradoxical notion for Wagner. As in the 1878 essay, he uses the example of Mozart's operas to show that an artist 'who sees his work treated as something monumental, something that may be performed indifferently at any given time before any given audience, must be exposed to every conceivable danger of misunderstanding', since the conditions which make that work, and its connection with 'real life', possible are inevitably denied (iv. 243).

There is no doubt that Wagner's critique of the tendency to monumentalize works of art, in other words, the tendency to divorce them from the time, place, and vital conditions that gave rise to them, inspired the second of Nietzsche's *Unzeitgemäße Betrachtungen*, 'Vom Nutzen und Nachteil der Historie für das Leben',[7] which Wagner read with great interest in February 1874 (*CT*, 22–4 February 1874). Here, too, a significant role is allotted to Nietzsche's critique of the closely related notion of 'monumental history'.

For Wagner, there was the same distinction between the authentic and the 'monumental' work of art as there is between a living person and a marble statue. The former is characterized by the fact that 'it reveals itself as something that is defined in the sharpest possible way by time, place, and circumstance; in other words, that it cannot manifest itself in its most vital and effective form unless it does so in a particular place, at a particular time, and in particular circumstances' (iv. 237). All these pre-conditions for the existence of a work of art are subsumed, for Wagner, under the concept of 'life', so that the most decisive way in which the 'tendency towards monumentalism' can be counterbalanced is through the immediate 'vital instinct' (iv. 238–9). It is this idea, more than any other in *A Communication to my Friends*, that points the way to the second of Nietzsche's *Unzeitgemäße Betrachtungen*.

In Wagner's view, the classic example of the way in which a previously non-monumental work of art could be monumentalized was a performance of Sophocles' *Antigone* which took place in Potsdam in 1841 at the behest of Friedrich Wilhelm IV. The incidental music was

---

[7] See Nietzsche, *Sämtliche Werke*, i. 243–334; translated into English by R. J. Hollingdale as *Untimely Meditations: On the Uses and Disadvantages of History for Life* (Cambridge, 1983), 57–123.

written by Mendelssohn. In 1851, in *Opera and Drama*, Wagner dismissed this antiquarian experiment as 'a crude and artistic white lie' (iv. 29). In *A Communication to my Friends* he poked fun at the idea that a work 'written two thousand years ago for Athenian democracy' could be performed today, without further ado, 'before the Prussian Court in Potsdam; in the opinion of our aestheticians, it must have exactly the same value, exactly the same essential qualities, no matter whether it be performed here or there, now or then'. And, Wagner adds sarcastically, people no doubt imagined 'that, like certain types of wine, it was improved by being laid down, and that only here today could it be properly and rightly understood' (iv. 236).

These ideas are taken up again in 'The Public in Space and Time', where Attic tragedy is said to have 'made a wholly different impression when it flourished in Syracuse than it did when performed in Athens'. And how different again, how much more alien, must its impact be on the modern stage! 'We see, in fact, that those same temporal circumstances which were so detrimental to the revelation of that great spirit also provided the sole conditions necessary for this product of the mind to manifest itself in physical form, so that, divorced from its proper time and circumstances, this product was robbed of the most important part of its vital effectiveness.' This was even more true of the Greek tragedians, inasmuch they were 'happily enclosed by the time and place of their surroundings, so that the latter, far from hindering them, exercised a creative influence on their works'. Wagner considers this fortunate state of affairs to be 'an exceptional phenomenon' in history (iv. 94–5).

It is against this background that we must see Wagner's theory of 'classical form'. It is a formal model conceived in the light of Greek art, but one which never loses sight of the latter's uniqueness and never underestimates the historical distance between the art of ancient Greece and that of nineteenth-century Germany. Attic tragedy, for example, is described in *The Destiny of Opera* (1871) as 'so specific and original a product of the Hellenic spirit and its religion, nay, even of its state, that to assume that it might be copied must necessarily lead to the greatest of errors' (ix. 151).

The essential features of classical form are described in Wagner's chief theoretical work, *Opera and Drama*, which will be examined in greater detail in the chapters that follow. Its principal characteristics are the concision, unity, and self-contained plasticity of design that distinguish Attic tragedy above all else. For the author of *Opera and Drama*, this, with its 'unified form' (iv. 34), was the most important structural model for the musical drama he was aiming to write. At the same time, it was the antithesis of two forms—the *opera* and the *novel*—

which Wagner considered representative of the modern period but which, from the standpoint of the art-work of the future, simply ought not to exist. The diffuseness of form of these two genres may well have mirrored the superficial structure of modern life, but, according to Wagner, such diffuseness could not survive his own awareness of form.

# 8

## Opera as an Immoral Institution

> Modern Italian opera music has been called, with singular
> appropriateness, a prostitute ... French opera music is rightly
> regarded as a coquette ... But there is a further type of degenerate
> woman who fills us with repugnance and loathing: I mean the
> prude, and it is to her that so-called German opera music has to be
> compared.
>
> Wagner, Opera and Drama, part I.

No art-form comes in for such violent criticism in Wagner's post-1848 reform essays as that of 'opera'. He appears to share all the feelings of resentment that have ever been harboured against this 'impossible' genre, particularly by the rationalist poets of the eighteenth century, describing it in *Opera and Drama* as 'a madhouse for all the follies of the world' (iii. 226). His account of its reprehensible form, the conditions which gave rise to it, and its subsequent reception forms a sombre background against which he elaborates his concept of what is intended to be a radically different kind of theatre, namely, musical drama. The latter, he insists, shall owe its structure neither to opera nor to modern 'literary drama', but to the living dramatic art of the Greeks and of Shakespeare on the one hand, and, on the other, to modern instrumental music, by which he means, first and foremost, symphonic form. When Wagner speaks of opera, he is generally thinking of the Italian and French music theatre and its specific audience; when he mentions spoken drama, it is, as a rule, the German post-classical literary drama that he has in mind, a genre which, by Wagner's day, had grown remote from theatrical reality. He himself attempts to steer his ship between the Scylla of a superficial musical dramaturgy and the Charybdis of its desensualized literary equivalent, guiding the beleaguered vessel towards the 'art-work of the future', which, in the form of 'musical drama', he sees as the only legitimate 'drama'. It is a vessel, moreover, which—to extend the composer's own maritime imagery—is built on the model of ancient tragedy, while its sails are filled by the breath of Beethoven's symphonies (cf. iv. 159–60).

'I shall write no more *operas*', Wagner announced in 1851 in *A Communication to my Friends* (iv. 343). Only in later essays such as *On the Destiny of Opera* (1871) did he adopt a more conciliatory attitude towards this generic description: even if one concedes, he writes, 'that opera has made the decline of the theatre plain for all to see', it is 'none the less clear from its present supremacy that it alone can be called upon to re-establish our theatre on a healthier basis' (ix. 135). This is a view which the Wagner of the earlier period would have refuted emphatically. Even as late as 1860, in *'Zukunftsmusik'*, he was still describing the operatic theatre as 'the most dubious and most ambiguous public institution of our day' (vii. 89), a value-judgement that is both aesthetic and moral.

Largely ignored hitherto, one of the corner-stones of Wagner's aesthetic theory is his identification of moral and aesthetic 'good', and his unmasking of artistic shortcomings as moral ones. In doing so, he denies that distinction between moral and aesthetic judgements which has constituted modern aesthetic theory since Karl Philipp Moritz, Kant, and Schiller. For Wagner, the stage was what Schiller had called a 'moral institution'. (Only later did Schiller revise his views under the influence of the aesthetic writings of Moritz and Kant.) Of course, in Wagner's case, we are dealing less with the identification than with the confusion of aesthetic and moral categories; judgements intended as moral ones repeatedly turn out to be grounded in aesthetics or cultural theory. At all events, there is scarcely a single essay by Wagner in which artistic conditions are not unequivocally equated with moral ones. The 'good in art', we read in 'Public and Popularity' of 1878, 'is synonymous with the morally good' (x. 75). And, according to the report with which he concluded his *Gesammelte Schriften und Dichtungen*, Wagner expected that the Bayreuth Festival would raise the level of 'national morality'. 'For it is certain that public morality can easily be judged by the character of a nation's public art.' (ix. 318.) Similar expressions may be found in almost all of Wagner's essays, from virtually every phase of his development as an artist. It is not surprising, therefore, that he even falls back on Enlightenment maxims which classical aesthetics had made to seem antiquated. Time and again, for example, we find him appealing to Joseph II's demand: 'The theatre should contribute to the ennoblement of the nation's morals and taste.' (vii. 274, 280–1, and *passim*). It is by this demand, he insists, that every artistic phenomenon must be judged.

By raising the theatre to the level of a moral institution, the Enlightenment had sought to pre-empt all moral outrage on the part of Protestant orthodoxy. It is extremely revealing, therefore, to follow the way in which Wagner, whenever he castigates the commercial theatre, and especially the 'frivolous institution' of opera (vii. 98), for offering mere entertainment, exchanges the garb of the Enlightenment philosopher, insisting on the stage's moral function, for the clergyman's cassock, and how, sometimes wagging his finger in remonstration, sometimes adopting the stance of the professional exorcist, he tries to do away with actors and all their troublesome ways. In 'German Art and

German Politics' (1867–8) he outlines the whole range of moral and aesthetic possibilities which the theatre has to offer, from the bloody indecency of gladiatorial games to the 'heavenly rainbow' of the *auto sacramentale*, very much justifying the Church's doubts in the face of this pandemonium:

If we enter a theatre, we shall, if we are capable of calm contemplation, look into a daemonic abyss whose possibilities range from the lowliest to the most sublime . . . With awe and dread have the greatest poets of all nations ever drawn near this fearful abyss; they devised the most ingenious laws, solemn spells to drive away the demon lurking there, and Aeschylus himself, with priestly dignity, led the tamed Erinnyes as divinely revered Eumenides to the place where they might be redeemed from baneful curses . . . But once the great hallowed sorcerers step back from its brink, the Furies of vulgarity, lowest concupiscence, and of the vilest passions, loutish gnomes of the most dishonouring pleasure, dance around the abyss. Banish hence the kindly spirits . . . and you will abandon the fields where gods once wandered to the filthiest offspring of Hell—and these latter will come of their own accord, uncalled—for they have always been at home in places whence only the advent of the gods could drive them away.—And this monster, this pandemonium, this terrible theatre you thoughtlessly leave to be run by mechanical routine . . . This theatre against which the Protestant clergy of the previous century perceptively warned you as a snare of the Devil . . .! (viii. 60–2.)

Opera in particular—that immoral institution *par excellence*—finds no favour when haled before this moral tribunal. The verbal excesses of which Wagner was capable in his social and moral condemnation of it emerge from the remarks he made on the occasion of a terrible fire at the Ringtheater in Vienna on 8 December 1881, when some four hundred members of the audience perished while waiting for a performance of Offenbach's *Tales of Hoffmann* to start. Two days later, when asked his opinion of the catastrophe, he replied: 'the most useless people frequented such an opera house; if poor workers are buried in a coal mine, that both moves and angers him, but a case like this scarcely affects him at all'. A few days later he was even more inexorably damning in his 'lack of sympathy in connection with the catastrophe in Vienna':

It sounds hard and is almost unnatural, but people are too wicked for one to be much affected when they perish in masses. As I have already said, when people are buried in coal mines, I feel indignation at a community which obtains its heating by such means; but when such-and-such a number of members of this community die while watching an Offenbach operetta, an activity which contains no trace of moral superiority, that leaves me quite indifferent. (*CT*, 16 December 1881.)

Verbal terrorism in the name of a social-critical message of sympathy!

But what was it that Wagner considered immoral about modern opera, especially the Italian and French variety? It was 'an institution whose public function was aimed, almost exclusively, at diverting and entertaining a population addicted to pleasure through utter boredom and which was dependent, moreover, upon earning money in order to cover the cost of the spectacles devised for that very end' (vii. 98). Opera as standardized by the repertory theatre had become the epitome of the modern consumer product. The very origins of opera—'at Italy's wanton courts' (iii. 231), and hence far removed from the *Volk*—were clear evidence, in Wagner's view, that the only audience for this genre was the pleasure-seeking 'man of luxury' (iii. 249). (Wagner had only the vaguest, not to say erroneous, ideas concerning the origins of opera: the name of Monteverdi, for example, is never mentioned in the whole of his prose writings.) It is this search for distraction and amusement which, according to Wagner, produces a diffuse form of opera, hostile to any sense of poetico-dramatic 'unity':

At opera houses in Italy an audience gathered which spent its evenings amusing itself; part of this amusement was the music which was sung on stage and which the audience would listen to from time to time during breaks in their conversation; the music continued during such conversations and while visits were paid from box to box, its function being that of table-music at grand dinners, namely, to encourage the otherwise timid talkers to speak up and drown its noise. The music that is played for this purpose and during these conversations fills out the vast bulk of any Italian opera score, while the music to which one really listens makes up perhaps a twelfth of it . . . Are we to blame this public if, suddenly confronted by a work which claims the same degree of attention throughout its entire length and for every one of its individual parts, it sees itself, at musical performances, wrenched from all its former habits? (vii. 124–5, *'Zukunftsmusik'*.)

According to this view, the structurally determinative feature of Italian opera is the division into conversational recitative (to be listened to in an absent-minded way) and aria (requiring close attention), whereas musical drama demands that the audience's concentration be directed at the entire dramatic work of art, not just at individual numbers. Musical drama is an integrated musico-poetic unity (its unity guaranteed by its leitmotivic structure) which thus demands the listener's undivided attention and a degree of absorption bordering on reverence. In other words, the concentrated form of musical drama results from the fact that the circumstances surrounding it, and the immediate causes behind it, are fundamentally different from those of 'number opera', which is essentially diffuse in structure. If opera, to quote Wagner, is 'the means' to a conversational end (conversation being the 'chief purpose of any operatic evening': vii. 125), the musical drama is an end in itself, that end being *contemplation* on the part of the *Volk* that has gathered for the purpose of self-recollection. Works of dramatic art, therefore, are no longer suited to pre-established, institutionalized social occasions, they themselves have become the occasion; they no longer go out in search of a 'public', they invite that public to come to them. To pick up Walter Benjamin's earlier remark, the public does not absorb the work of art but enters into it and is absorbed by it.

# 9

# The Birth of Opera from 'Absolute Melody':
# The Origins of Wagnerian Music Theatre

The absolute arts are a sad modern impertinence. Everything is falling apart. There is no organization to foster all the arts together as Art.

Nietzsche, *Nachlaß*, 1869.

Wagner's most detailed critique of traditional music theatre comes in the first part of his chief theoretical work, *Opera and Drama*, and is entitled 'Opera and the Essence of Music'. The titles of the other two parts ('Spoken Theatre and the Essence of Dramatic Poetry' and 'Poetry and Music in the Drama of the Future') make it clear that the train of thought in *Opera and Drama* follows the popular dialectical model of thesis, antithesis, and synthesis: opera and spoken drama are to be 'superseded' by the 'drama' which alone deserves that name.

Wagner submits here to the constraints of a system which elsewhere—most notably in his letters and in conversation with others—he repeatedly ignores. He sets out to argue, in the spirit of Hegel, from the standpoint of that 'absolute knowledge' which will find expression in the 'drama of the future'. This latter relegates all previous forms of musical and poetical drama—indeed, every form of music and poetry in general—to the realm of past history, and highlights the painful difference between them and the true telos of art: they are no more than approximations to an ideal which only now can be realized. Needless to say, Wagner's conformity to this system means that he believes that he can 'speak good only of the dead, but that the living must be persecuted with pitiless implacability' (iii. 295–6). His concern here is that of all such writers who seek to divine some grand design in history. The dead can be turned to face in any direction, but they themselves cannot turn aside or shake their heads in the way in which Wagner's musical and theatrical contemporaries were wont to do—reason enough for the latter to be brushed aside from the soteriological course of history. This was a road which grew ever narrower the closer it came to its goal. By the end, there was room for only one person.

This, of course, has nothing to do with personal arrogance. Wagner never allowed his own system (which became increasingly open in later years) to influence his spontaneous artistic impressions and/or his enthusiasm for the works of others. Cosima's *Diaries* confirm this on every page. Time and again we find remarks here which make it clear that neither in a purely musical nor a purely dramatic context did he regard his own works as the *ne plus ultra* of art history. Never for a moment did he doubt that Beethoven and, above all, Shakespeare were greater artists than himself. When he read an article in a Viennese newspaper on 7 May 1870, announcing that the 'Eroica' was a prophetic pointer towards his own works, he turned away in painful disgust: 'I find it horrible when people compare me with Beethoven; I always feel like saying, "What do you know of B.?"' In 1872, when he was preparing for a performance of Beethoven's Choral Symphony at the Margraves' Opera House in Bayreuth, he told himself: 'You have never done anything like that.' (*CT*, 2 May 1872.) And when someone spoke of him in the same breath as Beethoven and Shakespeare, he replied dismissively, saying that he was not even fit to tie their shoe-laces (*CT*, 13 September 1881 and *passim*).

Once he had completed *Parsifal*, he felt a very real sense of release at no longer having to concentrate on his own works. 'How nice it is that one's precursors always mean the most to one', he commented on 11 June 1882, having just read aloud his 'favourite scene' from *Henry IV* between Falstaff and the Lord Chief Justice, and played passages from Beethoven's Sonatas, Opp. 101 and 111: 'it is always the works of others which come into his mind, never his own', Cosima added. It is notable that it was relatively rare for Wagner to lavish such unqualified praise on examples of music theatre, a reticence due not least to his basic aesthetic belief that neither musically nor dramatically could opera come close to achieving the best that art history had yet produced.[1] That, as a genre, the musical drama which he himself had created was of a higher aesthetic order than any previous opera, whose musical perfections (even in the case of Mozart or Weber) were, in his opinion, frequently overshadowed by the new apocryphal genre, was a conviction repeatedly stressed in conversation with Cosima until the very end of his life.

In *Opera and Drama* Wagner had proclaimed not only the 'death of opera' (iii. 230) but of the spoken theatre, too (iv. 29), with almost Messianic fervour. The 'fundamental fallaciousness of the actual operatic genre' could no longer be denied, he noted later in '*Zukunftsmusik*', summarizing the views of his earlier *magnum opus*. Where did the basic error of this genre lie? In its belief that 'real drama could be achieved on the basis of absolute music' (iii. 233). Not even the opera reforms of Gluck and his successors could shake Wagner's

---

[1] As Egon Voss has pointed out, Wagner never studied operatic scores with the same intensity that he lavished on those of classical instrumental works, and it is significant that in later life he conducted only concerts but never operas. See Egon Voss, *Richard Wagner und die Instrumentalmusik: Wagners symphonischer Ehrgeiz* (Wilhelmshaven, 1977), 17–21, 23–4.

conviction that, in opera, 'a means of expression (music) had become the end, while the end (drama) had become the means' (iii. 231). (It is worth clearing up a long-standing misconception at this point: when Wagner describes 'real drama' as the end or aim of music, he does not mean the libretto—for this, too, is no more than a 'means'—but the whole expressive world of what takes place on stage. 'Drama, in its fullest development, will not be born', we read in the third part of *Opera and Drama*, until poet and musician 'are each absorbed the one by the other': iv. 207.)

Gluck's putative 'revolution', which, according to his 1769 preface to *Alceste*, gave primacy to the poetic text, had, according to Wagner in *Opera and Drama* (iii. 238), 'left things entirely as they were as regards the whole unnatural organism of opera'. 'Aria, recitative, and dance number are ranged alongside each other in Gluck's operas, entirely self-contained and just as unaccommodated as was the case before them and as remains the case, almost without exception, even today.' (iii. 238.) Of course, Wagner saw the operas written for Paris around 1800 as an essential step forward in the direction of musical drama. Here, indeed, was a genre which he admired right up to the end of his life, including, as it did, works by composers such as Luigi Cherubini, Gaspare Spontini, and Étienne Méhul (whose *Joseph* of 1807 could almost be described as Wagner's favourite opera),[2] together with the comic operas of Daniel Auber and Adrien Boieldieu, to which he devoted separate monographs,[3] and even Halévy's *La Juive*, which he saw as part of the same great tradition and of which he spoke in astonishingly effusive terms to Cosima.[4] What Wagner valued chiefly about these older French operas was the way in which they modified and differentiated traditional numbers, but he also admired their more organic structure and their introduction of a 'dramatico-musical ensemble' (iii. 239). He owed even his primitive use of the leitmotif—in the simple, tag-like form in which it appears in his early works—to operas written for Paris in the years before and after 1800.

Mozart's operas enjoyed something of a special position in Wagner's account of the history of the genre. Writers keen to expose his allegedly one-sided views generally cite his remark in *Opera and Drama* that 'only for the history of music in general, but certainly not for the history of opera as a separate genre, is Mozart of such surprising significance' (iii. 248). But there is little point in repeating this judgement unless its

---

[2] In addition to various remarks in Wagner's *Gesammelte Schriften*, see also *CT*, 27 June, 22 July 1872, 4 Mar. 1874, and *passim*.

[3] In addition to the *Gesammelte Schriften* (esp. 'Reminiscences of Auber': ix. 42–60), see *CT*, 27 Apr., 15 Dec. 1878, and 4 Aug. 1879.

[4] See *CT*, 25 May 1875, 4 June 1878, 17 Jan. 1880, 27 June 1882, and *passim*.

context is taken into account. For Wagner concedes that 'Mozart, that most absolute of all musicians, would long since have provided a clear solution to the problem of opera' if he had only found a sympathetic poet. In his 'truth of dramatic expression, in the infinite variety of his motivation', he had 'discovered the inexhaustible power of music to answer every demand that the poet made on its expressive potential, meeting those claims with the most unimaginably rich response and to a far greater degree than Gluck and all his successors had ever done' (i.e., more than the famous Paris-opera composers of the turn of the century). Of course, Wagner is forced by the constraints of his own argument to dispute that Mozart ever made 'fundamental' changes to the '*formal* framework of opera' (iii. 248). In the case of *Don Giovanni*, however, he was able to appeal elsewhere in his essay to E. T. A. Hoffmann's short story, *Don Juan*, and to speak of the 'surprisingly happy relationship between poet and composer' (iii. 288).

As he grew older, Wagner's enthusiasm for Mozart's dramatic masterpieces increased. He admired *Le nozze di Figaro* in particular, describing Beaumarchais' play as 'excellent' (*CT*, 12 February 1870). On 12 November 1878 he even referred to himself as 'the last of the Mozartians', and a few days earlier (3 November), when the conversation turned to Susanna's aria in Act IV and to the Count's words, 'Perdona, Contessa', he had said that he 'would have liked to have had Mozart as his contemporary'. 'How great is Mozart in comparison! Not only with his predecessors, but with his successors, too!', he exclaimed on 5 November, while discussing Spontini's *Fernand Cortez*. And he numbered himself among those 'successors' (*CT*, 1 December 1878), so that it struck him as absurd 'for people today to hold up Mozart against him' (*CT*, 5 November 1878). We even hear the diminutive form 'Mozartl' on his lips (*CT*, 11 February 1881), the same term of endearment which the dying Mahler is said to have whispered. In the conversations which he conducted with Cosima during the final years of his life, and in his 1879 essay, 'On Opera Poetry and Composition in Particular', he praised *Don Giovanni* and especially *Le nozze di Figaro*, describing them, in spite of a number of reservations, as consummate examples of music theatre, and declining—on this occasion—to stress the difference in principle between opera and musical drama. Wagner now recognizes that the ensemble passages in Mozart's finales are so extended that it is no longer possible simply to speak of 'number operas'.

With what self-assurance did he proceed . . . in *Le nozze di Figaro*! On the solid foundation of Italian *opera buffa* he erected an edifice of such consummate correctness that when his Emperor demanded cuts he was fully justified in declaring that he could not sacrifice a single note. What the Italians added by way of banal links and interludes between the actual numbers, Mozart used for the graphic animation of the scenico-musical events, creating the most appropriately effective harmony between those events and the text of the comedy which lay before him, a text, moreover, which had been worked out in such unusual detail. Just as in a Beethoven symphony the very pauses grow eloquent, so the noisy half-closes and cadential phrases which could conveniently have been omitted from a Mozart symphony enliven the musicalized events on stage in what appears to be a wholly irreplaceable manner, conjuring up the loveless conflict between cunning and presence of mind on the one hand, and passion and brutality on the other. The dialogue becomes all music here, while the music itself converses in dialogue form, something the master was able to achieve only by developing and deploying the orchestra to a pitch that was previously unsuspected and which perhaps even today remains unsurpassed [and this after *Tristan*!]. From this there might in turn appear to emerge a piece of music which fused together the once individual numbers to form a single complex, so that the admirable comedy on which it was based could be overlooked altogether and nothing heard but music. (x. 154.)

This astonishing homage to Mozart from the later Wagner represents a complete reversal of the teleological system propounded in *Opera and Drama*. The integral unity, the identity of the poetry on stage and the music in the pit, and the fundamental importance of the orchestra which he demanded of the musical drama have, according to this passage, already been fully attained by Mozart.[5]

In *Opera and Drama*, by contrast, his system had demanded that he see the culmination of a dramaturgy attainable by purely musical means not in Mozart (who is described as 'nothing but a musician': iii. 246), but in that trend in French opera which had started out from Gluck. As a result, it is Spontini (who, on a musical level, is far inferior to Mozart) whose operas are said to have pushed back the boundary of absolute music as far as possible. All that could be done for drama in that particular field had already been done by Spontini. Only beyond that

---

[5] Carl Dahlhaus sees Wagner's remarks on *Figaro* as proof of his thesis that the music drama is far more heavily indebted to the tradition of *opera buffa* than to that of *opera seria* (*Wagners Konzeption des musikalischen Dramas* (Regensburg, 1971), 23). Our quotation might give the impression that Wagner interpreted Mozart's opera as a 'loveless' piece involving much intrigue and plotting, a view which Nietzsche advanced in the course of a conversation with Wagner on 12 Feb. 1870: 'When Prof. N. remarks that Mozart is said to have invented the music of intrigue, R. replies that, on the contrary, he resolved intrigue in melody. One has only to compare Beaumarchais's (incidentally excellent) play with Mozart's opera to see that the former contains cunning, clever, and calculating people who deal and talk wittily with one another, while in Mozart they are transfigured, suffering, sorrowing human beings.' Wagner expressed himself in a similar vein at the beginning of Jan. 1873, when he undertook a comparative study of Beaumarchais and Mozart: 'Yesterday we went through *Le Nozze di Figaro* (last scene) and afterward read the same scene in Beaumarchais, and once again felt the transfiguring influence of the music. "In the play they are like beetles, struggling laboriously on the ground, in the opera they are butterflies playing in the air."' (*CT* 1–4 Jan. 1873.)

boundary, however, does true drama begin, a drama which does not exist for the sake of the music but in which the music exists for the sake of the drama. (In order to avoid the confusion between the means and the end, Wagner rejected the term 'music drama', and Nietzsche, too, was advised against using it in his *Geburt der Tragödie*: see *CT*, 11 June 1870.)

In Spontini there speaks the honest and convincing voice of the absolute musician who thereby announces: 'If the musician *per se*, as the one who is planning the opera, wishes to bring off the drama, then he cannot go a step further than *I* have gone, without exposing his total incapacity.' But the challenge has now been involuntarily uttered: 'If you want *more*, you must address yourselves not to the musician, but *to the poet*.' (iii. 241.)

In spite of all attempts at operatic reform, the poet has led a shadowy existence until now. In *'Zukunftsmusik'* Wagner sums up the relevant section of *Opera and Drama* as follows:

The poet who was not himself a master craftsman found in opera a firmly carpentered framework of musical forms which from the outset provided him with quite specific rules for inventing and elaborating the dramatic groundwork which he was required to furnish. Not he, but only the musician, could alter one iota of these forms; the nature of their content was involuntarily revealed only when the poet who had been called upon to help saw himself obliged, when inventing the plot and the verses, to degrade his poetic talent to so manifestly trivial a level that Voltaire took him to task for doing so. It will certainly not be necessary to expose the awkwardness and superficiality, not to say the absurdity of opera libretti; even in France the best attempts of their kind consisted rather in covering up this unfortunate state of affairs than in removing it. In consequence the actual framework of opera has remained an inviolable foreign body which the poet has treated subserviently, as a stranger, and it is because of this that, with few and unhappy exceptions, no truly great poets have ever had anything to do with opera. (vii. 102–3.)

It never ceased to amaze Wagner that Goethe and Schiller had looked to opera as a way of cleaning up the theatre. In his *Tag- und Jahreshefte* for 1789 Goethe describes 'pure operatic form' as 'perhaps the most favourable of all dramatic forms',[6] and Schiller, in his letter to Goethe of 29 December 1797, even takes his 'confidence in opera' so far as to believe that 'a more noble form of tragedy might develop from it, as from the choruses of the ancient Bacchic festival' (a remark which both Wagner and Nietzsche saw as heralding the rebirth of choral tragedy in the shape of musical drama). According to Wagner, however, the high hopes that were placed in opera were confounded by Goethe's own operatic texts: such hopes were bound to founder on the 'fundamental

---

[6] Johann Wolfgang von Goethe, *Gedenkausgabe der Werke, Briefe und Gespräche*, ed. Ernst Beutler, 2nd edn. (Zurich, 1961), xi. 623.

fallaciousness' of the genre as a whole (vii. 102). In Wagner's view, the 'ideal realization of opera' which Goethe and Schiller had envisaged demanded precisely that the limitations of the genre be transcended: what was required was 'a complete transformation in the nature of the part played by the poet in the work of art'. Only in the 'drama of the future' as conceived by Wagner himself could the poet's contribution be 'voluntary and desired by the poet himself' (vii. 103–4), now that he was no longer a slave to the form that was imposed upon him, but, rather, its master.

In *'Zukunftsmusik'* Wagner mentions in passing that in Germany it was Lessing who was 'the first to encourage' discussion about the way in which the 'ideal of drama' might best be achieved in opera (vii. 102). Wagner may perhaps have been referring here to the posthumously published material on *Laokoon*, which he had mentioned having studied shortly beforehand (vii. 100). Certainly, his Dresden library contained Karl Lachmann's twelve-volume edition of Lessing's works, and this in turn included the paralipomena to *Laokoon*.[7] It can scarcely have escaped his attention that Lessing was sketching out a sequel here to his investigations into 'The Boundaries of Painting and Poetry', to quote the subtitle of Lessing's essay, with its implied critique of the Horatian principle of *ut pictura poesis*. In his later piece, by contrast, Lessing was concerned to draw a generic comparison between poetry and music. Whereas painting and poetry, he argued, were wholly distinct as genres, poetry was closely bound up with music. Wagner was not altogether wrong, therefore, when he maintained in his introduction to the second part of *Opera and Drama* that his own theory of art had much in common with *Laokoon*, and when he stressed that to treat drama as a mere 'branch of literature' and to divorce it from music was to 'draw a conclusion from Lessing's definition for which there is not a single trace of justification' (iv. 4). 'Nature', Lessing explains, seems to have 'ordained that poetry and music should not so much be linked together as form one and the selfsame art.'

There was indeed a time when, together, they constituted but a single art. Yet I will not deny that their separation was not natural, still less will I complain if one of them be practised without the other, but I may perhaps be allowed to express some regret that, in consequence of this separation, we almost never think any longer of linking them together, or, if we do, it is to turn one of the arts into an ancillary of the other and to ignore the common effect which the two might produce in equal shares. It will also be recalled that but a single combination is practised in which poetry is the auxiliary art, namely opera, whereas the combination in which music would be the auxiliary art is still to be taken in hand.

[7] See Curt von Westernhagen, *Richard Wagners Dresdener Bibliothek 1842–1849* (Wiesbaden, 1966).

In a footnote to this passage (with its striking anticipation of *Opera and Drama*) Lessing none the less recalls 'a mark of essential difference between French and Italian opera'. As yet unaware of Gluck's opera reforms, he still refers, when writing of French opera, to the *tragédie lyrique* of the seventeenth century: 'In French opera, poetry is less of an ancillary art; and it is natural, therefore, that its music cannot be so brilliant. In Italian opera, by contrast, everything is subordinated to the music.'[8] The first part of *Opera and Drama* similarly alludes to the traditional distinction between French and Italian opera, but Wagner, of course, denies that the two are essentially different, since for him both imply the use of absolute music on stage. 'It is most important to note that everything which has exercised a real and decisive influence on the formation of opera right down to most recent times is derived *solely from the realm of absolute music*, certainly not from that of poetry or from a healthy interaction between the two.' (iii. 276.) All 'serious musical dramatists' between Gluck and Spontini were guilty of fundamental self-delusion 'when they ascribed the impact of their music less to the purely melodic essence of their arias than to their realization of those dramatic aims which they imputed to the arias in question' (iii. 257). Almost the same idea, albeit turned on its head, recurs in Eduard Hanslick's 1854 essay, *The Beautiful in Music*: 'Even Gluck, the most orthodox dramaturgist, although he originated the fallacy that opera music should be nothing but exalted declamation, did, in practice, often allow his musical genius to get the better of him, and this invariably to the great advantage of the work. The same holds good of Richard Wagner.'[9] In other words, Hanslick accuses Wagner of the very act of self-deception which Wagner himself had imputed to Gluck and Spontini: even the merits of his so-called music dramas lay in the fact that they were essentially absolute music. Hanslick thus denies the fundamental distinction between opera and musical drama.

According to Wagner, Spontini marks the end of opera's (misdirected) move in the direction of drama. For him, the antithesis of the Gluckian tradition was Rossini. Whereas Spontini deployed musical means in the interests of the drama, Rossini used dramatic means for purely musical effect. From the standpoint of aesthetic progress, therefore, Rossini was the typical 'reactionary', while Gluck and his

---

[8] *Lessings Werke*, ed. Georg Witkowski (Leipzig and Vienna, n.d.), iv. 309–10. Houston Stewart Chamberlain had already drawn attention to this fragment in *Richard Wagner*, 4th edn. (Munich, 1907), 274; translated into English by G. Ainslie Hight (Munich, 1897), 205. Highly illuminating is the article by Peter Horst Neumann, 'Einige Bemerkungen über Oper und Volkslied und die Idee der Einheit von Musik und Dichtung von Lessings *Laokoon*-Fragmenten bis zu Richard Wagner und Heinrich Heine', *Jahrbuch der Jean-Paul-Gesellschaft*, 7 (1972), 103–23, esp. pp. 104–13 (the passage on Wagner is, of course, somewhat non-committal).

[9] Eduard Hanslick, *Vom Musikalisch-Schönen: Ein Beitrag zur Revision der Ästhetik der Tonkunst* (Wiesbaden, 1980), 54; translated into English by Gustav Cohen as *The Beautiful in Music* (Indianapolis, 1957), 44.

successors were to be seen as 'revolutionaries' (however powerless they may have been). Wagner draws a direct parallel here with the political programmes of his day. Rossini was just as successful in opposing

Gluck's doctrinaire and revolutionary maxims as his great patron Prince *Metternich* ... was in resisting the doctrinaire maxims of those liberal revolutionaries who sought to establish humane and rational provisions *within* this state system without wholly abolishing that state's unnatural purport, but using, instead, the very forms that expressed that purport. (iii. 254–5.)

In other words, Wagner castigates both groups of revolutionaries, the political and the operatic, claiming that neither actually deserves the name, since they never really displaced the existing system. The first truly revolutionary act in the field of the theatre was therefore the conception of musical drama as initiated by the poet. In Wagner's view, what was 'reactionary' about Rossini's operas was that the Italian composer made the aria the nub of the work—the aria which had developed out of the 'folk melody', but which Rossini, so to speak, had decanted into perfume-bottles to amuse a bored theatrical audience, whereas Weber's 'folk-operas' (iii. 261) had attempted to liberate it and restore it to its natural form. (This was, of course, a pointless undertaking, inasmuch as opera audiences had sunk to the level of 'depraved elegance' and could no longer be regarded as the 'folk': iii. 254.) With Rossini, 'the actual *history of opera*' had come to a timely end (iii. 255). What followed (more especially, the eclectic operas of Meyerbeer, with their straining after theatrical effect) was no more than an attempt to resuscitate a corpse after it had already begun to decay (iii. 266). In declaring opera dead, Wagner was effectively sweeping the board clean in the hope that the 'poet' could establish the foundations of a new and authentic musical drama in the space which he believed had been cleared for it.

The essential element in existing music theatre, according to Wagner, was the aria or 'operatic melody', which owed its 'basic character' to 'absolute music' (iii. 249), in other words, to a four- or eight-bar periodic structure to which the librettist's verses had to conform. The latter, therefore, had 'merely to supply the necessary lines of verse required by the musical form of the aria' (iii. 232). The eight-bar period of the absolute musician—the 'four-square musician', as he is cynically called in the 1879 essay, 'On Opera Poetry and Composition in Particular' (x. 174)—is contrasted with what is termed the 'poetico-musical period' in *Opera and Drama* (iv. 154) and 'unending melody' in *'Zukunftsmusik'* (vii. 130), i.e., a period which is not determined immanently by the music but, rather, by the poetry. Its structure, therefore, is open rather than closed, and it has an uneven number of bars. In *Der fliegende Holländer*, Wagner noted in *'Zukunftsmusik'* (vii.

123), the lines of text had been tailored in such a way as to provide the 'basis' for a melody that was divided up a priori into regular groups of bars (eight-bar periods remain the norm as the basis of Wagner's musical syntax even as late as *Lohengrin*, of course),[10] whereas in *Tristan und Isolde* 'the entire extent of the melody was already mapped out in the fabric of the individual words and lines of verse; in other words, this melody was already structured poetically' (vii. 123).

Towards the end of his life, as his admiration for Bach continued to increase, Wagner more than once described the Leipzig cantor as the father of unending melody (*CT*, 13 November 1878, 20 February 1879, and 14 November 1882), an honour he had previously granted to Beethoven. Only a few months before his death, he played off the ostensible 'unendingness' of Bach's (and the late Beethoven's) melodic writing against that 'four-square melody' which followed the scheme 'four bars here, rum-ti-tum, then another four bars', and so on (*CT*, 14 November 1882).[11] Wagner was thinking here not only of the structure of operatic melody but also of the syntax of classical instrumental music. Even Mozart's symphonies were a source of constant irritation to him because of their allegedly conventional periodic structure and cadential schematism, which, he believed, trivialized even their most important melodic ideas. Thus we find him praising the 'magnificent, unsurpassed' fugal passage in the finale of Mozart's 'Jupiter' Symphony, while complaining (evidently taking Bach's fugues as his model[12]) that 'it is immediately followed by a banal "rum-ti-tum", which robs the whole thing of style' (*CT*, 29 October 1877). His complaint that there was a contradiction between the 'divine gracefulness of [Mozart's] themes' and the 'terrible formalism in which he sometimes clothes them' (*CT*, 27 November 1873) is typical of almost all of the later Wagner's remarks concerning Mozart's compositional technique. 'What we owe to Beethoven', he said on another occasion, is that 'he did away with the bridging passages [i.e., what is caricatured elsewhere as "rum-ti-tum"], in him everything is part of the melody' (*CT*, 31 March 1878). 'Unending melody' consists, therefore, in the avoidance of those 'half-closes and cadential phrases' (x. 154) which Wagner found in Mozart, but whose syntactic function he doubtless misunderstood.

In *'Zukunftsmusik'* Wagner confessed that 'those perpetually

---

[10] See Dahlhaus, *Wagners Konzeption des musikalischen Dramas*, pp. 52–4.

[11] Fritz Reckow's assertion ('Zu Wagners Begriff der unendlichen Melodie', in Carl Dahlhaus (ed.), *Das Drama Richard Wagners als musikalisches Kunstwerk* (Regensburg, 1970), 81–103) that the term has nothing to do with compositional technique is clearly refuted by Wagner's remarks as reported in Cosima's *Diaries*. See also Martin Geck's observations on Reckow's paper (Dahlhaus, *Das Drama Wagners*, pp. 104–5), and Klaus Kropfinger, *Wagner und Beethoven* (Regensburg, 1975), 133–5.

[12] See Wagner's remark on 15 Jan. 1872, concerning the fugal experiments of Mozart and Beethoven: 'As far as fugues are concerned, these gentlemen can hide their heads before Bach.'

recurring, pompously fussy half-closes in Mozart's symphonies' always gave him the impression that 'the music was expressing the rattle and clatter of a princely dinner' (vii. 126). According to this view, Mozart's alleged formalism was the result of the fact that his music was anchored in the world of courtly conventionality, from which it had never been able entirely to break free. By the end of his life, however, Wagner was convinced that Mozart had made a dramatic virtue of this musical necessity. In the passage quoted above from 'On Opera Poetry and Composition in Particular' it was said that those half-closes and cadential phrases 'which could conveniently have been omitted from a Mozart symphony' formed 'the most effective harmony' with the subject-matter of the opera (in this case *Le nozze di Figaro*), serving to provide 'graphic animation of the scenico-musical events', while at the same time reflecting the courtly world, with its conflict between cunning and passion (x. 154). Although outmoded from a musical point of view, the 'social' formulas of Mozart's compositional style are invested with an incomparable sense of rightness on stage, where it is precisely social rituals and tensions which form the theme of the work. The later Wagner now seems to want to invert his earlier thesis, adumbrated in *Opera and Drama*, whereby Mozart had played an innovatory role in the history of music in general but not in the field of opera.

As for Wagner's critique of the 'four-square' nature of 'conventional musical structure' (ix. 149), there was a significant shift of emphasis here following his reading of Schopenhauer. Whereas he had criticized it in *Opera and Drama* as undramatic, he later, under Schopenhauer's influence, came to see how it corresponded to the laws of the phenomenal world, so that periodic structure—and this emerges from his reassessment not only of Mozart but also of Rossini—no longer appears to be intrinsically irreconcilable with dramatic expressivity, at least where *opera buffa* is concerned. His *Beethoven* essay of 1870 sees periodic structure as being derived from the link between music and dance: as a result of a 'regular arrangement in the return of rhythmic periods' (ix. 80), music 'makes contact with the visible three-dimensional world, a contact established on the strength of its similarity to those laws according to which the motion of visible bodies reveals itself to our intelligence' (ix. 76). In consequence, Wagner goes on in the spirit of Schopenhauer, music loses 'its power to redeem from the curse of appearance, i.e., it no longer proclaims the essence of things, but itself becomes entangled in that illusive show which typifies the phenomenal world around us' (ix. 81). Unending melody, the abandonment of traditional periodicity, implies, therefore, that music no longer has an alienating effect once it conforms to the phenomenal world.

This metaphysical aspect is absent from *Opera and Drama*, where 'four-square melody' is still condemned exclusively from the point of view of the 'aim' of the drama. In Wagner's opinion, the periodic structure of the aria as the basic form of opera highlights the contradictory nature of the entire genre, at least to the extent to which the latter is thought of as something dramatic. 'Absolute, wholly self-sufficient melody and constantly true dramatic expression' are irreconcilable opposites (iii. 293). Since it cannot resolve this inherent contradiction, opera does not constitute a viable starting-point for the 'drama of the future'. Rather, that point of departure must be classical tragedy on the one hand, and, on the other, the symphonic writing of that composer—Beethoven—who, according to Wagner, took absolute music beyond its own limitations. It was Beethoven who, in his later works, first went beyond 'absolute music' and 'spoke in a language which, unrelated to any purely musical context, was bound only by the ties of a poetic intent which could not, however, be expressed in music with true poetic clarity' (iii. 279), since 'the expression of a quite specific, clearly intelligible individual content is impossible in this language, which is only capable of conveying feelings in their universal validity' (iii. 277). It is for this reason that the late Beethoven always gives the impression of 'having something to say to us that he cannot clearly communicate' (iii. 281).

This self-subsuming of absolute music within its own limitations—a speculative thesis which was violently refuted not least by Hanslick and Nietzsche—finds monumental and symbolic expression in the 'verbalization' of the symphony at the end of Beethoven's Ninth, a development which, in Wagner's view, signalled the end of the symphony as such. As was the case with opera, Wagner's own system forced him to dismiss all symphonic writing since Beethoven as a mere experiment in galvanization. ('No such symphonies will ever again be written', he told Cosima on 1 March 1873 after re-examining two of Beethoven's scores.) For Wagner, the only legitimate heir to the Beethoven symphony was the musical drama. (Of course, Wagner's attitude to the symphony, as to most other things, underwent a fundamental change in later years as a result of Schopenhauer's influence. As we have already noted, he told Cosima in countless conversations right up until a few days before his death that he intended writing only symphonies once he had finished *Parsifal*.)

The performance of the Ninth Symphony in the Margraves' Opera House in Bayreuth on 22 May 1872 lay the foundation-stone for the Bayreuth Festival in a spiritual as well as in a literal sense. It was Beethoven the symphonist, not Beethoven the opera composer, who was acknowledged as the 'father' of the musical drama. As late as 25 December 1880 Wagner was able to say to Cosima that *Fidelio*—

significantly, Beethoven's only opera—was 'unworthy of the composer of the symphonies'.

In the 1870 *Beethoven* essay Wagner insists that only the third *Leonore* Overture actually reveals

how Beethoven wanted the drama understood. Who can hear this thrilling piece of music without being filled with the conviction that the music contains within itself the most consummate *drama*? What is the dramatic action of the libretto to *Leonore* except an almost offensive watering-down of the drama that we experienced in the Overture, somewhat after the manner of a tedious commentary by Gervinus explaining a scene from Shakespeare? (ix. 105.)

In his early humorous short story, 'A Pilgrimage to Beethoven', written in 1840, Wagner had made the composer of *Fidelio* express his own misgivings about the genre of opera, and hence about his only attempt to write one. But, in the same breath, the fictional Beethoven goes on to justify his decision to write a 'symphony with choruses':

I am no opera composer—at least I know of no theatre anywhere in the world for which I would willingly write another opera! If I were to write an opera after my own heart, people would run away, for there would be none of your arias, duets, trios, and the rest of the rubbish with which people cobble together their operas nowadays; but what I'd write instead no singer would want to sing and no audience would want to listen to. Glittering lies, brilliant nonsense, and sugary tedium is all they understand. Anyone who wrote a true musical drama would be regarded as a fool, and so he would be, if he tried to get it performed, instead of keeping it to himself. (i. 109.)

The term 'musical drama' had already been used by E. T. A. Hoffmann in his short story, 'The Poet and the Composer', from the *Serapionsbrüder* cycle of 1819–21.[13] Hoffmann's tale, couched in dialogue form and set within the framework of a novella, deals with aesthetic theory, and had both a formal and a conceptual influence on the short stories which Wagner wrote during his years in Paris and which, in part at least, are entirely worthy of their model. Here it is the poet Ferdinand who expresses his discontent at having to comply with the pre-ordained forms and numbers of traditional opera. It is 'altogether burdensome', Ferdinand confesses to his friend, the composer Ludwig, for the poet 'to have to worry so much about your needs, about the structure of your trios, quartets, finales, etc., lest we sin, as happens (alas!) all too often, against the form which, by what right I know not, you yourself have adopted'. But, as Ludwig goes on, this clash between the claims of the poet and those of the musician is avoided in true opera—'romantic opera'—for here 'the music will spring directly

---

[13]  E. T. A. Hoffmann, *Werke* (Frankfurt, 1967), ii. 257.

from the poem as a necessary product of the same'.[14] Hoffmann appears to anticipate Wagner's own dramaturgy at this point, although the speaker is, of course, referring more to the content of the opera than to the way in which its language predetermines the musical structure. Ludwig's (and Hoffmann's) idea of 'musical drama' is influenced by the *fiabe dramatiche* of Carlo Gozzi: 'In his dramatic fairy-tales he was wholly successful in meeting the demands that I make of the opera poet, and it is beyond belief that this rich store of splendid subjects for operas has not been used more hitherto.'[15] Wagner later followed up this suggestion, and began his career as a music dramatist with an adaptation of Gozzi's fairy-tale drama *La donna serpente*, to which he gave the title *Die Feen*. In 'A Pilgrimage to Beethoven', however, his concern was not with the ideal operatic subject but with the scenic structure of the musical drama. And here the fictional Beethoven adduces the example of Shakespeare.

The extent to which Wagner's early writings are indebted to the musical aesthetics of E. T. A. Hoffmann is clear from the arguments which the latter places in his composer's mouth when discussing the problem of the relationship between the 'ineffable impact of instrumental music' and the rules which govern the stage: 'But now music must enter wholly into life, it must seize hold of life's apparitions and, embellishing word and deed, speak of specific passions and actions.'[16] When, in Wagner's novella, Beethoven discusses the relationship between the orchestral instrument and the human voice, his words seem to be almost a direct continuation of this idea:

The instruments represent the primal organs of creation and nature; what they express can never be clearly defined and set down, for they reproduce those primal feelings as they issued forth from the chaos of the first creation, perhaps even before there was any human heart to hear and feel them. The genius of the human voice is completely different: it represents the human heart and its self-contained, individual sensibility. Its character is therefore limited, albeit certain and clear. Imagine, now, these two elements brought together and united! Imagine those wild primal feelings encompassing the infinite and represented by the different instruments—imagine them beside the clear and certain sensibility of the human heart as represented by the human voice. (i. 110.)

These words from the fictional Beethoven, while intended to justify his conception of the Ninth Symphony, anticipate Wagner's later statement in his *Report on the Performance of Beethoven's Ninth Symphony in 1846* (ii. 61), as well as the thesis which he advanced in the reform essays he wrote between 1849 and 1851, namely, that absolute (instrumental) music outgrows itself in Beethoven's late works. According to Wagner's

---

[14] Ibid. 254–5.    [15] Ibid. 257.    [16] Ibid. 256.

principal theoretical work, Beethoven's symphony expounds the melodic 'shape' of the musical drama with archetypal clarity:

In his most important works he certainly does not present the melody as something finished from the outset, but allows it, so to speak, *to be born* from music's organs before our very eyes . . . But the most decisive statement that the master finally offers us is in his principal work, where it concerns the need which he feels *as a musician* to throw himself into the arms of the poet in order to consummate that act of *procreation* which will produce the true, unfailingly real, and uniquely redeeming melody. (iii. 312.)

It is within the framework of this sexual imagery that Wagner describes the structural rules governing the musical drama in *Opera and Drama*. The 'act of giving birth to melody' is inconceivable without the act of procreation: '*but every musical organism is by nature feminine*, it exists only *to give birth*, not to *procreate*; the generative force lies *elsewhere*, and unless it be impregnated by this force, it cannot give birth. Herein lies the whole secret of the barrenness of modern music!' (iii. 314.) It is 'madness', therefore, for the composer to believe that he can create 'the drama on his own, using merely the powers of absolute music and with *only ancillary* help from the poet' (iii. 286). In fact, this goal is attainable only as long as poetry and music are not 'absolute' and if one or the other does not set itself up as master over the other: it is a goal that will be realized only when both acknowledge a common master, which is *drama* as a scenic, poetic, and musical unity.

# 10

# 'Absolute Music' as a Covert or Overt Ideal: Nietzsche, Hanslick, and the Aesthetic Outlook of the Later Wagner

> The connection of poetry with music and with the opera is a sort of morganatic union, and the more closely we examine this morganatic union of musical beauty and definite thoughts, the more sceptical do we become as regards its indissolubility.
>
> Eduard Hanslick, *Vom Musikalisch-Schönen.*

The idea of 'absolute music' is older than the term. As Carl Dahlhaus has convincingly shown,[1] its natural home is the Romantic aesthetic of music. The term itself is not found, of course, until around the middle of the nineteenth century, when it appears to have been introduced by Wagner. It was then taken up by his antagonist Eduard Hanslick, who turned it into the corner-stone of his own aesthetic theory, speaking of 'pure, absolute music',[2] and subjecting the adjective 'absolute' (which for Wagner had had exclusively negative associations) to a radical revaluation. (We also see here the distance Wagner himself had travelled between his early Paris essays, influenced as they were by Tieck, Wackenroder, and, above all, by E. T. A. Hoffmann, and the reform essays of around 1850.)

For Wagner, absolute music resulted when the arts disintegrated and became separated from their 'primeval sisters', dance and poetry (iii. 67–71), with whom music had once been united in the 'total art-work' of the Greek *mousike*. 'We have grown used to interpreting the term "music" [*Musik*] in the more limited sense of the *art of tone [Tonkunst]*; we know that this is an arbitrary assumption, since the *Volk* which invented the name of "music" conceived of it ... as the artistic expression of the inner man himself, in so far as he communicated his feelings and intuitions ... through the organ of ringing speech', Wagner wrote in 1852 in his open letter to Franz Brendel, 'On Musical Criticism' (v. 59–60). 'Absolute' music, therefore, is merely the atrophied form of the

---

[1] Carl Dahlhaus, *Die Idee der absoluten Musik* (Kassel, 1978); see also Klaus Kropfinger, *Wagner und Beethoven* (Regensburg, 1975), 133 ff.

[2] Eduard Hanslick, *Vom Musikalisch-Schönen: Ein Beitrag zur Revision der Ästhetik der Tonkunst* (Wiesbaden, 1980), 34; translated into English by Gustav Cohen as *The Beautiful in Music* (Indianapolis, 1957), 29–30.

all-embracing *mousike* of the Greeks. In *The Art-Work of the Future* (1849) Wagner speaks in the same pejorative vein of 'absolute drama' as the 'isolated egotistical genre' of mime (iii. 80), while in *Opera and Drama* (1851)—this time in connection with the parallel mentioned above between Metternich's reactionary politics and Rossini's operas—he describes 'absolute monarchy' (i.e., monarchy divorced from the people) as the counterpart of 'absolute melody' (iii. 255). In *A Communication to my Friends*, finally, the 'absolute art-work' of the modern age is said to have become 'monumentally' isolated from life (iv. 235–9). The term 'absolute' always refers to an inferior abstraction, the separation of some phenomenon or other from its original context, which alone gives it meaning and in which it finds fulfilment. To gain a fuller understanding of Wagner's use of the term 'absolute music', we need to consider his critique of the 'absolute work of art' as contained in *A Communication to my Friends* (1851).

The *absolute art-work*, i.e., the art-work which is neither bound by time and place, nor portrayed by particular people under particular circumstances for the understanding of equally particular people, is a total nonsense, a phantom of aesthetic fantasy. The *idea* of art has been distilled from the *reality* of all those works of art that have been produced at various periods in history. (iv. 234–5.)

In fact, the singular form, 'art', is one that we owe to the eighteenth-century school of autonomist aesthetics and should not be confused with the ancient 'arts' or *artes*.[3]

In order to give this idea an imagined reality . . . it has been clothed with a fanciful body which, as the absolute work of art, is . . . the spectre that haunts the brains of our aesthetic critics. Just as this imaginary body has taken all the features of its supposedly physical form from the actual attributes of works of art from the past, so the aesthetic belief in it is essentially conservative, and the operation of this belief is therefore, in itself, an act of the most utter artistic barrenness. Only in a truly inartistic age could the belief in such a work of art enter into men's heads, for certainly it could never enter into their hearts. (iv. 235.)

The absolute work of art is therefore 'monumental' in the sense discussed above. What Wagner means by its 'conservatism' and by a 'belief in it which leads to artistic barrenness' becomes clear from a passage in Nietzsche's 1874 essay, 'Vom Nutzen und Nachteil der Historie für das Leben'. (As mentioned above, Nietzsche's inspiration in writing this passage was Wagner's idea of monumentalism in art.) As a result of 'a monumentalist history of artists', creative artists will find that 'their path will be barred, their air darkened, if a half-understood

---

[3] See Helmut Kuhn, 'Die Ontogenese der Kunst', in *Festschrift für Hans Sedlmayr* (Munich, 1962), reprinted in Wolfhart Henckmann (ed.), *Schriften zur Ästhetik* (Munich, 1966).

monument to some great era of the past is erected as an idol and
zealously danced around, as though to say: "Behold, this is true art: pay
no heed to those who are evolving and want something new!"' The
'canon of monumental art (that is to say, the art which . . . has at all times
"produced an effect"', prevents great art from developing in its own day.
Critics 'invoke the authority which the monumental derives from the
past', and exclaim: 'Behold, greatness already exists!'[4] This is what
Wagner means when he writes of the conservative, sterile nature of a
belief in the absolute (i.e., monumental) work of art.

For Wagner, the 'absolute artist' is the modern artist *par excellence*. His
account of the latter's aesthetic principles in *A Communication to my
Friends* corresponds in every detail to what Victor Cousin had already
described in 1836 as 'l'art pour l'art'. Inspired by German autonomist
aesthetics, the term was attached to a movement whose later
adherents—the *décadents*—included a number of the most passionate
Wagnerians. The realm of the absolute artist

is a world of art that is wholly cut off from life, a world in which the subject of
art is art and in which art shies sensitively away from all contact with reality, i.e.,
not only from the actuality of the modern present but from that of life in
general, regarding this latter as its *absolute* foe and adversary, and believing not
only that life everywhere and in every age is hostile to it but that every attempt
to fashion life is a wasted effort and therefore unbecoming to the artist.
(iv. 247.)

The absolute work of art, which Wagner equates by and large with
monumental art, is, on the one hand, a work which has been forcibly
torn from reality, a work which is no longer embedded in a concrete,
socio-historical context and which is 'unconditioned', in other words,
bound 'neither to time and place nor to particular circumstances' (iv.
236), while, on the other, it is the product consequent upon the
individual arts losing their 'original unity' (iii. 67).

The young Nietzsche took over Wagner's critique of the 'sad modern
impertinence' of absolute art and made it his own.[5] 'We are, as it were,
torn apart by the absolute arts and now enjoy things piecemeal, now
using only our ears, now our eyes', he wrote in 1870 in *Das griechische
Musikdrama*.[6] In one of his posthumously published fragments dating
from 1869 he compares the common organization of the 'arts as total art'
with a tree, while the individual arts are likened to its fruit.[7] The
'disintegration of the arts', 'absolute art', is a 'sign that the tree can no
longer hold the fruit; at the same time the arts decay'.[8] It is in the context

[4] Friedrich Nietzsche, *Sämtliche Werke: Kritische Studienausgabe in 15 Bänden*, ed. Giorgio Colli
and Mazzino Montinari (Munich, 1980), i. 263–4; translated into English by R. J. Hollingdale as
*Untimely Meditations: On the Uses and Disadvantages of History for Life* (Cambridge, 1983), 71–2.
[5] Ibid. vii. 22, 57.        [6] Ibid. i. 518.        [7] Ibid. vii. 22, 56.        [8] Ibid. 13.

of this criticism of the increasing autonomy of the individual arts (and of other social phenomena such as the 'absolute state' and 'absolute science'[9]) that Nietzsche's discussion of the idea of 'absolute music' must be seen. Of course, his views on the subject changed fundamentally between 1869 and 1871. Initially he used the term in a negative, Wagnerian sense: 'Absolute music and everyday drama—the two parts of music drama that have been torn apart', according to a note jotted down in the autumn of 1869.[10] In classical drama 'the music was never enjoyed absolutely, but always in association with ritual and surroundings or society. In short, it was occasional music.'[11]

In a further series of posthumously published fragments dating from 1870–1 and 1874 Nietzsche distinguished between this negative view of absolute music and a wholly different concept which, significantly— and long before his breach with Wagner—heralds a clear departure from the latter's musico-dramatic maxims. In a fragment from the spring of 1871, for example, he asks the question: 'What are we to make . . . of that monstrous aesthetic superstition according to which Beethoven, with the fourth movement of his Ninth Symphony, was himself making a solemn confession concerning the limits of absolute music, indeed, that he had, so to speak, unbolted the doors of a new art in which music was even enabled to represent images and concepts, thus opening it up to the "conscious spirit"?'[12] Although this final thought is wholly alien to Wagner, there can be no doubt that the quotation as a whole is directed against the composer's interpretation of the final movement of the Ninth Symphony. In a note dating from the spring of 1874 Nietzsche expressly rejects Wagner's thesis that the 'inclusion of words' was the 'principal achievement' of the Ninth Symphony, dismissing the idea as 'a bit much'.[13] (The 1871 fragment, it is true, does not mention the author of the disputed interpretation by name; indeed, Nietzsche even refers explicitly to Wagner's remarks on the *Missa solemnis* in his 1870 *Beethoven* essay in order to support his own view of the Ninth.) In fact, there is no denying that Wagner's own views on the relationship between words and music underwent a radical change under the influence of Schopenhauer. Immediately after the passage cited by Nietzsche, the *Beethoven* essay goes on to discuss this relationship, and Wagner reveals himself to be in astonishing agreement with Hanslick, who had argued along similar lines in *Vom Musikalisch-Schönen*:

Our experience that a piece of music loses nothing of its character even when set to very different texts shows . . . that the relationship between music and

[9] Nietzsche, *Sämtliche Werke*, 154.          [10] Ibid. 17, 25.          [11] Ibid. 26, 57.
[12] Ibid. 367. This fragment was reproduced by Jakob Kraus in his anthology, *Sprache, Dichtung, Musik* (Tübingen, 1973), and discussed by Dahlhaus in *Die Idee der absoluten Musik*, pp. 35 ff. Nietzsche's other posthumously published fragments concerning the problem of absolute music were not, however, taken account of by Dahlhaus.          [13] Nietzsche, *Sämtliche Werke*, vii. 766.

*poetry* is thoroughly illusory, for it transpires that in vocal music it is not the poetic thought which is apprehended, since this latter, especially when sung by a chorus, is not even intelligibly articulated, but at best whatever it was that that thought inspired in the musician in the form of music and by way of music. Any combination of music and poetry must therefore invariably lead to the latter's subordination, so that we can only wonder at our great German poets who time and again have considered the problem of how to combine these two arts, and who have even attempted to do so at all. (ix. 103–4.)

This quotation contains the clearest possible summary of the last-cited passage from Nietzsche's fragmentary *Nachlaß*. In other words, Nietzsche is attempting to refute Wagner by quoting Wagner back at him, contrasting the concept of music contained in *Opera and Drama* with that advanced in the *Beethoven* essay written almost two decades later. In a fragment from the spring of 1874 Nietzsche expressly distinguishes between the earlier and the later Wagner's definition of the relationship between music and poetry (drama): 'Means and end—music and drama—older doctrine. General and specific—music and drama—more recent doctrine.' Of the older doctrine, as expressed in *Opera and Drama*, Nietzsche notes: 'Wagner describes it as an error in the genre of opera that a means of expression, namely, music, was made an end, whereas the aim of the expression was made into a means. In other words, he regards music as the means of expression—very characteristic of the actor.'[14]

Wagner's 'more recent doctrine' had already been sketched out in various fragments which Nietzsche noted down in 1870–1. If we adopt Schopenhauer's position, that music expresses the 'will' or thing-in-itself whereas the other arts reproduce only the latter's appearance, it will become clear that 'the drama in relation to the music' is to be apprehended as 'a scheme, as the exemplum of a general concept'.[15] 'Music can create images from within itself, but these will only ever be schemata, images, as it were, of its actual general content. But how could the image, the representation, create music from within itself!' This final idea seems as absurd to Nietzsche as the notion that a son could sire his own father. 'What a topsy-turvy world!', he comments.[16] The pre-eminence of music which Nietzsche stresses here was also repeatedly emphasized by Wagner: it was the 'magic lantern' through which 'the drama is projected back' (*CT*, 7 March 1873). And in the essay 'On the Term "Music Drama"', written in 1872, the composer described his own dramatic works as 'acts of music made visible' (ix. 306).

Music, moreover, is said to be the 'mother's womb of drama, too' (a metaphor which had, of course, already played a central role in *Opera and Drama*). 'It sounds, and what it sounds you may see there on stage;

---

[14] Ibid. 770.  [15] Ibid. 360.  [16] Ibid. 362.

it is for this that it brought you together, for what it is you can only ever suspect; and that is why it reveals itself to your gaze through a scenic parable, just as a mother instructs her children in the mysteries of religion by recounting sacred legends.' (ix. 305.) (According to this interpretation, the opera *Fidelio* might be regarded as a failed legend or an unsuccessful visualization of those 'acts of music' which are successfully realized in the drama that we experience in the third *Leonore* Overture.) 'Music, which does not represent the ideas that are contained in the world's phenomena, but is itself an idea of the world, and a comprehensive one at that, naturally includes drama within itself', we read in *Beethoven* (ix. 105). Music therefore contains the potential for drama in the sense understood by Kantian transcendentalism (a philosophy of which Wagner had no first-hand knowledge but to which he came through the intermediary of Schopenhauer).

We should therefore not go far astray if we saw in music man's a priori ability to fashion drama. Just as we construct the world of appearances for ourselves by applying the laws of time and space which are present a priori in our brain, so this conscious representation, in drama, of the idea of the world would be pre-ordained by those inner laws of music which operate within the dramatist with the same degree of unconsciousness as those laws of causality which we unconsciously employ in apperceiving the phenomenal world. (ix. 106.)

This metaphysical reassessment of the relationship between music and drama no longer allows absolute music to be dismissed as it had been in *Opera and Drama*. This is something that Nietzsche expressly emphasizes. Adopting the arguments of the later Wagner, he spells out the conclusions which Wagner himself had avoided drawing in order not to have to refute altogether the principles contained in his main theoretical tract. If the 'more recent doctrine' sketched out above were true, Nietzsche wrote in 1874, 'then the general can in no way be dependent upon the specific, i.e., absolute music is in the right, even the music of the drama must be absolute music'.[17] In his 1887 polemic, *Zur Genealogie der Moral*, he commented on Wagner's 'conversion' to Schopenhauer, and gave ironic expression to the 'theoretical contradiction between his earlier and later aesthetic creed—the former set down, for example, in *Opera and Drama*, the latter in the writings he published from 1870 onwards':

He grasped all at once that with the Schopenhauerian theory and innovation *more* could be done *in majorem musicae gloriam*—namely, with the theory of the *sovereignty* of music as Schopenhauer conceived it: music set apart from all the other arts, the independent art as such, *not* offering images of phenomenality, as the other arts did, but speaking rather the language of the will itself, directly

---

[17] Nietzsche, *Sämtliche Werke*, 770.

out of the 'abyss' [i.e., Wagner's 'mystic abyss' in the Bayreuth Festspielhaus] as its most authentic, elemental, nonderivative revelation. With this extraordinary rise in the value of music that appeared to follow from Schopenhauerian philosophy, the value of *the musician* himself all at once went up in an unheard-of manner, too: from now on he became an oracle, a priest, indeed more than a priest, a kind of mouthpiece of the 'in itself' of things, a telephone from the beyond—henceforth he uttered not only music, this engastrimyth of God—he uttered metaphysics: no wonder he one day finally uttered *ascetic ideals*.[18]

(The final sentence is, of course, an allusion to *Parsifal*.) Nietzsche is no doubt guilty of overstating the theoretical contradiction in Wagner's aesthetic thinking, since the latter's views on the position of music did not alter as radically as the younger writer claims. Even for the Schopenhauerian Wagner, the 'older doctrine' never entirely loses its relative significance in terms of his musico-dramatic praxis, in other words, as a compositional maxim. Moreover, Nietzsche overlooks the fact that the relationship between the means and the end in music and drama is valid only on a dramaturgical plane. Even as early as *Opera and Drama* Wagner was developing a myth of music ('*Music* is the beginning and end of language just as . . . *myth* is the beginning and end of history': iv. 91) which raises the latter far above any purely functional relationship with the aim of the drama, and even goes so far as to describe it as the womb of the drama. The philosophy or, rather, the mythology of music already overlaps here with its empirical, dramaturgical evaluation.

The metaphysical outlook of the later Wagner which was the object of Nietzsche's ironical outburst of 1887 had in fact been Nietzsche's own position in 1872, when he wrote *Die Geburt der Tragödie*. The earlier essay takes Schopenhauer's philosophy of music to its most extreme conclusion, insisting that the music of drama must be 'absolute music'. In much the same vein, he had claimed in his posthumously published jottings of 1870–1 that the value of an opera would be 'all the greater if the music were freer, more unconditional, more Dionysian, and if it were to scorn all so-called dramatic requirements'. Even in his later fragmentary writings he always used quotation marks when referring to the concept of 'dramatic' music, in order to emphasize its illusory character and to indicate how remote it was from music as such (in other words, what he called 'pure music').[19] In a remarkable reversal of the cardinal thesis of *Opera and Drama*, he argues that the basic fault of opera, as a genre, was that it treated music 'as a means to an end', something which he describes as 'an impossibility'.[20] (According to

---

[18] Ibid. v. 345–6; translated into English by Walter Kaufmann as *On the Genealogy of Morals*, in *Basic Writings of Nietzsche* (New York, 1968), 539.

[19] Ibid. vii. 187–8.                                        [20] Ibid. 185–6.

Wagner, 'absolute music' was always the end to which the drama, as the means, had to be subordinated.) In diametrical opposition to the principal demand of *Opera and Drama*, Nietzsche states that 'Music *can* never be a means, however much it may be beaten, bullied, and tormented: as sound, as a drum-roll, in its crudest and simplest stages it still subverts the poetry and debases it to a mere reflection of itself.' The same is true of drama as stage action: 'The moment the Dionysian force of music strikes the listener, the eye mists over as it watches the action ... the listener now forgets the drama and only wakes up to it again when the Dionysian spell has released him from its power.'[21] In the fragment directed at Wagner's earlier interpretation of the Ninth Symphony we read that, as a result of the music, the listener is 'rendered wholly incapable of perceiving image or word'.[22] This is nothing less than an outright rejection of the idea of a 'total work of art' embracing poetry, dance (gesture), and music. Music is now invested with such metaphysical dignity that it is no longer able to form a unity with its sister arts, no longer able to be regarded as *prima inter pares*.

The last two quotations from Nietzsche's *Nachlaß* hark back to Wagner's theory of the way in which the spectator is 'rendered incapable of seeing' by the effects of music, a theory discussed in the *Beethoven* essay of 1870 (ix. 110). This piece already contains a detailed description of the laws of perception governing the music theatre, which, Wagner argues, are different from those that obtain in the spoken theatre. Starting out from Schopenhauer's theory of dreams, Wagner develops these laws by analogy with dreaming and somnambulistic clairvoyance. This notion of the stage action as a dreamlike vision was to have a decisive influence on Nietzsche's *Die Geburt der Tragödie*, and especially on his interpretation of the characters and events of Attic tragedy as 'phantom figures of the Apollonian fantasization of the chorus',[23] an idea which comes close to Stéphane Mallarmé's ideal of a theatre of the mind.

But just as the eye 'mists over', so, according to Nietzsche, the ear of the person listening to a piece of music becomes less sensitive, so that 'the meaning of the words is lost in the general sea of sound'. Citing Wagner's remarks on Beethoven's *Missa solemnis*, Nietzsche goes on to note that only someone singing the words in a piece of vocal music will understand the text, whereas 'the listener reacts to it as though to a piece of absolute music'.[24] Towards the end of his life Wagner, too, was saying much the same sort of thing. 'I am no poet', he told Cosima on 22 January 1871; 'to a certain extent it is a matter of indifference to me whether people understand my verses, since they will certainly

---

[21] Nietzsche, *Sämtliche Werke*, 188.          [22] Ibid. 366.
[23] Ibid. 191.          [24] Ibid. 368–9.

understand my dramatic action'. And on 27 December 1873: 'In the morning he plays the scene between Alberich and Hagen and looks forward to the impression it will make when Hill and Scaria sing it. "It will have the effect of two strange animals conversing together—one understands nothing of it, but it is all interesting."' Time and again Wagner emphasized 'how little words contributed to the drama' (*CT*, 29 April 1878): what was essential was the 'action' alone (*CT*, 19 November 1878); in other words, the *Handlung* or 'drama'.

We know that it is not the verses of a librettist, be he a Goethe or a Schiller, which can determine the music; that is something that *drama* alone can do, by which I do not mean a dramatic poem, but drama actually unfolding before our eyes, as a visible counterpart to the music, where word and speech no longer belong to the poetic thought, but solely and uniquely to the action [*Handlung*]. (*Beethoven*: ix. 111–12.)

Of course, this view is not as far removed from the central thesis of *Opera and Drama* as it initially appears to be. One of the basic misconceptions concerning Wagnerian theory is the belief that he wanted the music to serve the 'text'. Even Franz Liszt encouraged this opinion when he wrote in his essay, *Richard Wagner's Lohengrin und Tannhäuser*, that 'Wagner would certainly have written the dedication to *Alceste* if Gluck had not already done so'.[25] In fact, the text, no less than the music, was simply a means to an end for Wagner. The ultimate aim was 'drama', to which word, tone, and gesture were all subordinate as complementary means of expression.

Nietzsche thought that he was agreeing with Wagner when, in a posthumously published note dating from 1871, he wrote that the essential principle of Wagnerian dramaturgy was not the determinative influence of the text on the music, but the 'parallelism of music and drama': 'He sets store by the intrinsic intelligibility of the *action*, of the *mime*.'[26] The pre-eminence that Wagner grants to the mimic element (discussed above in the context of his theory of improvisation) corresponds, according to Nietzsche, to the primacy of the image within his dramatic poetry. 'The music in Wagnerian opera places the poetry in a new situation. What matters, rather, is the *image*, the animated and constantly changing *image*, which the word serves. In terms of their words, the scenes are no more than sketches.'[27]

Nietzsche did not allow Wagner's polemical attack on absolute music to mislead him or to blind him to the fact that Wagner was striving 'unconsciously' to create a form of art that breathed the spirit of absolute

---

[25] Quoted in Herbert Barth, Dietrich Mack, and Egon Voss (eds.), *Wagner: Sein Leben, sein Werk und seine Welt in zeitgenössischen Bildern und Texten* (Vienna, 1975), 178; translated into English by P. R. J. Ford and Mary Whittall as *Wagner: A Documentary Study* (London, 1975), 178.

[26] Nietzsche, *Sämtliche Werke*, vii. 275–6.  [27] Ibid. 303.

music. Wagner's unacknowledged goal, he wrote, was 'the greatest of all symphonies, whose principal instruments sing a song which can be rendered accessible to the senses by means of an action'.[28] For Nietzsche, the classic example of a 'symphony that coincides with drama',[29] even if it was disguised as an opera, was *Tristan und Isolde*,[30] 'the actual *opus metaphysicum* of all art', as he described it in the fourth of his *Unzeitgemäße Betrachtungen*.[31]

Towards the end of his life Wagner himself repeatedly noted that, in writing *Tristan und Isolde*, he had felt a need 'to go to the very limit musically, as if I had been writing a symphony' (*CT*, 28 September 1878), most of all because, 'in the *Nibelungen*, the requirements of the drama frequently forced him to restrict the musical expression' (*CT*, 1 October 1878). Or: 'He says he had felt the urge to express himself symphonically for once, and that led to *Tristan*' (*CT*, 11 December 1878); in this work he 'gave himself up entirely to music' (*CT*, 4 October 1881), and so on. That the symphony represented Wagner's musical ideal has been convincingly shown by a number of other writers, most notably by Egon Voss. Wagner not only conceived of his musical dramas as 'symphonies in disguise',[32] their thematic treatment apparently based on the model of classical instrumental music, but what Egon Voss has termed his 'symphonic ambition'[33] is also attested by his non-dramatic musical projects and, above all, of course, by his plans to write symphonies once he had completed *Parsifal*.

It goes without saying, however, that, unlike Nietzsche, Wagner did not automatically think of the symphony in terms of absolute music. 'Everything is either a march or a dance, there is hardly any absolute music', he told Cosima on 1 January 1881 in the course of a conversation about the introduction to the 'Eroica' Symphony, which he associated with the idea of a 'procession which I see so clearly and in such detail that I could stage it'. The finale of Beethoven's Eighth Symphony put him in mind of the 'Classical Walpurgis Night' in Goethe's *Faust*: 'Here comes Galathea! Then the dolphins and the ocean creatures, gambolling, making an uproar, and squabbling.' (*CT*, 3 October 1875.) Even as early as 1849, in *The Art-Work of the Future*, he had glossed the Seventh Symphony as the 'apotheosis of dance' (iii. 94)—dance, for Wagner, being the *fons et origo* of symphonic form (see v. 189 and *passim*). In conversation with Cosima he repeatedly compared the musical structure of the Seventh Symphony with the phases of a 'Dionysian festival', even going into considerable scenic detail. 'I could

---

[28] Nietzsche, *Sämtliche Werke* 323–4.     [29] Ibid. viii. 541.     [30] Ibid. 229, 329.
[31] Ibid. i. 479; English trans. (Hollingdale, *Untimely Meditations*), p. 232.
[32] Egon Voss, *Richard Wagner und die Instrumentalmusik: Wagners symphonischer Ehrgeiz* (Wilhelmshaven, 1977), 180.
[33] This is the subtitle of Voss's monograph cited above, n. 32.

actually draw the pictures it arouses in me', he told Cosima on 19 November 1878 (see also *CT*, 11 March 1873, 5 June 1875, and 12 January 1879). Of course, he constantly emphasized that Beethoven himself did not have these images in his mind: although it evoked them in the listener, his music was not itself produced by those images (*CT*, 19 November 1878).

In this instance Wagner's scenico-pictorial interpretation of Beethoven's symphony is entirely at one with Nietzsche's postulate of 'absolute music', inasmuch as the latter, expressly distancing himself from Hanslick, regards it as wholly appropriate that time and again 'a Beethoven symphony compels its individual auditors to use figurative speech to describe it'. Even the fact that 'the tone-poet expresses his composition in images' is something which Nietzsche—unlike 'certain other gentlemen' (by which he means Hanslick and his formalistic followers, of course) who exercise only their 'poor wit' on this phenomenon, often not even deigning to find it 'worth explaining'— regards as wholly legitimate as long as it involves 'symbolical representations born of music'[34], and that these representations correspond with the scenic visions of the Dionysian chorus of Attic tragedy. (This apologia for a musically inspired language of metaphor was taken over verbatim into *Die Geburt der Tragödie*.[35]) In 1874 Nietzsche countered Hanslick's theory that music consisted of 'sonorously shifting form' by arguing that music was 'the musician's agitated feelings expressed in sound', and that those feelings might easily be vented in images.[36] Only when such visual images did not follow the musical development but attempted, rather, to determine it was music alienated from itself. For Wagner, however, these 'musical images' (*CT*, 18 July 1871) never entirely lost their determinative function—even after his 'conversion' to Schopenhauer. On 1 March 1871, for example, he explained to Cosima that 'a musician is guided by an idea, an image, that he designs his music in accordance with that'.

Here Wagner still seems to share the point of view that he had advanced in 1857 in his open letter 'On Franz Liszt's Symphonic Poems', namely,

that music can impinge on our senses only in forms which, borrowed from life, are originally alien to music and which thereby obtain their deepest meaning as if through revelation of the music latent within them. Nothing is less absolute (as to its appearance in life, of course) than music, and the champions of absolute music clearly have no idea what they are talking about; it would be enough to reduce them to utter confusion to invite them to show us a piece of

[34] Nietzsche, *Sämtliche Werke*, vii. 185.
[35] Ibid. i. 50; English trans. (Kaufmann, *Basic Writings of Nietzsche*), p. 54.
[36] Ibid. vii. 771.

music without the form which (following the law of causal connection) it had borrowed from bodily movement or spoken verse. (v. 191.)

Wagner reminds his reader that 'march and dance form' constitute the 'unshakeable foundation of pure instrumental music'. 'On this point we are agreed, therefore, and admit that in this human world of ours it was necessary to afford divine music a point of attachment, nay . . . a determinative element, before ever it could appear to us.' (v. 191–2.)

The parenthetical qualifications in the above quotation show how difficult it was for Wagner, after his assimilation of Schopenhauerian thinking, to explain the extra-musical motivation behind a musical idea. He was never able to find a satisfactory compromise between what Nietzsche termed his older and his newer doctrines on the relationship between music and its determinants (or parallels) on the level of either the poetic word and image or the rhythmic and mimic gesture. It is a relationship which can be grasped only on the level of contradictions. Writing on the dramaturgical praxis of the later Wagner, Carl Dahlhaus has distinguished between a metaphysical and an empirical interpretation of the relationship between music and poetico-mimic motifs. 'The fact that, empirically, "in this human world of ours", music needs a causal formal motif before it can take shape does not preclude it from expressing, metaphysically, "the innermost essence of the world", to quote Schopenhauer. Empirically "conditioned", it is metaphysically "conditioning".'[37] Such formal motifs, therefore, may be one of the necessary conditions for the production of music, but they are not an 'essential factor'.[38] It was evidently this that Wagner had in mind when he wrote his open letter 'On Franz Liszt's Symphonic Poems', questioning the absoluteness of music only within the phenomenal world, a world that is governed by the principle of causality.

Of course, even before he had read a word of Schopenhauer, Wagner had already sought to justify the relationship between music and text in two different ways. On the one hand, the tonal language of the musical drama is said to be determined by the language of the text, while, on the other, it is the 'maternal element from whose womb . . . both word and verbal language' (iv. 102) have issued. In short, music is both conditioning and conditioned, even in *Opera and Drama*. Elaborating the sexual (and dramaturgical) metaphor mentioned earlier, whereby the musical principle is female and the linguistic principle male, Wagner compares music to Jocasta, who gave birth to Oedipus (i.e., the spoken language). Oedipus then married Jocasta and sired Antigone (i.e., 'drama') (iv. 102). (Wagner's attempt, if not to conceptualize the highly complicated interrelationship between music and poetry then at least to

---

[37] Dahlhaus, *Die Idee der absoluten Musik*, p. 32.    [38] Ibid. 134.

reduce it to a striking image, will form the subject of a later chapter, when we shall have occasion to look in closer detail at the implications of this metaphor in the context of his exegesis of the Oedipus myth in *Opera and Drama*.) So ambivalent is Wagner's definition of the dependent relationship between music and words in *Opera and Drama* that it will be difficult to agree wholeheartedly with Nietzsche's claim that this particular contradiction in Wagner's theory post-dates his reading of Schopenhauer. The composer was already familiar with the idea of music as a language expressing the very source of all things from the musical aesthetics of the Romantics (an aesthetic outlook which, in turn, had spawned Schopenhauer's metaphysics), even if he largely suppressed that view when writing his great reform essays. In many respects, his discovery of Schopenhauer merely revived a number of half-forgotten insights to which he had already given exegetical expression in the Romantically inspired essays of his earlier period.

According to *'Zukunftsmusik'*, the poet of the musical drama is required to be 'fully alive to the aim of music and its inexhaustible expressive potential, and to design his poem in such a way as to penetrate the finest fibres of the musical fabric' (vii. 112). Here Wagner posits the pre-existence of music, whose laws, he insists, will assert their involuntary hold on the poet. This passage recalls Wagner's letter to Karl Gaillard of 30 January 1844, in which the composer describes his 'method of production': 'I am attracted only by those subjects which reveal themselves to me not only as poetically but, at the same time, as musically significant. And so, even before I set about writing a single line of the text or drafting a scene, I am already thoroughly immersed in the musical aura of my new creation'; the opera, he goes on, was already finished with the completion of the text, 'and its detailed musical treatment is more a question of calm & reflective revision, the moment of actual creativity having already passed'.[39]

In other words, Wagner already had a vague musical idea of the overall piece at the moment of its conception. It was an overview which lacked any firm melodic and harmonic outlines (leaving aside any individual motifs, some of which may have been jotted down even before the text itself was drawn up), but which left its structural mark on the words and on the stage action. This vague idea of the work's form assumed more concrete shape under the influence of the text, so that one can speak, with Wagner, of an 'equal and reciprocal interpenetration of the poetry and the music' (vii. 116). The claim that Wagner invested music with a metaphysical apriority while subordinating it, aesthetically

[39] Richard Wagner, *Sämtliche Briefe*, ed. Gertrud Strobel and Werner Wolf (Leipzig, 1970), ii. 358; English trans. from *Selected Letters of Richard Wagner*, ed. Stewart Spencer and Barry Millington (London, 1987), 118.

and in practice, to extra-musical determinants is almost certainly an over-simplification. Even during the compositional process it was often the purely musical inspiration which came first: only later was it clothed in scenic or poetic guise. We must assume a constant interaction between musical and extra-musical influences not only in Wagner's theory but in his compositional praxis, too.

While he was working on *Parsifal*, Wagner—according to Cosima's *Diaries*—had a constant stream of musical ideas which he could not put to dramatic use and which he therefore 'saved up' for his symphonies. 'I should like to be writing symphonies, in which I could write down ideas as they come into my mind, for I have no lack of ideas.' (*CT*, 19 November 1878.) 'Recently he told me that themes came into his mind all the time, but they then vanished, since he made no use of them. He says he sometimes wishes he were just a musician and did not have other [dramatic] thoughts.' (*CT*, 22 September 1879.) 'In the evening he writes his score, though he keeps saying how much he would rather be writing symphonies: "all the time I am putting aside themes for the sake of the drama".' (*CT*, 7 February 1881.) 'He says once again that he is longing to do some instrumental compositions, adding that it was a similar mood which gave rise to *Tristan*.' (*CT*, 9 February 1881.) As we have already noted above, he wanted to 'go to the very limits musically', and write symphonies, because he felt himself to be a musical Prometheus, chained to the dramatic rock of the *Ring* (*CT*, 28 September and 1 October 1878).

In other words, Wagner was trying to withdraw from musical drama into the territory which makes that drama possible—the 'archetypal drama' of the symphony.[40] When, on 7 March 1882, he praised drama as the supreme artistic genre, Cosima added: 'And absolute music.' She was clearly using the term in a positive sense, and Wagner, astonishingly, allowed it to pass, while at the same time adding a rider in the form of a relative clause: 'Which is a kind of drama—I really believe that—a theme and a counter-theme, which combine in a dance.' What is remarkable, of course, is that in his own symphonies Wagner did not attempt to take up the 'dramatic' form of Beethoven's symphonies, preferring instead 'a melody spun out in a single movement' (*CT*, 13 January 1883). It was no more possible to write symphonies in four movements (*CT*, 19 November 1878) than to combine themes dramatically. 'If we write symphonies, Franz', he told Liszt on 17 December 1882, shortly before a performance of his C major Symphony of 1832, 'then let us stop contrasting one theme with another, a method Beeth. has exhausted. We should just spin a melodic line until it can be

[40] E. T. A. Hoffmann had already described the symphony as a kind of 'musical drama'; see Dahlhaus, *Die Idee der absoluten Musik*, p. 17.

spun no further; but on no account drama!' Wagner's final musical project dates from only a few weeks before his death (he returned to it on 13 January 1883), and is wholly indebted to that idea of 'absolute music' which he had formerly spurned. By now he was not even prepared to accept those structural analogies with drama which even Nietzsche had considered reconcilable with absolute music.

It might be claimed that Wagner's lifelong model, Beethoven, was now overshadowed by another, more 'absolute' composer, Johann Sebastian Bach, whom Wagner latterly came to regard as 'the voice of the thing-in-itself': 'in Beeth. everything is dramatic. I sometimes feel I don't want to hear anything more by Beeth.', he told Cosima on 11 November 1878. On another occasion he remarked that, whereas Mozart and Beethoven 'were closer to being poets', it was Bach who was 'a true musician' (*CT*, 24 April 1881), because his works, which, according to Wagner, were an expression of the 'pre-human' (in other words, a symbolic representation of a universe which was also pre-dramatic[41]), seemed totally to have broken free from the laws of that phenomenal world in which the poet and his dramatic relation, the composer, remained caught up. 'That is music in its true essence; everything we compose is applied music.' (*CT*, 18 December 1878.) That absolute music was now Wagner's secret ideal emerges unmistakably from this final remark; no less clear is his view that Bach came closer to this ideal than the 'dramatist' Beethoven.

To return to Wagner's plan to write symphonies, we may perhaps be justified in doubting whether he would have been successful at writing the sort of 'undramatic', monothematic composition that he had in mind. Against this assessment of himself as a quasi-symphonist must be set the view of a writer such as Egon Voss, who has shown, with the aid of structural analyses of such instrumental works as *A Faust Overture*, the *Siegfried Idyll*, and the Funeral March from *Götterdämmerung*, that their

[41] See *CT*, 12 Mar. ('he says that up to Mozart music remained in a vegetable state, but with M. and particularly with Beethoven "anima" had entered into it'), 6 July 1869 ('In this history of creation the venerable Bach appears somewhat like the entire planetary system, before it separated itself from the sun'), 12 Feb. 1871 ('Bach's music is certainly a conception of the world [the metaphysical definition of music which, according to Schopenhauer, distinguishes it from the other arts], his figurations, devoid of feeling, are like unfeeling Nature itself—birth and death, winds, storms, sunshine—all these things take place just like such a figuration . . . And it belongs to the organ, which is as devoid of feeling as the universal soul, yet at the same time so powerful'), 13 July 1872 ('A sphinx . . . One hears in it the lament of Nature (animals and plants)'), 7 Mar. ('Then R. plays the C sharp minor Prelude from [Bach's] *48 Preludes and Fugues*. An indescribable impression—it echoes within us like the quiet lament of a sphinx, or vanishing gods, or Nature before the creation of mankind!'), 9 June ('It is like a cosmic system, which moves according to eternal laws, without feeling; the sorrows of the world are indeed reflected in it, but not in the same way as in other music'), 14 Dec. 1878 ('music *eo ipso*'), 20 Feb. ('That is like Nature, uncomprehending and incomprehensible'), 18 Nov. 1879 ('These things are elemental forces, like planets, endowed with psychic life . . . There is the musician *par excellence*'), and 13 Oct. 1881 ('Like the world before the advent of man').

themes and motives are scarcely developed in a symphonic way, and that genuine thematic writing has been replaced by a system of repeating existing themes at different pitches or of introducing new motives.[42] This paratactical principle serves to underline the atmospheric or expressive quality of the themes, but at the same time it undermines their traditional formal function, which is to create superordinate musical links. What 'development' the motives undergo within their respective music dramas is more of a literary nature: in the course of the dramatic action, they acquire what Voss has termed an 'aura of meanings and associations'.[43] It is this which gives them their 'allusive magic', to quote Thomas Mann.[44] Even as early as 1878, in a posthumously published fragment, Nietzsche had spoken with cynical exaggeration of the lack of any potential for development in Wagner's themes: 'After each *theme* Wagner is always at a loss to know how to *continue*.' Another jotting reads: 'The *atmosphere* replaces the composition.'[45] Behind these remarks is the reproach which he was to repeat *ad nauseam* in his later anti-Wagnerian tracts, namely, that Wagner was unable to write 'absolute music' and that he was dependent upon scenic stimuli. 'Wagner begins from a hallucination—not of sounds but of gestures', we read in *Der Fall Wagner*. 'Then he seeks the sign language of sounds for them.' Only here is he truly 'worthy of our admiration'; his 'manner of "development"', by contrast, attests to his 'incapacity for giving organic form' and to his 'incapacity for any style whatever'. The whole was 'no longer a whole'. This, for Nietzsche, was 'the sign of every *literary decadence*' (in the sense in which Paul Bourget understood that term).[46]

'You will guess that I am essentially anti-theatrical—but Wagner was, conversely, essentially a man of the theatre and an actor, the most enthusiastic mimomaniac of all time, also as a musician!', Nietzsche wrote in *Die fröhliche Wissenschaft*.[47] All of Nietzsche's polemical essays against Wagner revolve around this same *idée fixe* (which contrasts ironically with Wagner's own declared antipathy towards the status and typology of the modern actor), echoing and re-echoing with the same jarring paradoxes and hyperboles. 'As a matter of fact, he repeated a single proposition all his life long', he claims in *Der Fall Wagner*: 'that his music did not mean mere music! . . . "motives", gestures, formulas, doing things double and even a hundredfold—he remained an orator even as a musician—he therefore had to move his "it means" into the

[42] Voss, *Wagner und die Instrumentalmusik*, pp. 129–31.

[43] Ibid. 143–4.

[44] Thomas Mann, *Wagner und unsere Zeit*, ed. Erika Mann (Frankfurt, 1963), 144; translated into English by Allan Blunden as *Pro and contra Wagner* (London, 1985), 187.

[45] Nietzsche, *Sämtliche Werke*, viii. 492.

[46] Ibid. vi. 27–8; English trans. (Kaufmann, *Basic Writings of Nietzsche*), pp. 626–7.

[47] Ibid. iii. 617; English trans., p. 325.

foreground as a matter of principle. "Music is always a mere means": that was his theory, that above all the only *practice* open to him.' Nietzsche is guilty here of consciously cocking a snook when he denies the significant shift of emphasis that took place in Wagner's theory under the influence of Schopenhauer, and when, a few lines later, he passes the composer off as the *'heir of Hegel'*.[48]

Nietzsche's anti-Wagnerian polemics veer constantly between dialectical extremes. Blatant contempt suddenly turns into emphatic adulation, or praise is transformed into vilification, all within the same account of a single phenomenon, simply by changing the terms of the evaluation. Thus, for example, we read in *Der Fall Wagner* that 'Here we may consider Wagner an inventor and innovator of the first rank—*he has increased music's capacity for language to the point of making it immeasurable'*, but then he goes on: 'Always presupposing that one first allows that under certain circumstances music may be not music but language, instrument, *ancilla dramaturgica*. Wagner's music, if not shielded by theatre taste . . . is simply bad music, perhaps the worst ever made. When a musician can no longer count up to three he becomes "dramatic", he becomes "Wagnerian".'[49]

Behind this overwritten polemic (which, as Thomas Mann has rightly observed, may be read against the grain as 'a panegyric in reverse, another form of eulogy'[50]) is the ideal of absolute music, an ideal which the young Nietzsche had already developed as a counter-thesis to *Opera and Drama*. Even in the fragmentary jottings from 1869–70 to which reference has already been made the heteronomous motivation of music is categorically rejected. Wagner's 'older doctrine' is simply invalidated by the newer, Schopenhauer-inspired doctrine. In Nietzsche's case the philosophical concept of music is identical with its empirical praxis. Music comes first not only metaphysically but creatively, too, through the process of musico-dramatic production; it is not merely absolute, therefore, but 'conditioning' within the phenomenal world. In this rigorous denial of all scenic and poetic motivation to musical development there are already clear signs of the later Nietzsche's anti-Wagnerian stance. Both as a Wagnerian and an anti-Wagnerian, Nietzsche was the unconditional ideologue of absolute music.

There is little doubt, however, that neither Schopenhauer nor Hanslick would have dignified Nietzsche's concept of music with the attribute 'absolute'. Schopenhauer (who had made it palpably clear to Wagner that, in his view, there was no such thing as a 'community of property' between poetry and music[51]) would have questioned whether it

[48] Ibid. vi. 35–6; English trans., pp. 633–4.      [49] Ibid. vi. 30; English trans., p. 629.
[50] Mann, *Wagner und unsere Zeit*, p. 72; English trans. (Blunden, *Pro and contra Wagner*), p. 100.
[51] See Kropfinger, *Wagner und Beethoven*, pp. 150–1.

was possible to include symphonically created drama under the heading of absolute music. Nietzsche's idea of drama as a visionary simile of music derives not so much from Schopenhauer's own metaphysics of music as from its extension and correction in Wagner's *Beethoven* essay, an extension to Schopenhauerian philosophy which is, of course, designed to legitimize the musical drama. Hanslick had consistently denied the validity of visual associations when listening to a piece of music, and he would therefore have regarded Nietzsche's philosophy of music as yet another variant of Wagner's own aesthetic outlook. Indeed, he included a specific critique of the latter's 1870 essay in later editions of *Vom Musikalisch-Schönen*.

Of course, Hanslick's treatise gave Wagner more to think about than he was prepared to admit. When he writes in *Beethoven* that his remarks on the 'illusory' relationship between music and poetry are based on the 'experience' that 'a piece of music loses nothing of its character even when set to very different texts' (ix. 103), there is little doubt that he is responding to Hanslick's own thoughts on the matter.[52] But even if the later Wagner moved relatively close to the ideal of absolute music, there was still an unbridgeable gulf between him and his Viennese arch-enemy on almost every fundamental question of musical aesthetics.

Hanslick's position was that of radical autonomous aesthetics, which regarded it as dangerous to deduce universal laws of beauty from the concept of art, since to do so prevented us from recognizing the 'technical limits' of the individual arts. In the later editions of his essay he quotes Franz Grillparzer on this point: 'Probably no worse service has been rendered to the arts than when German writers included them all in the collective name of art.'[53] From this standpoint, of course, Hanslick was bound to regard the total art-work as some sort of aesthetic Antichrist. By limiting himself to a purely musical aesthetic, he was giving absolute status to a *werkimmanent* approach.[54] In diametrical opposition to Wagner's critique of the ideology of the 'absolute work of art' (an ideology which Wagner criticizes for impermissibly isolating the work in question from its socio-historical context), Hanslick states with apodictic certainty: 'The aesthetic inquirer knows nothing (nor can he be expected to know anything) about the personal circumstances or the political surroundings of the composer—he hears and believes nothing but what the music itself contains.'[55]

---

[52] Hanslick, *Vom Musikalisch-Schönen*, pp. 37–9; English trans. (Cohen, *Beautiful in Music*), pp. 34–6.

[53] Ibid. 3; English trans., p. 8; the reference is to the 1872 edition of Grillparzer's *Gesammelte Schriften*, ix. 142.

[54] The *werkimmanent* approach to literary study is more normally associated with the New Criticism, and implies a close reading of the text and a disregard for the biographical and social background of the work.

[55] Hanslick, *Vom Musikalisch-Schönen*, pp. 81–2; English trans. (Cohen, *Beautiful in Music*), p. 63.

By restricting his aesthetic approach to the work *per se*, Hanslick also justifies his rejection of the 'aesthetics of sensation'. This rejection has two implications, one to do with content, the other with effect. On the one hand, Hanslick denies that the object or content of music is feeling: the only aspect of feeling which music is capable of expressing, he writes, is physiological and dynamic, a dynamism which is identical for the most heterogeneous 'affects' and which does not allow us to infer any one specific feeling; this latter is merely projected into the work by the listener in the course of the piece's development. On the other hand, Hanslick dismisses the traditional musical and rhetorical view that the aim of music is to arouse feelings or sensations. He rightly observes that support for the position of 'those older systems of aesthetics' has lasted far longer in the theory of music than in other specialist aesthetics: this is a view, he writes, 'which considered the beautiful solely in reference to the sensations aroused and the philosophy of beauty as the offspring of sensation (*aisthesis*)'.[56]

In his 1793 essay, 'Über das Pathetische', Schiller had used the 'music of more recent composers' to demonstrate the extent to which aesthetic 'freedom' was threatened when music affected the emotions, and how easy it was for listeners to suffer the 'symptoms of intoxication'.[57] Hanslick is advancing much the same idea when he writes that the products of no other art admit of such 'unreasoning enjoyment' as do those of music. 'We may drink in a melody, but not a picture, a church, or a drama.'[58] The view that aesthetics was founded on feelings gives theoretical support to this kind of response, a response which, for Hanslick, culminated in Wagner's music, with its 'intoxicating effect of opium'.[59] By defining music purely from the standpoint of the law of beauty, Hanslick was able to exclude such 'morbid sensitivity' from his calculations.[60] His analysis of the only kind of attitude which, he believed, it was appropriate to adopt towards the beautiful amounts to a kind of musical stoicism or quietism, tending towards the calm contemplation of works of fine art. Indeed, he even speaks of the 'pure contemplation [!] of a piece of music', and goes on to remark that, 'With a willing mind, calm but acutely sensitive, we enjoy the work of art as it passes before us', thus confirming Schelling's dictum of 'the sublime indifference of Beauty'.[61]

It is at this point in *Beethoven* that Wagner begins his assault on Hanslick's theory—without, of course, mentioning the Viennese critic

---

[56] Ibid. 1; English trans., p. 7.
[57] Friedrich Schiller, *Sämtliche Werke*, ed. Gerhard Fricke and Herbert G. Göpfert, 3rd edn. (Munich, 1962), v. 640.
[58] Hanslick, *Vom Musikalisch-Schönen*, p. 124; English trans. (Cohen, *Beautiful in Music*), p. 91.
[59] Ibid., p. vii; English trans., p. 7.
[60] Ibid. 131; English trans., p. 97.
[61] Ibid. 131–2; English trans., pp. 97–8; the reference is to Schelling's *Über das Verhältnis der bildenden Künste zu der Natur* (1807).

by name. In the spirit of Lessing's *Laokoon*, he condemns the tendency to confuse the laws of production and reception in the visual arts with those that obtain in music. In an aesthetic treatise which insists so strongly on the fact that each individual art has its own autonomous laws, this is certainly a remarkable position to adopt. Indeed, the roles seem to have been reversed, with the ideologue of the total art-work indulging in a veiled critique of the radical advocate of generic autonomy, and accusing him of confusing the different artistic genres. According to Wagner (who appropriates Schopenhauerian ideas here and adapts them to serve his own ends), the essence of all visual art is the pure contemplation of things unaffected by 'the will's emotion'. Only when we relate those things to the individual will is an emotion aroused. But it is the fundamental aim of visual art to avoid precisely this. To it alone belongs that 'calm' which makes it possible for us to 'contemplate, aesthetically and devoid of will . . . the *show* of things'. 'And it is this pacification of the will engendered by our sheer delight in appearance which, extended from visual art to all the arts, has been made a postulate for every kind of aesthetic pleasure and which, in consequence, has produced the *concept of beauty*.' This concept, according to Wagner, is justified only in the visual arts. The basis of music, by contrast, is the way in which it affects the will through the medium of the (aurally perceived) world around us, which is why it obeys 'wholly different aesthetic laws'. To derive an art from an 'expression of the will's emotion', in other words, from an allegedly 'purely pathological element', may be offensive to 'aestheticians', Wagner observes, plainly alluding to Hanslick. Music and painting have 'radically diverse effects', the former causing the 'profoundest pacification of the will', the latter its 'utmost excitation' (ix. 70–2). (The metaphysical consequences which Wagner drew from this distinction will be demonstrated in due course in the context of our interpretation of Act III of *Tristan und Isolde*.)

In order to distinguish his own philosophy of music from Hanslick's theory of the same, Wagner—borrowing chiefly from Schiller's theoretical writings—fell back on a concept which the aesthetic writers of the Enlightenment and of philosophical idealism in general had seen as a concomitant of the beautiful, namely, the sublime. Whereas 'taste in respect of the beautiful presupposes that the mind is in *restful* contemplation, and preserves it in this state . . . the feeling of the sublime involves as its characteristic feature a mental *movement* combined with the estimate of the object', we read in Kant's *Kritik der Urteilskraft*, written in 1790.[62] Nature is sublime 'in such of its

[62] Immanuel Kant, *Kritik der Urteilskraft*, ed. Karl Vorländer (Hamburg, 1924), 91; translated into English as *Critique of Judgement*, in Immanuel Kant, *Philosophical Writings*, ed. Ernst Behler, with a foreword by René Wellek (New York, 1986), 204.

phenomena as in their intuition convey the idea of their infinity' and 'transcend every standard of sense'.[63] For Wagner (but not for Kant, Schiller, or Schopenhauer), this aspect of the sublime becomes the basic definition of music, enabling him to distinguish it from the visual or 'fine' arts. But, at the same time, music is unharnessed from its self-evident union with the scenic arts, and hence from the 'total art-work'. In consequence, as we have shown, the absolute music which he once condemned has now become the later Wagner's covert ideal.

[63] Ibid. 99, 94; English trans., pp. 212, 207.

# 11

# The 'Redemption' of the Romance in the Musical Drama

In the slave, prose begins.

Hegel, *Ästhetik.*

The history of opera makes us aware of 'the inability of music itself to become genuine drama, in other words, to allow genuine drama (i.e., drama that is not merely tailored to meet the requirements of the music) to be assimilated into it, whereas it is the *music* which ought reasonably to merge with this genuine drama' (iii. 263). Here, in a nutshell, is the quintessential idea behind the first part of *Opera and Drama*. In Wagner's view, the predominance of 'absolute music' has led to a fragmentation of the dramatic form of opera, the *unity* of which had been demanded by the poetics of the spoken theatre ever since the time of Aristotle. But the absolute musician who ostensibly sets the tone in opera 'has never for a moment striven to impose a unified form upon the art-work as a whole: each individual vocal number was a self-contained and self-sufficient form, similar to the remaining pieces in the opera in terms of its superficial structure but certainly not connected with them through any formally determinative content. Thus, disconnectedness became very much a characteristic feature of operatic music' (iv. 201).

However, Wagner was fundamentally convinced that the 'realization of that consummate unified form' which would encompass the entire drama, providing a 'binding connection' between its different parts (iv. 202), could be achieved only when the musician joined hands with the poet. Even the unity of the *musical* form was similarly grounded in the 'poetic intent' (iv. 201). It is this, moreover, that legitimizes a leitmotivic technique which, in the form of a dense web, is designed to draw together all the elements in the dramatic action to create a referential whole. In one of the last of his dramaturgical writings, the essay 'On the Application of Music to Drama' (1879), Wagner returns to the central theses of *Opera and Drama* and, notwithstanding the differing views advanced in the essays of the intervening years, describes the 'unity of symphonic writing' as the ideal to which the composer should aspire in his search for dramatic unity:

This unity results from a web of basic themes [*Grundthemen*] which permeate the entire work of art and which, as in symphonic writing, contrast with and complement each other, allowing themselves to be re-formed, divided, and reunited, except that in this case the dramatic action which is elaborated and executed governs the laws of separation and association which were borrowed originally from dance movements. (x. 185.)[1]

The fact that, in spite of what Egon Voss has called his latent 'symphonic ambition', Wagner was unable to produce this sense of unity *except* by dramatic means, and that the specifically symphonic development of motives was essentially alien to his nature, was mentioned in the previous chapter. At the same time, Wagner's criticism of Mozart's compositional technique, for example, confirms that he was largely lacking in any understanding of how to create autonomous musical structures. The unity of Mozart's symphonic writing seemed to him to consist of a succession of individual 'four-square' periods separated by passages which were musically empty and which he described as 'rum-ti-tum'. Essentially, Wagner was able to conceive of 'unity' only as something poetical, and it is no longer possible to mistake the tone of the self-apologist when, in this late essay of his, he adduces one of the forms of 'absolute music' and seeks to extend its unity to the musical drama, too. Feeling threatened by the detested 'professors' of colleges of music, he attempts to prove that he, too, is fully conversant with the 'profession' of symphonic composer, albeit in the context of dramatic style.

The idea of unity is central to the dramaturgical system which characterizes *Opera and Drama*. Essentially, it means the same as Aristotle's understanding of the term as used in his *Poetics*. In Wagner's view, Greek tragedy was the poetic model on which the 'unified form' (iv. 34) of the musical drama should be based. It was, so to speak, a circular path that led to the 'drama of the future': following the example of the medieval stage and of the English and Spanish theatre which had grown out of that tradition (embodied in the figures of Shakespeare and Calderón), and conscious, therefore, of the 'barbarian advantages' resulting from the 'Romantic trend of uncultured centuries' (to quote, once again, one of Wagner's favourite Goethian expressions[2]), dramatic form had moved further and further away from Greek tragedy and yet, at the same time, was moving increasingly close to it from the other side by passing through the world of 'Romantic' forms, chief of which was Shakespearian drama. (This image may also shed light on the historico-dramaturgical structure of the second and third parts of *Opera and Drama*.)

Above the entrance to Haus Wahnfried in Bayreuth there is a sgraffito representing the art-work of the future;[3] it shows Wotan

---

[1] In contrast to his countless other remarks on the subject, Wagner refuses in this essay to consider that even Beethoven's symphonies might be 'dramatic' in character; cf. esp. x. 178.

[2] Johann Wolfgang von Goethe, *Gedenkausgabe der Werke, Briefe und Gespräche*, ed. Ernst Beutler, 2nd edn. (Zurich, 1961), xv. 1035; see also *CT*, 8 Feb. 1872.

[3] See Peter Wapnewski, *Richard Wagner: Die Szene und ihr Meister* (Munich, 1978), 22. The sgraffito is reproduced on the dust-jacket of Wapnewski's *Der traurige Gott* (Munich, 1978), and in

(described by Wagner as 'the sum total of present-day intelligence'[4]) with his two ravens whispering their runic lore in his ears; on either side are allegories of Greek tragedy and music. The former, like the muse Melpomene, holds a mask supported on a pedestal, whereas Music is seen holding a lyre in her left hand, while her right hand is held outstretched towards Wotan; beneath it is the figure of Young Siegfried, the 'man of the future',[5] who is shown looking up at Music. Greek tragedy, then, provides the formal model, while music is the essential medium of expression of the 'drama of the future'.

Wagner's theory of the spoken theatre sets out from the premiss that modern drama has a twofold origin. One of its sources is Greek drama, the other is the romance, of which Shakespeare's plays are the culminating development. This is, of course, a speculative thesis, but one whose historical justification is not at issue here. Clearly, Wagner did not wish to claim that Shakespearian drama was actually derived from romance; his aim was, rather, to show the structural affinity between the two genres (their 'epic' form) by using a metaphor according to which one of the genres developed out of the other. (It is in this same metaphorical sense that he speaks, for example, of the 'emergence of language from melody', a development which, by his own admission, he saw 'not as a chronological sequence but as an architectonic arrangement': iv. 93.) For Wagner, as for the German Romantic tradition as a whole, the romance or novel was the quintessential modern literary form, the counterpart of ('absolute') instrumental music. The drama of the future could ignore neither the former nor the latter, but had to justify itself by solving the structural problems which they posed. The musical drama could not retire behind the romance and symphony, but had to transcend them by 'superseding' them.

Whereas, in Wagner's view, the influence of Greek tragedy on the modern theatre is attributable merely to an act of theoretical capriciousness—'Greek drama, interpreted on the basis of a misunderstanding of Aristotle's rules', is said to have been grafted on to western Renaissance drama as the result of a process of 'reflection', which in turn had produced a foreign growth—the romance forms the modern theatre's 'natural' embryo, an embryo 'unique to our historical development'. While the fairest and finest form of romance was Shakespearian drama, the most influential product of classicizing

Herbert Barth, Dietrich Mack, and Egon Voss (eds.), *Wagner: A Documentary Study* (London, 1975), illus. 196.

   [4] Letter to August Röckel of 25/6 January 1854, in Richard Wagner, *Sämtliche Briefe*, ed. Hans-Joachim Bauer and Johannes Forner (Leipzig, 1986), vi. 69; English translation from Stewart Spencer and Barry Millington (eds.), *Selected Letters of Richard Wagner* (London, 1987), 308.

   [5] Ibid.

reflection was Racinian *haute tragédie*. 'The whole of the rest of our dramatic literature wavers indecisively and hesitatingly between these two extremes.' (iv. 6.)

'The true nucleus of our poetry lies in romance.' (iv. 6.) In advancing this claim (and in renouncing the classicistic tradition of drama which had enabled Greek tragedy to leave its mark on the modern theatre), Wagner appears to shift his ground in favour of a dramaturgy opposed to the antique model and geared instead to the principles of 'romantic' form, in other words, principles derived from romance. The subsequent argumentation, however, points in the opposite direction. Romance assumes an increasingly prosaic appearance in the course of *Opera and Drama*, while the 'classical art-form', ostensibly cleansed of its traditional classicistic elements, proves to be Wagner's poetic ideal. (Behind this view lies the belief that romance is specific to the modern age, an age whose autochthonous origins Romantic writers in France and Germany around 1800 had found in the Christian Middle Ages, contrasting it with Greek antiquity, which they saw as belonging to the irretrievable past.[6]) It is to this subsequent argumentation that we must now turn our attention.

'*Shakespeare's dramas* spring from life and from our historical evolution as a matter of utmost necessity', Wagner opines at the beginning of part II of *Opera and Drama* (iv. 8–9). The essential oneness of the Middle Ages and the modern period, as postulated by the German Romantics, is illustrated by what Wagner sees as a continuous process in which the romance is displaced by a form of drama which, unlike classicistic tragedy, where historical development has simply been cut short by theoretical capriciousness, is not in blatant contrast to the structural laws of romance but which seeks to subsume and supersede romance through a process of concentration. (As we shall see, this process of concentration must, in Wagner's view, be repeated by every musical drama, just as the history of the human race is repeated in the development of every human embryo.) The medieval romance, whose most important representative Wagner sees in the person of Ariosto (i.e. not a medieval poet in the modern sense of the term but an epic poet of the Renaissance), is distinguished by its wild variety of actions and settings, which, as soon as they were no longer evoked by narrative means but 'presented directly to the senses', were bound to become increasingly 'condensed'. It became necessary, therefore,

to master the mass of disparate material from the inside, investing its structure with a fixed centre and deriving that centre, as the axis of the work, from one's own intuition . . . From the tremendous mass of external phenomena, which

[6] See Hans Robert Jauss, 'Literarische Tradition und gegenwärtiges Bewußtsein der Modernität', in *Literaturgeschichte als Provokation* (Frankfurt, 1970), 11–57, esp. p. 40.

until now had never seemed sufficiently colourful and varied to satisfy the poet, those components that were interrelated were now singled out and the diversity of separate elements condensed in such a way as to provide a precise delineation of individual character. (iv. 8.)

'The mystery plays of the Middle Ages' and the 'popular theatre' which had survived in Switzerland right down to Wagner's own day (one thinks, for example, of the performance of Schiller's *Wilhelm Tell* recounted in Keller's *Der grüne Heinrich*) provided the historical link between the romance and the drama which came into being when the former was condensed in this way. It is to this process that the following passage refers:

The wooden stage of medieval mystery plays, erected in the open fields or in the squares and streets of towns, offered the assembled crowd a performance which lasted not merely a single day but, as may be seen even now, several days in succession: entire histories, whole life stories were performed, and it was left to the mass of spectators to choose, as they surged to and fro, what seemed to them to be most worth seeing. (iv. 10.)

This development marked the beginnings of a process which saw the romance adapted to the stage, imperfectly obeying the latter's rules, since the theatre's appeal to the spectator's 'senses' was confused with that appeal to the 'imagination' which constitutes the relationship between narrator and reader. What 'is presented to the senses' must be 'fully shown, from head to foot, and from start to finish'. What this means is that the playwright must 'compress' time, place, and action, and present them to the spectator as a manageable whole, intelligible to the senses and therefore 'completely self-contained' (iv. 10).

Ever at pains to impute a meaning to history, Wagner ascribes the goal of classically structured form to drama's developing course. Of course, Shakespeare's theatre, too, is palpably far removed from such a form, since his stage was still innocent of illusionistic sets.

As a result of this single appeal to the imagination (an appeal that was still unavoidably necessary, such was the state of contemporary stagecraft), the door remained open in drama for the romance, with its colourful multiplicity of themes, and the history play, with its over-abundance of action, to come and go as they pleased. If the poet ... did not yet feel the need to depict the surrounding scene in a way that was true to nature, he was no more likely to feel the need to condense the action that was to be depicted by limiting it, with increasing precision, to only its most important elements. (iv. 11.)

It was for this reason that Shakespeare, too, failed to realize that there were formal limits to the way in which romance might be translated into drama. It required the theatre of illusion to reveal that no romance could ever be condensed to the point at which it would assume the perfect artistic form of drama, in other words, that 'the nature of romance' differed from that of drama—'a discovery which *we* could not make until the undramatic multiplicity of themes contained in histories was borne in upon us *by the actualization* of those scenes which, requiring *only to be hinted at*, were uniquely capable of inspiring Shakespeare's dramatic romances' (iv. 17). There was, Wagner believed, only one conclusion that could be drawn from this, namely, that modern spoken drama, like opera, was an essentially illegitimate genre. On the one hand Wagner acknowledges only one dramatic tradition as 'natural'—the tradition that is based in romance—while, on the other, he insists that the 'nature' of drama is incompatible with that of romance. In short, Wagner's system obliges the reader to acknowledge that neither opera nor spoken drama, but only the musical drama, fully accords in essence with this highest of all artistic forms. The musical drama alone has the right to supersede the romance as a mirror of modern life, without its form being damaged in the process.

Wagner leaves us in no doubt, therefore, that Shakespeare, notwithstanding his matchless ability to create dramatic characters, is still some way short of the 'most perfect form attainable by the work of art', indeed, that he is 'the source and starting-point of the most unprecedented confusion that has plagued dramatic art for over two hundred years, right up to the present day' (iv. 11–12). This remark is part of a tradition of criticizing what Christian Grabbe, writing in 1827, had called 'Shakespeare mania', a tradition which, from Goethe to Nietzsche, was to provide a contrapuntal accompaniment to the enthusiasm for Shakespeare which was otherwise widespread in Germany. Wagner's criticism, however, is directed not so much at Shakespeare himself as at the generalized tendency to regard his incommensurable and unique dramatic form as a model worthy of imitation. It is striking that, however much it had fallen into disrepute since the time of Lessing, it was to *tragédie classique* that, in spite of their various reservations, writers frequently turned as an antidote to those of Shakespeare's successors who had sought a greater openness of form. Even Wagner, in his conversation with Cosima on 4 March 1869, had voiced a similar view when suggesting that 'with regard to artistic form we owe much to the French for having held so rigidly to the three unities, but one should be able to move around freely within these rules and project life into the prescribed magic circle. Sh[akespeare] had exploded the whole machinery, and what one sees in him is not the world in a magic mirror, but something so real that one is startled.' The criticism typically levelled by humanistic classicistic poets at what, from the standpoint of their own normative rules, they regarded as Shakespeare's doubtful status as a dramatist is suddenly transformed here into a panegyric of a genius who broke down every convention, and yet it is a panegyric which, as such, presupposes the universal validity of the classical formal model.

In his dramaturgical essays of the early 1870s (*On the Destiny of Opera* and *On Actors and Singers*) Wagner, as we have noted above, abandoned the Greek formal ideal and turned to the allegedly improvisatory irregularity of Shakespearian drama as a model for the art-work of the future. According to these essays, the theatre of illusion is far from being the ultimate goal in the history of the theatre, since a higher task is vouchsafed to the theatre of the imagination (at least as far as spoken drama is concerned), a form of theatre modelled on the Elizabethan stage. And it is equally clear that the logic of the musical drama (a logic which, under the influence of Schopenhauer's *Parerga und Paralipomena*, is described in the *Beethoven* essay of 1870 as being analogous to somnambulism) is now at odds with the pseudo-Aristotelian unities. Shakespearian drama, reborn out of the spirit of the Beethovenian symphony,[7] is subjected to the laws of dreams, with the result that Wagner's former objections to its open scenic structure have now become irrelevant. Cosima's *Diaries*—which bear eloquent witness to Wagner's emphatic, almost speechless, admiration for Shakespeare, *the great artistic experience of his old age*, far surpassing all other impressions, including even musical ones,[8]—contain no further trace, in their record of the conversations of his old age, of his earlier objections on the question of genre. No doubt Wagner would have felt such objections to be trivial, given his new-found enthusiasm for Shakespeare's 'invisible theatre', with its ability to transcend all stage reality.

Wagner's critical confrontation with the Elizabethan theatre in *Opera and Drama* attests to an overlap of two aesthetic systems. Whereas it is initially the romance which, in the spirit of Romanticism, is held up as 'the actual nucleus of our poetry', and Shakespearian drama interpreted accordingly as having sprung from that same tradition, what we find in the subsequent course of the argument, clothed in the garb of Feuerbach's materialist ideology,[9] is the old humanist prejudice against the (sub-literary) genre of romance and against Shakespearian dramatic

[7] On 3 Jan. 1881, in conversation with Cosima, Wagner described Shakespeare as 'a non-existent mirage of reality'.

[8] See, in particular, *CT*, 28 May 1878, 7 Nov. ('He is the greatest of them all'), 8 Nov. 1881 ('foolishness to compare him with anyone else'), 3 Jan., 27 Mar. ('he is completely unfathomable'), 27 May ('He is my only spiritual friend'), 4 June ('He was the greatest of them all'), 8 Sept. 1882 ('In the face of his ever-increasing admiration for Shakesp. his earlier predilection for Calderón is tending to diminish'), 11 Jan. 1883, and *passim*.

[9] See Feuerbach's *Grundsätze der Philosophie der Zukunft*, first published in 1843; translated into English by Manfred Vogel, with an introduction by Thomas E. Wartenberg, as *Principles of the Philosophy of the Future* (Indianapolis, 1986).

form. Drama is granted precedence over romance in the established hierarchy of the arts, since it is directed entirely at the senses whereas the latter appeals only to the imagination. But Shakespearian drama, through its renunciation of the illusionistic stage, has yet to complete the transition from the 'imaginary' world of the romance into the sphere of material perception, with the result that it is still some distance away from the perfect form of drama and from the true telos of art. In terms of Wagner's system in *Opera and Drama*, Shakespearian drama is therefore still some way short of the ideal.

Since Shakespeare 'did not yet feel the need to be true to life in his depiction of events on stage', he saw no reason to dispense entirely with the 'multiplicity of themes' (*Vielstoffigkeit*) and 'multiformity of action' (*Vielhandlichkeit*) which typify romance (iv. 9, 11). Wagner's choice of words here is clearly an attempt to render Aristotle's 'polymython' into German. In chapter 18 of his *Art of Poetry* the Greek philosopher had emphasized that the dramatic poet 'must be careful not to give his tragedy an epic structure', adding that by 'epic' he meant *tò polúmuthon*, 'one with a multiplicity of stories'. It would be intolerable, therefore, for a dramatic poet to rework the entire story of the *Iliad*. All attempts to reduce such a wealth of epic action to the confines of a tragedy had proved a failure.[10] Among the differences between tragedy and epic, we read in chapter 5, is the fact that 'tragedy tries as far as possible to keep within a single revolution of the sun, or only slightly to exceed it, whereas the epic observes no limits in its time of action'.[11] (It was from this observation that neo-classical poetics derived the rule concerning unity of time.) A story, Aristotle went on, was dramatic by virtue of the fact that it was 'complete and whole and of a certain amplitude' (*mían praxin olen kaì teleían*), and had a beginning, a middle, and an end.[12]

The epico-romantic multiplicity of action which was typical of Elizabethan drama and which, according to Wagner, revealed its natural descendancy from the 'actual nucleus of our poetry' was, at the same time, the very feature which prevented even Shakespeare's works from embodying the perfect art-form. 'In Shakespearian drama a door had been left open for romance and the loosely structured history . . . to go in and out as they pleased: this door was the stage presentation, which was left to the imagination.' But this door was 'relentlessly shut from the other side', in other words, by neo-classical tragedy (iv. 12). By investing 'stability of scene' with canonical status and by insisting upon Aristotle's ostensible 'rules', all those elements which Shakespeare 'had ignored as being an external factor' — a perfect visual realization of the scene, and

---

[10] *Poetics* 1456ᵃ, 11–19; translated into English by Ingram Bywater in T. S. Dorsch (ed.), *Classical Literary Criticism* (Harmondsworth, 1965), 57.

[11] Ibid. 1449ᵇ, 12–16; English trans., p. 38.    [12] Ibid. 1459ᵃ, 17–20; English trans., p. 41.

the identification of the fictional scene of action with the actual stage area—'became the standard for French drama, structuring it from the outside, so to speak, and forcing such drama to seek living form by means of a mechanical construct'. The dramatist was bound by the 'superficial unity of scene' to exclude the action proper from the stage and, almost without exception, to open up the latter to the *'superficiality of speech'*. 'In Racine's *tragédie*, therefore, we have discourse on stage, while all the action takes place off stage' (iv. 13–15). Like Shakespearian drama (but for the opposite reason), neo-classical tragedy also fails in its vital task of making the drama perceptible to the senses. In the visual splendour of opera, by contrast, with its frequent changes of scene, the senses are more than adequately regaled. Paradoxically, therefore, it is music theatre which (leaving aside Gluck's reform operas and their indebtedness to *tragédie classique*) has been transformed into a visual 'spectacle', whereas spoken drama is presented as though it is merely meant to be listened to (iv. 16).[13]

As a result of the unities, the romance, which, with its multiplicity of action, was 'the basic poetic element of medieval and more recent life', was excluded from the theatre of French tragedy. The dramatist was prevented from choosing subjects which first had to be 'reduced' to dramatic form, and had to restrict himself to those which already existed as a dramatic concentrate, so to speak. Since the neo-classical tragedian could not 'condense the vital poetic element of his time (which could only be mastered, as Shakespeare had done, in exactly the opposite way) and achieve a concentration commensurate with the standard imposed upon him from without', there was nothing left for him to do but to regurgitate the pre-digested themes of classical tragedy from which his rules were derived (iv. 14). As a result, the modern dramatist saw himself thrown back either on the, as yet, imperfect model of Shakespearian dramatic form or on the abstract, sterile, closed form of *haute tragédie*. Since there was no going back beyond the theatre of illusion (Tieck's 'revival of the Shakespearian stage' struck Wagner merely as an honourable experiment in antiquarianism: iv. 18), the modern dramatist was denied the possibility—for reasons of stage technology—of reproducing the Elizabethan theatre's multiplicity of scenes.

From now on the poet either renounced the desire to see his dramas presented on stage and calmly went on reproducing imaginary scenes based on Shakespearian drama (in other words, he wrote literary dramas to be read in silence), or else, in an attempt to realize his imaginary vision on stage, he turned more or less instinctively to a reflective form of drama, the modern origins of

[13] Wagner uses the terms *Schauspiel* and *Hörspiel*, literally 'a play intended to be seen' and 'a play intended to be heard'. In modern German the word *Hörspiel* is used exclusively to mean 'radio play'.

which we were bound to recognize in that pseudo-antique drama that is constructed along the lines of the Aristotelian unities. (iv. 19.)

This dilemma—and the consequent vacillation between anti-theatrical literary drama and hermetic stagecraft to which the musical drama would one day offer a legitimate solution—is one which Wagner demonstrates by adducing the example of Goethe's and Schiller's dramatic development (iv. 20–9). On the one hand he cites their early dramas which, inspired by Shakespeare, flout every formal convention; on the other, their later experiments in neo-classical form. According to Wagner, this reversion to classical myth in the works of both these dramatists proves that the poet whose concern is 'absolute artistic structure' must renounce all subjects drawn from contemporary life, for 'the substance of modern life, being capable of articulating itself intelligibly only through the novel, could not possibly be reduced to such plastic unity that, even assuming an intelligible, dramatic treatment, it could express itself in the form of Greek drama; nor, indeed, could it justify that form on its own terms, or even, necessarily, produce it' (iv. 22). Whenever it was a question of 'representing life itself', therefore, Goethe was obliged to forgo the ideal form of drama, turning instead to the novel, a genre which, even if it meant sacrificing the absolute art-form, was able to accommodate the whole of life 'in all its manifold ramifications' (iv. 23).

Schiller, it is true, did not write any further novels after his abortive *Der Geisterseher*, but, Wagner goes on, he too repeatedly fell from the 'heaven of a pure classical art-form' back to the 'earth' of the (dramatized) novel (iv. 27), writing plays which appropriated their specific subject-matter from history. In particular, the epic expansion of *Wallenstein*, originally conceived as a single drama, to a whole trilogy was evidence of the fact that it was 'impossible' for historical subjects to be 'represented in dramatic form' (iv. 23). Shakespeare was still able to use history for the (pre-illusionistic) theatre of his time without needing to curtail historical truth (by reducing the subject-matter in order to conform to the unities of place, time, and action), but, such were the conditions which obtained in the modern theatre of illusion, it was axiomatic that 'genuine history was not a suitable subject for drama'. 'Historical plays' either contravened the rules of dramatic form or they offended against historical truth (iv. 49–50).

History is only *history* because it depicts men's naked actions in all their unconditional truth: it does not give us men's inner cast of mind but allows us to infer that cast of mind from their actions. If we believe that we have identified that cast of mind correctly, and if we wish to represent history as justified by the same cast of mind, we can do so only through historiography pure and simple or—with the utmost artistic warmth—in the historical romance, i.e., in an art-form in which no external constraint obliges us to misrepresent the simple facts of history by any arbitrary sifting or compression. (iv. 24.)

There is no doubt that Wagner was thinking here of Sir Walter Scott,[14] who largely invented the form of the historical novel and whose works the composer read and admired to the very end of his life.

The true form of drama, according to Wagner, can be seen in only one historical manifestation, namely, Greek tragedy. 'Only the Greek view of the world has so far been able to produce the true art-work that is drama. The subject-matter of this drama, however, was myth, and only through the essence of myth can we grasp the supreme work of Greek art and its form which so enchants us.' *Myth*—the specific subject-matter of classical poetry—was itself a 'condensed image of the world's phenomena' (iv. 31), an image which, from the outset, tended towards the closed form of tragedy, whereas history or socio-political reality—the specific subject-matter of modern literature—naturally worked against that form. The perfect form of drama could be realized nowadays only at the cost of authenticity, by not reflecting modern reality but by drawing on ossified myth or on mythically condensed history, which presented the observer with the livid, shrunken features of a Hippocratic face. For the Greeks, by contrast, myth was the very substance of their lives. The result, according to Wagner, was that the closed form of Attic tragedy was still replete with authentic life, whereas the image which it presented now was of an artistic *caput mortuum*.

The reader may well ask in some bewilderment at this point: 'What has become of Wagner's own mythic dramaturgy? Has he not already sawn through the branch on which he was planning to sit? Having made a nonsense of mythic drama in the modern age, what arguments can he still adduce to change his present tack?' At the risk of pre-empting the later detailed discussion of this point, it is worth stating in advance that, according to Wagner's system, myth can be reborn in the musical drama—and only in the musical drama—since its 'naïve'[15] contours and constellations are reflected in an ever-changing pattern of light, thanks to the 'sentimental' medium of the symphonic orchestra, and thus provided with the whole allusive wealth of modern life. The orchestra is the counterpart of the novel's omniscient narrator: its scope for expression is extended, rather than reduced, by concentrating the work's dramatic form. The unendingness of the musical expression may add a Utopian dimension to the myth, transforming it into an image of perfect man at the end of time. For Wagner, the musical drama is the means by which to transcend history, for it alone is uniquely valid as a representation of

---

[14] See the frequent references to Scott in Cosima's *Diaries*, esp. the entries for 25 Jan.–17 Feb. and 14–17 Mar. 1878.     [15] See Chap. 7 n. 4 above.

that myth which, as the 'beginning and end of history' (iv. 91), is remythologized. In spoken drama the reproduction of classical or Germanic myth remains an act of mere restoration, forging a link which leads from modernity and the Middle Ages (with their characteristic art-forms) to the archaic world. In musical drama, by contrast, it is a kind of Utopia, creating a link which leads from the history of present and future generations to their eschatological culmination.

The crucial passage in Wagner's theory of myth comes in the second chapter of part II of *Opera and Drama*. His account of the genesis of Greek myth—a speculatively rationalist piece of writing, in the spirit of Feuerbach's critique of religion—is well calculated to disabuse all those who consider Wagner's addiction to myth to be a symptom of obscurantism. He characterizes myth as the product 'of the *Volk*'s common poetic ability'. Since archaic man was not yet capable of using 'intellect' to make causal connections between different phenomena, he sought to understand them 'imaginatively', substituting gods for the causes which lay behind those phenomena, but interpreting those gods, in the spirit of Feuerbach, as projections of 'his own human nature'. Hence he imagined the gods in human form. 'Just as the human form is the easiest for him to grasp, so the essence [and causal connection] of those natural phenomena which he has yet to recognize in reality becomes intelligible only when reduced to human shape.' Unlike the modern, godless, scientific world, therefore, the phenomenal world of the Greeks was imbued with anthropomorphic deities.

'In myth every formative urge on the part of the *Volk* is aimed at rendering the most remote links between the most manifold phenomena perceptible to the senses in the most concise [i.e., human] form possible.' Through the imagination's ability to visualize disparate and scattered phenomena 'in concise, clear, and graphic form, the *Volk* becomes the real creator of art in myth'. Greek tragedy was nothing less than the dramatic continuation and 'artistic culmination' of the formal tendency inherent in myth: 'thus, and entirely in accord with the nature of myth, the action that was now represented in reality was compressed to a greater degree of graphic density', creating that unity which, since Aristotle's time, has been regarded as the dramatic action's most important quality. Unlike the neo-classical drama of the modern period, the 'unified form' of Attic tragedy was therefore 'prefigured in the structural framework of myth', a structure which the dramatist needed only to 'elaborate to produce a living edifice, rather than having to take it to pieces and then reassemble it in order to produce some arbitrarily devised artistic construct. The tragic poet merely conveyed the content and essence of myth in the most convincing and intelligible way.' (iv. 31–4.)

As the aesthetic antithesis of drama, romance, according to Wagner, resulted from the corrosion of myth and of its cohesive, reductive force. The synthesizing imagination found itself in conflict with the dissecting intellect, which broke down the 'plastic' (i.e., vividly three-dimensional), mythic *Gestalt* into its constitutive parts:

From the moment that reflective understanding became diverted from the imaginary form and sought to investigate the reality of those phenomena which it comprised, it perceived only an ever-growing variety of details where poetic intuition had seen a complete whole. Anatomical science began its work, following a path which led directly away from the one which had been taken by folk-poetry: where the latter intuitively linked things together, the former intentionally tore them apart; where the latter sought to depict the overall context, the former strove only to acquire the most detailed knowledge of each individual part; and so, step by step, popular intuition had to be destroyed, dismissed as superstitious, and ridiculed as infantile. The natural intuition of the *Volk* has dissolved into physics and chemistry, its religion into theology and philosophy, its commonwealth [the Greek *polis*] into politics and diplomacy, its art into science and aesthetics, and its myths into historical chronicles. (iv. 34–5.)

Moulded by natural science, politics, and history, this 'view of life as shared by the modern world' is the basis and aim of the novel or romance.

In advancing this view, Wagner was following the idealistic tradition of a triadic structure to history. It is this tradition which lies, for example, behind Schiller's essay *Über naive und sentimentalische Dichtung*, written in 1795, a work which left a decisive mark on the composer's aesthetic thinking. In his notes on Humboldt's *Studium des Altertums* Schiller sketches a brief outline of this triadic structure: during the 'first period', at the time of the ancient Greeks, 'the object stood immediately before us' (in accordance with the integrational power of man's natural imagination); during the second—modern—period 'we differentiate individual features and make distinctions'; while the third period, which is 'still awaited', is characterized by the fact that 'the whole object will once again stand before us', but this time on a higher epistemological plane, no longer 'confluently' but 'lit from all sides'.[16] In much the same way, Wagner's eschatological myth is distinguished from primeval myth by the fact that it is 'lit from all sides', an illumination which, in the musical drama, is provided by the orchestra. In his essay *On Actors and Singers* (although the same point had already been made, albeit under a different aspect, in *Opera and Drama*) Wagner compares the function of the instrumental orchestra with the role of the chorus in the *orchestra* of the classical amphitheatre. Just as the chorus, together with the audience

[16] Friedrich Schiller, *Sämtliche Werke*, ed. Gerhard Fricke and Herbert G. Göpfert, 3rd edn. Munich, 1962), v. 1042.

as represented by that chorus, could observe the stage characters from three sides, so, in the musical drama, myth was transformed by the orchestra into a 'phenomenon which is borne along on every side by sound' (ix. 199). It is thus the omniscient orchestra which introduces into the musical drama that multifaceted modern spirit which is reflected in the novel. The ultimate aim of the musical drama was the 'emotionalization of the intellect' (iv. 78), an act comparable to that of transforming history into myth. (Myth, it will be recalled, is the 'beginning and end of history', just as feeling is the 'beginning and end of intellect': iv. 91.)

The romance was the art of the second period, therefore, the age of history and intellect. And just as this age was remote from the highest measure of humanity, so the romance fell short of the perfect form of art. But just as the new age of feeling could be reached only by passing through the age of intellect, so the art-work of the future would come about only through the supersession of the romance as the representative art-form of the modern period. Wagner's theory of the novel was clearly influenced by the aesthetic outlook of the Hegelian school. 'A romance in the modern sense of the word', Hegel had written, 'presupposes a world already prosaically ordered',[17] in other words, 'a firm and secure order of civil society and the state, so that police, law-courts, the army, political government replace the chimerical ends which the knights errant set before themselves.'[18] (Because of his premiss that the medieval romance and the modern novel were generically the same, Hegel is bound to interpret the theme of the latter as 'chivalry with a real subject-matter'.[19])

The prosaic outlook on life which typifies the modern period, and the banishing of the gods from the phenomenal world (in other words, the displacement of imagination and feeling by intellect, science, politics, and history), were developments which, in Wagner's view, must be laid at the door of Christianity. He was not, of course, the first writer to advance the idea that the world had been made godless through the dogma of a single transcendental God (and that it had also been aesthetically demystified and transformed into 'prose'), thus opening up the way to a scientific view of the world. ('Science, which broke down Nature into her constituent parts without as yet discovering the real connection between those parts,[20] could but support the Christian view of Nature': iv. 36.) It was an idea, after all, which had found

---

[17] G. W. F. Hegel, *Ästhetik*, ed. Friedrich Bassenge (Berlin, 1955), i. 452; translated into English by T. M. Knox as *Aesthetics: Lectures on Fine Art* (Oxford, 1975), 1092.

[18] Ibid. 567; English trans., p. 592.         [19] Ibid.

[20] Wagner is alluding here, of course, to Mephistopheles' satire of knowledge in the scene with the Student in part I of *Faust*: 'To docket living things past any doubt | You cancel first the living spirit out: | The parts lie in the hollow of your hand, | You only lack the living thing you banned.' (11. 1936–9; verse translation by Philip Wayne (Harmondsworth, 1949), 95.)

epoch-making expression in Schiller's philosophical poem, *Die Götter Griechenlands* (1788): 'That one alone might be enriched | This world of gods was doomed to die.' (ll. 155–6.) Nature has become 'empty' as a result of Christian demystification (l. 160). 'Lifelessly the fields and meadows mourn, | No god's made manifest to human gaze' (ll. 149–50).

> Gleich dem toten Schlag der Pendeluhr,
> Dient sie knechtisch dem Gesetz der Schwere,
> Die entgötterte Natur!                                    (ll. 166–8.)
>
> Like the pendulum's dull beat, she serves
> The law of gravity with servile nod,
> Nature reft of all her gods!

Much the same idea is found in Wagner. Whereas archaic man, governed by imagination and feeling, drew together disparate natural phenomena in myth, transforming those phenomena into visually striking human figures who were also gods, and declaring their causal concatenation to be a complex of human actions, modern man, being ruled by intellect, saw the world as a soulless chaos of isolated phenomena. Rendered godless and unpoetical as a result of Christianity, the phenomenal world had been turned into a political arena and an object for scientific enquiry. By devaluing life on earth and decrying sensuality (a sensuality which, for the Greeks, was the standard by which all else—including non-human Nature—was judged), and by glorifying death as a transition to 'life everlasting' (*'dying* and the longing for death are the only real subject of the art which has evolved from Christian myth': iv. 37[21]) Christianity has also violated the Germanic nations' autochthonous myth, a myth which, like its Hellenic counterpart, had developed an image of the phenomenal world condensed into human form. Of course, Wagner attempts to demonstrate a more enlightened mythic awareness in 'local legend': it was no longer a god who was central to Germanic myth, but a hero, the true human being. Myth, therefore, was no longer the expression of religious alienation from self (in the Feuerbachian and Marxian sense), but of an emancipated human consciousness. This was a point which Wagner sought to prove by reference to the original Siegfried legend, the musico-dramatic rebirth of which was intended to be heralded by the theorizing discourse of *Opera and Drama*.

---

[21] Naturally, the Christian cult of death was subjected to a radical reappraisal following Wagner's confrontation with Schopenhauer's quietistic thinking. The dramaturgical consequences of this encounter—in *Opera and Drama* Wagner describes the Christian philosophy as 'undramatic'—will become clear in the section on *Tristan* below. 'In Greek drama the sense of movement develops, right from the outset, at ever-increasing pace to culminate in the sublime storm of the catastrophe; the unadulterated, true Christian drama would have to begin with the storm of life, only for the sense of movement to fade away in a fanciful dying fall' (iv. 37), Wagner wrote in 1851 in a remarkable anticipation of Isolde's transfiguration.

What we see here are natural phenomena such as those of the day and night, the rising and setting of the sun, transformed by an act of poetic imagination into dramatic characters who are honoured or feared because of their actions, so that gods who were thought of as human were turned into heroes who were fully anthropomorphized, who are reputed to have once existed, and from whom living tribes and races vaunted their descendancy. Thus myth encroached on actual life, setting standards and providing structures, revindicating claims, and kindling in mankind the will to act. (iv. 38.)

This displacement of divine myth by heroic legend (in other words, the supersession of religious alienation in and through myth) provided the basic thrust to 'The Nibelung Legend (Myth)', as conceived in the autumn of 1848 for Wagner's planned adaptation of *Siegfrieds Tod*: the gods attempt to 'transfer their godhead to man'; 'their aim would be accomplished if they were to destroy themselves in creating mankind, in other words, if they were constrained to forgo their own immediate influence as a result of the new-found freedom of human consciousness' (ii. 158).

Christianity, however, had subverted Germanic myth, creating the 'chivalric romance' out of the 'corpse of old heroic myth'. The three-dimensional characters of legend, sprung from the *Volk*'s 'natural intuition', faded into 'phantasms of unbridled fancy', while heroic feats became fragmented as knightly 'adventures' which, once their illusionary character had become all too evident (as in *Don Quixote*), began to pursue material goals instead of the aims of chimerical knighthood:

Bold voyages of discovery, undertaken with a conscious aim, and the profound investigations of science which were based on the findings of those discoveries finally revealed the world to us as it actually is. The insights thus acquired marked the end of the medieval romance, and the description of imaginary phenomena was followed by the description of their reality. (iv. 42.)

Thus the modern novel was born. Like Hegel (for whom 'romance' was synonymous with 'knight-errantry' of a 'chimerical' or prosaically realistic nature[22]), Wagner forges a speculative link between medieval romance and the modern novel.

And Wagner, again like Hegel, argues that the structure of the novel reflects the prosaic state of the modern world, just as the perfect form of drama reflects a more poetic and mythical state. And, just as the mythic imagination reduces the entire phenomenal world to human (divine or heroic) form, so the dramatic poet concentrates suprahuman reality in his dramatic characters. The novelist, by contrast, has to leave reality — 'godless', soulless, and no longer personified by quasi-human figures — as such, retaining it in all its anonymity.

[22] Hegel, *Ästhetik*, i. 567; English trans. (Knox, *Aesthetics*), p. 592.

The dramatic poet condenses all that surrounds his protagonist, reducing it to an action that is easily taken in at a glance, and ascribing that action . . . to the individual's intrinsic cast of mind . . . The writer of romance, by contrast, must make the actions of his historical protagonist explicable in terms of environmental necessity . . . In the historical novel [which, for Wagner, was the representative modern form of the genre] we seek to make sense of that man whom we cannot understand from the purely human standpoint. (iv. 46.)

This objectified human being—an individual reduced 'to the narrowest confines of personal freedom'—can be adequately portrayed only by reproducing his 'surroundings' or environment as authentically as possible. But this environment is intelligible 'only when set forth in all its ramifications and full extent'. In other words, the novelist must be 'circumstantial in order to be intelligible. What the dramatist assumes to be unthematical constitutes the novelist's actual subject-matter, namely, his characters' socio-historical environment.

Drama, accordingly, moves from the inside to the outside, the novel from the outside to the inside. Beginning with a simple, universally intelligible environment, the dramatist rises to an ever richer development of individuality; the novelist, by contrast, takes as *his* starting-point a complex environment which requires an effort of understanding and from which he sinks, exhausted, to depict an individual too paltry in himself to be susceptible of individual interest without the aforesaid environment. In drama robust individuality, developed entirely out of its own resources, enriches its surroundings; in the novel it is the surroundings which satisfy the cravings of an empty individuality. In this way drama reveals the organism that is humankind, inasmuch as individuality is presented as the essence of the species; the novel, conversely, depicts the mechanism of history, a mechanism in which the species is made the essence of individuality. (iv. 47–8.)

It is no accident that this generic distinction echoes the one drawn by Schiller in his series of letters published in 1795, 'Über die ästhetische Erziehung des Menschen'. Here, too, a contrast is drawn between the ancient Greek and modern man. Whereas the 'whole of humankind' was embodied in each individual Greek, it was necessary now 'to ask around from individual to individual . . . in order to assemble the totality of the species'. The modern state prevented the individual from enjoying an 'independent life' and no longer allowed him to be a 'whole'; instead, it was the state itself which formed that 'whole', albeit an abstract whole replete with 'mechanical life', permitting the individual to play only a 'fragmentary part' and allotting that role according to its own best interests.[23] ('The state has set itself up as the educator of individuality', we read in similar vein in *Opera and Drama*. 'The citizen owes his individuality to the state; but that individuality is no more and no less

---

[23] Schiller, *Sämtliche Werke*, v. 582 ff.

than his pre-ordained attitude towards the state': iv. 68.) This contrast between the ancient Greek and his modern equivalent forms the basis of Wagner's distinction between the characters that appear in drama and those that figure in novels. 'Drama gives us the *human being*; the novel tells us about the *citizen*.' (iv. 48.)

Wagner leaves his reader in no doubt that the novel, notwithstanding its dubious status as a work of art, is 'no arbitrary phenomenon, but a necessary product of our modern development: it is an honest expression of circumstances which could be depicted in artistic terms only in a novel, not in a drama'. In striving to depict reality, it often went so far that it 'finally destroyed itself as a work of art' (iv. 48). It is unequivocally clear from this that Wagner was prepared to acknowledge only realistic historical and social novels as the legitimate forms of contemporary fiction, and that the two forms were essentially identical: 'The soil of history is *man's social nature*' (iv. 50); in other words, the historical novel is, as such, a social novel, just as the latter presents contemporary 'bourgeois society' as a historically conditioned state.

To the eye of the novelist seeking the 'unvarnished truth' about bourgeois society, the latter appears as a *'chaotic picture of ugliness and formlessness'* (iv. 51). To reflect that picture with rigorous consistency would, however, rob the novel of its beauty of form; indeed, in the end it would cease to be a work of art, and would become a piece of political propaganda. The more the novel fastened upon life and depicted 'its most vicious social basis', the more it was bound to become a 'revolutionary weapon against that social basis' (iv. 28).

The deep disquiet which he [the novelist] inevitably felt at his own account robbed him . . . of that tranquil mood of poetic contentment in which he was less and less able to delude himself, and persuaded him to espouse reality and fight for the real and recognized needs of human society. In the course of its progress towards practical reality, the novel, too, increasingly laid aside its artistic garb: the unity which it had shown to be possible as an art-form was bound to be displaced by the practical multiplicity of everyday phenomena if it was to remain at all intelligible. An artistic bond was impossible where everything strove for dissolution and where the coercive bond of the historical state had to be torn asunder. Novel-writing turned into *journalism*, its contents were scattered among *political articles*; its art became *platform oratory*, while the breath of its discourse inspired *an appeal to the people*. (iv. 53.)

This is the radical consequence of Heinrich Heine's prophecy that 'the end of the age of art' was at hand. The displacement of affirmative art by political journalism and revolutionary praxis is the final logical step which follows from the conceptual and formal aims of that paradigmatic modern literary genre, the novel.

If, in Wagner's system, the development of the novel was necessarily followed by the death of art, its rebirth could be justified only by a visionary transcendence of the present state of the world, by the anticipation of a new eschatological myth. It was the task of the musical 'drama of the future' to transcend the modern age in this radical manner. This was the only art-form which could still grant historical legitimacy to art as such. It is at this point that Wagner introduces his grand historico-philosophical excursus on the Oedipus myth, a myth which he interprets as crucial to the history of the world. (A more detailed analysis will be given below, in the section devoted to the *Ring*, not least because Wagner himself, in his *Epilogue to the 'Nibelung's Ring'*, indicated that this excursus was also a key to understanding the tetralogy.) Wagner uses the Oedipus myth to demonstrate the way in which the historico-political world has developed out of the mythical world and how state and history will be superseded in the age of the new myth, which will assimilate all the spiritual forces and historical experiences of the modern age with the same degree of concentration with which the magic ring of a new art-form will circumscribe the novel. And this new art-form will be the musical drama, which once again reduces its elements to concentrated, purely human form.

'The novel is the epic poem of a world that has been abandoned by God', Georg Lukács wrote in *The Theory of the Novel*.[24] To be abandoned by God was the inescapable fate of the novel and its form, since 'the great epic is a form bound to the historical moment, and any attempt to depict the utopian as existent can only end in destroying the form, not in creating reality. The novel is the form of the epoch of absolute sinfulness, as Fichte said, and it must remain the dominant form so long as the world is ruled by the same stars.'[25] There is no need to point out the extent to which these speculations coincide with the theory of the novel as set forth in *Opera and Drama*. What the novel is unable to achieve—'to depict the utopian as existent'—is for Wagner, of course, the historical mission of the musical drama. The latter 'redeems' the novel, so to speak, from its 'sinful' state by its dramatic concentration on the 'purely human'.

Wagner's view of the novel is far more heavily influenced by nineteenth-century English and French fiction than by the specifically German tradition of the *Bildungsroman*, the poeticized view of reality of which has little in common with the nineteenth-century French *réalistes* whom Wagner appears to have had in mind. For Wagner, the modern novelist *par excellence* was always Honoré de Balzac, whose *Comédie*

---

[24] Georg Lukács, *Die Theorie des Romans*, written in the summer of 1914 and first published in Max Dessoir's *Zeitschrift für Aesthetik und Allgemeine Kunstwissenschaft* in 1916; new edn. (Darmstadt, 1965), 87; translated into English by Anna Bostock as *The Theory of the Novel* (London, 1971), 88.     [25] Ibid. 157; English trans., p. 152.

*humaine* he read and reread with unfailing enthusiasm, as Cosima's *Diaries* make clear.[26] In his essay 'German Art and German Politics' Wagner praises the French novelist as 'a wholly incomparable phenomenon . . . in the field of literature'. No other writer had depicted the 'appalling chaos' of modern civilization 'with the unbelievable patience of a poet truly in love with his subject'. Balzac was a 'genius' who, by dint of his 'hitherto unheard-of realism and the tireless perseverance' with which he depicted corrupt social conditions, 'but chiefly by virtue of that state of utter hopelessness' to which that realism reduced his readers, was bound to seem a 'demon' to a society caught up in a permanent state of self-delusion concerning the 'terrible content' of nineteenth-century culture (viii. 91–2).

Did Wagner see a hidden correspondence between Balzac's cycle of novels and his own tetralogy? In his 1908 essay, 'Versuch über das Theater', Thomas Mann uses relevant passages from *Opera and Drama* to describe the *Ring* as a series of crypto-novels, before going on in 1933, in his public lecture *Leiden und Größe Richard Wagners*, to point out the 'family likeness' between Zola's *Les Rougon-Macquart* and *Der Ring des Nibelungen*.[27] And in his essay *Die Kunst des Romans* (1939) he claimed that the *Ring* was the only real equivalent in nineteenth-century German art to the great novels of European literature. 'The *Ring des Nibelungen* has much in common with the symbolic naturalism of the *Rougon-Macquart* series of novels by Émile Zola — even the "leitmotif"'[28] (which was, of course, an epic device which Zola owed originally to Wagner's influence). No doubt Wagner would not have disdained the comparison between the *Ring* and Balzac's *Comédie humaine*. The two cycles complement each other. Balzac's novels reflect, in Wagner's view, a world dominated by gold, a world whose derivation and supersession in the cyclical course of world history provides the *Ring* with its mythic structure and message.

It was the task of the 'drama of the future' to indicate the way in which history and politics would be superseded by myth. On the level of the work's musico-dramatic form, this occurs when the rationally based language of words is superseded by the language of music, a language defined by feeling. The 'emotionalization of the intellect' is therefore the principal aim of the musical drama. 'In drama we must become *knowing*'—but 'knowing' in the sense in which Brünnhilde attains to knowledge at the end of *Götterdämmerung* ('that I in grief might grow wise': vi. 252), or in which Parsifal grows wise in the third act of

---

[26] See esp. *CT*, 30 Dec. 1871, 11 Apr., 17, 27 July, 7 Dec. 1878, 23 Dec. 1880, and *passim*.

[27] Thomas Mann, *Wagner und unsere Zeit*, ed. Erika Mann (Frankfurt, 1963), 64; translated into English by Allan Blunden as *Pro and contra Wagner* (London, 1985), 93.

[28] Thomas Mann, *Gesammelte Werke* (Frankfurt, 1974), x. 361.

Wagner's final work, achieving insight not through 'the mediation of the intellect' but 'through feeling' or 'instinct', in other words, through the immediacy of experience. 'In the presence of a dramatic work of art there should be nothing left for the deductive intelligence to seek out: everything should come to a conclusion capable of setting our feelings at rest on the matter.' But the 'organs' which feeling employs in its quest for 'definitive comprehension' are the 'senses', which means that the dramatic action must be fully accessible to 'physical view' (iv. 78–9).

Wagner describes the poet's contribution to musical drama in the second part of *Opera and Drama*. If the poet appeals to the intellect (as he does in the novel, for example), he must proceed 'circumstantially', whereas if he addresses feeling 'directly', his approach must be 'simple', in other words, he must leave nothing to any 'deductive act . . . which cancels out all feeling' (iv. 69). But how can simplicity be guaranteed without the risk of over-simplifying? After all, drama is not intended to guide us back to some archaic state, but to do us justice in all our modern complexity. Accordingly, the dramatic poet must not reduce the 'wide circle' of human reality, but must draw it in towards its central point, compressing it in such a way that it becomes 'the outline which gives us our understanding of the hero' (iv. 80). 'This process of *condensation* is the actual work of the poeticizing intellect.' (iv. 80.) It is in this context that Wagner develops his dramaturgy of the 'wonder' (iv. 81–91), the practical realization of which can be seen in particular in the love-potion in *Tristan und Isolde*. Unlike the religious wonder, the aesthetic wonder appeals not to 'faith' but to 'emotional understanding', and is intended to represent a complex but easily comprehensible 'interrelationship between natural phenomena within a single, immediately intelligible, image' (iv. 82).

Those aspects of reality and other motives which were excluded when the material was compressed to form this 'immediately intelligible image' should not simply be discarded, but must be 'transferred to those principal elements which *are* retained; in other words, they must be subsumed by them in a way which may be clearly felt', so that they may appear to be 'fully motivated' (iv. 83). That this is no abstract theory is shown by *Tristan und Isolde*, where the 'wonder' of the love-potion is indeed an immediately intelligible image, revealing a complex emotional reality whose individual elements are poetically and musically encoded in a highly subtle way. Wagner uses the term *Verstärkung* ('intensification') to describe the process of charging a principal motive with implicit subsidiary motives: it is a process whereby '*many motives* are absorbed into *one*' (iv. 89). The action that is shaped by a motive 'intensified' in this way is a 'concentrated form of real life'. The more all-embracing the motivic complex which amplifies the principal motive

and action, the more 'wondrous' the latter will turn out to be, which is
to say, the further it will rise above the level of everyday reality (iv. 84).
The numinous—and myth as the system of numinousness—does not,
therefore, work against the natural order of things, but intensifies life to
the 'most animated degree, to a pitch unattainable in everyday life' (iv.
89). This 'intensification of motives', and the resultant pervasion of the
dramatic action by the mythically numinous, complements the realistic
reflection of the actual world. It seeks to grasp reality in all its totality,
not, of course, by realistic extensity but by lyric intensity.

If, as a result of this motivic intensification, life is raised above
ordinary human standards, so language itself (the organ of the
'poeticizing intelligence'[29]) must be subjected to a corresponding
process in order to intensify its powers of expression. This, however,
could be achieved only if the language of words were poured into the
language of music, from whose mother's womb it had originally issued
and to which it would one day return, just as intellect would be absorbed
by feeling, and history by myth. The one element of language still
directly related to music as the original 'language of emotion' is the
vowel. Wagner claims that vowels are a 'subjective expression of feeling',
whereas consonants are an 'objective expression of the object' (iv. 94).
Language, in the proper sense of the word, arose when feeling and
object, vowel ('expression') and consonant ('impression'), came together
to form a 'linguistic root'. The linguistic root, according to Wagner, was
originally a vocal expression of the inner man and his spontaneous
reaction to the objective world, an expression involuntarily accompanied
by 'physical gesture' and therefore the archetypal component of 'music'
in the Greek sense, in other words, a 'union of the language of gesture,
music, and words' (iv. 96). As such, it was the seed which, multiplied
and arranged together, provided the foundations for 'the whole
perceptual edifice of our infinitely diversified spoken language' (iv. 93).
Language became poetry the moment that its roots (signs which convey
expression and impression) began to alliterate. Alliteration or *Stabreim*,
Wagner believed, was 'the most ancient characteristic of poetic
language'. 'In *alliterative verse* cognate linguistic roots are joined together
in such a way that, sounding the same to the physical ear, they link
together similar objects to form one collective image in which feeling
seeks to express its conclusions concerning them.' (iv. 94.) In this way,
the use of alliteration creates what Thomas Mann called 'a veritable
feast of associations'[30] between different objects. The analogy with the

---

[29] On Wagner's theory of language, see Reinhard Gerlach, 'Musik und Sprache in Wagners
Schrift *Opera und Drama*', in Carl Dahlhaus (ed.), *Richard Wagner: Werk und Wirkung* (Regensburg,
1971), 9–39.
[30] Mann, *Wagner und unsere Zeit*, p. 145; English trans. (Blunden, *Pro and contra Wagner*), p. 188.

leitmotif is clear. 'These *rhyming roots* are distributed and arranged according to rules similar to those which persuade us, in the interests of understanding, to repeat those motives on which we place the greatest emphasis.' (iv. 94–5.) Alliterative verse and leitmotif reveal what the German Romantics called the secret 'sympathies' between things, and what the French *symbolistes* called '*correspondances*'.

Although it has been largely ignored by writers on Wagner, this idea of an analogy between the microstructure of the *Stabreim* and the macrostructure of the leitmotivic web reappears in the third part of *Opera and Drama*. Wagner does not use the term 'leitmotif', of course, referring instead to themes of 'presentiment and reminiscence', which he explains as 'emotional signposts through the whole convoluted structure of the drama'. They create semantic relationships between characters and actions, thus making us 'permanent accessories to the deepest secrets of the poetic intent' (iv. 200). By virtue of their 'suggestive, invariably well-motivated, rhyme-like [!] recurrence', these 'melodic elements', corresponding to the 'principal motives of the dramatic action', create an all-embracing, 'binding connection' between the different parts, extending over the entire drama and investing it with its 'unified artistic form' (iv. 202). In this way, the unity of the drama, achieved as it is by the use of a leitmotivic technique, finds, as it were, a microstructural counterpart in Wagner's use of *Stabreim*. This latter achieves in miniature what the dramatic poet achieves on a larger scale by 'intensifying' the motives and what the musician achieves by his use of those 'melodic elements' which are attuned to them, in other words, the 'poetic compression' of the disparate, non-uniform phenomenal world.

It goes without saying that, for Wagner, end rhyme was incapable of fulfilling this suggestive, reductive function, since end rhyme, unlike alliteration or initial rhyme, produced a (senseless) connection not between those substantial sounds which conveyed expression and registered impressions, but between their accidental echoes. The alliterative poet presented 'the countenance of the word', whereas the poet who used end rhyme offered only its 'faded obverse' to be 'dismissed' by the ear (iv. 133). (That Wagner later abandoned this theory is clear from his use of end rhyme in *Tristan* and *Die Meistersinger*.)

In the theatre, Wagner argues, a text employing a regular rhythm and end rhyme was of no value, since the melody broke down the line of verse into its constituent parts, reassembling them according to its own 'absolute judgement' and thus depriving end rhyme (which, in any case, is drowned by the music) of its acoustic characteristics (iv. 112). Only a musician like Gluck, who sought to intensify the natural speech accent by melodic means, was able to ignore the structure of the verse. 'In doing so, the musician not only broke down the verse into *prose*, he did the same to his melody, for all that was left of that melody which, by dint of tonal expression, emphasized only the rhetorical accent of a line of prosified verse was nothing more nor less than *musical prose*.' (iv. 114.) It is to precisely this that Wagner's critics pointed as a fault of his own compositional praxis.

There is, indeed, a consensus of opinion among present-day writers on Wagner that the *Ring* is written in 'musical prose'.[31] Needless to say, the term is not being used in the pejorative sense in which Wagner intended it[32] but in the positive sense as defined by Arnold Schoenberg. Wagner's emancipation from a periodic schema, from the four-square rhythmic and syntactical structure of 'absolute melody', together with his poetic practice of producing rhymeless, non-strophic verse and his establishment of a kind of *vers libre* with an irregular number of strong beats, all give his musical syntax the unmistakable character of prose. From the strictly compositional point of view, alliteration is largely irrelevant, or at least without influence on the work's rhythmic structure, in spite of Wagner's claims to the contrary in *Opera and Drama* (iv. 152–3). To quote Carl Dahlhaus: 'As the text for a musical composition, Wagner's alliterative poem is nothing more nor less than prose.'[33]

Although Wagner was obviously using the term 'musical prose' in a negative sense in the passage quoted above (iv. 114), only a few pages later he half concedes that the musico-dramatic language he was postulating was prosaic in structure. He rejects existing verse metres, with their regular rhythms, as inimical to the natural flow of the spoken language:

We must … invest *the prose of our ordinary language* with that heightened expression in which the poetic intent shall be revealed to feeling in all its potency. A form of linguistic expression which tears apart the bond that links it to everyday speech by basing its physical manifestation upon imported elements which, like those kinds of rhythmic prosody described above, are alien to the essential nature of our ordinary language—such a form can only confuse our feelings. (iv. 117.)

Wagner rejects the pre-established rules of strophic form and prosody, just as he rejects the ostensibly schematic, unrealistic closed form of Racinian tragedy, or the rigid periodicity of 'absolute' music. But this

---

[31] See Carl Dahlhaus, *Wagners Konzeption des musikalischen Dramas* (Regensburg, 1971), 50 ff.; Stefan Kunze, 'Über Melodiebegriff und musikalischen Bau in Wagners Musikdrama', in Carl Dahlhaus (ed.), *Das Drama Richard Wagners als musikalisches Kunstwerk* (Regensburg, 1970), 111–44; and Hermann Danuser, *Musikalische Prosa* (Regensburg, 1975), 67 ff.

[32] On the 18th-century origins of the term as a description of what Schlabrendorf has called 'beat-free music', see Danuser, *Musikalische Prosa*, pp. 51 ff.

[33] Dahlhaus, *Wagners Konzeption des musikalischen Dramas*, p. 61.

does not mean that closed dramatic form, or the individual line of poetry, or periodicity were in themselves anathema to him; rather, they had to be re-established on a new basis. End rhyme, with its regular rhythms, was to be replaced by free alliterative verse, conventional four-square writing was to give way to the 'poetico-musical period' (iv. 154) in which the harmonic development was to be governed by the poetic intent,[34] and the three unities were to be superseded by a unity of form organically achieved by the motivic concentration outlined above. In all three cases it may be said that prose is the actual basis of the musical drama. Wagner's dramaturgy is a theory of the novel, turned on its head. Just as, at the end of time, myth must be 'justified' by history, and just as feeling must be justified by intellect (iv. 91), so the musical drama must be legitimized by the novel, and verse by prose—no longer as a priori forms but as forms which issue a posteriori from the obverse element. Thus the 'course of this development'—from history to myth, from intellect to feeling, from the novel to drama, and from prose to poetry—involves 'not regression but progress, bringing with it the acquisition of the highest human potential' (iv. 91).

In the third part of *Opera and Drama* Wagner explains in detail how alliterative verse develops out of prose, a development which takes place by analogy with the dramatico-musical concentration of the romance or novel: in turn, this 'reduction and compression of the elements of the plot and their motives . . . can be achieved only by an equally concentrated and compressed mode of expression':

Just as we had to excise all that was fortuitous, trivial, and vague from these elements of the plot and, therefore, from the motives which determine those elements; just as we have to remove from the content of the drama all external distortions, all that has to do with the pragmatism of history, with the state, and with dogmatic religious belief in order to depict that content as something purely human and instinctively necessary, so we must now exclude from its linguistic expression all that derives from those distortions to the purely human and to instinctive necessity, and all that corresponds to these alone, and we must remove these features in such a way that only this kernel remains. (iv. 118.)

What this means is that the absolute 'language of intellect'—a language which, forming a counterpart to 'absolute music' (iv. 98), was coloured by 'religious, political, and historical convention'—had been increasingly broadened and syntactically complicated by a 'mechanistically mediating apparatus of words', and that this language must be reduced to its emotionally necessary elements, in other words, to its linguistic roots. In consequence of this process of contraction, language became closer to musical expression, just as, conversely, music could abandon its

---

[34] Its structural laws are analysed by Dahlhaus, ibid. 76 ff.

absoluteness and draw nearer to language again. Feeling re-entered the vocabulary, so to speak, after a period of musical exile.

According to Wagner, the necessary compression of the accents of the 'prose phrase' to the point at which they turned into alliterative verse mirrored the 'compressed expression' of the affection in question:

In any genuine affection, that is to say, when we abandon all those conventional considerations which produce the modern drawling phrase, we always seek to express ourselves with the utmost precision, briefly and to the point, and *in a single breath*: but in this compressed expression we also—because of the forcefulness of the affection—use far greater emphasis than usual, at the same time moving the accents closer together and lingering over those accents with an animatedly raised voice in order to give them weight and to impress them on the listener's feelings with the degree of emphasis with which we want to express our feelings in them. (iv. 119–20.)

Just as those elements which had been eliminated from the novel must be implicit in the principal motives of the musical drama, so the incidental words of prose phraseology which were eliminated from the poetic language must be implied by the nouns into which they have been compressed. In both cases, this process of compression signified an 'intensification', whether of the motive on the one hand or the speech accent on the other. The same was true, moreover, of the choreography and gesture used in the musical drama: the condensed action and intensified speech accent were mirrored by intensified gesture (iv. 178).

Just as there were stronger and weaker elements in the action, so there were stronger and weaker speech accents. These must be placed on the 'strong and weak halves of the musical bar', or on the 'strong and weak bars of a musical period' (iv. 122). In this way, the individual bar and period—in themselves semantically indeterminate—became 'significant'. Wagner knew, of course, that this semanticization of music was not possible in every language. Of the various 'operatic languages', German alone 'still accents the root syllables', in other words, German used accent to emphasize the meaning of a word (iv. 211–12). To place greater stress on an accent in German (in contrast to the Romance languages) was to highlight the sense of the word in question. This had fundamental repercussions for the musical setting and, by virtue of its links with vocal music, even for the stress patterns of instrumental music. In this respect, Wagner anticipated a number of insights of modern musicology. According to Thrasybulos Georgiades, the two archetypal forms of modern rhythmical structure in music, arsis and thesis, acquire a new sense as a result of German linguistic habits. They become 'sense realities which have something of the dignity of a semantically conditioned stress':[35] they become 'eloquent'. ('Music now

---

[35] Thrasybulos Georgiades, *Musik und Sprache* (Heidelberg, 1954), 58.

articulates as though it were speaking.'[36]) One of the examples which Georgiades uses to demonstrate this is the final movement of Beethoven's String Quartet, Op. 135, a work which rests, of course, on an association of two ideas, marked, respectively, by thesis ('Muß es sein?') and arsis ('Es muß sein!'). But he might also have cited the instrumental recitative in the final movement of Beethoven's Ninth Symphony, which Wagner himself used to expound his theory that absolute music becomes language here.

Time and again in his writings Wagner emphasized how little attention German opera composers had paid to the specific character of the German language and its stress patterns in their melodic writing.[37]

Absolute operatic melody, with its very definite melismatic and rhythmic peculiarities, such as had developed in Italy very much in harmony with an arbitrarily accentable language, had, from the outset, been the determining influence on German opera composers, too; this melody had been imitated and varied by them, and the singularity of our own language and its accent had had to conform to the demands of that melody . . . For the sake of the melody, even the normally conscientious Weber is often exceedingly careless with regard to language. (iv. 215.)

This disregard for natural speech accents is something which Wagner dealt with not only in theory but also in one of his dramatic works. The false emphases in Beckmesser's Serenade which Hans Sachs notes by striking the Marker's shoes with his hammer are typical errors on the part of German opera composers, who, influenced by the type of declamation found in Italian or French opera, did not notice that 'the speech accent is incomparably more adaptable there, in that it does not cling, as it were, to the root syllables' (x. 157), as Wagner perceptively observes in 'On Opera Poetry and Composition in Particular'. Hans Sachs interrupts Beckmesser after the first few lines of the Serenade with an alternative proposal in which the musical phrase reflects the sense of the words, but Beckmesser refuses to listen. Sachs retorts: 'Mich dünkt, 's sollt' passen Ton und Wort' (I think the music and words should be in accord: vii. 220); in other words, musical accent and speech accent should coincide.[38]

The way in which this problem affected Wagner's successors can be seen, for example, in the correspondence between Richard Strauss and Romain Rolland at the time of the first French performances of *Salome*

---

[36] Georgiades, *Musik und Sprache*, 80.

[37] See esp. x. 7–8 and, above all, 156–63 ('On Opera Poetry and Composition in Particular').

[38] See Egon Voss, '*Die Meistersinger* als Oper des deutschen Bürgertums', in Attila Csampai and Dietmar Holland (eds.), '*Die Meistersinger von Nürnberg': Texte, Materialien, Kommentare* (Reinbek 1981), 26–7; translated into English by Stewart Spencer as 'Wagner's "Meistersinger" as an Opera for the German Bourgeoisie', in *Wagner*, 11 (1990), 39–62.

in 1910. Schooled in the Wagnerian tradition, Strauss felt that what he called his 'feeling for linguistic roots' was being constantly offended by the variable stress patterns of the French language, a variability which had struck him especially while studying the score of Debussy's *Pelléas et Mélisande*. Rolland had to explain to him that the stress patterns of the German language could never be transferred to the French declamatory style, since the result would be a different sort of musical phraseology.[39] The very thing which puzzled Strauss ('Why does the Frenchman sing and speak in different ways?'), Wagner had already clearly recognized as an underlying principle of the Romance languages. He had proposed, therefore, in the course of his system, a thesis which, divorced from its linguistic context, is bound to appear as pure xenophobia: 'the consummate work of dramatic art . . . is possible only in the German language', because, alone of all the 'operatic languages', it is built on the 'power' of root syllables to 'coerce feeling' (iv. 128). For Wagner, of course, this was the *sine qua non* of musico-dramatic declamation and of the linguistic compression described above: the form of alliterative verse added, as it were, poetic highlights to the 'grey morass of prose' (iv. 97), and thus provided a germinal model for the structural laws of the musical drama as a whole. This emergence of linguistic roots through the use of initial rhyme is something which Wagner compares to buds shooting up through a blanket of snow. The poet still stood in the 'wintery frost of language', but shoots would soon begin to appear here and there on 'old roots which were thought to have died', until, finally, a 'new human springtide' would cause all the 'snow-flats of pragmatic prose' to melt clean away (iv. 127–8).

As we have already observed, there was clearly an analogy in Wagner's mind between alliteration on the one hand and the web of leitmotifs on the other. The 'force which enables even the most apparently disparate objects and sensations to strike the ear as though related to each other [through the "power of the same sound", which, in this case, means initial rhyme]' (iv. 133) links *Stabreim* with those 'melodic moments which are replete with presentiment or reminiscence' (iv. 200) and which reunite that which originally belonged together but which, in the age of prose, has become 'disunited and divided', restoring it to the 'purely human' (iv. 132–3) and, at the same time, re-establishing in a credible way the Aristotelian unity of the drama. It was in order to uphold this unity that Wagner declined to divorce these leitmotivic 'melodic moments' from their musico-dramatic structural context. Still less was he prepared to catalogue them. In his essay 'On the Application

---

[39] Stephan Kohler, '"Warum singt der Franzose anders als er spricht?" Richard Strauss über Claude Debussy und seine Oper *Pelléas et Mélisande*', *Jahrbuch der Bayerischen Staatsoper*, 2 (1978–9), 77–92.

of Music to Drama' (1879) he himself expressed doubts about Hans von Wolzogen's use of the term 'leitmotif', arguing that it ignored the importance of those basic melodic moments for the 'musical structure'. Indeed, Wagner's concern in writing this essay was very much to demonstrate that the 'unity of symphonic writing' provided the structural model behind the musical drama.

This unity results from a web of basic themes which permeate the entire work of art and which, as in symphonic writing, contrast with and complement each other, allowing themselves to be re-formed, divided, and reunited, except that in this case the dramatic action which is elaborated and executed governs the laws of separation and association which were borrowed originally from dance movements. (x. 185.)

This hypothesis no doubt conceals a twofold aim on Wagner's part: first, there is the problematical attempt to prove himself a professional musician in the eyes of academic critics by drawing a parallel between leitmotivic technique and the thematic writing of classical instrumental music, and, second, there is the justified desire to circumvent the misunderstanding which persists to this day among both critics and advocates of the composer that the leitmotifs are quasi-musical banners, a misconception of their function which destroys their 'allusive magic'. Wagner had little time for the lists of leitmotifs which were widely read even during his own day. When he came across labels such as 'wanderlust motive' and 'disaster motive' in a vocal score of *Götterdämmerung*, he remarked with some displeasure: 'And perhaps people will think all this nonsense is done at my request!' (*CT*, 1 August 1881.) People did indeed think so, and cynical comparisons between Wagner's themes and cloakroom tickets or labels on bottles are still to be found more than a century after his death. Emil Naumann, for example, dismissed these motives as superimposed 'slogans' in his 1876 pamphlet *Musikdrama oder Oper?*

The leitmotifs must be regarded as the most dubious aspect of Wagner's style, since they take us back to the infancy of art when words and labels were placed in the mouths of those persons whom we were not yet able to characterize from within: they announced whom they were intended to introduce, very much in the manner of Etruscan vases or the earliest experiments in medieval painting. We are reminded of these labels and inscriptions by leitmotifs in music, and, if many of them are heard at once, the impression which they evoke, given their persistent inflexibility [which Naumann has previously sought to demonstrate], is not of any artistic development, but at best of a kind of musical rebus which the listener is expected to solve and which, like those picture puzzles in which the image is merely a neutral symbol, signify something else but mean nothing in itself, being incapable of warming our hearts and souls.[40]

[40] Emil Naumann, *Musikdrama oder Oper? Eine Beleuchtung der Bayreuther Bühnenfestspiele* (Berlin, 1876), 17–18.

Naumann denies that the leitmotif is capable of symphonic development, and disputes the very quality which Wagner regarded as its most fundamental attribute, namely, its contribution to the unity and integrality of the musical drama.

The leitmotifs were a specifically dramatic device for Wagner, since they helped to 'compress' the action, a view which Thomas Mann rejected in his essay 'Versuch über das Theater'. For Mann, the leitmotif was 'epic through and through, and it starts with Homer'. He was convinced that it confirmed Wagner's own theory, according to which drama was derived from romance. At all events, it embodied that specifically epic spirit which permeated the musical drama.

I often find it difficult to see him [Wagner] as a dramatist. Is he not rather a practitioner of theatrical epic? An undercurrent of epic is present in all his creations, and what I have always loved most—apart from his descriptive musical preludes—are his great narrative passages, including the scene with the Norns in *Götterdämmerung* and the incomparably epic game of question and answer that is played out between Mime and the Wanderer. What is the dramatic Wotan whom we saw on stage in *Das Rheingold* compared with his epic counterpart in Sieglinde's account of the old man with the hat?[41]

This denigration of the narrative work of art in favour of its dramatic counterpart is one which Mann regards as 'base ingratitude' towards a genre to which Wagner owed so much.[42]

Here we find Mann playing a sophisticated game with his reader, a game which the reader will see through only if he is familiar with Wagner's theoretical writings. Mann's essay, after all, is directed against what he describes as the 'schoolmasterly' view that drama is the highest form of poetry, a view, moreover, which, in opposition to Wagner's theatromania, maintains that the novel is superior as a genre by virtue of its greater scope for delineation and its ability to convey a message. Both here and elsewhere in the essay Mann avails himself, without revealing his source,[43] of arguments and even expressions which Wagner himself had used in his essay *On Actors and Singers* to demonstrate the

---

[41] Mann, *Gesammelte Werke*, x. 27; English trans. (Blunden, *Pro and contra Wagner*), pp. 25–6.

[42] Ibid. 34 (the German passage quoted here is not included in Blunden's English translation).

[43] Mann adopts a similar attitude to Nietzsche: 'I am reliably informed (by a certain professor of philology) that the word "drama" is of Doric origin' (ibid. 47; English trans., p. 31). The 'professor of philology' is, of course, Nietzsche. Mann is referring here to a footnote in *Der Fall Wagner* (Friedrich Nietzsche, *Sämtliche Werke: Kritische Studienausgabe in 15 Bänden*, ed. Giorgio Colli and Mazzino. Montinari (Munich, 1980), vi. 32; translated into English by Walter Kaufmann as 'The Case of Wagner', in *Basic Writings of Nietzsche* (New York, 1968), 630). In addition to his arguments about the theory of the novel, Mann owes a number of other points to Wagner's essay *On Actors and Singers*, including the theory that the theatre was improvisatory in origin, his polemic against the way in which 'absolute poetry' had usurped the place of drama (an act of usurpation which had turned on its head the original relationship between the two genres), and his ideas on an anti-illusionistic style of production in the spoken theatre, based on the model of the Elizabethan stage. Even when polemicizing against Wagner, he avails himself of the latter's arguments.

superiority of the Attic and Elizabethan theatre (and of their legitimate heir, the musical drama of the future) over modern spoken drama, a genre indelibly marked by the French and Italian theatre, with its painted sets and proscenium stage. (Mann himself admits to having studied Wagner's essay in detail in chapter 4 of his 'Versuch über das Theater'.)

On the older stage, the performers were allowed to present themselves to the audience only in profile and from the front, but never from the back. The novel is more precise, more complete, more knowing, more conscientious, more profound than drama ... and, in contrast to the view that drama is the real graphic work of poetic literature, I confess that I see it far more as the art of silhouette, and that I feel the narrative figure to be uniquely rounded, whole, real, and graphically three-dimensional.[44]

It is precisely these arguments—which, in Mann's view, favour the novel—which helped Wagner in his advocacy of the symphonic, as opposed to the spoken, drama.[45] Through its association with the proscenium stage, which 'always showed the actors from only one side, namely, from the front', dramatic characters were typically 'one-sided'. In the classical amphitheatre, by contrast, both chorus and audience could see the actor from all sides, as a fully three-dimensional figure. In much the same way, the performers in the Elizabethan theatre were 'surrounded by spectators on all sides' (ix. 191–2). It was the autocratic rule of the proscenium stage which had turned modern drama into a kind of basso-relievo.

It is at this point that Wagner launches into a remarkable speculation by suggesting that the plasticity of Greek and Shakespearian drama could be restored by means of the orchestra. This suggestion makes sense only if considered against the background of an idea which will be treated in greater detail in the following chapter, namely, that the modern orchestra was, in Wagner's view, the legitimate successor to the chorus which, historically, was positioned in the *orchestra*, a semicircular space in front of the stage in the ancient Greek theatre. Constantly accompanying and reflecting on the dramatic action, the chorus was in a position to observe the performers from all sides. The 'magic spell which wells up from, and is led by, the *orchestra*' was able to 'extend in every conceivable direction wherever its individuality might manifest itself, and to do so, moreover, with the most exhaustive wealth'. 'Robbed of the magic of the omnipresent *orchestra*', modern spoken drama had

---

[44] Mann, *Gesammelte Werke*, x. 29 (the German passage quoted here is not included in Blunden's English translation).

[45] Much of the following section is taken from Dieter Borchmeyer, '*Tristan, Tasso* und die Kunst des "unendlichen Details": Zu Richard Wagners musikalischer Dramaturgie', *Jahrbuch der Bayerischen Staatsoper*, 3 (1979–80), 29–30.

become 'flatter' in the most literal sense of the word, since 'all that remains is the flat surface of the theatre on which the stage characters appear' (ix. 196–7). Through the participation of the instrumental orchestra as the modern metamorphosis of the ancient Greek chorus, however, the 'dramatic mime' would once more be 'sustained on every side by sound' (ix. 199).

This idea is undoubtedly behind the passage quoted above from Thomas Mann's 'Versuch über das Theater', where the role of the orchestra—Mann speaks here of the music 'ebbing and flowing at the feet of these happenings in a tide of song and narrative'[46]—is transferred to the narrator. Like the classical chorus, which many writers, including Victor Hugo in his *Préface de 'Cromwell'* and Bertolt Brecht, have regarded as an epic device, the narrator observes man from all sides, thus allowing his characters to appear 'plastic' or three-dimensional. Exactly the same function was performed by the orchestra, Wagner believed: by shedding light on the characters from every side, it overcame the one-sidedness or stereotypical flatness of modern drama, and so appeared to turn the musical drama into an art which was no less 'exact, complete, knowing, conscientious, and profound' than the novel was for Thomas Mann. The novel is thus revealed to be as much a crypto-music drama (one need think only of the influence of leitmotivic technique on Mann's narrative art) as Wagner's music dramas are crypto-novels.[47]

[46] Mann, *Gesammelte Werke*, x. 31; English trans. (Blunden, *Pro and contra Wagner*), p. 27.
[47] See n. 45 above.

# 12

## Choral Tragedy and Symphonic Drama: Wagner's Contribution to Nietzsche's *Die Geburt der Tragödie*

> A minute passed, filled with the ebb and flow of the music as it raced along at the feet of these events in a tide of song, of narrative, and of intimation . . .
>
> Thomas Mann, *Wälsungenblut*.

In the twenty-sixth section of his *Hamburgische Dramaturgie* Lessing puts forward the view that 'the orchestra at our stage plays takes the place, as it were, of the ancient choruses'.[1] Of course, Lessing's concern was not with music theatre but with the incidental music played at the theatre, for which he demanded a strict motivic link with the dramatic action, so that, like the chorus, such music could accompany and comment on the events taking place on stage. Lessing argued that instrumental music, which, unlike vocal music, he felt was essentially indeterminate in its 'expression', could gain in (semantic) clarity if particular motives were repeated, even if there were no words accompanying them. The musician

will therefore have to deploy his greatest strengths here; out of the various sequences of notes which can express an emotion, he will have to select those which express it most clearly; we shall hear these more often, we shall compare them with each other more often, and, by noting what they always have in common, we shall divine the secret of what they express.[2]

If the music were played only between the acts, this secret would, of course, never be revealed, since the musical motives could never be associated, unequivocally, with specific dramatic situations. Wagner's comments in part III of *Opera and Drama* seem to be a direct riposte to this remark of Lessing's:

A musical motive can produce a specific impression on feeling, inciting it to thought-like activity, only if the emotion expressed by that motive has been specifically conditioned by a specific object and if it is announced, before our eyes, by a specific individual. If any of these conditions is wanting, the effect which the musical motive has on our feeling is of something non-specific; and something that is non-specific may return in the same form as often as it likes

---

[1] *Lessings Werke*, ed. Georg Witkowski (Leipzig and Vienna, n.d.), v. 7.     [2] Ibid. 11.

[cf. Lessing], it will always remain a repetitious, non-specific entity ... The musical motive, however, into which the thought-inducing line of verse uttered by a dramatic performer is poured before our very eyes, so to speak, is something that is conditioned by necessity; when it returns, a *specific* emotion is discernibly imparted to us. (iv. 185.)

As a result of some specific dramatic situation in which its emotional meaning is articulated in words, the musical motive becomes semantically charged, so that, when repeated as an 'orchestral melody' (above all, in the overlapping of several motives), each dramatic situation appears in a 'more significant' light, thereby gaining a symbolic clarity which is virtually unattainable in spoken drama. The line of verse and even the verse melody are only the tip of an iceberg which reaches down far beneath the surface of the dramatic monologues and dialogues, penetrating the depths of the unspoken and of the unconscious. Each motive may, on its return, 'excite an emotion within us' of which 'the person currently conveying it [i.e., the performer] appears no longer conscious'. In this way, orchestral melody serves to 'complement a context, rendering each situation fully intelligible by interpreting motives which, although contained within that situation, cannot properly surface within its representable elements' (iv. 184).

The passage just quoted might give the impression that the leitmotif was firmly fixed from the very first moment and that its semantic content was irrevocably tied to the same linguistic definition. But this is not the case. Rather, the process of semanticization continues throughout the course of the musical drama, as the result of each new scenic contextualization and of the musical combination of the various leitmotifs. It must also be borne in mind that the orchestra acquires its 'linguistic ability' (iv. 173 and *passim*) not only through its 'recollection of the verse melody' but equally by its 'dependence on gesture' (iv. 186), in other words, by proclaiming that which is 'inexpressible' (i.e., that is not 'absolutely' non-communicable but which cannot be conveyed by rational means through the language of the spoken word). Through its 'ability to utter the inexpressible', the music of the orchestra is closer to gesture than it is to the spoken language (iv. 173–4). Moreover, the leitmotif functions not only as a motive of 'reminiscence' but also as one of 'presentiment' (iv. 186 and *passim*); the orchestral melody quite clearly comes first here, albeit with the aim of enabling what is presciently anticipated to achieve scenic autonomy at a later stage, for otherwise the leitmotif would remain no more than an 'unsolved cipher, an anticipation that is left unfulfilled', to quote Carl Dahlhaus.[3] Verse and orchestral melody form two 'languages' which, only when heard

[3] Carl Dahlhaus, *Richard Wagners Musikdramen* (Velber, 1971), 87; translated into English by Mary Whittall as *Richard Wagner's Music Dramas* (Cambridge, 1979), 86.

together, become a language in the full sense of the word—a sense no longer involving alienation. Wagner can demand that the language of words should transfer its telos to a blend of music and language, since, in his view, it is this amalgam which, in terms of its origins and ultimate aim, is the one true language. (This belief of Wagner's is the radical opposite of the doctrine of absolute music, whose most influential representative, Eduard Hanslick, would see it as one of the 'most important tasks' of the aesthetics of music to 'demonstrate with inexorable logic the fundamental difference between music and language'.[4])

As 'vowels dissolve into musical sound', verse melody becomes 'the binding and intelligible bond between the language of words and that of music', the 'moment of love incarnate' between poetry and music. Wagner uses the image of a boat on a lake to illustrate the 'proper relationship between this melody and the orchestra'. 'This boat, now launched upon the lake . . . is the *verse melody* of the dramatic singer, borne along by the orchestra's waves of sound.' (iv. 171–2.)

The image of water, albeit in a different metaphorical context, plays a further role in Wagner's description of the structure of the musical drama, where the music (or orchestral melody) is said not only to provide support but also to act as a mirror. Whereas the depth of the water symbolizes 'harmony in its vertical dimension', its surface signifies the 'horizontal dimension' of melody. It is that element 'which is still discernible to the poet's eye: it is the watery mirror which reflects back the poet's own image [i.e., the poet's words and phrases]'. It is the same Narcissus motif as the early German Romantics had used to describe the poet. The musician sees the image from beneath, as it were: 'from the depths of the sea of harmony' he rises up to the surface 'on which will be celebrated the rapturous marriage between the procreative poetic thought and music's infinite capacity for giving birth' (iv. 142). The image of a classical erotic sea festival, familiar to Wagner from the 'Classical Walpurgis Night' in part II of Goethe's *Faust*, serves here to allegorize the structural link between poetic intent and its musical realization in the association of poetic verse, vocal melody, and orchestral harmony in the musical drama. On the very last page of *Opera and Drama* Wagner once again draws on the image of the sea's mirror-like surface to describe poetry's sentimental desire for music, symbolized as its mother's womb:

We saw the poet, driven onward by his yearning desire to achieve a perfect expression of emotion, to the point where he saw his verse reflected on the

---

[4] Eduard Hanslick, *Vom Musikalisch-Schönen: Ein Beitrag zur Revision der Ästhetik der Tonkunst* (Wiesbaden, 1980), 92; translated into English by Gustav Cohen as *The Beautiful in Music* (Indianapolis, 1957), 70.

mirror of the sea of harmony in the form of musical melody: he had no choice but to make his way to this sea, only the mirror of this sea could show him the image he longed to behold; for he could not create this sea by his own will, rather was it that other aspect of his nature which he was destined to wed but which he could not produce from within himself or summon into existence. (iv. 228.)

The image of water's reflective surface was used by classical and Romantic poets to symbolize the essential nature of the poet's existence. Tasso, for example, exclaims at the end of Goethe's drama (11. 3443–5):

> In dieser Woge spiegelte so schön
> Die Sonne sich, es ruhten die Gestirne
> An dieser Brust, die zärtlich sich bewegte.
>
> How beautiful the sun's reflection
> In this wave, the very constellations
> Nestled at this breast, which gently rose and fell.

Whereas it is the poet's breast which represents the mirror-like wave in this example, Wagner's poet requires external melody to reflect *his* innermost self. Conversely, melody cannot, of course, produce a (poetic) reflection from within itself, since melody is 'a maternal element which can bring forth only that which it has received' (iv. 228).

This 'maternal element'—involving the incestuous ambiguity of an image in which music represents both the mother and wife of the poet's expressive potential (iv. 102)—is the central metaphor in Wagner's description of the genesis and structure of musical drama. It was from this metaphor, moreover, that Nietzsche derived his theory of the 'birth of tragedy from the spirit of music', the essential ideas of which—especially the idea of a functional affinity between the chorus of Greek tragedy and the modern orchestra—are already adumbrated in Wagner's writings. Leitmotivic technique enables the orchestra 'to play an uninterrupted part in the overall expression of the performer's every communication, supporting and elucidating on every hand: it is the moving matrix of the music from which the unifying bond of expression grows'. In this respect, the orchestra realizes the aim of the classical chorus: '*The chorus of Greek tragedy* has bequeathed its emotionally necessary significance in the drama *to the modern orchestra* alone.' (iv. 190–1.) Nietzsche, too, uses the same metaphor in describing 'the choral parts with which tragedy is interlaced' as the 'womb that gave birth to the whole of the so-called dialogue, that is, the entire world of the stage, the real drama'.[5] In much the same way, the metaphor in the

---

[5] Friedrich Nietzsche, *Sämtliche Werke: Kritische Studienausgabe in 15 Bänden*, ed. Giorgio Colli and Mazzino Montinari (Munich, 1980), i. 62; translated into English by Walter Kaufmann as *Basic Writings of Nietzsche* (New York, 1968), 65.

title of Nietzsche's essay turns out to be Wagnerian in origin, in that the idea of the rise and fall of Greek tragedy is already encapsulated in a note to Wagner's fragmentary essay of 1849, 'The Artists of the Future': 'Birth from music: Aeschylus. *Décadence*—Euripides.' (xii. 280.) Even at this early date we find Wagner questioning the traditional assessment of Attic tragedy: those later tragedians whom the writers of Weimar Classicism had held in highest esteem are clearly placed in the shade by Aeschylus.[6] Wagner blames Euripides for excluding 'music' from tragedy, although, unlike Nietzsche, he regards the resultant 'decline of Greek tragedy' (iv. 145) as an inevitable development in the history of art. According to *Opera and Drama*, the attenuation of the choric (i.e. musico-lyrical) element during the later period of Attic tragedy was the inescapable consequence of its emergence 'from the womb of lyricism into the world of intellectual reflection', in other words, from the 'chanting of the chorus to the iambic speech of actors who now spoke only words'. Euripides, Wagner went on, had revealed this reflective element and the spoken word as the actual nature of tragedy, exposing its 'lyric element' as a necessary lie.

Euripides had to suffer the bloody scourge of Aristophanic ridicule for so crudely exposing this lie. That poetry, growing ever more deliberately didactic, was bound to become the language of state rhetoric and, finally, the language of prose literature was the extreme, but entirely natural, consequence of a development which saw understanding evolve from feeling, and—in terms of artistic expression—the language of words emerge from melody. (iv. 145.)

The chorus, according to Wagner, could not achieve its intended aim: embodied as it was by a collective which contributed to the action while reflecting on that action, the musico-lyrical element could not unfold freely and independently. The death of the chorus was, therefore, a necessary historical development, in consequence of which its visible body became separated, so to speak, from its invisible soul. Once a real dramatic collective, it was disbanded to form a series of individual actors, while, as a musical organ, it was liberated from its alienated physical form to become the invisible modern orchestra

in order that, free from all constriction, it might here develop an immeasurably varied expressivity; its real, individually human form, however, has been transferred from the *orchestra* to the stage, where that germ of human individuality that lay in the Greek chorus may achieve the highest autonomous ascendancy as an immediate participant, acting and suffering, in the drama itself (iv. 191).

Like every other aspect of Greek tragedy, the chorus was evidence, therefore, of the fact that drama had hitherto existed only in an alienated

---

[6] See Curt von Westernhagen, *Richard Wagner: Sein Werk, sein Wesen, seine Welt* (Zurich, 1956), 132–44, esp. pp. 139–40.

form. In this case, the state of alienation would cease only when the chorus, as the musical basis of the tragedy, was transformed into the orchestra, its individualization as a series of discrete dramatic characters having already been effected by Shakespeare.

Without question, *Shakespeare*'s tragedy stands above that of Greece, to the extent that it has completely dispensed with the need for a chorus from the point of view of artistic technique. With *Shakespeare*, the chorus is broken down into various individuals personally involved in the action who act independently with the same inevitability of individual opinion and standpoint as is true of the principal hero himself. (iii. 268.)

In other words, Wagner attributes the fact that there are far more characters in Shakespeare than there are in Greek tragedy to the fragmentation of the chorus into individual figures.

In terms of the musical basis of tragedy, chorus and orchestra are scarcely comparable, the latter being the actualization of the former's potential. But the analogy between them is one to which Wagner returns on frequent occasions in his later dramaturgical writings, too. In his essay *'Zukunftsmusik'*, for example, he writes:

In the drama as I conceive it the orchestra's relation to the dramatic action will be roughly similar to that of the chorus in Greek tragedy. This latter was constantly in attendance, watching the motivation of the action unfold before its eyes and seeking to fathom the meaning of those motives in order thereby to form an opinion concerning the action. But this interest on the part of the chorus was essentially reflective in nature; the chorus itself stood apart from the action and from its motives. The modern symphony orchestra, by contrast, will be so intimately involved in the motivation of the action that, just as, on the one hand, it is uniquely able, as harmony incarnate, to invest the melody with a specific expression, it will, on the other hand, maintain that melody in a state of uninterrupted flux, and thus convey the motives to the audience's feelings with the most forceful conviction. (vii. 130.)

This distinction between the outward participation of the chorus and the orchestra's 'intimate involvement' in the dramatic action is something which Wagner had already illustrated in *Lohengrin*, where the chorus, following the model of Greek tragedy, supports and advances the action. But its mystified reaction to Elsa's silence in the face of Telramund's accusation ('How curious! What strange behaviour!': ii. 69) demonstrates how far it is from understanding the motivation behind that action. The orchestra, meanwhile, gives purely musical expression to that 'eloquent pause' which, according to Wagner, was the specific province of music in the drama (*CT*, 21 March 1878). In other words, it articulates Elsa's inner state of mind as words, quite literally, fail her.

In his reform essays Wagner castigates the use of the chorus on the operatic stage, attributing it to a false analogy with Greek tragedy. In doing so, he is critical not only of Gluck's reform operas but also of his own early music dramas, in which the chorus still plays a significant role, especially in *Lohengrin*, where the tenors in the chorus have more bars of music to sing than does the eponymous hero himself. The reason for this theoretical elimination of the chorus follows logically from Wagner's system. The role of the classical chorus had been divided up among the subsidiary characters of modern drama, each of whom appeared as an independent figure; having once been emancipated, they could not be turned back into a dramatic collective. At the same time, the ideal function of the chorus had passed to the orchestra, so that its reintroduction would be dramaturgically redundant. 'Even the *chorus*, as employed hitherto in opera, and taking account of the role assigned to it there in even the most favourable cases, would have to vanish from *our* drama.' (iv. 162.) The 'so-called chorus' should not be used 'as a symphonic body of sound to bring the harmonic requirements of the melody to the audience's attention'. Rather, the modern, 'independently developed art of music' should provide the tone-poet with an alternative means of 'bringing the harmony to the audience's attention'. Unlimited in its expressive potential, this organ possessed the ability to 'characterize the melody' in a way that was completely denied to the 'symphonic vocal mass': 'and this organ is none other than the orchestra' (iv. 164).

It is clear that the chorus, which in opera had already climbed up on to the stage itself, must now lose all the significance that it had had in ancient Greece; it can be conceived of now only as a participant in the drama, and where it is not required as such it is bound to strike us in future as disruptive and superfluous, since its ideal involvement in the action has passed entirely to the orchestra, where it is expressed in a way that is always immediate but never disruptive. (vii. 131.)

This quotation from *'Zukunftsmusik'* shows that Wagner does not entirely preclude the use of the chorus, but that he will accept its deployment—as an active crowd—only when it seems plausible from the point of view of the subject-matter.

In keeping with the maxim expressed in *Opera and Drama*, Wagner avoided the chorus almost entirely in the *Ring*. Only in *Götterdämmerung* does it again play a relatively significant role, but even here Wagner refused to accept that he had written a 'chorus': Hagen's liegemen, he told Cosima on 28 August 1871, were simply 'individual vassals who appear from the farmsteads nearby'. The fact that the chorus in *Die Meistersinger* and, above all, in *Parsifal* reacquires an almost 'antique' importance represents a remarkable departure from the earlier demand that the chorus should be largely avoided in musical drama.

Wagner never abandoned the idea that the orchestra was the successor of the classical chorus. It was a belief to which he returned time and again, not least in his conversations with Cosima. 'I have composed a Greek chorus', he told her on 29 September 1871, 'but a chorus which will be sung, so to speak, by the orchestra; after Siegfried's death, while the scene is being changed, the Siegmund theme will be played, as if the chorus were saying: "This was his father"; then the sword motif; and finally his own theme; then the curtain goes up.' In other words, Wagner thought of Siegfried's Funeral March as a kind of counterpart to the *stasimon* of Attic tragedy. A few months previously he had given Cosima a detailed explanation of the 'significance of the orchestra, its position as the ancient chorus, its huge advantage over the latter, which talks about the action in words, whereas the orchestra conveys to us the soul of this action' (*CT*, 16 January 1871). And on 23 April 1870 he spoke of 'the large orchestra which, like Nature, is all-embracing and within whose confines the human being can roam'.

He also discusses the choric function of the orchestra in his dramaturgical writings of the early 1870s. In his *Prologue to a Reading of 'Götterdämmerung' before a Select Audience in Berlin* (1873) he introduces a new argument which he clearly owes to Schiller's preface to his choral tragedy, *Die Braut von Messina*:

It is music which, by unceasingly revealing the innermost motivation of the action in its widest ramifications and by allowing us to sympathize with those motives, enables us at the same time to present that action with drastic specificity: since the characters do not have to use the language of reflective consciousness to explain their reasons for acting as they do, the dialogue thereby gains that naïve precision which constitutes the very life of drama. Whereas antique tragedy had to insert the dramatic dialogue between the choruses, dividing it off from them and thereby entailing a reduction in the amount of dialogue, this archetypally creative element of music, which had given drama its higher significance in the form of those choruses performed in the amphitheatrical *orchestra*, is no longer divorced from the dialogue in what is the greatest artistic achievement of our age, namely, the modern orchestra; it constantly accompanies the action, and may be said, in a profounder sense, to embrace the motives of the entire action as though in its mother's womb. It may thus be possible not only to restore a sense of naïve precision to the dialogue but also to extend that dialogue to cover the whole of the drama. (ix. 309.)

According to Wagner, the 'drastic specificity', precision, and concision of the action—in other words, 'closed' dramatic form—becomes possible only when there is no longer any need for the characters to reflect on their actions, or for those actions to be motivated, since it is precisely these features which have made modern drama so discursive. Dialogue is distinguished by its 'naïve precision' once the task of providing motivation is taken over by the *sentimental* organ of the orchestra. Thanks to the music, the action of the drama reacquires that 'ideal freedom, i.e., freedom from the need to provide motivation through reflection', which 'our great poets' had felt to be the aesthetic drawback of modern drama (ix. 309). Wagner will have been thinking here first and foremost of Schiller, who, in his preface to *Die Braut von Messina*, had expressed the conviction that tragedy was purified, in an aesthetic sense, by the introduction of the tragic chorus, to the extent that the latter 'separates reflection from the action and, by virtue of this act of separation, equips the action with poetic potency'.[7]

It was very much this function of the chorus which, in Wagner's view, had been taken over by the orchestra. Of course, its 'reflective' role was no longer expressed in conceptual form, but was 'condensed', in accordance with the basic aim of the musical drama (namely, the 'emotionalization of the intellect'), into a purely emotional utterance, *preceded* (and thereby 'justified') by rational reflection rather than *followed* by it (cf. iv. 91). 'Bound, as we are, to regard that art-form as ideal which can be grasped entirely without reflection', Wagner had written as early as in 1860 in '*Zukunftsmusik*', 'it must follow that, if we acknowledge the musical drama . . . to be that ideal art-form, the symphonic orchestra is the wondrous instrument uniquely capable of representing that form.' (vii. 130.)

The poetic element, according to Schiller, lies at the 'dead point between the material and the ideal'. It was not always possible, however, for 'the two elements of poetry, the material and the ideal . . . to work *together*'; but they must at least 'work *side by side* with each other, otherwise the poetry is nullified'. Schiller sought to achieve this juxtaposition in choral tragedy: dramatic action and chorus were contrasted with each other as the 'particular' and the 'general', the 'material' and the 'ideal', and as naïve immediacy and sentimental reflection. 'If the balance is not perfect, equilibrium can be achieved only by a *fluctuation* between the two scales.'[8]

This fluctuation or juxtaposition of dramatic dialogue and choric reflection is superseded, according to Wagner, by the orchestra's contribution to the musical drama. Here the ideal and the material work *together* and reach their 'dead point' (in the Schillerian sense). Dialogue is not segregated from, and delimited by, choral interjection any more than the musical element is separated from the action. Both are released reciprocally from their fetters in choral tragedy: the dialogue 'extends over the whole of the drama', and the 'archetypally creative element of music . . . constantly accompanies' the action. In this way, Wagner was

[7] Friedrich Schiller, *Sämtliche Werke*, ed. Gerhard Fricke and Herbert G. Göpfert, 3rd edn. (Munich, 1962), ii. 821.                    [8] Ibid.

later to write in 1872 in his essay 'On the Term "Music Drama"', the music of the orchestra became 'that part which initially was everything'. 'Invested with this dignity, it need not place itself either before or after the drama; it is not the drama's rival but its mother.' (ix. 305.)

There is no doubt that Nietzsche's book on tragedy was decisively influenced by Wagner's idea of the orchestra as a modern chorus. But it is equally clear that Nietzsche ignored the distinction which Wagner had drawn between the antique chorus and the modern orchestra, and that he chose to disregard Wagner's critical remarks concerning the function of the chorus in Greek tragedy, the musical significance of which, Wagner argued, was reduced by the dialogue, while, conversely, the action was 'disrupted' by the choral interjections (ix. 305). The starting-point for *Die Geburt der Tragödie* was not Wagner's critique of the Attic chorus but his theory of the orchestra: by equating the chorus with the orchestra, Nietzsche was guilty of a momentous but happy anachronism to which Wagner never lent his name, in spite of his passing enthusiasm for *Die Geburt der Tragödie* (cf. ix. 304–5 and 309).

When Wagner speaks of the 'birth' of tragedy from music, it is with the historical origins of Greek drama in mind: Attic tragedy developed out of the choral lyric, a genre from which it grew increasingly—and inevitably—remote. It is in a completely different sense, however, that the orchestra of the modern musical drama constitutes the 'matrix' or womb of the action and dialogue. Here the metaphor no longer has a diachronic significance but a synchronic one: the orchestra creates the constant harmonic and melodic background to the drama. With the Greeks, tragedy grew more and more distant from its musical well-spring the more it developed as drama; in the art-work of the future, by contrast, the involvement of the orchestra will enable drama to achieve its ideal purity of form. In a word, Attic tragedy grew increasingly remote from the womb of music the more it became drama; the art-work of the future, on the other hand, will be more perfect as a drama the more it regresses to the womb of music.

Nietzsche abandons this distinction, arguing, instead, that not only is the chorus of Aeschylean tragedy the womb from which the dialogue issues, so, too, is the modern orchestra. 'The chorus as orchestra', proclaims one of Nietzsche's posthumously published fragments from the spring of 1871.[9] In Chapter 10 we saw how his theory of the chorus as the 'beholder of the visionary world of the scene'[10] derives from Wagner's *Beethoven* essay, in which the latter, adducing the principle of Schopenhauer's metaphysics of music (albeit contradicting, as so often, the philosopher's own conclusions, inasmuch as Schopenhauer himself

---

[9] Nietzsche, *Sämtliche Werke*, vii. 373.
[10] Ibid. i. 59; English trans. (Kaufmann, *Basic Writings of Nietzsche*), p. 62.

refused to acknowledge a 'community of property'[11] between music and drama), had defined music as an a priori prerequisite of drama, while drama itself was the 'visible counterpart of music' (ix. 112), an analogical vision of music in keeping with Schopenhauer's theory of dreams and somnambulism.

There is no doubt that Nietzsche's idea of Attic drama as a graphically Apollonian 'discharge' and visionary 'transmission' of the Dionysian chorus, whereby the latter became the 'womb that gave birth to the whole of the so-called dialogue',[12] comes directly from Wagner. Nietzsche draws an explicit comparison between this discharge process and our experience of the way in which 'a Beethoven symphony forces its individual listeners to adopt a metaphorical language', so that even the composer himself (as in the Pastoral Symphony) was struck by 'symbolical representations born of music'.[13] It is on this basis that the musical drama, too, was justified. The translation of these visions into stage characters follows from the compulsive urge of symphonic music to discharge itself, cathartically as it were, in images. 'It sounds', Wagner had written in his essay 'On the Term "Music Drama"', 'and what it sounds, you may see there on the stage; it is for this that it brought you together', in other words, to give visual expression to the 'scenic parable' of itself (ix. 305). Of course, one cannot exclude the possibility that this remark of Wagner's was influenced retrospectively by Nietzsche's *Die Geburt der Tragödie*, but the idea that Wagner is developing here is essentially the same as that which can be found, differently formulated, in his commemorative essay on Beethoven.

Nietzsche explained the relationship between chorus and drama by reference to Schopenhauer's metaphysics of music (a metaphysics which he was later to hold in contempt). But it has not been noticed generally that Nietzsche's starting-point here was not so much Schopenhauer himself as Wagner's revision of Schopenhauer, a revision aimed at redeploying the philosophical apologist of absolute music as the advocate of that very genre—musical drama—which Schopenhauer had expressly condemned. Nietzsche made this revision entirely his own, even if, in fragmentary jottings dating from the time of *Die Geburt der Tragödie*, he was already criticizing Wagner's dramaturgy in the name of 'absolute music'. This criticism, however, affects only one aspect of *Opera and Drama*, namely, the way in which the music is determined by extra-musical factors; unlike Hanslick's definition of 'absolute music', it is not directed against musical drama as such, as long as the latter issues

---

[11] See Chap. 10 n. 51, and Wilhelm Roth, *Schopenhauers Metaphysik der Musik und sein musikalischer Geschmack* (Mainz, 1951).

[12] Nietzsche, *Sämtliche Werke*, i. 62; English trans. (Kaufmann, *Basic Writings of Nietzsche*), p. 65.

[13] Ibid. 50; English trans., p. 54.

purely from the 'womb' of music and provides a scenic analogy to what is going on in the music. For Nietzsche, not only was *Tristan und Isolde* absolute music, so too was Greek tragedy, at least to the extent that the chorus remained the musical well-spring of the action on stage.

Confirmation of this assumption comes from *Die Geburt der Tragödie*, where the term 'absolute music' is avoided altogether, no doubt out of consideration for Wagner's negative assessment of it. None the less, the *idea* of absolute music is very much the philosophical corner-stone of the work. The death of tragedy is also the death of absolute music for the Greeks. Nietzsche blames Euripidean tragedy and the new Attic dithyramb for debasing music to the point where 'the only thing left to it, as the slave of phenomena, was to imitate the formal character of phenomena'; and, in this respect, he compares it to that false doctrine which had been proclaimed by the founders of opera in the sixteenth century, the Florentine Camerata, to the effect that 'music is regarded as the servant, the text as the master'.[14] For Nietzsche, Wagner's musical drama signalled the rebirth of tragedy, since its symphonic basis meant that the drama (contradicting Wagner's own theory in *Opera and Drama*) was transformed back into absolute music.

In spite of their common appeal to *Die Welt als Wille und Vorstellung*, neither Wagner's nor Nietzsche's theory of music and musical drama can be reconciled with Schopenhauer's *magnum opus*. 'The music of an opera, as presented in the score', the latter observes unambiguously, 'has a wholly independent, separate, and as it were abstract existence by itself, to which the incidents and characters of the piece are foreign, and which follows its own unchangeable rules; it can therefore be completely effective even without the text.' However, since the music 'was composed with respect to the drama', it is,

so to speak, the soul of this, since, in its connexion with the incidents, characters, and words, it becomes the expression of the inner significance of all those incidents, and of their ultimate and secret necessity that rests on this significance ... Yet in opera, music shows its heterogeneous nature and its superior intrinsic virtue by its complete indifference to everything material in the incidents; and in consequence of this, it expresses the storm of the passions and the pathos of the feelings everywhere in the same way, and accompanies these with the same pomp of its tones, whether Agamemnon and Achilles or the divisions of an ordinary family furnish the material of the piece.

According to Schopenhauer, music 'stands to the text and the action in the relation of universal to particular, of rule to example' (which is why the text really has to be written to fit the music, rather than the music to fit the text). However, it is not necessary for music to discharge itself in

---

[14] Ibid. 126; English trans., pp. 118–19.

stage pictures (Nietzsche), nor is it so closely assimilated with the drama as is the case with Wagner's leitmotivic procedure. Rather, it hovers in 'absolute', godlike sublimity above the 'endless miseries of human life', and hence of the stage, too. That is why it is always best to 'interpret it purely and in its immediacy', untroubled by the tragic and comic vicissitudes of existence.[15]

We must never forget, according to Schopenhauer, that music, in spite of its 'analogies' with the ideas of the world of appearances (analogies which, for the later Wagner, legitimize the musical drama), 'has no direct relation to them [i.e., those analogies] but only an indirect one; for it never expresses the phenomenon, but only the inner nature, the in-itself, of every phenomenon, the will itself'. In every case, music 'expresses only the quintessence of life and of its events, never these themselves, and, therefore, their differences do not always influence it'. The extent to which Schopenhauer's 'metaphysics of music' is at odds not only with *Opera and Drama* but also with the later essay on Beethoven is shown by the following passage:

Therefore, if music tries to stick too closely to the words, and to mould itself according to the events, it is endeavouring to speak a language not its own. No one has kept so free from this mistake as Rossini; hence his music speaks its *own* language so distinctly and purely that it requires no words at all, and therefore produces its full effect even when rendered by instruments alone.[16]

Schopenhauer believed that music 'could still exist even if there were no world at all', since, like the latter, it was an 'immediate objectification' of the will as the essential being, whereas the other arts were an indirect copy of that essence, a copy which they achieved by means of the ideas of the 'phenomenal world'.[17]

Schopenhauer's conclusions are quoted at considerable length in chapter 16 of *Die Geburt der Tragödie*. The nub of this section is Schopenhauer's description of the specific relationship between music and the world (namely, that music is 'the heart of things' and that, therefore, it 'expresses the metaphysical to everything physical in the world, the thing-in-itself to every phenomenon'), a description which is couched in the language of scholasticism, suggesting that 'the concepts are the *universalia post rem*, but music gives the *universalia ante rem*, and reality the *universalia in re*'.[18] Nietzsche transfers this philosophical relativism to the relationship between chorus and dialogue in Attic

[15] *Schopenhauers sämtliche Werke*, ed. Max Frischeisen-Köhler (Berlin, n.d.), iii. 464–5; translated into English by E. F. J. Payne as *The World as Will and Representation* (New York, 1969), ii. 448–50.

[16] Ibid. ii. 300–1; English trans. i. 261–2.

[17] Ibid. 296; English trans., p. 257.

[18] Ibid. 302; English trans., pp. 262–3; also Nietzsche, *Sämtliche Werke*, i. 106–7; English trans. (Kaufmann, *Basic Writings of Nietzsche*), p. 100.

tragedy: the *orchestra*, so to speak, is the area of the *universalia ante rem*, while the stage reproduces the *universalia in re*. Chorus and dialogue are thus allotted to two different levels of existence. The metaphysical *ante* of the music is symbolized by the fact that the *orchestra* is positioned *in front of* the scene.

Nietzsche believed he had solved the 'riddle of the *orchestra* in front of the scene' by claiming that the latter was a mere vision on the part of the chorus, which was the only genuine 'reality' of the tragedy.[19] This separation of the *orchestra* from the stage is, of course, untenable from a historical point of view; Nietzsche has simply projected back on to the Attic amphitheatre the modern distinction between stage and auditorium, turning the former into the chorus's proscenium stage. The solution to the 'riddle of the *orchestra* in front of the scene' is provided by the orchestra pit in front of the opera stage. Nietzsche's anachronistic assumptions concerning the illusionistic conditions which obtain in the modern theatre also colour his view of the audience of antique tragedy. The force of the spectator's 'vision' (the object of which is the chorus, whose vision in turn forms the 'world of the stage') is 'strong enough', according to Nietzsche, 'to make the eye insensitive and blind to the impression of "reality", to the men of culture who occupy the rows of seats all around'.[20] The night of the darkened auditorium (protecting the spectator's eyes from reality and from the 'men of culture' all around him) descends over the sun-drenched terraces of the Attic amphitheatre, the *orchestra* sinks down into the 'mystic abyss' of the orchestra pit, the chorus is transformed into the orchestra, and all the disruptive influences between spectator and stage disappear, since there is no longer anything to see except for a stage picture 'removed to the unapproachability of a dreamlike vision' (ix. 337–8). In a word, the theatre of Dionysus anticipates the Bayreuth Festspielhaus.

The 'unity' between the world of the stage and the world of the audience, which Nietzsche claimed existed in the antique theatre but not in its modern equivalent—'there was at bottom no opposition between public and chorus', since the former 'found itself' in the latter[21]—was the *unio mystica* of Dionysian frenzy, and has nothing to do with the original unity between the reality of the stage and that of the audience in the classical festival theatre. Unity here lay in the fact that the dramatic action was fully integrated into the real world of the spectator, who was able to say to himself: 'tua res agitur.' With Nietzsche, by contrast, a sense of unity is achieved when the audience forgets itself and its concrete reality and is wholly identified with the visionary world

---

[19] Nietzsche, *Sämtliche Werke*, i. 62–3; English trans. (Kaufmann, *Basic Writings of Nietzsche*), p. 65.
[20] Ibid. 59–60; English trans., p. 63.      [21] Ibid. 59; English trans., p. 62.

depicted on stage. This idea of resolving the opposition between stage and audience is one which goes back to the Romantics and their aesthetic writings on the theatre. It is also closely associated with Wagner's contemporary theoretical attempts to devise a theatre of improvisation which would draw the spectator into the drama's dynamic action and thus remove him from prosaic reality. Wagner's observations on this point are to be found in his 1872 essay, *On Actors and Singers*. It is significant that Nietzsche—wrongly, no doubt—ascribed them to the influence of his own essay on tragedy.

However closely related the modernist thrust of *Die Geburt der Tragödie* to Wagner's aesthetic thinking, the two writers adopt radically different approaches when it comes to their historical assessment of Greek tragedy. As his post-1872 writings show, Wagner did not follow Nietzsche in abandoning the historical distinction between Attic tragedy and musical drama. According to *his* theory, chorus and dialogue did not belong to different levels of reality but coexisted on one and the same level in a state of rivalry from which the dialogue, as the vehicle of the real drama, finally emerged as victor. If one looks at the structure of tragedy rather than at the history of its origins, the chorus appears not so much the 'mother' as the 'rival' of the dialogue (cf. ix. 305). In Wagner's view, the chorus simply could not provide a basis for the action in the way in which the orchestra could, since music, as an emancipated art, was as yet unknown to the Greeks. Not only in *Opera and Drama* and *'Zukunftsmusik'* but elsewhere, too, Wagner repeatedly stressed that the 'inseparable and living combination of dance gesture and the language of words and sounds' (in other words, what the Greeks called 'music') prevented music from developing as an independent art. 'The Greeks felt obliged to cultivate music only to the extent that it had to serve as a support for gesture, whose meaning was already melodically expressed by language *per se*' (iv. 104). 'With the Greeks we know music only as the accompanist of dance', we read in *'Zukunftsmusik'*: the Greeks experienced the regular quantities of classical metre (quantities which distinguish it fundamentally from the 'accented' verse found in German: iv. 105) directly through the body.[22] The 'dancer's movements' gave the music 'the laws of rhythm, just as they gave them to the poem which the singer sang to a dance tune, and these rhythmic laws had so decisive an influence on verse and melody that Greek music (a term which almost always included poetry) can be regarded only as dance expressing itself in sounds and words' (vii. 106). It is clear that the unity of poetry, dance, and music which results from the rhythm of the Greek language is

---

[22] This emerges, in fact, from the Greek metrical terms *arsis* and *thesis*, literally, the 'lifting' and 'sinking' of the foot; it was entirely self-evident that one should speak of a (metrical) 'foot'. See Thrasybulos Georgiades, *Musik und Rhythmus bei den Griechen*, 5th edn. (Hamburg, 1958).

radically different from that of the modern *Gesamtkunstwerk*, with its voluntary integration of the individual emancipated arts. This is something that Wagner never underestimated.

Wagner's essay on Beethoven sets out from a belief in the original unity of the arts in Greek *mousike*, and concludes that music, as the voice of the thing-in-itself, had not yet broken free from its reproduction of the phenomenal world. Confirmation of this view came from the Pythagoreans' belief in the regular order of the cosmos and the resultant 'musical' harmony of the spheres. It was not yet true of Greek music that its kingdom was 'not of this world', since this world, having not yet sold its soul to science and been corrupted by civilization, was not yet alienated from man (ix. 121). Only when confronted by a 'modern world of appearance which, to his despair, hems him in on every side' did man feel the need for a redemptive force; and 'just as Christianity emerged from the midst of Rome's universal civilization, so music now bursts forth from the chaos of modern civilization. Both proclaim: "Our kingdom is not of this world."' (ix. 120.)

The power of music over 'the whole of our modern civilization' is something which Wagner illustrates by means of a metaphor, claiming that music 'nullifies it [civilization], as the light of day nullifies lamplight' (ix. 120). Nietzsche quotes this passage in *Die Geburt der Tragödie*, where he uses it to characterize the impact of 'Dionysian music': 'Similarly, I believe, the Greek man of culture felt himself nullified in the presence of the satyric chorus.'[23] Once again Nietzsche brushes aside the difference, not to say the contrast, between Greek tragedy and modern symphonic drama. After all, Wagner used this image to characterize not *classical* but *modern* music, contrasting the culturally nullifying effect of the latter with the impact of Greek music, which sustained and permeated every aspect of contemporary culture. Nietzsche, too, mentions the same forms of Greek music as those described by Wagner, but for him they are 'the music of Apollo' and, therefore, not genuine Greek music: they are merely 'architectonics in tones . . . the wave-beat of rhythm, whose formative power was developed for the representation of Apollonian states'.[24] For Wagner, by contrast, this Apollonian music was the only true music of the Greeks; its spirit was that of the choral chanting from which 'the drama was projected on to the stage':

It must seem to us as though the music of the Hellenes permeated the world of appearance itself and blended with its laws of perception. The numbers of Pythagoras are surely understandable only through music; the architect built according to the laws of eurhythmics, the sculptor conceived the human figure according to those of harmony; the rules of melody made the poet a singer, and

[23] Nietzsche, *Sämtliche Werke*, i. 55–6; English trans. (Kaufmann, *Basic Writings of Nietzsche*), p. 59.    [24] Ibid. 33; English trans., p. 40.

from out of choral chanting the drama was projected on to the stage. Everywhere we see how the inner law, conceivable only as having sprung from the spirit of music, determines that outer law which governs the visible world: the genuinely ancient Doric state which Plato sought to rescue from philosophy, nay, even the dispensations of war and battle were governed by the laws of music as surely as was dance. But that paradise was lost, the primal source of movement of a world ran dry. Like a ball once struck, the world span round in whirling vibration, but within it there no longer stirred a soul to give it movement; and so all movement was finally bound to flag until such time as the world's soul might be reawoken. It was the spirit of Christianity which breathed new life into the soul of music. (ix. 120–1.)

Nietzsche abandoned this historical reconstruction. It was not from the classical spirit of music, as described here by Wagner, but from its modern Christian counterpart that he anachronistically derived Attic tragedy. (It is significant that in chapter 19 of *Die Geburt der Tragödie* he draws a parallel between the relationship between Euripidean and Aeschylean tragedy on the one hand, and, on the other, the contrast between the operas of the Florentine Camerata and the 'ineffably sublime and sacred music of Palestrina ... which all medieval Christendom had been building up'.[25] In both instances, music loses the power to 'redeem' us from the world of appearance, a power which, according to Wagner, was the specific principle of modern Christian music.)

For Wagner, the essence of antique music was its ability to merge with the phenomenal world, an ability seen, above all, in dance. In the case of modern music, however, that same phenomenon was a sign of alienation, involving, as it did, the 'four-square' periodic structure derived from the rhythms of dance. 'In consequence, music leaves its state of lofty innocence; it loses the power to redeem from the curse of appearance, i.e., it no longer proclaims the essence of things, but itself becomes entangled in that illusive show which typifies the phenomenal world around us.' (ix. 81.) This power was still enjoyed by Greek music, since the appearance of things had not yet been alienated from the essence of things. On this point Wagner follows the tradition of those writers on classical Greece whose views owe more to myth than they do to historical fact, and whose idealizing tendencies prevailed time and again over the pessimistic view of antiquity which the findings of archaeology, familiar as they were to him, must otherwise have suggested. Although he repeatedly claimed that Schopenhauer's metaphysical pessimism had undermined his earlier Hellenic optimism, his picture of Greece remained largely free of pessimistic traits. More or less consciously, he relativized and historicized Schopenhauer's

---

[25] Nietzsche, *Sämtliche Werke*, 120; English trans., p. 114.

philosophy of the world-will, limiting its results to modern civilization. In the final analysis, his cultural pessimism was overtaken by the Utopianism of his reform essays of around 1850. (This will become patently obvious when we come to examine the end of the *Ring*.)

In terms of his pessimism, it was the author of *Die Geburt der Tragödie* who was the more consistent Schopenhauerian. His view of Greece remained free of all artificial attempts at transfiguration. Of course, it can scarcely be denied that the pessimistic features of Nietzsche's work are largely the result of his projecting Wagner's critique of civilization back on the world of ancient Greece. Just as Nietzsche identifies the spirit of modern music with that of ancient Greek music, so the world of Greek culture intended to be superseded by it assumes the characteristics of modern civilization. When Nietzsche writes of all that is 'nullified in the presence of the satyric chorus', in other words, 'the Greek man of culture . . . the state and society and, quite generally, the gulfs between man and man',[26] what he is thinking of is late nineteenth-century man, with his state institutions and social estrangements.

Nietzsche's first major essay is a system of images, therefore, reprojecting modern problems and conditions on to Greek tragedy—or, looked at from a different standpoint, a projection of these same problems and conditions on to Wagner's musical drama. The 'art-work of the future' finds legitimation and authentication in a reversion to the past and in the demonstration that, at bottom, it already existed. The final lines of Nietzsche's lecture on *Das griechische Musikdrama* anticipate and encapsulate the later *Geburt der Tragödie*, with its tendency to 'nullify' history:

Many arts in utmost activity and yet a *single* work of art—that is the antique music drama. But anyone who, on seeing it, is reminded of the ideal of him who would reform art today will also have to say to himself that that art-work of the future is certainly not a brilliant but deceptive mirage: what hopes we place in the future were already a reality—more than two thousand years in the past.[27]

[26] Ibid. 56; English trans., p. 59.
[27] Ibid. 531–2.

# III

## WAGNER'S DRAMATIC POETRY

The following comments on Wagner's dramatic poetry are concerned chiefly, but not, of course, exclusively, with those aspects of his works which have been examined in the preceding chapters in the context of his theoretical pronouncements. So that the following chapters may be read independently of the theoretical sections, without the need for constant turning back and forth, a brief summary of the relevant theoretical positions will be given at the appropriate point in the text. The occasional repetition of earlier formulations and quotations is unavoidable, but this ought not to disturb the Wagner-lover, accustomed as he (or she) is to the recapitulations of the *Ring*, a process which, far from harming the overall context, helps to throw light on its individual parts.

# 13

# Wagner's Début as an Operatic Composer:
## *Die Feen*

Entsage deinem Erdenreich,
mein Feenland beherrsche jetzt!

Renounce thy earthly realm
And rule my faery land!

*Die Feen*, Act III.

Wagner's first attempt to write an opera—apart from a pastoral opera about which we know nothing except that it was begun in 1830 and quickly abandoned—dates from 1832, the year of Goethe's death. In his *Autobiographical Sketch* (1843) he describes 'an opera text of tragic purport: *Die Hochzeit*. I no longer remember where I found the medieval subject-matter.' (i. 8.) (Later, in *Mein Leben*, he claimed that he had discovered it in Johann Gustav Büsching's *Ritterzeit und Ritterwesen*, published in Leipzig in 1823: *ML*, p. 75, English trans., p. 66.) 'A frenzied lover climbs up to the bedroom window of his friend's fiancée, where she is waiting for his friend; she struggles with the madman and hurls him into the courtyard below, where, his body shattered, he breathes his last. At his funeral his friend's fiancée utters a terrible cry and sinks lifeless upon the corpse.' (i. 8–9.) In *Mein Leben*, where Wagner recounts the story in greater detail, he describes it as 'the blackest nocturnal epic', written under the spell of E. T. A. Hoffmann and influenced by his 'pet musical mysticism' (*ML*, p. 75; English trans., pp. 67–8). The work was executed 'in black on black, with disdain for any ray of light and in particular for all operatic embellishments' (*ML*, p. 76; English trans., p. 68). This remark hints at two motives—one conceptual, the other formal—which were later to be of primary importance for Wagner's musico-dramatic œuvre: first, his rejection of opulent operatic conventions, and, second, his Romantic affinity with the night, a sympathy which was to influence not only his draft for *Die Bergwerke zu Falun* (sketched a decade later and directly inspired by E. T. A. Hoffmann) but more especially, of course, that great hymn to the night, *Tristan und Isolde*.

In writing *Die Hochzeit* (the completed libretto of which was unfortunately destroyed by the composer, although those parts which had already been set to music have survived), Wagner had renounced 'all operatic embellishments and treated the material in the darkest vein', to quote from his autobiography (*ML*, p. 81; English trans., p. 72). *Die Feen*, by contrast—a 'Romantic opera in three acts', written in 1833–4, and his first complete surviving work for the stage—was 'festooned . . . with the most manifold variety' (*ML*, p. 81; English trans., p. 72). Of the libretto, Wagner was to write in *Mein Leben* that he had been almost intentionally careless about the 'poetic diction and the verses themselves', since he was no longer anxious to make a name for himself as a poet, as had previously been the case. 'I had really become a "musician" and a "composer" and wanted simply to write a decent libretto, for I now realized nobody else could do this for me, inasmuch as an opera book is something unique unto itself and cannot be easily brought off by poets and literati.' (*ML*, p. 81; English trans., p. 72.) The terms enclosed in quotation marks are clearly used with ironic intent. Certainly, it was to be one of the basic aims of his later reform of the music theatre to overcome the dualism of text and music in opera, elevating the text to a level where it was no longer a mere means to the end of the music, and turning the 'composer' into a dramatist. In the 'art-work of the future', poetry and music were intended to be equally committed to upholding the aim of drama. According to Wagner, *Die Feen* was still a long way short of this ideal.

As with *Die Hochzeit*, *Die Feen* bears signs of the influence of E. T. A. Hoffmann, whose narrative 'The Poet and the Composer' from the *Serapionsbrüder* cycle was familiar to Wagner, as we have already noted, from the 1820s. In this imaginary dialogue Hoffmann advances his ideal of a 'musical drama' or 'Romantic opera' in which 'the music' would spring 'directly from the poem as a necessary product of the same'. These lines are placed in the mouth of the fictional composer Ludwig, who goes on to argue that the ten fairy-tale plays or *fiabe dramatiche* of Carlo Gozzi (1720–1806) would be ideal material for this kind of opera. In adapting Gozzi's fairy-tale drama *La donna serpente* (a work first performed in Venice in 1762), Wagner was clearly following Hoffmann's lead, and, in doing so, he was responsible for initiating a long series of Gozzi operas stretching down to the present century: suffice it to mention the *Turandot* operas of Busoni and Puccini, Prokofiev's *The Love for Three Oranges*, and Henze's *König Hirsch*. *La donna serpente* returned to the operatic stage in 1932 in an adaptation by the Italian composer Alfredo Casella, and two years later Gozzi himself became the main character in the opera *Die Familie Gozzi* by the pianist Wilhelm Kempff. Nor should we forget the Strauss/Hofmannsthal *Frau ohne Schatten*, which, although not a direct reworking of a Gozzi original, shares the same oriental atmosphere and contains several motifs and even a number of individual names taken over from the Italian poet's *fiabe dramatiche*.

Carlo Gozzi has gone down in the history of the theatre as an energetic advocate of *commedia dell'arte*, a brand of improvised comedy which he himself conserved and reformed. His antithesis—and the object of a number of violent attacks on his part—was Carlo Goldoni, who, believing that *commedia dell'arte* had become ossified through the constant repetition of the same schematic situations, sought to transform the genre by making it 'literary', in other words, by turning it into a realistic comedy of characters, with a strictly fixed text. Gozzi, by contrast, retained its essentially improvisatory character, breathing new life into it by adding a fantastical fairy-tale element and by introducing themes and motifs, in particular from *The Thousand and One Nights* and the *Cunto di li cunti*, the latter a collection of fairy-tales by Giambattista Basile. Gozzi's fairy-tales are, on the whole, examples of fixed literary form, but those of his scenes which include characters from the *commedia dell'arte* are merely sketched out as a basic scenario, thus allowing the characters greater or lesser scope for improvisation.

Gozzi's fairy-tale comedies were initially so successful that his rival, Goldoni, was forced to leave Venice and make his home in Paris, but they soon lost their appeal in Italy, enjoying their greatest and most influential success in Germany, not least through Schiller's adaptation of *Turandot* and, more especially, through the enthusiastic reception of the Romantics, who compared Gozzi favourably with Shakespeare. Wagner was probably introduced to Gozzi's writings by his erudite uncle and mentor Adolf Wagner, who had not only been personally acquainted with E. T. A. Hoffmann and Tieck, but had corresponded with Jean Paul and, in his youth, had even been introduced to Schiller. He was also responsible for the German translation of Gozzi's *Il corvo*. Throughout his life Wagner continued to enjoy reading Gozzi, as Cosima's *Diaries* make plain. In the course of a conversation with her on 13 October 1872 he expressly sided with Gozzi against Goldoni, although he was undoubtedly wrong to claim that Gozzi, unlike Goldoni, 'shared all the instinct of the people against the literary outlook': rather the opposite was the case, inasmuch as the aristocratic Gozzi felt only contempt for the mob, whereas Goldoni sought to enhance the status of his characters from the lower classes.

In his 'Letter to an Actor', written in 1872, Wagner praised Gozzi for having allowed so much scope for improvisation in his fairy-tale dramas. But in adapting *La donna serpente* for his own dramatic purposes, he either cut the improvisation scenes or else wrote them out in full. He could scarcely have done otherwise, of course. The *commedia dell'arte* masks are replaced by other, more or less comic, characters who, in keeping with the relocation of the half oriental, half Venetian fairy-tale world of masks in a Nordic setting, bear curious names such as Gunther and Gernot. The heroes of the *Nibelungenlied* are reduced to the role of comic servants. The irruption of comedy into the world of sublime tragedy, which is so typical of Gozzi's fairy-tale plays, and the predominance of grotesque elements which so fascinated the Romantics have been considerably reduced in Wagner's reworking of the text, although the interplay of tragic and comic scenes has substantially been retained.

By and large, Wagner has also retained the plot of Gozzi's tragicomedy. The most important difference is in the change to the theme of transformation, a change of which Wagner was particularly proud. In *A Communication to my Friends* (1851) he wrote: ' A fairy who renounces immortality in order to possess the man she loves can become mortal only if certain harsh conditions are met; failure to do so on the part of her earthly lover threatens her with the harshest of fates.' The ordeal—to which we shall return in due course—proves, however, to be too much for her lover. Whereas Gozzi transformed the fairy into a serpent, a shape from which she can be freed only by her lover's kiss, Wagner altered the ending so that 'the fairy is turned to stone, but the spell on her is broken by her lover's wistful singing' (iv. 252–3).

The transformation of an individual into stone or into a statue is an ancient mythical motif. One thinks, for example, of Lot's wife in the Bible, who is turned into a pillar of salt, or of the Grecian Niobe, whose grief at her children's murder causes her to turn to stone. The motif is found in the fairy-tales of every nation. It also recurs both in *Il corvo*, a work which Wagner valued very highly and which was summarized in detail in E. T. A. Hoffmann's 'The Poet and the Composer', and in Gozzi's *L'angellino belverde*, where, one after another, the characters are turned into marble statues before reverting back to their normal shapes. In short, Wagner's reworking of *La donna serpente* as *Die Feen* involved replacing one motif from Gozzi with another.

The meaning which Wagner has given to this motif suggests other sources, of course. The idea of restoring life to a statue by means of music is strikingly reminiscent of the ending of *The Winter's Tale*, with which Wagner was undoubtedly familiar. Here Leontes sees what he believes to be a statue of his wife Hermione—in reality, it is Hermione herself—turned back into her original human form to the sound of musical accompaniment. The motif is primarily associated with the classical myth of the sculptor Pygmalion, who falls so deeply in love with one of his statues that Venus gives life to it. From the eighteenth century onwards, this motif came to be regarded more and more as a symbol of the artist's existence, emblematic of his ability to breathe life into dead and artificial forms through the ardour of his love. Gozzi's original ideas, Shakespeare's *The Winter's Tale*, and the Pygmalion myth are linked at the end of *Die Feen* with the legend of Orpheus, whose singing not only tamed the savage beasts but could also move the very stones and trees. It is a deeply symbolic synthesis. Arindal is transformed into an artist who uses the power of music to break the spell which has turned his lover into a statue. (Musico-dramatically, this scene is based on the one in Hades in Gluck's *Orfeo ed Euridice*, in which the hero moves the unfeeling Furies by dint of his singing and playing.)

> Ja, ich besitze Götterkraft!
> Ich kenne ja der holden Töne Macht,
> der Gottheit, die der Sterbliche besitzt!
> Du, heiße Liebe, Sehnsucht und Verlangen,
> Entzaubert denn in Tönen diesen Stein!        (xi. 56–7.)
>
> Yes, I am strong as any god,
> I know sweet music's mighty power,
> The godhood which the mortal owns:
> Come, ardent love, desire and yearning,
> Break the spell that binds this stone.

The idea of a being from the spirit world who longs to become human and who is ready to sacrifice his or her mortality for the sake of human love, together with the motif of a tragic conflict between the spirit world and the world of humans, are central themes in many Romantic operas, ranging from E. T. A. Hoffmann's *Undine*, first performed in 1816, to Wagner's *Lohengrin*, premièred in 1850. Heinrich Marschner's operas *Der Vampyr* (1828) and *Hans Heiling* (1833) belong to the same tradition. The imposition of an almost unrealizable injunction to test the love of a mortal who is bound to a figure from the spirit world is a theme shared by three of Wagner's Romantic operas, namely, *Die Feen, Der fliegende Holländer*, and *Lohengrin*. In the case of *Die Feen* and *Lohengrin*, the test revolves around a forbidden question: the human lover must not seek to uncover the secret of the other-worldly being who has entered his or her realm. This, too, is a classical motif, as Wagner knew well: the examples of Zeus and Semele, and Amor and Psyche spring to mind here. In Gozzi's *La donna serpente* Farruscad offends against the decree by searching his wife's boudoir, while, in Wagner's case, Arindal—like Elsa in *Lohengrin*—importunes his lover 'to say who she is and whence she comes' (xi. 9).

According to Wagner's own account in *Mein Leben*, the fairy Ada has to subject her human lover to the sternest tests (the forbidden question is only one among several), 'by the mastering of which he alone can free her from the immortal world of the fairies and permit her to share his mortal destiny as a loving woman' (*ML*, p. 80; English trans., p. 71). This motif is strikingly reminiscent not only of *Undine* but also of an opera written in our own century, the above-mentioned *Die Frau ohne Schatten* by Hugo von Hofmannsthal and Richard Strauss. Hofmannsthal is known to have studied Wagner's music dramas intensively while working on the libretto to *Die Frau ohne Schatten*, and there is little doubt that *Die Feen* has left its mark on the later work in more than one respect, even if the numerous thematic parallels between the two operas—from the original animal shape of the fairy child brought down by her future human husband in the course of a hunt, to the idea of a test, and, finally, the statue motif—could be explained by the fact that both works derive from a common source. Strauss was certainly familiar with *Die Feen*, since it was as a young kapellmeister that he had prepared the first performances of the opera in Munich in 1888. He was deeply offended when he was then passed over and his superior, Franz Fischer, was asked to conduct the première. The production remained in the Munich Court Theatre repertoire for many years. (In 1895 the part of Ada was sung by Pauline de Ahna, who had become Strauss's wife in the September of the previous year.)

A comparison between *Die Feen* and Gozzi's *La donna serpente* shows to what extent the great poetical and musical impressions of his youth had encouraged Wagner to transform many of the situations that he found in his source. Shakespeare's influence is discernible not only in the parallel with the final act of *The Winter's Tale* but in several reminiscences of *A Midsummer Night's Dream*. Arindal's mad scene in Act II (for which there is no direct precedent in Gozzi) recalls *King Lear*, while Weber's *Oberon* has left its mark on many details of the work, not only musically but also poetically, including the appearance of the King of the Fairies at the end of the opera. The trial scene in the final act, with its 'chorus of iron men', is unmistakably inspired by the final trial of Tamino and Pamina. But there are other traces of *Die Zauberflöte* in *Die Feen*: the *buffo* scene between Drolla and Gernot in Act II is modelled on the duet between Papageno and Papagena, but it is impossible not to be reminded, too, of Pedrillo and Blonde in *Die Entführung aus dem Serail*, or Sherasmin and Fatima in Weber's *Oberon*. Even more important are the influences which Wagner himself admitted, namely, those of Beethoven—Ada's great *scena* and aria in Act II are clearly based on Leonore's 'Ha! Abscheulicher'—and, above all, Weber and Marschner, whose Romantic operas are the real inspiration behind both the words and music of *Die Feen*.

However numerous the reminiscences of Wagner's musical models in *Die Feen*, they go far beyond the mere epigonic repetition of tried and tested formulas, and, as with his next opera, *Das Liebesverbot*, not only hint at but even anticipate his more mature works. The rising semiquaver figure in the introductory section of the Overture looks ahead to *A Faust Overture*, perhaps Wagner's most important purely instrumental piece, and—to cite only one more surprising example—the horn-calls at the beginning of Arindal's mad scene, imitating the sound of barking dogs, anticipate Sieglinde's delirious vision of a baying pack in Act II of *Die Walküre*.

*Die Feen* is the only one of Wagner's thirteen operas not to be performed during his lifetime. When he began his practical career in the theatre in 1833 as chorus-master in Würzburg (where his brother was already engaged as tenor), he had already completed work on the libretto of the opera. Significantly, perhaps, it was while he was on his way to Würzburg that he interrupted his journey in Bamberg and, in his own words, 'recalled Hoffmann's stay in this place and how it had led to the writing of his tales' (*ML*, p. 81; English trans., p. 73), an indication of the extent to which Wagner was still under the spell of Romantic poetry at this time. He worked away on the score of *Die Feen* during his months in Würzburg—the full score was completed on 6 January 1834—and even planned a concert performance of the Overture and two vocal numbers from the work. (The performance appears not to have taken place: see *WWV*, p. 118.)

Following his return to his home town of Leipzig at the beginning of 1834, Wagner hoped to persuade the local theatre to stage a production of his first completed opera. Although the management agreed to consider the work, the date on which rehearsals were due to begin was repeatedly postponed, until finally the project was abandoned altogether. In the course of negotiations with the theatre, Wagner was persuaded to provide the work with spoken dialogue in the style of an *opéra comique*. These sections of dialogue are limited to the comic scenes—which in Gozzi's original were largely improvised—and they follow the Italian source much more closely than the accompanied recitatives. The coarsely comical and parodistic elements of the work are shown off to much greater advantage in this early reworking of the piece.

But *Die Feen* reached the stage neither in this form nor any other, an omission attributable not least to the fact that Wagner had already abandoned interest in the opera shortly after completing work on the score. 'But beginning the composition of *Das Liebesverbot* put me in a frame of mind in which I soon lost interest in the older work', Wagner later wrote in *Mein Leben* (*ML*, p. 104; English trans., p. 96). This new frame of mind finds unequivocal expression in Wagner's earliest theoretical essays, 'German Opera' and 'Pasticcio', both of which date from 1834. They are evidence of the composer's brusque renunciation of German Romantic opera, and his espousal of the Italian and French tradition. His earlier idol, Weber, is now contemptuously dismissed, particular opprobrium being reserved for the very opera to which he owed so much, not only in the past but also in the future, *Euryanthe*.

Wagner's aesthetic volte-face is closely bound up with his conversion to the Young German movement, a conversion which he probably owed to the movement's principal spokesman, Heinrich Laube, a family friend of some years' standing, whose journal, the *Zeitung für die elegante Welt*, had published his earliest essay, 'German Opera'. 'We must seize the opportunity offered by the present age and seek to develop its novel forms in all their purity', Wagner proclaims at the end of this essay. This is nothing less than a formal renunciation of the Romantic mysticism which he had embraced in *Die Feen*, and which finds expression in the way in which Arindal and Ada are transported to the faerie realm at the end of the opera, a significant deviation from Gozzi's *La donna serpente*, where Ferruscad and Cherestani share a common, mortal fate.

This flight from reality was now to be replaced by a living involvement in contemporary events and the praise of sensuality. It was in this spirit that Wagner conceived *Das Liebesverbot*, the text of which he completed in the same year (1834) that he put the finishing touches to *Die Feen*. If one were to compare the themes of his first two operas, Wagner wrote in *A Communication to my Friends*, one would see

that there existed within me the potential for developing in either of two fundamentally different directions: the deadly seriousness of my basic sentient self was countered [in *Das Liebesverbot*] by a lively inclination towards a wild and sensuous impetuousness, a defiant exuberance, which seemed in the liveliest contrast to my former mood. This becomes entirely clear to me when I compare the musical execution of the two operas . . . Anyone who were to compare this composition with that of *Die Feen* would be at a loss to explain how so striking a change of direction could have been achieved in so short a space of time. (iv. 255–6.)

Of course, Wagner has exaggerated this change of direction somewhat. Just as the influence of Italian opera, and especially of Rossini, can be felt at various points in *Die Feen*, so the composer of *Das Liebesverbot*—unlike the author of the derogatory essay on German opera—certainly did not deny the influence of Weber in several of its scenes.

Although Wagner later reverted to the tradition of Romantic opera with *Der fliegende Holländer*, dismissing as a complete aberration his enthusiasm for both Italian and French opera and for the world of ideas of the Young German movement, he consistently refused, right up until the end of his life, to agree to a performance of *Die Feen*, or even to consent to the publication of the work. Accordingly, he did not include the libretto in the edition of his *Collected Writings* which he superintended during the 1870s, although he did read parts of the work to a circle of friends a year before his death. Not until 1888, two years after the death of Ludwig II, to whom Wagner had donated the full score of the opera in 1865, did the work receive its first performance in the Court and National Theatre in Munich, a performance which took place against the wishes of Cosima Wagner, but since she did not possess the performing-rights to her late husband's first two operas, her claim that Wagner had never wanted the work to be staged went unheard. The première, produced by Karl Brulliot and with 'decorative arrangements, stage machinery, and lighting' by Karl Lautenschläger, was a spectacular success, not least because of its unprecedented lavishness, and the production remained in the repertoire until 1899. According to Theodor Helm's review of the first performance,

the final apotheosis of *Die Feen* in Munich struck us as the most beautiful and magical sight we have ever witnessed in this genre, indeed, it is impossible to describe the enchanting effect of the sculptural groups rising up to dizzying heights, the fantastical calyxes, seashells, and gemstone crystals opening up on every side, and, finally, the electric lighting that was used on such a massive scale.[1]

A second production of *Die Feen* was mounted at the Prinzregenten-theater in 1910, when it was conducted by Felix Mottl and given as part of the Munich Festival. On this occasion, however, the work proved a clear failure. Since then the number of productions can be counted on the fingers of one hand. Suffice it to mention only one of the most notable, an interpretation first seen at the Wuppertal Opera in 1981, when Friedrich Meyer-Oertel staged the work from an ironic perspective, seeing the Romantic fairy-tale world as an oneiric product of the nineteenth century. The opera was made to resonate with allusions to present-day reality, and seen as the projection of a society which seeks refuge from life's demands in a world of empty illusion. Thus the anti-Romantic stance which Wagner had temporarily adopted under the influence of the Young German movement was transferred back, so to speak, to his earliest completed opera. Romantic opera was called into question by means of its own conventions.

[1] Quoted in Richard Wagner, *Die Feen*, ed. Michael von Soden and Andreas Loesch (Frankfurt, 1983), 214–15. My interpretation of *Die Feen* is indebted in a number of respects to the documentation contained in this volume.

# 14

## The Transformations of Ahasuerus:
## *Der fliegende Holländer* and his Metamorphoses

> The world is the Wandering Jew. Death is nothingness but
> nothingness is impossible. 'Oh never more to die', as the song goes.
>
> Camille Desmoulins in Büchner's *Dantons Tod* (iii. 7).

In writing *Das Liebesverbot*, Wagner had brusquely turned his back on the tradition of German Romantic opera. Not only this work but his subsequent plans, from *Die hohe Braut* and *Männerlist größer als Frauenlist* (of which only the libretti were completed) to *Rienzi*, all attest to his predilection for the Italian and French type of opera. Not until 1840–1 did he return to Romantic opera with *Der fliegende Holländer*, where, as with *Die Hochzeit*, he renounced all those 'operatic embellishments' with which he had 'festooned' his operas from *Die Feen* to *Rienzi* (*ML*, p. 81; English trans., p. 72). '*Dutchman* disappointed many who awaited another *Rienzi*', Robert Gutman writes. 'Their objections were similar to those of the wealthy host in Strauss's *Ariadne auf Naxos*, displeased that his magnificently appointed mansion be the scene of an opera set on a desert island.'[1]

In his autobiographical essay, *A Communication to my Friends*, written in 1851, Wagner characterizes 'Senta's Ballad in the second act' as the corner-stone and 'thematic seed of all the music in the opera':

it was the poetically condensed image of the whole drama . . . and when I had to find a title for the finished work I was strongly tempted to call it a 'dramatic ballad'. When I eventually came to the composition, the thematic image I had already conceived spread out quite involuntarily over the entire drama in a complete, unbroken web; all that was left for me to do was to allow the various thematic germs contained in the ballad to develop to the full, each in its own direction, and all the principal features of the text were arrayed before me in specific thematic shapes of their own making. (iv. 323.)

This statement has been accepted at face value far too often. From the point of view of the work's genesis, however, it is untenable, as Carl Dahlhaus has shown in his analysis of the work's musical syntax. There can be no question, Dahlhaus argues, of a clearly contoured motivic

---

[1] Robert W. Gutman, *Richard Wagner: The Man, his Mind and his Music* (London and New York, 1968), 89.

complex spreading out over the entire work: at best, the Ballad contains 'a vague, though pervasive, poetico-musical mood'. And he goes on to point out, not without justification, that Wagner judged the musical structure of his early work from the standpoint of a fully developed leitmotivic technique, a technique for which there is very little evidence in his handling of the motives of reminiscence which are found in *Der fliegende Holländer*, where their use is still interpolatory rather than structurally determinative.[2]

In fact, Senta's Ballad contains only two thematic motives from the opera.[3] How little it corresponds, from a musical point of view, with Wagner's idea of a motivic cell is clear from the fact that, right up until the end of his life, Wagner planned to revise the score of the work, a revision whose starting-point was clearly to be the Ballad itself. The beginning of the Ballad, in particular, he told Cosima on 17 October 1878, was 'quite properly like a folk-song, but not characteristic of *Der Holländer*'. Indeed, a sketch exists from 1864–5 containing a substantially new melody for the first four lines of the Ballad[4]—clear evidence that the composer's claim that, genetically and structurally, the Ballad was the germ of the entire work belongs in the realm of Wagnerian fantasy—yet another of the 'myths of creation' with which he sought to account for the genesis of his various works.

But even if Wagner's claim appears invalid as far as the musical structure of his first 'Romantic opera' is concerned, it proves to be correct in terms of the work's poetical design: the Ballad is indeed 'the poetically condensed image of the entire drama'. It belongs to a genre which, thanks to its traditional poetic function, was especially suited to such an approach. Ballads, according to Hegel in his *Ästhetik*, 'comprise . . . the entirety of a complete event. It is true that they can sketch a picture of this event in its most prominent features, but at the same time they can bring out everywhere more fully, yet more concentratedly and fervently, both the depth of the heart which is interwoven with the event throughout and also the emotional tone of lament, melancholy, mourning, joy, etc.'[5] It is difficult to imagine a more telling description of Senta's Ballad.

---

[2] Carl Dahlhaus, *Richard Wagners Musikdramen* (Velber, 1971), 22–3; translated into English by Mary Whittall as *Richard Wagner's Music Dramas* (Cambridge, 1979), 18.

[3] Isolde Vetter, 'Der "Ahasverus des Ozeans"—musikalisch unerlöst? Der fliegende Holländer und seine Revisionen', in *Die Programmhefte der Bayreuther Festspiele 1979*, ii. '*Der fliegende Holländer*', 70–9, including English trans., pp. 27–33. The German text is reprinted in Richard Wagner, *Der fliegende Holländer: Texte, Materialien, Kommentare*, ed. Attila Csampai and Dietmar Holland (Reinbek, 1982), 116–29.

[4] The 1864 sketch is reproduced and transcribed in Isolde Vetter's article, 'Der "Ahasverus des Ozeans"', p. 76, and described in *WWV*, p. 240.

[5] G. W. F. Hegel, *Ästhetik*. ed. Friedrich Bassenge (Berlin, 1955), 1004; translated into English by T. M. Knox as *Aesthetics: Lectures on Fine Art* (Oxford, 1975), 1117.

Wagner's attempt to invest the macrocosm of an entire libretto with a sense of thematic unity derived from the microcosm of an interpolated poem—a kind of 'play within a play'—is evidence of a clear rejection of the additive form of 'number opera'. Although he had not yet achieved a rigorously consistent thematic structuring throughout the entire work, he was nevertheless aware from the very first that the mythic opera he was attempting to write required a new law of musical structure. 'From the outset I had to abandon the modern arrangement of dividing the work into arias, duets, finales, etc., and instead relate the legend in a single breath, just as a good poem should be', he wrote to Ferdinand Heine in early August 1843.[6]

The initial impulse to write *Der fliegende Holländer* came, as we know, from Heinrich Heine's *Aus den Memoiren des Herren von Schnabelewopski* (1834), with its parodistic description of a stage play about the Flying Dutchman. (Heine may have been thinking of Edward Fitzball's melodrama, *The Flying Dutchman; or The Phantom Ship.*[7]) Wagner probably read Heine's short story in Riga in 1837–8, since which date the legend of the Flying Dutchman refused to leave him in peace, assuming increasingly concrete poetic form in his imagination during a sea voyage from Riga to London in 1839. In his *Autobiographical Sketch* of 1843 he reports: 'Sailing between the Norwegian skerries made a wonderful impression on my imagination; the legend of the Flying Dutchman, as confirmed for me on the lips of the sailors, took on a definite, individual colouring in my mind such as only my adventures at sea could inspire.' (i. 13–14.)

The tale of the Flying Dutchman is a typically modern legend which did not achieve definitive form until the nineteenth century. Various accounts of captains ensnared by the Devil in consequence of their foolhardy hubris—the pact motif familiar from *Faust*—or condemned to sail the seas for all eternity, bringing misfortune to every ship they encounter, are found among seafaring nations from the seventeenth century onwards. Superstitious imaginations were fired more especially by floating wrecks, which sailors beset by the perils of the sea believed were phantom ships presaging disaster. Wagner himself saw evidence of

---

[6] Richard Wagner, *Sämtliche Briefe*, ed. Gertrud Strobel and Werner Wolf (Leipzig, 1970), ii. 314; English trans. from *Selected Letters of Richard Wagner*, ed. Stewart Spencer and Barry Millington (London, 1987), 114–15.

[7] It is doubtful whether Heine knew Kitzball at first hand. Fitzball's *The Flying Dutchman* opened at the Adelphi Theatre on 4 Dec. 1826 and was last performed there (prior to its 1829 revival) on 7 Apr. 1827. Heine did not arrive in London until 14 Apr. 1827. See William Ashton Ellis, 'From Fitzball to Wagner: A "Flying Dutchman" Fallacy', *The Meister*, 5 (1892) 4–21. Ashton Ellis doubts whether Heine had read Fitzball's play: 'A page or two, skimmed at random from the play, sufficed to convince me of the extreme improbability that Heine, or any one else, should ever have got *any* idea from such a jumble of burlesque and rant other than that of assaulting its author.' See also Fritz Mende, *Heinrich Heine: Chronik seines Lebens und Werkes* (Berlin, 1970), 60.

this superstition in 1839 in the course of his hazardous crossing from Pillau to London.

This widespread motif is regularly associated with the historical background of trade with the Dutch East Indies and with the geographical setting of the Cape of Good Hope, which was discovered in 1497 (thus providing students of the legend's history with a *terminus post quem*). The vow sworn by Captain van der Decken (one of the Dutchman's names) to sail round the Cape at any cost was transformed by popular tradition into a symbol of that hubristic spirit of discovery which transgressed the boundaries of knowledge and experience laid down by the Bible and by the Church. The Flying Dutchman is the maritime equivalent of Faust. It is impossible not to be reminded here of the Prologue to Marlowe's *Tragicall History of D. Faustus*, first published in 1604, in which the Chorus comments on Faust's presumptuous quest for knowledge:

> His waxen wings did mount above his reach,
> And melting, heavens conspir'd his over-throw.

And after Faustus has fallen into the Devil's clutches, the Chorus, in the final lines of the drama, exhorts the wise

> Onely to wonder at unlawfull things,
> Whose deepnesse doth intice such forward wits,
> To practise more then heavenly power permits.

These lines are as true of the Flying Dutchman as they are of Marlowe's Faustus. Even by the middle of the sixteenth century Vasco da Gama's rounding of the Cape of Good Hope in 1497 was being demonized and mythologized by historians such as Gaspar Correia (*c.*1550) and, more particularly, by Luis de Camoëns, whose *Os Luciades*, written in 1572, portrays the Spirit of the Cape as threatening to wreak vengeance on its discoverer for wresting its secret from it.

Literary adaptations of the legends dealing with the Flying Dutchman and his phantom ship are not found until the end of the eighteenth century. By and large they ignore what were originally the religious implications of the Captain's act of titanic defiance. The best-known poetic reworkings of the material are Coleridge's ballad, *The Rime of the Ancient Mariner*, first published in 1798, Wilhelm Hauff's 'Geschichte von dem Gespensterschiff' (from his 1826 cycle of oriental fairy-tales, *Die Karawane*) and 'Die Höhle von Steenfoll' (from the cycle *Das Wirtshaus im Spessart*), together with Captain Marryat's *The Phantom Ship* (1839), and, finally, the parodistic variant of the Dutchman theme in Heine's short story mentioned above.

Long condemned to an oral existence, the legend suddenly entered upon literary life during the so-called *Vormärz*, the period in German history between 1815 and the March Revolution of 1848. Clearly, the theme struck a topical note. But the most typical feature of these literary reworkings was their affinity with the legend of Ahasuerus, one of the great symbolic figures of the age. Like Hamlet, Faust, and Don Juan, Ahasuerus—the Wandering Jew—is one of those recurrent representatives of the mood of *Weltschmerz* or world-weariness which could be described as the underlying mood of the age and which is comparable with the *Empfindsamkeit* or *sensibilité* of the second half of the eighteenth century. In his novel *Epigonen*, first published in 1836, Karl Immermann places these words in Wilhelmi's mouth: 'Men of all ages have known misfortune in plenty, but it is the curse of the present generation to feel wretched through no particular suffering.' Existence as such becomes man's misfortune. In consequence, the yearning or unconscious illusion, felt by almost every individual, that he can somehow circumvent death is perverted to the point where it becomes the most terrifying of thoughts, namely, that he, like Ahasuerus or the Flying Dutchman, is damned to eternal life, 'the Wandering Jew of the ocean', to quote Heinrich Heine. In Pierre-Jean de Béranger's 1831 poem, *Le Juif errant* (translated into German by Adalbert von Chamisso in 1838), the curse of a life which will not end is strikingly symbolized by a refrain which, by dint of its constant repetition, reinforces the idea of perpetual existence:

> Je suis, je suis le Juif errant,
> Qu'un tourbillon toujours emporte. *(bis)*
> Sans vieillir, accablé de jours,
> La fin du monde est mon seul rêve.
> Chaque soir j'espère toujours;
> Mais toujours le soleil se lève.
>   Toujours, toujours, *(bis)*
> Tourne la terre où moi je cours,
> Toujours, toujours, toujours, toujours.

> I am, I am the Wandering Jew, I'm
> Borne along by the whirlwind of time, *(twice)*
> Stricken in years but ageing never,
> Dreaming aye of when the world ends.
> Each night I yearn these bonds to sever,
> But each new dawn new life portends.
>   Ever, ever, ever, ever *(twice)*
> Turns the earth in grim endeavour
> Ever, ever, ever, ever.

*Weltschmerz* is a form of anguish which does not need to have a specific cause, since it has a metaphysical basis. This is the 'breach in the world'—the German *Weltriß* was one of the most influential neologisms of the age—signifying the grievous breach in the very cause of creation. Individual pain is an embodiment of the pain inherent in the world itself, individual inner conflict an image of what Georg Büchner (born, coincidentally, in the same year as Wagner) refers to as the 'breach in creation'. By equating existence with suffering, Camille Desmoulins— one of the characters in Büchner's revolutionary drama, *Dantons Tod* (1835)—comes to the conclusion that, simply because it *exists*, the world is like the Wandering Jew, longing to die and to be engulfed in the peace of oblivion. But this annihilation is an ontological impossibility, as Danton points out: 'The accursèd argument: nothing that exists can cease to exist, something cannot become nothing. And I am something, more's the pity! Creation has spread itself so wide there is nowhere left empty. Everything swarms and seethes. The void has murdered itself, creation is its wound, we are its drops of blood, the world is the grave in which it rots.' (iii. 7.) A metaphysic of *Weltschmerz* illustrated by means of a nihilistic counter-mythology! The void—oblivion—bears the scars of being: all that exists is anguish. 'The stars prick the night like tears. There must be great grief in the eye that shed them', Danton says on the eve of his death (iv. 3). It is scarcely possible to say any longer whether it is the eye of God or the eye of oblivion: God and oblivion become as one, united in the pain of existence. The more man suffers pain, the sooner he will partake of mystic union with the God who is oblivion. 'We do not have too much suffering, we have too little, for it is through suffering that we attain to God', Büchner is believed to have said on his death-bed.

For all its ontological impossibility, oblivion remained an object of yearning: it was absolute 'peace'. Danton (alias Büchner) is a voluntaristic nihilist not an ontological one, and in this respect he is closely related to that quintessential philosopher of *Weltschmerz*, Arthur Schopenhauer, whose chief work, *Die Welt als Wille und Vorstellung*, ends with the word 'nothing'. This state of nothingness is nirvana, the state of peace from all desire and from the restless workings of the 'will'. It has often been asked, especially in recent years, whether Büchner had read Schopenhauer. In fact, Büchner is no more likely to have done so than the young Wagner, yet both of them were familiar with elements of his philosophy (as Wagner himself expressly claimed, following his introduction to *Die Welt als Wille und Vorstellung* in the autumn of 1854), a familiarity gained either through the unconscious and indirect assimilation of Schopenhauer's ideas, or else simply on the strength of their elective affinity in terms of all their sufferings.

'Peace' as the goal of voluntaristic nihilism is itself a Wagnerian concept. The Flying Dutchman longs to find this peace in love. Difficult though it is to imagine such an equation, the identification of love, death, and peace in oblivion is a further theme which links *Der fliegende Holländer* with Büchner's revolutionary drama, a work which, at first sight, must seem as far removed from Wagner's Romantic opera as is conceivably possible. 'I love you like the grave', Danton tells Julie in the opening scene. When she turns away in dismay, he explains: 'No, listen! It's said peace and the grave are as one. So, I lie in your lap and already I am underground. My sweet grave, your lips are my passing bells, your voice my death knell, your breast my mound of earth, your heart my coffin.'

Only one thing can lift the curse which weighs on the Dutchman—condemning him to eternal life—and that is a woman's pledge to be faithful unto death. It seems to be a condition which cannot be met. 'To hope is futile! Vain to dream of death!' The only hope left to the Dutchman is the end of the world, the Day of Judgement itself:

> Wann alle Toten aufersteh'n,
> dann werde ich in Nichts vergeh'n.
> Ihr Welten, endet euren Lauf!
> Ew'ge Vernichtung, nimm mich auf!     (i. 261.)
>
> And at the rising of the dead,
> the void will close about my head.
> You planets, you have run your course!
> Endless oblivion, I am yours!

Not 'redemption'—either through love or at the end of time, when all the dead rise up again—but 'oblivion' appears to be the Dutchman's fate, or so he believes in a moment of utter despair. He believes himself excluded from both salvation and damnation: he, alone of all men, will sink into 'oblivion'. His 'damnation' cannot be deferred to the 'Day of Judgement' but is something he must suffer even now, inasmuch as he is denied the salvation of death. What were originally religious ideas concerning death (as punishment for original sin), salvation (awakening to eternal life), and damnation (whether it be eternal death or the torments of hell after life on earth) are all turned on their head here.

In his opening monologue the Dutchman tells of the countless vain attempts he has made to end his life by force:

> Wie oft in Meeres tiefsten Schlund
> stürzt' ich voll Sehnsucht mich hinab:—
> doch ach! den Tod, ich fand ihn nicht!
> Da, wo der Schiffe furchtbar Grab,
> trieb *mein* Schiff ich zum Klippengrund:—
> doch ach! mein Grab, es schloß sich nicht!—
> Verhöhnend droht' ich dem Piraten,
> im wilden Kampfe hofft' ich Tod:
>
> .     .     .     .     .     .

Doch ach! des Meer's barbar'scher Sohn
schlägt bang' das Kreuz und flieht davon. —
Nirgends ein Grab! Niemals der Tod!      (i. 260–1.)

Engulf'd in ocean's deepest wave,
Oft have I long'd to find a grave;
But ah! a grave, I found it not!
I oft have blindly rush'd along,
To find my death sharp rocks among;
But ah! my death, I found it not.
And oft, the pirate boldly daring,
My death I've courted from the sword;

   .     .     .     .     .

Alas! the sea's rapacious son
But sign'd the cross and straight was gone!
Nowhere a grave! No way of death!

The same theme of repeated but futile attempts to put an end to life recurs in two ballads by Nikolaus Lenau, the *Weltschmerz* poet *par excellence*. In one of them, *Ahasver, der ewige Jude*, written in 1833, the Wandering Jew laments:

Ich stand, ein Bettler, weinend vor der Türe
Der Elemente, flehte um den Tod;
Doch ob ich auch den Hals mit Stricken schnürte,
Mein fester Leib erträgt des Odems Not.
Das Feuer und die Flut, die todesreichen,
Versagten das ersehnte Todesglück;
Ich sah die scheue Flamme rückwärts weichen,
Mit Ekel spie die Welle mich zurück.
War ich geklettert auf die Felsenmauer,
Wo nichts gedeiht als süßer Todesschauer,
Und rief ich weinend, wütend abgrundwärts:
»O Mutter Erde, dein verlorner Sohn!
Reiß mich zerschmetternd an dein steinern Herz!«
Der Zug der Erdentiefe sprach mir Hohn,
Sanft senkten mich die fluchgestärkten Lüfte,
Und lebend, rasend irrt ich durch die Klüfte.
»Tod!« rief ich, »Tod!« mich in die Erde krallend,
»Tod!« höhnte Klipp' an Klippe widerhallend.
Zu Bette stieg ich lüstern mit der Pest;
Ich habe sie umsonst ans Herz gepreßt.
Der Tod, der in des Tigers Rachen glüht,
Der zierlich in der giftgen Pflanze blüht,
Der schlängelnd auf dem Waldespfade kriecht,
Den Wandrer lauernd in die Ferse sticht,
Mich nahm er nicht!

I stood, a beggar, weeping at that gate
Where elemental forces promise death:

I tried to hang myself—defy my fate—
But sturdy limbs scarce felt the want of breath.
Both fire and flood, which often bring release,
Denied that happiness I sought in vain.
The flames recoil'd but left no sense of peace,
The floodtide spewed me out with grim disdain.
Tho' I might climb on beetling crag where naught
But death's sweet ecstasy were to be sought
And tho' I cried out, weeping at the smart,
'O mother earth, behold the prodigal!
Draw me, I beg you, to your stony heart!'
The earth made mock of me and caught my fall,
Curse-laden breezes, wafting me to earth,
Abandoned me to roam through barren lands.
'Death!' I cried and tore the earth with bloodied hands;
'Death' screamed the echo, mocking in its mirth.
I clasped the harlot death between my thighs—
The pox-infected whore ignored my sighs.
Death, which lurks in tiger's flashing maw, no less
Than belladonna's fatal loveliness,
Which worms its sinuous way through woodland glade
And lies in wait to bite the unwary, paid
No heed to me.

Elsewhere in the same poem we find Ahasuerus standing beside the bier
of a friend who has died prematurely and whose final resting-place he
longs to share:

O süßer Schlaf! O süßer Todesschlaf!
Könnt ich mich rastend in die Grube schmiegen!
Könnt ich wie *der* in deinen Armen liegen,
Den schon so früh dein milder Segen traf!
Den Staub nicht schütteln mehr vom müden Fuße!
Wie tief behaglich ist die Todesmuße!
Das Auge festverschlossen, ohne Tränen;
Die Brust so still, so flach und ohne Sehnen;
Die Lippen bleich, versunken, ohne Klage,
Verschwunden von der Stirn die bange Frage.

O gentle sleep, O gentle sleep of ages,
Could I find rest within that winding-sheet,
Could I but nestle in your arms, find sweet
Release like him whom early death assuages.
No longer shaking dust from weary limbs,
No longer subject to life's tedious whims,
His eye now firmly clos'd, wash'd free of tears,
His breast quite still'd, bereft of hopes and fears,
His uncomplaining lips are sunken now,
No anxious question clouds his tranquil brow.

The Ahasuerus myth was popular throughout the whole of Europe during the years when *Weltschmerz* was in vogue. Like every subject typical of its time, it was also adapted by writers of satire and parody bent on exposing the modish, posturing stance implied by such an attitude. Suffice it to mention here the 'Unterhaltungen des Satan und des ewigen Juden in Berlin' (1826) from Wilhelm Hauff's *Memoiren des Satan*. The Devil meets the Wandering Jew in Berlin's Tiergarten. His world-weary protestations are astonishingly reminiscent of the Flying Dutchman's monologue quoted above: 'O midnight! When, oh when, will your cooling shadows sink upon these burning eyes? When will the hour approach when the graves will ope, and space will be found for *one* who may then be granted rest?' He finally gets on Satan's nerves: '"To hell with you, you old grumbler!", I finally expostulated, annoyed at the eternal wanderer's lachrymose manner. "How dare you strike up such a poetic jeremiad? Believe me, you should count yourself lucky that you're so special. There's many a cheerful soul who's far worse off in a certain place than you are here on earth."'

In order to bring a little variety into the Wandering Jew's monotonous existence, Satan invites him to an 'aesthetic tea-party' at the home of an ageing spinster who, consumed by utter world-weariness, 'has the air of those melancholically sanctimonious nuns who, having bade farewell to the world with a broken heart, now devote the whole of their lives to a profoundly interesting *grande passion*'. (The extent to which Cosima Wagner had appropriated this attitude is clear from her published *Diaries*: for her, suffering had become a principle sustained by Schopenhauerian metaphysics.)

Motivated as they are by existential suffering, the suicide attempts by Lenau's Ahasuerus and Wagner's Flying Dutchman reflect the constant readiness of this world-weary age to shuffle off the mortal coil. Here, too, there are parallels with the age of *Empfindsamkeit* and with the suicide epidemic which followed in the wake of Goethe's *Die Leiden des Jungen Werther*. In 1839, in his book *Deutschlands jüngste Literatur- und Kulturepoche*, Hermann Marggraff described the contemporary craze for suicide in highly graphic terms:

For a time it was the pistol which was the order of the day with us, but now we have become more sophisticated and are no longer satisfied with shooting, hanging, drowning, and poisoning: more exquisite forms of death have been devised . . . A number of mystics have crucified themselves; unrequited lovers or young poets who were unsuccessful with their melodramas have, in this age of steam, choked themselves to death by inhaling coal fumes; Napoleonists have leapt to their deaths from the top of the column in the Place Vendôme; one girl swallowed sewing needles stuffed inside honey-cakes until her innards became a mass of incurable ulcers; a man in Birmingham crept inside a red-hot oven and burnt himself to a cinder; others chewed and swallowed glass; one ingenious suicide threw himself under the bone-crushing wheels of a heavily laden vehicle, a novel idea that was soon taken up by others; an Englishman hanged himself by decorating himself with candles and acting as a chandelier for the company he had invited to supper . . .

and so on. That this satirical account is no exaggeration is clear from the authentic reports of various suicide attempts made at this time, attempts which were as remarkable for their motivation as for the manner of their execution. The *Zeitgeist* clearly wanted to call it a day. It is against this background that we must see the death wish of Senta and the Flying Dutchman. Not only in literature but historically, too, there were many Sentas throughout the first half of the nineteenth century who would have liked to 'redeem' the man they loved by killing themselves. There is the famous case of Charlotte Stieglitz, who hoped that the shattering experience of her death would free her weak and sickly poet-husband from the writer's block from which he was suffering, and would set him on the road to literary creativity. (Her hopes proved ill-founded.) Theodor Mundt wrote a literary tribute to her in 1835, and the leading classical philologist August Boeckh compared her suicide with the myth of Alcestis, who went to her death so that her husband, Admetus, might live. The emotional egoism which not only Charlotte Stieglitz but society in general presupposed on the part of the husband is so typical of the age that we must beware of interpreting Senta's readiness to die as symptomatic of Wagner's own exploitative egoism as man and artist. (The tendency to interpret Wagner's music dramas—at all costs—in terms of his own personality is as deplorable as it is ineradicable, for all that the myth has long since been exploded in Wagnerian scholarship.) And Senta's penchant for hallucinations and somnambulistic trances, which strikes us today as merely 'operatic' and scarcely plausible from a psychological point of view, is entirely typical of its time, not only in literature but in real life, too. While the German Romantics played with the 'wondrous' in a wholly conscious way, turning it into the object of artistic experiment, that same element struck the period of restoration which followed as altogether hallucinatory. In other words, the materialization of the wondrous was in obvious contrast to the view of art held by the real Romantics, who were much closer to the Enlightenment than was long believed. From a historical point of view, *Der fliegende Holländer* is not so much a Romantic opera as an opera of the *Vormärz*.

Heine and Wagner were not the only writers to regard the legend of the Flying Dutchman as a variant of the Ahasuerus myth. In Levin Schücking's 1851 short story, *Die drei Freier*, the three suitors of the title are Ahasuerus, the Flying Dutchman, and the Wild Huntsman (another mythic figure denied the peace of the grave). The object of their courtship is a woman emancipated by her Young German ideals whom they attempt to convert to true womanhood. The Wild Hunt is also the subject of Heinrich Heine's *Atta Troll*, written in 1841 and published in its full and final form in 1847. One of the figures in the Hunt is Ahasuerus's female counterpart, Herodias, who, as we know, was to be reincarnated in *Parsifal* as Kundry: 'Herodias were you' (x. 346). What is not so well known is that the Wandering Jewess, Kundry—cursed to wander 'endlessly through life' (x. 360)—is by no means a pure invention of Wagner's. The idea that Herodias was condemned to a life of restless wandering was already familiar in the Middle Ages. (Ahasuerus and Herodias are both mirror images of John the Baptist, Jesus's favourite disciple, who, according to early Christian belief and legend, would not die until Christ's second coming.) This myth was taken up by Eugène Sue in his immensely successful novel, *Le Juif errant* (published in French in 1844–5 and immediately translated into German), a work which Wagner must have known. Here Herodias accompanies Ahasuerus on his restless wanderings through history, until, like Wagner's Kundry, she finally finds release. Yet another writer who gave a new interpretation to the medieval legendary motif was Karl Gutzkow, whose novel, *Die ewige Jüdin*, was first published in 1869.

There is no doubt that, in conceiving the character of Kundry, Wagner was indirectly influenced by Heine's *Atta Troll*. At the same time, it must be remembered that, throughout the nineteenth century, Herodias was often conflated with the figure of her daughter Salome. (One thinks, for example, of the versions by Heine and Mallarmé.) Similarly, Wagner's Kundry is a reincarnation of both Herodias and Salome. The 'she-devil' Herodias—Kundry is described as an 'arch-she-devil' in *Parsifal* (x. 345)—is the subject of the following strophes in *Atta Troll*:

> Auf dem glutenkranken Antlitz
> Lag des Morgenlandes Zauber,
> Auch die Kleider mahnten kostbar
> An Scheherezadens Märchen.
>
> Sanfte Lippen, wie Grenaten,
> Ein gebogenes Liliennäschen,
> Und die Glieder schlank und kühlig
> Wie die Palme der Oase.
>
> .     .     .     .     .
>
> Wirklich eine Fürstin war sie,
> War Judäas Königin,
> Des Herodes schönes Weib,
> Die des Täufers Haupt begehrt hat.
>
> Dieser Blutschuld halber ward sie
> Auch vermaledeit; als Nachtspuk

Muß sie bis zum jüngsten Tage
Reiten mit der wilden Jagd.

In den Händen trägt sie immer
Jene Schüssel mit dem Haupte
Des Johannes, und sie küßt es;
Ja, sie küßt das Haupt mit Inbrunst.

Denn sie liebte einst Johannem—
In der Bibel steht es nicht,
Doch im Volke lebt die Sage
Von Herodias' blutger Liebe—

Anders wär' ja unerklärlich
Das Gelüste jener Dame—
Wird ein Weib das Haupt begehren
Eines Manns, den sie nicht liebt?

On her glowing sickly features
Lay an oriental charm,
And her costly robes reminded
Of Scheherezade's sweet stories.

Soft her lips, just like pomegranates,
And her nose a bending lily,
And her members cool and slender
As the palms in the oasis.

.      .      .      .      .

And in truth she was a princess,
Was the queen of far Judæa,
Was the lovely wife of Herod,
Who the Baptist's head demanded.

For this deed of blood she also
Was accurs'd, and as a spectre
With the wild hunt must keep riding,
Even to the day of judgement.

In her hands she evermore
Bears the charger with the Baptist's
Head upon it, which she kisses,—
Yes, the head she kisses wildly.

For she once loved John the Baptist;
In the Bible 'tis not written,
Yet in popular tradition
Lives Herodias' bloody love.

Otherwise there's no explaining
That strange fancy of the lady,—
Would a woman ever ask for
That man's head for whom she cared not?[8]

[8] The translation of Heine's *Atta Troll* is by Edgar Alfred Bowring (London, 1872), 302–3.

Every reader will, of course, be reminded here of Oscar Wilde's *Salome*, first published (in French) in 1893; but Wilde's play was by no means the only version of the tale after Heine to give an erotic motivation to the relationship between Herodias/Salome and John the Baptist. The theme was extraordinarily popular, especially in France, during the whole of the second half of the nineteenth century, so much so that only the most important adaptations in literature and the visual arts can be mentioned here. (The popularity of the theme is further evidenced by Jules Laforgue's *Salomé*, a cynical parody of Flaubert's *Hérodias*, published posthumously in his *Moralités légendaires* of 1887.) One or more of these versions must undoubtedly have left its mark on the Kundry scenes in *Parsifal*, just as the latter were, in their turn, to influence the Herodias and Salome poems of such *fin de siècle* writers as Wilde and Villiers de l'Isle-Adam.

'Arch-she-devil, rose of hell! | Herodias were you, and what else?', Klingsor demands of Kundry (x. 345–6). The rose imagery is generally attributed to the influence of Baudelaire's *Les Fleurs du mal*, but, surprisingly perhaps, it is also found in Mallarmé's fragmentary dramatic poem, *Hérodiade*, and also in *Les Fleurs* (both written *c.*1864), where it has an important symbolic function, more especially in connection with the figure of Herodias:

> L'hyacinthe, le myrte à l'adorable éclair
> Et, pareille à la chair de la femme, la rose
> Cruelle, Hérodiade en fleur du jardin clair,
> Celle qu'un sang farouche et radieux arrose!

> The hyacinth, the myrtle with her flash of white
> And, like as any woman's flesh, the cruel rose,
> Herodias, the garden's blossoming delight,
> She in whose veins a wild candescent lifeblood flows!

It is the curse of Ahasuerus, as it is of Kundry/Herodias, to keep on committing the sin for which they were originally cursed. In Lenau's *Der ewige Jude*, written in 1839, one of the strophes runs as follows:

> Weh mir, ich kann des Bilds mich nicht entschlagen,
> Wie er um kurze Rast so flehend blickte,
> Der Todesmüde, Schmach- und Schmerzgeknickte,
> Muß ewig ihn von meiner Hütte jagen.

> Alas, that I might banish from my mind the sight
> Of one who begged to rest awhile and catch his breath,
> One whom, bowed down with shame and weary unto death,
> I must condemn for evermore to endless flight.

Just as Ahasuerus prevented Jesus from resting on the *via dolorosa* and struck him in order to hasten him on his way, so Kundry laughed at her

Saviour as he bore his cross. (This is a radical reversal of the message which forms the metaphysical and ethical core of *Parsifal*, namely, elemental compassion for those in pain: Parsifal's failure to show compassion constitutes the hero's tragic guilt.) This is why Kundry is condemned to repeat her 'accursèd laughter' with compulsive regularity, in addition to being compelled to keep on embodying the depravity of Herodias/Salome. The erotic frenzy which Parsifal's asceticism rouses in her is analogous to the frenzy which she felt when, as Herodias, she had demanded the head of John the Baptist. And it is just as futile now as it was then.

'Ahasuerus, the wandering Jew, is nothing but the personification of the whole Jewish race', Schopenhauer had written in his *Parerga und Paralipomena*.[9] It was the curse of this *'gens extorris'*, this 'John Lackland among the nations', to wander nomadically through history. In the nineteenth century a parallel was often drawn between the Ahasuerus myth and the homelessness of the Jewish nation, more especially with reference to the situation of Jewish writers. Both they and their contemporaries felt *Weltschmerz* to be their predestined role. Just as the Jew represented the quintessential *homo melancholicus* in the tradition of western melancholia, so 'inner conflict' became his specific distinguishing feature after 1815. There is a special affinity between him and the artist, who, more than anyone else, feels the Wandering Jew's rootlessness and the 'breach in creation' referred to above. All artists were Wandering Jews, Nietzsche was later to write in *Der Fall Wagner*.[10] Accordingly, Wagner was able to relate the Ahasuerus myth as much to himself as to the Jews. After all, his anti-Semitism is scarcely explicable without an awareness of this relationship between the artist and the Jew. On 21 June 1859 he wrote to Mathilde Wesendonck to tell her that he would have to beware of developing a passion for horses, since 'no horse was assigned to the Wandering Jew to accompany him on his wanderings'.[11] And, just as he saw himself reflected in the figure of Ahasuerus, so he undoubtedly saw himself in the Flying Dutchman and the Wanderer, who, he told Cosima on 23 January 1879, was 'a kind of Flying Dutchman'.

In his autobiographical apologia of 1851, *A Communication to my Friends*, Wagner interpreted the figure of the Flying Dutchman as a synthesis of Odysseus, Ahasuerus, and Christopher Columbus:

[9] Arthur Schopenhauer, *Sämtliche Werke*, ed. Arthur Hübscher (Wiesbaden, 1961), vi. 278; English trans. from E. F. J. Payne, *Parerga and Paralipomena* (Oxford, 1974), ii. 261.

[10] Friedrich Nietzsche, *Sämtliche Werke: Kritische Studienausgabe in 15 Bänden*, ed. Giorgio Colli and Mazzino Montinari (Munich, 1980), vi. 18; translated into English by Walter Kaufmann as 'The Case of Wagner', in *Basic Writings of Nietzsche* (New York, 1968), 617.

[11] *Richard Wagner an Mathilde Wesendonk: Tagebuchblätter und Briefe 1853–1871*, ed. Wolfgang Golther, 44th edn. (Leipzig, 1914), 198.

The figure of the 'Flying Dutchman' is the mythical poem of the people: a primeval trait of man's essential nature expresses itself here with heart-enthralling power. This feature, in its most universal significance, is the longing for peace from life's storms. In the bright Hellenic world we meet him in the wanderings of Odysseus and in the latter's longing for homeland, house, and hearth, but also for this wife who, for this civically minded son of old Hellas, was truly attainable and finally attained. Having no earthly home, Christianity embodied this feature in the figure of the 'Wandering Jew': there was no earthly deliverance for such a wanderer as he, damned for ever and eternity to the living death of a life devoid of purpose and joy; the only goal that was left to him was the longing for death, his only hope the prospect of no longer existing. As the Middle Ages came to an end, a new and active impulse drew all nations back towards *life*, an impulse which, within the context of world history, found its most successful expression in the urge for discovery. The sea became the terrain of life, no longer the tiny land-locked sea of the Hellenic world but the earth-encircling ocean. This marked a break with the ancient world: Odysseus's longing to return to his homeland, hearth, and wife, nurtured on the sufferings of the Wandering Jew, had become a yearning for death; it was now intensified in turn to become a desire for something new and unknown, something not yet visible but already dimly felt. This all but universal feature we find in the myth of the Flying Dutchman, that epic poem of a seafaring nation from that period in world history associated with the great voyages of discovery. What we encounter here is a remarkable mixture, produced by the spirit of the *Volk*, of the character of the Wandering Jew with that of Odysseus. As punishment for his temerity, the Dutchman is condemned by the Devil—a transparent image of the element of flood-water and storms—to roam the seas for all eternity. As an end to his anguish, he longs, like Ahasuerus, for death; this form of release, denied to the Wandering Jew, may be vouchsafed to the Dutchman through *a woman* who sacrifices herself to him out of love; yearning for death thus drives the Dutchman to search out this woman; this woman, however, is no longer the Penelope of Odysseus, wooed by him in ages past and caring for him at home; it is, rather, . . . *the woman of the future.* (iv. 265–6.)

Within this bold mythological synthesis, Wagner harnesses together classical antiquity (longing for one's homeland), the Middle Ages (longing for death), and the modern age (longing for the new) to create a Utopian myth. By the absurd perpetuation of the idea of being 'in transit', the modern expeditionary instinct is transformed into a yearning desire for oblivion, without the goal of the journey—the 'new'—ever being explicit. But what does Wagner mean by the 'woman of the future', the woman whose fate it is to redeem the wanderer from the absurdity of his sempiternal odyssey?

In *A Communication to my Friends* Wagner sees the homelessness of the Flying Dutchman as a symbolic projection of his own situation during his years in Paris from 1839 to 1842. 'An ardent, yearning patriotism awoke within me, such as I had never before suspected.'

Unlike the 'civically minded' Odysseus, however, Wagner did not really yearn to return to his homeland. Germany was certainly no political ideal for him,

for I was alive, at any rate, to the fact that political Germany did not have the slightest attraction to offer me as compared, say, with political France. It was the feeling of homelessness in Paris which aroused this yearning for my German homeland; yet this longing was not directed at old familiar haunts needing only to be rediscovered, but rather at a country pictured in my dreams, an unknown haven that was yet to be discovered ... It was the Flying Dutchman's longing for *womankind*, not, as I have said before, for the wife who waited for Odysseus, but for the woman who would redeem me, the woman whose features had never before presented themselves to me in any clear-cut form but who hovered before my mind's eye as the element of womanhood itself; and this element now found expression in the idea of *a homeland*, the idea of being enfolded by an intimately familiar community, a community, be it added, which I only learned to long for when I realized what the idea of a 'homeland' meant. (iv. 268.)

The same idea recurs in the closing sentence of Ernst Bloch's *Prinzip Hoffnung*, where 'homeland' is defined as 'something which shines into the childhood of all and in which no one has yet been'.[12] For Wagner, this homeland or *terra utopica* was encapsulated in the image of the *femme introuvable*. But in *Der fliegende Holländer*, of course, the woman who could never be found *is* found, and the 'not yet' becomes the 'now' in the moment of Utopian happiness that is the duet between Senta and the Dutchman in Act Two: 'Out of the mists of ages unremembered | her gentle image speaks to me: | for in my dreams of yearning long unnumbered | this was the face that I could see.' (i. 279.)

It would undoubtedly be a trivialization of the work to see the Flying Dutchman's homeless, dispossessed state as merely a reflection of Wagner's years of deprivation in Paris. Rather, it is the distinguishing mark of the modern 'absolute artist' *per se*. This idea, too, finds expression in *A Communication to my Friends*, where Wagner describes his Romantic operas (all of which are essentially symbolic works about the artist's life[13]) as disquisitions on the loneliness of the pure artist, a loneliness from which he seeks release through love. *Lohengrin*, in particular, is interpreted by Wagner himself as the tragedy of the absolute artist, a mythic account of its author's own life. According to this interpretation, the world of the Grail represents the hermetic world

[12] Ernst Bloch, *Prinzip Hoffnung* (Frankfurt, 1959), 1628; translated into English by Neville Plaice, Stephen Plaice, and Paul Knight as *The Principle of Hope* (Oxford, 1986), 1376.

[13] See the chapter 'Totenreich und Venusberg—Wagners "romantische Opern" als Künstlerdramen' in the German edition of the present book, *Das Theater Richard Wagners* (Stuttgart, 1982), 185–206. (The chapter in question is not included in the English translation.)

of art and the 'loneliness' of the artist who has withdrawn into that world to escape the trivial concerns of modern life. 'I felt myself outside the modern world and surrounded by a clear and sacred ethereal element which, in the ecstasy of my solitude, filled me with that voluptuous thrill we feel on Alpine peaks when, surrounded by an azure sea, we look down on the foothills and valleys.' There was, however, the very real danger that, 'affected by the colder atmosphere of these Alpine heights and in the midst of his self-absorption, he might finally be frozen to a monumental block of ice'. In other words, art threatened to become a kind of necropolis, a kingdom of the dead inimical to 'life'. But if the Wagner of this self-orchestrated mythic *vita* wanted to escape from life, it was not life as such he sought to evade, but only 'modern reality'. He longed to leave his hermetically sealed aesthetic existence behind him and live life once again, but a more perfect form of life:

Hardly had this blessed solitude enfolded me when it woke within me a new and overpowering desire, the yearning wish to descend *from peak to valley* ... From these heights my longing glance fell on *womankind*: the woman for whom the 'Flying Dutchman' yearned in the unfathomable depths of his misery; the woman who, like a star in the firmament, drew 'Tannhäuser' up from out of the Venusberg's concupiscent caverns [in both cases, the hermetic world must, therefore, be a subterranean world]; the woman, finally, who now drew *Lohengrin* down from sunny heights to the earth's warm breast. (iv. 294–5.)

Lohengrin wanted to be *loved* for his own sake, as a pure human being; he did not want to be *admired* on the strength of his sublime artistic nature. 'That is why he had to conceal his higher nature' (iv. 295), just as, in classical myth, Zeus concealed his divinity from Semele:

The god loves a mortal woman and, for the sake of this love, approaches her in human shape; but the lover learns that she does not know her beloved in his true estate and, urged by love's own ardour [thus Wagner justifies Elsa's insistence on asking the forbidden question: iv. 301], demands that her husband reveal himself to her in the full physical form of his being. Zeus knows that she can never grasp him, that his true aspect must destroy her; he suffers at this knowledge, suffers beneath the constraint of having to kill his lover in order to meet her demand: and so he condemns himself to death as the fatal splendour of his godlike presence destroys his beloved Semele. (iv. 289–90.)

In exactly the same way, Lohengrin wanted to be 'human, not a god, i.e., an absolute artist'. 'But there still clings to him the tell-tale halo of his heightened nature.' Elsa's doubts reveal that he has merely been 'worshipped' not loved, and so he 'confesses his divine nature, whereupon he returns, annihilated, to his former lonely state' (iv. 296).

Thus, in Wagner's view, the events depicted in *Lohengrin* reflect the absolute artist's hopes of finding a 'homeland', and the irretrievable dashing of those hopes. Unlike Lohengrin, the Flying Dutchman does not 'return, annihilated, to his former lonely state' at the end of the opera, but redemption comes about only because Senta joins him in his loneliness, a loneliness embodied in the sea into which she hurls herself in the closing moments of the work. Time and again in his prose writings—but principally in *The Art-Work of the Future*—Wagner described the sea as an image of the 'essence of music'. The image is frequently associated with a state of boundless isolation 'between sea and sky' and with the yearning desire to set foot on land, 'a homeland which constantly hovers before the mind's eye but which is never reached' (iii. 84). In this way, the seafarer becomes an existential symbol of the modern artist in general. It has not been noticed previously that one of the poems which Wagner set to music in Paris in 1839 (in other words, shortly before beginning work on *Der fliegende Holländer*) gives a central role to the motif of the seafarer who sees himself repulsed by every shore. The poem in question is Jean Reboul's *Tout n'est qu'images fugitives*:

> Navigateur d'un jour d'orage,
> jouet des vagues, le mortel,
> repoussé de chaque rivage,
> ne voit qu'écueils sur son passage,
> et rien n'est calme que le ciel!

> Sailor on a storm-tossed voyage,
> Mortal plaything of the oceans,
> Thrust back to sea, denied a moorage,
> Naught but reefs to guide his passage,
> Where is calm save in the heavens?

The image of sailing as a metaphor for writing verse has a long tradition, dating back to classical Latin and medieval poetry. According to Virgil's *Georgics*, 'to write verse' is *'vela dare'*, literally, to set sail.[14] Here, admittedly, it is poetic technique which is the principal idea behind the image. But from the late eighteenth century onwards the mariner becomes one of the most frequent and crucial symbols in the poet's repertoire of self-portrayal: Poe, Swinburne, Baudelaire, and Conrad Ferdinand Meyer all use the infertile realm of sea and water to symbolize a poetical cosmos far removed from life. In Franz Grillparzer's verse play *Sappho*, first performed in 1818, the poet is described in the following terms:

---

[14] See Ernst Robert Curtius, *Europäische Literatur and lateinisches Mittelalter* (Berne, 1948), 138–9; translated into English by Willard R. Trask as *European Literature and the Latin Middle Ages* (New York, 1953), 128–30; see also Rudolf Drux, 'Des Dichters Schiffahrt', in *Formen und Funktionen der Allegorie*, ed. Walter Haug (Stuttgart, 1979), 194–205.

Ein wild bewegtes Meer durchschiffet er
Auf leichtgefügtem Kahn. Da grünt kein Baum,
Da sprosset keine Saat und keine Blume,
Ringsum die graue Unermeßlichkeit.
Von ferne nur sieht er die heitre Küste,
Und mit der Wogen Brandung dumpf vermengt,
Tönt ihm die Stimme seiner Lieben zu.                (i. 5.)

A wild and storm-racked sea he ploughs aboard
His fragile bark. No trace of verdure here,
No seedling sprouts nor any flower grows,
Naught but a measureless expanse of grey.
From far away he sees the jocund shore
And, mingled with the booming breakers' roar,
The voices of his loved ones faintly hears.

Like Lohengrin and the Dutchman (Wagner's symbolic embodiments of the absolute artist), Sappho longs to escape from this barren realm and return to life's verdant pastures. She tries to cast aside the 'barren laurel' which condemns her to a life of isolation, and exchange it for love's garland, but she is finally forced to realize that art must always cut the poet off from life. This is the *malheur d'être poète*—thus Grillparzer's formulation, with its bold anticipation of Baudelaire.[15]

Ein Biß nur in des Ruhmes goldne Frucht,
Proserpinens Granatenkernen gleich,
Reiht dich auf ewig zu den stillen Schatten,
Und den Lebendigen gehörst du nimmer an!      (iii. 5.)

Bite but the golden fruit of glorious fame,
Like Proserpina's pomegranate seeds,
And silent shades will claim you as their own,
You'll nevermore be number'd with the living.

The kingdom of the dead or the 'shadow world' was a favourite symbol of absolute art from Schiller onwards. In his poem *An Goethe* the latter compares dramatic poetry with Charon's bark, which could ferry only 'shades and idols' over the Acheron but not men of flesh and blood. It is a symbol which recurs repeatedly in nineteenth-century poetry, especially in Symbolist verse. The sea and water generally are the abode of the dead. 'O Mort, vieux capitaine, il est temps! levons l'ancre!', Baudelaire apostrophizes death in the last of *Les Fleurs du mal*.[16]

[15] *Dichter über ihre Dichtungen: Franz Grillparzer* (Munich, 1970), 103. On *Sappho*, see Werner Vordtriede's important observations, drawing convincing links between Grillparzer's aesthetic as an artist and Romantic and Symbolist theories of art, in Werner Vordtriede, *Novalis und die französischen Symbolisten* (Stuttgart, 1963), 13–23.

[16] Charles Baudelaire, *Les Fleurs du mal*, ed. Antoine Adam (Paris, 1961), 160 ('Le Voyage', VIII. On the significance of water as a symbol of the kingdom of the dead, see Gaston Bachelard, *L'Eau et les rêves* (Paris, 1942), and Emil Staiger, 'Das Spätboot: Zu Conrad Ferdinand Meyers Lyrik', in Emil Staiger (ed.), *Die Kunst der Interpretation* (Zurich, 1955), 239–73.

At the end of Wagner's 'dramatic ballad' of the Flying Dutchman, the *poète maudit* of the title puts out to sea with a despairing cry of 'Unfurl the sails! Weigh anchor!' Grillparzer's Sappho, like Senta, throws herself into the sea from the top of a rocky promontory and thus returns to the realm of absolute art. 'Her home was not on earth with mortal men. | She has returned to dwell with her own kind.' Thus the final lines of *Sappho*, a work which anticipates many aspects of Wagner's early music dramas, with their symbolical treatment of the life of the artist.

Two symbols come together in the figure of the Flying Dutchman. He is the mythic incarnation of modern man, for whom the urge for discovery has become an aimless journey into the infinite void (whereby the modern optimistic belief in progress is transformed into a pessimistic view of history and world-weariness). As such, he exists only in terms of his quest for a *terra utopica* which can become his homeland. At the same time he is an existential symbol of the modern absolute artist in his alienation from life.

One of the most striking aspects of Wagnerian music theatre is its endless ability to provoke parody and travesty, caricature and satire. This is evidently connected with the latent comedy inherent in the contradiction between the naïvety of the mythic subject-matter and its modern 'sentimental' adaptation. The juxtaposition of naïvely graphic description and genuine sensitivity, of the crudely physical and the subtly psychological, has repeatedly tempted writers to parody Wagner's heroic store of legends and transpose it to a contemporary middle-class milieu. Nietzsche was one of the earliest writers to allow himself a joke at Wagner's expense: 'How can we test this content, this eternal content?', he asks in *Der Fall Wagner*.

The chemist replies: translate Wagner into reality, into the modern—let us be even crueller—into the bourgeois! What becomes of Wagner then?—Among ourselves, I have tried it. Nothing is more entertaining, nothing to be recommended more highly for walks, than retelling Wagner in *more youthful* proportions: for example, Parsifal as a candidate for a theological degree, with secondary school education (the latter being indispensable for *pure foolishness*). What surprises one encounters in the process! Would you believe it? All of Wagner's heroines, without exception, as soon as they are stripped of their heroic skin, become almost indistinguishable from Madame Bovary![17]

The ease with which mythic themes can be translated into a modern idiom (an ease well illustrated by the basic thrust of contemporary Wagner productions) is bound up with Wagner's repeated use of thematic material which had already been parodied even before he

---

[17] Nietzsche, *Sämtliche Werke*, vi. 34; English trans. (Kaufmann, *Basic Writings of Nietzsche*), pp. 631–2.

himself adapted it for his own dramatic ends. *Der fliegende Holländer* and
*Tannhäuser* are directly inspired by Heinrich Heine's parodies. Indeed,
all of Wagner's 'Romantic operas' might be described as parodistic
parodies: the negation of a negation produces a new position. The
reacquired tragic seriousness has already discovered its own comic
negation: to use Schiller's terminology, it is not a naïve seriousness, but
a sentimental seriousness born of reflection, more akin to parody than
that unrefracted seriousness which has yet to discover the opportunities
for irony.

That it is but a single step from the sublime to the ridiculous is very
much a pre-condition of the music drama which conjures up myth not
as something past but, rather, as something present. Parody and travesty
are the touchstone by which we judge the modernity of the mythico-
musical drama. A glance at Cosima's *Diaries* shows that Wagner himself
was very much an obsessive parodist. Not only other people's works but
his own, too, served constantly as the butt of his parodistic scorn. 'One
must be able to joke about the sublimest of things', he said on one such
occasion (*CT*, 24 December 1877). Wagner himself wrote French
parodies of Senta's Ballad and the Sailors' Chorus even as early as 1840,
showing how tragic themes immediately evoked parodistic associations
in his imagination. 'Oh, that is my salvation, this ability to convert the
most serious of things into nonsense in a flash—it has always kept me
from going over the brink', he told Cosima on 6 August 1878.

There is a little-known travesty of *Der fliegende Holländer* which, as it
were, restores Wagner's opera to the comic level of its parodistic source
in Heine's *Memoiren des Herren von Schnabelewopski*. One of three
'grotesque comedies' by Friedrich Huch, all of which date from 1911
(the other two are *Tristan und Isolde* and *Lohengrin*),[18] it features the
'Ahasuerus of the ocean' as a world-weary *décadent*. He suffers not only
from his interminable existence but also from the constant retelling of
his tale in literature. 'My fate is like that of a bad penny, forever passed
from hand to hand.' Like Helen of Troy in Goethe's *Faust*, he sees
himself as a literary figure, and discovers, to his annoyance, that nothing
ever happens to him that he has not already experienced as his own
fictional *doppelgänger*. 'A semi-historical being who is sung about in
ballads . . . A curious, almost eerie sensation, feeling oneself twice over.
For some time past I've been obsessed with the idea that my whole fate
were unfolding as though on stage and that I were performing my own
Passion play every seven years.' He wonders whether the picture of
himself contained in Wagner's opera is a true reflection of his character:
'Am I really as unsympathetic as I unfortunately appear to be there? So

---

[18] Huch's *Holländer* parody is reprinted in Dieter Borchmeyer and Stephan Kohler (eds.),
*Wagner-Parodien* (Frankfurt, 1983), 149–204.

passively demanding? So vampirically egotistical?' And he has to concede that 'A man who has nothing else to think about in the world except his own redemption is bound to grow egotistical.' This is one of the passages in which a comic reversal of the tragic myth is transformed into open criticism of Wagner's ideology of redemption, an ideology which Huch exposes by putting words in the mouth of the very figure who embodies the artist's own essential egoism.

In Huch's travesty it is old Mary, not Senta, whom Daland plans to marry off to the Flying Dutchman. Introduced into each other's presence, they stand stock-still, just like Senta and the Dutchman in Wagner's opera, but for quite a different reason: Mary was the Dutchman's lover on one of his earlier septennial visits. Now she is firmly resolved to 'redeem' the Dutchman, in other words, to lead him down the aisle. All attempts to discourage her, whether by persuasion or by force, are of no avail, until finally he succeeds in escaping with Senta and returning to sea once again.

As in the opera (which comes in for constant criticism), Senta has fallen in love with the Dutchman. But her playing of the 'Ballad from the Flying Dutchman', which she keeps tinkling away at on the piano, finally gets on the Dutchman's nerves: there is nothing he likes less, he says, than music which is 'badly performed'. He also feels uncomfortable at finding himself drawn into exactly the same situations as those he has seen on the operatic stage. Once again his rival is Erik, a 'sentimental lyric tenor' who has, of course, given up his uncertain life as a huntsman since Daland has said he can marry Senta only if he gets a steady job. He now works in a post office, a prosaic profession which Senta, eager for adventure, finds altogether tedious.

ERIK: Would you against love's simple pleasures rail?
SENTA: Away with you! Be gone! You smell of mail!

Huch's witty travesty was not written with the intention of exposing Wagner's Romantic opera to ridicule or satire; rather, he turns the tragic myth on its head, transferring it to a *fin de siècle* milieu and treating it as a subject for comedy. It is a satyr play performed, as it were, as an epilogue to the age between world-weariness and *décadence*.

Fritz Mauthner had a totally different aim in mind when writing his 1878 parody, *Der unbewußte Ahasverus*, a work which does not so much hit out at a particular music drama as deal with the Ahasuerus motif in Wagner's works generally. Unlike Huch, Mauthner pillories Wagner and his followers directly, mercilessly, and with caustic wit. The music, of course, is spared: 'If notes were all that you'd composed | To less contempt you'd be exposed'—thus the motto of the piece. Born in Bohemia in 1849, Mauthner was a linguistic philosopher and novelist, but he also published a whole series of parodies under the title *Nach berühmten Mustern* (1878–80), in which he satirized many aspects of Wagner's works, including what he regarded as the turgid language of Wagner's prose writings, the composer's sense of mission, his ideas concerning the 'total work of art', alliteration and his related etymological and semantic speculations, the philosophical ballast weighing down his musical theory and terminology (this aspect is alluded to in the second part of his title, 'The Thing-in-Itself as Will and Representation', and in the fact that the action takes place in 1781, the 'year of birth of the critique of pure reason'), the high-flown but essentially trivial and unreservedly admiring interpretations of writers such as Hans von Wolzogen, and, finally, the anti-Semitism of both Wagner and the Wagnerians, an anti-Semitism whose possible repercussions are evoked with terrifying clarity in Ahasuerus' closing lines:

> Erlöst durch die Länge des laubgrünen Liedes
> Wall' ich nach Walhall, wenn die Würgengel Wagners
> Den Hebräer Ahasver nicht hinterrücks hecheln.

> Released by the length of the leafy-green lay,
> I hie me to Valhall, when Wagner's grim Vandals
> Will heckle and hound Ahasuerus the Hebrew.

The subtitle, 'Bühnen-Weh-Festspiel' (Stage Woe Festival), is intended, of course, to recall the 'Bühnenweihfestspiel' (Stage Consecration Festival), the poem of which had just appeared in print (1877). But Mauthner's satire has little in common with *Parsifal*, unless we are to assume that the redemption of Ahasuerus is an allusion to the 'Wandering Jewess' Kundry and her redemption in death. On the whole, however, Mauthner does not parody the language of *Parsifal*, but rather the alliterative metre of the *Ring* and the style of Wagner's theoretical writings. Both here and in terms of its content, *Der unbewußte Ahasverus* has more to say about widespread preconceptions concerning the composer and the excesses of Wagnerism than it has about Wagner himself. But this kind of intentional distortion of the ideas of the author who forms the subject of the parody, together with a readiness to equate those ideas with current views on him (however much those views may, in turn, be grounded in prejudice), has always been both legitimate and crucial to parody as a genre. Parody can be successful, and will be understood as such, only if the audience recognizes its own prejudices and preconceptions in the work—and if it does so, moreover, with a smile of recognition.

On one point at least Mauthner understood Wagner exactly, and that is the extent to which the Wandering Jew Ahasuerus accompanied the composer throughout his life. That this theme also had serious ideological implications in the context of his rejection of 'Jewishness' is clear from the ending of his infamous essay, 'Judaism in Music', where 'the redemption of Ahasuerus—destruction' (v. 85) is held out as the only course of salvation open to the Jews. It must be stressed, however, that this 'destruction' has nothing to do with physical annihilation, as is often assumed. What Wagner meant by this was an end to the Jews' 'special status', whereby they, and modern man in general, will be 'redeemed as true human beings'. The aim of this process of redemption is that 'we' should become 'united' with, and 'indivisible' from, the Jews, as Wagner notes immediately before his mythic image of the redemption of Ahasuerus (v. 85). Mauthner's parody undoubtedly alludes to this final paragraph of Wagner's essay.

The action of *Der unbewußte Ahasverus* (which, its author claims, is the text of a Wagnerian music drama published, like *Parsifal*, in advance of its musical setting) is based on the conceit that Ahasuerus, the embodiment of the 'anti-musical' principle of Judaism *per se* (a further allusion to 'Judaism in Music'), will be granted redemption only 'when something exists that lasts somewhat longer | Than my lugubrious life', that 'something' being Wagner's famous 'unending melody'. 'It is so unending that the Wandering Jew reverts to childhood.' To this Mauthner adds a footnote, which he attributes to Heinrich Porges (himself, ironically, a Jew) and Hans von Wolzogen, whom he takes as representatives of the hagiographical school of Wagnerian 'scholarship': 'The Wandering Jew is redeemed by the Master's unending melody', in other words, he may die. 'Divine! And his wretched co-religionists do not even show themselves grateful. The Master is too good for them.' It is not so much a question here of adding a footnote as of putting the boot in, a malicious move on Mauthner's part intended to expose Wagner's arrogance in offering redemption to the Jews in the form of an offer which gives them only the chance of self-annihilation.

'Join unreservedly in this self-annihilatory and regenerative act of redemption, and we shall be united and indivisible!' (v. 85.) Again, it will be noted that Wagner speaks not only of 'self-annihilation' and 'destruction' in this final paragraph of his essay, but of 'regeneration' or redemption through annihilation. The Jew shall rise up out of the ashes like the phoenix, no longer a Jew but a true human being. This idea recalls Karl Marx's 1843 essay, *Zur Judenfrage*, a work no less infamous than Wagner's, which sets out from the notion that the Jewish question would not be solved if the Jew were assimilated into existing society, since he would simply be conforming to a lifestyle that was depraved, adopting, as it were, a corrupt existence. (Wagner shares the same conviction.) Assimilation would be achieved, Marx believed, only if the

Jews were 'superseded' in a process involving the whole of society, a process, moreover, in which individual self-alienation was itself overcome. What Marx describes as 'supersession' becomes a metaphysics of 'destruction' and 'redemption' with Wagner, an outlook explicable only in terms of the mood of *Weltschmerz* which characterized his age. The Ahasuerus myth is the myth of Wagner's existence as an artist. The fact that he includes the Jews in this myth is the clearest possible proof that the anti-Semitic use to which this theme increasingly was put from the second half of the nineteenth century onwards (including Franz Hippler's 1940 national socialist propaganda film, *Der ewige Jude*) has nothing whatever to do with Wagner. For him, the Ahasuerus legend was still a modern Christian myth of general human significance, the myth of a man who doubts in his own redemption but who is none the less redeemed from the depths of utter despair.

# 15

# Venus in Exile:
## *Tannhäuser und der Sängerkrieg auf Wartburg*

The old and fabled beings have all fled,
The charmèd race is gone for evermore.

Friedrich von Schiller, *Wallenstein* (*Die Piccolomini*, iii. 4).

Go to the frigid world of men,
From whose pretentious, flaccid dreams
We gods of pleasure long have fled,
Here in the earth's warm sheltering womb.

Richard Wagner, *Tannhäuser* (i. 2).

Wagner's various autobiographical writings offer a more or less detailed description of the way in which he was 'inspired' to write each individual music drama. Since then, word must have reached even the most dyed-in-the-wool Wagnerian that these 'inspirational myths' generally deserve our deep distrust. This is certainly true of *Tannhäuser*. One of the principal dogmas of Wagner's aesthetic ideology is that the musical drama is born out of the spirit of the *Volk*, and that its creator draws directly upon the figures of a mythopoeic popular imagination. From *Der fliegende Holländer* onwards, Wagner claimed that the basic idea for each of his works came from popular tradition, so that, in looking back over the history of each work, he either passes over in silence or else disparages the modern versions of the subjects which he himself has adapted. His reconstruction of the genesis of *Tannhäuser* is a case in point, and yet there can be no doubt that it was in modern adaptations that he first became familiar with the 'popular' subject-matter of all his 'Romantic operas', adaptations which were refracted, as it were, through a lens which was partly philological, partly poetical.[1] In the case of *Der fliegende Holländer* and, above all, *Tannhäuser*, the lens in question had the name of Heinrich Heine written all over it.

Heine published his essay 'Elementargeister' in 1837, in the third volume of *Der Salon*. (The first part of it had already appeared in French in 1835, in his *De l'Allemagne*.) It is unlikely, to say the least, that

---

[1] See Volker Mertens, 'Richard Wagner und das Mittelalter', in Ulrich Müller and Peter Wapnewski (eds.), *Richard-Wagner-Handbuch* (Stuttgart, 1986), 19–59; English trans. in preparation.

Wagner, who not only knew Heine's writings at first hand but imitated their style (as we know from his Paris *feuilletons*), was unfamiliar with this essay. The fact that he does not mention this source in either *A Communication to my Friends* or *Mein Leben* is no proof that he did not know it. His silence on the subject is part and parcel of his regrettable tendency, from the 1840s onwards, to repress all knowledge of Heine.

In the course of his essay Heine develops an idea to which he was to return in 1853 in 'Die Götter im Exil'. (Indeed, the idea might well be described as a recurrent theme in Heine's outcast life.) Some of the elemental spirits of the essay's title, Heine believed, had come into being through a 'transformation of the old pagan gods' who, following Christ's victory over them, had withdrawn into exile, 'dwelling in subterranean seclusion' and 'going about their demonic business with the other elemental spirits'. There then follows Heine's account of the Tannhäuser legend:

The strangest sounding tale of all those told by the German people is the romantic legend of the goddess Venus, who, when her temples were torn down, fled to a secret mountain where she now leads the most fantastical life of pleasure in the company of carefree spirits of the air, together with fair nymphs of woodland and water, and many a famous hero who had suddenly vanished from the face of the earth. As you draw near the mountain, you can hear, even from a distance, the sounds of contented laughter and the sweet strains of a harp stealing into your heart like an invisible chain that draws you into the mountain. But you are lucky, for close to the entrance an old knight keeps watch, known to all as the Faithful Eckart; he stands like a statue resting on his great broadsword, but his honest and hoary head nods unceasingly, and sadly he warns you of the tender dangers that await you within the mountain. Many have been frightened away in good time, but others have failed to heed the old man's bleating voice and hurtled blindly into the pit of accursed desire.[2]

Although Heine does not mention it, he must have been thinking of Ludwig Tieck's short story, *Der getreue Eckart und der Tannenhäuser* (1799), a tale which was also familiar to Wagner. It is here that we first encounter the idea of the ancient gods in medieval exile. Before taking up his position outside the Venusberg, where he warns others of the dangers that lurk within it, the faithful Eckart is told that 'devils' had fled inside the mountain, seeking 'refuge at the desolate centre of the earth when sacred Christianity, newly emergent, had cast out pagan idols. Here, it is said, Frau Venus holds court, gathering around her her hellish host of worldly desires and illicit wishes'.[3] Tannenhäuser reports in a similar vein: 'Thus the throng of smiling pagan gods approached

[2] Heinrich Heine, *Sämtliche Werke in vier Bänden*, ed. Werner Vordtriede and Uwe Schweikert (Munich, 1972), iii. 565.
[3] Ludwig Tieck, *Erzählungen des Phantasus* (Nuremberg, 1946), 42–3.

me, Frau Venus at their head, and all of them bade me welcome; they are held there in thrall by the power of the Almighty and are no longer worshipped here on earth; it is from here that they now exert their secret sway.'[4]

It is as an exiled goddess that Venus describes herself in Wagner's opera, when, 'in an outburst of violent anger', she gives Tannhäuser his freedom to leave:

> Hin zu den kalten Menschen flieh',
> vor deren blödem, trübem Wahn
> der Freude Götter wir entfloh'n
> tief in der Erde wärmenden Schoos.          (ii. 9.)
>
> Go to the frigid world of men,
> From whose pretentious, flaccid dreams
> We gods of pleasure long have fled,
> Here in the earth's warm sheltering womb.[5]

The 'blöder, trüber Wahn' (literally, 'purblind, sad illusion') refers, of course, to Christian morality, with its opposition to every form of sensuality. For its part, Christianity certainly did not dismiss the ancient gods as 'chimeras and monstrous products of deceit and error' (to quote Heine in 'Die Götter im Exil'), but as 'evil spirits plunged from their pinnacle of power by Christ's victory, and now carrying on their lives on earth in the gloom of temple ruins or magic groves, luring to their ruin the weak-willed Christians who have lost their way, and seducing them with their devilish wiles, with lust and beauty, and most of all with dancing and singing'.[6] This fraternization between the pagan gods and the hellish fiends of Christianity—an association which, significantly, plays no part in Wagner's opera—finds expression in Tieck's short story in the motif of Satan guiding lost souls to the Venusberg.

In his 1861 essay on *Tannhäuser* Baudelaire added a further variant to this idea of a link between Satan and the exiled Venus when he wrote: '*Tannhäuser* depicts a conflict between two principles which have chosen the human heart as their field of battle, and these two principles are the flesh and the spirit, hell and heaven, Satan and God.'[7]

The radiant Venus of classical antiquity, she who as Aphrodite was born of the waves' white spume, did not escape untouched by the terrible gloom of the Middle Ages. She no longer dwells on Mount Olympus nor on the shores of the fragrant Aegean, but has withdrawn to the depths of a cavern which, for all

---

[4] Tieck, *Erzählungen des Phantasus* 70.

[5] All translations from *Tannhäuser* are quoted, with permission, from Rodney Blumer's singing version of the text, in Richard Wagner, *Tannhäuser*, ed. Nicholas John (London, 1988), 61–93.

[6] Heine, *Sämtliche Werke*, ii. 707.

[7] Charles Baudelaire, 'Richard Wagner et *Tannhäuser* à Paris', in *Œuvres complètes*, ed. Claude Pichois (Paris, 1976), ii. 794.

its splendours, is lit by other fires than those of a smiling Phoebus Apollo. By descending to the nether world, Venus has drawn much closer to hell and, when certain awful rites are enacted, she never fails to offer up her sacrifice to the arch-fiend himself, the prince of the flesh, the lord of sin.[8]

The notion that Christianity drove the classical gods into exile recurs repeatedly in the poetry of the late eighteenth and nineteenth centuries. The supplanting of natural deities by Christian monotheism is the theme, for example, of Schiller's poem *Die Götter Griechenlands*, published in 1788, the first strophe of which begins:

> Da ihr noch die schöne Welt regiertet,
> An der Freude leichtem Gängelband
> Glücklichere Menschenalter führtet,
> Schöne Wesen aus dem Fabelland!
> Ach! da euer Wonnedienst noch glänzte,
> Wie ganz anders, anders war es da!
> Da man deine Tempel noch bekränzte,
> Venus Amathusia!

> While yet you ruled this beauteous earth of ours,
> Subjected to your sway a happier band
> Of men untrammelled by joy's leading strings,
> Oh beauteous beings from a fabled land!
> But ah! when men still worshipped you in awe,
> How diff'rent, oh so diff'rent was it then!
> When garlands decked your sacred fane,
> Oh Venus of Amathus!

(Amathus was the site of a famous temple dedicated to Venus on the island of Cyprus.) In the second part of his *Wallenstein* trilogy Schiller once again takes up the theme of the gods in exile, placing the following words in the mouth of Max Piccolomini:

> Die alten Fabelwesen sind nicht mehr,
> Das reizende Geschlecht ist ausgewandert;
> Doch eine Sprache braucht das Herz, es bringt
> Der alte Trieb die alten Namen wieder,
> Und an dem Sternenhimmel gehn sie jetzt,
> Die sonst im Leben freundlich mitgewandelt,
> Dort winken sie dem Liebenden herab,
> Und jedes Große bringt uns *Jupiter*
> Noch diesen Tag, und *Venus* jedes Schöne.
> (*Die Piccolomini*, ii. 4.)

> The old and fabled beings have all fled,
> The charmèd race is gone for evermore;

[8] Ibid. 790.

> And yet the heart must needs give tongue, old drives
> Bring back to mind old long-forgotten names,
> For in the starry firmament they dwell
> That once did walk on earth with friendly mien,
> Yet smiling down on lovers' heads, for e'en
> Today all greatness comes from *Jupiter*,
> All beauty, even now, is *Venus'* gift.

Samuel Taylor Coleridge, it may be added, adopted a much freer approach to Schiller's original in his translation of the trilogy, and it is this expanded version which is quoted by Walter Scott at the head of chapter 3 of *Guy Mannering*, and to which Keats alludes in lines 231–3 of his *Lamia* (1819):

> The intelligible forms of ancient poets,
> The fair humanities of old religion,
> The Power, the Beauty, and the Majesty,
> That had their haunts in dale, or piny mountain,
> Or forest by slow stream, or pebbly spring,
> Or chasms and wat'ry depths; all these have vanished.
> They live no longer in the faith of reason!
> But still the heart does need a language, still
> Doth the old instinct bring back the old names,
> And to yon starry world they now are gone,
> Spirits or gods, that used to share this earth
> With man as with their friend; and to the lover
> Yonder they move, from yonder visible sky
> Shoot influence down: and even at this day
> 'Tis Jupiter who brings whate'er is great,
> And Venus who brings every thing that's fair!

Here we have a variant of the theme of the gods in exile, reinterpreted in the spirit of classical humanism: the gods have migrated to the starry firmament, as projections of mankind. The neo-medieval Romantic tradition, conversely, demonizes the gods and transfers their place of exile to the nether world.

Both versions, however, deal with the continuing existence of the classical gods, and it is this theme, embodied in the contrast between a 'heavenly' and a 'demonic' Venus, which plays a part in Wagner's *Tannhäuser*. In this case, it is Wolfram von Eschenbach who, in contrast to the demonic underworld figure of Tannhäuser himself, is characterized by his special affinity with the starry vault. Thus his eulogy to love in the second act begins:

> Da blick ich auf zu *einem* nur der Sterne,
> der an dem Himmel, der mich blendet, steht:
> es sammelt sich mein Geist aus jeder Ferne,
> andächtig sinkt die Seele in Gebet.                    (ii. 22.)

> Then I look up to stars above me shining,
> One holds my gaze, more than all others fair:
> Its radiance fills my heart with chaste devotion,
> And reverently my soul sinks down in prayer.

Who is meant by this 'one' star? There is no doubt that it is Venus, the Star of Eve, the 'loveliest of all the stars', to whom Wolfram addresses his famous apostrophe in the third act. For him, the Star of Eve is the star of a 'noble', renunciatory love, transcending erotic desire. It is *Venus Urania*, sacred or heavenly love, in contrast to *Venus Cypria*, the earthly or profane love which—as a force of the nether world—Tannhäuser has tasted.

In *A Communication to my Friends* Wagner claims that the decisive impetus behind *Tannhäuser* came not from any modern reworking of the legend, but from 'the *Volksbuch* and the plain Tannhäuser Ballad'. Only here, he insisted, had he discovered in undistorted form 'the simple, genuine folk-poem that dealt with the figure of Tannhäuser' (iv. 269). But where had Wagner found this 'plain Tannhäuser Ballad'—by which he presumably meant the relevant poem in *Des Knaben Wunderhorn*? Certainly not in Arnim's and Brentano's anthology; still less in their source, Heinrich Kornmann's *Mons Veneris* of 1614. Quite simply, he must have read it in Heine's 'Elementargeister', where it was printed complete.

As for the *Volksbuch* or chap-book, no such work exists. What Wagner must have meant—as scholars have now established—is Ludwig Bechstein's collection of legends, *Die Sagen von Eisenach und der Wartburg, dem Hörselberg und Reinhardsbrunn*, the first part of which appeared in 1835.[9] Here Wagner not only found an account of the Tannhäuser legend, but the Venusberg, until then generally located in Italy, was transferred to Thuringia, while Tannhäuser was loosely associated with the Wartburg, 'where he, too, was no doubt invited by the Landgrave'. Bechstein's anthology also included, of course, an account of the Tournament of Song, which appears under the grammatically curious title of *Der Sängerkrieg auf Wartburg* (literally, 'The Minstrels' Contest on Wartburg'), an ellipsis which recurs in the subtitle of Wagner's opera. Bechstein, it may be added, is also mentioned in 'Elementargeister' as having sent Heine a copy of the older version of the 'Ballad of Danheüser' of 1515, a version to which we shall return in due course. ('The older version contains many variants and, to

---

[9] See Dolf Sternberger, 'Ein geheimer Sängerkrieg zwischen Richard Wagner und Heinrich Heine', in *Die Programmhefte der Bayreuther Festspiele 1973*, ii. '*Tannhäuser*', 69–80; English trans. by John Bell, 23–31. For a detailed examination of the sources, see Stewart Spencer, '*Tannhäuser*: Mediävistische Handlung in drei Aufzügen', in *Wagner 1976* (1976), 40–53; Mertens, 'Wagner und das Mittelalter', pp. 21–6; and Peter Wapnewski, 'Die Oper Richard Wagners als Dichtung', in Müller and Wapnewski, *Richard-Wagner-Handbuch*, pp. 223–352, esp. pp. 247–55.

my mind, bears a much more poetical stamp', was Heine's assessment of the Ballad.[10])

But there was even more for Wagner to learn from Heine's essay, for it also contains references not only to Eichendorff's 1819 short story, *Das Marmorbild* (a tale whose remarkable motivic parallels with *Tannhäuser* suggest, even if they cannot prove, that Wagner was familiar with this work, too), but also to Willibald Alexis's *Venus in Rom* (1828) and, finally, to the common source of both these tales, Heinrich Kornmann's compilation, *Mons Veneris: Fraw Veneris Berg*, published in Frankfurt in 1614. In other words, Heine's 'Elementargeister' contained virtually all that was worth knowing on the subject of Tannhäuser, including, not least, Heine's own parody of the legend.

Wagner met Tieck—the 'king of Romanticism', as Hebbel called him—in Berlin in 1847. The composer's autobiography contains a detailed account of his conversation with the 74-year-old poet, the sole surviving member of the first generation of Romantic writers in Germany. Tieck knew the libretti of both *Tannhäuser*—which had, after all, been inspired to a considerable degree by his own *Der getreue Eckart und der Tannenhäuser* of half a century previously—and of *Lohengrin*, and, according to Wagner's report of the meeting, he was most favourably impressed by them both. In his report of the conversation in *Mein Leben*, Wagner (who, as Cosima's *Diaries* repeatedly show, continued to show a lively interest in Tieck's poetry and prose writings right up to the end of his life) claimed that he had found this long meeting with the last surviving representative of classical Romanticism a valuable experience. Not that this prevented him from being positively rude about the elderly poet when he came to write his autobiographical self-defence, *A Communication to my Friends*, in 1851, when Tieck was still very much alive (he did not die until 1853). Although Wagner does not deny that he owed his first acquaintance with the Tannhäuser subject to Tieck's short story rather than to the bogus 'German Volksbuch' (i.e., Bechstein's account of the legend), he was forced by the constraints of his *völkisch* ideology to trivialize not only the debt he owed to Tieck but also the influence of E. T. A. Hoffmann's short stories:

Of course, Tannhäuser, in itself, was by no means wholly unfamiliar to me: I had first become familiar with it at an early age through Tieck's short story. At that time it had inspired me in the same fancifully mystical way as Hoffmann's tales had left their mark upon my youthful imagination; but never was any influence exerted on my artistic creativity from that particular quarter. (iv. 269.)

This is an altogether grotesque distortion of the truth, especially when we recall the 1842 opera draft, *Die Bergwerke zu Falun*, based upon

---

[10] Heine, *Sämtliche Werke*, iii. 569.

Hoffmann's homonymous tale, or the latter's 'Der Kampf der Sänger', to which Wagner owed not only his earliest knowledge of the legend of the Wartburg Tournament of Song but also (as we shall see) its specifically modern reworking. The passage just quoted then goes on: 'I now reread Tieck's entirely modern poem and understood why its tendency towards mystical coquettishness and Catholic frivolity had failed to inspire any interest in me.' (iv. 269.) This interest, Wagner claimed, was the result of his reading the factitious *Volksbuch* and the Tannhäuser Ballad in *Des Knaben Wunderhorn*.

That Wagner should accuse Tieck, of all people, of 'Catholic frivolity' is grossly iniquitous, given that Tieck was virtually the only Romantic writer who was not a convert to Catholicism and who was not even tempted to cast a glance in the direction of Rome. It is difficult to avoid the suspicion that Wagner was attempting to foist upon Tieck the very criticism which had been levelled at his own adaptation of the legend. But there is also an echo here of the Young Germans' polemical dismissal of Tieck, an attitude shared by Heine, too. Indeed, the fact that Heine fails to mention Tieck's tale of Tannenhäuser in his 'Elementargeister', in spite of deriving a number of important ideas from it, is no doubt due to malice aforethought. In his own parody of the legend, with which he concludes the essay, Heine imagines Tannhäuser returning from Rome via Dresden, where Tieck was then living. The old poet, who was a severe critic of the Young German movement, is likened to a vicious but toothless dog:

> In Dresden sah ich einen Hund,
> Der einst sehr scharf gebissen,
> Doch fallen ihm jetzt die Zähne aus,
> Er kann nur bellen und pissen.[11]

> In Dresden I beheld a dog
> Whose teeth are now all missing;
> It used to bite a lot but now
> It's reduced to barking and pissing.

Be that as it may, Tieck's 'entirely modern poem' left a far more indelible mark on Wagner's interpretation of the legend than the putative popular tradition. *Tannhäuser* is a kind of compilation of Tieck's *Tannenhäuser* and Hoffmann's 'Der Kampf der Sänger'. Wagner found the beginnings of a link between the two legends not in Bechstein but in the previously mentioned tale from Hoffmann's *Serapionsbrüder* cycle, where echoes of the Venusberg motif are already to be heard. Here it is the hell-hound Nasias, in league with Heinrich von Ofterdingen's mentor, Klingsohr, who seizes the opportunity of a nocturnal visit to

---

[11] Ibid. 575.

Wolfframb von Eschinbach to sing 'a song of fair Helen and of the rapturous joys of the Venusberg. In truth the song was seductive, and it was as though the flames which Nasias belched forth turned to vapours exhaling lustful desire and the pleasures of love, while dulcet strains surged back and forth like swaying cupids.'[12]

All that was required now was the final philological impulse, provided by a monograph brought to Wagner's attention by a friend in Paris, the philologist Samuel Lehrs. The book in question was C. T. L. Lucas's 1838 treatise, *Ueber den Krieg von Wartburg*. (Here, as with Bechstein, the definite article is missing before 'Wartburg'.) Wagner was now able to fuse both legends, equating the legendary figure of Heinrich von Ofterdingen (a central figure in all the accounts of the Wartburg Tournament of Song, from the late medieval *Wartburgkrieg* edited by Lucas to Hoffmann's 'Der Kampf der Sänger') with the figure of Heinrich (!) Tannhäuser, a historical figure who had himself become the subject of legend. It was an equation for which Wagner found spurious academic justification in Lucas's treatise:

There is no doubt that Heinrich von Ofterdingen or Afterdingen was thought of as a minstrel knight, famous in Wolfram von Eschenbach's day for the songs and, perhaps also, for the epic poems he wrote. But if he appears as a mysterious figure even in our own poem about the Wartburg Tournament of Song—a poem which, like the legend based upon it, is our chief source of information concerning Ofterdingen—he became an even more mysterious, not to say mythical, figure through his original affinity, or else through a later association, with the person of *Tannhäuser*. Although we may wish to distinguish between the poet Tannhäuser, who, under this name, is said to have sung songs of his own composition which have survived to this day, and the knight Tannhäuser, who betook himself to the Venusberg, it was inevitable that the two Tannhäusers should become fused together to form a single poetical figure, an amalgamation which makes it likely that Ofterdingen was related to both of them and subsumed by them in the poetical view of the *Volk*.[13]

Lucas seeks to demonstrate this identification with a wealth of speculation which no later scholar has seen fit to endorse. His monograph would have been forgotten long ago, had it not inspired Wagner to combine the figures of Ofterdingen and Tannhäuser. But, apart from this one idea, Wagner owed the Königsberg scholar next to nothing. The complete text of the Wartburg poem, which Lucas published and which he expounded in detail, barely influenced Wagner's opera at all. For the theme of the Tournament, as in Bechstein's account of the legend, is not the nature of love but the praise

---

[12] E. T. A. Hoffmann, *Poetische Werke* (Berlin, 1957), vi. 57.

[13] C. T. L. Lucas, *Ueber den Krieg von Wartburg* (Historische und literarische Abhandlungen der königlichen deutschen Gesellschaft zu Königsberg; Königsberg, 1838), 270.

of princes. Ofterdingen incurs the enmity of the other minstrels because he fails to praise the Landgrave Hermann of Thuringia, at whose court the Tournament takes place, but, 'in the face of all the other minstrels', insists upon 'praising the Duke of Austria' instead.[14] His life is threatened, and he has no alternative but to seek refuge beneath the protective mantle of the (unnamed) Landgravine: 'Als er zuo der lantgrefin floch | under iren mantell er ir kroch' (ll. 138–9) (And so he fled to the Landgravine's side | And crept beneath her mantle, there to hide.)

'Although I could use virtually none of this authentic version [of the Wartburg poem] for my own purposes', Wagner wrote in *Mein Leben*, 'it nonetheless showed me the German Middle Ages in a significant colouring I had not yet dreamed of.' (*ML*, p. 224; English trans., p. 213.) For all that, Wagner included very little of this 'significant colouring' in the opera, but borrowed a number of important motifs from Hoffmann's 'Der Kampf der Sänger' instead, while at the same time criticizing Hoffmann for having 'seriously distorted the old legend' (*ML*, p. 223; English trans., p. 212). Whereas Eros plays no part whatsoever in the medieval poem about the Tournament of Song, the theme of love occupies a central position in Hoffmann's tale. Wolfframb von Eschinbach and Heinrich von Ofterdingen are rivals for the hand of the Countess Mathilde, a rivalry in which Wolfframb repeatedly proves himself a magnanimous friend. When open hostility breaks out among the minstrels, he is the only one to stand by Heinrich. This same relationship has been taken over into Wagner's opera with scarcely any shift of emphasis.

It is strange, of course, that in Wagner's prose sketch (not published in its entirety until 1985[15]) there is as yet no hint of any love between Wolfram and Elisabeth. In the final libretto, by contrast, the reunion between Elisabeth and Tannhäuser ends with Wolfram's resigned words:

> So flieht für dieses Leben
> mir jeder Hoffnung Schein . . .   (ii. 20)

> My love remains unspoken,
> And every hope has gone!

whereas, in the prose sketch, Wolfram joins in the lovers' jubilant reunion.

The other important theme linking Wagner's *Tannhäuser* with Hoffmann's 'Der Kampf der Sänger' is the contrast between the

[14] Ibid. 43.
[15] Richard Wagner, *Der Venusberg*, in *Die Programmhefte der Bayreuther Festspiele 1985*, i. '*Tannhäuser*', 1–14; English trans. by Stewart Spencer, 95–105.

demonic and dissonant artistry of Heinrich von Ofterdingen (or Tannhäuser)—an artistry associated with the subterranean forces of hell or the Venusberg—and the well-tempered conventional art of the other minstrels at the Wartburg court. Ofterdingen behaves in an altogether boorish manner during the Tournament of Song, displaying overweening arrogance in letting his fellow-contestants see how little he thinks of their art. 'While the others sang, he stared at the ceiling, shifting around in his chair, twiddling his thumbs, and yawning; in a word, he showed his displeasure and boredom in every possible way.' His reaction to Wolfframb von Eschinbach's song—a song which leaves a deep impression on all the other listeners—is described in the following terms:

Heinrich von Ofterdingen, however, frowned and, turning away from Wolfframb, he took up his lute and struck a number of strange-sounding chords on it. He placed himself at the centre of the circle and began a song whose melody was so unlike anything that the others had sung, so unheard-of, that all were overcome by a sense of the greatest wonderment, and finally by utter astonishment. It was as though the powerful sounds which he struck from his lute beat at the gloomy portals of some strange and fateful realm, conjuring up the secrets of whatever unknown force might dwell there ... Now the chords thundered out more powerfully than ever, red-hot vapours wafted in, and images of wanton bliss burned in the Eden of all delights which now gaped open before them.

Of course, the reaction of Ofterdingen's audience is not one of general horror, as in Wagner's opera; instead, they burst into tumultuous applause, and Mathilde presses a laurel wreath on Ofterdingen's brow 'in guerdon of his singing'.[16] Only after some time has passed are the other minstrels struck by the 'infamy of his singing', and, with the exception of Wolfframb, 'who refused to pass judgement on it', they declare the tune with which Ofterdingen sings in praise of Mathilde's beauty to be 'a pagan abomination'.[17] We come very close here to the relationship between Tannhäuser and Elisabeth in Wagner's opera.

Hoffmann's reference to the 'Eden of all delights' is an allusion to the Venusberg which Nasias later apostrophizes in song. Of course, Ofterdingen himself has not been to the Venusberg. Instead, he projects all his erotic desires and ideas on to Mathilde. Unlike Wagner's Elisabeth, Mathilde is not, therefore, the antithesis of Venus. The idea of the hero vacillating between sacred and profane love, embodied in two antithetical female types, plays only a peripheral role in Hoffmann's tale, although this is so widespread a theme elsewhere in Romantic

---

[16] Hoffmann, *Poetische Werke*, vi. 39–40.
[17] Ibid. 42.

poetry that it could be described as one of Romanticism's leading motifs.

Ludwig Tieck had been the first writer to introduce 'another woman' into the story-line of *Der getreue Eckart*, a woman whom Tannenhäuser loves in vain. And, thirty years before Wagner's opera, Tieck's short story gave Clemens Brentano the idea for an opera about Tannhäuser which he intended to be set to music by Weber. Tieck knew about Brentano's plans, and one wonders whether he told Wagner about them when they met in 1847. In the event, of course, the idea was realized by two other, less important, figures: at almost the same time as Wagner was working on *his* opera, the poet Eduard Duller and the composer Carl Amand Mangold were writing their own *Tanhäuser* (*sic*), based upon Tieck's novella and first performed in Darmstadt in 1846. Here, too, the hero's redemption by a woman's pure love is central to the action.[18]

It may be added that Duller, like Wagner, recognized that, on its own, the story of Tannhäuser was too lightweight dramatically; but whereas Wagner combined it, much more compellingly, with the legend of the Wartburg Tournament of Song, Duller linked it to the legend of the Pied Piper of Hamelin. Lucas had been the first to equate Ofterdingen/Tannhäuser with the Pied Piper in his 1838 treatise, an equation based on the fact that the figure of the minstrel in the Venusberg legend lures men into the mountain with the strains of his music. Tieck's Tannenhäuser reported that, while still a child, he had heard of a minstrel who had come from a 'strange mountain', and that the minstrel's 'wondrous sounds had awoken such deep longing and such wild desires in the hearts of all his listeners that they had been drawn irresistibly along by the music, only to be lost inside the mountain. Hell then opened up its gates to these poor souls, accompanying their entry into the mountain with the sounds of lovely music.'[19] (The reader is involuntarily reminded here of the *Strömkarl*, that Nordic water-sprite who figures in Wagner's 1861 Venusberg ballet and whose playing incites the company to orgiastic dancing.) Mangold's opera also includes the character of Faithful Eckart, replaced by Wolfram von Eschenbach in the final scene of Wagner's opera, where Wolfram clearly assumes the admonitory role of the old man on guard outside the Venusberg.

The theme of two antithetical types of love embodied in two contrasting women is repeatedly associated in Romantic poetry with the myth of a demonic Venus, a myth which, in addition to the Venusberg legend, finds its principal expression in a medieval narrative concerning a statue of Venus which comes to life and becomes betrothed to a

[18] See Elisabeth Frenzel, *Stoffe der Weltliteratur*, 5th edn. (Stuttgart, 1976), 731–3; also Heleen Mendl-Schrama, 'The Other *Tanhäuser*', *Wagner*, 7 (1986), 83–94.
[19] Tieck, *Erzählungen des Phantasus*, p. 61.

passing knight. Heine gives a delightful account of this tale, in its various versions, in his 'Elementargeister':

The scene of action is generally Italy, and the hero . . . some German knight or other who, because of his youthful inexperience or because of his handsome figure, is beguiled by beautiful she-devils with especially charming wiles. He is to be found on beautiful autumn days walking alone, lost in his solitary dreams, thinking perhaps of the forests of oak-trees at home or else of the flaxen-haired girl whom he left behind, the carefree dandy! But suddenly he finds himself standing in front of a marble statue, the very sight of which arrests him in his tracks. It is perhaps the goddess of beauty, and he stands there face to face with her, and the young barbarian's heart is secretly ensnared by the age-old magic spell. What is it? Never before has he seen such slender limbs, and in this marble block he senses a life more intense than he ever found in the carmine cheeks and lips and in all the fleshly charms of his fellow countrywomen.[20]

The statue comes to life, and a dreamlike love-scene ensues. Above all, Heine recalls Eichendorff's 'beautiful tale' on the subject, *Das Marmorbild* (1819). In his own short story, 'Florentinische Nächte', published in 1837 in the same volume of *Der Salon* as his 'Elementargeister', Heine himself offers a variant on this theme, which he presents as a kind of summation of the various Romantic interpretations. The young Maximilian kisses the marble statue of a woman in an overgrown garden, and in later life he is repeatedly plagued by endless embodiments of an artificial and fatal beauty. On one occasion, for example, he falls in love with the painting of a 'Madonna of breath-taking beauty'. 'I then became a fervent church-goer, and my soul was sunk in the mysticism of the Catholic faith. Like some Spanish knight, I should have been glad to fight each day to the death in defence of the Immaculate Conception of the Virgin Mary, Queen of all the Angels, the fairest woman in Heaven and earth!'[21] These lines at once recall Wagner's famous letter to Ernst Benedikt Kietz of 6–10 September 1842, in which he writes of Carlo Dolci's *Madonna Addolorata* in the church at Aussig (Ústí nad Labem): 'It is a quite extraordinarily affecting picture, & if *Tannhäuser* had seen it, I could readily understand how it was that he turned away from Venus to Mary without necessarily having been inspired to do so by any great sense of piety.'[22] We are reminded, too, of Wagner's repeated comparison of Isolde with Titian's *Assunta* (a comparison which will be discussed at greater length in the chapter on *Tristan*, below): as Cosima noted in her

[20] Heine, *Sämtliche Werke*, iii. 560–1.

[21] Ibid. ii. 612.

[22] Richard Wagner, *Sämtliche Briefe*, ed. Gertrud Strobel and Werner Wolf (Leipzig, 1970), ii. 153; English trans. from *Selected Letters of Richard Wagner*, ed. Stewart Spencer and Barry Millington (London, 1987), 95.

diary on 22 October 1882, Wagner denied 'that the *Assunta* is the Mother of God, it is Isolde in the apotheosis of love'.[23]

The theme of religious devotion as a form of sublimated lust returns in Heine's 'Florentinische Nächte', where Maximilian maintains that images of saints excite the Italian populace's erotic imagination: 'And fruitful indeed is their reverence of those fair Madonnas, those lovely altar-pieces, which leave their mark on the mind of the bridegroom, while the bride herself thinks ardent thoughts of a handsome saint.'[24] This remarkable alternation of religious ardour and sinful lust, the synonymity of Virgin and Venus, is a widespread theme in Romantic poetry: thus the statue of Marie Wellner in Brentano's 1801 novel, *Godwi oder das steinerne Bild der Mutter*, contains reminiscences of the Virgin Mary, a suggestion explicitly realized by Brentano's friend, Achim von Arnim, in 1824 in his short story, *Raphael und seine Nachbarinnen*. Here the statue of Venus is identified with the hero's secret love, Benedetta. When Raphael is unfaithful to her and enters into an affair with the demonic Ghita, he rediscovers the statue as a Madonna in the nunnery where Benedetta lives as a painter.

It may be added that Heine's motif of Mariolatry as sublimated lust has a remarkable precedent in Schiller's *Maria Stuart*, first published in 1801. The religious zealot Mortimer confuses the images of Mary the Mother of Jesus and Mary Stuart, most obviously in his final prayer, 'Blessed Mary, pray for me' (l. 2819), a line which refers both to Mary Queen of Scots and to the Virgin Mary. And, following the disastrous encounter between Mary and Elizabeth, his allegedly purely platonic regard for the former turns out to conceal an erotic passion in which religious and sexual fantasies are inextricably linked.

The thematic link between the myths of Venus and the Blessed Virgin Mary continued right up to the turn of the century. The most famous example is Thomas Mann's short story, *Gladius Dei* (1902). In this case, a religious fanatic fired by the ideas of Savonarola attempts to persuade a fine-arts dealer to remove an image of the Madonna from his display and to destroy it, claiming that it bears all the signs of pagan lust. 'It was a Madonna, a piece of craftsmanship conceived in entirely modern terms and free of all conventionality. The figure of the Blessed Virgin was of bewitching femininity, undraped, and beautiful. Her large and languorous eyes were dark-rimmed, and her delicately, strangely smiling lips stood half open.'[25]

The work that comes closest to Wagner's *Tannhäuser* in this thematic

---

[23] On the significance of representations of the Madonna for Wagner, see Peter Wapnewski, *Der traurige Gott: Richard Wagner in seinen Helden* (Munich, 1978), 89–113.

[24] Heine, *Sämtliche Werke*, ii. 616.

[25] Thomas Mann, *Gesammelte Werke*, 2nd edn. (Frankfurt, 1974), viii. 202.

context is without doubt Eichendorff's *Das Marmorbild*. Although there is no proof that Wagner had read this tale, so many of the themes of the Romantic poetry with which he was familiar—from Novalis's *Hymnen an die Nacht* to Tieck's *Der getreue Eckart* and Brentano's *Romanzen vom Rosenkranz*—come together here that motivic parallels are not in the least surprising.

Like Wagner's Tannhäuser, the young poet Florio is torn between his pure love for the maidenly Bianka and his demonic attraction towards a marble statue of Venus which comes alive and seduces him. Just as he threatens to succumb to the goddess's blandishments, he is brought to his senses by the distant sounds of a song sung by his friend and guardian spirit, Fortunato. He utters a prayer and exorcizes the demonic spell. The story is set in Venus's garden, a setting significantly different, of course, from Wagner's Venusberg. Rather, it calls to mind Klingsor's magic garden in *Parsifal*. Even the flowermaidens put in a brief appearance here: 'As the strains of the lute and the rays of the evening sun glided over the flowery fields, beautiful girls rose up here and there from out of the flowers, as though awaking from their midday slumbers.'[26] The flowermaidens' motif had, in fact, been found even earlier, in Tieck's short story *Der getreue Eckart*: just like Parsifal, Tannenhäuser is surrounded by a throng of girls who beckon to him with inviting gestures. 'In the flowers there burned the charms of the girls and the lure of desire; in the women's bodies there blossomed the magic of the flowers; colours here spoke another language, sounds had new words to say, the world of the senses was held fast within a single bloom, and the spirits within it fêted the infinite triumph of rampant desire.'[27]

Eichendorff's tale culminates in a song sung by Fortunato, published in the 1841 edition of his works under the title 'Götterdämmerung'. But not only is it the title of the poem that causes the reader to prick up his ears: the two main themes of the poem also return in Wagner's opera. These themes are the motif of Venus rising up out of her subterranean realm each spring (a motif alluded to in the Shepherd's Song in Act I, 'Frau Holda kam aus dem Berg hervor', in which Frau Holda, according to Wagner's introduction to the first printed edition of the libretto, is the Germanic equivalent of Venus), and the appeal to the Virgin Mary, who is presented as the antithesis of the goddess of love.

> Wenn Frühlingslüfte wehen
> Hold überm grünen Plan,
> Ein leises Auferstehen
> Hebt in den Tälern an.

---

[26] *Joseph Freiherrn von Eichendorffs Werke*, ed. Gustav Karpeles (Leipzig, n.d.), ii. 100.
[27] Tieck, *Erzählungen des Phantasus*, p. 72.

Da will sich's unten rühren
Im stillen Göttergrab,
Der Mensch kann's schaudernd spüren
Tief in der Brust hinab.

.    .    .    .    .

Und unterm duft'gen Schleier,
So oft der Lenz erwacht,
Webt in geheimer Feier
Die alte Zaubermacht.

Frau Venus hört das Locken,
Der Vögel heitern Chor,
Und richtet froh erschrocken
Aus Blumen sich empor.

Sie sucht die alten Stellen,
Das luft'ge Säulenhaus,
Schaut lächelnd in die Wellen
Der Frühlingsluft hinaus.

Doch öd' sind nun die Stellen,
Stumm liegt ihr Säulenhaus,
Gras wächst da auf den Schwellen,
Der Wind zieht ein und aus.

.    .    .    .    .

Sie selbst muß sinnend stehen
So bleich im Frühlingsschein,
Die Augen untergehen,
Der schöne Leib wird Stein.

Denn über Land und Wogen
Erscheint, so still und mild,
Hoch auf dem Regenbogen
Ein ander Frauenbild.

Ein Kindlein in den Armen
Die Wunderbare hält,
Und himmlisches Erbarmen
Durchdringt die ganze Welt.[28]

When gentle springtime breezes
Waft o'er the verdant vale,
A sense of resurrection
Is felt in ev'ry dale.

Beneath the ground a stirring
Of gods long laid to rest
In silent tombs is welling
Within each human breast.

.    .    .    .    .

[28] *Eichendorffs Werke*, pp. 105–6.

And 'neath earth's scented mantle
At each awakening spring,
Of secret celebrations
The old enchantments sing.

Dame Venus hears them calling;
Birds carol all around;
She stirs in startled gladness
From out her grassy mound.

She seeks her former temples,
The airy columned fane,
And smiles to feel the breezes
Of springtime once again.

Forsaken are her temples,
Mute is the columned fane,
Grass grows upon a threshold
Exposed to wind and rain.

.     .     .     .

And bathed in spring's pale sunbeams
She stands there all alone,
Her eyes cast down in sadness,
Her body turned to stone.

For over land and ocean
A rival form is seen,
A rainbow-coloured vision
Both gentle and serene.

For lo, a new-born infant
The wondrous maiden holds,
And heavenly compassion
This world of ours enfolds.

In the version of the Tannhäuser Ballad printed in Nuremberg in 1515, Tannhäuser bids farewell to Venus in two lines which are missing from the later version of the Ballad reproduced in *Des Knaben Wunderhorn* and Heine's 'Elementargeister':

Maria, mutter, reyne maydt,
nun hilff mir von den weyben!

Mary, mother, purest maid,
Now help me flee from womankind!

The 1515 version of the Ballad was familiar to Wagner only from Bechstein, and it must have been from here, therefore, that he took the hero's appeal to the Virgin Mary and his exorcism of Venus's magic spell. At the same time, it must be said that Tannhäuser's reason for abandoning the goddess of love is totally different here. To understand why this is so, we need to examine the original meaning of the Tannhäuser legend, a meaning which has only relatively recently been convincingly elucidated, thanks to the researches of Dietz-Rüdiger Moser.[29] It is a meaning that had been misunderstood even before the Reformation swept across Germany; and it certainly remained a mystery to Wagner, too.

The Tannhäuser legend is part of a rich treasury of popular Christian morality tales which grew out of the Church's programme of doctrinal teaching and which therefore have a catechistical character. It was emphatically not their aim to denounce the pope as obdurate and self-righteous, or to play off God's all-forgiving mercy against the Church's evident lack of compassion, as was believed to be the case in the years before 1848. The pope's rejection of the penitent sinner is merely a temporary measure which, in reality, conceals the promise of redemption. In the popular catechistical tales in question, motifs such as the miracle of the papal staff putting forth green shoots are found again and again. There is one such tale, for example, in which the pope gives a particularly hardened sinner a black sheep, telling him that he will not find absolution until the sheep's black wool has turned white. Apparently denied forgiveness (a temporary measure which the pope conceals from the sinner lest his penance seem too easy), the latter begins to weep uncontrollably. As each tear falls on the sheep's black coat, it leaves a white stain, until finally the fleece is as white as snow. Like the barren staff which bursts into leaf in the papal hand, like the unseasonal blossoming of a tree, and like the countless other miraculous signs which comprise the topoi of Christian iconography, this miracle is the symbolic confirmation of a victory over nature, a victory which takes place against the background of divine mercy and which indicates the end of penance and the remission of sin.

But why does Tannhäuser seek out the pope in the first place? Carnal desire is such an everyday sin that the pope would have his hands full if he attempted to act as father-confessor to every sinner guilty of that particular failing. There are, however, certain mortal sins which, according to canon law, so threaten the Church's structure that the power of absolution remains the sole preserve of the Apostolic See itself. This is still the case in canon law today. Anyone familiar with its precepts will recognize at once that Tannhäuser's journey to Rome is simply to see the appropriate father-confessor. But what is the precise nature of that mortal sin of which only the pope can absolve him (for this is a feature which is part of the basic stereotype of all such legends

---

[29] The following section is based on Dietz-Rüdiger Moser, *Die Tannhäuserlegende: Eine Studie über Intentionalität und Rezeption katechetischer Volkserzählungen zum Buß-Sakrament* (Berlin and New York, 1977).

dealing with penitent sinners)? His stay in the Venusberg cannot, as such, be classed as a mortal sin, for the sin of 'evil desire' ('böse Lust' as Wagner calls it: ii. 36) is one which any priest would have pardoned without a moment's hesitation.

At this point we need to pause briefly to examine the history of the word 'Venusberg' and its Latinized form 'mons Veneris'. Wagner reports in his autobiography that it was the Dresden court music-dealer, Carl Friedrich Meser, who persuaded him finally to abandon the opera's original title of *Der Venusberg*: 'he told me that I simply didn't get round enough to hear the frightful jokes made about this title, which seemed to originate primarily from the staff and students of the Dresden medical school, as they attained heights of obscenity prevalent only in those quarters' (*ML*, p. 314; English trans., p. 301). It seems quite astonishing that Wagner had not realized until then that 'mons Veneris' is a technical term used in medical science for the mount of Venus[30] and that, colloquially, it occurs as a sexual metaphor apparently pre-dating the identification of the Venusberg as a geographical location. At all events, the German expressions 'in Frau Venus Berg fahren' (literally, 'to enter Lady Venus's mountain') and 'den Danhäuser spielen' ('to play at being Danhäuser') are both terms for sexual congress which are widespread in popular erotic language.[31] When Wagner had Tannhäuser invite his fellow-contestants to 'enter the Mount of Venus', he little suspected that he was placing in Tannhäuser's mouth so richly obscene an appeal.

But let us return to the question of Tannhäuser's mortal sin. Precisely what that sin entails emerges from the Tannhäuser Ballad in *Des Knaben Wunderhorn* only in passing, when Venus offers to give Tannhäuser one of her 'playmates' as his 'lawful wedded wife'. Tannhäuser replies:

> Nehme ich dann ein ander Weib,
> Als ich hab in meinem Sinne,
> So muß ich in der Höllenglut
> Da ewiglich verbrennen.

> And if I took another wife
> Than her for whom I yearn,
> Then in the flaming fire of hell
> Eternally I'd burn.[32]

The identity of the other woman is made transparently clear in the 1515 version of the Ballad. It is Mary, Mother of God. It is she to whom

---

[30] As Isolde Vetter has pointed out ('Wagner in the Light of Psychology', in *Wagner Handbook* (in preparation)), Wagner is being wilfully naïve here. The title of the opera had already been changed in 1843, years before there was any question of a vocal score being published (see also *WWV*, p. 287).

[31] See *Deutsches Wörterbuch von Jacob Grimm und Wilhelm Grimm* (Leipzig, 1956), xii/1, cols. 48–9.

[32] Achim von Arnim and Clemens Brentano (eds.), *Des Knaben Wunderhorn* (Heidelberg, 1819; repr. 1928), i. 86–7; trans. from J. W. Thomas, *Tannhäuser: Poet and Legend* (Chapel Hill, NC, 1974), 184–91, esp. p. 185.

Tannhäuser has sworn to be true. His sojourn in the Venusberg is, therefore, in violation of his vow of celibacy; and this is a sin which only the pope can absolve. The journey to Rome is interpreted by Wagner— and he was by no means the first to do so—as a penitential pilgrimage. And yet there can be no question of such a pilgrimage here, for what we are dealing with is a visit to the appropriate confessor, as laid down by canon law, a visit, moreover, which cannot have been so burdensome when we recall that, as a general rule, the Venusberg was located in Italy. The period of penance does not begin until after Tannhäuser's confession in Rome, where the pope's apparent refusal to absolve him amounts to no more than an expression of the fact that, so far, Tannhäuser has completed only two out of the three acts which comprise the sacrament of penance. These three acts are repentance, confession, and atonement (penance in the narrower sense). But Tannhäuser has still to atone, which is why the time is not yet ripe for the remission of his sins. Such is the severity of his guilt that confession in itself is not sufficient for absolution. It was not until the end of the fifteenth century that the practice of absolving the sinner *before* he had completed his penance began to gain acceptance. In the meantime, the pope promises Tannhäuser reconciliation, even though he appears to present it as an impossibility by making it dependent upon a miracle.

Even before the Reformation swept across Germany, this point had already been totally misunderstood. The hyperbolical 'impossibility' of reconciliation was seen as the sinner's definitive excommunication in an age no longer familiar with the rhetoric of the medieval Church. But the pope would never have been justified in excommunicating Tannhäuser in this way. Indeed, had he done so, he would have been guilty of heresy, for it is one of the fundamental dogmas of the Church that no sin is so great that it cannot be forgiven by virtue of Christ's act of redemption and the sacrament of atonement which he initiated. The author of the Tannhäuser Ballad of 1515 believed that the pope—Urban IV—had violated this elementary article of faith and that he was therefore condemned to eternal perdition:

> Des must der vierte Babst Vrban
> Auch ewigklich sein verloren.

> And so the pope, Urban the Fourth,
> Was lost for evermore.

These are the final lines of the Ballad. The version in *Des Knaben Wunderhorn* is rather more moderate in tone:

> Das soll nimmer kein Priester tun,
> Dem Menschen Mißtrost geben,
> Will er denn Buß und Reu empfahn,
> Die Sünde sei ihm vergeben.

> No priest should ever say such things,
> Nor leave a man unshriven,
> When offered penance and remorse,
> His sins should be forgiven.[33]

This is the Church's fundamental attitude, and one which has never been called into question, least of all by any pope.

This misunderstanding surrounding the original meaning of the Tannhäuser Ballad culminates in a hopeless contradiction in both versions of the poem known to Wagner. Of course, the miracle of the burgeoning staff duly takes place (as take place it must, given the basic stereotype of the catechistical tale of the penitent sinner), but it comes too late, for Tannhäuser has already made his way back to the Venusberg, overcome by despair at what he assumes to be the pope's sentence of damnation following his unforgivable 'sin against the Holy Ghost'. But this, of course, is absurd. In keeping with the original catechistical meaning of the legend, Tannhäuser's return to the Venusberg does not signify a relapse on his part, but simply the sinner's return to the place where he first incurred his sin and where he must now atone: only here can he do penance by being constantly reminded of his sin. This, too, is part and parcel of the well-established complex of motifs which make up the plots of all such penitential legends. Although only half-understood, an awareness of this fact can still be glimpsed in both Tannhäuser Ballads, for in each of them Tannhäuser's reaction to the pope's pronouncement is entirely appropriate: he seems to interpret the pope's words correctly as the imposition of a heavy penance, for when the latter announces:

> Wann dieser Stecken Blätter trägt,
> Sind dir deine Sünden verziehen,
>
> When this stick shall put forth shoots,
> Then all your sins shall be forgiven,

Tannhäuser replies:

> Sollt ich leben nicht mehr denn ein Jahr,
> Ein Jahr auf dieser Erden
> So wollt ich Reu und Buß empfahn
> Und Gottes Gnad erwerben.
>
> But if I live no more than a year,
> A year ere I expire,
> I'd fain be told to repent and atone
> And so God's grace acquire.[34]

---

[33] von Arnim and Brentano (eds.), *Des Knaben Wunderhorn*, 90.        [34] Ibid. 89.

He even justifies his return to the Venusberg as a directive from God, which would be wholly nonsensical if it were not meant to be interpreted, in the sense outlined above, as a practical admonition to atone. But this is something that the ballad-poet no longer understood, and so he also failed to understand that the miracle of the burgeoning staff signals the end of Tannhäuser's term of atonement in the Venusberg. Instead, the poet believed that Tannhäuser must remain there 'for ever and a day'.[35] That God has forgiven his sins—in spite of the fact that, in the meantime, he has returned to this hotbed of iniquity out of a sense of utter despair—is something he never discovers. It should now be clear that this ending makes theological nonsense.

It appears, therefore, that the 1515 Ballad and its later revision, as transmitted by Kornmann's *Mons Veneris*, Arnim and Brentano's *Des Knaben Wunderhorn*, and Heine's 'Elementargeister', is the product of a layman's misunderstanding of the earlier legend of a penitent Tannhäuser (or Danheüser), a legend already extant in a number of different versions even before it found written expression. Indeed, exactly when the legend first came into being is a matter for speculation. Its historical protagonist, a minnesinger from the Austro-Bavarian family of the lords of Tannhausen, was active around the middle of the thirteenth century and is believed to have taken part in the Crusade of 1228. His dance-poems, following the tradition of *nidere minne*, delight in the depiction of women's charms, and must themselves have inspired the legend of the Knight of Venus. A penitential hymn or *Bußlied* has also survived which has been attributed to him, although its authenticity has, not unnaturally, been called into question, so that it is impossible to say whether it was the hymn which inspired the legend or, conversely, whether the hymn is the reflection of an earlier legend.

Popularized by Arnim and Brentano in their 1806 anthology, the Tannhäuser Ballad of 1515 enjoyed a peculiar upsurge of interest among the Young German writers of the 1830s. (A clear indication of that interest is the appearance of the complete text of the Ballad in Heine's *Der Salon*.) Young German writers saw in it a reflection of their own theme of conflict; and in their polemical opposition to the mysticism of Rome, to reactionary Church orthodoxy, and to an old-fashioned morality inimical to sensuality, they could readily appeal to the Ballad in support of their cause. The values of Young Germany have also left their unmistakable imprint on Wagner's *Tannhäuser*. The young Wagner was linked to this literary movement (which suffered persecution at the hands of powerful political reactionaries) not only ideologically but personally, too, not least as a result of his friendship with Heinrich

---

[35] Ibid.

Laube. Artistically, the most important record of this relationship is, of course, Wagner's early opera *Das Liebesverbot*, first performed in 1836, to a libretto based on Shakespeare's *Measure for Measure*. According to his 'Autobiographical Sketch', Wagner's intention here was to allow 'free and open sensuality' to triumph over 'puritanical hypocrisy simply by being itself' (i. 10). The 'ban on love' (in other words, the declared illegality of a carnival and its attendant erotic permissiveness) is imposed on the population of Palermo by a Teutonic moralist, but is undermined by the Mediterranean sensuality of the Sicilian temperament. The governor, Friedrich, represents 'the very antithesis of love', to quote the text of the opera (xi. 97), but he finally succumbs to erotic desire. In this, he is, to a certain extent, supplanted by the pope in *Tannhäuser*, for in place of a ban on love and a death-sentence imposed on those who are guilty of falling in love, we find the hero condemned to eternal damnation for having abandoned himself to 'evil desire'.

There are, however, other parallels between *Tannhäuser* on the one hand and *Das Liebesverbot* and the Young German movement on the other. Tannhäuser flees from a state of servitude to social and poetic conventions which force him to repress his enjoyment of love and to seek refuge instead in the boundless erotic freedom of the Venusberg, fleeing, so to speak, from the Middle Ages into classical antiquity. The Wartburg poets, whose company he can no longer tolerate and who, following his return to the world, once more provoke him with their anti-erotic songs of love, glorify a desensualized type of *hôhe minne*[36] which denies all possibility of sexual fulfilment and which is symbolized by the limpid reflection in a fountain's glassy surface:

> Und nimmer möcht' ich diesen Bronnen trüben,
> berühren nicht den Quell mit frev'lem Muth!        (ii. 22.)
>
> I never could defile the fountain's beauty,
> Or cloud its purity with wanton deed.

Thus Wolfram sings in praise of love. For Tannhäuser, however, love is a single psycho-physical entity whose very essence is destroyed the moment that mind and body are divorced. That is why he approaches the fountain—which Wolfram introduces as an image of love—not in a spirit of 'reverential' contemplation but in order to drink from its waters:

> Des Durstes Brennen muß ich kühlen,
> getrost leg' ich die Lippen an.
> In vollen Zügen trink' ich Wonnen,
> in die kein Zagen je sich mischt.        (ii. 23.)

---

[36] The term *hôhe minne* describes the unconsummated love for a woman whom the poet places above himself in social standing. It is often—incorrectly, in the present translator's opinion—rendered into English as 'courtly love', a term coined by the French scholar Gaston Paris towards the end of the 19th century. The expression *nidere minne* describes a sexual relationship with a woman of lower social standing.

> I must cool a burning thirst
> And satisfy it with my lips.
> In long draughts I draw pleasure
> And will not tremble at the sight.

When Walther—the purest representative of an insipid and conventional view of love—presumptuously reproaches Tannhäuser for his ignorance of love's true nature, the latter scornfully replies:

> Wenn du in solchem Schmachten bangest,
> versiegte wahrlich wohl die Welt.                    (ii. 24.)

> While we were languishing so shyly,
> The world would wither and decay.

In other words, all humankind would perish if it were guided by a view of love which saw only 'impious passion' (ii. 23) in physical union. Worship befits only God and the world above.

> Doch was sich der Berührung beuget,
> euch Herz und Sinnen nahe liegt,
> was sich, aus gleichem Stoff erzeuget,
> in weicher Formung an euch schmiegt,—
> dem ziemt Genuß in freud'gem Triebe,
> und im Genuß nur kenn' ich Liebe!                   (ii. 24.)

> But all that we can touch and see
> Excites our hearts with restless fire;
> All that is flesh and blood as we are
> Is but an object of desire.
> Let us enjoy with fullest pleasure,
> For by enjoyment love I measure!

This is unadulterated Young German ideology. Provoked to the utmost by the arrogant impotence of the other court poets and by their mindless repetition of long-familiar clichés, Tannhäuser finally confesses his love for Venus as the ideal form of love. His hymn to Venus, which puts a premature end to the Tournament, causing the latter to break up in 'general disorder and horror' (ii. 25), is diametrically opposed to Wolfram's song, with which the Tournament had begun. This song, too, as noted earlier, is addressed to Venus—not, of course, to Venus Cypria, the goddess of sensual pleasure, but to Venus Urania, the goddess of a spiritual and renunciatory love, embodied for Wolfram in the evening star, Venus. This is the Venus who alone inspires self-composure and devotion.

Tannhäuser's earlier flight from a world which had conceived of love as something superficial and conventional may be said to signify his conversion from the sublimated view of love which was widespread during the Middle Ages to the hedonism of classical antiquity, a hedonism which now, as it were, leads an underground existence. The fact that, even in exile, the ancient gods still strive to interfere in our lives—indeed, that their apocryphal influence protects the world from desolation—is clear from Venus's words to Tannhäuser, which, in the version of the text published in Wagner's *Collected Writings*, run as follows:

> Ach! kehrtest du nicht wieder,
> dann träfe Fluch die Welt;
> für ewig läg' sie öde,
> aus der die Göttin schwand!   (ii. 10.)

> If you do not return,
> Then all mankind shall know my curse!
> Ever frigid and barren be
> The world that I have left.

This idea, which is also present in the pre-1861 versions of the libretto, albeit less explicitly formulated, is curiously—and almost paradoxically—confirmed by the Shepherd's Song at the beginning of the third scene:

> Frau Holda kam aus dem Berg hervor,
> zu ziehen durch Flur und Auen.            (ii. 11.)

> Dame Holda stepped from the mountain's heart,
> To roam through wood and through meadow.

Even the Shepherd, embodying the *paradis vert* of lost innocence in contrast to the *paradis artificiel* of the Venusberg,[37] dreams a 'lovely dream' ('einen holden Traum': ii. 12) about Holda/Venus. The first sounds which Tannhäuser hears on fleeing from the cave of lust and entering a world that is the complete antithesis of the Venusberg is a naïve song in praise of the beneficent powers of the goddess of love. For Holda is one and the same as Venus, as Wagner himself expressly emphasized in his introduction to the first printed edition of the libretto. The passage is clearly inspired by Heine's 'Elementargeister':

The ancient Germanic goddess Holda, benign, gentle, and merciful, whose yearly progress through the countryside brought prosperity and fruitfulness to the fields, was forced, at the advent of Christianity, to suffer a similar fate to that of Wodan and all the other gods whose existence and miraculous powers, being so deeply rooted in popular faith, could not be wholly gainsaid, but whose erstwhile beneficent influence was seen as suspect and reinterpreted as something evil. Holda was banished to subterranean caverns and mountain interiors; her emergence into the world was thought to herald disaster, her retinue likened to that of the Wild Hunt. Later (while the common folk continued to believe unconsciously in her gentle influence animating nature [cf.

---

[37] Hans Mayer, 'Tannhäuser und die künstlichen Paradiese', in *Richard Wagner: Mitwelt und Nachwelt* (Stuttgart and Zurich, 1978), 191–200.

the Shepherd's Song]), her name became merged with that of Venus, a name to which all ideas of an ill-starred magic being luring men to evil desire quickly became associated. The interior of the Hörselberg near Eisenach was designated one of her principal seats in Thuringia; there Frau Venus held court in wantonness and lust. (xvi. 186.)

Although condemned by Christianity as a place of evil, the Venusberg continued to exert a benign influence on the world of men. Venus succeeded Persephone, the goddess of the classical underworld. Both were granted the right to return to earth each spring and awaken Nature to a new life. This is the meaning of the Shepherd's Song: it too, therefore, is a secret hymn to Venus.

It will be seen that there is no strict antithesis in *Tannhäuser* between the world of classical sensuality and that of Christian spirituality, but that the two are dialectically interrelated. This is also true of the two women in the drama who personify this antithesis. Tannhäuser, who rebels against the dualism of spirit and sensuality, of sacred and profane love, originally sought out Venus because of Elisabeth, as it were. The latter was unattainable within the framework of *hôhe minne*, having become an object of mere veneration when Tannhäuser wanted to love her with both body and soul. In Venus he was looking for Elisabeth, just as, on his return to the Wartburg, he now looks for Venus in Elisabeth. For there can be no doubt that the hymn which Tannhäuser sings at the Tournament of Song in praise of 'enjoyment' in love is directed at none other than Elisabeth. It is not that he hesitates between the two women, for Venus is not a real *person* like Elisabeth, but that he thinks of Venus simply as an *idea*—the idea of a physically fulfilling love, which he looks for solely in Elisabeth.

Wagner suggested as much in his 1852 essay, *On Performing 'Tannhäuser'*. Following his return to the Wartburg, Tannhäuser's love for Elisabeth grips him like some 'all-consuming fiery force'. 'With this fire, this ardour, he once enjoyed Venus's love and must now involuntarily fulfil the vow he freely swore on leaving her, "henceforth to be her valiant champion against the entire world".' During the Tournament of Song 'his feelings struggle only for his love of Elisabeth, as he finally confesses, freely and openly, to being Venus's champion'. Prior to this confession, Elisabeth herself has tacitly accepted Tannhäuser's message of love. Even before he left the Landgrave's court, she had sensed how true to life Tannhäuser's songs were compared with the love-songs usually heard there:

> Der Sänger klugen Weisen
> lauscht' ich sonst gern und viel;
> ihr Singen und ihr Preisen
> schien mir ein holdes Spiel.

Doch welch' ein seltsam neues Leben
rief euer Lied mir in die Brust!
Bald wollt' es mich wie Schmerz durchbeben,
bald drang's in mich wie jähe Lust:
Gefühle, die ich nie empfunden!
Verlangen, das ich nie gekannt!
Was einst mir lieblich, war verschwunden
vor Wonnen, die noch nie genannt!                    (ii. 18–19.)

> When singers sang their songs here,
> I proudly praised their skill and fame;
> And yet their words and music
> To me were just a game.

But what a strange new world of feeling
Awoke in me when I heard you!
At times it seemed I'd die of sorrow,
And then my heart would burst with joy,
With feelings I had not experienced,
And longings I had never known!
All simple pleasures lay behind me,
My carefree innocence had flown.

Her reaction to Tannhäuser's song praising physical pleasure in love is significant: 'Elisabeth makes a gesture to show her approval but, as the whole of the rest of the audience maintains a solemn silence, she modestly restrains herself.' (ii. 23.)

But if Tannhäuser does not interpret his departure from the Venusberg as a radical break with the type of love which Venus embodies, why does he leave the Venusberg at all? In the first of his three great hymns in praise of Venus (each of which starts enthusiastically enough, only to develop a more melancholy tone), he announces:

Nach Freude, ach! nach herrlichem Genießen
verlangt' mein Herz, es dürstete mein Sinn:
da, was nur Göttern einstens du erwiesen,
gab deine Gunst mir Sterblichem dahin. —
> Doch sterblich, ach! bin ich geblieben,
> und übergroß ist mir dein Lieben;
wenn stets ein Gott genießen kann,
bin ich dem Wechsel unterthan;
nicht Lust allein liegt mir am Herzen,
aus Freuden sehn' ich mich nach Schmerzen:
aus deinem Reiche muß ich flieh'n, —
o, Königin, Göttin! Laß mich zieh'n!                   (ii. 6.)

The fruits of love my senses long to savour,
My heart cries out, my reason and my thought;

Once to the gods, our masters, you showed favour,
Now what they knew, a mortal has been taught.
　　From man's desires no god can spare me,
　　And all too rich the love that you bear me;
　　While gods through pleasure freely range,
　　I am a man, I yearn for change.
　　In joy alone lies no tomorrow:
　　I long to suffer in human sorrow.
　　So from your kingdom must I flee:
　　From endless love, Goddess, set me free!

Tannhäuser yearns to escape from the eternity of a *paradis perverti* and
return to a world of mortality, change, and pain, where time exists once
more:

　　Die Zeit, die hier ich weil', ich kann sie nicht
　　ermessen:—Tage, Monde—giebt's für mich
　　nicht mehr, denn nicht mehr sehe ich die Sonne,
　　nicht mehr des Himmels freundliche Gestirne;—
　　den Halm seh' ich nicht mehr, der frisch ergrünend
　　den neuen Sommer bringt;—die Nachtigall
　　nicht hör' ich mehr, die mir den Lenz verkünde:—
　　hör' ich sie nie, seh'ich sie niemals mehr?　　　　　(ii. 5–6.)

　　The time that I have been here
　　No longer can be measured;
　　Daytime, night-time, mean no more to me;
　　How long since I have felt the sunlight,
　　Or glimpsed the stars that glimmer in the darkness;
　　The grass no more I see, so fresh with promise
　　Of summer's healing warmth; the nightingale
　　No more I hear that sings of spring's awakening.
　　Am I to hear or see them nevermore?

Tannhäuser has grown weary of eternal bliss. In much the same way,
Tieck's Tannenhäuser had justified his departure from the Venusberg
with the words: 'I longed to lead the sort of life which people lead in all
unconsciousness, a life in which suffering alternates with joy; I was sated
with such glamour, and now sought out my former home once more.'[38]
Heine's Tannhäuser, too, in his parody of the legend, is similarly 'sick'
of always being happy: 'I pine for bitterness', he tells Venus:

　　Ich habe zu viel gescherzt und gelacht.
　　Ich sehne mich nach Tränen,
　　Und statt mit Rosen möcht ich mein Haupt
　　Mit spitzgen Dornen krönen.[39]

[38] Tieck, *Erzählungen des Phantasus*, p. 72.
[39] Heine, *Sämtliche Werke*, iii. 570.

> Too much have we jested, too much have we laugh'd,
> My heart for tears has long panted;
> Each rose on my head I fain would see
> By pointed thorns supplanted.

Not only the idea expressed here (an idea which is elaborated in the same writer's 'Elementargeister' essay) but, more especially, the Ecce Homo reminiscence in the final lines have clearly left a deep impression on Wagner. And they may well have continued to resonate in his subconscious, welling up to the surface not only in Siegmund's rejection of the joys of Valhalla as evoked by Brünnhilde during the *Todesverkündigung*, but in Parsifal's sudden vision of the tormented Amfortas as Kundry embraces him.

If Tannhäuser strives to flee from the Venusberg, it is not out of remorse or because he is conscious of his sin (for only at the very last moment, before he reaches the world above ground, does he once again apply Christian standards to himself and speak of repentance and salvation), but because he can no longer bear to be treated as a god—because, paradoxically, he suffers from a lack of suffering. To a certain extent, Tannhäuser is the opposite of those classical sinners, Tantalus, Sisyphus, and Ixion. Whereas *they* were cast out of Olympus and sent to Tartarus for failing to take account of human limitations (and failing to do so, moreover, in an erotic context), Tannhäuser ascends from the underworld, where the Olympian gods now live in exile, and re-enters the world above ground precisely in order to rediscover the limitations of humankind and to feel human suffering once again. At the same time, he longs to leave the *paradis artificiel* of the Venusberg and return to the *paradis vert* of lost childhood innocence amid the 'fresh green of the meadows' (ii. 7) and the fields of his homeland. Above all, however, he feels threatened as an artist by enslavement and sterility—the very qualities which he had found at the Landgrave's court in the empty conventionality of the Wartburg poets and which he had sought to avoid by fleeing to the Venusberg.

Whereas he was denied *enjoyment* within the world of self-contained feelings of Thuringian society, enjoyment now prevents him from *suffering*. But both these emotions—suffering and enjoyment in their fullest intensity—are what make him a poet. Thus he argues with Venus:

> .Bei dir kann ich nur Sklave werden;
> ˙nach Freiheit doch verlange ich,
> nach Freiheit, Freiheit dürstet's mich;
> zu Kampf und Streite will ich stehen,
> sei's auch auf Tod und Untergehen!     (ii. 9.)

> My life with you in slavery shames me;
> For freedom, yes, my senses yearn,
> For freedom, freedom, still I burn.
> The world waits there to be explored,
> Even though death be my reward.

An idea which had been merely hinted at in the pre-Paris versions[40] now emerges with unmistakable clarity from the 1861 revision of the Venusberg scene: Tannhäuser is related spiritually to the Flying Dutchman. Both suffer from the eternity of existence and from their inability to die:

> O Göttin, woll' es fassen,
> mich drängt es hin zum Tod!
>
> O Goddess, understand me,
> I long to suffer death!

Whereupon Venus reveals to him that the terrible fate of Ahasuerus may well await him, too:

> Wenn selbst der Tod dich meidet,
> ein Grab dir selbst verwehrt? (ii. 11.)
>
> But when death has turned you away,
> When the grave closes shut in your face . . .

At no point is it ever suggested that this Wagnerian Venusberg is a kind of hell, that the exiled gods are in league with Satan, or that this underground realm is a world of evil. The system of values associated with medieval Christianity has, so to speak, been suspended here. Venus's realm is a world of eroto-aesthetic beauty which insists upon its apocryphal rights in the face of Christianity's prevailing demands, rights which are also guaranteed to the exiled gods of classical antiquity in Heine's *Die Götter Griechenlands*, which is, as it were, a *contrafactum* of Schiller's similarly entitled poem. (This emerges with particular clarity from Wagner's 1860 sketch for the Venusberg ballet, a sketch which is a kind of synoptic vision of erotic myths from ancient times, from Diana and Endymion to the Rape of Europa and the myth of Leda and the Swan. At the same time, this whole new scene is an astonishing anticipation of Nietzsche, with a Dionysian procession in which all the requisite properties and mythological characters irrupt with orgasmic frenzy into the Apollonian world of Venus's hedonistic court.)

[40] In view of the complex history of the various versions of the opera, it is, of course, an over-simplification to speak of the 'Dresden Version': see Reinhard Strohm, 'Zur Werkgeschichte des "Tannhäuser"', in *Die Programmhefte der Bayreuther Festspiele 1978*, iii. '*Tannhäuser*', 12–13, 64–76; English trans. by John Bell, 21–9.

Up to this point, *Tannhäuser* could be seen as the work of any Young German dramatist: the artist flees from an anti-epicurean, illiberal society characterized by its rigid conventionality, and seeks the emancipation of the flesh in the classically inspired sensuality of the antithetical world of the Venusberg. He abandons the latter because the shadowless, erotic pleasures it has to offer cause him to sink into inactivity, although it is never his intention to deny the experience of physical love which he has gained there. Following his return to society, he finds himself torn between his desire to praise a physically fulfilling love and the established forces of a society hostile to Eros. The conflict is irreconcilable, and the artist is driven from society.

This model does not, of course, exhaust the whole range of meanings contained in Wagner's opera. The 'Young German' chain of motivation and course of action is contrasted with a 'Romantic' chain, so to speak, and the two cannot be linked together without a certain sense of strain. It should be clear by now that when Tannhäuser leaves Venus, he does not disown her altogether. The principle of physical love which she embodies, and the shadowless, timeless, erotic pleasures which she offers, cannot—by virtue of their total one-sidedness—provide Tannhäuser with a satisfactory basis for his life and art. He does not attempt to exclude this principle from his life, but seeks to reincorporate it within the original framework of his existence, in which permanence and change, pleasure and pain, spirit and sensuality are interrelated as polar opposites. That is why, in all the versions of the text, he can assure Venus:

> Nie war mein Lieben größer, niemals wahrer,
> als jetzt, da ich für ewig dich muß flieh'n!　　　(ii. 8.)
>
> Never was love more fervent, never truer
> Than now, when I must beg you to set me free!

And (also in all the versions):

> Ja, gegen alle Welt will unverdrossen
> fortan ich nun dein kühner Streiter sein!　　　(ii. 8.)
>
> Yes, out into the world your banner raising,
> Your loyal champion I will ever be.

It is a promise which he keeps during the Tournament of Song. This explanation of Tannhäuser's departure from the Venusberg, however, is overshadowed by a second reason, suddenly introduced at the end of the scene, without any previous warning, when Tannhäuser abruptly announces (in the 'Dresden Version'):

> Vom Bann werd' ich durch Buß' erlöst!
> Repentance shall forgiveness buy!

and (in every version):

> Mein Heil ruht in Maria!
> My hope lies in Mary!

This, of course, prepares the way for an effective *coup de théâtre* in which the Venusberg suddenly disappears from sight, but, from the standpoint of the Venusberg scene and in the context of the foregoing dialogue, this sudden turn of events in the direction of orthodox Christianity is altogether unjustified.

This superimposition of two unconnected motives leads to a fundamental contradiction in the conception of the Wartburg scene. In the libretto Wagner has drawn a discreet veil over the reason why the Landgrave has organized the Tournament of Song at all. In the prose draft it is the Landgrave himself (in the libretto, Wolfram) who informs Tannhäuser of Elisabeth's love and bluntly invites him to 'sue for Elisabeth's hand'.[41] Indeed, he even points out the best way of doing so ('Tannhäuser, let me show you the way to win this noble girl'): Tannhäuser must win the Tournament of Song, and Elisabeth must hand him the coveted prize.[42] She herself, of course, will be that prize. It is impossible to overlook the parallel with *Die Meistersinger* here, a work which, as we know, was originally intended to 'follow on from my *Sängerkrieg auf Wartburg* as a richly allusive satyr play' (iv. 284), in other words, as a bourgeois comedy which would form a pendant to the courtly tragedy of *Tannhäuser*. Even in the completed libretto there is no mistaking this original reason for holding the Tournament of Song: whoever sings most worthily of love, the Landgrave declares, will receive the prize from Elisabeth's hand:

> er ford're ihn so hoch und kühn er wolle,
> ich sorge, daß sie ihm gewähren solle.          (ii. 21–2.)

> However high the prize, let him demand it:
> I promise on my honour she will grant it.

It is impossible, therefore, to agree with Hans Mayer when he claims[43] that there is a parallel between Tannhäuser and Goethe's Tasso, inasmuch as both poets transgress the social limitations imposed upon them as a result of the love they feel for their respective princesses.

---

[41] Wagner, *Der Venusberg*, p. 4; English trans. (Spencer), p. 97.
[42] Ibid. 6–7; English trans., p. 99.
[43] Mayer, 'Tannhäuser und die künstlichen Paradiese', p. 60.

Elisabeth is the prize which persuades Tannhäuser to take part in the Tournament.

Wagner had good reasons for drawing a veil over the motivation behind the Tournament in the libretto (he was unable to remove it entirely), since it would have revealed all too clearly the fundamental contradiction at the root of the opera's conception. For how are we to explain the fact that, following his homage to Venus, Tannhäuser suddenly falls into line with the values of Wartburg society and sets off, in a spirit of penance, on his way to Rome—the selfsame man who, on leaving Venus, had sworn that he would face the world unflinchingly as Venus's 'loyal champion'? Tannhäuser himself gives the following reason for his change of heart:

> Zum Heil den Sündigen zu führen,
> die Gott-Gesandte nahte mir:
> doch, ach! sie frevelnd zu berühren
> hob ich den Lästerblick zu ihr!          (ii. 28.)

> To save a sinner from damnation
> An angel came to guard my days,
> But I, I saw her, and desired her,
> Soiled her with sly and lustful gaze.

It is at this moment that Tannhäuser's love, together with his longing for physical fulfilment and his Young German glorification of erotic love, suddenly assumes a sinful aspect. Elisabeth, who had been an attractive first prize in the song contest, is now expected to play a totally different role as divine intercessor. It is not his sojourn in the Venusberg, but the fact that he had 'dared to profane the messenger God sent' and that he had projected his erotic desires on to her which is now to be seen as his actual sin. Wagner insisted on this interpretation. The passage quoted above, he wrote to Franz Liszt on 29 May 1852 (anticipating ideas shortly to be expressed in his essay *On Performing 'Tannhäuser'*), encapsulates 'the entire meaning of Tannhäuser's catastrophe, nay, it is the unique expression of Tannhäuser's entire being'. 'All his suffering, his bloody pilgrimage, everything stems from the sense contained within these strophes: unless we hear them at his point, and precisely at this point, and unless we hear them, moreover, as they must be heard, Tannhäuser as a whole remains incomprehensible, an arbitrary, vacillating—pitiful figure.'[44]

Whenever Wagner lays especial emphasis upon a point, we do well to mistrust him. And the same is true on this occasion. A glance at the prose draft shows that the lines in question are not a part of the original complex of motives. That they later grew in importance for Wagner is,

---

[44] Wagner, *Sämtliche Briefe*, iv. 377; English trans. (*Selected Letters of Richard Wagner*), p. 258.

of course, understandable. Without them—in other words, without the wholesale re-evaluation of Tannhäuser's relationship with Elisabeth— his 'bloody pilgrimage' to Rome, his outward appropriation of the code of values held dear by the other members of Thuringian society, would be insufficiently motivated. (If his 'sin' had not been committed against Elisabeth, he could have set off to Rome immediately after leaving the Venusberg, as in the original legend.) The new motivation behind his pilgrimage destroys almost entirely the meaning of all that has gone before it. Up to this point, Elisabeth had appeared to Tannhäuser not as an intercessor but as a lover who, like Tannhäuser, had yearned for the physical fulfilment of her love. Indeed, the Landgrave had made a veiled promise of marriage to them both. Only after the scandal has broken over the Wartburg is Elisabeth transformed into an ascetic figure who, in her prayer to the Virgin, dismisses physical love as 'foolish illusion' and 'sinful longing' (ii. 32).

The ethos of renunciation proclaimed by Wolfram in the second act achieves a victory in the final act over the Young Germans' cult of Eros. Venus Urania triumphs over Venus Cypria, while the world of convention, in the shape of medieval Thuringian society and the Church in general, is inevitably placed in the wrong. Divine clemency overrides their rigid norms, and the sinner is forgiven. *Tannhäuser* thus assumes a remarkable position midway between Wagner's earlier opera, *Das Liebesverbot*, and his final music drama, *Parsifal*: on the one hand it looks back to the cult of Eros of the earlier opera, on the other, it anticipates the renunciatory ethos of the later work. The tale of the Young German artist who, transported back to the Middle Ages, sets out to learn all about the emancipation of the flesh in the sensual world of an 'exiled' antiquity is transformed at the end of the second act into a Romantic opera of renunciation and redemption.

# 16

# Improvisation and Vocational Skill:
# The Poetics of *Die Meistersinger*

> So führen wir vor Aug und Ohr
> Euch heut einen alten Dichter vor.
> Derselbe war nach seiner Art
> Mit soviel Tugenden gepaart,
> Daß er bis auf den heutgen Tag
> Noch für'n Poeten gelten mag,
> Wo deren doch unzählig viel
> Verderben einer des andern Spiel.
>
> Goethe, 'Ein Meistersänger als Prologus' to
> Deinhardstein's *Hans Sachs* (1829).

> And so if you with eye and ear
> Attend, you'll see a poet here
> Who, in the manner of his day,
> Was blest with virtue, so they say,
> That even in the present age
> He'd still be deemed a bard, I wage,
> Though now their number is so great
> Each would his fellow's game frustrate.

Wagner completed the full score of *Tannhäuser* in April 1845, and in early July he set off for Marienbad (Mariánské Lázně) in order to take the waters. It was here that he sketched out the first prose draft of a 'comic opera in three acts', *Die Meistersinger von Nürnberg*, a work which was not to receive its first performance until twenty-three years later in Munich. 'Just as, with the Athenians, a comic satyr play followed the tragedy', Wagner wrote in *A Communication to my Friends* six years after this first draft was completed, 'so I was struck by the idea for a comic play which could indeed follow after my "Wartburg Tournament of Song" as a richly allusive satyr play.' (iv. 284.) Originally, then, *Die Meistersinger* was intended as a parodistic variant of Wagner's Romantic opera about the artist Tannhäuser, a comic interlude in the series comprising *Der fliegende Holländer*, *Tannhäuser*, and *Lohengrin* (the latter conceived and executed immediately after the *Meistersinger* sketch). Hans Sachs, recently elevated to the status of an operatic hero by Deinhardstein and Lortzing, seemed to Wagner to represent 'the final manifestation of the artistically creative spirit of the *Volk*': as such, he contrasted with the 'petty bourgeois Mastersingers, to whose altogether comical poetical pedantry, with its insistence on the *Tabulatur*', Wagner 'gave concrete expression in the figure of the "Marker"' (iv. 284–5).

In his 1851 essay Wagner explains his initial reluctance to versify this draft and set it to music. It was, he claims, because he felt able to tackle the subject only from an 'ironical' standpoint (iv. 287), and 'irony' was incapable of stimulating him as poet or musician. The word 'irony' does indeed occur repeatedly in the Marienbad draft, and always in connection with Sachs. Since the latter was responsible for 'maintaining the rules' at the time that the action is set, it was his task in Act I to read the rules of the guild to the young knight (as yet unnamed) and to explain them to him. 'Hans Sachs does all this with a dash of irony—the Masters sometimes find his attitude questionable.' Indeed, the Masters' doubts emerge in conversation even before Sachs appears on stage, since 'they do not really trust him and doubt whether he is being honest with the guild' (xi. 345–6). Even his song in 'praise of the Mastersingers' guild' at the end of the opera is said to be 'half ironic, half serious' (xi. 355). Clearly, Wagner found no way of reconciling Sachs and the young knight with the guild, since all he could see in the latter was a 'petty bourgeois society', while the positive aspects of their rules concerning art—a fixed 'style' and a universally valid 'art-form' which complemented the more subjective expressive abilities of the young knight—were evidently not yet amenable to adequate evaluation. There is an antagonism between Sachs and the young knight on the one hand and the Mastersingers on the other which is not yet dialectically accommodated and which can scarcely be reconciled convincingly through the medium of humour and comic opera. Only later, when Wagner had developed a more positive attitude to the 'craftsmanlike' qualities of art, would such a reconciliation be possible.

In his letter to Richard Strauss of 1 July 1927 Hugo von Hofmannsthal attributes the 'great appeal and great strength of *Die Meistersinger*, purely as a poem', not least to the poetic association of the German Romantics' myth of Nuremberg with the revival of that myth through Wagner's own experiences in the town as related in his autobiography:

This town, as a whole, still existed, completely unspoilt, in the 1830s, not merely reflecting the intellectual, emotional, and everyday world of the German burghers of 1500 but actually bringing that world to life. As such, it provided one of the great decisive experiences for all the Romantics, from Tieck and Wackenroder's *Herzensergießungen eines kunstliebenden Klosterbruders*, with the figure of Dürer in the background, to Achim and Bettina von Arnim, E. T. A. Hoffmann, and, finally, to Richard Wagner, who rounded off the Romantic age [!].

Hofmannsthal speaks of the 'Homeric' aspect of *Die Meistersinger* and compares it, as the realization of a closed civic world, to Goethe's *Hermann und Dorothea*, drawing a link between Wagner's opera and those of Goethe's works—*Faust*, I, *Götz von Berlichingen*, and *Hans Sachsens poetische Sendung* (1776)—which, like the opera, seek to evoke the historical atmosphere of the sixteenth century and which undoubtedly left their mark on Wagner's work.

The spirituality in which Hans Sachs is shrouded, and, at the same time, the national element, the ceremonial: these are things that Wagner owes to Goethe's wonderful interpretation of the figure of Sachs . . . you will also find the two allegorical female figures of the Prize Song prefigured here—the Muse as the humanistic element and, contrasting with her, the simple domesticity and sensuousness of the soul, embodied in a woman. And, finally, the idea of having a knight among craftsmen, the splendid combination of the world of chivalry with that of the burgher, you will find has been borrowed from E. T. A. Hoffmann's fine novella, *Meister Martin der Küfner und seine Gesellen*.

The *Herzensergießungen eines kunstliebenden Klosterbruders* of Wackenroder and Tieck contains a section in honour of Albrecht Dürer, and it is here that we find a tribute to ancient Nuremberg, whose mythic (gold) background has left its unmistakable traces on *Die Meistersinger*, not least in the authors' roll of honour, with its list of Nuremberg's great men, a list which also includes the name of Hans Sachs:

Nuremberg! O town of erstwhile universal fame! How happy I was to wander through your narrow crooked streets; with what childlike love I observed your ancestral houses and churches which bear the firm imprint of our fatherland's ancient art! What heartfelt love I feel for the creations of that age, creations which speak so vigorous, powerful, and true a language! How they draw me back to that grey century of yours when you, O Nuremberg, were the life-teeming school of our fatherland's art and when a truly fruitful and prodigal spirit flourished within your walls: when Master Hans Sachs and Adam Kraft the sculptor, and, above all, Albrecht Dürer and his friend Wil[l]ibaldus Pirckheimer and so many other highly praised men of honour were still alive! How often I longed to return to that age!

All this continues to reverberate in Sachs's declaration of love for 'his' Nuremberg at the end of the *Wahn* Monologue (vii. 234). And if, in Wackenroder's text, it is the eponymous 'art-loving monk' who recalls how he 'sat in some cramped corner in one of your venerable library halls, in the fading light of your small bull's-eye windows, brooding over a folio volume of the valiant Hans Sachs or over some other old and yellowing, wormeaten paper',[1] it is Hans Sachs himself who, at the

---

[1] Wilhelm Wackenroder and Ludwig Tieck, *Herzensergießungen eines kunstliebenden Klosterbruders*, with an afterword by Richard Benz (Stuttgart, 1955), 50–1.

beginning of Wagner's third act, 'is engrossed in reading a large folio volume which he has open before him on his lap' (vii. 230). This fictional Sachs can, of course, distance himself from his own time and from the world around him with the objectivity of Schiller's 'sentimental' poet. He is a reprojection of the typical modern artist, a 'sentimental' figure among purely 'naïve' fellow-artists, having, as it were, read Wackenroder's essays on art and music and come to share the latter's regret that their 'fatherland's art' has disappeared.

In the Marienbad draft, nostalgic grief is the only emotion registered by Sachs in his monologue at the beginning of Act III. At this juncture, of course, he had not studied *Die Welt als Wille und Vorstellung*. Whereas, in the finished work, his reflections on the *Wahn*[2] embodied in that 'chronicle of local and international events' (vii. 233) dictated by the blind world-will are clearly influenced by Schopenhauer, he limits himself in the 1845 draft to 'philosophizing on the decline of poetry': 'Is beautiful poetry really coming to an end?' (xi. 351.) How can such a question have occurred to him? The volume which he has taken down from 'among the great books around him' and which lies open 'on his lap' must be the fifth volume of Gervinus's *Geschichte der poetischen National-Litteratur der Deutschen* (1835–42; 2nd edn., 1844), a tome to which the composer owed the immediate stimulus behind *Die Meistersinger*. Hence Gervinus announces the end of 'beautiful poetry', which he sees as a positive development. 'The competition of art is over; we ought now to set ourselves a different target, a target which none of our marksmen has hit as yet, and discover whether here, too, Apollo will grant us that praise which he did not deny on that other occasion [i.e., in Goethe's works].' The *Volk*, Gervinus goes on, was 'addicted to the quiet life'. For them, the only life worth living was 'the intellectual life'. The goal which mankind must set itself was therefore to lead the *Volk*

into the realm of history, to show them deeds and actions of greater value, and make the disciplining of the will [!] as sacred a duty as the disciplining of emotion and intellect has already become. Our young people, too, have no doubt felt this need. Poets in their masses have been resisting the quietism of Romanticism ever since the most recent upheavals shook the political world: attitude and action have acquired a reputation with them that they had never had before among our Romantic nihilists [a term invented by Jean Paul].[3]

---

[2] The German word *Wahn* embraces a multiplicity of meanings. It is normally translated into English as 'illusion' or 'self-delusion', but, as used by Wagner, it resonates with ideas of madness, folly, and fancy, but also self-actualization and determinism: see Iris Gillespie, 'The Theory and Practice of "Wahn"', *Wagner*, 5 (1984), 79–85; and Richard Turner, '"Die Meistersinger von Nürnberg": The Conceptual Growth of an Opera', *Wagner*, 3 (1982), 2–16.

[3] Georg Gottfried Gervinus, *Geschichte der poetischen National-Litteratur der Deutschen*, 2nd edn. (Leipzig, 1844), v. 732–5. There is no doubt that it was these last 3 pages that Wagner read.

Hans Sachs must feel that he is very much this kind of Romantic quietist and nihilist, which is why, after the young knight has failed to satisfy his judges at the *Singschule*, he lectures the latter in terms which, partly inspired by the irony of resignation and partly by his sceptical attitude to art, proclaim the activistic ideas of the *Vormärz*. Indeed, when he 'cheerfully' advises the knight to give up poetry, to read Hutten and Luther, and to fight with his sword in the name of reason against foolishness and superstition, the note of irony gives way to utter seriousness. 'We need . . . a man like Luther', Gervinus had exclaimed in this very context (alluding to Goethe's famous remark about Lessing), a man 'who would finally take up this task now, a task which the great reformer had already been pleased to begin'.[4] Wagner's Marienbad Sachs explains to the youthful poet:

You are a poet! But you cannot survive any longer now! . . . Believe me, poetry will be forgotten for a long, long time. There will be other weapons against foolishness and superstition—not songs but reason and philosophy, indeed, these new weapons will themselves be defended by the sword; you, with your fine and noble ideals, shall play a part in the coming struggle, for you'll achieve far more in that way than by exploiting a talent which no one values today. One day, hundreds of years from now, when a new world has begun [a world which no longer has to be fought for, since it is now secure in the here and now], people may stop for a moment and begin to look round for what they have lost; perhaps they will then rediscover Hans Sachs, who in turn will point them further back and direct them to Walther, Wolfram, and the heroic lays . . . Go home to your castle, study what Ulrich von Hutten and the Wittenberger wrote, and, if need be, defend what you have learnt with the sword! (xi. 352.)

How could such scepticism towards historical chance and the legitimacy of art be put into words and music (a scepticism, moreover, inspired by Hegel,[5] Heine, and the literary figures of the *Vormärz*)?

But Wagner's scepticism did not last. After all, the final verses of the work (for all the misunderstanding that has attached to them) are positivistic in tone: 'Zerging' das heil'ge römische Reich in Dunst, | uns bliebe doch die heil'ge deutsche Kunst.' (xi. 355; or, in Ernest Newman's translation: 'Though should depart the might of holy Rome, | No harm will come to holy German art!') Admittedly, these lines were not originally included in the Marienbad draft: they do not square with

---

[4] Wackenroder and Tieck, *Herzensergießungen eines Kunstliebenden Klosterbruders*, 734–5.

[5] 'The spirit of our world today . . . appears as beyond the stage at which art is the supreme mode of our knowledge of the Absolute. The peculiar nature of artistic production and of works of art no longer fills our highest need . . . Thought and reflection have spread their wings above fine art . . . The beautiful days of Greek art, like the golden age of the later Middle Ages, are gone . . . In all these respects art, considered in its highest vacation, is and remains for us a thing of the past.' (G. W. F. Hegel, *Asthetik*, ed. Friedrich Bassenge (Berlin, 1955), i. 21–2; translated into English by T. M. Knox as *Aesthetics: Lectures on Fine Art* (Oxford, 1975), 10–11.)

the ending conceived there, with Sachs's 'half ironical, half serious' praise of *Meistersang*, or with the (historically qualified) affirmation of art. They were added later, in pencil, to the Marienbad manuscript, perhaps as late as 1851, when Wagner wrote *A Communication to my Friends*, where they were published for the first time (iv. 286). They express the political resignation which Wagner felt following the failure of the Revòlution of 1848–9, together with his disappointed hopes for the rebirth of the German Reich.[6] Now that the Reich has gone up in smoke ('zerging in Dunst'), all that remains is German art. If it is described as 'holy', this has less to do with any idea of sanctification than with the fact that 'holy German art' forms a consciously anachronistic parallel to the 'might of holy Rome'. It is one of the more absurd aspects of Wagner literature that these lines have been singled out for (mis)interpretation, and regarded, in flagrant contradiction of their literal meaning, as a glorification of the Reich. They are, in fact, wholly unpolitical, expressing rather, in Thomas Mann's words, 'a downright anarchic indifference to political structures, as long as German intellectual and spiritual values—"German Art"—are preserved intact',[7] a reading confirmed by the fact that it is no longer the Emperor who is glorified at the end of the work (as it had been in Deinhardstein's drama), but the artist Hans Sachs. In 1925 the Bayreuth Festival administration found itself obliged to post notices in the auditorium discouraging the audience (who clearly thought the work ended with the lines: 'May the Holy German Empire yet remain') from singing the German National Anthem at the end of the opera. 'What matters here is *art*!',[8] Siegfried Wagner insisted, quoting from the text of the opera (vii. 200). (The national socialists' misuse of *Die Meistersinger* as a panegyric to the Third Reich at its annual Nuremberg rallies is a chapter to itself.)

In his diary jottings of 1865, published under the title 'What is German?' in 1878, Wagner has, as it were, provided a prose commentary on the lines in question: 'Only with the loss of external political power, i.e., with the abandoned significance of the Holy Roman Empire, whose demise we lament today as the decline of German glory: only now [!]

[6] On this point we agree with Reinhold Brinkmann, 'Über das Kern- und Schlußwort der *Meistersinger*', in Klaus Schulz (ed.), *Programmheft zur Neuinszenierung der 'Meistersinger' im Münchener Nationaltheater* (Munich, 1979), 82–91. The pencil addition cannot, of course, be dated unequivocally. None the less, it is written, like the rest of the Marienbad draft, in Gothic script, whereas Wagner began to write in roman script at the end of 1848: see Richard Wagner, *Sämtliche Briefe*, ed. Gertrud Strobel and Werner Wolf (Leipzig, 1970), ii. 628 n. 1, and *WWV*, pp. 483–4.

[7] Thomas Mann, *Wagner und unsere Zeit*, ed. Erika Mann (Frankfurt, 1963), 113–14; translated into English by Allan Blunden as *Pro and contra Wagner* (London, 1985), 141.

[8] See Dietrich Mack, 'Die Bayreuther Inszenierungen der "Meistersinger"', in Richard Wagner, *'Die Meistersinger von Nürnberg': Texte, Materialien, Kommentare*, ed. Attila Csampai and Dietmar Holland (Reinbek bei Hamburg, 1981), 162–3.

does the essential German character really begin to develop.' (x. 39.) Both this quotation and the lines from the end of *Die Meistersinger* cited above have a remarkable parallel in the prose sketch of a poem by Schiller, dating from 1797 and given the title *Deutsche Größe* by its first editor: 'The Germans have established their own independent worth, quite apart from any political worth, and even if the Holy Roman Empire were to vanish into dust, German dignity would still remain unchallenged'; and, 'while the political empire totters, the spiritual empire has become increasingly solid and more perfect'.[9] Although Wagner cannot have known Schiller's fragment, he *was* familiar with the closely related *Xenien*, a collection of satirical epigrams including *Deutscher Nationalcharakter, Das deutsche Reich*, and the poem *Die deutsche Muse*, which he quoted and provided with a historical commentary in his essay 'German Art and German Politics' (viii. 33), completed in 1868, the year in which *Die Meistersinger* received its first performance. So Schiller's idea that Germany was somehow out of alignment, aesthetically, with its political counterpart must have been one of the sources of what Thomas Mann described as 'that key statement at the end of *Die Meistersinger*'.[10]

There is, of course, another literary reminiscence here which comes more readily to mind. The 'key statement' to which Mann was referring and which Wagner consciously adds to the end of the opera is clearly a response to Heinrich Heine's thesis that the 'end of the age of art' was at hand, a thesis which was much quoted in its day (as well as being repeated frequently by Heine himself), so that Wagner, too, must certainly have been familiar with it. Indeed, the speech by Hans Sachs quoted above from the Marienbad draft seems to us to presuppose Heine's famous *aperçu*. 'Present-day art must perish', Heine wrote in 1831, 'because its principle is still rooted in the superannuated *ancien régime*, in the Holy Roman Empire's past.' Wagner's counter-thesis is that, even if the Holy Roman Empire *is* a thing of the past, its art is always with us. When the portals of art are thrown open, it will not be to that 'new art' prophesied by Heine, an art in 'enthusiastic concord' with the 'new age' and with the 'politics of the day' which 'does not need to borrow its symbols from the insipid past',[11] but to an art which is both old *and* new, an art divorced from 'politics' and yet (or precisely because of that fact) in perfect accord with 'life'. 'Es klang so alt, und war doch so neu' (It sounded so old, and yet was so new), Sachs says of Walther's first attempt at *Meistersang* (vii. 198).

[9] Friedrich Schiller, *Sämtliche Werke*, ed. Gerhard Fricke and Herbert G. Göpfert, 3rd edn. (Munich, 1962), i. 473–7.

[10] Mann, *Wagner und unsere Zeit*, p. 113; English trans. (Blunden, *Pro and contra Wagner*), p. 141.

[11] Heinrich Heine, 'Gemäldeausstellung in Paris 1831', in *Werke*, ed. Eberhard Galley (Frankfurt, 1968), iii. 45–6.

This aesthetic paradox is mirrored in Walther's social standing. In the Marienbad draft he is still 'the son of an impoverished knight' (xi. 344), whereas by 1861 he has become the 'last living member of his family' (xi. 359) and has sold his family estate in Nuremberg.

> Als seines Stammes letzter Sproß,
> verließ er neulich Hof und Schloß
>    und zog nach Nürnberg her,
>    daß er hier Bürger wär'.          (vii. 177.)
>
> As last descendant of his line,
> He lately left his home and lands,
>    And came to Nuremberg here
>    To join our burghers' guild.

The reader may well be reminded here of Attinghausen's prophecy in Schiller's *Wilhelm Tell*: 'The nobleman descends from ancient castles | And as a burgher swears a civic oath' (ll. 2430–1). By renouncing his privileges, Walther is clearly aiming to break down the old order both socially and aesthetically. Of course, this does not mean that he now denies all knowledge of the past, but rather that he is concerned to free that past from ossifying tradition, incorporating 'history' into the living present so that it is 'superseded' by a new form of life, namely, that of the middle-class burgher. Where this form itself is already ossified, he turns away abruptly; he has not come with the aim of exchanging one form of superannuated existence for another, but with the intention of rediscovering the living past in the living present.

Although Walther wants to become a burgher, he is not thinking of denying his background as a knight. His ideas about poetry are entirely orientated towards the courtly poetry of the Middle Ages, something which emerges even more clearly from the prose drafts than it does from the finished opera, where only Walther von der Vogelweide is named as his mentor. The Marienbad draft mentions 'Walther, Wolfram, and the heroic lays' (xi. 352), in other words, *Minnesang*, courtly romance, and heroic epic, the very genres whose representatives had been denounced in *Tannhäuser* as conventional court poets. The affinity between Walther and Sachs is explained in the first draft by reference to the fact that the latter had also borrowed from medieval authors. (The historical Sachs's plays about Siegfried and Tristan were in Wagner's library in Dresden.) In his monologue at the beginning of Act III Sachs complains: 'Am I, a shoemaker, the only one to have breathed the spirit of our German past?' (xi. 351.) He regards *Meistersang* as the heir to the courtly poetry of the Middle Ages, just as the young knight believes initially that he can rediscover the earlier genre in the later one. Indeed, it is precisely for this reason that he has come to Nuremberg 'to apply for entry into the

Mastersingers' guild' (xi. 344). This is his immediate aim. (Only in the later version of the opera does his motivation change, when his desire to become a Mastersinger is prompted by his love for Eva.) 'I thought I would find traces of the spirit of Thuringia, etc. here: but what a disappointment awaited me!', he says in Sachs's workshop, articulating the latter's regrets that the Mastersingers have lost touch with medieval poetry. Before starting the Trial Song, the knight asks: 'In what tone shall I sing? That of Siegfried and Grimmhilde?' The Masters' reaction is one of shock and much shaking of heads. He encounters a similar response with his second question: 'Well, then, shall I sing of Parzival in Wolfram's tone?' In the second and third drafts, both written in 1861 after Wagner had made a detailed study of the rules of *Meistersang*, Konrad (as the knight is now called) 'begins in the tone of the old minnesingers', and once again incurs the Mastersingers' instant disapproval (xi. 383).

Konrad (or Walther) is no less courtly in his lifestyle than he is in his poetry. Having, as it were, lived in the heroic Middle Ages on the family estate in Franconia, he is bound to come into conflict with the closely knit municipal world of late medieval Nuremberg. His meeting with Eva in Act I, the Trial Song, the plan to elope, and the idea of mugging Beckmesser while the latter plucks away at his lute, show repeatedly that he is projecting the figments of his knight's imagination on to the world of Nuremberg's burghers. In this, he shares definite characteristics with the titular hero of Cervantes' *Don Quixote*, a work which Wagner greatly admired and which he frequently reread.[12] This is particularly striking in Act II, Scene 5, where Walther suddenly sees himself in his mind's eye in some enchanted place, surrounded by the Masters as though by 'evil spirits', so that, misjudging the situation just as Don Quixote would have done, he mistakes the sound of the Nightwatchman's horn for a signal for battle.

> WALTHER. Und ich ertrüg' es, sollt' es nicht wagen
> grad' aus tüchtig drein zu schlagen?

> And I must bear it, swallow my passion,
> Not fall to in knightly fashion?

[*The Nightwatchman's horn sounds. Walther reaches for his sword with an exaggerated gesture and stares wildly about him.*]

---

[12] This has already been observed by Adorno, Ernst Bloch ('Paradoxa und Pastorale bei Wagner', in Dietrich Mack (ed.), *Richard Wagner: Ausgewählte Schriften* (Frankfurt, 1974), 22–3; translated into English by Peter Palmer as 'Paradoxes and the Pastorale in Wagner's music', in *Essays on the Philosophy of Music* (Cambridge, 1985), 146–82, esp. pp. 156–7), and Egon Voss ('*Die Meistersinger* als Oper des deutschen Bürgertums', in *Die Meistersinger von Nürnberg*, ed. Csampai and Holland, pp. 9–31, esp. p. 24; translated into English by Stewart Spencer as 'Wagner's "Meistersinger" as an Opera for the German Bourgeoisie', *Wagner*, 11 [1990], 39–62, esp. 54).

Ha! ...
Ha! ...
EVA [taking his hand soothingly]. Geliebter, spare den Zorn;
    's war nur des Nachtwächters Horn.                          (vii. 207.)

> Beloved, waste not your scorn;
> That was the Nightwatchman's horn!

It is also significant that, in the Marienbad draft, Wagner directs his
knight to enter in Act II like some hidalgo in a Spanish cloak-
and-dagger drama: 'The lover enters from the street, wearing a cloak
and armed with a sword; his beloved has seen him from her window and
hurries anxiously to meet him: "Dearest!"' (xi. 347.)

Walther and the Masters confront each other like thesis and antithesis
in some Hegelian construct. It is Sachs who mediates, dialectically,
between them, stage-managing the confrontation as both a comedy of
intrigue and a play of ideas. From the mass riot to the genesis of the
Prize Song, everything that enfolds in the second and third acts, whether
on the seamy level of violent farce or on the sublime heights of aesthetic
calculation, is manipulated by the cobbler-poet. 'Ein Schuster in seinem
Laden | zieht an des Wahnes Faden: | wie bald auf Gassen und Straßen
| fängt der da an zu rasen!' (A cobbler in his workshop | Draws on the
threads of folly: | How soon in alleys and streets | People are shaken by
rage!), he sings in the *Wahn* Monologue (vii. 234). But this shoemaker
draws on the threads not only of folly but also, and more especially, of
art: he makes the impulsive Walther von Stolzing (a *Sturm und Drang*
poet if ever there was one) a true *reflective* poet, a transformation effected
not by mere instruction but by means of a didactic game. The
juxtaposition of farce and dialectical calculation to which we must now
turn our attention lends Sachs an almost Socratic air. (After all, the
Platonic dialogues which Wagner admired so much are philosophical
comedies in which Socrates attempts to make his interlocutors see the
truth by both reasoning and playing with them.)

One of Wagner's fundamental beliefs in the realm of aesthetics was
that all great forms of art developed out of the 'creative popular spirit' or
*Volksgeist*. In *A Communication to my Friends* he singles out Hans Sachs as
the 'final manifestation' of that spirit, while in his appraisal of Goethe's
*Faust* in his later essay, *On Actors and Singers* (1872), he claims that 'the
rough-hewn art of our old national poet Hans Sachs' forms the 'popular'
basis of Goethe's masterpiece, too. The 'wondrous edifice' erected by
Goethe, metrically, on the basis of the *Knittelvers*[13] which the historical

---

[13] *Knittelvers* is normally, if unhelpfully, translated as 'doggerel verse'. It describes a verse-form
found from the 15th century onwards and believed to have developed out of a specifically Germanic
metre in which 4 stresses occur with an irregular number of unstressed syllables. The lines rhyme
in pairs. The form was revived in the 18th century by Goethe (in *Faust*) and Schiller (in *Wallensteins*

Sachs had, in his turn, taken over from existing models was such that the Nuremberg poet 'seems never to leave this foundation of the most perfect popularity, while yet soaring above it to the highest art of antique metre' (ix. 214–15). The inspiration which Sachs provided was the reason for the 'immense popularity' of *Faust*, Wagner told Cosima in the course of a conversation on 13 December 1878. Of course, Wagner was secretly thinking here of his own *Meistersinger*, in which Sachs not only appears in person but is celebrated in the 'Wach' auf' Chorus (to words by the historical Sachs), while interpreting his own 'sad piece' about Tristan and Isolde as an example of the illusory constraints of a love which he himself renounces (vii. 254). Equally certainly, this Sachs is no longer the historical Mastersinger but his 'sentimental' reflection as conjured up by Goethe and the German Romantics. None the less, the 'rough-hewn' art of the Nuremberg cobbler-poet was, in Wagner's view, the common, popular basis of both *Faust* and his own *Die Meistersinger*.

Wagner, however, believed that the earliest aesthetic expression of the popular spirit was improvisation. As the first part of this study has shown, improvisation became a structural principle of the musical drama, too, at least in Wagner's later aesthetic writings. In his 1871 address, *On the Destiny of Opera*, he defined 'the work of art which we ourselves envisage' as one involving 'mimic and musical improvisation of consummate poetic value, fixed, moreover, by supreme artistic, conscious recollection' (ix. 149–50). Paradoxical though the idea of fixed improvisation or calculated spontaneity must sound, it harks back to Novalis's idea of 'intentionally random creativity'. Like Wagner's 'improvisation', it is an aesthetic fiction, a hypothetical construct, or, rather, the metaphor for a structure which breaks down the conventional schemata of existing forms of art. Judged by traditional norms, the musico-dramatic structures conceived in this way seem genuinely improvisatory and unpredictable, even though they were not devised in any extempore fashion. Although such a calculatedly aleatoric technique naturally evolves on a highly artificial level, Wagner believed it would enable him to achieve the spontaneity of the creative popular spirit (just as Schiller's 'sentimental', reflective poetry would ideally coincide with 'naïve' poetry at its point of ultimate perfection, and just as all progress around the circumference of a circle ultimately leads back to the point from which we started out).

Genuine improvisation is, of course, out of the question in the musical drama. But it is significant that all the poetico-musical products

Lager), and in the 19th century by Wagner (in *Die Meistersinger*). The irregular nature of the metre will be apparent from the English translations accompanying quotations from Wagner's poem. These are mostly taken from the Frederick Jameson translation revised by Norman Feasey and Gordon Kember and performed by the English National Opera. Occasionally, the Corders' more accurate, but less musical, translation has been preferred.

presented within the context of Wagner's music dramas are improvisatory products inspired by the moment, apparently unforeseen and, because they offend against the listener's (professional) expectations, likely to provoke a sense of puzzlement or shock. Although Senta's Ballad pre-dates, in a sense, the beginning of the action, its ending issues spontaneously from the heat of the moment. That Tannhäuser's eulogy to love in the Tournament of Song does not turn out as his listeners—and he himself—had expected, goes without saying. Siegfried forges the sword without having learnt how to do so, while the professional smith, Mime, fails in the task. That the act of forging a sword symbolizes the process of artistic creation is clear from *Wieland der Schmied*, a drama based on the life of the artist-smith Wieland which Wagner sketched in 1849–50: 'a vigorous fiery song is heard on his lips to the hum of the bellows, the sputter of sparks, and the beat of the hammer' (iii. 197).

Although this theory of improvisation was conceived in the years following the first performance of *Die Meistersinger*, it is well illustrated by the genesis of Walther's Prize Song in Act III of the opera. His Trial Song in Act I is a completely free fantasia, as it were, lacking the element of 'supreme artistic, conscious recollection' which is the *sine qua non* of fixed improvisation. The knight is entirely guided by the inspiration of the moment. The Marker's 'Fanget an' (Begin) gives him, so to speak, the cue for his hymn to Spring. Beckmesser's 'disgruntled sighs' and the noise of the chalk on the blackboard encourage him to sing of the envious Winter 'lying in wait' in the hope of somehow 'destroying' the woodland's 'song of Spring'—a side-swipe which is directed, of course, at the Marker and his attempts to interrupt Walther's song. (As in Siegmund's and Sieglinde's Spring Song in Act I of *Die Walküre*, Spring and Winter symbolize the contrast between natural freedom and rigid order.) And in the midst of the uproar which finally breaks out, Walther sings the final strophe of his hymn, comparing the Masters to a chorus of crows, while he himself is 'borne aloft' on 'golden pinions', rising above 'the city's tomb' and heading home 'To meadows where the song of birds | The Master [Walther] first revealed in words', in other words, to the Thuringian equivalent of Mount Parnassus. 'Der Noth entwachsen Flügel' (From need do pinions spring: vii. 182–9), Walther concludes in another reminiscence of *Wieland der Schmied*, whose hero had forged a pair of wings for himself in order to escape his servile state: 'Need! Need beat its wings, breathing inspiration into my brain!' (iii. 201.)

'Unpredictability' in art strikes the Masters merely as an infringement of their rules. Their objections are similar to the criticisms levelled at 'the music of the future': 'I found no sense! I must confess | None there could find an end', the Mastersingers complain, echoing criticisms of Wagner's 'unending melody', while Beckmesser objects: 'No cadences or coloratura, | Not a single trace of melody!', an objection which follows inevitably from the breakdown of 'four-square' periodic structure (vii. 184–5). Sachs alone recognizes that Walther's song is not simply formless but that it obeys other laws, laws which reveal careful thought, even if they have not been consciously formulated.

> Des Ritters Lied und Weise,
> sie fand ich neu, doch nicht verwirrt;
> verließ er uns're G'leise,
> schritt er doch fest und unbeirrt.
> Wollt ihr nach Regeln messen,
> was nicht nach eurer Regeln Lauf,
> der eig'nen Spur vergessen,
> sucht davon erst die Regeln auf!          (vii. 185.)

> The singer's bold intention,
> I found it new, but hardly wrong.
> Though he has scorned convention,
> His step was firm and ever strong.
> If by the rules you'd measure
> What does not with your rules agree,
> Forget the laws you treasure.
> Seek out first what his rules may be.

Sachs astutely emphasizes the historical necessity of all artistic rules, recalling with astonishing accuracy the outcome of the *querelle des anciens et des modernes*. This *querelle* flares up again here between Walther and the Masters, where it is resolved and settled amicably by Sachs's dialectical and didactic intervention - a poetological intrigue, one might almost say.

The Masters ignore the genesis and historical development of their norms, acting as though those rules were eternally valid. The idea of judging a work of art according to rules effected by a specific historical situation, especially when the work in question has been conditioned by quite different factors (Walther, after all, is a knight who has come to poetry via a fundamentally different route from the one adopted by the burghers of Nuremberg), is ironically called into question by Sachs when he challenges the Masters to justify the rules underpinning their judgement. This, of course, is impossible, since their standards are simply anachronistic.

Sachs clearly feels that the art of the Mastersingers runs the risk of becoming fossilized and academic, and of losing its popular foundation. It needs a change of style, it needs to be reinvigorated by the popular spirit. Hence his suggestion that, once a year, the townsfolk should be

allowed to judge the prize song and to put the rules to the test: 'Daß
Volk und Kunst gleich blüh' und wachs' (that folk and art both bloom
and grow: vii. 175). It is a genuinely revolutionary concept. The
Masters should decide on the rules only during their annual term of
office, after which they would submit those rules to the townspeople to
be ratified, even though (or, rather, precisely because) the populace does
not have legal competence in such matters.

> Gesteht, ich kenn' die Regeln gut;
> und daß die Zunft die Regeln bewahr',
> bemüh' ich mich selbst schon manches Jahr.
> Doch einmal im Jahre fänd' ich's weise,
> daß man die Regeln selbst probir',
> ob in der Gewohnheit trägem G'leise
> ihr' Kraft und Leben sich nicht verlier':
> > und ob ihr der Natur
> > noch seid auf rechter Spur,
> > das sagt euch nur
> wer nichts weiß von der Tabulatur.                      (vii. 174–5.)

> Confess, the rules right well I know;
> And that those rules should suffer no slight
> Has been my endeavour day and night.
> But once every year it might be better,
> To put those rules themselves to a test,
> To find out if following custom forever
> Their force and life be still at their best!
> > And if you would be sure
> > You follow Nature's law,
> > Ask folk unskilled
> Who don't know of the rules of our Guild.

*Meistersang* runs the risk of becoming an 'aristocratic' art, remote from
the *Volk*, and hence of suffering the fate of all the noble arts, which is to
die out. That, after all, is why Walther von Stolzing has sold his family
estate: 'Was mich nach Nürnberg trieb, | war nur zur Kunst die Lieb' (I
came to Nuremberg | For love of art alone: vii. 166). The burghers of
Nuremberg feel proud of the fact that their art has replaced the courtly
art of the earlier period. Pogner announces, self-importantly: 'daß wir
im weiten deutschen Reich | die Kunst einzig noch pflegen' (Though in
our country's spacious bounds | The arts we alone have tended: vii.
172). But a paradoxical situation now arises, whereby the middle-class
burghers have become aristocrats as a result of the ossification of their
art, while the aristocratic knight becomes a burgher who breaks down
convention by means of improvisation and who rejuvenates art by
deriving it from the popular spirit.

It is on St John the Baptist's Day that the Mastersingers exchange the hermetically sealed and academic world of the *Singschule* for the public arena of popular celebration; the 'church chancel' gives way to the 'open meadow'. Their gaining of the 'layman's ear' in this way (vii. 171) is intended to demonstrate the popular basis of their art, as Hans Sachs proposes:

> D'rum mocht's euch nie gereuen,
> daß jährlich am Sankt Johannisfest,
> statt daß das Volk man kommen läßt,
> herab aus hoher Meister-Wolk'
> ihr selbst euch wendet zu dem Volk'.          (vii. 175.)

> I'm sure you will not regret it,
> If only on each Midsummer day,
> Turning aside from custom's way,
> You leave your realm of mist and cloud
> And turn yourselves towards the crowd.

But if the Masters wish to 'please' the *Volk*, and if the festivities are not to be meaningless ceremonial and mere window-dressing (as they appear to have become with the passage of time), the townsfolk must be allowed to have a say in judging the singing competition, rather than simply acclaiming whatever decision the Masters have already reached. This suggestion by Sachs is rejected, but he consoles himself with the thought that Eva's casting vote is enough, since 'a woman's thoughts, wholly untaught [i.e., ignorant of the *Tabulatur*], seem to me at one with the people's mind' (vii. 174, 176). Sachs, of course, is fully aware that the rules of the guild and the spirit of free improvisation reflect too stark a contrast to offer any immediate prospect of future development. A balance must be found—and it is this which Sachs achieves in Act III. Although Nietzsche was at first profoundly influenced by Wagner's theory of improvisation,[14] as his admiration for the 1872 essay, *On Actors and Singers*,[15] demonstrates, he later distanced himself from such a view. As early as 1874 we find him noting in his diary: 'False the possibility of an art which is pure improvisation.'[16] Evidently he saw in this theory an excuse for dilettantism. But Nietzsche's criticism is wide of the mark. In the course of the private lesson in poetics which Sachs gives Walther in his workshop, the cobbler himself makes it clear that the latter's Trial Song was immature, even dilettantish, however much he may initially have admired its bold spontaneity. Feeling alone does not make an artist. We are reminded of Goethe's and Schiller's criticism of dilettantism.

---

[14] See Friedrich Nietzsche, *Sämtliche Werke: Kritische Studienausgabe in 15 Bänden*, ed. Giorgio Colli and Mazzino Montinari (Munich, 1980), vii. 311–12 and *passim*.

[15] Ibid. viii. 218.

[16] Ibid. vii. 762; see also viii. 433.

'Dilettantism negates the master', Goethe told Riemer in July 1810.[17] There was nothing to resist it, 'except firm principles and the strict application of the same'.[18] It is precisely this 'mastery' and the application of 'firm principles' which Sachs attempts to teach Walther. 'Lenzes Gebot, | die süße Noth, | die legten's ihm in die Brust', Sachs reflects on Walther's song in the *Flieder* Monologue: 'nun sang er, wie er mußt'! | Und wie er mußt', so konnt' er's' (Spring's sweetest strain, | Its wondrous pain, | These taught him what he must say: | He sang just as he must! | And as he must, so could he: vii. 198). But this 'need', this idea of *having* to do something, which Wagner always describes as 'spontaneous' in his post-1848 writings, fell under the heading of the blind 'will' following his reading of Schopenhauer in the autumn of 1854 (cf. iii. 4). It was the function of art to release us from the constraints of that will by means of 'rules' and 'conscious recollection'. In his 1981 essay on *Die Meistersinger* Egon Voss offers a penetrating interpretation of Sachs's apologia for the Mastersingers' rules and his explanation of those rules in terms of an image of middle-class family life. This image, Voss argues, is a kind of exorcism and domesticization of the will, the focal point of which is the compulsive nature of erotic love.[19] Just as Walther (according to Sachs) sings 'as he must', so Eva describes her love as 'compulsive and constraining'. Had she had any 'choice', Sachs would have been her husband, but, as it is, she is left with no alternative. She has been overwhelmed by the 'torment' of erotic love, a torment which recalls the compulsive effect of the love-potion—hence the score's verbal and musical reminiscence here of the 'sad piece' about Tristan and Isolde (vii. 254).

Free improvisation is the aesthetic counterpart of the power of erotic love. The analogy between improvisation and the constraints of love on the one hand, and marriage and artistic 'mastery' on the other, recurs with leitmotivic regularity in the course of the second and third acts. Alluding to Walther's planned elopement and to the way in which he provoked the Masters with his Spring Song, Sachs makes it clear to the young knight that

> Eu'r Lied, das hat ihnen bang' gemacht;
> und das mit Recht: denn wohl bedacht,
> mit solchem Dicht- und Liebesfeuer
> verführt man wohl Töchter zum Abenteur;
> doch für liebseligen Ehestand
> man and're Wort' und Weisen fand.          (vii. 236.)

---

[17] Johann Wolfgang Goethe, *Gedenkausgabe der Werke, Briefe und Gespräche*, ed. Ernst Beutler (Zurich, 1949), xii. 597.

[18] Ibid. xiii. 199.

[19] See n. 12, above.

Your song has filled them with dark dismay;
And with good cause, for, truth to say,
A song so full of poet's passion
May kindle our daughters in wicked fashion.
But to praise long-lasting married bliss
We've other words and tunes than this.

The fires of poetry and love (which for Sachs—and Wagner—are one and the same thing) have a deeply unsettling, not to say chaotic, effect. A protective wall must be erected to keep them out, a bulwark of bourgeois and aesthetic order. The fragility of this order is confirmed by the riot on Midsummer Eve. Forces which seem to be reconciled in the 'Wahnfried' of art break out here in the form of a *bellum omnium contra omnes*. According to the stage directions in the full score, the neighbours who strike out at each other, venting aggressions which previously have been held in check by the constraints of communal life ('I've been wanting to do that for a long time!', and 'That's for complaining!': vii. 225), are none other than the Mastersingers themselves, with that guardian of the guild's rules, Fritz Kothner, leading the way.[20]

Sachs's lesson in poetics takes place on the morning after the *Wahn*-induced riot, and is aimed (in the Schopenhauerian sense) at providing aesthetic release from that *Wahn*, whether expressed in aggression and violence, in passionate love, or in an art which defies all the rules. Before the start of the lesson Sachs asks himself:

warum gar bis auf's Blut
die Leut' sich quälen und schinden
in unnütz toller Wuth!
　　Hat keiner Lohn
　　noch Dank davon:
　　in Flucht geschlagen,
　　meint er zu jagen.　　　　　　(vii. 233–4.)

Why people strive and fight
Both in and out of season
In fruitless rage and spite.
　　What do they gain
　　For all their pain?
　　They fly the foe
　　Yet think they pursue him.

This is given striking musical expression in the Midsummer Eve riot, which is written as a fugue, a style which, in keeping with the etymology of the word (Latin *fuga*, 'flight'), was used throughout the nineteenth

---

[20] See the text of the full score as reproduced in *Die Meistersinger von Nürnberg*, ed. Csampai and Holland, pp. 94–102.

century as the typical musical expression of flight and conflict.[21] (The claim, frequently made, that Wagner wanted to tame chaos by depicting it in the strictest of all musical forms misses the point, not least because the *Meistersinger* fugue is by no means strictly developed.) Who can give a name to this mutual torment, confusion, and self-deception, Sachs asks? To which he replies: 'The folly's still the same.' (vii. 234.) Of course, he himself has been pulling the threads of *Wahn*: the previous night's riot is part of his lesson in poetics, since he knows that in matters of love and art a certain amount of *Wahn* is indispensable:

> Jetzt schau'n wir, wie Hans Sachs es macht,
> daß er den Wahn fein lenken mag,
>     ein edler Werk zu thun.                    (vii. 235.)
>
> Now let us see what Sachs can do
> So that the folly may be turned
>     And used for nobler work.

This manipulation of the threads of *Wahn* consists in his social and aesthetic instruction of Walther, a form of instruction which, to quote Egon Voss, involves his 'introduction to bourgeois life'.[22] Walther, who promises to become a burgher, socially and economically, by selling his ancestral estate, by concluding a business deal with Pogner, by acquiring civic rights, and by marrying into Nuremberg's bourgeoisie, is now to become a burgher in a spiritual or intellectual sense, too, namely, as an artist. It is partly for this reason (but also to tempt him into accepting the right course, since love and marriage appear initially to him to be more important than art) that Sachs 'familiarizes' the form of the *Meisterlied* with such rhetorical and didactic skill, describing its tripartite strophic structure in terms of the image of husband, wife, and child, and thus seducing Walther into channelling his inspiration into an existing form.

Walther tells Sachs about his dream, yet he hesitates to recount it, still less to 'think' it (in other words, to interpret it): 'I dare not think what it could mean | For fear that it should fade away.' But this is not the way to become a poet. 'My friend, that is the poet's art | To seek in dreams what he may impart', Sachs informs him (vii. 235). The unconscious must be made conscious, and the unstructured given proper structure. Recording and interpreting dreams echoes the way in which improvisation is consciously 'fixed', and Walther's 'beautiful song' is formally transformed into a *Meisterlied*. Like his Trial Song in Act I, this derives from the immediate inspiration of youth ('The gift of song is given | To all by kindly Heaven: | 'Tis spring that sings, not we': vii.

---

[21] Voss, '*Die Meistersinger* als Oper des deutschen Búrgertums', p. 29; English trans. (Spencer, 'Wagner's "Meistersinger" as an Opera for the German Bourgeoisie'), p. 60.
[22] Ibid. 13; English trans., p. 43.

237). The beauty of such a song is 'merely natural beauty, as it were', to quote Egon Voss again.[23] There can be no question of a *Meisterlied* until life's hardships have dulled the joyful exuberance of feeling:

> Kam Sommer, Herbst und Winterzeit,
>  viel Noth und Sorg' im Leben,
>  manch' ehlich' Glück daneben,
> Kindtauf', Geschäfte, Zwist und Streit:
>  denen's dann noch will gelingen
>  ein schönes Lied zu singen,
>  seht, Meister nennt man die.   (vii. 237.)

> Through summer, fall, and winter's chill
>  When cares of life are pressing,
>  Though marriage brings its blessing,
> Children and business, strife, ill-will,
>  Only those who still have kept then
>  This gift of song from Heaven
>  Then Masters they will be!

The true poet, Wagner will have read in Schiller's review 'Über Bürgers Gedichte', does not sing of feeling in the midst of feeling. 'He may write his poetry on the strength of a gentler and more distant memory, and then it will be better for him, the more he himself has experienced of that which he sings; but never under the present sway of the affection which he is to present to us in all its beauty.'[24]

When Walther digresses from the subject in hand, telling Sachs, 'I love a woman and want to woo her', the latter replies, once again, in poetological terms:

> Die Meisterregeln lernt bei Zeiten,
> daß sie getreulich euch geleiten,
>  und helfen wohl bewahren,
>  was in der Jugend Jahren
>   in holdem Triebe
>   Lenz und Liebe
> euch unbewußt in's Herz gelegt,
> daß ihr das unverloren hegt.   (vii. 237.)

> The Masters' rules then learn and ponder,
> To guide your footsteps when they wander,
>  To help you keep with rigour
>  What in your youthful vigour,
>   In hasty fashion
>   Spring and passion
> Placed secretly within your heart,
> That it may never thence depart!

---

[23] Voss, '*Die Meistersinger* als Oper des deutschen Bürgertums', 15; English trans., p. 45.
[24] Schiller, *Sämtliche Werke*, v. 982.

It is the merit of learnable form that it grants permanency to experience and that, as a result, the world of the unconscious can be reproduced consciously (or 'reflectively', as Wagner would prefer to say). Form is the 'likeness' or reflection of experience, summoning the latter into present consciousness even when it no longer lives on in the poet's heart.

> Das waren hoch bedürft'ge Meister,
> von Lebensmüh' bedrängte Geister:
> in ihrer Nöthen Wildniß
> sie schufen sich ein Bildniß,
> daß ihnen bliebe
> der Jugendliebe
> ein Angedenken klar und fest,
> dran sich der Lenz erkennen läßt.          (vii. 238.)

> By certain sorely troubled Masters,
> Their hearts oppressed by life's disasters:
> By sore distress o'erweighted,
> A likeness they created,
> That they might take it
> And ever make it
> A memory of youthful love
> In which the soul of Spring doth move.

Sachs now invites Walther to improvise his 'Morgentraum', while he, the shoemaker, gives it 'fixed' form: 'I'll write as you dictate to me!' It is a vivid demonstration of Wagner's theory of improvisation, albeit realizable only within the world of art. Sachs aims to show Walther the virtues of artistic form, in other words, its ability to revive forgotten experiences, through the latter's recollection of a dream which, in typically dilettante fashion, has already slipped from his mind while Sachs has been explaining the rules to him.

> Grad' nehmt die Dichtkunst jetzt zur Hand:
> Mancher durch sie das Verlor'ne fand.          (vii. 238.)

> The art of poetry essay:
> Oft what was lost has been found that way.

To Walther's question, 'How should I by rule begin?', Sachs characteristically replies:

> Ihr stellt sie selbst, und folgt ihr dann.
> Gedenkt des schönen Traum's am Morgen;
> für's And're laßt Hans Sachs nur sorgen!          (vii. 239.)

> First make your rules, then follow them.
> Think only of your dream of beauty:
> All else shall be Hans Sachs's duty.

What this means is that the rules should not be a rigid a priori schema, but a variable norm which must be applied afresh to each new work of art. Walther should simply get on and improvise, and leave Sachs to worry about the way in which that improvisation is channelled and fixed. This is the ideal (or paradox) of an art-form which is both pre-conditioned and inspired by the moment, both free and strictly bound.

Sachs notes down only the first two Bars (which Beckmesser takes with him to the Festival Meadow); the later section is produced entirely without Sachs's help, being inspired, instead, by the sight of Eva: Walther has now 'internalized' Bar-form as a medium of expression. The baptism of the song as the 'selige Morgentraumdeut-Weise' (literally, 'blessed Morning Dream-Interpretation Melody'), although a parody of the rite which permeates the whole work as a leitmotif, is at the same time the culmination of Sachs's half serious, half humorous attempt to familiarize Walther with the Masters' rules. In spite of its parodistic and anachronistic features in terms of both words and musical setting, this baptism represents the legitimization of Walther's artistry, a rite of passage completed shortly afterwards in the public arena of the Festival Meadow.

When he performs the Prize Song in public, Walther departs from the fixed text, altering it, once again, in an improvisatory spirit by adding the formula 'Parnassus and Paradise', and thereby providing the dream with an interpretation merely hinted at hitherto. The interaction of subjective and predetermined form (a form which is universally binding and which recalls Wagner's 'sentimental' search for a lost common style), the interplay of fixed and free improvisation which breaks down convention without violating it, the happy balance between the old and the new, and between an adherence to the academic tradition and the claims of popular appeal—this is Wagner's aesthetic ideal, the Utopian goal of art, a goal which is, however, only approximatively attainable. Wagner's own aspiration to the status of Master is bound up with the tendency of his later aesthetic writings to seek to legitimize the form of his musical drama by appealing, in particular, to the tradition of symphonic music, and to show himself to be a 'professional' musician, in contrast to his popular image as the 'musician of the future'. Behind those Masters whose praises are sung at the end of the opera are Bach, Haydn, Mozart, and Beethoven—the very composers to whom Wagner felt indebted musically.

Walther's Prize Song is the product of Sachs's dialectical outlook, but the latter necessarily involves a victim, namely, Beckmesser, the doctrinaire pedant who prevents tradition from forging ahead. In recent writings on *Die Meistersinger*, as well as in productions of the work, Beckmesser's rehabilitation has become *de rigueur*. An essay by Joachim

Herz is significantly entitled 'Beckmesser Reconciled After All',[25] while Walter Jens parades an impressive knowledge of cultural history in a scintillating article' 'Salvaging a Critic's Reputation':[26]

The Master [Beckmesser who, according to Wagner's stage directions, disappears 'among the townspeople': vii. 265] must return, brought back by Sachs, who points to him as he sings of those German Masters who must be honoured. To the left (from the audience's point of view) is Stolzing, with Sachs in the middle, while, right at the edge on the extreme right, approaching only hesitatingly but encouraged to do so by Sachs, is the Town Clerk, who finally joins in with the townspeople. This, I think, is the only logical way to arrange the finale ... The Town Clerk must remain on stage. He is still needed.[27]

It is an attractive *aperçu*, but, like the essay as a whole, it rather misses the point. There is little to be gained by demonstrating how town clerks played a highly respectable role in community life from the sixteenth century onwards, since Wagner offers only a parodistic distortion of that role. No more is it possible to turn Faust's servant, Wagner, into a figure of respectability by showing that he represents the tradition of humanist rhetoric, a tradition which had commanded respect in its day but for which Goethe felt nothing but satirical scorn. In spite of Walter Jens's claims to the contrary, Beckmesser is never great; like Goethe's Wagner, he is a permanently ridiculous figure, however much we may regret the damage done to the reputation of the historical town clerk. The assertion, put about by Křenek and Bloch[28] and repeated ever since, that Beckmesser's music and nonsense poem, with its alleged anticipation of Christian Morgenstern and Ernst Jandl, are far more advanced than Walther's Prize Song is simply untenable from the standpoint of aesthetic logic, ingenious though it is otherwise. It goes without saying, of course, that the *depiction* of artistic failure cannot itself be allowed to fail, but that, as art, it can aspire to a very high level of artificiality. The 'progressiveness' of Beckmesser's poem is not to be laid at *his* door, therefore, but at that of his creator, who presents the failure with such artistic skill. This is merely the paradox of aesthetic form. After all, no one will admire the appreciation of art on the part of the Midsummer Eve rioters simply because they sing a fugue while laying into one another.

No less eccentric than the idea of rehabilitating Beckmesser is that of interpreting him as a Jewish caricature. It was only *after* his altercation

---

[25] Walter Felsenstein and Joachim Herz, *Musiktheater: Beiträge zur Methodik und zu Inszenierungskonzeptionen* (Leipzig, 1976), 245–8.

[26] *Die Meistersinger von Nürnberg*, ed. Csampai and Holland, pp. 249–57.

[27] Ibid. 256–7.

[28] Ernst Bloch, 'Über Beckmessers Preislied-Text', ibid. 257–62.

with Eduard Hanslick that Wagner identified the figure of the Marker with his Viennese critic, turning the latter into a Jew in the process.[29] At the time of the Marienbad draft Wagner can scarcely have had his later arch-enemy in mind, not least because Hanslick had just written a highly appreciative review of *Tannhäuser*, which had received its first performance that same year. And this draft reveals the figure of the pedantic Marker already clearly defined in all the basic comic situations.

The learned pedant was not only a favourite object of moralistic satire from the time of the Renaissance onwards (Montaigne, for example, devoted one of his *Essais* to him), he is also one of the traditional stereotypes of European comedy. He appears most notably as the *dottore* in the *commedia dell'arte* tradition, where he is always a figure of ridicule. If we accuse Wagner of carrying on a witch-hunt against intellectuals and 'outsiders' (although, as Marker and Town Clerk, Beckmesser is certainly no outsider, but a highly respected individual in the eyes of his fellow guild-members), we must therefore draw the logical conclusion, and regard every comedy of intrigue ever written as representing part of a pogrom against the Jews. Of course, this genre has never had a chance in Germany, hence the heavy-handed, anti-theatrical views expressed time and again by writers discussing the character of Beckmesser. Schiller was one of the first to complain that 'pure comedy' (by which he meant the comedy of intrigue) had been almost driven out of existence in Germany by the *comédie larmoyante*. No doubt he was thinking primarily here of Lessing's *Minna von Barnhelm* and its imitators. In pure comedy, by contrast, moral judgement (which 'always introduces a note of seriousness') and philanthrophic feelings are suspended, he argued in his *Dramatische Preisausgabe*. The goal of the comedy of intrigue could be attained 'only through absolute moral indifference'.[30] 'In comedy everything must be transferred from the moral forum to the physical one, for the moral forum admits of no indifference.' But it is precisely this indifference which is the law underpinning both the genre of comedy and its reception: comedy has the task of 'neutralizing moral feelings'.[31]

Only on the strength of premises such as these can a character like that of Beckmesser be grasped adequately. Of course, the plot of *Die Meistersinger* as a whole cannot be reduced to the single dimension of a comedy of intrigue. The greatness of this Everest of German comedy consists in the fact that it does *not* merely introduce a farcical and emotionally neutral element into that specifically German type of

---

[29] On Hanslick's family origins, see the detailed account by Peter Wapnewski in *Tristan der Held Richard Wagners* (Berlin, 1981), 47–9.

[30] Schiller, *Sämtliche Werke*, v. 845.                              [31] Ibid. 1017.

sentimental and realistic comedy whose unassailable model Lessing had created with his *Minna von Barnhelm*. Rather, its merit lies in linking the two genres together in a constant dialectic interplay. Within the framework of farce, Wagner reveals sovereign mastery of the stereotypes and motifs which make up the storehouse of European comedy. The ageing lover, not infrequently a learned pedant whose bride-to-be is snatched from his grasp by a younger lover as the result of some intrigue or other, is an integral element of improvised comedy and its 'literary' successors, recurring in countless different variants. That Wagner's central act also draws on the lively comedy of situation found in sixteenth-century Shrovetide plays from Nuremberg, in which riots are the order of the day, is entirely to be expected. Spanish cloak-and-dagger comedies have already been mentioned; but Beckmesser's Serenade, the disguises and mistaken identities, and the ensuing riot also recall the nocturnal scene beneath Donna Elvira's balcony in Mozart's *Don Giovanni*, which, like Wagner's opera, is indebted, of course, to Spanish models.

Criticism has frequently been levelled at the psychological implausibility of the farcical sub-plot for which Beckmesser serves as the victim, but this is to apply an inappropriate standard of realism to the opera. In a comedy of intrigue, Schiller rightly remarks, 'the characters are there merely for the sake of the events that befall them'.[32] In his delight at the imbroglio, at the pure comedy of situation, Wagner moved effortlessly away from all demands that the action be plausible. The various prose drafts tell a very different story. Beckmesser's requisition of a song he believes to be by Sachs of all people (especially after Sachs has treated him so badly the previous night) is additionally motivated in the Marienbad draft by the fact that it is not the guild which awards the prize in the public competition, but the townspeople (xi. 344–5). Since the Marker knows how popular Sachs is as a poet, it is understandable that he should try to win the townspeople's favour with one of Sachs's poems.

In the draft his humiliation is not yet the result of his garbling the text, merely that, failing to appreciate its poetic novelty, he tries to force it into the procrustean bed of his own pedantic rules, rendering the words unintelligible to the listener by setting them to a nonsensical melody. 'The song [i.e., the text] is in striking contrast to the way in which it is delivered . . . Its effect is comical because of the Marker's style of delivery.' (xi. 354.) Even as late as the third prose draft we read that 'He now delivers Konrad's tender and fiery verses in a way which altogether distorts them and which makes them appear ridiculous.' The Masters

---

[32] Ibid. 846.

are bewildered by the 'incoherency of the delivery' (xi. 370). If, in the definitive version of the libretto, Sachs observes:

> Ich sag' euch Herrn, das Lied ist schön:
> nur ist's auf den ersten Blick zu erseh'n,
> daß Freund Beckmesser es entstellt,          (vii. 265)

> I tell you, sirs, the song is fine:
> But it is not difficult to divine
> That friend Beckmesser sang it wrong,

it is not easy to square this with the nonsense poem with which Beckmesser has just regaled his listeners: no one could guess from the distortions to which it has been subjected that the song is as fine as he says. Sachs's remarks are intelligible only in the light of the prose drafts, in which the song is indeed distorted by false musical declamation.

It may be added that, in Wagner's first draft of the libretto (completed on 25 January 1862), Walther's Prize Song, here with a substantially different content, is textually garbled by Beckmesser. There are already some of those surreal insanities which characterize the involuntary travesty of the definitive Prize Song. As sung by Walther, the *Abgesang* of the first *Stollen* includes the following lines:

> goldene Wogen
> auf den Bergen reih'ten sich;
> Türme und Bogen,
> Häuser, Straßen breiten sich.
> Durch die Tore zog ich ein,
> dünkte mich,
> ich erkenn' sie wieder:
> auch der alte Flieder
> lud mich ein, sein Gast zu sein.          (xvi. 214.)

> Golden billows
> On the mountains were ranged;
> Towers and arches,
> Houses, streets stretched before me.
> Through the gates I entered,
> It seemed as though
> I'd seen them before:
> Even the ancient elder
> Invited me to be its guest.

In Beckmesser's rendition this becomes:

> Goldene Wagen
> auf den Bergen ritten sie;
> Würste und Magen
> auf den Häusern brieten sie:

und mich Thoren zog man ein,
        tünchte mich;
ach! ich brenne nieder!
Brau't mir kalten Flieder!              (xvi. 217–18.)

        Golden waggons
On the mountains they rode;
        Sausage and stomach
On the houses they brewed:
And me, a fool, they drew in,
        Whitewashed me;
Ah! I'm burning down!
Brew me cold elder!

(Since a literal translation misses the point of the travesty, it is, perhaps, worth adding an alternative version in keeping with the *spirit* of the original: 'Golden pillows | On the mountains were strange; | Blows and aches, | Hearses, sheets retched before me. | Though the girls I enticed, | I seethed as though | I'd seen their buttocks: | Even the ancient elder | Invited me to see a ghost.')

In his literary history, Gervinus had claimed that the Mastersingers were principally concerned with innovations of melody rather than of text. From this, Wagner may have concluded that there was the same unbalanced relationship between text and music here as there was, he believed, in modern opera. Thus Beckmesser becomes a caricature of the 'absolute musician' who disregards, and thus does violence to, the structure of his poetical source (in other words, the poem which he assumes to be by his 'librettist' Hans Sachs, although it is, in fact, by Walther). In much the same way, Beckmesser's Serenade is criticized by Sachs for its nonsensical declamation and accentuation. As the central section of the present study has pointed out, Wagner repeatedly insisted in his theoretical writings that the natural speech accent should be observed in musical declamation. Whereas the accent was 'incomparably more flexible' (x. 157) in Romance languages, so that it could wander from syllable to syllable, in German it always attached itself to the semantically important root syllable. It was inevitable, therefore, that 'absolute operatic melody, with its quite specific melismatic and rhythmic peculiarities', should offend against the 'uniqueness of our language and of its accent' (iv. 215). In Wagner's view, German translations of Italian and French operas had exercised a harmful influence on the language of those libretti written originally in German. (It was for this reason that, whenever he discussed the matter with Cosima, Wagner always insisted that Italian and French operas should be performed only in the original language.)

Beckmesser, too, is an 'absolute musician' who does violence to the language by his nonsensical phrasing. 'Mich dünkt, 's sollt' passen Ton und Wort' (I think the music and words should be in accord: vii. 220), Sachs reproaches Beckmesser. In other words, musical accent and speech accent should coincide. But Sachs's counter-suggestion for the opening lines of his Serenade, with semantically justified accentuation, is ignored by the inflexible Marker, obsessed as he is with his rigid musical rules and with the pursuit of rhyme at all costs. Sachs's lesson in the art of poetics—so well received in Walther's case—makes no impression on Beckmesser, who turns himself into an outsider by being the only character in the opera to remain unaffected by Sachs's carefully stage-managed game of mediating between the old and the new.

In Act I David tells Walther about the Mastersinger's triple role as singer, poet, and Master, the first two of which fit into neither Walther's nor Wagner's aesthetic universe. Singer and poet stand in the same relationship to one another as absolute musician and librettist. The poet's task is to ensure that the rhymes and the words fit together:

> füget ihr selbst nun Reim und Wort',
> daß sie genau an Stell' und Ort
> paßten zu einem Meister-Ton,
> dann trüg't ihr den Dichterpreis davon.　　　　　(vii. 163.)

> If you yourself in true accord
> Find and unite both rhyme and word
> So that they fit some Master tone:
> Then you've made the poet's prize your own.

In other words, words and rhyme-scheme must be adapted to fit the predetermined formal schemata of the music—a creed wholly at odds with Wagner's musico-dramatic aesthetic. The Master, according to David, is

> der Dichter, der aus eig'nem Fleiße
> zu Wort' und Reimen, die er erfand,
> aus Tönen auch fügt eine neue Weise.　　　　　(vii. 163.)

> The poet who by faithful striving
> To words and rhymes he himself has found
> A melody adds of his own contriving.

This is how the musical dramatist operates. Significantly, Walther replies:

> So bleibt mir nichts als der Meisterlohn!
> 　　Soll ich hier singen,
> 　　kann's nur gelingen,
> find' ich zum Vers auch den eig'nen Ton.　(vii. 163–4.)

> One path alone then to Master's name!
>> If I sing here,
>> Victory I'll wring here
> Only through verse with the proper strain.

But what this signifies is that Walther refuses to accept the prescribed way of becoming a Mastersinger. For him, the synthesis of singer and poet offers the only way of singing and writing poetry. By professing his own idea of the ideal Mastersinger, he breaks down the existing system of *Meistersang*. From David's contemptuous point of view, this is very much a case of

> Der war nicht 'Schüler', ist nicht 'Singer',
> den 'Dichter' sagt er, überspring' er;
>> denn er ist Junker,
>> und mit einem Sprung er
> denkt ohne weit're Beschwerden
> heut' hier 'Meister' zu werden.      (vii. 164.)

> Who's not a scholar, nor a singer,
> As poet, too, he's a beginner;
>> A gallant knight,
>> He, in single flight
> Now hopes without ruin or disaster
> Today to be a Master.

That man will become Master who devises a new melody to fit a poem of his own composition. Beckmesser, by contrast, is capable neither of writing a poem of any significance nor even of inventing a melody to fit the words of the song he has plagiarized. He has failed in every respect.

> Sitzt ihr nur immer! Leimt zusammen,
> Braut ein Ragout von andrer Schmaus,
> Und blast die kümmerlichen Flammen
> Aus eurem Aschenhäufchen 'raus.      (ll. 538–41.)

> Well, well, keep at it: ply the shears and paste,
> Concoct from feasts of other men your hashes,
> And should the thing be wanting fire or taste,
> Blow into flame your little heap of ashes.[33]

Thus Faust's side-swipe at his servant Wagner, Beckmesser's spiritual brother and undoubtedly one of the models for the figure of the Marker. Like Beckmesser, Faust's servant is a caricature of the pedant who, living in his ivory tower and completely obsessed with the norms and conventions of the 'school' of humanist rhetoric, senses his own sterility and attaches himself to the heels of some genuinely creative figure. Just as Beckmesser is 'always with Sachs' (vii. 170), even allowing himself to

---

[33] Translated by Philip Wayne (Harmondsworth, 1949), 49.

be led into disaster by him, like a rabbit held by the snake's hypnotic gaze, so Goethe's Wagner never leaves Faust's side.

Beckmesser is the only non-artisan among the Masters, the only one of them to have a Latin forename (Sixtus), a sure sign of his purely academic scholastic education and of his remoteness from the spirit of the *Volk*. In spite of his secret admiration for Sachs, he feels exactly the same reservations towards the shoemaker-poet as led seventeenth- and eighteenth-century humanist writers, with their insistence on a formal art of poetics, to reject and ridicule the historical Sachs. The line which Wagner places in his character's mouth: 'Hans Sachs, ein Schuh- | macher und Poet dazu' (Hans Sachs, a shoe- | maker and a poet too: vii. 213), is taken from a seventeenth-century satirical poem intended as a parody of the allegedly inelegant doggerel of the Nuremberg shoemaker-poet.

As early as Act I Beckmesser has already given repeated and unconcealed expression to his mistrust of Sachs's popularity. When Kothner protests that art is running after 'the people's favour', Beckmesser observes, with a glance at Sachs:

> D'rin bracht' er's weit, der hier so dreist:
> Gassenhauer dichtet er meist.                    (vii. 175.)
>
> Shame has he brought who talks so loud:
> Writing doggerel rhymes for the crowd.

This satirically barbed remark is turned against Beckmesser in the second act, when Sachs reminds the Marker:

> Nur Gassenhauer dicht' ich zum meisten;
> drum sing' ich zur Gassen, und hau' auf den Leisten.   (vii. 216.)
>
> If nought but doggerel rhymes I can stammer
> Then doggerel I sing as my leather I hammer.[34]

(The remark gains added significance when we recall that Beckmesser had compromised Sachs earlier, in the presence of the other Masters, by claiming that the quality of Sachs's work as a shoemaker was suffering from his pretensions as a poet.)

Walther had already said, somewhat laconically, that the Mastersingers' rules could certainly be used to produce 'a pair of well-made shoes' (vii. 161). Sachs now proceeds to give a literal demonstration of this in Act II. One by one, he parodies every stage of the Marker's activities, from 'Fanget an' (Begin) to the final peremptory

---

[34] As so often, Wagner's penchant for paronomasia gets the better of his translator. The word 'Gassenhauer', meaning a popular melody or 'hit', is made up of two elements, *Gasse*, 'alley', and *hauen*, 'to hit'. The literal translation of these two lines, therefore, is: 'For the most part I write only hits: | so I sing to the alley and hit my cobbler's last.'

question: 'Seid ihr nun fertig?' (Say, have you finished?). Almost grotesquely, Beckmesser even replies to this question with the same words as Walther had used earlier: 'Wie fraget ihr?' (Why do you ask?: vii. 183, 222). The fact that he asks 'in extreme fear' shows how keenly sensible he is of his own failure. The work as a whole is full of verbal correspondences which make it clear how much Wagner improved the poem even while he was setting it to music. For example, Nachtigall's exclamation of 'Merkwürdiger Fall!' (Strange is the case!: vii. 180), which he sings at Walther's entrance in Act I and which is repeated in the murmurings of the Mastersingers on hearing Beckmesser's nonsensical rendition of the Prize Song in Act III ('Höchst merkwürdiger Fall!',[35] (Most strange is the case!)), makes Beckmesser's failure seem to mirror Walther's, but it is a situation which, remarkably, has been reversed: the rigid representative of artistic normality now provokes the same bewilderment as the courtly outsider had done initially. The latter's poetry, moreover, is integrated into the world of bourgeois ideas in the following final scene, so that the horizons of that world are imperceptibly broadened. The gateway to the 'art-work of the future', previously locked, is now thrown open.

Walter Jens is convinced that, according to the laws of Hegelian dialectics which he assumes to underpin the structural model of the opera's plot, the presence of Beckmesser is logically necessary in the work's final tableau. But it is easier to demonstrate the dialectical necessity of the opposite point of view: as an intractable member of the *ancien régime*, Beckmesser may no longer appear on stage at the end of the work, since his antithesis, radical 'modernism', has ceased to exist now that Walther has agreed to take part in Sachs's dialectical (and successful) attempt to mediate in the *querelle des anciens et des modernes*. Beckmesser, by contrast, wanted nothing of this quarrel, and has little alternative now but to disappear 'among the townspeople'. Sachs's warning: 'Verachtet mir die Meister nicht | und ehrt mir ihre Kunst' (Do not disdain our Masters thus, | But honour well their art!), would be absurd if it were spoken in Beckmesser's presence, more especially when Sachs continues: 'Was ihnen hoch zum Lobe spricht, | fiel reichlich euch zur Gunst' (That which they love and prize the most | Has made them take your part), and: 'Wie kann die Kunst wohl unwerth sein, | die solche Preise schließet ein?' (Who could an art like ours despise | That brings him such a noble prize?: vii. 270). The Marker would never have accorded Walther this prize or this favour.

The final tableau of *Die Meistersinger* represents a monumental, aesthetic Utopia in which tradition is reconciled with progress and art

---

[35] *Die Meistersinger von Nürnberg*, ed. Csampai and Holland, p. 133; because this line was added at the time of the musical setting, it is not included in Wagner's *Collected Writings*.

with reality. Not only are the individual arts reunified on the Festival Meadow, but the entire life of the community is concentrated in a 'total work of art' from which the individual work of genius no longer needs to be divided by a 'mystical abyss'. Rather, it emerges from the total work of art as a flower grows from a plant: both are part of a single entity. Old ideals of Wagner's are once again revived here. We are reminded, for example, of his 1851 project, *A Theatre in Zurich*, in which he speaks of the possibility of allowing the theatre to develop on the basis of folkloristic traditions. 'Whatever the occasion for a public festival, be it cheerful or more solemn, there is a spontaneous desire . . . to organize processions in characteristic costumes: representations of scenes from the life of the people or from history . . . form the principal fare at these pageants.' (v. 47.) It is impossible not to recall here the procession of the guilds in *Die Meistersinger*, more especially since Wagner was clearly inspired by the *Sechseläuten*, a traditional procession of guilds held in Zurich every year on the third Monday in April. Wagner himself must almost certainly have seen this while he was living there. At a later date, too, in the speech he delivered to mark the foundation-stone-laying ceremony in Bayreuth in 1872, he recalls those 'festival halls run up in wood' which, as distant models of his own 'temporary theatre', were 'sometimes erected in German towns for choral meetings and similar co-operative festivals, and then taken down again immediately after the festival is over' (ix. 326). It would not be going too far, therefore, to claim that the Festival Meadow outside Nuremberg constitutes the Utopian counterpart to Wagner's festival in Bayreuth, a festival conceived for the present prosaic state of the world and barely able to bridge the gulf between art and reality.

But Walther's Prize Song, with its increasingly explicit structuring and exegesis of his 'Morgentraum', represents a second aesthetic Utopia. In Sachs's workshop he unfolds an elaborate image of Paradise in the opening Bar, in which the tree of life (Genesis 2: 9) figures prominently, with the biblical Eve offering him its fruit. (That the garden of which he dreams is Paradise and that the woman is Eve becomes fully clear to Walther only on the Festival Meadow, as the result of his increasingly penetrating hermeneutic exploration of the vision.) Eve tendering the fruit of the tree of life is by no means the temptress luring Adam to his ruin, as Hans Mayer assumes in an otherwise highly important essay on *Die Meistersinger* published in 1979.[36] The fruit has been picked not from the fatal tree of knowledge but from the tree of life. Walther's vision is like a mirror image of Dürer's 1504 copper engraving of *Adam and Eve*, a work which Wagner

---

[36] Hans Mayer, 'Parnaß und Paradies: Gedanken zu den *Meistersingern von Nürnberg*', in Klaus Schulz (ed.), *Programmheft der 'Meistersinger'*, pp. 23–38, esp. p. 29.

must certainly have known. In it, Adam can be seen offering Eve the apple from the tree of knowledge, already poisoned by the serpent's bite. In Walther's dream, by contrast, Paradise is not lost.

The vision of Paradise gives way to the complementary image of Mount Parnassus, with its laurel tree and that Castalian spring which was sacred to the Muses. (Once again this vision is recounted in the shoemaker's workshop but its meaning is not yet fathomed by Walther.) In the later version (after the Beckmesser scene, and inspired by the sight of the real-life Eva) Eve is replaced by Walther's Muse, with a garland of stars around her head, a garland which, at the same time, is also an attribute of Our Lady of the Assumption. Eva places the laurel wreath on the brow of her husband-poet. In the final form of the Prize Song, where the imagery is much more condensed than in the earlier, somewhat discursive, dream, the Muse additionally baptizes (!) the poet with water from the Castalian spring. Paradise in Walther's vision is literally a 'morning land' or Orient, while Parnassus, curiously enough, is the Occident. What this shows is that we are not dealing here simply with the contrast between Judaeo-Christianity and paganism, between the biblical world and its classical counterpart, but that the Hellenistic Parnassus has been relocated in the West, where it signifies modern art in its dialectical opposition to life, whose promise of happiness is symbolized by the tree of life in Paradise.

Paradise is not lost in Walther's dream, but is merely replaced in the concluding Bar of the Prize Song (a Bar which is now freely improvised) by the real Paradise, that Utopian day when the dialectical opposition between Paradisal morning and Parnassian evening is superseded and annulled. The Castalian spring suggests this new Paradise in which the beloved is both Eve/Eva and the Muse, 'Parnassus and Paradise' in one. Throughout all this, the listening townspeople feel 'cradled by the fairest of dreams' (vii. 268). That this is not, in fact, a dream—unless life itself has become a Utopian dream here, as indeed appears to be the case—is clear from the episode which comes immediately after it, when Walther is crowned as poet not only with a laurel wreath but also with a garland of myrtle. The 'wreath of laurel and myrtle' (vii. 269) which Eva places on his brow is the singer's prize and also a token of love, a symbol of both Paradisal life and Parnassian art. And when, in the final tableau, Eva 'takes the wreath from Walther's brow and places it on Sachs's' (vii. 271), she does so not only in honour of the poet, but as a tender confession of love. If love had been a matter of 'choice' and not of 'will', Eva might have become Sachs's wife.

The brave Utopian dream enacted in the final tableau of the opera imposes a sense of harmony on all those elements in Wagner's life and art (or, more specifically, those of his works which, in the form of short

stories or music dramas, are centred on the life of the tragic artist) which
are in a state of tension and disharmony. The laurel wreath, it is said in
Goethe's *Tasso*, is an 'infertile branch' (l. 2032), unlike the statesman's
reward, which is said to be as 'effective and alive' (l. 2052) as the service
which it recompenses. Hence Leonore's description of the laurel wreath
as 'A token more of suffering than of happiness' (l. 2039). And the
heroine of Grillparzer's *Sappho* (a work as familiar to Wagner as
Goethe's play about the life of Tasso) is forced to admit: ''Tis not for
naught the choir of Muses chose | The barren laurel as an ornament, |
A cold, infertile, scentless weight upon | The poet's brow' (ll. 271–4).
Sappho, too, had dreamt of exchanging 'the myrtle for the laurel' (l. 95),
of 'weaving both these wreaths about my brow, | Drinking life from art's
intoxicating cup | And sipping art from out the hand of life' (ll. 281–3).
In the end, however, she is bound to pay for this error with her life, for
the poet can be at home in only *one* of these two worlds. Anyone who has
chosen the kingdom of the dead (for such is the aesthetic world) can no
longer return to life, a message underlined by the allusion to
'Proserpina's pomegranate seeds', which, once partaken, symbolize a
living death (Act III, Scene 2).

For Romantic poets such as Tieck, Brentano, and E. T. A.
Hoffmann, tasting Proserpina's pomegranate seeds was often seen as
tantamount to eating of the fruit of the tree of knowledge: the decision
to espouse art signified not only the loss of happiness but also the loss
of life's innocence. The artist's existence was weighed down with a
demonic sense of guilt; time and again the poet longs to escape from the
*paradis artificiel* to which he is condemned, and return to the *paradis vert*
of a life not stigmatized by art. 'Art is perhaps a great crime', Wagner
told Cosima on 24 January 1869. Is it possible that this experience of art,
gained at the time of *Tannhäuser*, should be denied in *Die Meistersinger*?
Could the *paradis artificiel* be green as well? There is no doubt that the
unadulterated idyll of the Prize Song and of the final tableau on the
Festival Meadow would be a dubious escape into an ideal world if there
were not a complement to Walther's Utopian hymn, a complement
which describes the true, current state of art, contrasting the poet's
wreath of laurel and myrtle with his crown of thorns, and confronting *ars
triumphans* with *ars patiens*. It is Sachs's 'popular melody', first heard on
Midsummer's Eve and taken up, as it were, the following morning, when
it is introduced into the wordless Paradisal bliss of Eva and Walther with
a brusque and painful humour calculated to destroy the illusion and to
provide a conscious counterpart to the lovers' 'selige Morgentraumdeut-
Weise':

> Immer Schuster! Das ist nun mein Loos;
> des Nachts, des Tags—komm' nicht davon los! . . .
> Säng' mir nur wenigstens Einer dazu!
> Hörte heut' gar ein schönes Lied:—
> wem dazu ein dritter Vers gerieth'?                    (vii. 251.)

> Always cobbling, that now is my fate,
> By night, by day, both early and late . . .
> If only someone would sing me a song!
> Only today one charmed my ear!
> Ah, if only a third verse I could hear.

(The reference, of course, is to Walther's as yet incomplete song.)

Sachs's complaint that he is 'always cobbling' reminds us of the song of a lost Paradise which he had sung the previous night not only to annoy Beckmesser but as a silent reproach to Walther and Eva: 'Als Eva aus dem Paradies | von Gott dem Herrn verstoßen' (When Eve from Paradise was cast | Her sin she soon repented). Here Eve is not the innocent temptress, as in Walther's dream of Paradise, but the embodiment of the erotic world-will, luring him to his ruin: 'O Eva! Eva! Schlimmes Weib!' (O Eve, for shame you now should weep). For it was Eve who brought *labor improbus*—toil in the sweat of one's brow—into the world. The angel whom the Lord commissioned to make shoes for Adam and Eve, and who was thus obliged to exchange the idleness of the blessed spirits for the misery of earthly labour, is a symbol of the poet who, like Hans Sachs, must divide his time between alienated labour and poetry. At the same time, however, there is an allusion here to the fact that Sachs must sacrifice his happiness to Eva Pogner and 'Adam' Stolzing. Eva understands this perfectly: although she rejects Walther's spontaneous suggestion that Sachs's song is aimed at her, she knows that Walther is right: 'Mich betrübt das Lied' ('Tis the song that wounds); and, later: 'Mich schmerzt das Lied, ich weiß nicht wie! (His song so pains me, I know not why!: vii. 212–14).

Like the artists in E. T. A. Hoffmann's *Meister Martin der Küfner* who have chosen the anonymity of cooperage merely out of their love for the fair Rosa, Sachs, too, regards art and shoemaking as alien activities.

> Gäb' nicht ein Engel Trost,
> der gleiches Werk erlos't,
> und rief' mich oft in's Paradies,
> wie dann ich Schuh' und Stiefeln ließ'!
> Doch wenn der mich im Himmel hält,
> dann liegt zu Füßen mir die Welt.          (vii. 213.)

> Without an angel there
> To drive away my care
> And call me up to Paradise,
> I'd leave this work that I despise!
> But when enthroned in Heaven on high
> The world beneath my feet will lie.

This Paradise differs, of course, from the Paradise of Walther's dream. It is not the sense of earthly joy which is identified with artistic joy but, as Hans Mayer has made clear, that 'contrary joy', a *paradis artificiel* closer to the Parnassus relegated to the kingdom of the dead than Walther's 'Paradise'. According to Mayer, Gottfried Benn had, as it were, provided a sequel to Hans Sachs's closing words to Walther in his poem, 'Einsamer nie als im August':

> Wo alles sich durch Glück beweist
> und tauscht den Blick und tauscht die Ringe
> im Weingeruch, im Rausch der Dinge—
> dienst du dem Gegenglück: dem Geist.[37]

> When others revel in life's happiness,
> Exchanging glances and their wedding rings
> While drunk on wine and worldly vinousness,
> You serve the spirit of unworldly things.

By espousing the world of the spirit, Sachs escapes, of course, from that *Wahn* which is characteristic of life and in which the lovers, Walther and Eva, remained enmeshed. But is not that art also an expression of *Wahn* which, like Walther's Prize Song, denies the Fall, seeking to regain a Paradise that was never lost? Is not the whole of the vision enacted on the Festival Meadow called into question by a pessimistic scepticism on Sachs's part which speaks of angels with flaming swords barring the way back into Paradise? Only at the price of bitter atonement are those who devote themselves to art granted even momentary access to a Paradise which is not the old familiar Paradise, but a new one, a Paradise which can never be won on a permanent basis but which, time and again, must be gained by an act of hubristic defiance and which always bears the stigma of original sin. The splendour of the final scene is doubtless overshadowed by a sense of resignation. Utopianism and pessimism, always intermeshed in Wagner's view of the world, overlap on this occasion, too. And when, at the end of *Die Meistersinger*, the townspeople acclaim Sachs as 'Nuremberg's loyal Sachs' (vii. 271), and Eva crowns him with the poet's garland, this is a moment of sorrow rather than of happiness for him, since the myrtle signifies the joys he has renounced, while the laurel—'a symbol more of suffering than of joy'—reminds him

[37] Mayer, 'Parnaß und Paradies', 32.

that his fame is not as great as Walther's. The Festival Meadow is a *terra utopica*, a blessed isle in the midst of a sea of melancholy.

Like Goethe's *Hermann und Dorothea* and Schiller's *Die Glocke*, Wagner's *Die Meistersinger* has given rise to a sort of myth of German civic life, a lifestyle which has never actually existed and which, in the case of *Die Meistersinger*, is consciously opposed to contemporary middle-class life. It *is* mythic to the extent that the world of everyday reality, presented with the stylistic attributes of classical antiquity or Renaissance Germany, allows a glimpse of the archetypes of Greek myth in the case of Goethe's poem, and of biblical myth in the case of Wagner's. But the interweaving of classical myth and prosaic modernity also provides an ironic device which lends itself to humour. It is the predominance of this element which, not least, has kept Goethe's epic poem and Wagner's opera alive, while the monumental seriousness of Schiller's *Die Glocke* has failed to survive the collapse of nineteenth-century bourgeois cultural illusions.

The plot of *Die Meistersinger* is characterized by a wealth of biblical allusions. The baptism motif has already been mentioned: Hans Sachs appears as a latter-day John the Baptist (the forerunner and precursor); Eva has already seen a likeness of Walther—in a painting of the young David—even before she sets eyes on him (a motif which recurs in almost every work by Wagner); Eva herself has a biblical name, a name with which she is repeatedly associated on a symbolical level; and much else besides. That all these mythical reminiscences are an aesthetic attempt to secularize religion or else to sanctify art is only half the truth, since both are also used, again and again, in an ironical and parodistic way. The myth is present not only in all its original seriousness but also in the form of a travesty. When Eva, for example, describes 'her' David ('with sword in his belt and a sling in his hand'), the real David, Sachs's apprentice, appears 'with a ruler in his belt and dangling a large piece of white chalk on a piece of string' (vii. 155).

Wagner was at constant loggerheads with the bourgeois audiences of his day. His works deal constantly with the tragic disposition of the artist in a prosaic age. His *Tristan und Isolde* had ended with the drunken affirmation of a love which destroys all sense of social order, while *Die Meistersinger* was to be followed by a return to the anarchical Utopia of the *Ring*. But this is the same Wagner who, in *Die Meistersinger*, created a myth for the German middle classes, a myth which, no matter how relativized by tragic seriousness or ironic parody, shows the German burgher offering a festive home to art. Is this merely another mask assumed by the born 'actor' that Wagner was alleged to be, a *'histrio'* who, in his transcendental homelessness, can slip into every past, into divergent philosophies, who was an anarchist yesterday, a burgher today, and a religious fanatic tomorrow—all of them masks behind which lurks nothing but emptiness?

The middle-class aspect of *Die Meistersinger* involves a Utopianism at immediate odds with the social reality of the German and European middle classes of the time. The ideal of the *burgher* is contrasted with that of the *bourgeois*, who casts his long shadow over Pogner's lines, with their echo of a prejudice held both at court and among the unpropertied classes:

> An Höfen, wie an nied'rer Statt,
> des bitt'ren Tadels ward ich satt,
>     daß nur auf Schacher und Geld
>     sein Merk' der Bürger stellt'.     (vii. 172.)
>
> In castle and in humble hut
> The evil slander ended not,
>     That only treasure and gold
>     Our burghers' dreams can hold!

In the knowledge that this bourgeois mentality dominates the present state of the world, Wagner holds out its antithesis, the burgher whose art will banish the *Wahn* of money. *Die Meistersinger* thus complements *Der Ring des Nibelungen*. No one was more fascinated than Thomas Mann by this concept of the ideal burgher, an ideal which Wagner himself aimed to realize at Wahnfried by adopting its outward forms, including the famous velvet beret. Mann's essay, 'Lübeck als geistige Lebensform',[38] contains unmistakable traces of this middle-class outlook in its account of the historical dimension to that late medieval city-state oligarchy whose poeticized image is embodied in Wagner's *Meistersinger*. How difficult Mann found it to break free from that fascination is clear from the fact that, in his *Betrachtungen eines Unpolitischen*, he apologizes in five different ways for having more or less 'slept through the transformation of the German burgher into the bourgeois'.[39]

---

[38] Thus the title of Mann's 1926 speech, published in 1930 in *Die Forderung des Tages*.
[39] See Michael Zeller, *Bürger oder Bourgeois? Eine literatursoziologische Studie zu Thomas Manns 'Buddenbrooks' und Heinrich Manns 'Im Schlaraffenland'* (Stuttgart, 1976), 16–17.

# 17

## Oedipus and *Der Ring des Nibelungen*

> Nor need this mother-marrying frighten you;
> Many a man has dreamt as much.
>
> Sophocles, *King Oedipus*, ll. 980–1.

One of Germany's leading Greek scholars, Wolfgang Schadewaldt, has described Wagner's music dramas as 'mythic palimpsests'[1] in which the underlying script of Greek myth is constantly decipherable beneath the surface layer of Germanic and Christian legend.[2] Wagner himself gave frequent emphasis to the importance of Greek myth and Attic tragedy whenever he was discussing the type of subject-matter he felt appropriate to the musical drama. Nowhere is this truer than in his self-apologia, *A Communication to my Friends*, although it must be added that if, in this essay, he claims to derive the themes of even his Romantic operas from classical archetypes, it is because of his palpable wish to reconcile his earlier ideas with his present beliefs as influenced by Feuerbach and revolutionary ideology. If he did have recourse to subjects from the Christian Middle Ages, he insisted, what had attracted him to them were the classical myths which lay behind them:

it is a fundamental error of our superficial way of observing things to consider the specifically Christian outlook as somehow essentially creative in its manifestations. Not one of the most characteristic and affecting of the Christian myths belongs originally to the Christian spirit, as we commonly understand it; this latter inherited them all from the purely human notions of prehistory, merely moulding them to fit its own unique particularity. (iv. 289.)

Wagner then goes on to illustrate this by reference to *Der fliegende Holländer*, *Tannhäuser*, and *Lohengrin*:

Just as the basic feature of the myth of the 'Flying Dutchman' finds an earlier embodiment, still clearly intelligible to us, in the Hellenic Odyssey; just as, in wresting himself from the arms of Calypso, in fleeing Circe's blandishments, and in yearning for his homeland's mortal wife, this same Odysseus gave expression to fundamental features of a longing which, familiar to the Hellenic

---

[1] Wolfgang Schadewaldt, 'Richard Wagner und die Griechen', in Wieland Wagner (ed.), *Richard Wagner und das neue Bayreuth* (Munich, 1962), 167.

[2] The present chapter is an expanded and revised version of an article originally published under the title 'Der Ödipus-Mythos und der Ring des Nibelungen', in *Die Programmhefte der Bayreuther Festspiele 1980*, iv. *'Das Rheingold'*, 1–12, 91–100.

spirit, we rediscover, immeasurably enhanced . . . in the figure of Tannhäuser, so we already encounter in Greek myth . . . the essential feature of the Lohengrin myth. Who does not know the story of 'Zeus and Semele'? (iv. 289.)

In his essay 'Versuch über Schiller' Thomas Mann suggests that Schiller's 1782 'operetta', *Semele*, already contains perceptible pre-echoes of *Lohengrin*,[3] while Baudelaire, for his part, had pointed out 'a striking similarity' between the Lohengrin legend on the one hand and, on the other, the 'classical myth of Psyche' who, like Elsa, was a victim of demonic curiosity and who, refusing to respect her godlike spouse's anonymity, forfeited all her happiness when she penetrated his secret. Elsa lent an ear to Ortrud, as Eve did to the serpent. Eternal Eve falls into the eternal trap.'[4] Wagner himself gives a matchless account of this archetypal, mythic motif of demonic curiosity and its Christian metamorphosis in *A Communication to my Friends*, in one of many passages which Nietzsche numbered 'among the most beautiful in all German prose':[5]

The ethereal realm from which the deity longs to descend in order to live among men had expanded, through Christian longing, to utterly inconceivable bounds. To the Hellenes it was still the cloud-girt world of thunderbolts and lightning from which the shaggy-haired Zeus descended and cunningly took on human form: to the Christian, the azure sky dissolved in an infinite sea of sensuous yearning in which the forms of all the gods grew blurred in outline, until at last his own likeness alone, that of the yearning human being, could rise towards him out of the sea of his own imagination. A primal feature, repeated in manifold forms, permeates the legends of those nations who dwelt by the sea or by rivers that emptied into the sea: on the billows' azure mirror a stranger was seen to draw near, a man of utmost grace and purest virtue who charmed and won each heart by the irresistible spell which he wove; he was the fulfilment of that desire which fills the yearning breast of him who dreamt of happiness beyond the sea in a land he could not discern. The stranger disappeared again, withdrawing over the ocean waves, as soon as he was questioned about his innermost being. (iv. 290–1.)

The motif recurs, transformed, in Wagner's 1849–50 prose draft, *Wieland der Schmied*, where Schwanhilde reports that her father, the Prince of the Light-elves, had approached her mother in the form of a swan, just as Zeus had appeared before Leda. For three years they had lived together, until her mother 'desired to know, in her foolish zeal, who her husband was, a question that he had forbidden her to ask. Then

    [3] Thomas Mann, *Gesammelte Werke* (Frankfurt, 1960), ix. 929.
    [4] Charles Baudelaire, 'Richard Wagner et *Tannhäuser* à Paris', in *Œuvres complètes*, ed. Claude Pichois (Paris, 1976), ii. 799.
    [5] Friedrich Nietzsche, *Sämtliche Werke: Kritische Studienausgabe in 15 Bänden*, ed. Giorgio Colli and Mazzino Montinari (Munich, 1980), i. 502; translated into English by R. J. Hollingdale as *Untimely Meditations: Richard Wagner in Bayreuth* (Cambridge, 1983), 248.

the Prince of the Elves assumed the form of a swan and swam away through the flooding waves.' (iii. 182.) Elements of the myths of Leda, Semele, and Lohengrin are intertwined here in a wholly idiosyncratic way. (Wieland, or Wayland, the Smith is also, of course, a Germanic variant of Daedalus, the skilled Athenian metalworker.)

It is in the *Ring* that the majority of parallels with classical myth are to be found. Wolfgang Schadewaldt has pointed out a profusion of reminiscences of Aeschylus's Prometheus trilogy, a work which, as we shall see, has left its mark on *Parsifal* as well, where there is also evidence of a motif from the myth of Achilles, in the form of the wound which can be cured only by the spear which dealt it. Wagner planned a drama on the life of Achilles in 1849, and must have known of the motif from the legend of King Telephus, who was wounded by Achilles and later healed by him:

> Nur eine Waffe taugt:
>     die Wunde schließt
> der Speer nur, der sie schlug.   (x. 375.)

> One weapon only serves:
>     The Spear that smote
> Must heal you of your wound.

Hans Pfitzner was the first to suspect that these lines from *Parsifal* contain a reminiscence of the scene in Goethe's *Tasso* in which Antonio seeks to placate the poet whom he has offended, and Tasso draws an analogy between Antonio's aim and the action of Achilles in healing Telephus: 'The poet tells us of a spear which yet | Might cure the wound that it itself had dealt | If friendly hand were but to place it there.' (ll. 2576–8.)[6]

There is one mythic parallel, however, which, for all its immense significance, has, remarkably, remained unnoticed. But its importance is suggested by Wagner's principal theoretical work, *Opera and Drama* (1851), the second part of which contains an analysis of the 'Oidipus myth' (Wagner always uses the Greek form of the name) conducted from the standpoint of the history of philosophy and based on the plots of Sophocles' *King Oedipus* and *Antigone* (*Oedipus at Colonus* is only briefly mentioned), together with that of Aeschylus's *Seven against Thebes*. He pieces together the disparate parts of this cycle of legends, producing a self-contained, causally coherent system of myths in which he sees 'an image of the whole of human history, from the beginnings of society to the necessary downfall of the state' (iv. 65). In other words, the Oedipus myth not only illustrates events which are past, including those

---

[6] Hans Pfitzner, 'Der Parsifalstoff und seine Gestaltungen' (1914), in *Gesammelte Schriften* (Augsburg, 1926), i. 160.

which reach back to the origins of the process of socialization, it also encompasses the immediate present, together with events which are still to take place. It is a 'total' myth of lasting actuality which embraces the whole of humankind. It is clear, therefore, that if Wagner appealed to myth, it was not to escape from the present and to seek refuge in some remote archaic past; it was an attempt to capture chronological specificity within the medium of musical drama. Shaw was right to describe the *Ring* as 'a drama of today, and not of a remote and fabulous antiquity'.[7] But it would be equally correct to describe the work as a drama of tomorrow. 'All our wishes and burning desires which, in truth, carry us over into the future, we seek to make intelligible to the senses by using images from the past in order to give them the form with which the modern present cannot provide them', Wagner himself declared in *A Communication to my Friends*. The future is prefigured in an image of the past.

'What is incomparable about myth', Wagner insists in *Opera and Drama*, 'is that it is true for all time, and that its content, however densely compressed, is inexhaustible throughout the ages.' (iv. 64.) In other words, it is the poet's task to keep on reinterpreting that content on the strength of every new experience. Whereas, in his Romantic operas, Wagner had treated myth as a means of expressing the problematical existence of the modern, absolute artist, his concern in *Siegfrieds Tod*, the work for which audiences were to be prepared by the theoretical self-justification of *Opera and Drama* and which was later to develop into the Nibelung tetralogy, was far greater, for his aim here was the musical realization of a myth which embraced both the world's primeval origins and the end of time itself, a 'musical cosmogony', in Thomas Mann's words, in which a 'passion for the past' is permeated by a 'yearning for the future'.[8]

This holistic intent links the myth of the *Ring* with the 'world-historical' myth of Oedipus (iv. 62) as expounded by Wagner in *Opera and Drama*. The very fact that, in the essay intended to prepare the way for the *Ring*, he included a speculative exegesis of the Sophoclean and Aeschylean tragedies mentioned earlier, and that he invested them with so crucial a significance, suggests that, in his view, there was a genuine affinity between Greek and Germanic myth. The most striking link between the two is the incest motif embodied in the figures of Oedipus and Jocasta on the one hand, and Siegmund and Sieglinde on the other. A close examination of Wagner's exegesis of this motif within the

---

[7] Bernard Shaw, *The Perfect Wagnerite: A Commentary on the Ring of the Niblungs* (London, 1898), 1; the 4th edn. of 1923 is reprinted in *Shaw's Music: The Complete Musical Criticism of Bernard Shaw*, ed. Dan H. Laurence, 2nd edn. (London, 1989), iii. 421.

[8] Thomas Mann, *Wagner und unsere Zeit*, ed. Erika Mann (Frankfurt, 1963), 137; translated into English by Allan Blunden as *Pro and contra Wagner* (London, 1985), 180.

context of the Oedipus myth underlines the importance of the incestuous relationship between the Volsung twins, in addition to revealing a whole series of surprising parallels between these two major cycles of myths.

Oedipus's incestuous relationship with his mother is never once described by Wagner as 'unnatural' or as a 'violation of human nature' (iv. 56). Quite the opposite: it is said to be the expression of a physical inevitability at odds with society's moralistic outlook. This interpretation is equally true, we may assume, of the incest between the Volsung twins in *Die Walküre*, an act which is certainly not 'counter to the order of nature', as Nietzsche claims in the fourth of his *Unzeitgemäße Betrachtungen*.[9] What society sees as a monstrous crime in the case of Oedipus (a moralistic view to which both Oedipus and Jocasta subscribe, as is clear from the fact that, on acknowledging their incestuous marriage, the former blinds himself and the latter takes her own life) is, in Wagner's view, an example of the way in which the individualistic 'instinctiveness' or spontaneity of sexual love irrupts into the world of family life, a world which is necessarily kept inviolate. Within the family—which Wagner sees as 'the most natural, but also the most restricted basis of society'—sexual love is reduced to the relationship between husband and wife, since the family is held together not by natural instinct but by the 'ties of custom'. Sexual love, however, is 'a goad' whose spontaneity conflicts with predictable custom. Of course, the revolution which love wages against the family is, so to say, a social necessity, since it breaks down the latter's 'narrow confines' in order to 'extend them to include a wider human society', without, however, encroaching on existing family relationships. 'Oedipus, who married his mother and fathered children upon her, is a phenomenon which fills us with horror and loathing precisely because it offends, irreconcilably, against our *customary* relations with our mother and against the views which have been formed by those relations.' (iv. 56.)

That Oedipus and Jocasta violate custom rather than Nature, indeed, that Nature gives her blessing to their union is clear from the fact that their marriage is fertile and that they produce a family. 'Oedipus and Jocasta . . . had acted unconsciously, according to the natural instinct of the purely human individual; and from their union sprang an enrichment of human society, in the shape of two strong sons and two noble daughters.' (iv. 57.) But society, for all that it had been enriched by their marriage, cursed the couple and their issue, since society, like the family, was based on 'custom', so that interference in family life was mercilessly punished.

---

[9] Nietzsche, *Sämtliche Werke*, i. 508; English trans. (Hollingdale, *Untimely Meditations*), p. 253.

The individual vital instinct *always* expresses itself in *new* and *immediate* ways, whereas the essence of society is *custom*, its mode of perception *mediated*. Until such time as society gains a perfect understanding of the essence of the individual and the way in which it has developed out of that essence, its outlook must remain limiting and inhibiting, and it will become increasingly tyrannical the more the individual, animative and innovative by nature, contends instinctively with custom. (iv. 54.)

'Natural necessity', manifesting itself in the 'individual's physical, vital instinct', was misinterpreted by the Greeks as 'fate', a misunderstanding which Wagner believed could be ascribed to society's moral outlook and its grounding in 'custom'. The individual's instinctive actions, 'acknowledged as being disruptive from the standpoint of moral custom', were derived

from a conjuncture in which the individual agent was deemed possessed by an influence which robbed him of that freedom to act according to which he would have done what was morally customary. Since, as a result of the deed committed in defiance of moral custom, the individual had compromised himself in the eyes of society, but since, being conscious of his action, he was able to return to society at least to the extent that he accepted society's condemnation [as was the case with Jocasta and Oedipus], the act of unconscious transgression appeared explicable only as the result of some curse which lay upon him through no particular fault of his own. This curse was portrayed in myth as divine punishment for a primordial crime, a punishment which clung to a particular family until that family had all been destroyed [Wagner may have been thinking here of the curse which weighed on the House of Tantalus, and its poetic explication in Goethe's *Iphigenie*]. But in truth it is none other than the power of instinct which is embodied here, a power which informs the individual's unconscious, physically inevitable actions. (iv. 54.)

Paradoxically, then, the individual's radical autonomy is interpreted by society as the cause of his divinely ordained undoing.

Having misconstrued physical inevitability as fate, the Greeks, according to Wagner, sought refuge from it in the political state, whereas modern man (whose fate, to quote Napoleon's remark to Goethe, was to become a political animal: iv. 53) seeks to break free from the 'tyrannical political state' and return to a life of 'natural necessity', which is now recognized as the 'pre-condition for our existence' (including that of society) and which acknowledges the power of individual instinct (iv. 56–64). Similarly, Wagner believed, this modern inversion of the classical relationship between the individual and the state was already prefigured in the Oedipus myth, as his speculative exegesis of *Seven against Thebes* and *Antigone* demonstrates. Indeed, his interpretation of the latter provides an original alternative to Hegel's famous interpretation of the play. Hegel derives the tragedy of the Sophoclean drama from the dialectical process of equally justified material forces—family and religion on the one hand, and authority and state on the other—even though, in doing so, he misses the point of the work (which clearly places Creon in the wrong) just as surely as Wagner does in *his* interpretation. According to this latter view, Antigone's actions are motivated by instinctive human feelings, whereas the truth of the matter is that she is obliged to act as she does by her commitment to the family's ties of blood. But this is not the place to discuss the myth's authentic meaning.

Following Oedipus's banishment from Thebes, his two sons, Eteocles and Polynices, decided to rule the city alternately, each for a period of a year. Eteocles was first to assume the succession, but when Polynices demanded his right to the throne, his brother refused to grant it. The outcome was the War of the Seven against Thebes. According to Wagner, the Thebans fought on the side of Eteocles, since they disapproved of the 'change of ruler and constant innovation', so much had 'custom already become the true legislator'. This custom guaranteed peace and safeguarded that power of 'property' which everybody 'wanted to enjoy on his own and not to share with anyone else'—just as Eteocles revelled in the possession of power. 'Every citizen who saw in property the guarantee of customary calm must, for that very reason, bear part of the blame for the unbrotherly act committed by that supreme property-holder, Eteocles. In other words, the power of selfish custom lent support to Eteocles; and against it, betrayed Polynices fought with all the hot-headedness of youth.' Although he showed himself an 'unworthy patriot' in waging war on his home town, he and his army, assembled from a host of different nations, betrayed a 'purely human interest', embodying 'society in its widest and most natural sense in contrast to that limited, narrow-minded, selfish society which shrank imperceptibly, under their attacks, into the ossified state' (iv. 59).

But this state was embodied in the figure of Creon, to whom power over Thebes accrued following the war between the sons of Oedipus. According to Wagner, Creon bolstered up that power by ordering that the body of the 'unpatriotic Polynices' should not be buried—an 'act of supreme political sagacity' to the extent that it was fully in accord with 'public opinion', the nucleus of which Creon regarded as 'custom, care, and resistance to change', all qualities associated in his mind with the figure of Polynices.

Here we see the *state*, which had developed imperceptibly out of the community, battening on to the latter's habitual outlook and representing that custom to the extent that it represented custom alone, abstract custom whose nucleus is fear and abhorrence of all that is *not* customary. Armed with the power of custom, the state now rounds on society with annihilating force by denying it the natural sustenance of its being in the most instinctive and holiest social feelings. (iv. 58.)

Wagner is thinking here, of course, of the piety due to the dead. In his view, the state arises out of the victory of ossified 'absolute custom' (which he distinguishes from its original 'naïve' prototype, the necessary embodiment of 'socio-moral concepts'), in other words, out of the triumph of 'communal self-interest' over 'moral consciousness' and society's 'purely human' aspirations. Society's conscience is appeased by prophylactic rituals and surrogate rites, while its 'praxis', determined by 'utilitarian' considerations alone, hardens to the point at which it becomes the 'state' (iv. 59–60).

'The political state lives only through the vices of society, its virtues being provided solely by human individuality.' (iv. 66.) The immoral origins of the state are already hinted at, Wagner believed, in Oedipus's exposure by his father Laius. The discovery of what had taken place left the Theban population unmoved, since it had been carried out in the interests of securing power and establishing calm. '*Calm* and *order*, gained even at the price of the basest crime against human nature and against customary morality itself . . . were at any rate more worthy of consideration than that most natural of human sentiments which bids the father sacrifice himself to his children, not them to *him*.' (iv. 61.) A line can be traced from Laius to Eteocles and, finally, to Creon which mirrors the state's evolution from utilitarianism and abstract custom to moral indifference, while a parallel line, from Oedipus to Polynices and thence to Antigone, charts the progress from natural instinct to autonomous individuality and, finally, to a society or community characterized by moral consciousness. Whereas Creon is the 'state personified', Antigone embodies 'pure human love' (iv. 63), a love which gives rise to the Utopian hope that the 'state will one day perish' (iv. 72).

Antigone sees herself at odds with a society in which the 'poison' of 'custom' has tainted our 'natural feeling for morality'.

The craving for custom and unconditional calm misleads [society] into blocking off the well-spring by which it could have kept itself forever fresh and healthy; and this spring was the free, self-determining individual. Only when the individual acted in accordance with the involuntary urge of natural necessity and denied society through his moral supremacy was morality—in other words, that which is truly human—restored to a society which was utterly corrupt. (iv. 61–2.)

Wagner is referring here, of course, to Antigone's action in ignoring Creon's refusal to allow her to bury her brother's body and in thereby risking her own life. Creon 'struck out at humanity and cried, "Long live the state"', whereas Antigone acted out of 'loving necessity', a necessity greater than any previously known, involving, as it did, that 'pure human love' which emerged 'from the ruins of that sexual, parental, and sibling love denied by society and disclaimed by the state'. As such, her action brought about the downfall of the state as embodied in the figure of Creon. On seeing the body of his dead son, who had followed Antigone to her death, 'the ruler became a father once again . . . Wounded to its innermost depths, *the state* came crashing down, to become in death *a human being*.' (iv. 62–3.) But 'a human being', or 'man', was also the answer which Oedipus found to the Sphinx's riddle, a solution which Wagner saw as central to the whole of the Oedipus myth (iv. 57).

For Wagner, the end of Antigone's tragedy is the mythic embodiment of the ultimate telos of history, namely, the 'downfall of the state'. 'The necessity of this downfall is something we feel in advance in myth; it is the task of actual history to realize that goal.' (iv. 65.) Whereas the Greeks had misinterpreted the force of individuality as the workings of fate, arming themselves against it by inventing the city-state, our fate today is that abstract political state 'in which free individuality perceives its destiny of self-denial'. But the 'destruction of the state' will enable us to reorganize society on the basis of 'the free self-determination of the individual' as a 'necessity common to all members of society' (iv. 66–7). The state drew its life from the death of free individuality, while the latter will draw new life from the death of the state. This, for Wagner, is the quintessential meaning of the Oedipus myth, which he saw as one of the key myths in the history of the world.

Disapproving as it is of the state and of society, Wagner's mythology draws on an earlier aesthetic tradition of criticizing the state, the most important example of which he regarded as being Schiller's series of open letters, 'Über die ästhetische Erziehung des Menschen,' first published in 1795. No less influential, however, was the political philosophy of the Young Hegelians and of the young Karl Marx. Concrete individuality is destroyed by the 'elaborate mechanism' of the modern state, in which 'a mechanical life is formed out of the fragmentation of an infinite number of lifeless parts'. Each 'individual concrete life' is irrelevant for the 'abstraction of the whole', and 'the state remains eternally remote from its citizens since it cannot be discovered by feeling', Wagner could have read in Schiller's essay.[10] (According to Wagner's later tract, 'Shall We Hope?', Schiller was the 'first to recognize how utterly inimical to art' is the modern state constitution: x. 121.) Other contemporaries of Schiller, notably Schelling, Hölderlin, and Hegel in his *Ältestes Systemfragment des deutschen Idealismus*, demanded the 'abolition' of the state, arguing that it was 'mechanical' and that it treated human beings as 'cogs in a machine'.[11] But, however much Wagner was indebted to

[10] Friedrich Schiller, *Sämtliche Werke*, ed. Gerhard Fricke and Herbert G. Göpfert, 3rd edn. (Munich, 1962), v. 584–5.

[11] Friedrich Hölderlin, *Sämtliche Werke*, ed. Friedrich Beißner (Frankfurt, 1961), 1014.

those of his aesthetico-idealistic predecessors who had criticized the state as an institution, there are even more direct links between Wagner's thinking and the writings of the young Marx, who had advocated the supersession of that abstract political state which 'deprived' man of 'his real individual life'.[12]

It may be added that Wagner returns to his exegesis of the Oedipus myth in a revealing footnote at the end of the second part of *Opera and Drama*, where he interprets the myth as a symbol of the relationship between language and music in the musical drama. Antigone is very much cast in the role of the patron saint of musical drama, as Wagner draws on the familiar image of sexual polarity to describe the relationship between the language of words and that of music; music being the feminine, emotional element, language the male, rational element. The expressive potential of music precedes that of language, just as feeling precedes understanding, which is why the female element is also described as the maternal one: the language of words issues from the 'womb of that expressive potential for primal melody' and, therefore, stands in the same relationship to it as a son does to his mother. The reunification of feeling and understanding, of words and music in the musical drama is now described in highly graphic terms using the image of sexual congress. The 'poetic intent' is the seed with which music *qua* womankind is impregnated in order that it may 'give birth' to the musical drama. The mother/son relationship becomes a sexual one. 'Would it be thought trivial of me', Wagner asks, 'if I were to remind the reader—with reference to my exposition of the myth in question—of Oedipus, who was born of Jocasta and who fathered on her the redeeming figure of Antigone?' (iv. 102–3.) Thus, incestuous love is seen to symbolize the structural relationship of the musical drama.

Just as Antigone's act of redemption leads to the destruction of the state as embodied in the figure of Creon (mythically paralleling the historical future and the twilight of that state of the world so fatally dominated by politics), so the mythico-musical drama is the Utopian harbinger of a purely human society free from politics and political rule (and hence the counterpart of the novel which reproduces the existing, politically determined, state of society). Music drama is, as it were, the Antigone of the arts. Myth is 'the beginning and end of history'. Its dramatic representation does not, therefore, merely delve into prehistory, it also extends beyond it into the future, since the 'return' of history into the matrix of myth is also 'a form of progress, leading to our acquisition of the highest human potential' (iv. 91).

---

[12] Karl Marx, *Die Frühschriften*, ed. Siegfried Landshut (Stuttgart, 1964), 181; translated into English as 'On the Jewish Question', in *Karl Marx and Friedrich Engels: Collected Works* (London, 1975), iii. 154.

The work to which all these speculations ultimately lead is *Siegfrieds Tod*, the precursor of the later *Ring*, and, in a certain sense, Wagner's 'Antigone' not only in terms of its formal aesthetics but also in terms of its content. That there was originally an analogy between the 'decline of the state' at the end of Sophocles' tragedy and the twilight of the gods at the end of the *Ring*, and that both of these are symbolic pointers to that mythical state of the world when, at the end of time, political domination is no more, ought, by now, to be self-evident, in spite of later attempts by Wagner to reinterpret the tetralogy in the light of Schopenhauerian metaphysics. No less obvious is the fact that these two 'world-historical myths' (the Sophoclean and the Wagnerian) presuppose a future state in which the individual will be freely self-determining, finally superseding all those outer influences on him (or her) which find expression in the mythic images of fate, divine rule, the curse on the gold, and the treaties engraved on Wotan's spear. In this sense, both the Oedipus myth and the Nibelung myth are Utopian political parables for Wagner.

The fate which dominates the lives of both gods and humans, although embodied in the primeval mother-goddess Erda and her three daughters, the Norns, derives less from Germanic sources than from the *moira* of Aeschylus's *Prometheus* and the three Moerae or Parcae who spin the thread of destiny in Greek mythology. This fate, so powerfully proclaimed in Erda's oracular pronouncement at the end of *Das Rheingold*, is superseded even before the downfall of the gods as prophesied by her. Just as the end of the gods is implied by mankind's autonomous action, so the power of fate is already destroyed by the chief of the gods himself. It is surely significant that the scene in which Siegfried triumphs over Wotan, in Act III of *Siegfried*, follows immediately after the Wanderer's conjuration of Erda, and that, after their great altercation, he dismisses her to the realm of eternal sleep. Essentially, Erda's power is already broken when she succumbs to the spell of Wotan's love:[13] 'Mich Wissende selbst | bezwang ein Waltender einst', she tells him (Even I in my wisdom | was once abused by a god); to which Wotan retorts: 'Dein Wissen verweht | vor meinem Willen' (Your wisdom scatters | before my will: vi. 154, 156). Those feelings which he reduces to endless silence—'Urmütter-Furcht! | Ur-Sorge! | Zu ewigem Schlaf | hinab! hinab!' (Primeval mothers' fear! | Primeval care! | To endless sleep | Return!: vi. 157)—are the universal principles of

[13] In a conversation with Cosima on 8 May 1874 Wagner commented as follows on this very point: 'What a strange night that must have been when Wotan subjugated Erda! That is my own invention entirely—I know nothing [analogous] about Zeus and Gaea, for instance, and nothing struck me in another poet, the way we are sometimes much struck by some feature which escapes other people. The night when Brünnhilde was begotten—it can only be seen as something divine; the urge to subjugate this prophetic woman, to learn all from her! Such outbreaks of natural force I have witnessed in the animal world—our only analogue for the divine is in the animal world.'

care and fear, principles ascribed to a future which, already known and predetermined, threatens to engulf the world.

> Urwissend
> stachest du einst
> der Sorge Stachel
> in Wotan's wagendes Herz:
> mit Furcht vor schmachvoll
> feindlichem Ende
> füllt' ihn dein Wissen,
> daß Bangen band seinen Muth.     (vi. 155.)

> Primevally knowing,
> you thrust ere now
> the thorn of care
> through Wotan's venturous heart:
> with fear of a shamefully
> adverse end
> your wisdom filled him,
> and dread enmeshed his mind.

Fear and care have suddenly paralysed Wotan's actions, actions which were formerly characterized by the unbroken will to live. 'Wie besiegt die Sorge der Gott?' (How can the god overcome that care?). It is a question which Erda can no longer answer but to which Wotan himself provides the response: 'Urmütter-Weisheit | geht zu Ende' (Primeval mothers' wisdom | ends ere long: vi. 155–6). The end of the gods is what he himself desires now: care has given way to *amor fati*. (The supersession of the gods in human self-awareness is the mythic counterpart of Feuerbach's supersession of religion.)

Fear and care can paralyse individual action not only because of a numinously ordained future but also by virtue of self-inflicted fate. The idea behind such a fate is one which Wagner explains in *Opera and Drama* in connection with Napoleon's remark that politics had replaced the fate of classical antiquity. Karl Marx, in his turn, described the predominance of economic concerns, the law of supply and demand, as the fate of modern man.[14] Politics, economics, and those other socially coercive forces of power and dominion, the desire for possessions and contractual constraints, form another kind of fate in the *Ring*, a fate which is similarly conquered by autonomous, 'purely human' actions.

The extent to which this fate 'thrusts the thorn of care' into the hearts of all on whom it weighs is clear from Alberich's curse on the ring: 'Wer ihn besitzt, | den sehre Sorge, | und wer ihn nicht hat, | nage der Neid!' (May he who owns it | be blighted by care, | and he who has it not | be

---

[14] Marx, *Die Frühschriften*, p. 363; translated into English as 'German Ideology: Feuerbach', in *Karl Marx and and Friedrich Engels: Collected Works* (London, 1976), v 52.

gnawed by envious spite: v. 254). Only the man who is innocent of care
and fear can break the power of such a fate. Siegfried's carefree nature
and his fearlessness (at least until such time as he learns the meaning of
fear in the *mysterium tremendum* of sexual love) suggest that he himself is
untouched by any fate, be it that of the Norns or of the ring itself. 'An
dem furchtlosen Helden | erlahmt selbst mein Fluch', Alberich admits
to Hagen: 'denn nicht weiß er | des Ringes Werth, | zu nichts nützt er |
die neidlichste Macht' (Over the fearless hero | even my curse is
unavailing: | not a whit does he know | the worth of the ring, | and makes
no use | of its baleful power: vi. 210–11). He knows no fear, since the
desire for power and possessions is alien to him. As he lightheartedly
tells the Rhinemaidens: 'Der Welt Erbe | gewann mir ein Ring: | für der
Minne Gunst | miss' ich ihn gern' (The world's riches | I won with a
ring: | for a woman's favours | I'd gladly forgo it). And when they warn
him of the 'curse' which the Norns have woven by night into the rope of
'eternal law', their attempts to sow the seeds of care in his heart are
countered by an anti-fatalistic defiance:

> Des Urgesetzes
> ewiges Seil,
> flochten sie wilde
> Flüche hinein,
> Nothung zerhaut es den Nornen!
> Wohl warnte mich einst
> vor dem Fluch' ein Wurm,
> doch das Fürchten lehrt er mich nicht.          (vi. 238.)

> Primeval law's
> eternal rope,
> although wild curses
> were woven within it,
> Nothung will hew it from the Norns' hands!
> A dragon once warned me
> beware of the curse,
> but it failed to teach me fear.

Fearlessness, therefore, is a sign of human autonomy and of freedom
from all forms of fatally deterministic action, whether manifest in the
form of a curse or symbolized by the rope of destiny.[15]

---

[15] On Wagner's attitude towards care, cf. his conversation with Cosima on 19 Apr. 1869: 'If a
human being were to act with the certainty of truth and to look neither to the right nor to the left,
no one could really do anything to him, and he would be as safe from other men as the bird's nest
from the most violent gale. Christ's words—"Fear not, for the Father, who clothes the lilies, who
protects the sparrows on the roof, for whom the very hairs of your head are numbered, will also care
for you"—are difficult to understand (R. said), but of profound truth; the human being who truly
lives for his own calling alone, has nothing to fear. This vision of an inwardly secure being has been
perpetuated for mankind in the legend of Siegfried and the fairy tale of Tom Thumb.'

The image of the Norns' fraying rope had already been mentioned in Brünnhilde's dithyrambic confession of love in the closing pages of *Siegfried*. In the ecstasy of that love, she tears down all those barriers which inhibit the 'purely human', triumphing over the hand of fate and undermining the might of the gods:

> Leb' wohl, prangende
> Götter-Pracht!
> Ende in Wonne,
> du ewig Geschlecht!
> Zerreißt, ihr Nornen,
> das Runenseil!
> Götter-Dämm'rung,
> dunk'le herauf!              (vi. 175–6.)

> Fare well, glittering
> godly pomp!
> End in delight,
> you race of immortals!
> Rend, you Norns,
> the rope of runes!
> Dusk of the gods,
> gather around!

The next scene of the tetralogy is the Prelude to *Götterdämmerung*, in which the image of the fraying rope of destiny becomes a reality, long before Siegfried announces his intention of hacking it from the hands of the Norns. Binding the pieces of broken rope around their bodies, the latter now return to their mother, Erda, already sunk in eternal sleep:

> Zu End' ewiges Wissen!
> Der Welt melden
> Weise nichts mehr:—
> hinab zur Mutter, hinab!              (vi. 182.)

> Eternal wisdom is ended!
> Wise women no longer
> tell the world their tidings:—
> descend to our mother, descend!

The age of fate and oracles, of seers and prophets, of apparently suprahuman knowledge is over. (We may be reminded here of the end of Goethe's essay, *Plato als Mitgenosse einer christlichen Offenbarung*, where the poet speaks out against the presumptions of oracular irrationalism and against the idea of suprahuman inspiration: 'For the time is past when sibyls prophesied under the earth'.[16]) But the end of omniscience and of the predetermined course of all human action (whatever form that predetermination may take) must also herald the

---

[16] *Goethes Werke* (Hamburger Ausgabe), ed. Erich Trunz (Hamburg, 1959), xii. 249.

end of those emotions and states of mind related to them, in other words, the sense of care and fear.

But although the rope of destiny has broken and the power of the gods has been destroyed, a fatal force remains, for all that it, too, should have ceased to exist. It is the cunning of the world and the intrigue of men, a force which Siegfried fails to perceive and which is the reverse side of his fearlessness. He who has not learnt fear should not venture into the 'cunning' world, Mime tells him. In the more detailed version of the opening scene of *Siegfried* (a passage not set to music but included in the 1853 privately printed edition of the libretto) we read:

> fühltest du noch
> das fürchten nicht:
> in der list'gen welt
> verlierst du dich;

> Wem die furcht die sinne
> neu nicht schuf,
> in der welt erblindet
> dem der blick:
> Wo nichts du siehst
> wirst du versehrt;
> wo nichts du hörst
> trifft es dein herz.

> wem die furcht die sinne
> nicht scharf gefegt,
> blind und taub in der welt
> schlingt ihn die welle hinab![17]

> If even now
> you have felt no fear,
> in the cunning world
> you will lose your way;

> He whose senses are not
> newly stirred by fear
> will blink in the blinding
> light of the world:
> where you can see nothing,
> you'll suffer harm;
> where you can hear nothing,
> your heart will be hurt.

[17] Reproduced from Otto Strobel (ed.), *Richard Wagner: Skizzen und Entwürfe zur Ring-Dichtung* (Munich, 1930), 115.

> He whose senses are not
> made keen by fear,
> blind and deaf in the world,
> will be swallowed up by the surging wave!

It is precisely this fate which befalls Mime's ward. And that is why it is
not Siegfried, the carefree, naïve 'pure fool', who can accomplish that
'deed which redeems the world', but only Brünnhilde, Erda's 'knowing
child' (vi. 156).[18] For it is to her, the Norns' half-sister, that Erda's
'primeval mothers' wisdom' has been transferred and transformed into
a purely human understanding no longer dependent on fate. Borrowing
from the language of Schiller, one might almost say that this supreme
wisdom is a new naïvety acquired by sentimental means (in other words,
by the character's passing through a period of reflection), in which the
opposition of pure folly and reflective wisdom is ultimately reconciled.
(The wisdom denied to Siegfried will finally be acquired by the 'pure
fool' Parsifal, initially Siegfried's equal in terms of conscious awareness
but later destined to become '*wise* through pity'.)

The universal principle of care can be overcome only by supreme
human self-awareness, when divine wisdom dissolves into human
knowledge. The thematic centrality and symbolism of care also provides
a remarkable link between the two greatest poems of the modern period,
which take universal myth as their starting-point, Goethe's *Faust* and
Wagner's *Ring*. Faust (who, in part II of the drama, shares many features
with those *Sturm und Drang* heroes who insist upon 'self-help') is the
enemy of care. In the final act of *Faust*, II, the allegorical embodiment of
care confronts Faust with words reminiscent of Alberich's curse on the
ring:

> Wen ich einmal mir besitze,
> Dem ist alle Welt nichts nütze;
>
> .    .    .
>
> Bei vollkommnen äußern Sinnen
> Wohnen Finsternisse drinnen,
> Und er weiß von allen Schätzen
> Sich nicht in Besitz zu setzen.
> Glück und Unglück wird zur Grille,
> Er verhungert in der Fülle;
>
> .    .    .

[18] On Wagner's view of Siegfried, cf. his remark to Cosima in the course of a conversation on
13 Oct. 1882: 'it is indeed curious that though one claims that men are intelligent, in legends
they are always foolish', and he cites the examples of Siegfried and Tristan. On 4 July 1873 he
noted that Siegfried was 'not a tragic figure, since he does not become conscious of his position . . .
Wotan and Brünnhilde are tragic figures'.

Ist der Zukunft nur gewärtig,
Und so wird er niemals fertig.       (ll. 11453–66.)

He finds, once within my power,
His world is useless, from that hour.

.    .    .

Though in his outward senses whole,
He harbours darkness in his soul;
No matter what the treasure is,
He lacks the power to make it his.
Pleasures or ills mock him, forlorn
He starves in sight of plenty's horn;

.    .    .

Always on the future waiting,
Nothing ever consummating.[19]

The lines which follow on from these are a convincing psychopathological portrait of a person consumed by care, describing the paralysation of his resolves and activities, and the 'painful sloth and hateful action' of his existence. As such, they could almost be a characterization of Wotan. Faust, by contrast, refuses to recognize Care's 'creeping power', so that she breathes on him and blinds his vision. The carefree man is the one who is blind: while the Lemures dig his grave, he believes that the sounds he hears come from his great life's work, the dyke intended to reclaim land for a Utopian community. Like Faust, Siegfried is destroyed by his defiant rejection of care—and their joint aspirations are salvaged from oblivion only by a woman's love, with all the risks that that love entails.

In Wagner's 1848 prose draft, 'The Nibelung Legend (Myth)', the teleological aim of the myth is defined as the self-annihilation of the gods, who, as it were, offer living proof of Feuerbach's critique of religion, renouncing 'their own immediate influence in the freedom of human consciousness' (ii. 158). In other words, religious consciousness is traced back to human self-awareness. 'Man is god perfected', Wagner had written in a similar vein when jotting down ideas for a drama on the life of Achilles.[20] 'The eternal gods are only the elements which create man. Creation thus finds its ultimate expression in man. Achilles is higher and more perfect than the elemental Thetis.' (xii. 283.) In *Opera and Drama* Wagner advances the view that Germanic myth is superior to Greek myth to the extent that the heroes here (in other words, true human beings) have increasingly displaced the gods. The 'Siegfried legend' in particular is said to attest to the way in which 'gods conceived of as human' have been transformed into 'truly anthropomorphized

---

[19] English translation by Philip Wayne (Harmondsworth, 1959), 265–6.
[20] *WWV* (p. 340) casts doubt on the authenticity of the 'fragment' published under this title.

heroes' (iv. 38). If the gods seek to transfer their divinity to humankind, in accordance with 'The Nibelung Legend' scenario, they are merely conforming to the underlying aim which Wagner ascribed to Germanic myth in general. 'Their aim would be accomplished if they were to destroy themselves in creating humankind' (ii. 158): thus the Feuerbachian reading of *ragnarök*,[21] the twilight of the gods.

Of course, it was only when Wagner republished the poem of the *Ring* in 1863 that he gave the final part of the tetralogy the title *Götterdämmerung*. In the privately printed edition of 1853 it had still been called *Siegfried's Tod* (the apostrophe was later dropped). To impute this change of title to a shift in the work's essential thrust following his reading of Schopenhauer in 1854 is to miss the point, since the idea of the downfall of the gods is already clearly explicit in the first edition of the text. It cannot be emphasized often enough that the poem as a whole had already been finished and privately published *before* the shock of reading Schopenhauer persuaded Wagner to reassess his view of the work. The philosopher's *magnum opus* was without any influence on the mythic or poetic substance of the *Ring*, always ignoring the specific problem posed by the ending, of course. The Buddhist variant of Brünnhilde's peroration, inspired by Schopenhauer, was never set to music by Wagner, unlike the Feuerbach ending, which he wrote out in short score as a private gesture for Ludwig II.[22] The alleged inconsistency in the conception of the *Ring* after 1854 is a legend which, though long since exposed, appears to be indestructible.[23] That the twilight of the gods inspired mixed feelings in Wagner even before he had read a word of Schopenhauer (though he will have known the philosopher's name from Eckermann's *Gespräche mit Goethe*) is clear from his letter to Liszt of 11 February 1853, in which he describes the 'flames of Valhalla' (not provided for in the 1848 scenario or in the original version of *Siegfried's Tod* but clearly implied in the idea of the gods' 'self-annihilation') as the end of the world. Whether it is the end of *the* world or only of *a* world is a question which Wagner never resolved, as he continued to vacillate between the two alternatives following the abandonment of his revolutionary illusions in the early 1850s. In a conversation with Cosima on 25 November 1873 he spoke of the 'idea in Scandinavian mythology of a new world to follow the

---

[21] Old Norse *ragnarök*, 'the doom or destruction of the gods'; *ragnarøkkr*, 'the twilight of the gods'. Both terms were used to describe the end of the world. Interestingly, Wagner did think of renaming *Götterdämmerung* 'The Judgement of the Gods' (*Göttergericht*) following his researches into the etymology of the Old Norse term (*CT*, 3 Aug. 1872).

[22] Cf. Carl Dahlhaus's important article, 'Über den Schluß der *Götterdämmerung*', in *Richard Wagner: Werk und Wirkung*, (Regensburg, 1971), 97–115.

[23] Cf. Joachim Herz, 'Die *Nibelungen* auf unserer Bühne', in Walter Felsenstein and Joachim Herz, *Musiktheater: Beiträge zur Methodik und zu Inszenierungskonzeptionen* (Leipzig, 1976), 249.

downfall of the gods'. And is there not a presentiment of this new world
at the end of *Götterdämmerung*, when the human survivors watch 'in
speechless consternation' as disaster overtakes the world of men and
gods, a catastrophe which they evidently survive as the inhabitants of a
new world order freed from the curse of gold? Certainly, Wagner
referred explicitly to his exegesis of the Oedipus myth in the second part
of *Opera and Drama*, when, in his 'Epilogue' of 1871 (vi. 257), he
suggested a solid basis on which to interpret the *Ring*. It is a reference
which perhaps entitles us to suppose that the end of the work may,
indeed, be Utopian in character. And this supposition becomes a
certainty when we hear the instrumental theme which concludes the
work as a whole, the 'redemption motive' which had first been stated in
Act III of *Die Walküre*, where it had accompanied Sieglinde's words, 'O
hehrstes Wunder' (Sublimest wonder: vi. 69), following the announce-
ment that she was with child. In Dahlhaus's view, this theme 'looks
forward in hope to reconciliation in the future' and echoes the idea,
advanced in 'The Nibelung Legend', that the gods will be superseded by
the newly created race of mortals. The closing bars of *Götterdämmerung*
attest to the fact that, in Dahlhaus's words, '[Wagner's] first conception
was also his last'.[24] Carlo Schmid offers a matchless account of the
ending of the tetralogy in a conversation published in the 1977 Bayreuth
Festival programme for *Das Rheingold*: 'The river Rhine at the end of
*Götterdämmerung*—what we see here is Nature before the advent of
historical man: the world of Wotan is swallowed up by Nature just as the
dead are buried, only to return to that earth which will one day put forth
the shoots of new life.'[25]

Ever since Erda prophesied their downfall in the final scene of *Das
Rheingold* (a prophecy paralleled by the oracle in classical myth), the end

---

[24] Carl Dahlhaus, *Richard Wagners Musikdramen* (Velber, 1971), 140; translated into English by
Mary Whittall as *Richard Wagner's Music Dramas* (Cambridge, 1979), 141. Patrice Chéreau
attempted to do justice to the problems inherent in the ending of the tetralogy in his 1976
production at Bayreuth: 'The "redemption motive" is a message addressed to the whole world, but,
like all prophetesses, the orchestra is unclear [Chéreau is alluding here to the comparison which
Wagner drew between the orchestra pit at Bayreuth and the sulphurous rocky cleft at Delphi in
which the oracle resided: ix. 338], and its message can be interpreted in various ways. This is my
way of taking account of the *impasse* in which, it seems to me, Wagner found himself twenty-five
years after beginning work on the *Ring*: what was there to complete, and how was it to be
completed?' (*Die Programmhefte der Bayreuther Festspiele 1977*, vi. '*Siegfried*', 87.) In conversation with
Carlo Schmid, Chéreau remarked: 'I simply wanted those who were there, those human beings who
were present [the crowd of onlookers which stands by as disaster engulfs the world], to listen to the
music, and to listen to it as they would listen to an oracle, an oracle which may reach you or may
not reach you, and whose meaning you may or may not understand. I wanted these human
spectators to stand as though on the edge of an abyss ... and to have to interpret the oracle.'
('Mythologie et idéologie: Échange de vues sur la mise en scène de la tétralogie en 1976 entre Carlo
Schmid, Pierre Boulez et Patrice Chéreau', in *Die Programmhefte der Bayreuther Festspiele 1977*, iv.
'*Das Rheingold*', 1–23, 102–10, esp. p. 7.)

[25] 'Mythologie et idéologie', p. 110.

of the gods has provided the overall action with a dark and lowering background. The tragic irony of the Oedipus myth, where attempts to evade the oracle merely serve to make it come true, recurs in the *Ring*, where Wotan's grand idea of averting the downfall of Valhalla by means of a hero who, free from 'divine decree' (vi. 32), will slay the dragon that watches over both the hoard of gold and the ring (a feat which Wotan himself is prevented from encompassing by virtue of the fact that he is 'lord of treaties') precipitates the very disaster he was seeking to avoid. 'Ihrem Ende eilen si zu, | die so stark im Bestehen sich wähnen' (They are hurrying towards their end, | though they think they'll endure forever: v. 264), Loge observes at the end of *Das Rheingold*, displaying a cynicism worthy of Mephistopheles. The very thing which is intended to demonstrate and bolster up the possession of power leads directly to its loss. Dahlhaus is right in drawing attention to the parallel between the tragic dialectic dominating these closing pages of *Das Rheingold* and the dialectics of the state as sketched out in *Opera and Drama*.[26] Appealing directly to the Oedipus myth and to the necessary destruction of the state which he believed that myth to symbolize, Wagner himself had observed: 'Since the political state has come into being, not a single step has been taken in history which, no matter how decisively aimed at its consolidation, has not led to its downfall.' According to the composer, the *fons et origo* of the collapse of the state as embodied in the Oedipus myth was Laius's exposure of his son, an act undertaken with the aim of securing his own position of power. 'In Laius's *rule* we see the seed of all offences, for it was to possess this power undiminished that he became an unnatural father. From this desire to *possess*—a desire which, strangely enough, is seen as the basis of all good order and which has led to the development of ownership—there issue all the crimes of myth and history.' (iv. 65.) Here we already find Wagner generalizing on the basis of a single incident in myth, and it may not be too bold a speculation to suggest that he was thinking of that central symbol of the Nibelung myth, the ring, which signifies, after all, the economic possession of power, a possession, moreover, which is turned into private property and which, by being egoistically indivisible, excludes all other persons, and subjects them to its sway. It would be true to say that all the crimes committed in the course of the myth derive from the ring and the power of which it is a symbol.

The curse which clings to the ring is a curse on love, the purest of human emotions. It immediately becomes clear from *Das Rheingold* that all 'purely human' relationships are blighted by the ring, and that the

---

[26] Dahlhaus, *Wagners Musikdramen*, pp. 97–8; English trans. (Whittall, *Wagner's Music Dramas*), pp. 97–8.

relationships which are formed involve 'unnatural fathers', sons, and siblings: Alberich enslaves his brother Mime; Wotan, the father of the gods, is only just prevented by Erda from 'selling' Freia in order to keep the ring for himself; and Fafner kills his brother Fasolt for the sake of the golden circlet. In Wagner's view, a similar line of development can be traced through the Oedipus myth, with its chain of family relationships broken and estranged. (One thinks especially of Laius and Oedipus, and of Eteocles and Polynices.) The return of the ring to the waters of the Rhine, and the freeing of the world from the curse which weighs upon it, signify the end of 'property' or, in Marx's words, an end to that all-powerful 'sense of *having*',[27] from which Wagner believed the state to derive. It is Brünnhilde who brings about that end. She is the only character for whom the ring is not a 'possession' but, in total contradiction of that essential quality which it owes to the curse on love, a token of Siegfried's love: 'Denn selig aus ihm | leuchtet mir Siegfried's Liebe' (For from it shines | the blessed light of Siegfried's love: vi. 205). Brünnhilde is, as it were, the Antigone of the Nibelung myth. It is she who is destined to accomplish that which neither Siegmund nor Siegfried can do: Siegmund was fated to be destroyed by the paradox in which he found himself, since his apparent self-determination was, in fact, determined in advance by Wotan; while Siegfried failed because, although his actions were genuinely independent of the divine will and of the ring's despotic sway, he fell into a web of fatal intrigue as a result of his 'involuntary' and naïvely unreflecting actions. It is Brünnhilde, therefore, who performs that 'freest of deeds' which liberates the world from all the constraints of both destiny and society.

In mythology we often encounter the motif of the gods needing the help of mortals to exorcize a danger which threatens their whole existence. The most famous example of this is the conflict between the gods of Olympus and the giants, a conflict which the immortals finally win with Heracles' support. In exactly the same way, Wotan needs a mortal hero who will act involuntarily:

> Noth thut ein Held,
> der, ledig göttlichen Schutzes,
> sich löse vom Göttergesetz:
>     so nur taugt er
>     zu wirken die That,
> die, wie noth sie den Göttern,
> dem Gott doch zu wirken verwehrt. (vi. 32).

---

[27] Marx, *Die Frühschriften*, p. 240; translated into English by David McLellan as 'Economic and Philosophical Manuscripts', in *Karl Marx: Early Texts* (Oxford, 1971), 152.

A hero is needed
who, lacking godly protection,
breaks loose from the gods' decree:
thus alone he is fit
to perform that feat
which, however needful to the gods,
the god is forbidden to do.

He attempts to create this hero in Siegmund, but the result is a contradiction in terms, since Siegmund's actions are not genuinely independent, not 'fremd dem Gotte, | frei seiner Gunst, | unbewußt, | ohne Geheiß' (far from the god, | and free of his gift, | all unwitting, | without his bidding: vi. 40): they are divinely predetermined and, as such, entirely predictable. Only Siegmund's incest with his sister is an involuntary act not foreseen by Wotan, which is precisely why the latter welcomes it so emphatically as a sign that his hopes may yet be realized. It is, however, a groundless hope, as his confrontation with Fricka in Act II of *Die Walküre* makes pitilessly plain.

Fricka is 'the guardian of wedlock' (vi. 24), the personification of moral 'custom'. To such a person, the 'power of instinct which guides the individual's unconscious, physically inevitable actions' (to quote from *Opera and Drama*: iv. 54) and which is manifest in the incest of both Oedipus and the Volsung twins is bound to appear as nothing less than a return to that state of chaos which seemed to have been averted by the gods' well-ordered rule.

Stets Gewohntes
nur magst du versteh'n,

Constant custom
is all you can understand,

Wotan remonstrates with Fricka, very much in the spirit of the passage from *Opera and Drama* cited above:

doch was noch nie sich traf,
danach trachtet mein Sinn!                    (vi. 31.)

but what has yet to come to pass
is what my mind aspires to!

What Wotan wants is something that has never been witnessed before, something unpredicted, unforeseen by godly wisdom, and 'involuntary': the wholly free action of a mortal hero is the only hope for the survival of the world of the gods (although, as Wotan has yet to discover, the gods will 'survive' only by being superseded by human self-awareness). Fricka obstinately refuses to listen to this argument of Wotan's, or, if she does listen to it, it is to refute it with striking finality: divinely willed spontaneity is logically impossible.

The family, we read in *Opera and Drama*, is held together by the 'ties of custom', and it is these ties which give rise to 'a natural affection between siblings'. This affection, however, rules out the possibility of sexual love. Oedipus's incestuous marriage arouses a sense of 'dread and loathing' at the breakdown of 'normal family relationships' (iv. 56) which also informs Fricka's reproaches in her argument with Wotan:

> Mir schaudert das Herz,
> es schwindelt mein Hirn:
> bräutlich umfing
> die Schwester der Bruder!
> Wann—ward es erlebt,
> daß leiblich Geschwister sich liebten?
>
> My heart quakes,
> my head reels:
> a brother embraced
> his sister as bride!
> When were siblings ever seen
> to love each other carnally?

To which Wotan replies:

> Heut'—hast du's erlebt:
> erfahre so
> was von selbst sich fügt,
> sei zuvor auch nie es gescheh'n.        (vi. 27.)
>
> Today you have seen it happen:
> Learn thus
> that a thing may come to pass,
> though it never happened before.[28]

---

[28] In his chapter on 'The Consanguine Family' in *The Origin of the Family, Private Property and the State*, Friedrich Engels refers to a letter from Karl Marx, written in 1882, in which the latter had expressed himself 'in the strongest terms about the complete misrepresentation of primitive times in Wagner's text to the *Nibelungen*'. (This, of course, begs the question of whether Wagner had ever seriously intended to present an authentic picture of primitive Germany on the Bayreuth stage.) Marx considered the lines quoted above to be a classic example of this misrepresentation: 'To Wagner and his "lecherous gods" who, quite in the modern manner, spice their love affairs with a little incest [cf. Mann's *Wälsungenblut*], Marx replies: "In primitive times the sister *was* the wife, *and that was moral*."' For the 4th edition of the text, Engels was encouraged by 'a French friend of mine who is an admirer of Wagner' to modify his criticism and to alter the note: 'If one wants to find excuses for Wagner, it would perhaps be better to cite Goethe instead of the Edda, for in his ballad of God and the Bayadere Goethe commits a similar mistake in regard to the religious surrender of women, which he makes far too similar to modern prostitution.' Of course, Engels is still applying inappropriate standards of historical authenticity to what Hegel termed the 'necessary anachronism' of poetry. See Friedrich Engels, *Der Ursprung der Familie, des Privateigentums und des Staats* (Stuttgart, 1910), 609; translated into English by Lewis H. Morgan as *The Origin of the Family, Private Property and the State*, 2nd edn. (London, 1941), 36–7.

Wotan's revolutionary gesture, his radical break with 'custom', ensnares him, of course, in a contradiction which Fricka, 'breaking out in extreme indignation', exposes without pity:

> hin wirfst du alles,
> was einst du geachtet;
> zerreißest die Bande,
> die selbst du gebunden;
> lösest lachend
> des Himmels Haft!          (vi. 28–9.)

> you cast away
> what once you cared for;
> rend the bonds
> which you yourself bound;
> laughingly loosen
> heaven's hold!

It is on custom that the order created by Wotan rests. As Fasolt had reminded him in the second scene of *Das Rheingold*:

> Was du bist,
> bist du nur durch Verträge:
> bedungen ist,
> wohl bedacht deine Macht.          (v. 219.)

> What you are,
> you are through treaties alone:
> fixed and
> well-defined is your power.

In order to reinforce his power, Wotan has created the cosmos of a contractually safeguarded social order out of the chaos of the state of nature. Its symbol is his spear:

> Treu berath'ner
> Verträge Runen
> schnitt Wotan
> in des Speeres Schaft:
> den hielt er als Haft der Welt          (vi. 179),

> The runes of loyally
> counselled treaties
> Wotan carved
> on the shaft of his spear:
> he held it as his grip on the world,

the Second Norn sings in the Prelude to *Götterdämmerung*. The *contrat social* initiated by Wotan bears within it the seed of evil from the very outset, since it is not (as in Rousseau's classic theory) the result of an amalgamation of free individuals but the product of a single person's desire for power and possessions. From the very beginning, therefore, disaster is already bound up with the 'state of treaties', as Schiller called the social condition in his 'Über die ästhetische Erziehung des Menschen', distinguishing it from the state of nature which he termed the 'state of independence'. Wotan himself admits as much to Brünnhilde in the second act of *Die Walküre*:

> Als junger Liebe
> Lust mir verblich,
> verlangte nach Macht mein Muth.

> When youthful love's
> delights had faded,
> my mood demanded power.

(Power is therefore a substitute for love. An even more striking example of this same motif had already been seen when Alberich, in order to be able to forge the ring, had placed a curse on the love which was denied him by the Rhinemaidens. It is a motif which is later turned on its head by Siegfried's indifference to power and by Brünnhilde's love-inspired curse on the ring.)

> Von jäher Wünsche
> Wüthen gejagt,
> gewann ich mir die Welt.
> Unwissend trugvoll
> übt' ich Untreue,
> band durch Verträge,
> was Unheil barg.          (vi. 37.)

> Impelled by the rage
> of impulsive desires,
> I won for myself the world.
> Unwittingly false
> I acted unfairly,
> binding by treaties
> what boded ill.

The fact that the very establishment of the social contract is attended by a crime is further suggested by the motif of the spear, which, cut from the trunk of the world ash-tree, is both a symbol and a guarantee of the treaties into which Wotan enters. The wound inflicted on the world ash-tree causes the whole of nature around it to wither:

> In langer Zeiten Lauf
> zehrte die Wunde den Wald;
> falb fielen die Blätter,
> dürr darbte der Baum:
> traurig versiegte
> des Quelles Trank.   (vi. 178–9.)

> In the course of many ages
> the wound consumed the wood;
> fallow fell the leaves,
> barren, the tree grew rotten;
> sadly the well-spring's
> drink ran dry.

These are striking symbols of the way in which both human and suprahuman nature have been alienated by the world of social contracts.

Qualities which in the natural order of things are self-evident—spontaneity and independence—are transformed into injustice and immorality by the 'statutes of cold moral treaties' (to quote from *Opera and Drama*: iv. 75). The sexual love between the Volsung twins which, like the marriage between mother and son in the Oedipus myth, is sanctioned by nature (which, in the case of the *Ring*, means the birth of the hero Siegfried) is condemned by Fricka not just because it involves adultery but because it is an act of 'incest' (vi. 26). Natural necessity is morally stigmatized as a sinful and unbridled action dictated by 'pleasure and whim'.

Custom is the naïve 'record of socio-moral concepts' and, as such, is necessary if we are to coexist, Wagner argues in *Opera and Drama* (iv. 74). But, in Fricka's attitude towards Hunding and the Volsungs, custom becomes that ossified moral attitude for which possessions and peace of mind are the highest of all values. As Fricka herself says, in lines which, in the event, were not set to music:

> Wo nach Ruhe
> der Rauhe sich sehnt,
> wo des Wechsels
> sehrender Wuth
> wehre sanft ein Besitz,—
> dort steh'ich lauschend still. (vi. 27.)

> Wherever the ruffian
> longs for rest,
> wherever possessions
> may gently oppose
> the harmful fury of change,—
> I stand and listen in silence.

This is a type of morality which denies individual spontaneity, denies what Wagner, in *Opera and Drama*, calls 'the purely human'. This emerges clearly from Fricka's deafness (at least in the final version) to Wotan's objection that Hunding's marriage was brought about by force and 'coercion' and solemnized against Sieglinde's wishes. The 'sacred oath', he insists, is 'unholy' here, because it 'binds unloving hearts'

(vi. 26). In Fricka and Wotan the conflicting forces of legalistic rigour and outright spontaneity find powerful expression—but not for long, since Wotan is soon obliged to realize that his position is untenable. As Fricka exclaims, in horror and admonition, in the earlier version of this same scene:

> Wohin renn'st du,
> rasender Gott,
> reißest die Schöpfung du ein,
> der selbst das Gesetz du gab'st?                (vi. 30.)

> Where are you running to,
> desperate god,
> destroying the world you created,
> a world whose laws you made yourself?

The laws which he gave to the world, and the treaties which he concluded in order to add to his power base, reveal themselves now as the fetters which bind him:

> In eig'ner Fessel
> fing ich mich:—
> ich unfreiester Aller!                (vi. 36.)

> In my own fetters
> I caught myself fast:—
> I, least free of all things living!

he complains to Brünnhilde in the scene that follows.

This dialectic reversal from total freedom to its total absence, from domination to slavery, and from power to impotence not only finds expression in the topos that treaties are self-defeating ('der durch Verträge ich Herr, | den Verträgen bin ich nun Knecht' (I who am lord of treaties, | to those treaties am now a slave): vi. 40), it also returns in the symbolism attached to the ring: 'des Ringes Herr | als des Ringes Knecht' (the lord of the ring | will be the ring's slave: v. 255), Alberich curses the ring in the final scene of *Das Rheingold*. Ownership becomes a fetish, leading to the domination of objects over men: the owner of an object becomes 'possessed' of that object in a twofold sense. The peripeteia in Wotan's great confrontation with Fricka is grandiosely underlined by gesture, according to the stage directions published in the score: 'Another violent gesture on Wotan's part, after which he sinks into an awareness of his own powerlessness.'[29] This says it all: the whole of Wotan's earlier revolt against the force of habit is nothing but a violent, futile gesture. Powerlessness is the god's true position: it is this that forces him to side with the law, with treaties, marriage, and traditional

---

[29] Dover score, p. 223; Eulenburg pocket score, p. 327; Breitkopf & Härtel vocal score, p. 110.

norms. His impotence obliges him to sacrifice the Volsung clan, if he is not to sacrifice himself.

Fricka is also in a stronger, more rational, position than Wotan, for the reason already given.

> Wie wollt' ich listig
> selbst mich belügen?
> So leicht entfrug mir
> ja Fricka den Trug!
> Zu tiefster Scham
> durchschaute sie mich,    (vi. 42)
>
> How subtly I sought
> to delude myself!
> How easily Fricka
> exposed the fraud!
> To my deepest shame
> she saw through my scheme,

Wotan himself admits in his ensuing conversation with Brünnhilde. The deception lies in the paradox of willing something that ought to be in conflict with his own will, and of seeking to create someone who ought to create himself:

> denn selbst muß der Freie sich schaffen—
> Knechte erknet' ich mir nur!                    (vi. 41.)
>
> for the free man must create himself—
> slaves are all I can fashion!

Exposed to the cruel light of reason by Fricka's unanswerable arguments, Wotan sees the absurdity of his search for a non-ego, which is, after all, merely another side of himself:

> Wie macht' ich den And'ren,
> der nicht mehr ich,
> und aus sich wirkte,
> was ich nur will?                    (vi. 41.)
>
> How could I make another
> who is no longer myself,
> one who, of himself, would do
> what I can only will?

Wotan thus sees through the veil of his previous illusion:

> Zum Ekel find' ich
> ewig nur mich
> im Allem, was ich erwirke!
> Das And're, das ich ersehne,
> das And're erseh' ich nie.    (vi. 41.)

> To my disgust I only
> ever find myself
> in all that I effect!
> That other thing I seek,
> that other thing I'll never see.

And later:

> Einen Freien kann ich nicht wollen.   (vi. 43.)
> I cannot will a free man.

All that remains is suicidal despair—'Auf geb' ich mein Werk: | Eines nur will ich noch: | das Ende!' (My work I abandon: | one thing alone I still desire: | the end!: vi. 42)—and to give his blessing to Alberich, to whom he now bequeaths his godhead with nihilistic cynicism. Of course, his total resignation entails a second paradox, which is very much a reversal of the earlier one: only now that he has given up his search for his 'other' self, can that self come into being. Brünnhilde defies the god of contracts by following that self which was 'estranged' (vi. 76) by Fricka, the representative of 'custom'. The offspring of the abandoned Volsungs, Siegfried, is the hero who is truly free. Untutored by the gods, he grows up in a state of nature (a state traditionally evoked through the literary genre of an idyll), entering the world of treaties, and standing up to the god when the latter attempts to bar his way—just as Wotan himself had willed when he had voiced his desire for a free hero who 'entgegen dem Gotte, | für mich föchte' (opposing the god | would fight for me: vi. 41). The spear on whose shaft Wotan's treaties were carved and which once shattered the sword of natural necessity must now, in its turn, fragment when struck by a blow from the latter.

The conflict between legalistic and natural morality which divides the world of the gods is replicated on a human level in the contrast between Siegmund and Hunding. Hunding's marriage flies in the face of natural affection and was clearly concluded for reasons of kinship. In the bloody confrontation between himself and Siegmund, he stands, significantly, on the side of kinship's 'customary' law. The case in question is identical to his own. A marriage is to be concluded against the woman's wishes:

> Ein trauriges Kind
> rief mich zum Trutz:
> vermählen wollte
> der Magen Sippe
> dem Mann ohne Minne die Maid.
> Wider den Zwang
> zog ich zum Schutz.          (vi. 10).

A hapless child
called for my help:
her kinsmen's clan
were wanting to wed
the maid to a man without love.
In the face of such force
I flew to her aid.

Siegmund is very much the child of his father Wälse (or Wotan), therefore, who, when Siegmund himself is under duress, calls on the Valkyrie to shield him 'against such force', defending the law of nature against the arbitrary institution of marriage in his argument with Fricka. And, like Fricka, Hunding represents the 'sacred' law of wedlock. When he calls on her to avenge him, she assures him of her protection. Wotan is somewhat less fastidious about the inviolability of marriage as an institution, as the catalogue of transgressions with which Fricka now confronts him makes abundantly plain. She is referring, of course, to those by-blows of the father of the gods which are a typical feature not only of Germanic myth but of its classical counterpart, too. The Volsung twins are described, significantly, as the 'wanton fruit' of Wotan's 'infidelity' (vi. 29).

The sense of estrangement between husband and wife is made worse by the Valkyrie Brünnhilde, also fathered out of wedlock and, as such, the object of Fricka's hatred and scorn. In this respect, her relationship with her father reminds us of Jung's hypothesis of the Electra complex. It is striking, certainly, that Fricka describes Brünnhilde to Wotan as 'deines Wunsches Braut' (the bride of your wishes: vi. 30), and there does, indeed, appear to be some affinity between the subliminally erotic father–daughter relationship and the incest of the Volsung twins. Fricka and Hunding, therefore, are the party of 'custom', Wotan, Brünnhilde, and the Volsungs that of 'natural necessity'. The hatred felt by such creatures of habit for those social outcasts who cut themselves off from established norms of behaviour and live according to laws of their own devising finds expression in Hunding's view of the Volsung race. It is a judgement which, in its hubris, brings to mind those heroes of classical antiquity whose families, according to Wagner's account in *Opera and Drama*, were forced to commit some necessary action which, viewed as a crime, brought down a curse on the whole of the rest of their family. (The House of Tantalus is the classic example of such enforced atonement.)

Ich weiß ein wildes Geschlecht,
nicht heilig ist ihm
was And'ren hehr:
verhaßt ist es Allen und mir.          (vi. 11.)

> I know an unruly race
> which does not revere
> what others deem holy:
> it is hated by all, and by me.

The irruption of natural spontaneity into the world of custom and patriarchal domesticity is overwhelmingly illustrated in the great love scene between Siegmund and Sieglinde in Act I of *Die Walküre*, when the door of Hunding's hut flies open and the springtime night invades this human habitation. In Siegmund's image of cosmic incest, with its apostrophization of irresistible spring breaking down all barriers in order to free captive love and unite with her as his 'bride and sister', Sieglinde recognizes her lover and rediscovers herself, even before she and Siegmund know that they are brother and sister: 'Du bist der Lenz' (You are the spring: vi. 18), she sings, not needing to add that she herself is captive love. By identifying with those natural forces of spring and love, and by personifying the latter as brother and sister, the Volsung twins commit an act of metaphorical incest which, following their mutual recognition, is re-enacted in real life with all the irresistibility of a natural event. That Nature herself sanctions the act of incest is patently clear from the birth of Siegfried himself, the offspring of the Volsung twins, but it has already found expression in the symbolic identification of the lovers' sexual congress with the cosmic coupling of natural forces.

The incest between brother and sister finds a later parallel in Siegfried's awakening love for Brünnhilde, with its interaction of erotic passion, fear, and mother-fixation, all of which anticipates the later findings of psychoanalysis. When Brünnhilde alludes to her rescue of the pregnant Sieglinde with the words,

> Dich zarten nährt' ich,
> noch eh' du gezeugt;
> noch eh' du geboren
> barg dich mein Schild            (vi. 167),

> I fostered you, you tender child,
> even before you were fathered;
> before you were born
> my shield was ever your shelter,

Siegfried misunderstands her, taking the maternal metaphor literally, and believing he has rediscovered his mother in the woman he has just awoken with his kiss. With a smile, she corrects his misapprehension:

> Du wonniges Kind,
> deine Mutter kehrt dir nicht wieder.          (vi. 168.)

> You blithesome child,
> your mother will not come back to you.

But the form of address she uses shows that she has not abandoned her maternal feelings towards him: she remains the knowing woman beside the inexperienced child, which is precisely why Siegfried falls prey to her charms. Figuratively speaking, she is both wife and mother in one. The same interaction of sexual love and mother-fixation recurs in the original version of Walther's Prize Song in *Die Meistersinger* (xvi. 218–21), while it is the erotic mother complex which is to pose the greatest danger for Parsifal, with Kundry's seduction consisting in her offer to kiss him as a mother. Sophisticated psychologist that she is, she knows how to play with the Oedipus complex:

> Die Liebe lerne kennen,
> die Gamuret umschloß,
> als Herzeleid's Entbrennen
> ihn sengend überfloß:
> > die Leib und Leben
> > einst dir gegeben,
> der Tod und Thorheit weichen muß,—
> > > sie beut'
> > > dir heut'—
> als Muttersegens letzten Gruß
> > der Liebe—ersten Kuß.                    (x. 358.)

> Of love now learn the rapture
> that Gamuret once learned,
> when Herzeleide's passion
> within him fiercely burned!
> > For love that gave you
> > life and being,
> must death and folly both remove,
> > > love sends
> > > you now
> a mother's blessing, greets a son
> > with love's first kiss.[30]

This subtle mixture of myth and psychology helps to explain why Thomas Mann admired the Wagnerian music drama as much as he did: it is the immediate model for his own art of mythico-psychological novel writing.

What an interweaving of double meanings—what a penetrating insight into the complex depths of an emotion! . . . What we have here, rising up from the dark depths of the unconscious, is a presentient complex of mother fixation, sexual desire and *Angst* (by which I mean that fairy-tale fear that Siegfried seeks to know)—a complex, therefore, that bears witness to the most extraordinary

---

[30] Here, and later, the translations of *Parsifal* are from Andrew Porter's singing translation, in Richard Wagner, *Parsifal*, ENO Opera Guide 34, ed. Nicholas John (London, 1986) 85–126.

intuitive affinity between Wagner the psychologist and that other characteristic son of the nineteenth century, the psychoanalyst Sigmund Freud. The way that Siegfried's thoughts of his mother slide into eroticism in his reverie beneath the linden tree, or the way in which, in the scene where Mime tries to instruct his ward in the meaning of fear, the motif of Brünnhilde slumbering in the fire moves through the orchestra like a dark, distorted presence—this is pure Freud, pure psychoanalysis. And let us not forget that as in Wagner so in Freud ... the psychological interest goes hand in hand with an interest in myth, in primitive humanity and precivilization.[31]

The Volsungs' act of incestuous love, the erotic mother-fixation of Siegfried and Parsifal, and Wagner's interpretation of mythical incest in *Opera and Drama* have left clear traces on Thomas Mann's work, and nowhere more so than on his 1906 short story, *Wälsungenblut*. Feeling isolated in an anti-Semitic environment which they arrogantly despise, the Jewish twins Siegmund and Sieglinde Aarenhold embrace that feeling of isolation with a kind of *amor fati*, acting out the incestuous relationship between the Volsung twins from whom they take their names.

Decades later, following his study of Freud, Mann returned to the incest motif, introducing it, with greater psychological insight, into his novel *Der Erwählte*, a work which takes as its starting-point the life of an apocryphal medieval Saint Gregory. As with Wagner's Volsung myth, Grigorß is the incestuous offspring of the union between the twins Wiligis and Sibylla. But in Grigorß's case, Siegfried's act of would-be incest becomes a living reality: he suffers the fate of Oedipus—a fate unconsciously desired—and marries his own mother. The double incest, however, is the symbol and pre-condition of the fact that he is 'elect'. In a letter to Karl Kerényi of 5 July 1950 Mann described the incestuous relationship of the 'affectionate little sibling couple' as a necessary consequence of the idea that 'they alone are equal to each other in their sophistication'. This 'rapturous delight in their coequality'—the aesthetico-aristocratic awareness of being 'elect'—also typifies the Aarenhold twins in *Wälsungenblut*. Both here and in *Der Erwählte*, the incest committed by the different twins is paradigmatic of a narcissistic isolation and sense of self-absorption: each twin seeks his own identity in his opposite number.

Astonishingly, this narcissistic aspect of incestuous love, intensified by the physical similarity between the twins, can already be found in the first act of *Die Walküre*:

> den heut' zuerst ich erschaut,
> mein Auge sah dich schon          (vi. 19),

[31] Mann, *Wagner and unsere Zeit*, p. 69; English trans. (Blunden, *Pro and contra Wagner*), pp. 97–8.

> you whom I first beheld today
> my eye had seen ere now,

Sieglinde tells her lover, even before recognizing her brother in him. It could be the 'dream of love' of which Siegmund now goes on to speak ('Du bist das Bild, | das ich in mir barg' (Yours is the likeness | locked in my heart)), an idea which returns again and again in Wagner, whether it be in *Der fliegende Holländer*, *Lohengrin*, *Tristan*, or *Die Meistersinger*: the partner's likeness is already familiar to the lover either through a dream or because it has been glimpsed in the depths of his or her soul. But in Sieglinde's case there is a further aspect to this prescient vision:

> Im Bach erblickt' ich
> mein eigen Bild—
> und jetzt gewahr' ich es wieder:
> wie einst dem Teich es enttaucht,
> bietest mein Bild mir nun du!

> In the brook I glimpsed
> my own likeness—
> and now I see it again:
> as once it rose from the pool,
> so now you show me my likeness.

Here is Narcissus admiring his own reflection.

> O still! lass' mich
> der Stimme lauschen:
> mich dünkt, ihren Klang
> hört' ich als Kind—
> doch nein! ich hörte sie neulich,
> als meiner Stimme Schall
> mir wiederhallte der Wald.            (vi. 19–20.)

> O hush! let me
> listen to your voice:
> it seems I heard
> its sound as a child—
> but no! I heard it of late
> when the woods re-echoed
> with my ringing voice.

It is the myth of Echo and Narcissus, but in reverse. Condemned by Hera to repeat the final words of whatever was said to her, the nymph Echo fell in love with Narcissus but, when her love was spurned, pined away until only her voice remained. For Sieglinde, by contrast, echo and reflection symbolize that part of herself which she loves in Siegmund, and that part of Siegmund which she loves in herself.

This, of course, has nothing to do with the auto-erotic withdrawal from reality of the Aarenhold twins. It can, however, be explained in terms of Freud's concept of 'primary narcissism' which precedes the antagonistic relationship between ego and external world. In his 1930 essay, *Civilization and its Discontents*, Freud was to write: 'Originally the ego includes everything, later it detaches from itself the external world. The ego-feeling we are aware of now is thus only a shrunken vestige of a far more extensive feeling—a feeling which embraced the universe and expressed an inseparable connection of the ego with the external world.'[32] Herbert Marcuse takes up this point in his book, *Eros and Civilization*, where he writes: 'Primary narcissism is more than autoeroticism; it engulfs the "environment", integrating the narcissistic ego with the objective world.' According to Freud, Marcuse goes on, this primary ego-feeling can recur even in the mature ego, expressing itself in that 'oceanic feeling' which proclaims a sense of 'limitless extension and oneness with the universe'.[33] It is very much this primary narcissism which seems to us to be expressed in these lines of Sieglinde. And the 'oceanic' feeling of 'oneness with the universe' is transformed by feelings of narcissism into incestuous love, as the cosmic metaphor cited above makes clear.

Freud himself refers to the incestuous nature of the originally psychosexual relationship between men and women in his chapter, 'The Horror of Incest', in *Totem and Taboo*, first published in German in 1913. (This chapter in particular was of importance for Thomas Mann.) 'It is regularly found', writes Freud, that the man

chose his mother as the object of his love, and perhaps his sister as well, before passing on to his final choice. Because of the barrier that exists against incest, his love is deflected from the two figures on whom his affection was centred in his childhood on to an outside object that is modelled upon them . . . Psychoanalysis has taught us that a boy's earliest choice of objects for his love is incestuous and that those objects are forbidden ones [because of the inculcated horror of incest]—his mother and his sister.[34]

How close Wagner came to this insight requires no further demonstration here. He brings the true psychoanalyst's insights to bear on the naturally incestuous origin of the individual's choice of object in matters of sexual love. 'A youth who sets out in search of his mother and wins a wife for himself who, however beautiful, could be his mother

[32] Sigmund Freud, *Civilization and its Discontents* (London, 1949), 13.
[33] Ludwig Marcuse, *Eros and Civilization: A Philosophical Inquiry into Freud*, 2nd edn. (Boston, 1966), 168.
[34] Sigmund Freud, *Totem und Tabu* (Frankfurt, 1956), 23; translated into English by James Strachey and Anna Freud as *Totem and Taboo* (London, 1955), 16–17.

must reckon on the fact that it is actually his mother whom he marries', Thomas Mann writes in *Der Erwählte*.[35] Siegfried very much reckons on doing so, as his misunderstanding of Brünnhilde's words, quoted above, makes plain.

The more recent production history of the *Ring* has been characterized above all by psychological and socio-critical approaches, two lines of interpretation which continue to be regarded by Wagnerians of the old school as an act of sacrilege against the Master's work. That Wagner himself regarded myth as a medium for social criticism and for advancing a Utopian programme of social reform is clear from his exegesis of the Oedipus myth and its manifold links with the *Ring*. For a long time the composer himself refused to acknowledge these aims. Only during the final years of his life did he admit to holding them, reaffirming his earlier beliefs with astonishing frankness in his conversations with Cosima. His almost daily indignation at the adoption of Bismarck's social legislation,[36] his regular statements of sympathy for revolutionary movements such as that of the Russian nihilists[37] — 'I am always on the side of the rebels' (*CT*, 17 June 1881) — and his repeated conviction that 'the future belongs' to the socialist movement (*CT*, 31 May 1878) recall his former revolutionary ideas. 'As then, he is still expecting socialism to take over, the only difference being that he does not foresee its happening at any particular time', Cosima noted in her diary on 2 June 1879. She was not always able to share her husband's views, however. On 24 March 1881, for example, their differing attitudes to the Russian nihilists led to a lively altercation: even after Wagner's 'violent displeasure' had abated, he still continued to tease his wife on the subject of her '"golden-mean" views'. Not infrequently, these and similar remarks are found in connection with the *Ring*. His 1881 essay, 'Know Yourself', interprets its central symbol as a 'stock-exchange portfolio' and a 'frightening image' of the way in which the world was dominated by money (x. 268). Four years previously, he and Cosima had visited the London docklands: 'This is Alberich's dream come true', he told her: 'Nibelheim, world dominion, activity, work, everywhere the oppressive feeling of steam and fog.' (*CT*, 25 May 1877.) The seed is already being sown here for those socio-philosophical interpretations of the *Ring*, the most brilliant of which remains Bernard Shaw's *The Perfect Wagnerite* (1898). How delighted Shaw would have been to read the above entry in Cosima's diary. That it was in London that Wagner saw the realization of Alberich's dream is

---

[35] Mann, *Gesammelte Werke*, vii. 253.

[36] See *CT*, 24, 30–1 May, 3, 11 June, 6 July, 9, 23, 25 Sept., 23 Oct., 5 Nov., 4 Dec. 1878, 2 June, 7 Aug., 18 Nov. 1879, 13 Jan. 1880, and *passim*.

[37] *CT*, 23–4 Mar., 12 Apr. 1881, and 5 Jan. 1882. On Wagner's socialist feelings, see also *CT*, 10 Feb. 1870, 20 June 1872, 6 Jan. 1877, and *passim*.

very much in keeping with Shaw's own exegesis of the *Ring*, which shifted Valhalla, Nibelheim, and the home of the giants to London, turning Wagner's mythical society into a reflection of contemporary British society. His characterization of Alberich, for example, is followed by the laconic remark: 'Such dwarfs are quite common in London.'[38] And, on the very first page of the book, the perfect Wagnerite learns that: 'First, The Ring, with all its gods and giants and dwarfs, its water-maidens and Valkyries, its wishing-cap, magic ring, enchanted sword, and miraculous treasure, is a drama of today, and not of a remote and fabulous antiquity.'

Feature by feature, Shaw decodes the *Ring*, interpreting it as a nineteenth-century allegory, his wittily ironic comments turning repeatedly into a bitter indictment of the social evils of his day. 'And now, what forces are there in the world to resist Alberic, our dwarf, in his new character of sworn plutocrat?', Shaw, the rigorous socialist, asks, commenting not only on *Das Rheingold* but also on that contemporary social reality which he saw reflected in Wagner's *Ring*:

He is soon at work wielding the power of the gold. For his gain, hordes of his fellow-creatures are thenceforth condemned to slave miserably, overground and underground, lashed to their work by the invisible whip of starvation. They never see him, any more than the victims of our 'dangerous trades' ever see the shareholders whose power is nevertheless everywhere, driving them to destruction. The very wealth they create with their labor becomes an additional force to impoverish them; for as fast as they make it it slips from their hands into the hands of their master, and makes him mightier than ever.[39]

*The Perfect Wagnerite* combines a perceptive analysis of the text, based on an excellent knowledge of both Wagner's life and his literary sources, with ironic and parodistic paraphrases of it, but also with an attempt to write an allegorical sequel to the work, in other words, to relate it to the changed historical and social conditions of the end of the nineteenth century. At the end of the work, Shaw suggests with an eye to the present age, Alberich 'had got the ring again, and was marrying into the best Valhalla families with it'.[40] In order to increase his capital even further, he must

make himself an earthly Providence for masses of workmen, creating towns, and governing markets . . . Alberic, as the pursebearer, [is], under Destiny, the real master of the situation. Consequently, though Alberic in 1850 may have been merely the vulgar Manchester factory owner portrayed in Friedrich Engels' Condition of the Working Classes, in 1876 he was well on the way

---

[38] Shaw, *The Perfect Wagnerite*, p. 8; 4th edn., p. 426.

[39] Ibid. 9–10; 4th edn., p. 427.

[40] This passage was not added until the 3rd edn. of 1913. It is included in the 1989 reprint (see n. 7, above), p. 502.

towards becoming exoterically a model philanthropic employer and esoterically a financier.[41]

Shaw was not the first to see an allegory of the modern industrial world in Wagner's *Ring*, nor was he the first to suggest a semi-serious, semi-parodistic sequel to it. Not long after the first Bayreuth Festival, the Berlin writer Paul Pniower published (pseudonymously) a parody, *Der Ring der nie gelungen*, in which Wagner's tetralogy is transformed into a drama about the contemporary world of city life and big business. Fasolt and Fafner are building contractors, Alberich and Mime are the founders of the banking firm of Albrecht & Co. Both, of course, are Jews, described by the gods as 'Zwiebeljungen' (literally, 'onion boys'), whence the corruption 'Nibelungen'. During the boom years of the early Reich (a period known as the *Gründerjahre*), the gods had an official residence built for them which was far beyond their means, and they are now on the verge of bankruptcy. 'Wodann', the father of the gods, complains: 'O how I sigh for the green *Gründerjahre*, | Where one could build as one wanted!' The plight of the gods reflects the 'great depression' which overtook the German Reich following the collapse of the Vienna Stock Exchange in 1873. Thus the twilight of the gods becomes a symbol of economic depression. (The final part of *Der Ring der nie gelungen* is headed 'Katzenjämmerung', a play on Wagner's title derived from the German *Katzenjammer*, meaning 'hangover' or 'depression'.) As such, the piece appears more of a parodistic actualization of political events than a satire on Wagner's myth of the Nibelung's ring.[42]

Independently of Shaw, there were socialist interpretations of the *Ring* in both Germany and France, where one thinks above all of Jean-Léon Jaurès's *L'Art et le socialisme*. In their popular study, *Richard Wagner in der Karikatur*, published in 1907, Ernst Kreowski and Eduard Fuchs described Wagner as the cultural heir of the French Revolution, just as 'Marx was in historical economics'. The *Ring* is said to contain

a wealth of socio-revolutionary ideas ... Siegfried, the fearless individual, splitting Wotan's spear with the sword which he himself has forged, and killing the monster Fafner which lies in supine possession of the world, is he not the embodiment of a free nation seeking to conquer ... the age of capitalism? Who could deny the German proletariat the right to see its most venerable symbol in Siegfried the dragon-killer?[43]

[41] Shaw, *The Perfect Wagnerite*, 504.

[42] Pniower's parody is quoted in Dieter Borchmeyer and Stephan Kohler (eds.), *Wagner-Parodien* (Frankfurt, 1983), 299–300. (Pniower published his satire under the pseudonym Paul Gisbert.)

[43] Ernst Kreowski and Eduard Fuchs, *Richard Wagner in der Karikatur* (Berlin, [1907]), 2, 12.

The other forward-looking element in Wagner's mythology, apart from the socio-philosophical aspect just described, is that unprecedented 'blend of mythical primitivism and psychological, not to say psychoanalytical, modernity', of which no one has written more penetratingly than Thomas Mann.[44] The twofold nature of the mythological music drama, as both socio-political parable and psychological exemplar, was made possible for Wagner—as the example of the Oedipus myth makes clear—by his synoptical treatment of classical Greek and Germanic myth, a synthesis which, here too, points the way to the future and to Mann's syncretizing mythology. But it is the diaphanousness of the situations and relationships between the different characters which, borrowed from Greek mythology and tragedy, invest the *Ring* with its greatest psychological and poetic effects. 'You will find', Gottfried Keller wrote to Hermann Hettner in his famous letter of 16 April 1856, 'that a powerful sense of poetry, essentially German, but purified by the spirit of classical tragedy, imbues this work.

---

[44] Mann, *Wagner und unsere Zeit*, p. 148; English trans. (Blunden, *Pro and contra Wagner*), p. 191.

# 18

# The World in a Dying Light:
## *Tristan und Isolde* and the Myth of Night

> Musical sounds are the life and form of night, the sign of all that is invisible, and the children of yearning desire.
>
> Clemens Brentano, *Godwi*.

*Tristan und Isolde* was 'the end of all Romanticism', Richard Strauss wrote to Joseph Gregor on 8 January 1935: 'the yearning desire of the whole of the nineteenth century' was 'captured here in a single focus'.[1] For Thomas Mann, too, *Tristan und Isolde* was 'a Romantic work, deeply rooted in Romantic thought and sensibility', since night was 'the true domain and dwelling place of all Romanticism, its real discovery'.[2] It was the early Romantics in Germany who had created the *myth* of night, contrasting the raven down of darkness with that light of reason which they associated with the Enlightenment. This latter, after all, was a movement which saw itself, as no other, as being transfigured by light. The very term 'Enlightenment' says it all: light must be shed on things, all things must be progressively illumined. (In German the term is *Aufklärung*, deriving from the Latin *clarus*, while the French refer to this rationalistic age as 'le Siècle des lumières'.) The metaphysical metaphor of light on which this concept is based is expressed with particular potency by Leibniz's *Monadologie*, first published in German in 1720. Monads are simple, windowless entities which, by a process of entelechy, strive to achieve a state of greater and greater brightness until they are united with the brightest, and most enlightened, monad, God.

In his treatise 'Die Christenheit oder Europa', written in 1799 but not published until 1826, Novalis reproached the Enlightenment writers for treating light as 'their darling because of its mathematical tractability and freedom. They were pleased that it could be fragmented more readily than would have been possible with colour, and so they named their great enterprise, the Enlightenment, after it'.[3] It was Novalis, too, who

---

[1] The present chapter is an expanded and, in certain sections, amended version of an article published under the same title in the 1981 Bayreuth Festival programme, pp. 1–38.

[2] Thomas Mann, *Wagner und unsere Zeit*, ed. Erika Mann (Frankfurt, 1963), 97; translated into English by Allan Blunden as *Pro and contra Wagner* (London, 1985), 125.

[3] Novalis, *Werke*, ed. Gerhard Schulz, 2nd edn. (Munich, 1981), 509.

wrote what is perhaps the greatest of all European poems to the night, the *Hymnen an die Nacht* of 1799–1800. This work has long been suspected as having been one of the principal sources of Wagner's *Tristan und Isolde*, although there is no incontrovertible evidence that Wagner ever read Novalis.[4] None the less, there are unmistakable reminiscences of the *Hymnen an die Nacht* in the *Tristan* libretto, as Thomas Mann was one of the first to point out: Novalis's 'Der Nacht Geweihte' (Dedicated to the Night) reappears verbatim when Wagner's lovers describe themselves as 'Nacht-geweihte' (vii. 43).[5] Mann also drew attention to the almost word-for-word parallels between *Tristan* and another work of early Romanticism, which Wagner demonstrably knew, Friedrich Schlegel's *Lucinde* (1799). 'O eternal longing!': thus Lucinde and Julius declare their love for one another. 'Yet at last the day's fruitless yearning, its empty glare, will fade and die, and a great night of love will feel at peace forever.' Lucinde, too, describes herself as 'der Nacht geweiht', a parallel overlooked by Mann.[6]

Novalis's *Hymnen an die Nacht* begins with the question: 'Where is the man who is living and sensible to the world, who, in preference to all the wondrous phenomena in the whole vast space around him, does not love the all-gladdening light with its colours, rays, and waves, its mild ubiquity, like the wakening day?' This praise of light (reminiscent as it is of the ecstatic cry of the awakening Brünnhilde in the final scene of *Siegfried*: 'Heil dir, Sonne! | Heil dir Licht! | Heil dir, leuchtender Tag!' (Hail to you, sun! | Hail to you, light! | Hail to you, radiant day!: vi. 166) is continued for a while before the perspective abruptly changes: 'I turn away to sacred, ineffable, secretive night.' Night causes the wonders of the day to fade away like insubstantial dreams. 'How poor and childish the light now seems! how gladsome and blessed the day's farewell!'[7] The Enlightened hymn to light with which the poem begins is called into question by the Romantic vision of night, and dismissed as something which, by contrast, is impoverished and childish.

The degree to which poets were unimpressed by the *mysterium tremendum* of night, even as late as the second half of the eighteenth century, is clear from their use of a device which, ever since Roman

---

[4] It was not until 1879 that Wagner read Carlyle's 1829 essay on Novalis, an essay which he read 'with great enjoyment' and which, independently, no doubt also helped to introduce the French *symbolistes* to the most important of the early Romantic poets in Germany (cf. Werner Vordtriede, *Novalis und die französischen Symbolisten* (Stuttgart, 1963), 41–2). Wagner's remarks on Novalis in subsequent conversation with Cosima (*CT*, 16–18 Apr., 19–20 May 1879) make it likely that he had known the poet's writings previously, but this can certainly not be taken for granted, since Novalis had virtually fallen into oblivion by the later 19th century.

[5] Mann, *Wagner und unsere Zeit*, p. 96; English trans. (Blunden, *Pro and contra Wagner*), p. 124; Novalis, *Werke*, p. 42, l. 26.

[6] Friedrich Schlegel, *Lucinde*, ed. Karl Konrad Polheim (Stuttgart, 1963), 107, 104 (3rd line from foot of page).                         [7] Novalis, *Werke*, pp. 43–4.

antiquity, had been used to motivate the end of a poem or of one of its sections. This was the topos of the setting sun, which obliged the poet to draw to a close. It is a formula for ending a poem which was particularly popular in medieval Latin literature, so much so that Ernst Robert Curtius has seen it as symptomatic of that 'fear of the night which was felt throughout the Middle Ages'.[8] Admittedly, the lyric poetry of this period includes a genre—the *alba, aubade*, or *tagesliet*—which reviles the dawning day as something evil. 'Gevluochet wart dem tage' (They cursed the day), we read in a dawn song by Wolfram von Eschenbach, arguably the greatest poet of the genre.[9] It is significant that Wagner picks up the tradition of the *alba* in the second act of *Tristan und Isolde*, no doubt inspired, in part, by Act III, Scene 5 of Shakespeare's *Romeo and Juliet* or, more probably, by the corresponding scene in Bellini's *I Capuleti e i Montecchi*, a work which he had heard in his youth with Wilhelmine Schröder-Devrient in the role of Romeo, and which, as such, was one of the great artistic experiences of his early years. Wagner himself indicated as much in the course of a conversation with Cosima about *Tristan* on 23 March 1878: 'How did I ever achieve the rapture of the 2nd act? I know, it was through seeing Schröder-D. as Romeo, and it isn't so silly to have a woman in that role, for those little runts of men, and particularly tenors [it might almost be Richard Strauss speaking here], can never do those lovely wild embraces.'

The situation depicted in Act II of *Tristan*, with the disquisition on love between the two adulterous lovers, and the warnings uttered by their look-out, reflects that of the *aubade* in many ways. There is, however, a significant difference. Tristan and Isolde are now impervious to Brangäne's words of warning. Deaf to the need to part from each other's embrace, they live only for that *summum bonum* of mystic union when night and death and love become one, whereas the lovers in the *aubade* never doubt life's unconditional value for a moment.

The *aubade*, moreover, is set, significantly, on the cusp between night and day, unlike the second act of *Tristan*, which unfolds entirely at night. There are, as far as we are aware, only two traditions in the history of European poetry prior to German Romanticism which anticipate many of the essential features of that mystical cult of night which is found in *Tristan*. The first of these (to which we shall return in due course) goes back to Spanish mysticism, while the second dates back to the *dolce stil nuovo* and the Petrarchan tradition, more especially in France, where its chief representative was Pierre de Ronsard. To posit a link between Petrarch and Ronsard on the one hand and *Tristan* on the other is not

---

[8] Ernst Robert Curtius, *Gesammelte Abhandlungen zur romanischen Philologie* (Berne, 1960), 5.

[9] *Wolfram von Eschenbach*, ed. Karl Lachmann, 6th edn. (Berlin and Leipzig, 1926), 8,22; translated into English by Marion E. Gibbs and Sidney M. Johnson in Wolfram von Eschenbach, *Titurel and the Songs* (New York and London, 1988), 75.

so eccentric as it may appear at first sight. Wagner's uncle, Adolf Wagner, a man whom the composer admired greatly throughout his life and to whom he owed the decisive educational experiences of his youth, edited a volume entitled *Parnasso italiano* in 1827. Dedicated to Goethe and well received by him, it was an anthology of poetry by Dante, Petrarch, Tasso, and other *stilnuovisti*. Wagner naturally learnt a great deal about this work from his uncle. Nor should we forget, in this context, Liszt's three Petrarch settings of 1838–9 and, more especially, Wagner's own setting of Ronsard's *Mignonne, allons voir si la rose* (first published in 1553), completed during his early months in Paris at the end of 1839. Although there is no reason to believe that Wagner had any deeper knowledge of Ronsard, there are astonishing pre-echoes of *Tristan* in some of the *Amours de Cassandre* (first published in 1552) and *Amours de Marie* (1555–6). In one of the former, for example, we read:

> Je voudroy bien pour alleger ma peine,
> Estre un Narcisse et elle une fontaine,
> Pour m'y plonger une nuict à sejour;
>   Et si voudroy que cette nuict encore
> Fust eternelle, et que jamais l'Aurore
> Pour m'esveiller ne rallumast le jour.[10]

> To dull my pain I wish that I might be
> Narcissus, and a woodland fountain she
> Wherein I'd plunge and sojourn overnight.
>   I wish that night would never end; my hope
> Is that Aurora n'er again will ope
> The gates of heaven, nor wake me with her light.

Or in one of the *Amours de Marie*: 'Le jour m'est odieux, la nuit m'est opportune, | Je crains de jour l'aguet d'un voisin ennemy' (Though day be hateful to me, night is opportune; | By day I fear the wiles of some close enemy).[11] (This same sonnet also speaks of the poison of love as

[10] Pierre de Ronsard, *Œuvres complètes*, ed. Gustave Cohen (Paris, 1950), i. 11 (*Le Premier Livre des Amours: Amours de Cassandre*, xx, 'Je voudroy bien richement jaunissant'). On this sonnet and the Petrarchan origins of its motivic language, see Hugo Friedrich, *Die Werkinterpretation*, ed. Horst Enders (Darmstadt, 1967), 294–311. The Narcissus motif also appears in the lyric poetry of the German Middle Ages. A poem by Heinrich von Morungen, for example, begins: 'Mirst geschên als eime kindelîne, | daz sîn schônez bilde in eime glase ersach | unde greif dar nâch sîn selbes schîne | sô vil biz daz ez den spiegel gar zerbrach' (It befell me as it would a child who saw his fair reflection in a glass and grasped so much at his own semblance that the mirror lay in shards). The poet goes on to compare the 'unhappiness' of the child with the suffering he feels on seeing his *frouwe* or lady. The mirror motif returns at the end of the poem: 'daz ich durch mîn ouge schouwe solche nôt, | sam ein kint daz wîsheit unversunnen | sînen schaten ersach in einem brunnen | und den minnen muose unze an sînen tôt' (that I see such suffering with my own eyes, like a child who, bereft of wisdom, saw his shadow in a pond and was bound to love it till the day he died); see *Des Minnesangs Frühling*, ed. Carl von Kraus, 33rd edn. (Leipzig, 1964), 191 (145, 1–24).

[11] Ronsard, *Œuvres complètes*, i. 131 (*Le Second Livre des Amours: Amours de Marie*, xxv, 'Cache pour ceste nuit ta corne, bonne Lune!').

'l'amoureuse poison'.) The Narcissus motif was later to fascinate the Romantic poets as well as Wagner himself. Here it is related to the lover who, as in the water's glassy surface, reflects the lover's image. Once again it is worth recalling Sieglinde's lines from Act I of *Die Walküre*:

> Im Bach erblickt' ich
> mein eigen Bild—
> und jetzt gewahr' ich es wieder:
> wie einst dem Teich es enttaucht,
> bietest mein Bild mir nun du!     (vi. 19.)

> In the brook I glimpsed
> my own likeness—
> and now I see it again:
> as once it rose from the pool,
> so now you show me your likeness.

The same symbol is used in *Opera and Drama* to characterize the relationship between poetry and music in the musical drama: the surface of the sea of melody reflects the poet's image back at him, embodying the erotic union of the male element of poetry with the feminine element of music (iv. 142).

According to classical books on dreams, to see a reflection of oneself signified death. Hence the death of Narcissus when he saw his own reflection.[12] It was a brilliant idea on the part of Jean-Pierre Ponnelle, the producer of the 1981 Bayreuth Festival staging of *Tristan*, to associate the Narcissus motif with the fatal attraction which binds the lovers to one another in life and death. At the moment in Act I when they seize the goblet containing the potion, their gaze is caught and held by their own reflection in the broad-brimmed vessel. As though dumbfounded, they suddenly become aware of their love for one another. The motif is repeated in the second act, when the lovers observe their reflections in a woodland spring. At the same time, and in keeping with ancient mythic experience, the reflection in the drinking-bowl and in the spring suggests staring into the face of death. The reflection becomes a drink of love *and* death. Although Ponnelle's idea does not derive from Wagner's text, the Narcissus motif is closely bound up symbolically with the spirit of the poem—indeed, it heightens its mythic associations so significantly that one might almost assume that Wagner would have incorporated this production idea into his work if only he had thought of it himself. In his 1942 study, *L'Eau et les rêves*, Gaston Bachelard gives a fascinating account of the way in which water symbolizes death in nineteenth-century poetry, and especially in the writings of Edgar Allan Poe. For the latter, looking at water always

---

[12] Herbert Hunger, *Lexikon der griechischen und römischen Mythologie* (Reinbek, 1974), 265–6.

meant dying, approaching the mother-figure. Hence Bachelard's description of water as an 'invitation to die'.[13]

It would, of course, be anachronistic to project the Symbolist rediscovery of ancient mythic experiences in nineteenth-century poetry back on to Ronsard's sonnets, where the motivic handling of the themes of Narcissus, mirrors, and night is still embedded in the solid tradition of Petrarchan topoi. But, be that as it may, Thomas Mann's thesis that night was a 'discovery' of Romanticism is one that needs to be treated with a certain caution.

The poetic *moods* associated with night had already been discovered by the Age of Sentimentalism in the years after 1740. This was an age which, as it were, provided a contrapuntal accompaniment to the Enlightenment, making up for the latter's one-sided emphasis on reason by stressing the cult of feeling, without, however, lapsing into irrationality. This is clear from the first great work of European poetry to treat the subject of night, Edward Young's *The Complaint, or Night Thoughts on Life, Death and Immortality*, published in 1742–5. Here the traditional epic closing formula mentioned above is literally turned on its head, as the onset of day becomes the reason for ceasing meditation. Young's *Night Thoughts* exerted an enormous influence on European poetry of the period, and especially on the German writers of the time. There was scarcely a single sentimental poet after the middle of the century who did not follow Young's example and beg the moon for pity, weeping 'lonely tears' as the midnight hour began to strike.[14]

In his 1779 'dramatic maggot', *Der Triumph der Empfindsamkeit*, Goethe pokes fun at this modish infatuation with night. The central figure in this satirical comedy is one Prince Oronaro, who orders a specimen of 'artificial nature' to be made, a piece of machinery with all the attributes of the sentimental poetry of the period, which he takes with him on all his travels. He also has a model of his lover made, a doll which exerts such 'magic power' over him that, like some perverse Pygmalion, he finally prefers it to the original.[15] When Wagner and Cosima read Goethe's play on 1 November 1870, they were astonished to find how much the narcissistic Prince Oronaro resembled King Ludwig II. Thomas Mann draws a parallel between the cult of night to be found in *Tristan* and what he describes as the arch-Romantic 'primacy of the night' in Ludwig's royal castles, with their artificial grottoes and natural paradises.[16] Wagner himself would certainly have felt this

---

[13] See Emil Staiger (ed.), *Die Kunst der Interpretation* (Zurich, 1955), 250.

[14] See Lawrence Marden Price, *Die Aufnahme englischer Literatur in Deutschland 1500–1960* (Munich, 1961), chap. 9.

[15] Johann Wolfgang von Goethe, *Frühes Theater*, ed. Dieter Borchmeyer (Frankfurt, 1982), 402–3, 432.

[16] Mann, *Wagner und unsere Zeit*, pp. 97–8; English trans. (Blunden, *Pro and contra Wagner*), p. 125.

parallel to be a trivialization of his work. After all, would it not be truer to claim that Ludwig (as Wagner rightly recognized) was a latter-day Prince Oronaro transported to the nineteenth century?

The phenomena described in these pre-Romantic poems of the night are almost always portrayed *in* the night. In other words, it is not so much the darkness of night that matters as the effects of its light—the light of the moon and the stars. The night itself rarely figures as a mythic, symbolic whole, and, if it does, it is with recourse to the traditional topoi of mythological allegory. In the *Tageszeiten* by Friedrich Wilhelm Zachariä (1755), for example, Night appears (as in Young) mounted on a wain, wearing a veil and a star-studded mantle, and with a crown on her head whose crescent horns radiate light. Or else she sits on a throne, holding out her 'anarchical' sceptre over the globe. With her 'black-woven veil' in front of her face, the attributes of the 'star-blazing' Queen of Night in Mozart's *Die Zauberflöte* belong, at least in part, to this same mythological tradition.

For the poets of the Age of Sensibility, night was chiefly thought of as a stimulus to emotional outpourings and as an opportunity for reflection. The complex of ideas associated with time, life, death, and immortality is one which dominates not only Young's *Night Thoughts* but also all those poets of *Empfindsamkeit* in Germany who wrote about the night. Above all, the night was a time of solitary 'complaint' (as the title of Young's poem suggests), a lament at the death of the poet's dearest relations or friends. Well-known examples include Klopstock's poems, *Die frühen Gräber* and *Die Sommernacht*, where the motif of night is associated with another widespread theme of the time, the idea of grave-side meditation, a theme inspired in particular by such works as Thomas Gray's *Elegy Written in a Country Church-Yard*, first published in 1751.

Night was pre-eminently a time for meditation, therefore. Thus Young describes the stars:

> By them best lighted are the paths of thought:
> Nights are their days, their most illumin'd hours.
> By day, the soul, o'erborne by life's career,
> Stunn'd by the din, and giddy with the glare,
> Reels far from reason, jostled by the throng.[17]

This moral contemplation of the starry night-time sky as though it were some divine hieroglyph is part of a baroque tradition. But, more than the stars, it was the moon, of course, and the magic of light and atmosphere cast by her rays, to which the German poets of the Age of Sensibility paid particular homage: she was the favoured 'friend' of the poet's thoughts, to quote Klopstock's significant description of her in his ode, *Die frühen Gräber*.

---

[17] *The Poetical Works of Edward Young* (London, 1896), i. 81.

There is a world of difference between this atmospheric poetry of night, sicklied o'er as it is with the pale cast of thought and moonstruck melancholy, and the mythic vision of night which is typical of the Romantic poetry of the nineteenth century. This latter vision presupposes a new way of seeing things and involves the 'inner light' of the mystic tradition.[18] It was no longer a question of admiring the play of the moonlight with the same eyes that admired the light of day, or of paying homage to the stars as the poets of the Age of Sensibility had done. (Essentially, the latter were merely poets of daytime experience transported to a different setting.) The poet now had to become 'nacht-sichtig' (night-sighted), to quote Wagner's neologism from Act II of *Tristan* (vii. 42). Such a poet sees things which escape the notice of those poets who have only 'daytime vision'. He perceives sounds and the symbolic images of states of soul, revealing a musical way of seeing things in which ear and eye become one. 'Durch die Nacht, die mich umfangen, | Blickt zu mir der Töne Licht' (Through the night whose arms enfold me | Sounding light looks up at me), are the famous closing lines of Brentano's *Abendständchen*, a synaesthetic vision which looks forward to Wagner's third act, in which Tristan, too, will 'hear the light'.

For the poet of the *Hymnen an die Nacht*, the stars are merely signposts of the day. The poet who sings their praises bows to day's dominion over night:

Therefore, only because the night turns your servants away from you did you sow those spheres of light in the vast expanses of space, proclaiming your all-powerful might—the certainty of your return—at those times when you are absent. More heavenly than those incandescent stars we deem the eternal eyes which night has opened for us. [Novalis is referring here to the *oculi cordis* of the Bible and of mysticism.] They see further than the palest of those countless hosts: needful of no light, they penetrate the depths of every loving soul, filling a higher sphere with their ineffable delight. (Hymn I.)[19]

Novalis's repudiation of the light of the stars links his *Hymnen an die Nacht* with Baudelaire's 'Obsession' from *Les Fleurs du mal*. Symbolist poetry, too, reveals what Paul Claudel describes as 'une sympathie avec la nuit'.[20]

> Comme tu me plairais, ô nuit! sans ces étoiles
> Dont la lumière parle un langage connu!
> Car je cherche le vide, et le noir, et le nu![21]

---

[18] See Vordtriede, *Novalis*, pp. 146–57.
[19] Novalis, *Werke*, p. 42.
[20] On the following section, see Vordtriede, *Novalis*, p. 152.
[21] Charles Baudelaire, *Les Fleurs du mal*, ed. Antoine Adam (Paris, 1961), 82 (LXXIX); translated into English by Roy Campbell in *The Flowers of Evil*, selected and edited by Marthiel and Jackson Mathews (London, 1955), 94.

> How you would please me, Night, without your stars
> Which speak a foreign dialect, that jars
> On one who seeks the void, the black, the bare.

To the Age of Sensibility, such praise of darkness would have been unthinkable. Only Edward Young, far bolder than his German imitators, dares to revile the light (albeit the light of the sun, not of the stars) in the name of darkness:

> Darkness has more divinity for me;
> It strikes thought inward; it drives back the soul
> To settle on herself, our point supreme!
> There lies our theatre! there sits our judge.
> Darkness the curtain drops o'er life's dull scene.

And Young refers to 'the fam'd Athenian', Socrates, who kept vigil through the night, 'till the sun | (Rude drunkard rising rosy from the main!) | Disturbs his nobler intellectual beam, | And gives him to the tumult of the world'.[22] The true poet is described by Young as one who is night's intimate and who, as such, is played off against those poets who sing day's praises: 'Take Phoebus to yourselves, ye basking bards.'[23] Here we do indeed appear to hear a pre-echo of those Romantic writers for whom night would be the central symbol of their lives as poets.

In the second of his hymns Novalis contrasts the Enlightenment's belief in the omnipotence of light with the myth of eternal night, a darkness which is both the night of primordial chaos and that of the end of time. 'Light was granted its dominions; but the dominion of night is beyond time and space.'[24] To a certain extent, Novalis is giving a positive gloss here to Mephistopheles's nihilistic and cynical conviction in *Faust*, I, that 'in the beginning' was the void, that darkness of which he himself is a part. (Thus the Devil's mythological account of the origins of the world.) It was darkness which was 'mother of the light, | Proud light, that seeks a sway imperial, | Outranking far the ancient realm of night'. But, like the material world to which it cleaves, light must 'with matter share the general wreck',[25] leaving night and darkness to reassert the solitary sway which they had enjoyed at the beginning of time (ll. 1349–57). This myth runs counter to Goethe's own view of the world, since, as we know, he always numbered himself among those people 'who strive from darkness into light'.[26] The clearest manifestation of this trend is the redemptive mystery of the very last scene in *Faust*, II, set in a mountain gorge: rising up through the hierarchically ordered transcendental

---

[22] Young, *Poetical Works*, i. 81, 83.
[23] Ibid. 36.     [24] Novalis, *Werke*, p. 42.
[25] Translated by Philip Wayne (Harmondsworth, 1949), 75.
[26] See Curtius, *Gesammelte Abhandlungen*.

regions, Faust's monadic soul breaks free from materiality and darkness before dissolving finally into spirituality and light. The movement towards light is upwards, whereas the poet who espouses night always appears to sink into subterranean depths, as in the *Hymnen an die Nacht*: 'I turn away to sacred, ineffable, secretive night ... I would fain sink down in drops of dew' (Hymn I); or: 'Down into the womb of the earth | Away from the realms of light!' (Hymn VI).[27] We shall see how, in the case of Isolde's transfiguration, upward and downward movements overlap and cancel each other out in the most remarkable way, so that all idea of concrete space is lost.

For Novalis, night is more than just an *état d'âme*, since it symbolizes a particular state of the world. His *Hymnen an die Nacht* contain a detailed historical myth which links his work with Hölderlin's contemporary elegy, *Brot und Wein*. 'Night' (it was under this title that the opening strophe of Hölderlin's elegy first appeared in print) is the cosmic night between the day of the ancient gods and that Utopian day associated with the Hesperian gods. (On this point, Hölderlin differs from Novalis, for whom the night of the world was the eschatological aim of history.) In the *Hymnen an die Nacht*, too, the end of the 'ancient world' and the disappearance of the gods are mirrored in the symbol of the end of the day. 'Into the deeper sanctuary, into the mind's higher reaches, the soul of the world withdrew with its powers ... No longer was light the gods' abode, no longer a heavenly sign: they cast the veil of night upon themselves. Night became the mighty womb of revelations to which the gods returned.'[28] This is the hour at which Christianity was born. The ancient world, ruled by the gods and flooded by light, collapses into the nocturnal world of inwardness. Night becomes a 'homeland', the sphere in which to experience, mystically, the union of erotic love and death (Novalis speaks of 'death's ecstatic joys'), mystic union with Christ, and reunion with the dead beloved ('Down to the sweet bride, | To Jesus, the beloved!').[29]

Here, in aesthetico-erotic guise, is that mystic notion of the dark night of the soul which finds expression elsewhere in *En una noche obscura* by the Spanish mystic, Saint John of the Cross. Written *circa* 1577, this poem (which is part of a longer treatise) depicts the poet's ecstatic union with God using a series of images and concepts which recur in Novalis and Wagner, albeit with a somewhat different emphasis. (In the prose draft of *Tristan*, for example, Isolde speaks of the 'heart's nocturnal depths' in which the beloved's image rests: xi. 335.[30]) For the Spanish

---

[27] Novalis, *Werke*, pp. 41, 52.    [28] Ibid. 47–8.    [29] Ibid. 44, 53.
[30] Leo Spitzer has drawn a perceptive comparison between *En una noche obscura* and Isolde's transfiguration in 'Drei Gedichte der Ekstase', in *Eine Methode Literatur zu interpretieren* (Munich, 1966), 9–51.

mystic, eroticism—including clandestine love and the type of situation depicted in the *aubade*—becomes an image of mystic union, whereas for Novalis and, above all, for Wagner, religious symbolism is used for different ends, serving, rather, to portray a new erotic mysticism.

En una noche obscura
Con ansias en amores inflamada
    o dichosa uentura
    sali sin ser notada
Estando ya mi casa sosegada

    A escuras, y segura
Por la secreta escala disfraçada
    o dichosa uentura
    a escuras y ençelada
Estando ya mi casa sosegada

    En la noche dichosa
En secreto que nadie me ueya.
    Ni yo miraua cosa
    Sin otra luz y guia
Sino la que en el coraçon ardia

    O llama de amor uiua
    que tiernamente hieres
De mi alma en el mas profundo centro
    pues ya no eres esquiua
    acaba ya si quieres
Rompe la tela deste dulce enquentro.


    Once in the dark of night
when love burned bright with yearning, I arose
    (O windfall of delight!)
    and how I left none knows—
dead to the world my house in deep repose;

    in the dark, where all goes right,
thanks to a secret ladder, other clothes,
    (O windfall of delight!)
    in the dark, enwrapped in those—
dead to the world my house in deep repose.

    There in the lucky dark,
none to observe me, darkness far and wide;
    no sign for me to mark,
    no other light, no guide
except for my heart—the fire, the fire inside!

    O living flame of love!
    how soothingly you wound

my soul in its profundity—that centre
you once made havoc of.
O finish! Take me soon!
Tearing the veil away in love's encounter.[31]

For the wanderer who has walked for some length of time through a gloomy forest, it is an impressive moment when he emerges from the darkness of a wood into a clearing and suddenly sees the sun's rays breaking through the trees. The Enlightenment was a movement within the glade of reason: it believed it could conquer progressively the darkness all around it. For Romantic writers, by contrast, this clearing was no more than a patch of light wrested from infinite darkness: at any time, night could envelop it once again, drawing it back into the engulfing chaos.

According to Thomas Mann, *Tristan* is so firmly bound up with what Novalis had called the Romantics' 'enthusiasm for night'[32] that the work 'as such had no need of Schopenhauer to stand godfather'.[33] Of course, Novalis's myth of the night differs in certain essential respects from Wagner's: the latter's music drama lacks, for instance, the former's historical background and, more especially, the mysticism associated with the figure of Christ. The Romantic elements are refracted through the philosophy of Schopenhauer, while the latter, in turn, is invested with a Romantic symbolism which leads to a significant shift of meaning. Night becomes nirvana, the realm of 'primeval oblivion' (vii. 61), a realm which cannot, of course, be reached by denying that 'will' whose 'focus' is erotic desire (in other words, by renouncing sex),[34] but by intensifying and sublimating sexual love until that point is reached where individuation ceases to exist. When, in Act III, Tristan recovers from his faint (and it will be recalled that, according to Schopenhauer, fainting is the 'twin-brother' of death[35]), he tells Kurwenal:

> Ich war—
> wo ich von je gewesen,
> wohin auf je ich gehe:
> im weiten Reich
> der Welten Nacht.    (vii. 61.)

---

[31] *The Poems of St John of the Cross*, trans. John Frederick Nims, 3rd edn. (Chicago, 1979), 18–23. (The first 3 strophes are from *En una noche obscura*, the 4th from *O llama de amor uiua*.)

[32] Novalis, *Werke*, p. 43, l. 16.

[33] Mann, *Wagner und unsere Zeit*, p. 97; English trans. (Blunden, *Pro and contra Wagner*), p. 125.

[34] Arthur Schopenhauer, *Sämtliche Werke*, ed. Arthur Hübscher (Mannheim, 1972), ii. 390; translated into English by E. F. J. Payne as *The World as Will and Representation* (New York, 1969), i. 330.

[35] Ibid. iii. 535; English trans., ii. 468.

> I was—
> where I have been forever,
> where I must ever go:
> the boundless realm
> of endless night.[36]

Night, therefore, is the beginning and end of all existence, or, to borrow an image from Schopenhauer, it is 'the abundant womb of that nothing which is pregnant with worlds',[37] which in *Tristan* bears clear traces of the classical underworld. Life is the flashing foam on the wave of night, created by it and returning to it. This image of the night as some primordial Great Mother is, of course, Romantic through and through and, as such, foreign to Schopenhauer, for whom night is the state of nirvana and hence only a goal, not a source of anything.

Night and day are in the same relationship in *Tristan und Isolde* as being and appearance. There are night-people, who live a life of truth, and there are day-people, who are forever caught up in a series of metaphysical deceptions. At the beginning of the drama, of course, all the parties involved are victims of appearance; only the ostensible cup of atonement wrests Tristan and Isolde from their metaphysical night-blindness, estranging them in a twinkling from those people around them who are denied all insight into the nature of the world, since they are blinded by the light of day. It is now no longer possible to build a bridge of understanding between them and the 'night-sighted' lovers: although words may pass between them, these simply lead to greater, and more fatal, misunderstandings than silence would have done.

The potion does not awaken the love between Tristan and Isolde, it merely brings their silent and suppressed passion into the open. Since both believe they are drinking poison, they no longer feel held back by the dividing wall of illusionary moral concepts and defiant self-preservation. Only the belief that it is a *death*-potion which they are drinking makes it possible for them to confess their love so unconditionally. As Thomas Mann points out in his essay *Leiden und Größe Richard Wagners*, Brangäne could just as well have offered the lovers a glass of water: the outcome of the first act would have remained the same.[38] Thus the potion symbolizes a metaphysical process of cognition (in the Schopenhauerian sense) and, at the same time, encapsulates a complex psychological process at which the three-dimensionality of the stage action can merely hint, but whose subtly differentiated motivation and 'epic' exposition are left to the music to depict.

The drink of love and death corresponds exactly with Wagner's

---

[36] Verse translations from Wagner's libretto are taken from Andrew Porter's singing translation, published in ENO Opera Guide 6, ed. Nicholas John (London and New York, 1983), 47–92.

[37] Schopenhauer, *Sämtliche Werke*, iii. 546; English trans. (Payne, *World as Will*), ii. 477.

[38] Mann, *Wagner und unsere Zeit*, p. 68; English trans. (Blunden, *Pro and contra Wagner*), p. 97.

description of the poetic device of the 'wonder' in *Opera and Drama*, where he writes that 'it serves the aim of the poet who ... must compress life's manifestations by reducing them from their unmanageable multiplicity to a dense and easily manageable form' (iv. 81).

It has often been shown how, in writing *Tristan*, Wagner radically reduced and simplified the complex and many-stranded plot of his medieval source, internalizing it, so to speak, and, in his own words, concentrating on the 'focal point' of its 'purely human emotional content' (v. 173).[39] All that remains of the original epic source, in terms of the musical and dramaturgical composition of the work, are three situations of concentrated emotion which, according to Wagner's aesthetic beliefs, could be articulated and amplified only in music. The way in which he highlighted these three emotional peaks and linked them together has always been a source of wonderment. (The concentrated nature of the plot brings *Tristan* astonishingly close, dramaturgically, to Racinian tragedy, a genre which Wagner described in *Opera and Drama* (iv. 6) as the formal antithesis of Shakespeare's open structure.)

By offering Tristan the death-potion, Isolde admits to him in Act II, she had hoped to draw him with her into the night:

> wo der Täuschung Ende
> mein Herz mir verhieß,
> wo des Trug's geahnter
> Wahn zerrinne. (vii. 41.)

> where my heart had told me
> delusion would die;
> where deceit and lies
> could make no capture.

The lovers are concerned here not only to demonstrate a love which has been concealed by self-delusion and by the insistence on merely apparent values, but to reveal the truth as such, a truth which hitherto has been hidden behind the veil of *maya*. Truth, therefore, does not 'come to light'; it is revealed exclusively *by* night, a revelation which turns on its head the traditional western metaphysics of light. At the very moment when Tristan suspects that the cup of atonement which Isolde has offered him portends his death,

> da erdämmerte mild
> erhab'ner Macht
> im Busen mir die Nacht;
> mein Tag war da vollbracht. (vii. 42.)

---

[39] These remarks of Wagner's are taken from his essay, 'Beethoven's Overture to *Coriolan*' (v. 173–6), written in 1852.

> then there dawned in my heart
>   with tender might
> the wondrous charm of night;
>   my day would lose its light.

Thus Tristan recalls the earlier events from the vantage-point of the
second act. The cup of atonement becomes the Acheron on which he
passes to a realm beyond the world of things:

> Durch des Todes Thor,
>   wo er mir floß,
>   weit und offen
>   er mir erschloß,
> darin sonst ich nur träumend gewacht,
> das Wonnereich der Nacht.                         (vii. 42.)[40]

> Through the doors of death
>   there flowed a tide,
>   when those portals
>   were opened wide,
> then they revealed my dream of delight,
> the enchanted realm of night.

This is a realm beyond the boundaries of individuation.

In his chapter 'On Death and its Relation to the Indestructibility of
our Inner Nature', which he wrote as a supplement to book IV of *Die
Welt als Wille und Vorstellung* (and which is the most important single
philosophical source of *Tristan*), Schopenhauer writes that: 'Death is the
great reprimand that the will-to-live, and more particularly the egoism
essential thereto, receive through the course of nature ... Egoism really
consists in man's restricting all reality to his own person, in that he
imagines he lives in this alone, and not in others.' Dying is 'the moment
of that liberation from the one-sidedness of an individuality which does
not constitute the innermost kernel of our true being, but is rather to be
thought of as a kind of aberration thereof. The true original freedom
again enters at this moment which ... can be regarded as a *restitutio in
integrum*'.[41] It is very much this experience which the potion vouchsafes
to Tristan and Isolde in the instantaneity of the symbolic 'wonder'. That
which the novelist would have had to describe gradually, within the
limitations of psychological probability, is visualized here using an image

---

[40] Here and elsewhere, quotations are based on the text as it appears in Wagner's *Collected
Writings*. In a number of instances, this version of the text was superseded when Wagner set the
libretto to music: 'darin sonst ich nur träumend gewacht, | das Wonnereich der Nacht', for example,
became 'darin ich sonst | nur träumend gewacht, | das Wunderrich der Nacht' (Eulenburg pocket
score, pp. 523–4; the Peters full score, pp. 330–1, reprinted by Dover, retains the erroneous
'Wonnereich'). The present translator is grateful to Dr Isolde Vetter of the Richard Wagner-
Gesamtausgabe, Munich, for sorting out this particular crux.

[41] Schopenhauer, *Sämtliche Werke*, iii. 581–3; English trans. (Payne, *World as Will*), ii. 507–8.

which is 'readily intelligible' on the level of feeling (iv. 82). The potion, one might say, enables the lovers to imbibe the philosophy of Schopenhauer.

It would be wrong, of course, to explain this metaphysical potion in wholly Schopenhauerian terms. The fact that, although it was thought to be poison, it was actually a love-potion sets it apart from a philosophy preaching the denial of the will. Erotic love, according to Schopenhauer, was the most powerful expression of the will-to-live. 'Self-preservation and maintenance' are man's 'first aim', 'egoism' his guiding principle.[42] With Wagner, by contrast, erotic love ceases to serve existential ends and becomes one with the longing for death, for the delimitation of the individual, and for his union with the universe. Tristan and Isolde confess their love for one another precisely because they believe they are drinking poison. 'Oblivion's healing draught' is first and foremost a drink to jolt the memory, a drink which brings back into the open a love which they had concealed and with which they had come to terms. It eases that existential convulsion in whose thrall 'Tristan the hero' (vii. 8) had lived hitherto.

At this juncture it is perhaps worth quoting a poem by Friedrich Rückert which mirrors the inner action of the first act right down to its metaphorical associations. It is called *Nach Dschelaleddin Rumi* and refers to Mawlânâ Jalâl al-Dîn Rûmî, the most famous of Persian mystic poets:

Wohl endet Tod des Lebens Not,
Doch schauert Leben vor dem Tod.
Das Leben sieht die dunkle Hand,
Den hellen Kelch nicht, den sie bot.
So schauert vor der Lieb ein Herz,
Als wie vom Untergang bedroht.
Denn wo die Lieb erwachet, stirbt
Das Ich, der dunkele Despot.
Du laß ihn sterben in der Nacht,
Und atme frei im Morgenrot.[43]

Though death no doubt will end all pain and strife,
The thought of it must needs affrighten life,
Which watches as the darkling hand enfolds
It, heeding not the chalice that it holds.
Thus hearts beset by love beat faster still
As though destruction threatened them with ill.
For when love wakens, then that self that I
Abhor as despot of the dark must die.
So let the night contrive the tyrant's death
And at each day's new dawning draw new breath.

---

[42] Ibid. ii. 389, 446; English trans. i. 329, 377.
[43] Friedrich Rückert, *Gedichte*, ed. Johannes Pfeiffer (Stuttgart, 1963), 24.

'The kiss of love', Wagner told Cosima on 15 August 1869, 'is the first intimation of death, the cessation of individuality, that is why a person is so terrified by it.'

Tristan represses his love for Isolde because of courtly convention, an attachment to life which refuses to countenance night and death, refuses to acknowledge that painful mystery which once unfolded between them when the sword she had drawn to avenge Morold's death sank weakly to her side. Here is that archetypal dramatic situation, endlessly repeated since classical antiquity, which Wolf Hartmut Friedrich has called the 'miraculously deflected fatal blow' or 'the enemy's life unexpectedly spared'.[44] Wagner owes this motif, of course, to the medieval *Tristan* romance, but he has altered it in a significant way. In Gottfried von Straßburg's original, the heroine raises the sword three times, allowing it to fall again on each occasion without knowing why. Nor is she alone with Tristan when this confrontation takes place.

The intimacy and psychological ambivalence of Wagner's reworking recall another dramatic model, the scene between Joan and Lionel (Act III, Scene 10) in Schiller's *Die Jungfrau von Orleans*, a work which Wagner much admired. Schiller's heroine may never love a man. She fights with Lionel, but at the very moment when she raises her arm to strike the fatal blow, 'she looks into his face, the sight of which moves her; she stands motionless, then slowly allows her arm to sink'. Joan turns aside her face, until Lionel's importunity causes her to raise the sword a second time but, 'as she contemplates his features, she quickly lets it fall once more'. In her monologue at the beginning of Act IV, she seeks to justify her behaviour: 'Sollt ich ihn töten? Konnt ichs, da ich ihm | Ins Auge sah?' (Should I have slain him? Could I, when I looked | Into his eyes?). She clearly realizes that it was not 'the voice of mercy' which prompted her to spare her enemy's life. 'Warum mußt ich ihm in die Augen sehn! | Die Züge schaun des edeln Angesichts! | Mit deinem Blick fing dein Verbrechen an, | Unglückliche!' (What power made me gaze into his eyes? | Behold the features of that noble face? | That glance it was from which thy guilt did grow, | O hapless maid!: ll. 2564–80).

The similarity between this episode and Isolde's recollection of the moment when she spared *her* enemy's life is unmistakable, particularly when we consider the glance motif itself. (In the course of a conversation on 17 November 1873 Wagner and Cosima advanced the view that this motif could be expressed only in narrative form: if depicted on stage, as it was in Schiller's drama, it would cease to be effective.)

    [44] Wolf Hartmut Friedrich, *Vorbild und Neugestaltung: Sechs Kapitel zur Geschichte der Tragödie* (Göttingen, 1967), 57–87, esp. pp. 67–70.

Von seinem Bette
blickt' er her, —
nicht auf das Schwert,
nicht auf die Hand, —
er sah mir in die Augen.
Seines Elendes
jammerte mich;
das Schwert — das ließ ich fallen:
die Morold schlug, die Wunde,
sie heilt' ich, daß er gesunde,
und heim nach Hause kehre, —
mit dem Blick mich nicht mehr beschwere.    (vii. 11.)

But as he lay there
he looked up
not at the sword,
not at my hand,
he gazed in my eyes.
And his anguish
wounded me so;
the sword then fall before me.
The Morold wound I tended
in hope that when it was mended,
for home and house he'd leave me,
where his glances no more would grieve me.

An action which appears from the outside (to Brangäne, for whose benefit Isolde recalls these events) to be an act of mercy is revealed unmistakably by the music ('very expressive and tender', according to the score) as 'love at first sight'. From this moment onwards, Isolde knows (and there can be no doubt that Tristan shares that knowledge) that the two of them are destined for each other. What is so appalling from Isolde's point of view is that Tristan suppresses that knowledge: 'Mir erkoren, — | mir verloren' (Destined for me, — | lost for ever: vii. 4). As a result, allowing the sword to slip from her hand assumes traumatic proportions: time and again her mind harks back to that moment; she is incapable of grasping that an action which, for her, was so unprecedented, could yet have been so futile.

It was Nietzsche who made one of the most penetrating remarks about Wagner when, in *Nietzsche contra Wagner*, he described the composer as the 'Orpheus of all secret misery'.[45] Nowhere is this more true than in that silent scene in which Isolde allows the sword to fall, and Tristan, that 'glorious' hero, gazes up into her eyes in unutterable grief. It is

[45] Friedrich Nietzsche, *Sämtliche Werke: Kritische Studienausgabe in 15 Bänden*, ed. Giorgio Colli and Mazzino Montinari (Munich, 1980), vi. 417–18.

almost always such moments of animal-like vulnerability which reveal true humanity for Wagner, and almost never those scenes of heroic splendour which remain, for the most part, mere outward deception. Man's true face reveals the indelible marks of suffering, and the highest goal he can ever achieve, not only in *Parsifal*, is knowledge through pity, that 'clairvoyance of pain' which Gerhart Hauptmann once described as the fundamental feature of all his own writings, initiation into the world's essential suffering.

Such is its cause and the nature of its origins that the love between Tristan and Isolde bears the marks of fellow-feeling from the very outset. It is that same fellow-feeling whose origin and nature, according to Schopenhauer, is 'seeing through the *principium individuationis*' and through the suffering inextricably bound up with it. 'All love is compassion or sympathy', he writes, by which he means not sexual love but 'pure affection' or *caritas*, erotic love being, for Schopenhauer, 'selfish', although he admits that 'combinations of the two occur frequently'.[46] It is precisely such a combination that we find, from the very beginning, in the love between Tristan and Isolde.

But how can we explain the fact that, in Tristan's case at least, so profound an experience of love, related as it is to a metaphysical knowledge of compassion, is buried and 'betrayed'? The word 'betrayal' has a double meaning here: it signifies both the betrayal of a secret and a breach of trust, both of which Tristan is guilty of committing. As Isolde says:

> Wie anders prahlte
> Tristan aus,
> was ich verschlossen hielt!
> Die schweigend ihm
> das Leben gab,
>
> mit ihr—gab er es preis.          (vii. 12–13.)

> Yet Tristan boldly
> cried aloud
> what I in silence hid!
> My silent care
> had healed his wound
>
> yet he cried it aloud!

In other words, Tristan praised Isolde to King Marke in a voice both 'loud and clear'. Like Hebbel's female characters, Isolde feels wounded in her woman's dignity, seeing herself demeaned to the level of an

---

[46] Schopenhauer, *Sämtliche Werke*, ii. 442–4; English trans. (Payne, *World as Will*), i. 374–6.

object, albeit one which is held in high esteem. While, out of pity, she had mastered her feelings and allowed the sword to fall, Tristan, she believes, was simply 'measuring her up' to see whether she would make a suitable husband for Marke (vii. 23–4).

The image Isolde uses here is that of 'stealing her likeness'. The symbolism attached to the image, with its idea of a secret which must be locked away and guarded within the heart's dark portals and not allowed to be revealed to the light of day, also determines Tristan's disquisition on love in Act II. He depicts the blossoming of his affection for Isolde as the acceptance of a likeness at which, his eyes not yet 'hallowed' by night, he had initially not dared to look. Before his transformation by the potion, Tristan had devoted himself to 'day', with its attributes of honour, fame, and the resplendent life of chivalry. The mystery of love, and the woman who revealed that mystery to him, he could grasp only by recourse to concepts from courtly life. Hence his description of the way in which Isolde was stolen away by day:

> dahin, wo sie
> der Sonne glich,
> in hehrster Ehren
> Glanz und Licht.          (vii. 39.)
>
> Where you shone
> like the glorious sun
> in highest honour's
> dazzling ray.

And, even more pointedly: 'in lichten Tages Schein | wie war Isolde mein?' (In day's resplendent shine | how could Isold' be mine?: vii. 39). How could Tristan still believe that she was destined for him, that the woman who was the perfect embodiment of 'honour's show and fame's proud sway' could belong to anyone other than the most high-ranking of all the men at court?

This is the reason why he praises her to King Marke, abandoning the image locked within his heart and allowing all to see it. The 'noonday blaze of worldly glory' entered

> bis in des Herzens
> tiefsten Schrein.
> Was dort in keuscher Nacht
> dunkel verschlossen wacht',
> was ohne Wiss' und Wahn
> ich dämmernd dort empfah'n,
> ein Bild, das meine Augen
> zu schau'n sich nicht getrauten,—
> von des Tages Schein betroffen
> lag mir's da schimmernd offen.          (vii. 40.)

> down to my deepest,
> inmost soul.
> And in that holy dark
> there I perceived a spark, —
> unknown and unexpressed,
> a vision scarcely guessed;
> a vision, whose enchantment
> I scarcely dared to gaze on;
> but when daylight shone before me,
> that vision shone in glory.

The 'heart's shrine' is an ancient mystic and erotic symbol, and, as such, was chosen by Karl Lachmann to open his anthology of medieval German lyric poetry:

> Dû bist mîn, ich bin dîn:
> des solt dû gewis sîn.
> dû bist beslozzen
> in mînem herzen:
> verlorn ist daz slüzzelîn:
> dû muost immer drinne sîn.[47]

> You are mine, I am thine:
> Of that you may be sure.
> You are locked
> Within my heart:
> The little key is missing:
> You must remain forever mine.

In *Tristan und Isolde* the symbol of the heart's shrine is invested with a special significance, in that the contents of the shrine (love's likeness) must remain hidden. The shrine must not be opened lest the image within it be caught in the glare of the sun's rays. 'Let it rest in the night, do not snatch it into the light, what blooms in the heart's silent depths', we read in Schlegel's *Lucinde*.[48] At the same time it is impossible not to recall the important symbolical role of the shrine or casket in Goethe's poetic œuvre, and especially the countless variants of the motif in *Wilhelm Meisters Wanderjahre*, a work which Wagner often reread: for Goethe, it symbolized something secret and deeply hidden, particularly in an erotic context, and, as such, something which elicited awe and inspired silence. To open the shrine prematurely or without authority, and thus to betray its secret content, invariably brings disaster.

    Tristan, too, is guilty of a similar act of betrayal by opening his heart's shrine. The disaster which looms over him is described by Isolde in highly symbolic terms:

[47] *Des Minnesangs Frühling*, p. 1 (3, 1–6).
[48] Schlegel, *Lucinde*, p. 106.

> was dir gezeigt
> die dämmernde Nacht,
> an des Tag-Gestirnes
> Königs-Macht
> mußtest du's übergeben.                    (vii. 43.)

> what you perceived
> in glory of night,
> to the empty pride
> of kingly might
> you were forced to surrender.

In other words, Tristan had no choice but to woo the woman destined for him, but to do so on another's behalf:[49] the image of love contained within the dark night of the heart must be entrusted to the sun or to the king (the two are equated symbolically).

The lines just quoted recall the symbolism of *Die Zauberflöte*, but with a significant reversal of the values adumbrated there. Tamino, too, receives a portrait, in his case from the Queen of Night, and, like its original, it passes into the sphere of influence ruled over by the 'orb of day'. Sarastro's realm is ruled by the sun, into whose image the whole stage is transformed during the final scene of the opera. This kingdom of the sun increasingly divests night of all its powers, an act symbolized by the transfer of all the magical attributes of the Queen of Night—flute, glockenspiel, and the Three Boys—into the service of the brotherhood. When, immediately before the final chorus, Sarastro sings the words: 'Die Strahlen der Sonne vertreiben die Nacht, | Zernichten der Heuchler erschlichene Macht' (The sun's golden splendour now sunders the night, | And shatters the hypocrites' ill-gotten might), what we hear is the Enlightenment hope that the light of reason will triumph over obscurantism, and that the forces of darkness will be defeated. 'Bald prangt, den Morgen zu verkünden, | Die Sonn' auf goldner Bahn' (Soon shall the sun to herald morning | In splendour gild the sky), the Three Boys sing at the beginning of the second-act finale: 'Bald soll der Aberglaube schwinden, | Bald siegt der weise Mann' (Parted the clouds of superstition | And wisdom victor be). It is a victory over all forms of dark superstition and obscurantism.

In proclaiming the end of spiritual night, *Die Zauberflöte* remains entirely within the spirit of the Age of Reason, with its metaphorical treatment of light. *Tristan und Isolde*, by contrast, reverses the traditional values of light and darkness, inverting the symbolism of day and night

---

[49] In his *Epilogue to the 'Nibelung's Ring'* Wagner compares Tristan to Siegfried in this respect: what they have in common is that each of them, 'under the constraint of a delusion which makes this deed of his not free, woos, on another's behalf, the woman destined for him by primeval law, meeting his death as the result of the ensuing *mésalliance*' (vi. 268).

and thus becoming a kind of anti-*Zauberflöte* (no less so than Novalis's *Heinrich von Ofterdingen*, whose eponymous hero 'destroys the kingdom of the sun'[50] in the unfinished final section of the work). That part of himself which had been revealed to Tristan by 'darkening night', and entrusted to its care, is now transferred to the power of the 'orb of day'; this transfer does not signify the latter's definitive victory, however, for what has been handed over on an outward level is still withheld on an inner level by the potion. The alienation and profanation of the likeness of his beloved which he holds within his heart also alienates the image in Isolde's heart following his act of 'betrayal':

> Den dort ich heimlich barg,
> wie dünkt' er mich so arg
> wenn in des Tages Scheine
> der treu gehegte Eine
> der Liebe Blicken schwand,
> als Feind nur vor mir stand. (vii. 41.)

> He whom my love concealed
> traitor he stood revealed,
> there to my gaze so tender
> he blazed in day-lit splendour
> within that burning glow,
> defied me as his foe!

The death-potion is intended to end this sense of estrangement: Isolde offers it to Tristan in the hope that her lover, mistaking and mistaken, will be drawn by it out of the 'light of day', in which he stands as a 'traitor', and into the night, where all deception will cease. When she drinks what she takes to be poison, Tristan's likeness, formerly estranged, returns to her heart, just as, conversely, the image of Isolde which had been forfeited to the 'orb of day' returns to Tristan's heart:

> Von dem Bild in des Herzens
> bergendem Schrein
> scheucht' er des Tages
> täuschenden Schein,
> daß nacht-sichtig mein Auge
> wahr es zu sehen tauge. (vii. 42.)

> From the dream that my inmost heart
> did enshrine
> gone was the daylight's
> false lying shine,—
> and, night-sighted, before me
> I saw the truth in glory.

[50] Novalis, *Werke*, p. 284.

Only now is Tristan's vision 'hallowed', so that he can see the likeness undistorted, without the deceptive glare of courtly chivalry and pomp.

Previously estranged by day, the lovers suddenly find a whole new perspective has opened up for them. 'Was träumte mir | von Tristan's Ehre?' (What dream was mine | of Tristan's honour?), Tristan asks, to which Isolde replies: 'Was träumte mir | von Isolde's Schmach?' (What dream was mine | of Isolde's shame?: vii. 27). Totally reversing all the values they had formerly held dear, day now becomes the sphere of dreaming and of 'empty illusion' (in the prose draft we even find the striking neologism 'sun-dreams': xi. 336), while night becomes the matrix of truth. The daily world of the courtly code of virtue, with its insistence on 'fame and honour, | power and gain'—the feudal manifestations of the will-to-live—are now just as unimportant to Tristan as is Isolde's offended dignity to *her*. Both are now consumed by the longing to rediscover the heart's dark shrine in which that mystic union for which they yearn may be consummated at last. It is a yearning for the 'holy night' of death, when the 'I' and 'You' will no longer be held apart (vii. 43–4).

A similar sentiment invests the opening lines of Clemens Brentano's poem, 'Heil'ge Nacht', from the play *Die Gründung Prags*, first published in 1814: 'Heil'ge Nacht, heil'ge Nacht! | Sterngeschloßner Himmelsfrieden! | Alles, was das Licht geschieden, ist verbunden' (Holy night, holy night! | Star-girt peace of heaven! | All that light had sundered now is joined together).[51] In much the same way, the second act of Wagner's *Tristan und Isolde* is imbued with that mystic darkness where all distinctions cease to exist. Isolde's passionate wish to see extinguished the torch which the anxious Brangäne guards as a 'warning flame', even though death itself should be the result, is doubtless, as Peter Wapnewski has emphasized,[52] a reminiscence of Lessing's 1769 essay, *Wie die Alten den Tod gebildet*. Here Lessing advances the thesis that in classical antiquity, unlike the later Christian tradition, death was depicted not as a frightening skeleton but as a guardian spirit with an inverted torch. 'What can describe the end of life more clearly than an extinguished, inverted torch?'[53] Wagner did not need to have read Lessing's essay, since the idea cited here was a part of the general cultural heritage. In Schiller's poem *Die Götter Griechenlands*, for example, we read:

> Damals trat kein gräßliches Gerippe
> Vor das Bett des Sterbenden.

[51] Clemens Brentano, *Werke*, ed. Friedhelm Kemp (Munich, 1966), iv. 721.
[52] Peter Wapnewski, *Der traurige Gott: Richard Wagner in seinen Helden* (Munich, 1978), 53.
[53] *Lessings Werke*, ed. Georg Witkowski (Leipzig and Vienna, [n.d.]), vi. 80.

> Still und traurig senkt' ein Genius
> Seine Fackel.[54]

> No hideous skeleton would come
> To stand before the sick man's bed.
> In silent grief a genius
> Would let his torch sink to his side.

An identical image recurs in Novalis's *Hymnen an die Nacht*:

> Mit kühnem Geist und hoher Sinnenglut
> Verschönte sich der Mensch die grause Larve,
> Ein sanfter Jüngling löscht das Licht und ruht—[55]

> With bold and burning sensuality
> Man sought to beautify the fearful spectre:
> A gentle youth would douse the light and rest—

In Act III of *Tristan und Isolde* the image of the dying torch becomes the direct expression of Tristan's fervent death-wish:

> Ach, Isolde!
> Süße! Holde!
> Wann—endlich,
> wann, ach wann
> löschest du die Zünde?     (vii. 62–3.)

> Ah, Isolde!
> Sweetest! Dearest!
> When—at last,
> when, ah when
> will you quench its burning?

Night is the symbol of that death which brings an end to individuation, revealing that I and You are indivisible. It is around this idea of the lovers' identity, the oneness of self and world ('selbst dann | bin ich die Welt' (I myself | am the world): vii. 45), that the love duet in Act II revolves, taking up the mystery of oneness in ever new variations:

> Stünd' er vor mir,
> der mächt'ge Tod,
> wie er mir Leib
> und Leben bedroht',—
> die ich der Liebe
> so willig lasse!—
> wie wär' seinen Streichen
> die Liebe selbst zu erreichen?   (vii. 46.)

---

[54] Friedrich Schiller, *Sämtliche Werke*, ed. Gerhard Fricke and Herbert G. Göpfert, 3rd edn. (Munich, 1962), i. 166.
[55] Novalis, *Werke*, p. 47.

> Though I confronted
> mighty death,
> threatening both
> my limbs and my life,—
> which I so freely
> to love have yielded,—
> what though his stroke descended,
> could love itself then be ended?

This, to quote Schopenhauer, is the 'indestructibility of our inner nature', for this thing-in-itself is the 'endless and beginningless' will in all its original unity,[56] before it fell under the law of 'appearance', the *principium individuationis*. Tristan names this will 'love' (just as Schopenhauer had described erotic love as the 'focus' of the will).

It is not love, therefore—that cosmogonical primeval force, or, to quote Wagner, 'des Welten-Werdens | Walterin' (literally, 'the mistress of the worlds' becoming': vii. 34)—which is subject to death, but only the lovers in the one-sidedness of their individuality. It is through death that they revert to the womb of the Great Mother:

> Stürb' ich nun ihr,
> der so gern ich sterbe,
> wie könnte die Liebe
> mit mir sterben!
> Die ewig lebende
> mit mir enden?                    (vii. 46–7.)

> Though I should die,
> find the death I long for,
> yet how could the love
> within me perish?
> the ever-living
> with me be ended?

As 'will', love is, after all, the indestructible thing-in-itself, the same in all phenomena. This belief, to which the lovers keep on returning, is one of the original ideas behind the *Tristan* poem. Even in the earliest prose sketches, dated the end of 1855,[57] Tristan is already made to ask: 'Were I to die, all that would disappear is what prevents me from loving you with all my being ... What does not end with me, is it no more than I? Would I thus become love without end?'[58] In much the same way, Lucinde and Julius in Friedrich Schlegel's novel describe themselves as 'immortal ... as love'; and Julius remarks: 'I can no longer say, "my

---

[56] Schopenhauer, *Sämtliche Werke*, iii. 573; English trans. (Payne, *World as Will*), ii. 500.
[57] But see *WWV*, pp. 442–3, for a dating 12 months later.
[58] First published in *Programmheft zur Neuinszenierung des 'Tristan' an der Bayerischen Staatsoper am 27. Juli 1980* (Munich, 1980), 29–30.

love" or "your love"; both are the same and utterly one.'[59] This last quotation shows to what extent the metaphysics of Romantic love is interwoven in Wagner's *Tristan* with Schopenhauer's philosophy of the will.

For Schopenhauer, death was 'the great opportunity no longer to be I'.[60] But this is also the aim of the love between Tristan and Isolde, which is why it can be achieved only in death. The lovers want to be nothing but *love*, or, in their own words, to die for love. Hence their exchange of identity: 'You Isolde, | Tristan I, | no longer Isolde!', Isolde sings, to which Tristan answers: 'You Tristan, | Isolde I, no longer Tristan!' (vii. 50);[61] and hence, too, their desire for the end of the 'sweet little word "and"' (vi. 47) which separates their names, expressing the fact that they are not yet one, but still I *and* you.

The love-potion 'reveals what was bound to be exposed', Isolde tells Brangäne in the 1857 prose draft (xi. 334), while Tristan exclaims in the second-act love duet: 'O Heil dem Tranke! | Heil seinem Saft!' (I praise the potion! | bless that draught): it had opened the gates of death and revealed the 'enchanted realm of night' to the lovers (vii. 42). But is it not also this potion which prevents Tristan and Isolde from entering the nocturnal kingdom of the dead and which hands them back to day? In Act III Tristan curses the 'fearful drink' (vii. 67). How can this be reconciled with his former praise of it? There is little doubt that this earlier encomium was directed not at the actual love-potion but at the deception of the poisoned cup. Only the approach of what they believed to be death revealed to the lovers what had been hidden from them previously: the love-potion is not only absurd in itself (since what it is intended to awaken has long since existed), it very much prevents their love from finding fulfilment in death. It simply replaces old illusions with new ones. As Isolde says:

> Doch ach! Dich täuschte
> der falsche Trank,
> daß dir von Neuem
> die Nacht versank;
> dem einzig am Tode lag,
> den gab er wieder dem Tag.          (vii. 42.)

> But ah, deceit lay
> within the drink,
> night once again
> from my grasp did sink,
> no death in the potion lay,
> it drove thee back to the day!

[59] Schlegel, *Lucinde*, pp. 12–13.
[60] Schopenhauer, *Sämtliche Werke*, iii. 582; English trans. (Payne, *World as Will*), ii. 507.
[61] On the motif of 'exchange of persons' in Gottfried's *Tristan*, see Wapnewski, *Der traurige Gott*, pp. 71–9.

The love-potion also forces the lovers to commit new acts of deception and to betray their friends and their allegiance to Marke. Indeed, it makes the 'night-sighted' lovers blind to the day, so that they are no longer aware of the real state of affairs and of the dangers to which they are now exposed.

It is *this* potion which is 'fearful', its remedial properties deriving only from the lovers' misconception of its true nature. And this is the meaning behind Tristan's curse in Act III: the 'poison', by drinking which he hoped to 'recover completely', throws him back into life, 'so that I may never die' (vii. 67). It is worth remarking on the notable paradox whereby the hoped-for poison signifies recovery for Tristan, whereas the true, life-enhancing effect of the potion reduces him, like death, to despair. But it would be wrong to attribute Tristan's curse on the potion to Schopenhauer's philosophy of the denial of the (erotic) will, and hence to interpret it as the renunciation of love, as has recently been done.[62] Admittedly, Wagner speaks of the 'curse on love' in his early sketches for Act III of *Tristan* ('then renewed desire, increasing more and more to consuming longing'),[63] while in the prose draft Tristan breaks out in a desperate cry of 'Accursed love, release me!' (xi. 341). But we are dealing here with a paroxysmal outburst which, like the curse on love in the finished libretto, is worlds removed from the ascetic impassivity involved in denying the will.

The curse is aimed exclusively at a love which becomes a 'torment' through the lover's absence, a love which forces the lovers back into life, denying Isolde death and recalling Tristan from the kingdom of the dead, since only in and with Isolde can he suffer that death which is the ultimate aim of their love, the *Liebestod* or 'love-death' (vii. 50). (In the prose draft we read: 'Isolde—ah! in her alone can I die!': xi. 339.) Tristan's curse is the ultimate expression of what, in Act II, is called 'der Tage | Trennungs-Klage' (the days' | lament of separation: vii. 50). In other words, it is not directed at that love which Tristan and Isolde praise in the second act, but that passion which is estranged by the magic potion and therefore cut off from death. It is directed at the constraints of love as a life force. It is entirely consistent, therefore, that, in the definitive version of the text, the potion is no longer praised but only cursed.

Tristan feels recalled to life by Isolde, who is not yet allowed to follow

[62] Egon Voss, 'Tristan ohne Mythos', in *Programmheft zur konzertanten Aufführung des ersten Tristan-Aufzugs unter Leonard Bernstein im Bayerischen Rundfunk am 11.–13. Januar 1981*. Voss repeats his (to the present writer) problematic interpretation of the love motif in *Tristan* in his otherwise convincing analysis of *Die Meistersinger* in Richard Wagner, *'Die Meistersinger von Nürnberg': Texte, Materialien, Kommentare*, ed. Attila Csampai and Dietmar Holland (Reinbek, 1981), 11; translated into English by Stewart Spencer as 'Wagner's "Meistersinger" as an Opera for the German Bourgeoisie', in *Wagner*, 11 (1990), 41–2.

[63] *Programmheft des 'Tristan'*, p. 29.

him into the 'land of night' (vii. 55), for only in life can she die in him, and he in her.

> Krachend hört' ich
> hinter mir
> schon des Todes
> Thor sich schließen:
> weit nun steht es
> wieder offen;
> der Sonne Strahlen
> sprengt' es auf.          (vii. 62.)

> Crashing once I
> heard the gates
> of oblivion
> close behind me;
> wide once more
> the gates are open;
> the streaming sunlight
> forced them wide.

We are involuntarily reminded here of those classical myths which tell of a return from Hades. 'Here the inferno is thrown open which we can bear to gaze at only when holding Virgil's hand', we read in one of Nietzsche's posthumously published notes written in 1871.[64] Of course, the normal relationship between life and death, the upper world and the underworld, is radically reassessed here. Tristan is, as it were, Orpheus in reverse: it is not Isolde's death which he laments but her life, and he does not follow her to Hades in order to bring her back to the world of the living, but returns from the nocturnal kingdom of the dead to guide her back with him from the world of day. He is not afraid of the terrors of Hades; it is the dazzling light of the sun which torments him:

> mich wirft die Nacht
> dem Tage zu,
> um ewig an meinen Leiden
> der Sonne Auge zu weiden.          (vii. 67.)

> Cast back by night
> to burning day,
> that at pangs in whose pow'r I am maddened
> the eye of the sun may be gladdened.

What a magnificently powerful image this is! It is not the night, nor even the sun, which rejoices, but the night which gladdens the eye of the sun.
  Tristan's deathly faint has so estranged him from the visible world

---

[64] Nietzsche, *Sämtliche Werke*, vii. 324. For reminiscences of the Hades myth, cf. Hans Mayer, 'Tristans Schweigen', in *Richard Wagner: Mitwelt und Nachwelt* (Stuttgart and Zurich, 1978), 220–1.

that he can no longer make out its forms; more than that, he can no longer even grasp where he is. The Shepherd's piping is the only sound he recognizes at the moment of waking. Although his other senses may be clouded and confused, his hearing is unimpaired. 'Sound comes from the night', runs a note of Nietzsche's dating from 1869–70.[65] Sounds are the only thing that Tristan, resurfacing from 'the night of the world', can still identify, for the *alte Weise* or 'old tune' was always a harbinger of death for him: he associates it with the final hours of both his father and his mother, and with what he thought was his own approaching death when he lay stricken by the wound Morold had dealt him. In *Mein Leben* Wagner tells us that the Shepherd's mournful melody was inspired by the overwhelming impression evoked by the melancholy cries of gondoliers on Venice's night-enshrouded waterways. And in his 1870 *Beethoven* essay he asks: 'What could daytime Venice, lit by the sun's bright rays, tell me about itself that that resonant night-time dream could not have brought directly to my consciousness with infinitely greater profundity?' (ix. 74.)

Tristan, too, sinks into a resonant night-time dream in the third act. His perceptions are no more than inner forms. Not even Isolde's ship appears to him in reality (his view of the sea, after all, is blocked off), but with what Novalis called the 'infinite eyes which night has opened within us'.[66] Various fields of vision overlap in the phantasmagoria of a ship transporting Isolde to him. She approaches on a sea of flowers:

> Auf wonniger Blumen
> sanften Wogen
> kommt sie licht
> an's Land gezogen.                    (vii. 69.)
>
> The waves are like
> flow'ring fields before her,
> gently t'ward the land
> they draw her.

And finally, just before his dying cry of 'Isolde', he thinks he hears the light ('Wie hör' ich das Licht?': vii. 73)—the light of life which begins to resonate at the very moment when, as he had longed that it would, it starts to fade from sight. Night, death, and music become a symbolical unity, the forms of the inner and outer worlds grow blurred, what was visible turns to sound, while the audible takes on visual form. In his *Beethoven* essay Wagner set out to interpret this phenomenon on the basis of Schopenhauerian metaphysics. The outer world, he argued,

---

[65] Nietzsche, *Sämtliche Werke*, vii. 70. See also the similar remark of Brentano's at the beginning of this chapter, quoted in Richard Benz (ed.), *Lebenswelt der Romantik* (Munich, 1948), 295.
[66] Novalis, *Werke*, p. 42.

could not be distinguished from the inner world as being something which communicated itself to our sense of hearing ('I myself am the world'). The individual's deluded belief that he is distinct from the 'essence of things outside him' fades away when he hears the world. (It is in this context that Wagner recalls his sound-filled dream in the depths of the Venetian night: ix. 71–7.)

In his short story *Abdias* (which Cosima translated into French in 1859) Adalbert Stifter describes a blind girl whose sight is suddenly restored during a thunderstorm and who, as a result, can no longer distinguish between 'the daytime world and the life of dreams'. She retains a remarkable empathy with the nocturnal world, allowing objects from the external world to merge with her inner visions—a striking link with the final act of Wagner's *Tristan*. 'With others, day is the rule, night the exception: with her it was day, rather, which was the exception. Each of her long and intimate nights extended into the following day . . . It was no doubt because of that long night that she did not like fiery colours, preferring ones, including blue [the Romantic colour *par excellence*], that were cool and subdued.' She 'preferred singing to speaking', and her words were synaesthetic, even, one might say, imbued with symbolic poetry. She heard with her eye and saw with her ear. 'And so she also spoke of purple sounds, and said that these were dearer to her than those which stood erect and which were as offensive to her as bars of red-hot metal . . . Thus she lived in a world of sight and blindness'[67]— just like Tristan on his return from the 'land of night'.

That the world should start to resonate when night begins to fall is a specifically Romantic notion. Eichendorff, for example, writes:

> Schläft ein Lied in allen Dingen,
> Die da träumen fort und fort,
> Und die Welt hebt an zu singen,
> Triffst du nur das Zauberwort.[68]

> Since songs do sleep in every thing
> That dreams and dreams away unheard,
> So shall the world begin to sing
> If you but speak the magic word.

And in his *Gesang zu zweien in der Nacht* Mörike notes how, as soon as

> . . . der freche Tag verstummt,
> Hört man der Erdenkräfte flüsterndes Gedränge,
> Das aufwärts in die zärtlichen Gesänge
> Der reingestimmten Lüfte summt.[69]

---

[67] Adalbert Stifter, *Gesammelte Werke*, ed. Max Stefl (Frankfurt, 1959), ii. 102–3.

[68] Joseph Freiherr von Eichendorff, *Neue Gesamtausgabe der Werke und Schriften*, ed. Gerhart Baumann (Stuttgart, 1957), i. 80.

[69] Eduard Mörike, *Sämtliche Werke/Briefe*, ed. Gerhart Baumann, 2nd edn. (Stuttgart, 1961), i. 55.

The brazen day falls mute at last,
You'll hear earth's forces' whisp'ring throng
Surge upwards as their tender song
Bestirs the pure-toned firmament.

One of the most important poetic reflections of this mystic belief that the night-time world was transformed into music is Stifter's description of the solar eclipse which took place on 8 July 1842. Stifter believed that at the moment when the sun received its 'kiss of death'[70] and the light began to fade, he was able to hear an 'ineffably tragic music of colours and lights' which could not be reproduced in language but only in music. Only Beethoven, he concluded, could have 'translated' it.[71]

As a result of the eclipse, light and colours began to move in a musical way, a movement which gave Stifter the idea for a new art:

Would it not be just as possible to devise a music for the eye using a simultaneity and succession of lights and colours as it is to produce music for the ear using sounds? Until now light and colour have not been used independently but only as an accessory of drawing, for fireworks, transparent pictures, and lighting effects are still too crude a prelude to that music of light for them to deserve to be mentioned here. Might it not be possible that, by a combination of light-chords and melodies, something just as powerful and shattering could be produced as can now be achieved through sounds?[72]

Stifter is astonishingly far-seeing here in his anticipation of the way in which modern art was subsequently to develop. One thinks, for example, of Skryabin's colour keyboard, used in a performance of his *Prométhée* in 1916, which allowed coloured light to be projected in time with the music according to precisely calculated analogies between colour combinations and chords. (The work had first been performed in Moscow in 1911, but without the colour keyboard.) Similar experiments with the music of colour were undertaken, of course, by Vassily Kandinsky in *Der gelbe Klang* (a 'stage composition' written in 1909 and published in *Der blaue Reiter* in 1912) and also by Arnold Schoenberg.

The colour keyboard, it may be added, is an eighteenth-century idea (one thinks, for example, of Louis-Bertrand Castel's 'ocular harpsichord' described at length by Goethe in his *Farbenlehre*) which found a lively echo in the Romantics' theory of synaesthetics. It was, moreover, an idea which reflected speculations on a vowel scale or on what August Wilhelm Schlegel called a 'vowel colour scale', but it also recalls the symbol of a keyboard of images. To quote Novalis: 'The poet uses things and words like the keys of a musical instrument.' Similar considerations are found among the French *symbolistes*, most notably in Rimbaud's sonnet on the different vowels ('A noir, E blanc, I rouge, U

[70] Stifter, *Gesammelte Werke*, vi. 587.
[71] Ibid. 592.          [72] Ibid. 594–5.

vert, O bleu, voyelles'), Mallarmé's 'word keyboard', and René Ghil's idea of an 'audition colorée'.[73] The arts appear as the different registers of one and the same universal keyboard. And it is Wagner and his integration of the arts which, time and again, was the avowed starting-point for the synaesthetic speculations of the *symbolistes* and late Romantic writers on the theory of colour and light in music. Of no one is this more true than of Skryabin. His *Prométhée* was intended not only as a 'poème du feu' but as a mystery of sound, colour, smell, and touch, the realization, as it were, of Isolde's vision at the end of *Tristan*, with its appeal to all the different sense-organs.

It is in the context of all these ideas for a music of colour that we must see Adolphe Appia's attempt to use light in staging Wagner's music dramas. Appia advanced his epoch-making ideas in *La Mise en scène du drame wagnérien*, first published in 1895, where he argued that it was necessary to dispense with the pseudo-realism of painted sets, since the theatre of illusion contravened the specific laws governing our perception of the stage action of the Wagnerian drama, with its musical underpinning. Light—'active', musicalized light—was to make it possible to realize that 'illusion suprême' for which no work is better suited than *Tristan und Isolde*. And it was for a production of *Tristan*—that 'opus metaphysicum', as Nietzsche called it[74]—that Appia designed the sets in 1896.[75] (In the event, the designs were not executed until 1923.) Wagner himself, in his *Beethoven* essay, had spoken of a 'deactivation' of the sense of sight while listening to music, and had shown how, in consequence, visions of the inner, 'night-sighted' eye are superimposed on the natural occurrences of everyday life (ix. 75–6). This idea ought, in fact, to have led Wagner to reject theatrical realism, with its painted flats and costumes. (Only in the case of the spoken drama did he do so, however, when, in his later theoretical remarks, he advocated a theatre of 'allusion'.) Appia sought to free light from its traditional but limited role of lighting backcloths, but at the same time he was concerned to make the sets themselves less inflexible. In this way, he hoped to use stage technology to realize Wagner's metaphorical idea of music breaking down 'the rigid motionless floor of the actual stage into a fluidly yielding ethereal surface sensitive to impressions' (*The Art-Work of the Future:* iii. 157). What we see in Appia's use of light is the triumph of those 'Romantic' qualities described by Friedrich Schlegel in his *Romanze vom Lichte* and *Philosophische Vorlesungen*: light causes space to

[73] On this, see Vordtriede, *Novalis und die französischen Symbolisten*, pp. 168–71.

[74] Nietzsche, *Sämtliche Werke*, i. 479; translated into English by R. J. Hollingdale as *Untimely Meditations* (Cambridge, 1983), 232.

[75] On Appia, see Curt von Westernhagen, *Richard Wagner: Sein Werk, sein Wesen, seine Welt* (Zurich, 1956), 190–2.

dissolve, its billowing movement transforming it from a state of steadfast solidity to one of movement and freedom, while at the same time 'spiritualizing' the physical world in the idealistic sense of the term.[76] As Baudelaire wrote in his 1861 *Tannhäuser* essay:

It would be extremely surprising if sound *were not capable* of suggesting colour, that colours *could not* give an idea of melody, and that sound and colour were not suited to rendering ideas, since things have always been expressed by reciprocal analogy since that day when God created the world as a complex and indivisible unity.[77]

Wagner's music struck the French poet very much as a product of his own imagination (Nietzsche was later to describe Baudelaire as 'a kind of Richard Wagner without the music'[78]), in support of which he cites some lines from his own poem, 'Correspondances', the second strophe of which runs as follows:

> Comme de longs échos qui de loin se confondent
> Dans une ténébreuse et profonde unité,
> Vaste comme la nuit et comme la clarté,
> Les parfums, les couleurs et les sons se répondent.

> Like dwindling echoes gathered far away
> Into a deep and thronging unison
> Huge as the night or as the light of day,
> All scents and sounds and colours meet as one.[79]

It must be added, however, that in the aphorisms to his aesthetic essays of 1849–51 Wagner himself was critical of the search for analogies between colour and sound:

It has happened to me in the case of (intelligent) people who had no appreciation of music whatsoever that they sought to interpret those tonal structures which seemed so inexpressive to them by analogy with the impressions made by colours; but I have never met a musical person who has seen colours when listening to sounds, except in a figurative sense. (xii. 280.)

Wagner repeated this view in conversation with Cosima on 10 November 1879, when they touched on 'the connection between colour and key'. Wagner referred explicitly to Baudelaire on this occasion,

[76] Fritz Strich, *Deutsche Klassik und Romantik*, 5th edn. (Berne and Munich, 1962), 121.

[77] Charles Baudelaire, *Œuvres complètes*, ed. Claude Pichois (Paris, 1976), ii. 784.

[78] Nietzsche, *Sämtliche Werke*, xi. 476 (unpublished note from 1885). Nietzsche repeatedly drew a parallel between Wagner and Baudelaire, most notably in his letter to Peter Gast of 26 Feb. 1888. Here he also quotes Wagner's letter to Baudelaire, which he appears not to have known previously. (Evidently Baudelaire never played a role in his conversations with Wagner; see Nietzsche, *Werke*, ed. Karl Schlechta, 6th edn. (Munich, 1969), iii. 1280.) Cf. Karl Pestalozzi, 'Nietzsches Baudelaire-Rezeption', *Nietzsche-Studien*, 7 (1978), 158–88.

[79] Baudelaire, *Les Fleurs du mal*, p. 13 (IV); translated into English by Richard Wilbur in *The Flowers of Evil*, ed. Mathews, p. 12.

saying that he 'very wittily translated the Prelude to *Lohengrin* into colours, but he was not a musician'. There is little doubt that Wagner was thinking of the passage from the *Tannhäuser* essay quoted above, a passage which does indeed relate to the *Lohengrin* Prelude. In the case of *Tristan*, Wagner himself argued that the work had 'a colour all its own, it is mauve, a sort of lilac' (*CT*, 3 June 1878). And is not that mighty synaesthetic hymn which brings the work to an end—Isolde's Transfiguration—a confirmation of Baudelaire's own aesthetic? These closing pages could also be given the title 'Correspondances'. Certainly Baudelaire would have sensed his own affinity with them.

Once Isolde has sunk down over Tristan's body, she no longer speaks, being far removed from all that is going on around her. The arrival of King Marke's ship and Kurwenal's death pass her by, unnoticed. Only now does she speak again, ignoring Brangäne's questioning, but fixing her eyes on Tristan 'with growing transfiguration',[80] raising her voice not in lamentation but in a panegyric directed less at her dead lover than at the cosmos as a whole. In accordance with the pantheistic belief that (to quote Leo Spitzer) 'two souls that have consumed one another in yearning for each other merge with the universe',[81] Isolde sees herself united with Tristan in death's ecstasy. He, of course, disappears from her field of vision in the second half of her peroration, their union appearing now as no more than a reassimilation with those elements to which he has returned in a flood of perfume and sound, fading away like some dying breath or sound of distant music, a 'sweet breath' and wondrous 'melody' in one. (It is the first half of this closing section which describes Tristan's dispersal among the elements.)

Isolde is now, quite literally, 'beyond herself'. She is in that state of 'clairvoyance' which Wagner repeatedly describes in his aesthetic writings and in which the real world sinks down like a wall before the inner eye, revealing a view of the deeper, true nature of the world. But if Isolde is oblivious to her surroundings, who are the 'friends' to whom she appeals with almost ritualistic regularity: 'Do you see it, friends?'— 'Do you not see it?' It is impossible not to be reminded here of the *eidete* (See!) with which the heroes of Greek tragedy appeal to the attendant chorus in scenes of high emotion (Antigone's farewell lament is perhaps the most obvious example of this). But who is Isolde addressing? Certainly not Marke, Brangäne, or Melot, whose arrival she has not even noticed. It is an invisible chorus of all those who are dedicated to night. That which they see is hidden from the everyday eye; for 'to see' here means to perceive with every sublimated sense.

---

[80] See Eulenburg pocket score, p. 994; Dover score, p. 633; Peters full score, p. 633; Breitkopf & Härtel vocal score (V. A. 1262), p. 269.
[81] Spitzer, *Eine Methode*, p. 47.

The all-sensuous eye perceives Tristan's soul rise up and leave his body. This separation of body and soul is expressed as a glint of light streaming from his eye, as a breath of air wafting gently over his lips, and as a mysteriously beautiful melody rising up from his body. The harmony of the spheres, momentarily hushed, now rings out afresh from Tristan's breast (this, too, is a motif from Romantic poems of the night):

> Höre ich nur
> diese Weise,
> die so wunder-
> voll und leise,
> Wonne klagend
> Alles sagend,
> mild versöhnend,
> aus ihm tönend,
> auf sich schwingt,
> in mich dringt,
> hold erhallend
> um mich klingt?          (vii. 80.)[82]

> Can it be
> that I alone
> hear this wondrous
> glorious tone?
> Softly stealing,
> all revealing,
> mildly glowing,
> from him flowing,
> through me pouring,
> rising, soaring,
> boldly singing,
> round me ringing?

(There is no mistaking how close these verses are, stylistically, to the short lines of Goethe's *Faust*, a point to which we shall return below.) There arises the impression of a sea of sound enveloping Isolde, but, in the following lines, this image is overlaid by that of billowing air and clouds of perfume. Just as Tristan, in his feverish vision, saw Isolde approach on an ocean of flowers, so she feels herself sinking finally into a sea of blossom. In the earliest prose sketches we read: 'Isolde bent over Tristan, recovers consciousness and listens with growing delight to intensifying melodies of love which seem to rise towards her from Tristan's soul, swelling like a sea of blossom—into which she plunges to sink down and die.'[83] Here we already find that overlapping of the two

---

[82] When Wagner set this passage to music, he altered the last four lines to: 'in mich dringet, | auf sich schwinget, | hold erhallend, | um mich klinget'.

[83] *Programmheft des 'Tristan'*, p. 29.

different fields of vision associated with rising and falling, an overlap which is so typical of these closing pages of the work and which evokes the idea of billows rolling up and down.

Isolde feels enveloped by the seething and surging of sounds, breezes, waves, and perfumes: the constant repetition of the particle 'um' (around), both as prefix and as preposition, suggests some elemental medium which encloses her on every side and into which she and Tristan both dissolve. This disintegration is described in terms of a perfume-laden exhalation, a 'sinking and drowning' in 'the world-breath's wafting universe' with which the 'sweet breath' from Tristan's lips is mingled: mystic union with the dead Tristan becomes communion with that element which floods from within him, union with that divine universe which, in the musically and poetically spellbinding rhythms of the closing lines, takes on physical form, revealing itself as a powerfully pulsating wave-like movement which finally ebbs away.

There is no suggestion here, Leo Spitzer argues, of any movement upwards, but rather of a sinking downwards. In this, the work appears to differ from *Der fliegende Holländer*, where two souls rise heavenwards 'in transfigured form'. But, as we have seen, Spitzer's claim is not strictly true, since upward and downward movements do overlap in the later work, with Isolde's final note, the upward octave leap to the word 'Lust' (bliss), with its pianissimo suspiration, reintroducing, as it were (and as Spitzer himself supposed), a sense of ascent after the sinking expressed in the previous lines. At all events, it is clear from Cosima's *Diaries* that Wagner interpreted Isolde's transfiguration as an apotheosis, which suggests that he imagined a movement similar to, rather than different from, the upwards movement in the final tableau of *Der fliegende Holländer*, although it must be conceded, of course, that the overlapping of the two fields of vision means that all sense of space is essentially abolished here.

On several occasions Wagner compared Isolde with Titian's *Assunta*, a work which fascinated him anew each time he visited Venice. Cosima's diary entry for 22 October 1882 contains the remarkable statement that Wagner even denied 'that the *Assunta* is the Mother of God; it is Isolde, he says, in the apotheosis of love'. Possibly Wagner had a vague recollection here of a remark which Cosima had made three years previously: on 4 September 1879, while Wagner was working on his 'Religion and Art' treatise, in which he had dealt at length with Raphael's *Sistine Madonna*, she had expressed the opinion that 'the beauty of Raphael [is] free of desire; I compare Titian's *Assumption of the Virgin*, on the other hand, with Isolde's transfiguration'. In the later conversation, too, Titian's *Assunta* is compared with the *Sistine Madonna*, this time by Wagner himself: in the latter, he maintained, 'one sees, for all the consummate beauty, her utter unapproachability'.

Whereas, for Wagner, Raphael's Madonna symbolized that redemption which follows from the 'innermost denial of the world' and of the erotic will (to quote from 'Religion and Art': x. 217), Titian's *Assunta* represented redemption as the sublimated 'ecstasy of love' (*CT*, 8 December 1880). If this is so, we must question the link which Peter Wapnewski has sought to establish—with remarkable perspicuity, it should be added—between the inspirational experience of Titian's painting reported in *Mein Leben* and the renunciatory theme of *Die Meistersinger* (especially evident in the figure of Sachs):[84] for Wagner, the *Assunta* embodied not the denial of the will but that mystical intensification of erotic love which finds expression in Isolde's *Liebestod*.

Time and again, from *Tannhäuser* onwards, we find traces of a remarkable veneration for the Virgin Mary in Wagner's œuvre. In his 1867–8 essay, 'German Art and German Politics', he even defends the 'dogma of the Immaculate Conception' which had 'recently been elevated to canonical status' and which, much to the indignation of the Protestant world, Pope Pius IX (whom Wagner normally vituperated) had proclaimed in 1854. Wagner, by contrast, was convinced that the Catholics of the Romance world were incapable of understanding this dogma. He even reproached them for not taking it seriously enough. There had, he claimed, been 'many a frivolous witticism' on the subject in the French and Italian press, whereas 'the greatest German poet had concluded his greatest poem with the beatific invocation of the Mater Gloriosa as the loftiest ideal of spotless purity' (viii. 101).

The fact that Wagner took over two lines from the invocation of the Mater Gloriosa at the end of *Faust*, and repeated them, almost word for word, in *Tristan*, has largely escaped attention. Goethe's Chorus of Penitent Women apostrophizes the Queen of Heaven as 'Du Ohnegleiche, | Du Gnadenreiche!' (Thou, mercy bearing, | Past all comparing: ll. 12035–6), while Gretchen's prayer some lines later begins with almost identical words, 'Neige, neige, | Du Ohnegleiche, | Du Strahlenreiche' (Look down, look down, | Thou rich in heaven's renown, | Thou who art past comparing: ll. 12069–71). Wagner's affinity with these lines is clear from an entry in Cosima's diary for 27 June 1878: '"Look down, thou, mercy bearing", he whispers to me as we part in the afternoon.'[85] And in their hymn to love in Act II Tristan and Isolde sing: 'Ohne Gleiche! | Überreiche!' (Past comparing! | Richness bearing!: vii. 36). This example may also serve to show how far the rhythmic structure of the lines in *Tristan* is inspired by the short lines in *Faust*, and especially by those in the final scene, where they are very much lines from an imaginary opera.

[84] Wapnewski, *Der traurige Gott*, pp. 89–113.
[85] Wagner was particularly fond of seeing Cosima as a Madonna figure: see *CT*, 25 Apr. 1882 and *passim*.

There is also a reminiscence of the Assumption in Isolde's final speech, but, remarkably, with reference not to herself but to Tristan:

> seht ihr's nicht?
> Immer lichter
> wie er leuchtet
>
> .    .    .
>
> Stern-umstrahlet
> hoch sich hebt?          (vii. 79.)[86]
>
> See you not?
> Ever brighter,
> brightly shining
>
> .    .    .
>
> borne in starlight
> high above?

In the final scene of *Faust* Doctor Marianus sees the Mater Gloriosa in the midst of the female saints soaring high above him:

> Die Herrliche mitteninn
> Im Strahlenkranze,
> Die Himmelskönigin,
> Ich seh's am Glanze.          (ll. 11993–6.)[87]
>
> With them the heavenly Queen,
> Majesty tender,
> In wreath of stars is seen,
> Clear in her splendour.

The wreath of stars is the Assunta's traditional attribute. Even today, the introit for the Feast of the Assumption of the Blessed Virgin Mary contains the words: 'And there appeared a great wonder in heaven, a woman clothed with the sun, and the moon under her feet, and upon her head a crown of twelve stars.' (Revelation 12: 1.) This is the woman of the Apocalypse, whose symbols are transferred to the Virgin Mary. The same symbols are also found in the eighteenth century, when they were related to the allegory of night (as with Edward Young) or to the Queen of Night (as in Mozart's *Die Zauberflöte*). (In Goethe's and Schinkel's famous designs for the entry of the 'star-blazing Queen', the latter is depicted as a Virgin on the Crescent.) And, finally, the fifth of Novalis's *Hymnen an die Nacht* culminates in an appeal to the Mother of God: 'To thee, O Mary, hearts | Have risen in their thousands.'[88]

---

[86] The suspension points indicate two lines ('wie er minnig | immer mächt'ger') published in Wagner's *Collected Writings* but not set to music.

[87] On the significance of the Virgin Mary in *Faust*, II, see Ilse Graham, '"Fiat mihi": Der *Faust*-Schluß in mittelalterlicher Sicht', *Atken des VI. Internationalen Germanistenkongresses I* (Berne, 1981), 85–113. (This article is surprisingly reminiscent of Wagner at many points.) All translations from *Faust* are by Philip Wayne (Harmondsworth, 1959), 284–7.          [88] Novalis, *Werke*, p. 50.

There is no doubt that Wagner's 'Mariolatry' is a question not of faith but of art, and that it accords with his conviction, expressed in 'Religion and Art', that it was 'reserved to art to salvage the kernel of religion, inasmuch as the mythical images which religion would wish to be believed as true are apprehended in art for their symbolic value, and through ideal representation of those symbols art reveals the concealed deep truth within them' (x. 211). What Wagner saw as the 'truth' in the case of the *Assunta* emerges from a long conversation which he and Cosima held in Venice on 25 April 1882, when they stood before the Titian canvas in the Belle Arti: 'The glowing head of the Virgin Mary recalls to him his idea of the sexual urge: this unique and mighty force, now freed of all desire, the Will enraptured and redeemed.'

The idea which Wagner 'recalled' on this occasion is, I believe, self-evident. It was his attempt to revise Schopenhauer's 'Metaphysics of Sexual Love',[89] which he undertook in 1858 while working on the score of *Tristan* and which assumed the form of a letter to the philosopher. In this letter (which was neither completed nor sent) he seeks to expound his view that it is 'our predisposition to sexual love' which 'represents a way to salvation leading to self-knowledge and self-denial of the will'. Wagner emphasizes that Schopenhauer alone had provided him with the 'material for those concepts which allow me to communicate my insight along philosophical lines . . . and if I attempt to clarify my own thoughts on the matter, it is only by trusting in what I have learnt from you yourself' (xii. 291).

The implications of this 'correction' to, and extension of, Schopenhauer's 'system' are spelt out in a letter to Mathilde Wesendonck of 1 December 1858: 'It is a question, you see, of pointing out the path to salvation, which has not been recognized by any philosopher, and especially not by Sch[openhauer], but which involves a total pacification of the will through love, and not through any abstract human love, but a love engendered on the basis of sexual love.' Just as supreme understanding comes to us when we are in a state of 'enthusiastic joy and ecstasy' (and not in a state of total emotional calm,

---

[89] This part of Schopenhauer's system must have been a constant irritation to Wagner, since the former makes no attempt to conceal his sarcasm in exposing the lofty feeling of love as an illusion, a pure ruse on the part of the will and as a 'means to its ends' (*Sämtliche Werke*, iii. 632; English trans. (Payne, *World as Will*), ii. 551), those ends being the preservation of the human species. None the less, a number of passages in Schopenhauer's 'Metaphysics of Sexual Love' provided inspiration for Wagner's *Tristan*, as when the philosopher comments as follows on Calderón's *Zenobia the Great*: 'Here honour, which hitherto outweighed every interest, is driven from the field, as soon as sexual love, i.e. the interest of the species comes into play, and sees a decided advantage before it. For this is infinitely superior to any interest of mere individuals, however important it be. Therefore, honour, duty, and loyalty yield to this alone, after they have withstood every other temptation, even the threat of death.' (Ibid. iii. 633; English trans. ii. 552.) For Schopenhauer, of course, this *amor vincit omnia* is merely a ruse on the part of the will, in other words, the means whereby to preserve the species.

as Schopenhauer believed), so Wagner argued that in love lay 'the possibility of raising oneself above the individual impulse of the will to a point where total mastery over the latter is achieved, and the generic will becomes fully conscious of itself, a consciousness which, at this level, is necessarily synonymous with total pacification'.[90] This is the meaning behind Wagner's remark to Cosima that the sexual urge is 'enraptured' and freed of all desire.

This remark also contains the key to our understanding of Isolde's 'declaration of love' at the end of *Tristan*. It is not renunciation, not the ascetic denial of the will, which is the *summum bonum*, but its ecstasy and redemption. It is an idea extrapolated from the heart of Schopenhauer's philosophy but diametrically opposed to its ethical aim. That the highest metaphysical knowledge is reserved for the lover, and not for him who renounces love, is clear from King Marke's blindness. It is Marke who, by renouncing sexual congress with Isolde ('der mein Wille | nie zu nahen wagte, | der mein Wunsch | Ehrfurcht-scheu entsagte' (literally, 'whom my will [!] | never dared approach, | whom my wish renounced | in reverential awe'): vii. 54), corresponds to Schopenhauer's ideal of the ascetic saint; but it is also Marke who, precisely because he renounces love, is denied an insight into the essence of the world.

But is the telos of *Tristan* not to fade away into 'nothing', to quote the final word of Schopenhauer's principal work? Does not the sense of ebbing away, in the final lines of Isolde's peroration, the stilling of that surging movement which had invested its earlier section, express that extinction of all desire in nirvana which, according to Schopenhauer, could be attained only through renunciation? Wagner's text precludes this conclusion. For the state of nirvana coincides here with that of the 'enraptured will'. This idea of Wagner's reveals a fundamental difference between *his* assessment of the will and that propounded by the Sage of Frankfurt. Schopenhauer's pessimism gives way to a drunken affirmation of the world which finds overwhelming musical and poetical expression at the end of *Tristan und Isolde*. Isolde's transfiguration is a *trionfo della morte* (to quote the title of D'Annunzio's novel), the triumphal progress of the senses into death's eternal night of love. 'Love in *Tristan* is not to be interpreted as Schopenhauerian, but as Empedoclean', Nietzsche wrote in one of his posthumously published fragments from 1875: it was 'the symptom and guarantee of an eternal unity'.[91]

[90] *Richard Wagner an Mathilde Wesendonk: Tagebuchblätter und Briefe 1853–1871*, ed. Wolfgang Golther, 44th edn. (Leipzig, 1914), 130–1; English translation from *Selected Letters of Richard Wagner*, ed. Stewart Spencer and Barry Millington (London, 1987), 432.

[91] Nietzsche, *Sämtliche Werke*, viii. 191.

With the final bar of *Tristan* Wagner 'closed the door on Romanticism', Richard Strauss remarked in a letter to Curt von Westernhagen in 1935. And in a diary entry of 1946 he expressed the belief that Eichendorff could never have guessed that, only a few years after his death in 1857, a work would appear that 'absorbed the whole of Romanticism, leading to its supreme culmination, redeeming all . . . the songs of the night by the Schlegels, Novalis, Brentano, Arnim . . . in an immortal A flat major love duet, and placing a divine coping-stone upon it with the most beautifully orchestrated B major chord in the history of music'.[92] At the end of the chapter 'Tragik und Ende' in Rudolf Bach's book, *Tragik und Größe der deutschen Romantik*, published that same year, Strauss appended four bars of music (reproduced here in facsimile) in which the beginning and end of *Tristan*—for Strauss, the 'beginning and end of all music'—were entwined with one another:[93]

[92] Quoted in Curt von Westernhagen, *Richard Wagner*, pp. 180, 532–3.
[93] Reproduced from Strauss's *Nachlaß* by kind permission of his heirs.

# 19

## Summation and Consummation:
### *Parsifal*

> Oh, art and religion are just what is left in human beings of the
> monkey's tail, the remains of an ancient culture.
>
> Wagner to Cosima, 27 June 1878.

One of the earliest Wagnerians was Hans Christian Andersen. An
ardent admirer of the composer's, he visited the latter in Zurich in 1855
on Liszt's recommendation, and left an enthusiastic account of the
meeting in the second part of his autobiography.[1] In one of his fairy-
tales, *The Garden of Eden*, he recounts the story of a Prince who, from
childhood onwards, is consumed by the wish to regain Paradise and
abrogate the original sin of tasting the forbidden fruit. 'Why, why, did
Eve pick from the Tree of Knowledge! Why did Adam eat of the
forbidden fruit! If it had been me, it would never have happened—and
sin would never have come into the world!' As good fortune would have
it, the Prince makes the acquaintance of the four winds, and the East
Wind tells him that, following the Fall, the Garden of Eden had sunk
beneath the earth; it was now inhabited by a Fairy Princess, 'and there,
too, is the Island of the Blest, where death never comes'. At his earnest
entreaty, the East Wind transports the Prince to Asia, to an underground
kingdom where the Garden of Eden continues to bloom (Andersen is
clearly following the German Romantics' myth of the underworld here).

The Princess invites him into her castle and, in one of the windows,
shows him a tableau vivant burnt into the pane by Time, depicting
Paradise before the expulsion of Adam and Eve. This is the Prince's
opportunity to pre-empt the loss of Paradise. 'As long as you don't, like
Adam, allow yourself to be tempted to do what is forbidden, you may
certainly remain here.' And what is he forbidden to do? Every evening
the Princess, against her will, has to appear before him in some new

---

[1] This was revealed by Lotte Eskelund, '"Groß durch Verstand und Willen": Andersens
Begegnung mit Richard Wagner in Zürich', *Neue Zürcher Zeitung*, 176, 2–3 Aug. 1975; see also
Martin Gregor-Dellin, *Richard Wagner: Sein Leben, sein Werk, sein Jahrhundert* (Munich and Zurich,
1980), 403–4; translated into English by J. Maxwell Brownjohn as *Richard Wagner: His Life, his
Work, his Century* (London 1983), 263. Andersen's tale, *Paradisets have*, appears in H. C. Andersen,
*Eventyr og historier*, ed. Hans Brix (Copenhagen, 1953), 147–60; the English translation by R. P.
Keigwin is from Hans Christian Andersen, *Fairy Tales* (Odense, 1955), ii. 215–44.

seductive guise beneath the Tree of Knowledge. But if he kisses her lips, the paradisal vision will disappear in an instant, and 'sorrow and tribulation' will be his lot.

And the Fairy led him into a great hall of transparent white lilies ... The loveliest girls, slender and graceful, clad in billowy gauze that revealed the beauty of their limbs, swayed in the dance and sang of the sweets of living and how they would never die and the Garden of Eden would bloom forever. And the sun went down, the whole sky became a sheet of gold, which gave the lilies a tinge of the loveliest rose. And the Prince drank of the foaming wine handed him by the girls, and he felt a happiness he had never known before. He saw how the far end of the hall opened. There stood the Tree of Knowledge in a shining splendour that dazzled his eyes. The singing that came from it was soft and beautiful like the voice of his mother, and it was as though she sang to him, 'My child, my darling child!'.

His senses confused by seductive scents and sounds, the Prince follows the Fairy as she beckons him after her:

And at every step the Prince's cheeks burned hotter, his blood ran faster. 'I must!' he said. 'There's no sin in that—cannot possibly be! Why not follow beauty and joy? I only want to see her asleep. It will be none the worse, as long as I don't kiss her; and I shan't do that! I am strong, with a firm will!' And the Fairy threw off her glittering robe, bent back the branches, and a moment later was hidden among them. 'Not yet have I sinned', said the Prince, 'nor will I!'— and he drew aside the branches. There she lay, already asleep, beautiful as only the Fairy in the Garden of Eden can be. She smiled in her dreams, and as he bent over her he saw the tears trembling between her eyelashes. 'Is it for me you weep?' he whispered. 'O loveliest of women, do not weep! Now at last I have learnt to know the happiness of Eden. It streams through my blood, through my thoughts; in my mortal limbs I can feel angelic power and immortal life. Doom me to eternal night—one moment like this is wealth enough!' And he kissed the tear from her eye, his mouth touched hers ...

Everything collapses around him with a crash of thunder. Dismayed, the Prince realizes that he has 'sinned like Adam!' As he opens his eyes, he sees the lost Paradise sink into the dark night and reappear in the sky as the morning star. The black-winged figure of Death appears to the sinner, and marks him out with his scythe.

Although Andersen's fairy stories were read to the children at Tribschen and Wahnfried, it is unclear whether Wagner knew *The Garden of Eden* at first hand. The motivic parallels are certainly remarkable and cannot be altogether explained by the fact that both Andersen and Wagner owed many of their ideas to the German Romantics. (The Danish poet's enthusiasm for Wagner was sparked off, significantly, by *Tannhäuser*, that most Romantically indebted of all Wagner's operas.) The sexual nature of original sin, the disillusionment at the moment of the kiss, the sudden disappearance of the Garden of Eden, the flowermaidens, the reluctant seductress, the erotic mother-fixation—all these motifs recur in Wagner's *Parsifal*, albeit differently motivated.

In his letter to King Ludwig II of 7 September 1865 Wagner takes up the question which his 'royal friend' had put to him two days earlier on reading the prose draft of *Parzival*:[2] Why is it not until Kundry kisses him that Parzival is converted?' Wagner rehearses the traditional mythological account of Paradise, the serpent, and the Tree of Knowledge, before going on to explain that Eve's seduction of Adam is re-enacted in the kiss which Kundry (that 'old primeval woman' as Wagner described her to Cosima on 17 April 1878) implants on Parsifal's lips, while Adam's original sin is repeated by Amfortas. At the same time, Kundry is like the serpent in Paradise. Just as the latter promises Eve: 'Ye shall be as gods, knowing good and evil' (Genesis 3: 5), so Kundry, even in the 1865 prose draft, invites Parsifal: 'Enfold me now with your love and this very day you will be God Himself!' (xi. 409.) Christ's redemptive act is mirrored by Parsifal's act of salvation in redeeming Amfortas and Kundry. Wagner's formula is 'Adam—Eve: Christ . . . Anfortas[3]—Kundry: Parzival'. (It is, however, an analogy which, as Wagner emphasizes, should be drawn only 'with considerable caution'.[4]) As a result of Kundry's kiss, Parsifal becomes 'Welt-hellsichtig' (literally, 'having a clear insight into the world': x. 361): he becomes conscious of sin and enters the ranks of those who are *scientes bonum et malum*. Not yet having tasted the fruit of the Tree of Knowledge, he knew nothing of good or evil until he was kissed by Kundry. (This is a distinction which he heard for the first time in Act I, although on that occasion he had not understood it. To his question: 'Who is afraid of me?', Kundry had replied: 'The wicked', to which Parsifal had responded in surprise: 'Were those who threatened me wicked?' And, completely confused by Gurnemanz's laughter, he had then gone on to ask: 'Who is good?' (x. 337).)

This sense of yearning for a lost Paradise, for a love neither corrupted by *concupiscentia* nor interpreted as a fatal and demonic constraint passed on from one generation to another, had already been a poetic motif in *Die Meistersinger*. Walther's Prize Song is the dream not of Paradise regained but of a Paradise which has not yet been lost and which can be

---

[2] The familiar spelling was not adopted until Mar. 1877 (see *CT*, 14 Mar. 1877).

[3] The forms 'Anfortas' and 'Amfortas' coexist in the manuscript tradition of Wolfram's *Parzival*. Wagner later settled on the second alternative and shifted the stress from the first to the second syllable.

[4] Cf. his criticism of Wolzogen's essay, '*Bühnenweihfestspiel*': Wolzogen had 'gone too far in calling Parsifal a reflection of the Redeemer: "I didn't give the Redeemer a thought when I wrote it" '( see *CT*, 20 October 1878).

translated directly from his dream into life: the Fall of Man has been avoided. Unlike the Prince's illusory vision in Andersen's tale of *The Garden of Eden*, Walther's dream is not destroyed—the comedy is more fairy-tale-like than the fairy-tale—but provided with a contrapuntal accompaniment in the form of Sachs's popular melody about Eve's wickedness, the expulsion from Paradise, and man's obligation to work in the sweat of his brow: in moments of great good fortune and happiness, an angel's ladder will lead the artist out of his misery and into a new 'artificial' Paradise bought at the cost of his tears. Hans Sachs has, as it were, already received Kundry's kiss: he knows that love is *Wahn*,[5] and that the sinless carnality of Walther and Eva/Eve is a fairy-tale dream. The true—eternal—Eve returns in Kundry. The inherited compulsion to commit evil is a force to which the human race is condemned by *eros*, the focus of the world-will, and can be resisted only by renunciation. The metaphysics of love which finds affirmative expression at the end of *Tristan* appears to be rescinded not only in *Parsifal* but also, to a certain extent, in the music drama which preceded it, *Die Meistersinger von Nürnberg*. 'Hans Sachs was wise and would not | Through King Marke's torments go' (vii. 254). Marke, too, abjures love—as he himself admits, his 'will' renounced Isolde 'in reverential awe' (vii. 54)—but in this case, of course, we are not dealing with an act of renunciation stemming from the highest metaphysical insight, as is the case with Sachs and Parsifal. As a result, it pales into insignificance beside the awareness of love *and* death vouchsafed to Tristan and Isolde.

Although we have described Wagner as having 'revoked' the ideas contained in *Tristan und Isolde*,[6] we do not mean to imply that he simply dismissed as a momentary aberration his revision of Schopenhauer's metaphysics of sexual love (a revision undertaken in the light of *Tristan und Isolde* and developed both in his letter to Mathilde Wesendonck of 1 December 1858 and in his fragmentary letter to the philosopher himself). His conversation with Cosima on 25 April 1882 (in other words, *after* completing *Parsifal*) makes it clear that he still espoused the philosophical belief in redemption *through* love, not *from* it. Wagner's own 'Metaphysics of Sexual Love' is intelligible, therefore, only as something contradictory, and certainly does not lead to an unambiguous philosophical solution, presenting, rather, an irreconcilable contrast between Schopenhauer's original metaphysics of love and his own

---

[5] See Chap. 16 n. 2.

[6] Hans Mayer (*Richard Wagner: Mitwelt und Nachwelt* (Stuttgart and Zurich, 1978)) was one of the first writers to describe *Parsifal* as a 'recantation' (p. 170), a description which is itself an allusion to Leverkühn's 'recantation' of the Ninth Symphony in Thomas Mann's *Doktor Faustus*. A similar view has been advanced more recently by Peter Wapnewski, *Tristan der Held Richard Wagners* (Berlin, 1981), 173–91.

proposed alternative to it. The projected sequence of works—*Tristan, Die Sieger, Parsifal*—does, however, give the Schopenhauerian original clear predominance, although Wagner, of course, did not adopt the tone of metaphysical cynicism with which the Sage of Frankfurt dismissed love's ecstasy as a mere ploy on the part of the will to preserve the species. This essential aspect of Schopenhauer's 'Metaphysics of Sexual Love' remained without significance for Wagner. But if we accept that there is a conceptional consistency in the order in which Wagner's works were planned, we shall find it hard to escape the conclusion that, in terms of their metaphysical principles, it was Schopenhauer who triumphed over Wagner in the latter's dramatic œuvre.

From the very outset, *eros* was Janus-faced for Wagner, half divine and half demonic. In the dialectical and dramatic interplay of light, the spectator's gaze is directed now at one aspect, now at the other, often in one and the same work—most notably in *Tannhäuser.* Just how close the blessings and the curse of love are to one another became clear when we looked at *Tristan und Isolde.* There, of course, it was the redemptive power of love which triumphed unequivocally at the end, in spite of the inevitable curse placed upon it in the earlier course of the opera, when the magic potion had forced the lovers back from the brink of death into the arms of a life of intrigue and suffering. This, however, is the only one of Wagner's works to end with a paean to love which is in no way overshadowed. But the *dramatist* in Wagner concluded otherwise: renunciation was the consummation devoutly to be wished. The Grail Castle is the Utopian emblem of a world from which original sin has been exorcized by neutralizing eroticism. But is this only one of the masks assumed by Wagner the *histrio*—Wagner the erotomaniac, with his Klingsor-like propensity for denying sexuality and, at the same time, his magic gift for conjuring up a hell of wanton pleasure? The yearning for a world released from the sway of erotic love is one which we find, of course, precisely in those creative individuals who have felt its power most of all, a power which drives them to the very brink of self-destruction. Even Casanova wrote a fantastic novel, *Icosaméron*, first published in 1788, which locates Paradise in a subterranean realm whose inhabitants are the Megamicri, their men- and womenfolk joined together as hermaphroditic beings. Male and female eroticism is thus effectively neutralized. These double beings lead prelapsarian lives, for (to quote Ernesto Grassi) man 'is not yet conscious of his sexuality and knows no instinctive passion'.[7]

This negation of the erotic element in man, the ban and curse on love, are themes which recur with leitmotivic regularity throughout the composer's œuvre, from *Das Liebesverbot* of 1834–6 to the projected

[7] Casanova, *Memoiren* (Reinbek, 1958), i. 304 (Afterword).

Buddhist opera *Die Sieger*. Based on Shakespeare's *Measure for Measure*, the first of these operas centres on Friedrich, the governor of Palermo, who, as 'love's enemy' (xi. 97), is subjected to Young German opprobrium for his puritanical ban on public displays of love, but, although he denies erotic love, he is none the less (or precisely because of that fact) firmly in its power. As such, the governor is more than a mere caricature of some German Puritan discomfited by *italianità*. His monologue in Act II contains astonishing pre-echoes of Amfortas's inner conflict:

> Was hat ein Weib aus dir gemacht!
> Armseliger, wohin ist das System,
> das du so wohl geordnet, hingeflohen?
> Ein Hauch von ihrem warmen Atem nur,
> und wie ein frost'ger Wintertraum zerflossen!
>
> .    .    .
>
> Ja, glühend, wie des Südens Hauch
> brennt mir die Flamme in der Brust;
> verzehrt mich auch die wilde Glut,
> genieß' ich doch die heiße Lust!                    (xi. 106.)

> What has a woman done to you?
> Where is that system now which you,
> You wretch, once ordered with such care?
> The merest sigh of her warm breath
> And lo! it melts like winter's dreams!
>
> .    .    .
>
> Yea, glowing like the southern breeze,
> A flame burns brightly in my breast;
> Though wildest ardour may consume
> Me, I'll enjoy love's keen delights.

The ban on enjoyment in love, imposed on the poet by courtly convention, the condemnation and anathemization of sexuality (the Venusberg as hell, and the curse which the pope calls down on the hero), are central to *Tannhäuser*. A ban on love of a different kind is implied by Torbern's words to Elis in *Die Bergwerke zu Falun*: 'If he wished to behold the true wonders of the subterranean world and obtain a glimpse of the Mountain Queen herself, he must put from his mind all thoughts of love.' (xi. 128.) (In this context, the 'subterranean world' symbolizes art, that 'kingdom of the dead' which demands the sacrifice of life.) Another character who denies love is Alberich, but his curse is directed only at love itself, not sexual desire: 'Erzwäng' ich nicht Liebe, | doch listig erzwäng' ich mir Lust?' (Though I cannot gain love by coercion, | I may gain its pleasures by cunning: v. 212). (It is in this way—by obtaining pleasure by force, in other words, by rape—that Alberich fathers Hagen.) That Tristan's curse on the potion was originally a 'curse on love' was mentioned in the previous chapter. *Parsifal* (and the related project for *Die Sieger*, which was also intended to centre upon a seduction scene) is virtually a summation of all these motivic variants.

In the course of a conversation with Cosima on 12 June 1878, Wagner drew a revealing comparison between Parsifal and Schiller's Maid of Orleans in terms of the ban on, and victory over, love. Both characters had been 'deprived forever of sensual urges by a great impression made on them in their adolescent years'. In a later conversation on the subject of the myth of Eros and Anteros, Wagner remarked: 'Anteros is Parsifal' (*CT*, 20 September 1881). This latter is the radical antithesis of all those Wagnerian characters who risk their lives for love and lose the wager. (Wagner was in error when he imagined Anteros triumphing over sexual love; Anteros is, in fact, the god of reciprocal love who avenged those lovers who were spurned.)

Love as *eros* is contrasted in *Parsifal* with love as *agape*, that love which, according to Schopenhauer, 'has its innermost origin in a certain degree of seeing through the *principium individuationis*'. Just as *eros* is egoism, so *agape* is compassion, grounded in the Vedantic insight: 'Tat twam asi' (This art thou!). 'Whoever is able to declare this to himself with clear knowledge and firm inward conviction about every creature with whom he comes into contact', writes Schopenhauer, 'is certain of all virtue and bliss, and is on the direct path to salvation.'[8] Such a person, we may add, borrowing a phrase from *Parsifal*, is 'made wise by pity'. Paradoxically, Parsifal himself experiences the sensation of *tat twam asi*—and thus becomes 'Welt-hellsichtig'—at the very moment when he is kissed by Kundry. This kiss—the experience of egotistical *eros*—allows him to see through the *principium individuationis* in a sudden flash of insight, arousing in him that 'clairvoyance of pain' which Gerhart Hauptmann (perhaps with *Parsifal* in mind) once described as an underlying idea in his own tragic view of the world.

It has repeatedly been observed that, in almost all its characters and the essential elements of its plot, *Parsifal* constitutes a recapitulation of Wagner's earlier œuvre.[9] But not only is it a recapitulation, it can also be seen as a *contrafactum* and (as is clear from the motif of compassionate love already discussed) as a polar opposite. A mere glance at Cosima's *Diaries* for the time when Wagner was working on the score shows the remarkable frequency with which he related each of the characters of his 'last work' (*CT*, 21 March 1879) to the dramatis personæ of his earlier musical dramas. A few examples must suffice. In

    [8] Arthur Schopenhauer, *Sämtliche Werke*, ed. Arthur Hübscher (Mannheim, 1972), ii. 439, 442; translated into English by E. F. J. Payne as *The World as Will and Representation* (New York, 1969), i. 371, 374.
    [9] See Mayer, *Richard Wagner*, pp. 243–4.

the course of a conversation with Cosima on 19 February 1878 he asked: 'Who is Titurel?' And he promptly gave her the answer: 'Wotan. After his renunciation of the world, he is granted salvation, the greatest of possessions is entrusted to his care, and now he is guarding it like a militant god.'[10] Indeed, Wagner even attempted to link the names of Wotan and Titurel on the strength of their etymological derivation (*CT*, 19 February 1878). On 2 March 1878 a comparison suggested itself to him 'between Alberich and Klingsor'. Power at the price of love, and as revenge for its loss! 'R. sees a resemblance between Wotan and Kundry', Cosima noted on 4 June 1878: 'both long for salvation and both rebel against it, Kundry in the scene with P., Wotan with Siegfried.' And on 29 April 1879 Wagner observed that 'in fact Siegfried ought to have turned into Parsifal and redeemed Wotan, he should have come upon Wotan (instead of Amfortas) in the course of his wanderings—but there was no antecedent for it, and so it would have to remain as it was'.

As early as 30 May 1859, in a letter to Mathilde Wesendonck, Wagner had already called Amfortas 'my third-act Tristan inconceivably intensified'.[11] The sight of the life-giving Grail reduces the King, bent upon dying, to the same overwhelming despair as Tristan is forced to suffer when, returning from the night of death, he is brought back to life by the power of the love-potion. Of course, it scarcely needs to be added that the reason for, and the meaning of, their deaths, and, by analogy, the significance of the Grail and the potion, are diametrically opposed in the two works in question. Tristan and Amfortas, to quote Peter Wapnewski, are

destroyed by love. Both desired death as a way of recovering from it. Both are destroyed by love *in* this world and *for* this world. But one of them wants to forsake the world that he may purge himself of love and cast aside his lovelorn fate, while the other wants to forsake it in order to belong exclusively to love, finally falling prey to the very fate that love decrees. One of them wants to conquer the world in order to conquer love as well. The other wants to conquer the world in order that love may triumph wholly over him.[12]

Wagner originally planned to introduce Parsifal into the final act of *Tristan*, during the course of his quest for the Grail. Parsifal's fellow-feeling for the tormented Amfortas ('Die Wunde sah ich bluten:— | nun blutet sie mir selbst' (The wound, I saw it bleeding— | it's bleeding now in me: x. 358[13]) would no doubt have allowed him to have had a

[10] There is a misprint in the English edition of Cosima Wagner's *Diaries* at this point; 'mortal' should read 'militant'.

[11] *Richard Wagner an Mathilde Wesendonk: Tagebuchblätter und Briefe 1853–1871*, ed. Wolfgang Golther, 44th edn. (Leipzig, 1914), 191; English translation from *Selected Letters of Richard Wagner*, ed. Stewart Spencer and Barry Millington (London, 1987), 457.

[12] Wapnewski, *Tristan der Held*, p. 173.

[13] See Chap. 17 n. 30. When Wagner came to set this passage, he changed the line 'nun blutet sie mir selbst' to 'nun blutet sie in mir'.

comforting word with the stricken Tristan and to have consoled him for what Wagner, in conversation with Cosima, described as our propensity for being 'utterly consumed by love' (*CT*, 2 March 1869). For Parsifal, the sufferings of others are a form of self-suffering (*tat twam asi*): he becomes aware of the 'pain of loving', of 'Das Sehnen, das furchtbare Sehnen, | das alle Sinne mir faßt und zwingt' (The yearning, the wild fearful yearning | that fills my senses and holds them fast: x. 358). But, for Parsifal, Tristan's suffering would have been only 'sündiges Verlangen' (sinful, guilty yearning: x. 359), whereas the latter exists beyond the categories of sin and purity, seeking salvation and redemption in the very love (of death) from which Parsifal ought, instead, to have cured and redeemed him, just as he heals and redeems the sinful Kundry. Two different worlds, two different systems of values, would have come into violent conflict here, only to bounce off each other again without having any effect. It was only logical, therefore, that Wagner should have refrained from introducing Parsifal into the earlier work.

There is a further work with which Parsifal's name is linked: *Lohengrin*. Here, of course, the Grail king has a son, who is none other than Lohengrin himself, a parentage explicable only in terms of the fact that, at the time of *Lohengrin*'s conception, Parsifal had not yet read the works of Schopenhauer and Buddha and, therefore, had yet to renounce the pleasures of erotic love. Only the name, but not the character, of the later Grail king is heralded here. Yet one can scarcely fail to notice how the Grail mysticism of *Parsifal* is related to *Lohengrin* (musically, too), and that, in a certain sense, the later work is an amplified version of the earlier one. (Wagner's thoughts were revolving around the subject of *Parsifal* even as early as 1845, the period between the conception of *Tannhäuser* and that of *Lohengrin*.) But Wagner's final work also harks back to his other Romantic operas. Kundry is a female variant of the 'Wandering Jew', as Wagner himself explained in the 1865 prose draft (xi. 404). She is therefore a counterpart not only of the Flying Dutchman (that 'Wandering Jew of the ocean', as Wagner called him in *A Communication to my Friends*: iv. 265), but also of Wotan, whom he similarly described to Cosima as 'a kind of Flying Dutchman' (*CT*, 23 January 1879).

But it is in *Tannhäuser*, of course, that the most striking parallels are to be found: Klingsor's *paradis artificiel* recalls the Venusberg; Kundry is a second Venus (ideally, Wagner wanted her 'lying there naked, like a Titian Venus': *CT*, 4 January 1881); and the flowermaidens even provide a direct link with Wagner's source for the earlier opera, Ludwig Tieck's short story, *Der getreue Eckart und der Tannenhäuser*. Here, too, the 'flowers of evil' encircle the new arrival. ('In the flowers there burned the charms of the girls and the lure of desire; in the women's bodies there blossomed the magic of the flowers.'[14]) In both works the cave of wanton delight disappears at a stroke, in the one case at the sound of the blessed name of 'Maria' (in other words, the Virgin Mary), and, in the other, at the sign of the Cross. Tannhäuser experiences the same duality of heavenly and earthly love as Parsifal does, and is torn apart by the same conflict between Venus Cypria and Venus Urania, between erotic desire and that ascetic willingness to atone which is felt by Amfortas. And just as Tannhäuser abandons the god-like status conferred on him by erotic ecstasy in order to experience human suffering, so Parsifal, in a spirit of renunciation and for the sake of fellow-suffering, rejects the supposed apotheosis promised him by the serpent of 'evil desire'. Tannhäuser is concerned exclusively with self-suffering, Parsifal with fellow-suffering. It is for this reason that we may be justified in calling him an 'intensified Tannhäuser', in the sense that Goethe called his *Tasso* an 'intensified *Werther*'.

But Parsifal is also a more intense version of Siegfried. Like the latter, he is characterized by an erotic mother complex, an 'inexperienced fool' and unthinking muscleman who soon renounces violence and heroic aspirations. His breaking of his bow and throwing away his arrows in Act I (x. 335) represents an act of purification whereby physical strength is spiritualized and an ancient Germanic hero becomes a compassionate Christian anti-hero whose very existence is marked out for suffering in the sense of the Latin *passio*. And if, in his *Perfect Wagnerite*, Shaw always calls Siegfried 'Bakunin', we ought by rights to christen Parsifal 'Schopenhauer'. But the most basic difference between the two heroes is that Siegfried remains 'stupid Siegfried' (as Nietzsche called him[15]), never attaining to that supreme wisdom which is the prerogative of Brünnhilde, daughter of the sibylline Erda, and half-sister of the Norns, whereas Parsifal becomes worldly wise following Kundry's kiss: made wise by pity, he ceases to be a fool.

The Grail (interpreted above as a kind of sacred counterpart to the love-potion) had already been mentioned by Wagner in 1849 in his essay *The Wibelungs*,[16] when he had associated it with the Nibelung hoard. In the section headed 'The Merging of the Ideal Meaning of the Hoard with the "Holy Grail"', he writes: 'The quest for the Grail now replaces man's striving for the Nibelung hoard.' (ii. 150–1.) The hoard is now reduced to its 'real meaning', which is 'actual possessions', 'property', and capital. 'Whereas, according to the most ancient religious beliefs,

---

[14] See Chap. 15 n. 27.
[15] Friedrich Nietzsche, *Sämtliche Werke: Kritische Studienausgabe in 15 Bänden*, ed. Giorgio Colli and Mazzino Montinari (Munich, 1980), vii. 75.
[16] Dating from *WWV* (p. 329).

the hoard appeared as the earth's splendour revealed to us by the full
light of day' (which is how the Rhinemaidens sing its praises with the
words: 'Rheingold! | Rheingold! | Leuchtende Lust, | wie lach'st du so
hell und hehr!' (Rhinegold! | Rhinegold! | Radiant delight, | how
brightly and nobly you laugh!): v. 209), 'we later see it in concentrated
form as the booty which gives the hero his power.' (ii. 153.) In other
words, the Holy Grail complements the Nibelung's ring: whereas the
Rhinegold, whose ideal and real meanings have not yet been divorced
from one another, is reified as the ring or as a 'possession granting
power to its owner' (ii. 153), the *ideal* meaning of the gold passes over
into the 'anti-capital' of the Grail. Not only the *Ring* tetralogy but
*Parsifal*, too, might thus be said to envisage an anti-capitalist Utopia.
(Both ring and Grail can be obtained only by renouncing sexual love.
Just as, with Parsifal, *eros* is replaced by *agape*, by that brotherly love or
*caritas* which, according to Schopenhauer, is identical with compassion
and which is symbolized by Parsifal's brotherly kiss on Kundry's *brow* (x.
372), so Alberich replaces erotic love with sex, supplanting love with
those of its pleasures which can be obtained by force.)

There is thus a symbolic web of allusion between *Parsifal* on the one
hand and the 'Romantic operas' and 'musical dramas' on the other. It is
an allusive magic which Carl Dahlhaus has compared with the
composer's leitmotif technique, a 'mythological systematization' which
extends beyond any one individual drama.[17] Mythic recapitulation finds
its counterpart in the music of *Parsifal*. 'It is from the waning of primary
inventiveness [?] that Wagner's power creates the virtue of a style which
is typical of old age and which, to quote Goethe, withdraws behind the
phenomenon', Adorno observes in his essay, *Zur Partitur des Parsifal*.
'This character is revealed by a comparison between the sombre and, as
it were, toned-down fanfare motive in *Parsifal* and the motive associated
with Siegfried: it is as though the former motive were already a
quotation cited from memory.'[18] The comparison with Goethe's late
style (with which Wagner was intimately familiar) is certainly an obvious
one to draw. Goethe once said that the late Titian had ended up painting
velvet purely symbolically. (This is the 'withdrawal behind the
phenomenon' to which Adorno was referring.) In much the same way,
the impression which objects left on him, even in old age, was
increasingly that of pure symbols, emblems which can no longer be
explained solely in terms of the conceptual context of one individual
work but which are used in a more general way, especially in the later
lyric poetry, where they are juxtaposed with a certain glassy rigidity

---

[17] Carl Dahlhaus, *Richard Wagners Musikdramen* (Velber, 1971), 143; translated into English by
Mary Whittall as *Richard Wagner's Music Dramas* (Cambridge, 1979), 144.

[18] Wieland Wagner (ed.), *Richard Wagner und das neue Bayreuth* (Munich, 1962), 176.

which allows only muted colours to show through, their significance remaining inexplicit within the individual work. This explains the symbolic laconism and tendency towards abbreviation which we find in Goethe's later style.[19] To the reader who is not initiated into this style and who is not familiar with the system of references in which objects and images are embedded, these features often seem strange and enigmatic. Similar feelings must be roused in the listener who hears *Parsifal* for the first time without knowing Wagner's œuvre as a whole. For here, to quote Adorno, 'the fragmentary motives' appear 'much more exposed than, say, in *Tristan*, much less interwoven with each other, less drawn into the development of the composition, and also less varied. They are often placed alongside each other, intentionally and unconcernedly, like little pictures.' (Adorno emphasizes that this is not meant at all pejoratively, since the 'sophistication of this simplicity' is 'altogether without equal'.)[20]

Nietzsche seems to have been thinking of something similar when he described the Prelude to *Parsifal* thus in a rhapsodical letter to Peter Gast of 21 January 1887:

The greatest possible psychological awareness and certainty in relation to what has to be said, expressed, and *communicated* here, the briefest and most direct form for it, every nuance of feeling expressed with epigrammatic concision; a clarity of music as a descriptive art which makes one think of a shield with *rilievo* work embossed on it.

(Faced with this epigrammatic simplicity, even Nietzsche asked himself: 'Has Wagner ever done anything *better*?')

Adorno's and Nietzsche's remarks on the style of *Parsifal* are confirmed by Wagner's own characterization of it, as recorded by Cosima. On 22 September 1880 he said of the Prelude: 'Nothing here and nothing there—it was from nothing that God made the world', an enigmatic remark to which Cosima adds the following gloss: 'What he means is that he has simply placed his themes side by side, like a preacher his Bible passages.' (Wagner's use of this simile to explain the Prelude's paratactical structure recalls Nietzsche's praise of its epigrammatic and 'communicative' character.) Themes and motives become gnomic utterances in music, so that, once again, it is possible to see links between Wagner and the later Goethe, whose final works reveal much the same sort of tendency towards a gnomic style. (That this is true not only of the music but of Wagner's poetry, too, is clear from the language of *Parsifal*, with its manifest tendency towards hieratic utterance.) Suffice it to mention here Goethe's late cycles, *Maximen und*

[19] See Dieter Borchmeyer, *Die Weimarer Klassik* (Königstein, 1980), 324–6.
[20] Wagner (ed.), *Richard Wagner und das neue Bayreuth*, p. 176.

*Reflexionen* and the *Zahme Xenien*, both of which express, in verse and prose, that wisdom which, specific to old age, aims to achieve 'results' by seeking to fathom life's basic phenomena in terse didactic form. But, first and foremost, we are reminded of those gnomic anthologies in *Die Wahlverwandtschaften* and in *Wilhelm Meisters Wanderjahre*, where, as in the Prelude to *Parsifal*, themes are juxtaposed, with the links between them obscured ('nothing here and nothing there').

Wagner spoke repeatedly not only of the 'simplicity of the Prelude' — it was, he said, 'just a few contrasted themes' (*CT*, 1 October 1878) — but of the conscious simplicity of the work as a whole. 'He must always keep it very simple', Cosima noted on 24 November 1878 while discussing the latest few bars that Wagner had written: 'he told me recently that he could never be too simple.' And on 27 April 1879 she observed: 'Perhaps the most wonderful thing about the work is its divine simplicity, comparable to the Gospels.' That this observation was directly related to the musical structure of the work is clear from Wagner's remark that 'the orchestration would be completely different from that of the *Ring*, no figurations of that kind; it would be like cloud layers, dispersing and then forming again'. Hence his fear, frequently repeated, that the orchestration would be too dense (*CT*, 30 December 1881 and 16 July 1882). The tendency towards simplification of the compositional material, described above by Adorno and illustrated, for example, by the archaizing reminiscences of the different Church modes, is mirrored by the tendency towards *conceptual* simplification also referred to above. Poetically and musically, *Parsifal* represents a recantation of *Tristan und Isolde*. It is characteristic of this development that the notion of love's yearning, now deemed to be something sinful, is banished to the hell of wanton desire, together with its whole chromatic range of expression. As Adorno noted: 'The *Tristan* chord in the lower woodwind now symbolizes Klingsor's world.'[21]

This tendency towards simplification results in a kind of spatialization of the poetico-musical structure. Time and again, Gurnemanz's adage, 'Zum Raum wird hier die Zeit' (Here time is one with space), has been described as the 'structural principle behind the *Bühnenweihfestspiel*'.[22] Ernst Bloch recalls Friedrich Schlegel's remark to the effect that architecture is frozen music,[23] while Reinhold Brinkmann has described 'apparent statis, detemporalization, the figure of a circle' as the

---

[21] Wagner (ed.), *Richard Wagner und das neue Bayreuth*, 177.

[22] Mayer, *Richard Wagner*, p. 251; *Bühnenweihfestspiel* can be translated as 'Stage Consecration Festival Drama'.

[23] Ernst Bloch, 'Paradoxa und Pastorale bei Wagner', in Dietrich Mack (ed.), *Richard Wagner: Ausgewählte Schriften* (Frankfurt, 1974), 36–7; translated into English by Peter Palmer as 'Paradoxes and the Pastorale in Wagner's Music', in *Essays on the Philosophy of Music* (Cambridge, 1985), 167.

characteristic features of Wagner's late style.[24] Much the same could be said of the poetry of Goethe's old age: in his letter to Zelter of 11 May 1820 he explains his fascination with medieval Persian poetry by claiming that what he found there was a 'serene overview of the earth's restless activity, an activity which keeps on returning in the form of a circle or spiral', while 'everything real' appeared 'purified, dissolving symbolically'. Here Goethe gives perhaps the best description of the most essential features of his later style—its cyclical character (the circular repetition of the same typical elements and, at the same time, their spiralling 'intensification') and the symbolical purification of all those material phenomena which, now viewed only at a distance, are faded out, as it were, like the fanfare motive in *Parsifal*. 'Dein Lied ist drehend wie das Sterngewölbe, | Anfang und Ende immerfort dasselbe' (Your song is turning like the starry vault, | Beginning and end forever the same), we read in 'Unbegrenzt', one of the poems from the *West-östlicher Divan*.

The stylistic features which have been described or touched on here suggest a proximity to ritual, with its endless ability to be repeated.[25] 'I believe that the secret longing of the theatre, its ultimate ambition, is that ritual from which it first emerged among both Christians and heathens', Thomas Mann wrote in his 'Versuch über das Theater',[26] and he appeals to 'a certain professor of philology' by whom he has been 'reliably informed' that the word 'drama' originally meant a 'sacred action'. (The unnamed professor is, of course, the Professor of Classical Philology at the University of Basle, Friedrich Nietzsche.)

Just as the first dramatic action was *ritual* action, so it appears that the drama at the summit of its ambitions always aspires to take on that original meaning once again. The scene on the Rütli meadow [in Schiller's *Wilhelm Tell*] is after all 'action' only in the sense of a ritual ceremonial; while in *Parsifal* we witness the return to the stage of religious cult, in the form of baptism, foot-washing, the Eucharist and the exposure of the reliquary.[27]

Wagner's final work, Mann argued, was his 'most theatrical' one when seen from the standpoint of the theatre's sacral origins. It was the

---

[24] Stefan Kunze (ed.), *Richard Wagner: Von der Oper zum Musikdrama* (Berne and Munich, 1978), 62.

[25] See Dahlhaus, *Wagners Musikdramen*, pp. 148–9; English trans. (Whittall, *Wagner's Music Dramas*), pp. 150–1.

[26] Thomas Mann, *Gesammelte Werke* (Frankfurt, 1960), x. 54; translated into English by Allan Blunden as *Pro and contra Wagner* (London, 1985), 31.

[27] Ibid. 47–8; English trans., p. 32. The remark on the part of the 'professor of philology' to which Mann alludes here is a footnote in *Der Fall Wagner* (Nietzsche, *Sämtliche Werke*, vi. 32; translated into English by Walter Kaufmann as 'The Case of Wagner', in *Basic Writings of Nietzsche* (New York, 1968), 630).

'logical' consequence of his development as a dramatist: 'An art of sensuousness and of a symbolically formulaic language (for the "leitmotif" is a formula; more than that, it is a monstrance, since it claims almost religious authority for itself) necessarily leads back to ecclesiastical celebration.'[28]

No other work by Wagner comes as close as *Parsifal* to the model of Aeschylean tragedy, a model with which Wagner felt a particular affinity when working on the score of this final work of his (see *CT*, 23–5 June 1880). Wolfgang Schadewaldt has shown that the dramatic action of Attic tragedy is set within a sequence of basic preformed patterns drawn from cultic, legal, and state ceremonial which take up the flow of the action, conducting it on to the following phase like buckets in a mill-race. Schadewaldt goes on to claim that all the major forms of world theatre continued to bear the signs of this ritual structuring of the individual dramatic action until well into the eighteenth century. Indeed, Schadewaldt (like Thomas Mann, for whom the 'theatre of naturalism' was 'a crude contradiction in terms'[29]) even declared this to be a structural principle of the theatre in general.[30] And Schiller, in whose classical dramaturgy the ritualization of the action played an equally important role,[31] declared in his preface to *Die Braut von Messina* that, in so far as the theatre was a form of public ceremonial, those elements best suited to the formation of a 'natural theatre' were the ones with an inherent public aura to them.[32] This was especially true of those elements in the action which required the presence of the chorus, in that the latter was originally a liturgical instrument ('liturgy' in the sense of action of the people for the people).

Even the listener only superficially acquainted with Wagner's music dramas will be able to recall a host of rituals in his works, be they cultic, magic, legal, courtly, social, folkloristic, or whatever. Simply providing a list of them would run to several pages, but mention must at least be made of the many forms of incantation ritual (invocations, especially in the case of names which exert a magic force,[33] prayers, oaths and curses, blessings, enchantments, exorcisms, and natural magic), love rituals (perverted to a ritual of seduction), and rituals associated with baptism,

---

[28] Mann, *Gesammelte Werke*, pp. 53–4.

[29] Ibid. 54.

[30] Wolfgang Schadewaldt, *Hellas und Hesperien: Gesammelte Schriften zur Antike und zur neueren Literatur* (Zurich and Stuttgart, 1960), 253, 584–5.

[31] See Dieter Borchmeyer, *Tragödie und Öffentlichkeit: Schillers Dramaturgie* (Munich, 1973), 174–5.

[32] Friedrich Schiller, *Sämtliche Werke*, ed. Gerhard Fricke and Herbert G. Göpfert, 3rd edn. (Munich, 1962), ii. 823.

[33] Suffice it to mention here Kundry's invocation of Parsifal in Act II; cf. Harald Fricke, '"Wie mein Nam' und Art": Zur Zentralstellung der Personennamen im Werke Richard Wagners', in *Die Programmhefte der Bayreuther Festspiele 1981*, iv. '*Lohengrin*', 14–33.

marriage, death, the law, contracts, atonement, playing, riddles,[34] and battle; but it is also worth including here all those encounters and scenes of recognition or farewell which assume ritualistic proportions through the use of repetition, generally involving a three-part question made up of invocation, answer, and action. The means used to portray such ceremonial procedures are hieratically or emotionally intensified words, formulas, aphorisms, and gestures, linguistic or situational images, stylized actions (especially those which are mythologically transparent), and symbolic objects such as spears, swords, drinking vessels, and rings, together with their leitmotivic musical equivalents. Thomas Mann compares the leitmotif with a raised monstrance, a characterization which is particularly true of *Parsifal*, a work which bears the hallmarks, both linguistically and musically, of a tendency towards sacral utterance and gesture. (Suffice it to mention here the Grail motif itself. It is a quotation, of course, of the 'Dresden Amen', in other words, a musical formula from the Protestant liturgy which was also used by Mendelssohn as the principal subject of the first movement of his 'Reformation' Symphony and whose thematic variants had already been found in *Das Liebesverbot* and *Tannhäuser*.) Action, language, and thematic writing are all distinguished in *Parsifal* by the same hieratic and gnomic character.

The great narrations in Wagner's music dramas, from the Rome Narration in *Tannhäuser* and the Grail Narration in *Lohengrin* to those epic reports and lengthy recapitulations in the *Ring* (often felt to be so undramatic) and, finally, to Gurnemanz's narrations in *Parsifal*, are, moreover, almost ritual 'numbers' which Schadewaldt has compared, in terms of their content and theatrical function, to the epic reports in Aeschylean tragedy.[35] Although they are not 'dramatic' in the modern sense, they are certainly so in the classical sense, since, at least in the composer's later works, they recall sacred history by providing an epic recapitulation of the myth in a way entirely in keeping with the reading of lessons and of the Gospels during the liturgy, not to mention the ritualized silence and intensive listening on the part of the congregation, and the interruption to the sacred 'action'. Among Wagner's 'Romantic operas', it is *Lohengrin* which bears the clearest marks of ritual, while *Parsifal* shares that honour among the later musical dramas. Significantly, these are his two Grail operas. In both these works the chorus plays a role influenced partly by Aeschylean tragedy, partly by the

[34] Cf. the Wanderer/Mime scene in Act I of *Siegfried*. Riddle contests have a long tradition going back to the Orient (as evidenced by the biblical contest between Solomon and the Queen of Sheba). This scene in *Siegfried* is a classic example of the life-or-death riddle found, for example, in Gozzi's *Turandot*, a work which, in Schiller's German translation, may well have inspired Wagner.

[35] Wolfgang Schadewaldt, 'Richard Wagner und die Griechen', in Wagner (ed.), *Richard Wagner und das neue Bayreuth*, pp. 172–3.

Christian liturgy. In *Parsifal* it no longer has the character of a mass comprised of many individuals who, as it were, enter together by chance and sing with a single voice. (It was only in this form that Wagner had been prepared to tolerate the chorus in the *Ring*, as his handling of Hagen's vassals shows.) Once again it becomes that 'ideal' collective which, for Wagner the radically individualistic disciple of Feuerbach, had previously been an absurdity. But now that he had seen through the *principium individuationis*, Wagner seems to have abandoned his earlier reservation about this type of chorus as an instrument of the drama. When, on 27 November 1879, he told Cosima that 'one could write a whole book' about Aeschylus's chorus, he was evidently thinking of his own use of the chorus in *Parsifal*. The antiphonal dirge by the two processions which make up the chorus in the final scene—recalling the lament of the two semi-choruses in the final act of Schiller's *Die Braut von Messina*—is, emotionally, the most powerful choral scene to be found in any piece of world theatre since the time of Aeschylus.

Wagner also reduced the language of the orchestra in *Parsifal* to one of archaic and lapidary simplicity. The 'endless detail' of the earlier works is replaced, according to Adorno, by a 'choric process' often reminiscent of Anton Bruckner.[36] A style of writing which Wagner had once condemned as pleonastic in the choral operas of Gluck and other composers—the way in which that fundamental vehicle of classical tragedy, the chorus, was duplicated by being combined with an instrumental orchestra itself derived from that chorus—is no longer deemed opprobrious.

It is not only in terms of form that Wagner is indebted to Attic tragedy. Although the most obvious parallels between the Wagnerian œuvre and Aeschylus's works are to be found in the *Ring*, there is one particular work by the older dramatist which shows through the Christian legend of *Parsifal* as though on some ancient palimpsest. That work is *Prometheus*.[37] In her diary entry of 28 February 1877 Cosima refers to *Parsifal* under the title 'The Redeemer Unbound', a clear allusion to *Prometheus Unbound*. Parsifal, who responds to his Saviour's appeal, 'Erlöse, rette mich aus schuldbefleckten Händen!' (Redeem me, rescue me from hands defiled and guilty!: x. 359), has much in common with Heracles, who frees Prometheus from the Caucasian mountains. But Parsifal not only frees his Saviour (immanent in the Grail), he also rescues Amfortas, who, even more clearly than Parsifal, points to Prometheus as his prototype. For it is with this saviour of the world of Greek antiquity that the Grail king shares a wound in his side which

---

[36] Wagner (ed.), *Richard Wagner und das neue Bayreuth*, p. 176.
[37] See Werner Diez, 'Prometheus, Luzifer und die Gralsutopie', in *Die Programmhefte der Bayreuther Festspiele 1972*, vii. *'Parsifal'*, 12, 56–68.

refuses to heal. In Amfortas's case, the torment he suffers as a result of his wound is always renewed by the sight of the Grail, while the bound Titan is harrowed by Zeus's eagle which tears at his liver every day. Just as Amfortas is the very antithesis of a Christ-figure[38]—he has been wounded by the lance of Longinus, that same lance which had wounded Christ, but the meaning of the Saviour's wound has been traduced—so Christian tradition has repeatedly regarded Prometheus as a *typus Christi* or Christ-figure. Gerhart Hauptmann, for example, notes that 'the crucified Christ, with the open wound in his breast, looks very much like Prometheus, bound to a rock in the Caucasian mountains'.[39]

Parsifal, however, not only resembles Heracles, he also recalls Achilles, who heals Telephus with the very spear which had wounded him, thus confirming the oracle's pronouncement that 'He who dealt the wound will heal it.'[40] (Of course, Telephus's wound is in his thigh, which is also where Amfortas had been wounded, according to Wagner's 1865 prose draft. Indeed, the composer even went to the absurd lengths of relocating Christ's wound in order to underline the similarity between them: Longinus, he wrote, transfixed 'the Saviour's thigh': xi. 409, 413.[41])

The syncretization of myth which Wagner offers in *Parsifal*, therefore, is a mixture of Hellenic mythology and Christian legend. Not only is the action channelled into ritual procedures, it is, at the same time, modelled on scenes from the New Testament, including the Commmunion and Last Supper, Mary Magdalene's anointing of Jesus, the washing of his feet, and Gurnemanz as John the Baptist—all motifs which go back to Wagner's dramatic sketch, *Jesus von Nazareth*, drafted in Dresden in 1849, and all of them visual scenes which, once again, show how time becomes space in this work. The action becomes a tableau. In much the same way, Amfortas's scenes of high emotion remain scenes from the Passion, isolated from the action proper. As such, they are strikingly reminiscent, dramaturgically, of the structure of the laments uttered by Prometheus when chained to his rock in the Caucasian mountains.

[38] Peter Wapnewski, *Der traurige Gott: Richard Wagner in seinen Helden* (Munich, 1978), 256.
[39] Quoted in Diez, 'Prometheus, Luzifer und die Gralsutopie', pp. 61, 64.
[40] See Herbert Hunger, *Lexikon der griechischen und römischen Mythologie* (Reinbek, 1974), 394. The present author has been able to find only a single reference to this mythic parallel, in Franz Muncker, *Richard Wagner* (Bamberg, 1909), 148. See also, of course, Hans Pfitzner, 'Der Parsifalstoff und seine Gestaltungen', in *Gesammelte Schriften* (Augsburg, 1926); Pfitzner does not appear to have noticed, however, that the lines from *Tasso* quoted here also refer to the Telephus myth.
[41] The thigh wound might also, of course, be an allusion to the fact that, in Wolfram's original, the spear had struck the Grail king 'durch die heidruose sîn' (through his testicles) (*Wolfram von Eschenbach*, ed. Karl Lachmann, 6th edn. (Berlin and Leipzig, 1926), 230 (479, 12)); see Wapnewski, *Der traurige Gott*, p. 220.

In his 1880 essay, 'Religion and Art', Wagner sets art the task of 'salvaging the kernel of religion, inasmuch as the mythical images which religion would wish to be believed as true are apprehended in art for their symbolic value, and through ideal representation of those symbols, art reveals the concealed deep truth within them' (x. 211). What this appears to mean is no more and no less than that, in the best Hegelian tradition, religion is subsumed by art. 'No matter how excellent we find the statues of the Greek gods, no matter how we see God the Father, Christ, and Mary so estimably and perfectly portrayed: it is no help; we bow the knee no longer', Hegel confirms.[42] Whereas the artist was formerly 'bound up with the specific character of such a world-view and religion, in immediate identity with it and with firm faith in it', we are nowadays 'not seriously in earnest with this material'.[43] According to Hegel, today's artist 'stands above specific consecrated forms and configurations and moves freely on his own account, independent of the subject-matter and mode of conception in which the holy and eternal was previously made visible to human apprehension . . . Today there is no material which stands in and for itself above this relativity.'[44]

Art 'conveys to the emotions the truth behind the dogmas', Wagner told Cosima on 9 May 1880, adding that, in doing so, it did not inspire faith in the letter of them. And yet, throughout the time he was working on *Parsifal*, he never let it be doubted for a moment that his final work was a Christian work. Cosima's *Diaries* contain countless remarks attesting to his preoccupation with the New Testament, the Christian mystics, Luther, and various writings on the science of religion, all of which inspired him to characteristic confessions of faith. Not only did he marry Cosima in the Protestant Church in Lucerne, he later went to Communion, defended the sacraments, and even played the missionary: in December 1873 he scolded the free-thinking Malwida von Meysenbug for

not having her ward [Olga Herzen] baptized. This was not right, he said, not everyone could fashion his religion for himself, and particularly in childhood one must have a feeling of cohesion. Nor should one be left to choose; rather, it should be possible to say, 'You have been christened, you belong through baptism to Christ, now unite yourself once more with him through Holy Communion.' Christening and Communion are indispensable, he said. No amount of knowledge can ever approach the effect of the latter. People who evade religion have a terrible shallowness. (*CT*, 9–13 December 1873.)

---

[42] G. W. F. Hegel, *Ästhetik*, ed. Friedrich Bassenge (Berlin, 1955), 139–40; translated into English by T. M. Knox as *Aesthetics: Lectures on Fine Art* (Oxford, 1975), 103.

[43] Ibid. 566; English trans., p. 603.          [44] Ibid. 568; English trans., p. 605.

And he went on to proclaim: 'There are no great men without religious feeling', and, again: 'Christ is our intermediary, he leads us out of this life.' Cosima, continuing the entry, records how Wagner 'recalled Fidi's [Siegfried's] baptism with emotion' and said that he would 'never forget the occasion, how beautiful, how comforting it had been; how earnest the faces of the people who were present—only in a common faith can people come together like that. Religion is a *bond*, one cannot have religion by oneself.' Remarks of this kind are to be found especially during the time when Wagner was working on *Parsifal*.[45] But reactions to ecclesiastical customs alternate, inconsistently, with ideas on a pure form of Christianity attainable only when existing Churches have been disbanded, a Christianity 'freed of all sectarianism', he told Cosima on 30 January 1880.[46]

In his book *Abenteuer und Fahrten der Seele* the Indologist Heinrich Zimmer (1890–1943) offers an interpretation of *Parsifal* which comes as close as any to Wagner's view of Christianity. In the words 'Erlösung dem Erlöser' (Redemption to the Redeemer: x. 375), Zimmer sees a formula for extending an ossified cult until it embraces the whole of

---

[45] On 27 Apr. 1879 he once again became 'annoyed with M[alwida] for speaking out against religious acts ... He says he cannot understand how one can hold out against baptism ... He can think of nothing more unbearable than a priest, but that has nothing to do with the act of baptism or the symbol of redemption.' That Wagner himself went to Communion is clear from *CT*, 31 Oct. 1872 (see also *CT*, 2 Nov.), 9 Apr. 1882, and, indirectly, from 28 Apr. 1880, on which date Wagner announced his intention of taking Hermann Levi to Communion in order that the blood of Christ might redeem him of his Jewishness ('I cannot allow him to conduct *Parsifal* unbaptized, but I shall baptize them both, and we shall all take Communion together'). On Wagner's positive, not to say devout, attitude to Christianity, see *CT*, 27–8 Oct. 1873, 31 May, 27 Dec. 1874, 17 May 1875 ('one must accept the four Gospels in the way one accepts a lava formation, nothing in them should be touched or altered'); 11 ('These donkeys who do not believe in God and who think that such figures as Jesus of N. or a great creative genius move according to the ordinary processes of Nature!'), 12, 15 ('[R.] believes that Christianity can still be rescued for future ages'), 16–17 (these remarks were inspired by Blandine's Communion on the 16th, an event which elicited Wagner's lively sympathy and forced him to adopt a stance towards 'Peter's recognition of Christ'), 22 June, 2, 7 July, 16 Sept., 20 Oct. 1878, 12 Apr., 12 May 1879, 13 Jan., 27 Apr. 1880, and *passim*.

[46] See some of the remarks quoted in the previous note; also *CT*, 15, 27 Nov. 1878, 15 July 1879 ('For me Christianity has not yet arrived, and I am like the early Christians, awaiting Christ's return'), 10 Feb. 1880 ('Renan's book [*L'Église chrétienne*] provides him with another opportunity to talk about "the most horrible thing in history", the church, and the victory of Judaism over all else: "I can't read two lines of Goethe without recognizing the Jewish Jehovah; for him Jesus was a problematical figure, but God was as clear as crystal"'). This last remark confirms that Wagner professed to a Schopenhauerian Buddhistic Christianity, with anti-Judaic features. He hoped that this particular brand of Christianity would cleanse it of its Old Testament affiliations (13 Nov. 1878) and of the Jewish conception of God (10 Feb. 1880). If, on 20 Sept. 1879, he observed that 'I do not believe in God, but in godliness, which is revealed in a Jesus *without sin*', one cannot conclude from this (as Gregor-Dellin has done in his life of Wagner (*Richard Wagner*, p. 743; this section is not included in Brownjohn's English translation)) that Wagner was secretly an atheist. After all, the previous year he had dismissed as 'donkeys' all those who did not 'believe in God' or who wanted to demythologize the 'great creative genius' as a force of nature (*CT*, 11 June 1878). Wagner's lack of faith was directed solely at 'Jehovah', a figure whom he regarded with contempt.

humanity,[47] a process analogous to the Christian spread of the Jewish tribal religion to the point where, thanks to the effusion of the Holy Ghost, it became a world religion.

Richard Wagner shows us this theme, developing it as the pivotal point of his later works. Here we find that the Saviour, the Jesus Christ of the New Testament, must now be saved in turn: Parsifal helps to restore to its former power that divine principle of Christ's blood which is present in the Grail chalice. What had become feeble and ineffective he causes to flow once again, and the chorus of angels rejoices, 'Redemption to the Redeemer!' These are the final words of this mystic work. The hero in human guise has revitalized the revitalizing essence of the Holy Ghost. The human spirit has restored the power of the divine. Thus Wagner's Brünnhilde—the symbol of humanity incarnate, the suffering and compassionate 'fallen goddess'—releases Wotan, the father of the gods, from the thraldom of spiritual impotence. In a spirit of renunciation and self-sacrifice, she leaps into the refining fire, singing her dying song as she goes to her own destruction: 'Rest, O rest now, you god!' The words of a requiem, they are also a liberating incantation.[48]

The final formula, 'Redemption to the Redeemer!', is by no means as baffling as has repeatedly been claimed. It needs no special interpretative powers to deduce a meaning which is unmistakably clear from the dramatic context in which the expression occurs. That the 'Redeemer' in *Parsifal* is none other than Christ emerges unequivocally from every passage in which the term occurs. (There is a single notable exception here, which will be discussed below, but it is one which, in any case, does not contradict our present findings.) There is no other 'redemption' in *Parsifal* except that which relates to Christ's redemptive act. But does this not imply that Jesus must redeem himself? Allowing for certain, as yet undefined, assumptions, the answer to this question must be an unequivocal 'yes'.

This final line of the work, 'Redemption to the Redeemer', expresses

---

[47] Cf. Wagner's professions of a Christianity which would transcend all existing Churches (n. 45 above). This Christianity was the polar opposite of the fatalistic racial doctrine of a man like Gobineau, which he had discovered two years earlier. But, in spite of widespread claims to the contrary, Wagner never made this racial teaching wholly his own. See e.g. his remark on 23 Apr. 1882: 'He reproaches Gob. for leaving out of account one thing which was given to mankind—a Saviour, who suffered for them and allowed himself to be crucified.' Christianity could abolish all racial differences. 'But one thing is certain: races are done for, and all that can now make an impact is—as I have ventured to express it—the blood of Christ.' (*CT*, 17 Dec. 1881). Hence his wish to attend Communion with Levi (*CT*, 28 Apr. 1880) and hence his remark, immediately after hearing about Gobineau's *Essai sur l'inégalité des races humaines*, that, whenever one thought of the Gospels, one knew 'that what really matters is something different from racial strength' (*CT*, 14 Feb. 1881). It is impossible, therefore, to turn Wagner into a forerunner of national socialist racist thinking, in spite of his undeniably anti-Jewish sentiments.

[48] Heinrich Zimmer, *Abenteuer und Fahrten der Seele: Mythen, Märchen und Sagen aus keltischen und östlichen Kulturbereichen. Darstellung und Deutung* (Düsseldorf and Cologne, 1977), 63–4.

the fact that Parsifal has now fulfilled the request vouchsafed to him in his vision of his Redeemer which followed Kundry's kiss. When, in horror, he tears himself from Kundry's arms and feels Amfortas's wound in his heart, he is (according to the stage directions) 'completely lost to the world'. He sees the Grail before him and hears the 'Saviour's cry':

> die Klage, ach! die Klage
> um das verrath'ne[49] Heiligthum: —
> 'erlöse, rette mich
> aus schuldbefleckten Händen!'        (x. 359.)
>
> lamenting, ah, lamenting
> for the profaned sanctuary: —
> 'Redeem me, rescue me
> from hands defiled and guilty!'

The hands which are 'defiled and guilty' are those of Amfortas, the 'sinful guardian of the sanctuary', as Wagner called him in a programme note dating from 1882 (xii. 349). Redemption comes about when Parsifal, having resisted Kundry's attempt at seduction, brings back the sacred lance and replaces Amfortas as head of the Grail community. In this way he brings 'redemption to the Redeemer'. This, and this alone, is the meaning behind the phrase.

But does this not also mean that Parsifal himself is a redeemer, greater, moreover, than Christ, who, it would appear, needs to be redeemed by Parsifal? The answer is 'no'. With the single exception already mentioned, Wagner painstakingly avoids depicting his hero as the initiator of the redemptive act, at least in the finished poem. In the 1877 draft, for example, Parsifal still tells Kundry: 'I want to love you and redeem you',[50] whereas in the completed text he says: 'Lieb' und Erlösung soll dir lohnen'[51] (Love and redemption will be granted: x. 362). In other words, Parsifal sees himself not as the instigator of redemption, but as its medium. But not even in the earlier draft does Parsifal think that he can redeem Kundry by himself. Redemption emanates from the one true Redeemer who uses the pure individual as his instrument. That Parsifal, entrusted with the task of redeeming the Christ who is immanent within the Grail, remains, as it were, confined within the limitations of his humanity, and that he himself is conscious of the immense distance between himself and his Saviour, is clear from his reaction to his Saviour's lament. Overcome by remorse at his failure in the Grail Castle, he sinks to his knees: 'Erlöser! Heiland! Herr der

[49] When Wagner set this text, he changed 'verrath'ne' (betrayed) to 'entweihte' (profaned).
[50] Quoted in Richard Wagner, *Sämtliche Werke*, ed. Martin Geck and Egon Voss (Mainz, 1970), xxx. 84.
[51] When Wagner set this text, he changed 'lohnen' (reward) to 'werden' (become).

Huld! | Wie büß' ich Sünder solche Schuld?' (Redeemer! Saviour! Lord of grace? | Can I my sinful crime efface?: x. 359).

Parsifal remains prey to human frailty, but, ever since his vision of the Saviour, he knows that Christ regards him as an instrument of salvation and redemption. 'Auch dir bin ich zum Heil gesandt' (For your salvation I was sent: x. 361), he tells Kundry, leaving her (and us) in no doubt who is to be seen as 'des einz'gen Heiles wahren Quell' (the fount whence truly healing flows: x. 361). It is he with whose symbol—the sign of the Cross—he exorcizes the magic of Klingsor's world. Christ remains the instigator of redemption, using Parsifal as his instrument to bring redemption to himself. This is the paradox of the final formula, 'Redemption to the Redeemer', a paradox which, to a certain extent, recalls Wotan's existential problem in the *Ring*: the god must leave it to a human hero 'zu wirken die That, | die, wie not sie den, Göttern, | dem Gott doch zu wirken verwehrt' (to perform that feat | which, however needful to the gods, | the god is forbidden to do: vi. 32). This hero, of course, must act entirely by himself and of his own initiative, 'ledig göttlichen Schutzes' (lacking godly protection), whereas Parsifal always acts with an eye to Christ's redemptive act. (Christ himself is no longer active; having committed himself into the hands of mankind in the form of the Grail, he finds expression as a holy relic which is handled by others but which does not itself act.)

Reified as a holy relic, the Saviour uses a pure human being to redeem him. This redemption is a *restitutio in integrum* symbolized by the reunion of two objects which had become separated, the spear and the Grail, the former the weapon which had wounded Jesus in his side, the latter the vessel into which his blood had flowed. Parsifal sums up this sense of restitution when he says to Amfortas:

> Die deine Wunde durfte schließen,
> ihr seh' ich heil'ges Blut entfließen
> in Sehnsucht dem verwandten Quelle,
> der dort fließt in des Grales Welle!     (x. 375.)

> The holy weapon that has healed you,
> upon its point fresh blood is flowing
> and yearning to join the kindred fountain,
> that darkly in the Grail is glowing!

*Restitutio in integrum* is the teleological thrust of the action in *Parsifal*, an appropriate formulation for that circular or helical line of development which mirrors the work's formal structure: its end marks a return to the beginning, to a heightened point of return. The blood which flows from the lance is the blood of the Redeemer not that of the sinner; spear and

Grail become one again in this sacred blood; Amfortas's wound is healed when it is touched by the spear whose blow once caused it to fester; the Grail community is re-established, Klingsor's contrastive world is exorcized, and nature is restored to its Paradisal innocence.

One of the central ideas in *Parsifal* is taht of *apokatástasis pánton* (a term borrowed from Acts 3:21, where it is translated as 'the restitution of all things'). It is an idea which, traceable to the Stoics, was of particular importance for the Christian tradition, and refers to the renewal of the world through the cyclical restitution of a perfect primordial state. The end of the *Ring* could, of course, be interpreted in a similar way. With the self-annihilation of the gods (in other words, with the supersession of a world order which stemmed from Wotan's despoliation of nature, and with the return of the ring to the natural elements), the world itself is restored to its integral natural state. As the world ends, so it begins anew. The so-called 'redemption motive', first heard at Sieglinde's words: 'O hehrstes Wunder' (Sublimest wonder: vi. 69) in Act III of *Die Walküre*, symbolizes the restitution of all things, when it is heard again at the end of the cycle. This, of course, has nothing to do with the idea of 'more of the same.' Anyone who, at the end of a circuit, returns to the point from which he set out, sees that point, so to speak, from behind; and he bears within him a knowledge of the route he has travelled, so that what has been recovered is a higher form of what had been lost. The idea of *apokatástasis*, therefore, is better expressed by the symbol of a spiral rather than by the image of a circle. The new beginning contains the hope that the evil of the previous state of the world will not be repeated. And this hope is contained in the redemption motive or, rather, in the motive of promise which we hear at the end of the cycle.

In exactly the same way, the cosmic conflagration at the end of *Götterdämmerung* points to a tradition, behind the Scandinavian myth, which is closely linked to the doctrine of *apokatástasis*. This is the idea of *ekpýrosis* found in the Stoics and signifying a 'burning-out' of the world, its disintegration into the primal element, fire, from which it first arose. (Fire, in this context, must be understood to mean the sperm— *spérma*—of the world, from which a new world will arise.) The fire that is kindled by Brünnhilde, therefore, is intended to 'cleanse' the ring— and hence the world—from the curse which lies upon it.

The theologian Hans Küng has pointed out, quite rightly, that at no stage in the *Bühnenweihfestspiel* does Parsifal regard himself as a 'Christ-substitute or divine figure'. (The major theme of *Parsifal*, according to Küng, is our own 'participation in the process of redemption, with a clear emphasis on active involvement in that process, without God's earlier redemptive action in Christ being thereby negated or superseded'.[52]) We spoke earlier, however, of an exception, a passage in the text where Parsifal is described unmistakably as 'Redeemer', and, moreover, as 'Redeemer' in his own capacity. It is Kundry who addresses him thus in Act II:

> Bist du Erlöser,
> was bannt dich, Böser,
> nicht mir auch zum Heil dich zu einen?
> Seit Ewigkeiten—harre ich deiner,
> des Heiland's, ach! so spät,
> den einst ich kühn verschmäht.　　(x. 360.)

> If you're a saviour,
> then what restrains you
> from joining with me in my salvation?
> Through endless ages you I awaited,
> My saviour, ah! so late!
> Whom once I dared revile!

Parsifal really does appear to become the Redeemer here, the Saviour, a reincarnation of Christ, at whom Kundry once laughed on his way to be crucified. But it must be remembered that it is Kundry the seductress who is speaking here: to her, redemption and salvation assume the guise of sexual congress with Parsifal. He must feel himself to be a saviour; indeed, she even promises him: 'Mein volles Liebes-Umfangen | läßt dich dann Gottheit erlangen' (The full embrace of my loving | surely to godhead will raise you: x. 361). What the serpent promised Eve, Kundry now promises Parsifal—just as Venus once promised Tannhäuser that he, too, would be 'a god' (ii. 6). But just as Tannhäuser retains an awareness of being 'mortal', and just as he yearns to suffer pain in the midst of pleasure, so Parsifal's fellow-feeling for Amfortas's sufferings prevents him from being seduced into gaining apparent divinity. In vain the temptress seeks to foist on him the role of Redeemer, Saviour and Christ-figure. Never for a moment does he himself—or his creator Wagner—see him in such a role.

Parsifal is not himself a redeemer but the agent of redemption, of Christ's continuing act of salvation. But who is it that is redeemed? To begin with, it is the alienated Grail and hence Christ himself, inasmuch as 'the relic [i.e. the Grail through which he has realized himself] is freed from the care of sullied hands' (to quote from the 1865 prose draft: xi. 408); but it is also Amfortas, who is cured of his wound and whose 'yearning desire', caused by 'love's torment', is finally stilled; and,

---

[52] Hans Küng, 'Sehnsucht nach Erlösung', in *Die Programmhefte der Bayreuther Festspiele 1982*, i. *'Parsifal'*, 1–38, esp. p. 34.

last of all, it is Kundry, whose baptism and death release her from the torment of her eternal peregrinations. Both Amfortas and Kundry are redeemed through Christ's agency, by the spear from which his blood flows and by the sacrament which he initiated and gave to mankind as a token of faith: 'die Taufe nimm | und glaub' an den Erlöser!' (baptized be, | have faith in the Redeemer!: x. 371).

In the 1865 prose draft Wagner wrote that 'The span of Kundry's life cannot be measured, for she lives under constantly changing rebirths, in consequence of a primeval curse which condemns her, like the "Wandering Jew", to assume different forms and bring men the suffering of love's seduction.' (xi. 404.) Klingsor identifies her as the re-incarnation of the biblical Herodias, who, as we saw in the chapter on 'The Transformations of Ahasuerus', appears in legend and poetry from the Middle Ages onwards as the female counterpart of Ahasuerus, condemned, like the Wandering Jew, to a restless and nomadic existence. But, as she wanders through history, Kundry, for all her similarity with the mythical figure of Ahasuerus, is depicted not as a Jewess but, rather, as a heathen. This is how the Squires describe her: 'Eine Heidin ist's, ein Zauberweib' (She's a heathen maid, a sorceress: x. 329). In *Parsifal* her eternal wanderings mean that she does not always remain the same figure, like the Wandering Jew. Instead, Wagner associates the idea of those wanderings with the Buddhist belief in metempsychosis, the endless succession of rebirths, and, more importantly, with the eternal cycle of Nature. Kundry, after all, literally hibernates, reawakening every spring to a new life. At the beginning of Act III Gurnemanz drags her out of an overgrown thicket of thorn-bushes, rubbing her limbs to relax her wintery stiffness. The Squires compare her with a 'savage beast', to which she retorts: 'Sind die Thiere hier nicht heilig?' (Are the creatures here not holy?: x. 329). But she is also the most beautiful of all the 'flowers of evil', those tropical blooms in Klingsor's magic garden. 'Rose of Hell' the latter calls her. There is no doubt that Kundry embodies heathen nature, as yet unredeemed. Her redemption through baptism, therefore, is associated, symbolically, with the redemption of extrahuman nature in the Good Friday scene, one of the most moving and inspired of all Wagner's mythico-musical syntheses, in which age-old motifs from Christian mysticism and legend are given new life.

The Good Friday music begins at the moment when Kundry is baptized and her tears bedew the ground. It is now that woodland and meadow begin to grow brighter. Parsifal notices this 'in gentle ecstasy', comparing this radiant beauty with the 'morbid' charms of the 'magic flowers' in Klingsor's garden. But, he asks Gurnemanz in dismay, ought not Nature to join with the rest of humanity in grieving for the Redeemer's death on this 'day of deepest agony'? Gurnemanz replies:

> Du sieh'st, das ist nicht so.
> Des Sünders Reuethränen sind es,
>     die heut' mit heil'gem Thau
>     beträufet Flur und Au':
>     der ließ sie so gedeihen.
> Nun freut' sich alle Kreatur
> auf des Erlösers holder Spur,
>     will ihr Gebet ihm weihen.
> Ihn selbst am Kreuze kann sie nicht erschauen:
> da blickt sie zum erlös'ten Menschen auf;
> der fühlt sich frei von Sünden-Angst und Grauen,
> durch Gottes Liebesopfer rein und heil:
> das merkt nun Halm und Blume auf den Auen,
> daß heut' des Menschen Fuß sie nicht zertritt,
> doch wohl, wie Gott mit himmlischer Geduld
>     sich sein' erbarmt und für ihn litt,
>     der Mensch auch heut' in frommer Huld
>     sie schont mit sanftem Schritt.
> Das dankt dann alle Kreatur,
> was all' da blüht und bald erstirbt,
> da die entsündigte Natur
> heut' ihren Unschulds-Tag erwirbt.        (x. 371–2.)

>     You see, it is not so.
> The sinner's tears of true repentance
>     today with holy dew
>     bedeck the flowery mead
>     and make them glow so brightly;
> while all created things rejoice
> to see the Saviour's sign of grace,
>     and raise a prayer to praise Him.
> Himself, the Saviour crucified, they see not:
> and so they raise their eyes to man redeemed,
> the man set free from sin, set free from terror,
> by God's most loving sacrifice made pure:
> today each blade and bloom upon the meadow
> knows well the foot of man will do no harm;
> in truth, as God with heavenly loving care
>     endured for man and for him bled,
>     so man now will repay that love
>     and walk with gentle tread.
> And grateful, all creation sings,
> all things that bloom and pass away;
> nature her innocence has won,
> all is renewed once more this day.

The symbolic relevance which this whole speech holds for Kundry—for is it not her tears of remorse which conferred on Nature its present radiance; is it not she who is the redeemed figure to whom all those creatures in need of redemption now raise their eyes in turn?—is clear from her reaction to it: 'Kundry has slowly raised her head again and gazes up at Parsifal with tearful eyes filled with calm and earnest entreaty.' Parsifal himself recognizes the secret correspondence between Kundry's redemption and Nature, which, freed from the taint of sin, is restored to a state of Paradisal innocence: here, too, we find an example of *apokatástasis*, a *restitutio in integrum*. 'Ich sah sie welken, die einst mir lachten' (I saw them withering when once they mocked me: x. 372), Parsifal says, referring, of course, to the flowers in Klingsor's magic garden whose pagan spell he had broken by making the sign of the Cross. 'Ob heut' sie nach Erlösung schmachten?' (Are they now for redemption yearning?). And he turns to Kundry: 'Auch deine Thräne ward zum Segensthaue: | du weinest—sieh! es lacht die Aue!' (A dew of sorrow from your eyes is flowing: | you're weeping—look, they smile, the meadows!: x. 372).

The Good Friday spell is a mystic realization of the Pauline doctrine of the sigh uttered by those creatures suffering at their fatal destiny, a sigh which had been heard in the 'dull groaning' uttered by Kundry when she was hidden in the thorn-thicket at the beginning of Act III. (Wagner himself speaks of 'nature's lament' in his essay 'Religion and Art': x. 249.) According to chapter 8 of Paul's Epistle to the Romans, Adam's rejection of God affected not only humankind but the whole of creation.

For the earnest expectation of the creature waiteth for the manifestation of the sons of God. For the creature was made subject to vanity, not willingly, but by reason of him who hath subjected the same in hope, because the creature itself also shall be delivered from the bondage of corruption into the glorious liberty of the children of God. For we know that the whole creation groaneth and travaileth in pain together until now. (Romans 8: 19–22.)

This passage in Paul's Epistle to the Romans has always fascinated poets. Suffice it to recall Annette von Droste-Hülshoff's 1846 poem *Die ächzende Kreatur*:

> Da ward ihr klar, wie nicht allein
> Der Gottesfluch im Menschenbild,
> Wie er in schwerer, dumpfer Pein
> Im bangen Wurm, im scheuen Wild,
> Im durst'gen Halme auf der Flur,
> Der mit vergilbten Blättern lechzt,
> In aller, aller Kreatur
> Gen Himmel um Erlösung lechzt.

> She saw that she was not alone
> And that God's curse on humankind
> Afflicted with its dull-edged moan
> The timid worm and fearful hind,
> And that parched grass upon the lea
> Whose yellow leaves refreshment craved.
> In each and every beast she'd see
> Eyes raised in hope of being saved.

The human race bears a guilt of which it is barely conscious, as the final strophe suggests:

> Das ist die Schuld des Mordes an
> Der Erde Lieblichkeit und Huld,
> An des Getieres dumpfem Bann
> Ist es die tiefe, schwere Schuld,
> Und an dem Grimm, der es beseelt,
> Und an der List, die es befleckt,
> Und an dem Schmerze, der es quält,
> Und an dem Moder, der es deckt.

> This is the price we have to pay
> For butchering earth's loveliness.
> Beasts we subjected to our sway
> And guilt must bear for their duress
> And for the fury which they feel
> And for the trick which taints them still
> And for the pain which grips like steel
> And for the mould which suits them ill.

The guilt that is incurred for 'butchering earth's loveliness' is expunged on the Good Friday Meadow in the final act of *Parsifal*. Man and Nature celebrate their reconciliation under the sign of the Cross. 'Das merkt nun Halm und Blume auf de Auen, | daß heut' des Menschen Fuß sie nicht zertritt' (Today each blade and bloom upon the meadow | knows well the foot of man will do no harm: x. 372), Gurnemanz sings. Rather, man spares them by walking with gentle tread. This enactment of man's reconciliation with Nature is in symbolic contrast to Parsifal's entry in Act I, when his killing of the swan had shattered the sacred natural peace of the Grail's domains.

> Du konntest morden? Hier im heil'gen Walde,
>     dess' stiller Frieden dich umfing?
> Des Haines Thiere nahten dich nicht zahm,
>     grüßten dich freundlich und fromm?                    (x. 335.)

> So you can murder, here, within this forest,
>     where quiet, holy peace should reign?
> The woodland creatures, are they not your friends?
>     Are they not gentle and tame?

In his essay, 'Religion and Art', written three years after the poem of *Parsifal*, Wagner described the violation of Nature and ill-treatment of animals as altogether typical of western 'militant civilization'. Throughout the 'regeneration essays' of his later years he adopts a radical pacifism which is in the greatest possible contrast to his militaristic attitude at the time of the Franco-Prussian War. For Wagner, this pacifism was in part an attempt to escape his own aggressiveness and to put behind him the errors of the years around 1870, errors of which he became increasingly aware after 1874.

'Let us recognize, with the Redeemer in our hearts, that it is not their actions but their sufferings which bring the men of the past closer to us, making them worthy of our remembrance, and that it is not to the victor but to the vanquished hero that we owe our sympathy.' (x. 247.) This is the message which Wagner contrasts with the law of history, a history which hitherto had been governed by the law of the jungle. The 'rudest barbarian, no less than the artistically creative Greek', says Wagner in 'Religion and Art', regarded this law as

the only law that shaped the world: there is no blood guilt which even this nation, with its sense of formal beauty, did not bring down upon itself in rabid hatred of its neighbour, until one stronger than they fell upon them, that stronger nation falling in turn before a yet more powerful enemy, so that, as century gave way to century, ever fresh and cruder forces have been brought into play, finally forcing us back, for our own protection, behind giant cannons and armoured walls which, year by year, continue to grow in size. (x. 330.)

In its sequel, 'What Use Is This Knowledge?', Wagner openly extends his criticism of the modern hegemonic state to the German Reich and to the policies of Bismarck, whom he came to despise in the final years of his life. German unity, he argued, was purely the result of political calculations; it had no other meaning. 'German unity must be able to show its teeth everywhere, even if there is nothing for it to chew.' Whereas 'true peace' could be achieved only 'by peaceful means', the treaty which was concluded with France in Frankfurt in 1871 was leading only to 'new preparations for war'.

Here, however, recognition of the need for, and the possibility of, a real regeneration of the human race—now crushed beneath an embattled civilization—could have inspired a peace agreement which might very well have opened up the way to universal peace: in consequence, fortresses would not have had to be taken by storm, but razed to the ground, pledges would not have had to be taken for future war securities, but pledges would have been given in order to safeguard peace; whereas only historical rights are now weighed up against historical claims, all founded on the right of conquest ... They all dream about world peace; even Napoleon III had this idea in mind, except that, in his case, peace was intended to benefit his dynasty in France: for these powerful figures cannot imagine it other than under the widely respected protection of an extraordinary number of cannons. (x. 254–5.)

(If he were alive today, Wagner would have written 'nuclear warheads' instead of 'cannons'.)

Wagner contrasts this progressively embattled civilization with the picture of a culture imbued with the spirit of peace. 'Violence may civilize, but culture must spring from the soil of peace, just as it draws its very name from the tillage of the actual soil. It is from this same soil that knowledge, science, and art have grown in every age.' (x. 234.) Wagner's regenerated world is in stark opposition to that civilization which is characterized by war, power, egoistical possessions, and the exploitation of both Nature and the weaker sections of society. 'Violence is utterly excluded from such a course', he writes (x. 251–2).

Wagner's concrete programme of regeneration is certainly one of the stranger lunacies among his journalistic writings. It culminates in the suggestion of a 'mass migration' to southern climes, where that 'lost Paradise' might be rediscovered in which men would live together in a state of universal peace not only with each other but with nature, too (x. 238, 242). Only the rich would suffer as a result of such a general exodus. 'But, if they chose to raise a hue and cry, the grabbing, grasping money-bags of modern civilization, fattened on the sweat of our brow, would be turned upon their backs like pigs and reduced at once to astonished silence by the surprising sight of a heaven which they had never seen before.' (x. 243.)

As forerunners and instruments of this idea of regeneration, Wagner sees the international 'peace groups' of vegetarians, temperance societies, animal protection leagues—and socialists. It was Wagner's dream that 'present-day socialism' should unite with these peace groups to form 'a true and intimate union' which, he hoped, would also help to win back 'true religion'. For Wagner, however, this religion was none other than the Christian faith—the religion of the Cross—merged with the ethics of Buddhism. He plays Christianity off against the Jewish religion, using historically untenable arguments. Significantly, the figure who fascinated him above all others was the early Christian heretic, Marcion, who 'wished to separate the New from the Old Testament' (*CT*, 23 January 1880). Like Marcion, Wagner drew a distinction between Christianity as a religion of love and compassion and the Old Testament Jewish religion of law and terror, which had, he believed, fatally eclipsed the Christian religion of peace. 'Wherever we saw Christian armies set out in quest of pillage and bloodshed, even under the sign of the Cross', it was not the names of Jesus and the New Testament that were invoked, but Moses, Joshua, Gideon, and other generals.

How else would it have been possible, without this involvement of the old Judaic spirit and without its identification with that of the purely Christian Gospels, to make ecclesiastical demands on the 'civilized world' even today, a world whose nations, armed to the teeth as though for mutual extirpation, squander their peacetime resources in order to fall on one another, methodically tearing each other apart, at the first sign from their generals? (x. 232–3.)

When Gurnemanz explains to him the crime that he has committed against the tranquillity of Nature, Parsifal breaks his bow and throws away his arrows. When he leaves Klingsor's realm with the recaptured spear, he offers himself, defenceless, to his enemies. Just as Christ, to use Gurnemanz's words,

> bar jeder Wehr,[53] sein heilig Blut
> der sündigen Welt zur Sühne bot      (x. 366),
>
> bare of defence, His holy blood
> once shed to redeem the sinful world,

so must Parsifal guard the sacred lance, suffering wound upon wound, 'denn nicht ihn selber | durft' ich führen im Streite' (the Spear itself | could not be wielded in battle). This spear no longer exists to inflict wounds but to heal them: it is a symbol of peace. Was it not Amfortas who initiated the sequence of crimes when he used it as a weapon against his enemy, Klingsor?

*Parsifal* is a poem about peace, about the need for man to be at peace not only with himself but also with Nature. In his penetrating study of the work, Hans Küng has described its central idea as the 'rejection, in favour of fellow-feeling with man and Nature, of our tendency to think in terms of power and self-assertiveness'. It is an idea which, in a world 'whose power structures still function largely in a socio-Darwinian and Machiavellian way',[54] is more than ever valid today as a regulatory principle. But this principle was a specifically Christian one for Wagner, as he made unambiguously plain.

Even in his detailed dramatic draft of 1849, *Jesus von Nazareth*, Wagner had felt that what was truly revolutionary about Christ's act of redemption was the fact that it had overturned that law of history according to which violence could be defeated only by further acts of violence. 'When Jesus was baptized by John', Wagner wrote, 'the people recognized him as the heir of David: but he went into the wilderness and took counsel with himself: should he assert his descent from David in the sense desired by the people? Were he to succeed in this, would he then be anything other than a confederate of those great men of the

---

[53] In the 1877 prose draft Wagner wrote 'jeder Waffe sich entledigend' (ridding himself of every weapon); see Wagner, *Sämtliche Werke*, xxx. 85.

[54] Küng, 'Sehnsucht nach Erlösung', p. 36.

world who rely on the rich and heartless?' Would not the result be to exchange one form of violence for another, especially if, as the people expected, he supported Roman tyranny? The outcome of Christ's meditations in the wilderness was that

Jesus repudiated the line of David: through Adam he had come from God, and all men were his brothers; not through any earthly kingdom could he free them from their misery, but only by fulfilling that supreme divine vocation which he recognized as his, in which God became man in order that, through that one man who first recognized him in himself, he might bring himself to the consciousness of *all* mankind: the most wretched and most afflicted must be closest to him: through them would knowledge enter the world. (xi. 285.)

By regarding his descent from David as secondary to his descent from Adam, Christ renounces a national and political mission in favour of a purely human one. His assertion that 'My kingdom is not of this world' (John 18: 36) was, according to Wagner, a rigorous rejection of that 'earthly hegemony' (xi. 279).

Wagner was no doubt reminded of this dramatic fragment in 1874–5, when, as preparation for *Parsifal*, he studied August Friedrich Gfrörer's monumental, multi-volume work on the history of early Christianity. First published in 1838, Gfrörer's study is a highly demanding work of critical exegesis, consisting in no small part of quotations in Hebrew and Greek, but it introduced Wagner to the origins of Christianity and to the essentials of historico-critical biblical studies, and did so, moreover, so thoroughly that we should be wary of reproaching him for his ignorance of theology.[55] Gfrörer's main concern was to counteract the destruction of the Christian faith by modern biblical criticism (whose methodology he uses none the less, albeit in a wholly positive sense). His work culminates in an apologia for St John's Gospel, the only historically authenticated one, in his opinion. On this point he had Wagner's lively support, and the picture of Christ's teachings which Gfrörer paints on the strength of this 'most spiritual' of the Gospels is one which Wagner took over in its entirety, not least because, on many points, it reflected ideas which he himself had held for decades.

In conversation with Cosima on 3 September 1880 Wagner described Gfrörer as 'the most sensitive of writers in his handling of religious matters'. And, indeed, Gfrörer offers a very similar interpretation of Christ's 'My kingdom is not of this world' to the one which Wagner

---

[55] Wagner also studied other theological and scholarly texts in connection with *Parsifal*; these include Renan's life of Christ and (a source of displeasure) Overbeck's essay *Über die Christlichkeit unserer heutigen Theologie*. It is remarkable, however, that (as emerges from Cosima Wagner's *Diaries*) it was the first volume of Gfrörer's *Geschichte des Urchristentums* that gave him particular pleasure, a volume which portrays Jewish theology and national education at the time of Christ and which also includes a detailed account of mysticism and the cabbala.

himself had given in 1849: 'Purely spiritual is my kingdom: dominion, slavery, state institutions in general do not affect its inner core, its strength lies in what binds it to the eternal root of its existence, to God.' This is the kernel of Christ's message, and Gfrörer concludes: 'Without incurring the charge of presumptuousness, we may say, therefore, that the Lord spoke these words to *us* in particular.'[56]

It has been pointed out, with some justification, that, in the highly unorthodox Christianity of Wagner's old age, no role is allotted to Christ's resurrection. It is a Christianity which centres on Good Friday not on Easter Day. There is no doubt that the composer was strongly influenced by Gfrörer on this point, since the latter makes no secret of his disquiet concerning the Resurrection and Ascension. It was this, he claimed, 'which bequeathed to Christianity those Judaic teachings of a ruling Messiah, of a thousand-year empire, of Christ's second coming, of the Last Judgement, and so forth, all of them errors long since refuted by experience'. These ideas, Gfrörer goes on, are nothing but a 'protective cover, which was necessary to shield the pure kernel of Christianity during the decay of the Roman Empire and the tempests of the Middle Ages, and to commend it to that more modern Europe which is being driven towards a more spiritual outlook by a thousand considerations over which we have no control'.[57] In other words, Gfrörer attempts to eliminate the Resurrection from the Christian viewpoint, never actually denying it, but arguing that it is immaterial to our understanding of Christ's act of redemption. 'Only this much seems to me to be beyond dispute, that the Lord considered his mission complete when he died on the Cross. What happened afterwards was unexpected even by him and was not a part of his plan.'[58]

Like Gfrörer, Wagner, too, looked forward to a time when Christianity would be restored to its original, purely spiritual, form. To accompany it and strengthen it on its progress was, for the later Wagner, the task of art and, above all, of music—the 'only art wholly in keeping with the Christian faith', as he himself described it in 'Religion and Art' (x. 221). It was in this sense that Wagner intended his *Bühnenweihfestspiel* to be a 'Christian work' which, for that very reason, should not be desecrated by repeated performances in an ordinary repertory theatre.[59]

[56] August Friedrich Gfrörer, *Geschichte des Urchristentums* (Stuttgart, 1838), iii. 104–6.

[57] Ibid. 250–1.                            [58] Ibid. 254.

[59] Needless to say, Wagner did not want the Christian character of his work to be seen as 'ecclesiastical'. When, at the beginning of 1878, Nietzsche sent the Wagners an interpretation of *Parsifal* written by his doctor, Otto Eiser, Cosima replied on 20 Feb. 1878 (doubtlessly in complete agreement with her husband, as the latter's remarks on the relationship between art and religion in her *Diaries* suggest) that the comparison which Eiser had drawn between *Parsifal* and the *autos sacramentales* of Calderón was misguided. 'Calderón used his genius to dramatize Church dogmas for the people, but *Parsifal* has nothing in common with any Church, nor indeed with any dogma,

Wagner's idea of a 'true religion' was of a pure form of Christianity identical with the ethical nucleus of Buddhism, and, as we have seen, it was radically pacifistic. In spite of his susceptibility to the pessimism of Schopenhauer and Gobineau, Wagner hoped that humanity might yet be regenerated in a spirit of peace and that it might still be possible to restrore man's integrity and his relationship with Nature. His essay 'Religion and Art' culminates in his revival of the myth of a Paradisal harmony between mankind and Nature. Wagner does not leave his reader with this picture of peace, of course, but with a vision of terrifying actuality, describing an apocalyptic catastrophe which humanity risks bringing down upon itself by engaging in an increasingly dangerous arms race and which may be triggered off by a mere 'mistake'. It must 'give cause for concern', Wagner begins this final section of his essay,

that the advancing art of war is turning increasingly away from the guiding principles of moral forces and towards the development of mechanical forces! The most brutish powers of Nature's lowly forces are involved here in an elaborate game in which, despite all mathematics and arithmetic, the purblind will could one day interfere by breaking loose with elemental force. Even now the armoured monitors,[60] against which the proud and glorious sailing ship cannot hold her own, offer a sight of spectral horror: mutely dedicated men, no longer with the looks of men, operate these monsters, and will nevermore desert their posts, though they are in the terrible stokehole; but, just as in nature everything has its destructive foe, so art invents torpedoes for the sea, and dynamite cartouches and the like, elsewhere. It is altogether conceivable that

for here the blood turns to bread and wine, whereas it is the other way round in the Eucharist. *Parsifal* picks up where the Gospels leave off, and its poet continued to structure and create his material, heedless of all that already existed. The poet of the *autos* always set out from an existing faith and dogma, allowing the latter to be demonstrated by allegorical characters through actions which are certainly wonderfully alive.' As an autonomous work of art, *Parsifal* cannot allow its meaning(s) to be determined by any one existing religion; rather, art must freely approach religion and avail itself of the latter's symbols. 'The path from religion to art bad, from art to religion good', Wagner told Cosima on 13 Jan. 1880. It was 'permissible for art to use' the symbols of religion, 'but in a free spirit and not in the rigid forms imposed by the church'; since art was 'a profound form of play', it freed those symbols from all dogmatic earnestness (*CT*, 27 Apr. 1880). As for the 'change' to the meaning of the Eucharist which Cosima mentioned in her letter to Nietzsche, Wagner himself had already told her, in the course of a conversation on 26 Sept. 1877, that the transformation of blood into wine 'permits us to turn our gaze refreshed back to earth, whereas the conversion of wine into blood draws us away from the earth'. Hans Küng is right to remark here that this 'reversal of the Eucharistic process of transubstantiation' does not involve a 'radical reversal, but gives us, rather, a sense of consistency in our practical lives' a 'process of humanization, an "earthing" of heavenly mysteries' ('Sehnsucht nach Erlösung', pp. 31, 33). (This is an idea very close to the modern understanding of the Eucharist.) This transformation of the Eucharist as described by Küng is undoubtedly what the different choruses describe at the end of Act I: the reversion of the blood and body of Christ to wine and bread serves to strengthen us for an active life in the spirit of the Communion, encouraging us 'zu wirken des Heiland's Werke' (to do the Saviour's works here: x. 344). As Küng points out (p. 31), 'this element of active Christianity is overlooked by the majority of interpreters'.

[60] Monitors were armoured warships used for reconnaissance. Wagner no doubt read newspaper reports about the frequent fatalities in the stokeholds of these and other steamships.

not only this, but art and science, bravery and points of honour, life and property could one day explode as the result of some incalculable error. Once our peaceful prosperity has gone up in a puff of smoke, a time of general famine will surely follow, a time of dearth prepared for slowly and yet with blind infallibility: and so we would once more find ourselves standing at the point from which world history first set out, and might indeed receive the impression that 'God created the world in order for the Devil to take it', to use the expression which our great philosopher [Schopenhauer] found in Jewish-Christian dogma. Then the will would reign in all its brutality. (x. 252–3.)

And Wagner ends his vision with an anxious reminiscence of a line from Goethe's *Faust*, I (l. 1117): 'Blessed are we who have turned to the realm of our noble forebears!' (x. 253).

# 20

# Afterword:
# A Note on Wagner's Anti-Semitism

The pacifistic Christianity of Wagner's old age which we examined in the previous chapter represents a renewed attempt on the composer's part to come to terms with the Jewish question. As we noted, he played off the New Testament message of love and compassion against what he saw as the Old Testament emphasis on law and terror, the embodiment of that Judaic religion said to have eclipsed the Christian religion of peace and to have become the spirit of modern militarism. (Thus Wagner turns on its head the traditional prejudice against the Jews, that, as a race, they were wholly unfit for war.) Notwithstanding his fascination with Jewish music and the cabbala, which he had learned about from the first volume of Gfrörer's *Geschichte des Urchristentums*, Wagner's aim in reviving a 'true religion' was, therefore, to eliminate all genuinely Jewish elements from Christianity.

There is no doubt that ideas such as these were mirrored in many respects by a movement which, ever since the publication of Wilhelm Marr's pamphlet, *Der Sieg des Judentums über das Germanentum*, in 1879, had come to be known as 'anti-Semitism' and which had found particularly unsavoury expression in the markedly anti-Semitic tendencies of that 'Christian Social Party' founded in 1878 by the Prussian court chaplain, Adolf Stoecker. Nor can it be doubted that Wagner's essay 'Judaism in Music,' first published in 1850 and reprinted in 1869 as a separate pamphlet, belongs in the forefront of the anti-Semitic movement. But, as Jacob Katz has recently pointed out in his book *The Darker Side of Genius*,[1] there are, somewhat surprisingly, no anti-Jewish remarks in any of Wagner's letters or prose works before 1850, as a comparison of the composer's earlier relationship with Heinrich Heine and the embarrassment of his later remarks, in which he attempts to distance himself from the poet whom he had once defended passionately at the time of his exile from Germany, ably demonstrates.[2]

---

[1] Jacob Katz, *Richard Wagner: Vorbote des Antisemitismus* (Königstein, 1985); translated into English by Allan Arkush as *The Darker Side of Genius: Richard Wagner's Anti-Semitism* (Hanover, New Hampshire, 1986).

[2] Wagner's article, the 4th of his *Parisian Reports*, was dated 6 July 1841 and published in the Dresden *Abend-Zeitung* of 2–4 Aug. 1841. It was republished in his *Collected Writings*, xii. 96–103.

If Wagner began to harbour anti-Jewish feelings, it was quite clearly as a consequence of the years he spent in Paris from 1839 to 1842. The capital's artistic life, strongly influenced as it was by Jews, his lack of success there, the humiliation which he suffered through constant setbacks, the tension generated by his rivalry with Meyerbeer, whom he accused of having failed to help him, his own material misery against the background of that metropolitan luxury which, having assimilated the views of outspokenly anti-Jewish early socialist writers, he regarded as the product of exploitative Jewish capitalists, and the explosive mixture of a deep-seated envy and an inadequately assimilated ideology—all this is sufficient to explain Wagner's increasingly idiosyncratic stance towards all things Jewish. It was a stance, moreover, encouraged by violent anti-Semitic tendencies in French intellectual life for which there was no counterpart in contemporary Germany. Certainly, Wagner's phobia towards the Jews was far more French than German in origin.

In later life, too, his attitude towards things Jewish, now increasingly influenced by racial ideology, remained indebted to French sources, an indebtedness due not least to the intermediation of his wife Cosima, who, like Wagner himself, brought her hatred of the Jews with her from Paris as part of her intellectual baggage. It is surely significant that the most extreme expressions of Wagner's hostility towards the Jews are found in the pages of Cosima's *Diaries*. Of course, we also find charitable remarks about Jews here, the gamut of affirmation running from ironic acknowledgement to undisguised admiration. On 22 December 1880 Wagner told Cosima that, thanks to the power of their capital, the Jews were no longer enslaved by the state: they were 'the only free people'. They had 'preserved a feeling of genuineness which the Germans have entirely lost, and that is why so many of them cling to him' (*CT*, 22 November 1881). As representatives of the oldest religion, they were 'the most superior of all' (*CT*, 2 July 1878), an idea which recurs in a conversation about Joseph Rubinstein: 'Jews like him behave quite differently from us Germans, they know the world belongs to them, we are *déshérités*' (*CT*, 15 May 1878). These and other remarks attest to the way in which Wagner saw the Jews not as outsiders but as cultural superiors. The remark just quoted reveals what almost amounts to a metaphysical jealousy of the Jews, a jealousy grounded in the conviction that (as he told Nietzsche in a letter of 23 October 1872) the 'only possible counterpart' to Judaism was *Deutschsein*, 'being German': like Jewishness, it was, he believed, a 'purely metaphysical concept' rather than a sense of merely national identity.

A view which recurs repeatedly in Wagner's conversations with Cosima is that 'the Jews have been amalgamated with us at least 50 years too soon': 'we must first be something ourselves', he told Cosima. In other words, the Germans ought to have broken free, culturally, from that Romance model on which they had been dependent for so long (*CT*, 1 December 1878). 'If ever I were to write again about the Jews, I should say I have nothing against them, it is just that they descended on us Germans too soon, we were not yet steady enough to absorb them.' (*CT*, 22 November 1878.) Since the Jews 'intervened too early in our cultural condition', the 'human qualities which the German character might have developed from within itself and then passed on to the Jewish character' had been prevented from evolving properly (*CT*, 13 January 1879). That the 'essential German character' was destined to guide humanity to a world beyond national and racist barriers, uniting all nations in the spirit of a universal humanity which would transcend all ethnic, social, and political particularities, is an idea which links Wagner with the cosmopolitan idealism of late eighteenth-century Germany, and especially with the figure of Schiller. Jewishness, too, would be superseded by this sense of universal humanity, a notion reminiscent of the conclusion of Wagner's essay 'Judaism in Music', discussed in detail above, in the chapter on 'The Transformations of Ahasuerus'. In this essay Wagner had written that the Jew and non-Jew could become 'united and indivisible' only if the Jew chose 'to become human in common with us', in other words, if he neither insisted on his Jewishness nor strove to be assimilated with that alienated humanity of the present day. The Jew could find redemption only 'when we too are redeemed as true human beings' (v. 85).

But there is no doubt that, in Wagner's view, the starting-point for this act of redemption was the 'art-work of the future'. As we know, numerous Jews in his own immediate circle subscribed to this aesthetic doctrine of salvation, not least because of the indisputable fact that he kept his musico-dramatic œuvre free of anti-Semitic tendencies. In all the countless commentaries on his work, there is not a single remark which would allow us to interpret as Jewish any of the characters or situations in his music dramas. Admittedly, he compares both the Flying Dutchman and Kundry with the Wandering Jew, but in both cases the third element in the comparison is the motif of endless wanderings on the part of a character unable to die. The Flying Dutchman is not, of course, a Jew, and although Kundry was the Herodias of the Bible in an earlier incarnation—the female counterpart of Ahasuerus, according to a traditional legend stretching back to the Middle Ages—she has undergone countless rebirths among other nations since that time. As we have seen, she is not portrayed as a Jewess but described explicitly as a 'heathen'. Her membership of any one tribe or race is simply not an issue in *Parsifal*, and the potential for inspiring compassion with which

Wagner has invested her both poetically and musically precludes all attempts to interpret her as an anti-Semitic type. That Wagner, finally, did not reinterpret the Ahasuerus myth from an anti-Semitic point of view has already been pointed out.

Ever since 1952 and the publication of Theodor W. Adorno's *Versuch über Wagner* it has been claimed again and again that the Nibelungs — and especially Mime, the delineation of whose character is said to recall Wagner's description of the physical appearance and language of the Jews in his 1850 pamphlet — are ill-concealed Jewish caricatures. This, at best, is idle speculation, rendered implausible not least by the fact that on 2 March 1878 Wagner himself admitted to Cosima that he had 'once felt every sympathy for Alberich'. Certainly, Brünnhilde's freeing of the Nibelungs, including Alberich, was part of the original conception of the Nibelung legend as early as 1848.

We may also discount the view that Beckmesser is a caricature of the Jewish intellectual, an interpretation based on the argument that, in the 1861 prose drafts of *Die Meistersinger*, the Marker bore the name Veit Hanslich. Quite apart from the fact that, in their professional status and social roles, town clerks and Jews had nothing whatever in common, it can only have been *after* his altercation with the Viennese critic that Wagner (as noted in the chapter on *Die Meistersinger*) identified Hanslick with the Marker. When he first sketched the opera in 1845 Wagner was on the best of terms with Hanslick, as is clear from the latter's favourable review of *Tannhäuser*, which had received its first performance earlier that same year.[3] This sketch confirms that, even as early as 1845 the character of the Marker was already firmly established in every essential detail.

Beckmesser is the embodiment of the academic and purist critic from the tradition of humanist satire, where the pedant is regularly exposed to ridicule. As such — but not as a Jew — Hanslick later became the butt of Wagner's satire. Had he intended to invest Beckmesser with Jewish characteristics of the kind encouraged by prevailing anti-Semitic prejudice, he would have had little difficulty in doing so. Beckmesser is a figure from the stock-in-trade of the European improvised comedy of intrigue. (The reader will recall the *dottore* from the *commedia dell'arte* tradition.) The ageing husband from whose grasp both wife and dowry are snatched by a younger man is a type of character which recurs in countless variants in traditional comedies of intrigue. The motive of greed almost always plays a determinative role here: the suitor, who is

---

[3] Hanslick's review appeared in 11 issues of the *Allgemeine Wiener Musik-Zeitung* between 28 Nov. and 29 Dec. 1846. It is republished in Helmut Kirchmeyer, *Situationsgeschichte der Musikkritik und des musikalischen Pressewesens in Deutschland dargestellt vom Ausgange des 18. bis zum Beginn des 20. Jahrhunderts*, iv. *Das zeitgenössische Wagner-Bild* (Regensburg, 1968), iii. 147–83.

already advanced in years, is attracted less by the nubile bride than by her wealth. What is remarkable, of course, is that Wagner has dispensed with this traditional theme in *Die Meistersinger*. There is not a single line in the entire libretto which might force us to conclude that Beckmesser had his eye on Eva Pogner's not inconsiderable dowry. On the contrary, it is his adversary, Hans Sachs, to whom Beckmesser imputes this motive for getting married. If it had ever been Wagner's intention to turn Beckmesser into a Jew, whether openly or otherwise, he would certainly not have let slip an opportunity like this to emphasize his 'Jewish' greed as the real reason for wooing Eva.

How many leading nineteenth-century writers depicted Jews as negative characters without thereby incurring the imputation of being anti-Semitic! And yet the very writer who repeatedly proclaimed his ideological hostility towards the Jews (and who, at the same time, numbered so many Jews among his close circle of friends and acquaintances)—Wagner himself—avoided doing so. Or perhaps it would be truer to say that to foist his anti-Jewish ideology on to his artistic œuvre was as remote from his field of interest as it was beneath him as an artist. There are no Jewish characters in his music dramas, still less any anti-Semitic tendencies. His hatred of the Jews was excluded from the inner sanctum of his artistic personality. The fundamental reason for this undoubtedly lies in the fact that Wagner would have given the lie to his promise of aesthetic salvation if the 'art-work of the future', which promised 'redemption' to Jews as well as Gentiles, had been turned into an instrument of anti-Jewish satire and polemical prejudice. Within the Utopian framework of the mythic musical drama, the Jewish question had been solved for Wagner by his mystic doctrine of redemption.

In his *Betrachtungen eines Unpolitischen*, Thomas Mann remarks: 'where there is no common conceptual ground, there can be no enmity, and what prevails will be a sense of strange indifference. Only where people think the same but feel differently will there be enmity, only there will hatred thrive.'[4] Is this not also true of Wagner's relationship with the Jews? Time and again his opponents reproached him for the fact that, to quote the once popular novelist, Gustav Freytag, Wagner himself was 'the greatest Jew of all' in the sense propounded by his 1850 pamphlet.[5] Time and again Wagner was forced to hear such things said about himself. Indeed, his critics felt themselves confirmed in their opinion by the considerable following he had among Jews. None the less, Wagner's attitude towards the Jews is characterized by a neurotic and obsessive

    [4] Thomas Mann, *Gesammelte Werke in Einzelbänden*, ed. Peter de Mendelssohn, *Betrachtungen eines Unpolitischen* (Frankfurt, 1983), 46.
    [5] Gustav Freytag, 'Der Streit über das Judenthum in der Musik', *Die Grenzboten*, 28 (1869), 336.

belief that he and his works were being 'persecuted' by them. In his *Remarks on 'Judaism in Music'*, written in 1869, this obsession finds unconcealed expression. Virtually all opposition to his work is interpreted as an unacknowledged vendetta against his 1850 essay on Judaism, even though that essay had provoked only a limited stir among a mere handful of readers and had long since been forgotten. During the final years of his life, Wagner's persecution mania became so extreme that he once assured Cosima that the Jews were 'just waiting for his death, for then, as they well know, all will be ended' (*CT*, 15 May 1879)—an altogether insane belief when one thinks of the tremendous impact that he and his works have had on Jews right up to the present day. Wagner himself often commented on this appeal, his reactions extending from irony and surprise to genuine emotion, depending on the circumstances. On one occasion he told Cosima that he would have to build a synagogue in Bayreuth for all his Jewish friends there (*CT*, 13 January 1879). (There had been few Jews in Bayreuth before his arrival in the town.) And on another he remarked that 'we ought to give Fidi [their son Siegfried] a crooked nose' (*CT*, 7 August 1879). Essentially, however, the very real desire for redemption which brought so many Jews into his orbit mirrored his own metaphysical and aesthetic plan of salvation as outlined in the foregoing chapter. At all events, Wagner never made any attempt to relate his theoretical hostility towards the Jews to the practice of his personal dealings with them.

No doubt the Christian-Buddhist beliefs of the later Wagner also played a role here. It was in this spirit that he judged the racial (but by no means anti-Semitic) theories of his friend Count Gobineau, with whose *Essai sur l'inégalité des races humaines* (1853–5) he became familiar only two years before his death, in other words, after his life's work had already been completed. (Gobineau's influence on the composer has been hugely overestimated.) Although he accepted Gobineau's central thesis of racial inequality, he spurned its fatalistic consequences. On this point his criticism coincided with that of Alexis de Tocqueville, who had rejected the idea that man was wholly dependent on his racial constitution, arguing from a humanistic liberal standpoint in his correspondence with Gobineau. With Wagner we find a related critique, but one which was conducted along religious lines. If one thinks of the Gospels, he remarked in conversation with Cosima on 14 February 1881, still fresh from the impression left by Gobineau's *magnum opus*, which he had just begun to read, 'one knows that what really matters is something different from racial strength'. A year later: 'He reproaches Gob. for leaving out of account one thing which was given to mankind— a Saviour, who suffered for them and allowed himself to be crucified' (*CT*, 23 April 1882): in other words, Christ had triumphed over the racial principle, replacing it with the principle of a universal humanity. On 17 December 1881 Wagner noted: 'But one thing is certain: races are done for, and all that can now make an impact is—as I have ventured to express it—the blood of Christ [in the form of the Communion].'

Wagner is referring here to 'Heroism and Christianity', an essay written in August–September 1881, where he had stressed that the blood of Christ had not been shed for one particular 'race, however preferred it may be', but for 'the human race as a whole' (x. 283). The natural inequality of the races—which had led to a 'thoroughly immoral world order' as a result of the 'domination and exploitation of the inferior races'—must be compensated for by a moral equality 'of a kind which true Christianity must seem to us uniquely destined to develop' (x. 284–5). It was not simply diplomacy, therefore, that persuaded Wagner to write to his Jewish friend, the Berlin impresario Angelo Neumann, dissociating himself from the anti-Semitic movement, and especially from the 'Mass Petition against the Rampancy of Judaism' initiated by Nietzsche's brother-in-law, Bernhard Förster, in 1880: 'I have absolutely no connection with the present "anti-Semitic" movement', Wagner informed Neumann on 23 February 1881; his regeneration essays made this so palpably plain, he went on, that 'it will be impossible for anyone of *intelligence* to associate me with that movement'.[6] Of course, Wagner hoped that by distancing himself in this way he could salvage Neumann's grandiose plans to mount the *Ring* in Berlin (plans which were being jeopardized by rumours of an anti-Semitic campaign in Bayreuth), but the idea advanced here also corresponds with a deeper insight on Wagner's part. For who can deny that his superficial chauvinism remains very much on the surface, while the humane essence of his work is left unaffected, an essence which, transcending its time and rising above all ideological hatred and conceptualized hostilities, retains its relevance as never before, filling the hearts of men of all nations and races.

[6] Angelo Neumann, *Erinnerungen an Richard Wagner*, 2nd edn. (Leipzig, 1907), 139; English translation from *Selected Letters of Richard Wagner*, ed. Stewart Spencer and Barry Millington (London, 1987), 906.

# BIBLIOGRAPHY

The following bibliography contains only those primary and secondary texts which bear directly on Wagner. For general works on literary history, the history of music, and other specialized topics, the reader is referred to the annotation to the individual chapters.

ADORNO, THEODOR, *Versuch über Wagner* (Frankfurt, 1952); translated into English by Rodney Livingstone as *In Search of Wagner* (London, 1981).

BARTH, HERBERT (ed.), *Internationale Wagner-Bibliographie* (Bayreuth, 1956 ff.).

—— , MACK, DIETRICH, and VOSS, EGON (eds.), *Wagner: Sein Leben und seine Welt in zeitgenössischen Bildern und Texten* (Vienna, 1975); translated into English by P. R. J. Ford and Mary Whittall as *Wagner: A Documentary Study* (London, 1975).

BEKKER, PAUL, *Wagner: Das Leben im Werke* (Stuttgart, 1924); translated into English by M. M. Bozman as *Richard Wagner: His Life in His Work* (London and Toronto, 1931).

BORCHMEYER, DIETER, 'Inspiration durchs Kasperltheater: Richard Wagners Idee des improvisatorischen Dramas', *Euphorion*, 74 (1980), 113–33.

BOUCHER, MAURICE, *Les idées politiques de Richard Wagner: Exemple de nationalisme mythique* (Paris, 1948).

CHAMBERLAIN, HOUSTON STEWART, *Richard Wagner*, 4th edn. (Munich, 1907); translated into English by G. Ainslie Hight (Munich and London, 1897).

CONRAD, MICHAEL GEORG, *Wagners Geist und Kunst in Bayreuth* (Munich, 1906).

DAHLHAUS, CARL, *Wagners Konzeption des musikalischen Dramas* (Regensburg, 1971).

—— , *Richard Wagners Musikdramen* (Velber, 1971); translated into English by Mary Whittall as *Richard Wagner's Music Dramas* (Cambridge, 1979).

—— (ed.), *Das Drama Richard Wagners als musikalisches Kunstwerk* (Regensburg, 1970).

—— (ed.), *Richard Wagner: Werk und Wirkung* (Regensburg, 1971).

DEATHRIDGE, JOHN, GECK, MARTIN, and VOSS, EGON (eds.), *Wagner Werk-Verzeichnis (WWV): Verzeichnis der musikalischen Werke Richard Wagners und ihrer Quellen. Erarbeitet im Rahmen der Richard Wagner-Gesamtausgabe* (Mainz, 1986).

DONINGTON, ROBERT, *Wagner's 'Ring' and its Symbols: The Music and the Myth* (London, 1963).

EINSTEIN, ALFRED, 'Verdi und Wagner', *Melos*, 18 (1951).

FEHR, MAX, *Richard Wagners Schweizer Zeit* (2 vols.: i, Aarau and Leipzig, 1934; ii, Aarau and Frankfurt, 1953).

FRIES, OTHMAR, *Richard Wagner und die deutsche Romantik* (Zurich, 1952).

FURNESS, RAYMOND, *Wagner and Literature* (Manchester, 1982).

GAUTIER, JUDITH, *Richard Wagner et son œuvre poétique* (Paris, 1882).

GECK, MARTIN, *Die Bildnisse Richard Wagners* (Munich, 1970).

GLASENAPP, CARL FRIEDRICH, *Das Leben Richard Wagners*, 5th edn. (6 vols.; Leipzig, 1910–23); English trans. of the 3rd edn. by William Ashton Ellis (London, 1900–8; repr. 1977) (vols. iv-vi are by Ellis alone).

GREGOR-DELLIN, MARTIN, *Wagner-Chronik: Daten zu Leben und Werk* (Munich, 1972).

——, *Richard Wagner: Die Revolution als Oper* (Munich, 1973).

——, *Richard Wagner: Sein Leben, sein Werk, sein Jahrhundert* (Munich and Zurich, 1980); translated into English by J. Maxwell Brownjohn as *Richard Wagner: His Life, his Work, his Century* (London, 1983).

GUTMAN, ROBERT W., *Richard Wagner: The Man, his Mind and his Music* (London and New York, 1968).

HANSLICK, EDUARD, 'Richard Wagners Bühnenfestspiel in Bayreuth', in *Musikalisches und Literarisches*, 2nd edn. (Berlin, 1889); translated into English by Henry Pleasants as 'Richard Wagner's Stage Festival in Bayreuth', in *Music Criticisms 1846–99* (Harmondsworth, 1963), pp. 129–56.

HILDEBRANDT, KURT, *Wagner und Nietzsche: Ihr Kampf gegen das neunzehnte Jahrhundert* (Breslau, 1924).

JÄCKEL, KURT, *Richard Wagner in der französischen Literatur* (2 vols.; Breslau, 1931–2).

KARBAUM, MICHAEL, *Studien zur Geschichte der Bayreuther Festspiele (1876–1976)* (Regensburg, 1976).

KIRCHMEYER, HELMUT, *Situationsgeschichte der Musikkritik und des musikalischen Pressewesens in Deutschland*, iv. *Das zeitgenössische Wagner-Bild* (Regensburg, 1967 ff.).

KOPPEN, ERWIN, *Dekadenter Wagnerismus: Studien zur europäischen Literatur des Fin de siècle* (Berlin and New York, 1973).

KREOWSKI, ERNST, and FUCHS, EDUARD, *Richard Wagner in der Karikatur* (Berlin, [1907]).

KROPFINGER, KLAUS, *Wagner und Beethoven* (Regensburg, 1975).

KUNZE, STEFAN (ed.), *Richard Wagner: Von der Oper zum Musikdrama* (Berne and Munich, 1978).

KURTH, ERNST, *Romantische Harmonik und ihre Krise in Wagners 'Tristan'* (Berne and Leipzig, 1920).

LOOS, PAUL ARTHUR, *Richard Wagner: Vollendung und Tragik der deutschen Romantik* (Munich, 1952).

LORENZ, ALFRED, *Das Geheimnis der Form bei Richard Wagner* (4 vols.; Munich, 1924–33).

MACK, DIETRICH, *Bayreuther Festspiele: Die Idee, der Bau, die Aufführungen*, 22nd edn., revised by Matthias Theodor Vogt (Bayreuth, 1988).

MANN, THOMAS, *Wagner und unsere Zeit*, ed. Erika Mann (Frankfurt, 1963); translated into English by Allan Blunden as *Pro and contra Wagner* (London, 1985).

MAYER, HANS, *Richard Wagner: Mitwelt und Nachwelt* (Stuttgart and Zurich, 1978).

MENDÈS, CATULLE, *Richard Wagner* (Paris, 1886).

MÜLLER, ULRICH and WAPNEWSKI, PETER (EDS.), *Richard-Wagner-Handbuch* (Stuttgart, 1986) (English trans. forthcoming).

MUNCKER, FRANZ, *Richard Wagner: Eine Skizze seines Lebens und Wirkens* (Bamberg, 1909).

NAUMANN, EMIL, *Musikdrama oder Oper? Eine Beleuchtung der Bayreuther Bühnenfestspiele* (Berlin, 1876).

NEWMAN, ERNEST, *Wagner as Man and Artist* (London, 1914).

——, *The Life of Richard Wagner* (4 vols.; New York, 1933–46; reset Cambridge, 1976).

NIETZSCHE, FRIEDRICH, *Der Fall Wagner: Schriften und Aufzeichnungen über Richard Wagner*, ed. Dieter Borchmeyer (Frankfurt, 1983).

PORGES, HEINRICH, *Die Bühnenproben zu den Bayreuther Festspielen des Jahres 1876* (Leipzig, 1896); translated into English by Robert L. Jacobs as *Wagner Rehearsing the 'Ring'* (Cambridge, 1983).

SCHÜLER, WINFRIED, *Der Bayreuther Kreis von seiner Entstehung bis zum Ausgang der Wilhelminischen Ära. Wagnerkult und Wagnerreform im Geiste völkischer Weltanschauung* (Münster, 1971).

SCHURÉ, ÉDOUARD, *Souvenirs sur Richard Wagner* (Paris, 1900).

SHAW, GEORGE BERNARD, *The Perfect Wagnerite* (London, 1898).

STEIN, HERBERT VON: *Dichtung und Musik im Werk Richard Wagners* (Berlin, 1962).

STEIN, JACK M., *Richard Wagner & the Synthesis of the Arts* (Detroit, 1960).

VORDTRIEDE, WERNER, 'Richard Wagners Tod in Venedig', *Euphorion*, 52 (1958), 378–96.

VOSS, EGON, *Richard Wagner und die Instrumentalmusik: Wagners symphonischer Ehrgeiz* (Wilhelmshaven, 1977).

WAGNER, COSIMA, *Die Tagebücher 1869–1883*, ed. Martin Gregor-Dellin and Dietrich Mack (2 vols.; Munich, 1976–7); translated into English by Geoffrey Skelton as *Cosima Wagner's Diaries* (2 vols.; London and New York, 1978–80).

WAGNER, RICHARD, *Gesammelte Schriften und Dichtungen*, 2nd edn. (10 vols.; Leipzig, 1888).

——, *Briefe an August Röckel*, ed. La Mara (Leipzig, 1894); translated into English by Eleanor C. Sellar as *Richard Wagner's Letters to August Roeckel* (Bristol [1897]; repr. Ann Abor, 1969).

—— *Briefwechsel zwischen Wagner und Liszt*, ed. Erich Kloss, 3rd edn. (2 vols.; Leipzig, 1910); the English trans. by Francis Hueffer, revised by William Ashton Ellis (London, 1897; repr. New York, 1973), is based on Hueffer's incomplete German edition of 1887.

——, *Sämtliche Schriften und Dichtungen* (16 vols.; Leipzig, 1911–14).

——, *Richard Wagner an Mathilde Wesendonk: Tagebuchblätter und Briefe 1853–1871*, ed. Wolfgang Golther, 44th edn. (Leipzig, 1914); the English trans. by William Ashton Ellis (London, 1905) is based on the first German edition of 1905.

——, *König Ludwig II. und Richard Wagner: Briefwechsel*, ed. Otto Strobel (5 vols.; Karlsruhe, 1936–9).

——, *Briefe: Die Sammlung Burrell*, ed. John N. Burk (Frankfurt, 1953); translated into English by Hans Abraham, Henry Lea, and Richard Stoehr as *Letters of Richard Wagner: The Burrell Collection* (London, 1951).

WAGNER, RICHARD, *Sämtliche Briefe*, ed. Gertrud Strobel and Werner Wolf (vols. i-iv), Hans-Joachim Bauer and Johannes Forner (vols. vi-vii) (Leipzig, 1967 ff.).

——, *Sämtliche Werke: In Zusammenarbeit mit der Bayerischen Akademie der Schönen Künste, München*, ed. Carl Dahlaus (Mainz, 1970 ff.).

——, *Das Braune Buch: Tagebuchaufzeichnungen 1865 bis 1882*, ed. Joachim Bergfeld (Zurich and Freiburg, 1975); translated into English by George Bird as *The Diary of Richard Wagner: The Brown Book 1865–1882* (London, 1980).

——, *Mein Leben*, ed. Martin Gregor-Dellin (Munich, 1976); translated into English by Andrew Gray as *My Life* (Cambridge, 1983).

——, *Die Musikdramen* (Munich, 1978).

——, *Selected Letters of Richard Wagner*, ed. Stewart Spencer and Barry Millington (London, 1987).

WAGNER, WIELAND (ed.), *Richard Wagner und das neue Bayreuth* (Munich, 1962).

WALZEL, OSCAR, *Richard Wagner in seiner Zeit und nach seiner Zeit* (Munich, 1913).

WAPNEWSKI, PETER, *Richard Wagner: Die Szene und ihr Meister* (Munich, 1978).

——, *Der traurige Gott: Richard Wagner in seinen Helden* (Munich, 1978).

——, *Tristan der Held Richard Wagners* (Berlin, 1981).

WESTERNHAGEN, CURT von, *Richard Wagner: sein Werk, sein Wesen, seine Welt* (Zurich, 1956).

——, *Vom Holländer zum Parsifal: Neue Wagner-Studien* (Zurich, 1962).

——, *Richard Wagners Dresdener Bibliothek 1842–49* (Wiesbaden, 1966).

——, *Wagner*, 2nd edn. (Zurich, 1969); translated into English by Mary Whittall as *Wagner: A Biography* (Cambridge, 1978).

WOLZOGEN, HANS VON, *Thematischer Leitfaden durch die Musik zu Richard Wagners Festspiel 'Der Ring des Nibelungen'* (Leipzig, 1876); translated into English as *Guide through the Music of R. Wagner's 'The Ring of the Nibelung'* (London and Leipzig, 1882).

——, *Erinnerungen an Richard Wagner* (Vienna, 1883).

ZLINSKY, HARTMUT, *Richard Wagner: Ein deutsches Thema. Eine Dokumentation zur Wirkungsgeschichte Richard Wagners 1876–1976* (Frankfurt, 1976).

Also of general interest are the programme booklets issued by the Bayreuth Festival from 1951 onwards, together with the Bavarian State Opera programmes for its productions of *Lohengrin* (1978), *Die Meistersinger von Nürnberg* (1979), *Tristan und Isolde* (1980), and *Der fliegende Holländer* (1981). The rororo series of opera guides, edited by Attila Csampai and Dietmar Holland, includes volumes on *Der fliegende Holländer* (1982), *Tannhäuser* (1986), *Lohengrin* (1989), *Tristan und Isolde* (1983), *Die Meistersinger von Nürnberg* (1981), and *Parsifal* (1984). A series of opera guides in English, published jointly by the English National Opera and the Royal Opera House, and edited by Nicholas John, covers all Wagner's mature operas with the exception of *Lohengrin*.

# GENERAL INDEX

# INDEX OF RICHARD WAGNER'S WORKS